The Law of Restitution

The Law of Restitution

Second edition

Andrew Burrows   MA (Oxon), BCL, LLM (Harvard)

Norton Rose Professor of Commercial Law in the
University of Oxford; Fellow of St Hugh's College, Oxford;
Honorary Bencher of the Middle Temple.

Butterworths
LexisNexis™

Members of the LexisNexis Group worldwide

United Kingdom	LexisNexis Butterworths Tolley, a Division of Reed Elsevier (UK) Ltd, Halsbury House, 35 Chancery Lane, LONDON, WC2A 1EL, and 4 Hill Street, EDINBURGH EH2 3JZ
Argentina	LexisNexis Argentina, BUENOS AIRES
Australia	LexisNexis Butterworths, CHATSWOOD, New South Wales
Austria	LexisNexis Verlag ARD Orac GmbH & Co KG, VIENNA
Canada	LexisNexis Butterworths, MARKHAM, Ontario
Chile	LexisNexis Chile Ltda, SANTIAGO DE CHILE
Czech Republic	Nakladatelství Orac sro, PRAGUE
France	Editions du Juris-Classeur SA, PARIS
Hong Kong	LexisNexis Butterworths, HONG KONG
Hungary	HVG-Orac, BUDAPEST
India	LexisNexis Butterworths, NEW DELHI
Ireland	Butterworths (Ireland) Ltd, DUBLIN
Italy	Giuffrè Editore, MILAN
Malaysia	Malayan Law Journal Sdn Bhd, KUALA LUMPUR
New Zealand	LexisNexis Butterworths, WELLINGTON
Poland	Wydawnictwo Prawnicze LexisNexis, WARSAW
Singapore	LexisNexis Butterworths, SINGAPORE
South Africa	LexisNexis Butterworths, DURBAN
Switzerland	Stämpfli Verlag AG, BERNE
USA	LexisNexis, DAYTON, Ohio

A CIP Catalogue record for this book is available from the British Library.

ISBN 0 406 93244 1

Printed and bound in Great Britain by Butler & Tanner Ltd, Frome Somerset

Visit Butterworths LexisNexis *direct* at **www.butterworths.com**

For Edward, Tom and John

Preface to the second edition

It has recently been said (by Webb and Akkouh [2002] Restitution Law Review 235) that 'Writing a ... text on the law of restitution must be a daunting task'. Not surprisingly, I agree. But I would add that producing a new edition ten years after the first has proved almost more daunting. The judicial developments in the English law of restitution since the first edition of this book in 1993 have been enormous; and they have been matched and even outstripped by an explosion of academic writing. Readers who would like to see an immediate overview of these developments should refer to pp 2–4 below. Combine all this with the revolution in information retrieval over the last decade, not to mention the Woolf reforms, and one can readily understand why this second edition has required very significant amendments and rewriting.

Having said that, those readers familiar with the first edition may be relieved to see that, with one main exception, the structure and basic approach of this book remains unchanged. Indeed, in many areas the courts have refined, and filled in, the detail of what was outlined and discussed in the first edition. The exception is proprietary restitution. In the light of persuasive criticism of my original views, I have come to see that, first, it is important to distinguish between, on the one hand, the recovery of what one previously owned and still owns and, on the other hand, the creation of new proprietary rights in response to unjust enrichment; and, secondly, that a lien or trust imposed after tracing is not best rationalised as the continuation of a pre-existing proprietary right. Chapter 13 in the first edition has therefore been excised and the question of when unjust enrichment does trigger proprietary, as well as the more usual personal, restitution has been considered throughout the book under the different 'unjust factors' (as well as in chapter 1 at pp 60–75). The number of chapters has, nevertheless, remained the same because undue influence has now been given its own chapter separate from exploitation of weakness.

As with the first edition, while this is primarily a student text, it is hoped that it will also meet the needs of practitioners. A feature of the last decade has been the willingness of the courts to cite academic writings on the law of restitution. Nowhere else in the development of English private law has the working relationship between judges, practitioners and academics been so fruitful.

I would like to thank Adrian Briggs for his comments on the conflict of laws section in chapter 16; Daniel Tividar for his help with the references; Katherine Frisby for all her hard work in typing up the new script; and the editorial team at Butterworths for their skill and patience in seeing the book through from manuscript to publication. I am also grateful to Francis Rose and Gareth Jones for allowing me to see the proofs of, respectively, this year's Restitution Law Review and the 6th edition of Goff and Jones.

Incidentally, for those many who have asked (which only goes to show that people do read prefaces!) Edward is fine and appears not have been scarred for life by his early excessive exposure to Restitution.

The law is stated as at 30 September 2002, subject to a few amendments at proof stage.

The abbreviations 'Birks' and 'Goff and Jones' refer respectively to Birks, *An Introduction to the Law of Restitution* (revised edn 1989) and Goff and Jones, *The Law of Restitution* (6th edn, 2002).

Andrew Burrows
1 November 2002
Oxford

Preface to the first edition

When the late Alfred Wainwright completed his classic seven volume guide to the mountains of the English Lake District, he described himself as happy, sorry, and relieved. Happy because he had successfully reached the end of a 13 year road; sorry because it was a long road he had enjoyed travelling; and relieved because a broken limb during those years would have also meant a broken heart. That mixture of emotions well describes my own on completing this book.

I first studied restitution as a postgraduate student in the seminars given in Oxford by Peter Birks and Jack Beatson in 1979. It has held a fascination for me ever since and, while I can clearly remember the day over two-and-a-half years ago when I started to write this book, it is in a sense the product of 13 years of thought.

Traditionally English law sought to manage without a law of restitution based on reversing unjust enrichment. Its case law was dispersed into areas treated as having no relationship to each other such as quasi-contract, subrogation, tracing, and a fiduciary's liability to account for unauthorised profits. As a result similarities and inconsistencies between like cases, both at common law and in equity, were hidden, the importance of the subject matter was obscured, and rational development of the law was hindered.

Over the last 25 years or so, that traditional view has come under increasing attack and it has become widely accepted, by academics and practitioners alike, that there is a coherent and principled English law of restitution. In 1991 any argument to the contrary was authoritatively silenced by the House of Lords' momentous recognition of the principle of unjust enrichment in *Lipkin Gorman v Karpnale Ltd.* It cannot now seriously be denied that the subject is as important and central as, say, contract and tort. With the subject's existence secure, all attention can rightly be focused on its content.

There are only two books on the English law of restitution: Goff and Jones, *The Law of Restitution* (3rd edn, 1986), hereinafter referred to as 'Goff and Jones' and Peter Birks, *An Introduction to the Law of Restitution* (revised paperback edn, 1989), hereinafter referred to as 'Birks'. Both are superb and it will soon be apparent that I owe an enormous debt to them (and also to several outstanding judgments of Lord Goff). Goff and Jones is essentially a practitioners' work, while Birks represents a highly theoretical analysis of the structure of the subject. This book aims to steer a middle course. It is more theoretical than Goff and Jones, less theoretical than Birks. Although I have sought to provide answers to many of the problems increasingly encountered by practitioners in advising in this difficult area, my principal target has been students. This book can perhaps justifiably lay claim to be the first *textbook* on the English law of restitution. I have attempted to present the law, and the intriguing issues raised by it, in a clear and coherent manner: and throughout I have explained how the black-letter law is tied to the underlying principle of reversing the defendant's unjust enrichment at the plaintiff's expense. The views of leading writers are critically assessed and various proposals for improving the law are suggested. Above all it is hoped that the book conveys the fascination, excitement, and importance of this long-neglected subject.

Perhaps because the law of restitution has been so little explored, many of the questions raised by it are unresolved and difficult. My own perception is that parts of chapter 1, and chapters 2 and 4, contain the most complex material. A reader who is unfamiliar with the subject and wishes to gain a flavour of what it is about would perhaps be well-advised to read chapter 3 first. Chapter 1 on Fundamental Ideas is, in many senses, the most important chapter for it underpins what follows: but the significance of some of the issues may not be fully appreciated until one is more familiar with the detailed content of the law.

Over the years I have benefited greatly from discussing points with Jack Beatson and Stephen Moriarty and, more recently, with Ewan McKendrick. I would also like to thank Ewan for his valuable comments on several chapters of this book. Since my return to Oxford in 1986, six years of BCL students have provided the challenge and stimulus for much of my thinking. I would also like to thank my colleagues at Fountain Court Chambers, London. Several of the practical problems discussed in this book are a direct product of my part-time practice there. I also owe a special debt for her kindness and help to my closest college colleague, Ann Kennedy.

My overwhelming intellectual debt is to Peter Birks, Regius Professor of Civil Law at Oxford. As a tutor it was he who first taught me the excitement and importance of rigorous legal analysis. More recently, as a colleague and friend, he has always been available to help and encourage. The power of his thinking and his academic generosity and passionate commitment mark him as one of the greatest scholars and teachers of our times. Although, as will become clear, we disagree on much, several of his ideas are now basic to the subject. In particular I have drawn on his central division of the subject between unjust enrichment by subtraction and unjust enrichment by wrongdoing and I have also used some of his distinctive terminology (eg 'unjust factor', 'subjective devaluation', and 'counter-restitution').

During the past three years I am all too aware that I have been unduly obsessed with this book. I am not exaggerating when I say that the first three words of our eldest son Edward (now aged four) were 'Mummy', 'Daddy', and 'Restitution'. Through it all my wife, Rachel, has been a source of encouragement and strength. Although I dedicate this book to our three young children, it is to her that I owe my greatest thanks.

The manuscript was submitted at the end of September 1992 and, subject to a few minor amendments at proof stage, the law is stated as at that date.

Andrew Burrows
5 November 1992
Oxford

Contents

Table of statutes

Table of cases

PAGE

Decisions of the European Court of Justice are listed below numerically. These decisions
are also included in the preceding alphabetical list.

Chapter 1

Fundamental ideas

The purpose of this chapter is to introduce and explain the principles, concepts and ideas that, it is believed, run through and underpin the law of restitution; and several of the key theoretical controversies concerning the subject will be addressed. In many senses it is the most important chapter in the book for the detailed analysis of the law undertaken in the following 15 chapters is built on the framework set out here. Some of the material in this chapter is complex and its significance may only be fully appreciated on reading later chapters.

1. UNJUST ENRICHMENT AND COMPETING THEORIES

(1) A law of restitution based on unjust enrichment

There are different opinions as to the exact ambit of the law of restitution. The view taken in this book is that it is the law concerned with reversing a defendant's unjust enrichment at the claimant's expense. Although it incorporates elements of the law of property as well as the law of obligations, restitution is most akin to, and belongs alongside, contract and tort; and, just as the principles underlying and giving coherence to contract and tort can be said to be, respectively, the fulfilment of expectations engendered by binding promises and the compensation of wrongful harm, so the underpinning principle of restitution is the reversal of unjust enrichment. Like the former two principles the principle of reversing unjust enrichment is not intended to be a vague reference to individual morality. For although the principle itself is, and must be, morally justifiable[1] its essential role is as an organising tool for existing legal decisions. It enables one to see which are the like cases that

---

1   For a call for the philosophical foundations of the law of restitution to be carefully exposed and analysed, see Barker, 'Unjust Enrichment: Containing the Beast' (1995) 15 OJLS 457. See also McBride and McGrath, 'The Nature of Restitution' (1995) 15 OJLS 33; Ho, 'The Nature of Restitution – A Reply' (1996) 16 OJLS 517; Lionel Smith, 'Restitution: The Heart of Corrective Justice' (2001) 79 Texas LR 2115; Stephen Smith, 'Justifying the Law of Unjust Enrichment' (2001) 79 Texas LR 2177.

should be treated alike. One is therefore not primarily concerned with what any one individual or commentator may think is unjust enrichment but rather with what the law regards as unjust enrichment. Just as textbooks on contract and tort have for the last century sought to explain their respective territories by a readily intelligible framework of more specific principles and doctrines leading from the root principle to the legal decisions, so the primary task that has faced writers on the law of restitution in recent times has been to do the same for this long-neglected subject.

Traditionally English lawyers were hostile to a law of restitution based on unjust enrichment. Until recently powerful dicta of great judges like Lord Mansfield[2] and Lord Wright tended to fall on deaf ears. In *Fibrosa Spolka Akcyjna v Fairbairn Lawson Combe Barbour Ltd*[3] the latter said:

> 'It is clear that any civilised system of law is bound to provide remedies for cases of what has been called unjust enrichment or unjust benefit, that is to prevent a man from retaining the money of or some benefit derived from another which it is against conscience that he should keep. Such remedies in English law are generically different from remedies in contract or in tort, and are now recognised to fall within a third category of the common law which has been called quasi-contract or restitution.'

However, following ever-increasing judicial references to restitution and unjust enrichment, authoritative blessing was finally given to the subject in 1991 by the House of Lords in the momentous decision of *Lipkin Gorman v Karpnale Ltd*.[4] In the light of that decision it is no longer necessary to become embroiled in the long-running but arid debate as to whether the subject exists. All attention can rightly be focused on its content.

Indeed, since *Lipkin Gorman*, there have been several decisions of the House of Lords in which aspects of the law of restitution have been developed or clarified. For example, *Woolwich Equitable Building Society v Inland Revenue Commissioners*[5] on taxes demanded ultra vires by public authorities; *Westdeutsche Landesbank Girozentrale v Islington London Borough Council*[6] on restitution of money paid under void contracts; *Kleinwort Benson Ltd v Glasgow City Council*[7] on the jurisdiction of the English courts to hear restitutionary claims; *Stocznia Gdanska SA*

---

2   See, esp, *Moses v Macferlan* (1760) 2 Burr 1005, 1012.
3   [1943] AC 32, 61.
4   [1991] 2 AC 548.
5   [1993] AC 70.
6   [1996] AC 669.
7   [1999] 1 AC 153.

v Latvia Shipping Co[8] on total failure of consideration; *Banque Financière de la Cité v Parc (Battersea) Ltd*[9] on non-contractual subrogation; *Kleinwort Benson Ltd v Lincoln City Council*[10] on restitution of payments made by mistake of law; *Foskett v McKeown*[11] on tracing and on the problematic relationship between property law and the law of restitution; *A-G v Blake*[12] on restitution for breach of contract; and *Royal Bank of Scotland plc v Etridge (No 2)*[13] on rescission of a contract for undue influence. There have also been influential judgments of the Privy Council in, for example, *A-G of Hong Kong v Reid*[14] on proprietary restitution in respect of bribes and *Dextra Bank and Trust Co Ltd v Bank of Jamaica*[15] on change of position. Add to all these, important decisions of the Court of Appeal, such as *Bishopsgate Investment Management v Homan*[16] on tracing, *Kleinwort Benson v Birmingham City Council*[17] on passing on, and *Scottish Equitable plc v Derby*[18] on change of position, and numerous decisions at first instance, and one can see that the English law of restitution has finally, albeit belatedly, come of age. As Gerhard Dannemann has powerfully expressed it, 'Preceded and helped by scholarly work, English courts have unfrozen the law of restitution and have, particularly over the last ten years, achieved a rapid development which might have taken a century in other areas of the law'.[19]

The last decade has also seen an explosion of academic writing on the law of restitution. When the first edition of this book was published, there were only two texts on the English law of restitution (Goff and Jones, *The Law of Restitution*[20] and Birks, *An Introduction to the Law of Restitution*)[1] and a few collections of essays.[2] In addition to this book, Goff and Jones and Birks, we now have one other 'practitioner work' (*The Law of Restitution*, edited by Hedley and Halliwell),[3] three other

---

8   [1998] 1 WLR 574.
9   [1999] 1 AC 221.
10 [1999] 2 AC 349.
11 [2001] 1 AC 102.
12 [2001] 1 AC 268.
13 [2001] UKHL 44, [2001] 3 WLR 1021.
14 [1994] 1 AC 324.
15 [2002] 1 All ER (Comm) 193.
16 [1995] Ch 211.
17 [1997] QB 380.
18 [2001] EWCA Civ 369, [2001] 3 All ER 818.
19 Dannemann, 'Unjust Enrichment by Transfer: Some Comparative Remarks' (2001) Texas LR 1837, 1843.
20 Then in its 3rd edition but now in its 6th edition (2002).
1   Revised edition, 1989.
2   *Essays on Restitution* (ed Finn, 1990); Beatson, *The Use and Abuse of Unjust Enrichment* (1991); *Essays on the Law of Restitution* (ed Burrows, 1991).
3   (2002). There is also a succinct and important chapter headed 'Unjust Enrichment' written by Birks and Mitchell in *English Private Law* (ed Birks, 2000), ch 15.

textbooks (Tettenborn, *The Law of Restitution in England and Ireland;*[4] Virgo, *The Principles of the Law of Restitution;*[5] and McMeel, *The Modern Law of Restitution*)[6] as well as the first texts in Australia[7] and New Zealand.[8] In addition to several casebooks,[9] and numerous collections of essays,[10] the last decade has also seen the publication of a series of important monographs on particular aspects of the English law of restitution: these have included, for example, Mitchell's *The Law of Subrogation;*[11] Lionel Smith's *The Law of Tracing;*[12] Chambers' *Resulting Trusts;*[13] Alison Jones' *Restitution and European Community Law,*[14] Panagopoulos' *Restitution in Private International Law;*[15] Edelman's *Gain-Based Damages;*[16] and Rotherham's *Proprietary Remedies in Context.*[17] Hundreds of articles on the law of restitution have been published in recent years and the subject has had its own dedicated law journal, the *Restitution Law Review,* since 1993. There is a very helpful Restitution web-site run by Steve Hedley from Cambridge[18] and a thriving internet discussion forum organised by Lionel Smith from Canada. In sharp contrast to its earlier neglect, the law of restitution can lay claim to have been the most debated subject in English private law over the last ten years.[19]

A further feature of the last few years has been the increased interest shown, both amongst academics and judges, in the comparative law of restitution, especially comparisons with Germany and other

---

4   Now in its 3rd edition (2002).

5   (1999).

6   (2000).

7   Mason and Carter, *Restitution Law in Australia* (1995). This is reviewed at length by several commentators at [1997] RLR 229.

8   Grantham and Rickett, *Enrichment and Restitution in New Zealand* (2000). The first text in Canada was Maddaugh and McCamus, *The Law of Restitution* (1990).

9   Eg, McMeel, *Casebook on Restitution* (1996); Burrows and McKendrick, *Cases and Materials on the Law of Restitution* (1997); Grantham and Rickett, *Restitution: Commentary and Materials* (2001).

10 Eg, *Laundering and Tracing* (ed Birks, 1995); *Restitution and the Conflict of Laws* (ed Rose, 1995); *Restitution: Past, Present and Future* (eds Cornish, Nolan, O'Sullivan and Virgo, 1998); *Restitution and Banking Law* (ed Rose, 1998); *Lessons of the Swaps Litigation* (eds Birks and Rose, 2000); *Restitution and Insolvency* (ed Rose, 2000); *Restitution and Equity* (ed Birks and Rose, 2000); Birks, *The Foundations of Unjust Enrichment* (2002).

11 (1994).

12 (1997).

13 (1997).

14 (2000).

15 (2000).

16 (2002).

17 (2002).

18 www.law.cam.ac.uk/restitution

19 The experience in the United States has been very different. Until a recent mini-revival led, for example, by Professor Andrew Kull of Boston University, the subject had virtually disappeared as a separate law school course (albeit sometimes taught as part of a Remedies course) and rarely featured in law journals. See Langbein, 'The Later History of Restitution' in *Restitution: Past, Present and Future* (eds Cornish et al, 1998), pp 57, 60–62.

codified civil jurisdictions.[20] A particularly important aspect of this is the ongoing work of the 'Study Group on a European Civil Code' headed by Walter van Gerven. The proposed code would include unjust enrichment. Also worthy of close attention in this regard is the formidable work of Eric Clive in producing a draft code on the Scottish law of unjustified enrichment.[1] Views differ as to the purpose and consequent merits of such codes. A legislative European code would be highly controversial in England as being contrary to the common law tradition. A non-binding European code, on the model of the Restatements of the American Law Institute, would seem to offer a more beneficial, and less contentious, way forward.

(2) Quadrating restitution and unjust enrichment

As has been said above, the view taken in this book is that the law of restitution is the law concerned with reversing a defendant's unjust enrichment at the claimant's expense. That is, the view taken is that the law of restitution and the principle against unjust enrichment are two sides of the same coin. Following Peter Birks' early work,[2] the law of restitution may be regarded as having a central divide between unjust enrichment by subtraction (or autonomous unjust enrichment) and unjust enrichment by wrongdoing. This division is marked by the two meanings of 'at the expense of' the claimant; 'by subtraction from' and 'by a wrong to'. The divide is one between where unjust enrichment is the cause of action or event to which restitution responds and where a wrong is the cause of action or event to which restitution responds.

In recent years Peter Birks has favoured abandoning the automatic link – the quadration – between restitution and unjust enrichment.[3]

---

20 See, eg, Zimmermann and Du Plessis, 'Basic Features of the German Law of Unjustified Enrichment' [1994] RLR 14; Dickson, 'Unjust Enrichment Claims: a Comparative Overview' [1995] CLJ 100; Zimmermann, 'Unjustified Enrichment: The Modern Civilian Approach' (1995) 15 OJLS 403; Markesinis, Lorenz, Dannemann, *The German Law of Obligations* (1997), ch 9; *The Limits of Restitutionary Claims: A Comparative Analysis* (ed Swadling, 1997); Verse, 'Improvements and Enrichment: A Comparative Analysis' [1998] LR 85; Mitchell, 'Claims in Unjustified Enrichment to Recover Money Paid Pursuant to a Common Liability' (2001) 5 ELR 186; Krebs, *Restitution at the Crossroads: A Comparative Study* (2001); *Unjustified Enrichment: Key Issues in Comparative Perspective* (eds Johnston and Zimmermann, 2002); *Kleinwort Benson Ltd v Lincoln City Council* [1999] 2 AC 349.

1 *Draft Rules on Unjustified Enrichment and Commentary* published as an Appendix to Scottish Law Commission, *Judicial Abolition of the Error of Law Rule and its Aftermath*, Discussion Paper No 99 (1994).

2 Birks, at pp 26, 44–45.

3 'Misnomer' in *Restitution: Past, Present and Future* (eds Cornish, Nolan, O'Sullivan and Virgo, 1998), pp 1–29; 'Unjust Enrichment and Wrongful Enrichment' (2001) 79 Texas LR 1767. See similarly Lionel Smith, 'The Province of the Law of Restitution' (1992) 71 Can BR 671.

On his new approach, one should classify the law by cause of action (or event). This book should therefore be confined to the law concerning the cause of action (or event) of unjust enrichment and should be called the law of unjust enrichment. Restitution for wrongs should be excluded and seen as part of the different subject of wrongs.

While in the long-term it may be that Birks' new approach proves to be justified, it is submitted that at least at this stage in the law's development (and, in particular, before we can be sure of the scope of restitution for wrongs or of the change of position defence), it would be premature to abandon the quadration between the law of restitution and the principle against unjust enrichment.[4] That quadration approach has served the subject well. It has been the basis upon which the Anglo-American law of restitution has been developed since 1937;[5] and in England it is an approach, pioneered by Goff and Jones[6] and built on by Birks,[7] which has produced an astonishing advance in the understanding of the relevant law over the last twenty years or so. There is a danger that some of this ground will be lost if the quadration approach is abandoned. Moreover, while elegance or neatness of structure may be enhanced by such an abandonment, it is hard to see its practical advantages. This book therefore adopts the position of '[continuing] to sing to the old hymn-sheet which quadrates the principle against unjust enrichment and restitution'.[8]

It should be added here that in his excellent book, *The Principles of the Law of Restitution*[9] Graham Virgo also advocates abandoning the quadration approach. In his view, the law of restitution is founded not upon one principle but upon three different principles, namely the reversal of unjust enrichment, the prevention of a wrongdoer from profiting from his or her wrong, and the vindication of property rights with which the defendant has interfered.[10] But, with respect, Virgo's third principle cuts across the first because, crucially, property rights may be created to reverse an unjust enrichment.[11] The other essential difference between us is, again, in relation to whether one regards

---

4   For a detailed defence of the quadration approach, see Burrows, 'Quadrating Restitution and Unjust Enrichment: A Matter of Principle?' [2000] RLR 257. See also McInnes, 'Restitution, Unjust Enrichment and the Perfect Quadration Thesis' [1999] RLR 118.

5   This was the date of publication of the *Restatement of Restitution* by the American Law Institute. Professor Andrew Kull is the Reporter for the (Third) Restatement of Restitution (the second having been abandoned while in draft form): his work, which is ongoing, is expected to take several years to complete.

6   *The Law of Restitution* was first published in 1966; the 6th edition was published in 2002.

7   Especially in *An Introduction to the Law of Restitution* (1989).

8   [2000] RLR 257, 269.

9   (1999).

10   *The Principles of the Law of Restitution*, esp pp 6–17.

11   See below, pp 60–75.

restitution for wrongs as helpfully underpinned by the principle against unjust enrichment (Virgo thinks not). It should also be noted that if one recasts Virgo's principles, using Birks' distinction between events and responses, one can clearly see that Virgo's anti-quadration approach leads him to the diametrically opposite conclusion to Birks; that is, that the law of restitution is a useful category concerned with the response of restitution to various events (only one of which is unjust enrichment).

(3) Competing theories

Over the years, various theories have been advanced that have sought to challenge the relevance and importance of the principle against unjust enrichment. In giving an outline of the most important of these theories,[12] it is convenient to consider them under five sub-headings: (a) implied contract; (b) Stoljar's proprietary theory; (c) unjust sacrifice; (d) the views of Dietrich, Jackman and Jaffey; (e) Hedley's critique.

(a) Implied contract

The 'implied contract' theory was the main reason why, traditionally in England, restitution was pushed into the shade of contract and tort. According to this theory, most of the common law part of restitution[13] (which comprises the bulk of the subject) was satisfactorily explained as resting on an implied promise by the defendant to pay the claimant. This area of the law was therefore seen merely as an adjunct to the law of contract: hence the label 'quasi-contract'. By this theory, if the claimant paid the defendant £100 under a mistake of fact, his legal remedy to recover the £100 rested on the defendant's implied promise to him to pay it back. But this approach was fictional and said nothing about why the promise should be implied. By masking the underlying basis for recovery the theory obscured the important similarities and differences between the cases reversing benefits received. Moreover it was contrary to the rule of law for judges to

---

12 One should also note the views (albeit, in my opinion, profoundly mistaken!) of the distinguished Australian judge, Gummow J. While not developing an alternative theory (albeit that he seemed to favour 'unconscionability') he used his judgment in *Roxborough v Rothmans of Pall Mall Australia Ltd* [2001] HCA 68 to attack the 'theory' of unjust enrichment. See also Finn, 'Equitable Doctrine and Discretion in Remedies' in *Restitution, Past, Present and Future* (eds Cornish, Nolan, O'Sullivan and Virgo, 1998) pp 251–274, esp pp 251–253. For persuasive criticism of Gummow J's judgment see, eg, Beatson and Virgo, 'Contract, Unjust Enrichment and Unconscionability' (2002) 118 LQR 352; Birks, 'Failure of Consideration and its Place on the Map' (2002) 2 OUCLJ 1.

13 More specifically, that part of common law restitution concerned with the actions for money had and received to the claimant's use, money paid to the defendant's use, *quantum meruit* and *quantum valebat*.

reach decisions without properly explaining their reasoning. This is not to say that judges applying the implied contract theory reached results that were inconsistent with unjust enrichment reasoning. On the contrary, it is believed that, whatever language was overtly adopted, the courts were throughout applying the principle of unjust enrichment. It follows that the implicit rejection of the implied contract theory in *Lipkin Gorman*, and its explicit rejection in *Westdeutsche Landesbank Girozentrale v Islington London Borough Council*,[14] has not altered, and will not alter, decisions at a stroke.

Nevertheless the acceptance of the unjust enrichment principle can occasionally lead to differences in the results of cases. This is for three main reasons. First, the recognition of unjust enrichment in *Lipkin Gorman* was combined with the Lords' acceptance of a change of position defence which, at the defence stage, allows a more rigorous examination of the defendant's enrichment than was possible under the previous law. Moreover, with that important defence in place, the courts feel less constrained in pushing forward the scope of prima facie restitutionary liability. Secondly, recognising unjust enrichment has enabled the courts to see clearly that certain areas of the law (most obviously, the mistake of law bar and the general insistence that a failure of consideration be total)[15] represent restrictions on the pure principle of unjust enrichment that do not withstand close scrutiny. Thirdly, recognition of the principle brings together areas of the law (for example, restitution for common law and equitable wrongs) that might otherwise have appeared disparate and may reveal inconsistencies that require eradication. In the words of Maddaugh and McCamus, 'Giving a rational structure to the material ... serves to expose anomalies in the past treatment of restitutionary questions and facilitates the development of doctrine which will afford similar treatment to cases which can now more clearly be seen to be similar in material respects.'[16]

The weakness of the implied contract theory has long rendered it easy prey for those who support unjust enrichment. Of far more interest

---

14 [1996] AC 669. Lord Browne-Wilkinson, with whom Lords Slynn and Lloyd agreed said, at 710: 'The common law restitutionary claim is based not on implied contract but on unjust enrichment: in the circumstances the law imposes an obligation to repay rather than implying an entirely fictitious agreement to repay ... In my judgment, your Lordships should now unequivocally and finally reject the concept that the claim for moneys had and received is based on an implied contract. I would overrule *Sinclair v Brougham* [1914] AC 398 on this point.'

15 *Kleinwort Benson Ltd v Lincoln City Council* [1999] 2 AC 349 (rejection of the mistake of law bar); *Westdeutsche Landesbank Girozentrale v Islington London Borough Council* [1996] AC 669, *Goss v Chilcott* [1996] AC 788, *Stocznia Gdanska SA v Latvian Shipping Co* [1998] 1 WLR 574, *Guinness Mahon & Co v Kensington and Chelsea Royal London Borough Council* [1999] QB 215 (all casting doubt on, while not removing, the general need for a failure of consideration to be total).

16 *The Law of Restitution* (1990), p 14.

and difficulty are the modern challenges to the unjust enrichment approach that we shall now turn to consider.[17]

(b) Stoljar's proprietary theory

The late Professor Stoljar put forward his proprietary theory in *The Law of Quasi-Contract*.[18] He argued that much of the law that has traditionally been classified as quasi-contractual, for example that dealing with the recovery of money paid by mistake or under duress, is best viewed as giving the claimant a remedy because, without the claimant's consent, the defendant received property that at the time of receipt belonged to the claimant. In the first edition of his book Stoljar presented his theory as the antithesis of unjust enrichment thinking[19] but by the second edition he saw it rather as a more concrete clarification of what is meant by unjust enrichment. It is possible to argue that the theory is consistent with the common law on personal restitution from an indirect recipient of money that belonged to the claimant (ie, where the claimant's money has been paid to the defendant by a third party).[20] But as an explanation of the usual case of restitution, where the claimant has itself paid its money to the defendant, the theory is seriously deficient for in only a limited number of cases does the property in the money not pass to the payee. For example, it is only where a mistake is fundamental that it prevents property passing. Yet for restitution a mere causative mistake is sufficient. Moreover the proprietary theory clearly cannot explain the recovery of money on a total failure of consideration for it is trite law that property passes to the payee; Stoljar was therefore unsatisfactorily forced to see that area as some sort of off-shoot of contract. Nor can the proprietary theory explain the award of a *quantum meruit* for services rendered, necessitating yet a third Stoljar theory – all the time impairing the unity of the subject – namely that loss to the claimant not enrichment of the defendant is in issue in the services cases.[1]

---

17 See also Atiyah, *The Rise and Fall of Freedom of Contract* (1979), p 768. He does not appear to dispute the importance of the unjust enrichment idea but considers it misconceived to treat its study as a separate subject rather than running through several subjects, for example, property, tort, family law, company law, and, most importantly for his work, contract. This view is convincingly rejected by Birks 'Restitution and the Freedom of Contract' (1983) 36 CLP 141. For Atiyah's reply to Birks see Atiyah, *Essays on Contract* (1986), pp 47–52.

18 (2nd edn, 1989) pp 5–10, 113, 250. See also 'Unjust Enrichment and Unjust Sacrifice' (1987) 50 MLR 603.

19 (1st edn, 1964) p 6.

20 *The Law of Quasi-Contract* (2nd edn, 1989), pp 9–10, 250. See also (1987) 50 MLR 603; *International Encyclopedia of Comparative Law*, vol X chapter 17 (*Negotiorum Gestio*) pp 15–17. A somewhat similar approach to Stoljar's, albeit differing in its detail, is put forward by Watts, 'Restitution – a A Property Principle and a Services Principle' [1995] RLR 49.

(c) Unjust sacrifice

The above discussion leads directly on to a further theory put forward by scholars, including Stoljar, who argue that 'unjust sacrifice' is a better explanation than unjust enrichment of many of the so-called restitution cases, especially those involving services.[2] The argument is that one should not use an overinclusive concept of benefit and thereby artificially force into the unjust enrichment framework cases that are better viewed as concerning loss not benefit.

There are three main difficulties with this approach. The first is that it appears to adopt an unnaturally narrow view of benefit. So, for example, Muir thinks that for restitutionary purposes 'benefit' must mean 'a positive accretion to wealth'.[3] However, if the receipt of £100 is indisputably a benefit to the defendant, how can one deny that the claimant's payment of the defendant's debt of £100, which the defendant was about to pay, is not equally a benefit to the defendant? Muir finds himself having to distinguish standard uses of the term benefit so that only some count as restitutionary; for him unjust enrichment is concerned only with actions which *confer benefits* on defendants and not actions which are merely *of benefit* to defendants. He writes, '... situations in which an action is a benefit to the defendant without involving the conferral of a benefit upon him require ... a compensatory remedy rather than disgorgement'.[4] With respect, this is to take an underinclusive approach to benefit.

The second difficulty is that, without the element of *gain* inherent in the unjust enrichment principle, it is not easy to see the moral justification for legal intervention outside breach of promise or tortious or equitable wrongdoing. What is the moral force behind an autonomous principle of 'unjust sacrifice'? Why should a defendant be made to pay for loss suffered by the claimant unless he is causally responsible for it or has benefited from it? Muir is aware of this for he writes, 'It is in fact very difficult to explain why there is any obligation to reward or compensate an unjust sacrifice and the reality is probably that no one explanation is sufficient'.[5] By contrast the unjust enrichment principle has an intuitively appealing force for, leaving aside cases of wrongdoing, it principally rests on the claimant's loss

---

2   Apart from Stoljar, see, eg, Beatson, *The Use and Abuse of Unjust Enrichment* (1991), pp 21–44; Muir, 'Unjust Sacrifice and the Officious Intervener' in *Essays on Restitution* (ed Finn, 1990), pp 297–351; Hedley, 'Unjust Enrichment as the Basis of Restitution – An Overworked Concept' (1985) 5 Legal Studies 56, 60–63. Some of Hobhouse J's reasoning in *The Batis* [1990] 1 Lloyd's Rep 345, 353 could also be interpreted as supporting this approach.
3   *Essays on Restitution* (ed Finn, 1990), p 301.
4   Ibid.
5   Ibid at 308.

becoming the defendant's gain. This gives it a force lacking in a principle concentrating solely on the claimant's position.

The third difficulty is that the 'loss only' view appears, ironically, to ignore the importance of loss in the unjust enrichment principle. That principle dictates that the enrichment must be 'at the expense of' the claimant. As is explained later in this chapter, 'at the expense of' may mean wrongdoing by the defendant in which case there is no need for the claimant to suffer any loss. But for the bulk of restitution one is principally concerned with the claimant's loss becoming the defendant's gain.

(d) The views of Dietrich, Jackman and Jaffey

In recent books, Dietrich, Jackman and Jaffey have rejected the unjust enrichment principle by arguing that the law of restitution is best structured and categorised in ways that do not rely on that principle. Although their basic approach may therefore be regarded as somewhat similar, the suggested restructuring differs significantly from author to author and it is best to look at each of the three separately.

(i) Dietrich

Joachim Dietrich, in *Restitution – A New Perspective*,[6] argues that no part of the so-called law of restitution is best explained by the principle against unjust enrichment. Rather the law of restitution largely comprises four separate and unlinked categories. First, fault-based liability, akin to breach of contract and tort, where the primary emphasis is on compensating loss. This covers liability for losses incurred in anticipation of a contract or under an invalid or unenforceable contract. It also covers liability for the defendant's duress, undue influence or exploitation of weakness. Secondly, a principle of 'just sharing' which applies where parties, having a common interest, have not provided for particular events. It applies, for example, where contracts are frustrated, where domestic relationships have failed, or where the law imposes an obligation to make 'contribution' to another. Thirdly, a principle of 'justifiable sacrifice' which applies in cases where a person performs necessitous services. Fourthly, there is liability based on a 'fair outcome'. Here strict liability is imposed on an innocent person who has received money, services, or goods from another that was or were transferred, for example, by mistake or for a consideration that has failed.

---

6   (1998). For a helpful review, see Rotherham [2000] RLR 254.

A major difficulty with Dietrich's thesis is that his fourth category is very vague and seems artificial in rejecting an unjust enrichment explanation. Indeed the notion of a 'fair outcome' can be regarded as underpinning all law. Moreover, as regards his first three categories, to recognise unjust enrichment is not to deny that there could be situations where, outside breach of contract and tort, the law compensates loss. But, traditionally, the law has not required a person to compensate another's loss unless he or she has committed a civil wrong against the other person. The present law does not regard, for example, the breaking off of contractual negotiations or undue influence as the commission of a wrong triggering compensation. Even if the law were to move to that position, a less controversial first position is that (non-wrongful) unjust enrichments should be reversed.

(ii) Jackman

Ian Jackman in *The Varieties of Restitution*[7] argues that, apart from restitution for wrongs, there are two main principles in play in the law of restitution. Neither concerns the reversal of an unjust enrichment. They are first, the reversal of a non-voluntary transfer of money or another incontrovertible benefit; and, secondly, the fulfilment of non-contractual promises where benefits in kind have been voluntarily conferred on the promisor. The first category comprises, for example, the restitution of money paid by mistake or for a total failure of consideration or under duress or undue influence and restitution for necessitous intervention and compulsory discharge of another's liability. The second category covers, for example, the restitution of the value of benefits in kind conferred under invalid or discharged or anticipated contracts.

However, it is submitted that, while there is nothing inaccurate about Jackman's description of his first category, it rests, at a higher level of generality than Jackman explains it, on the reversal of unjust enrichment. That is, if one asks, 'why does the law reverse non-voluntary transfers of money or other incontrovertible benefits?' the answer is because such transfers unjustly enrich the defendant at the claimant's expense. Moreover, Jackman's second category is better viewed as linked to his first because benefits in kind, such as services, may benefit a particular defendant (for example, because it requested them) even though the benefit is not 'incontrovertible' like money. And once the common link of benefit is seen across these two categories, it naturally follows that, whether or not the law should move to enforcing non-

---

7   (1998). Jackman's book is critically analysed by Birks, 'Equity, Conscience and Unjust Enrichment' (1999) 23 Melbourne ULR 1.

contractual promises as Jackman advocates, the law should (and does) accept the (less controversial) position of reversing the value of unjust benefits in kind received at the claimant's expense.

(iii) Jaffey

Peter Jaffey in his complex book *The Nature and Scope of Restitution*[8] argues that, apart from restitution or disgorgement for wrongs, the so-called law of restitution comprises two main categories neither of which is best viewed as reversing unjust enrichment. A first category, which Jaffey argues should be treated as part of an expanded law of contract, comprises so-called restitutionary remedies in respect of a contract discharged for breach or frustration, pre-contractual liability, liability under ineffective contracts, necessitous intervention, discharge of another's liability, or use of another's property. In these situations, the repayment of money or a reasonable payment for, for example, work done rests on imposing liability for reliance loss under an actual contract (which has been discharged) or an 'imputed contract'. A second category, which Jaffey argues should be tied to the law of property, is restitution for vitiated transfers, such as transfers made by mistake, lack of authority or duress.

Two main comments on Jaffey's approach can be made. First, the second category relies on unconventional and difficult views of the law of property. With respect, the argument fails to defeat the claim that at a higher level of generality this category is underpinned by the principle against unjust enrichment. Secondly, the first category seems to rely on the fiction of an imputed contract. Like the rejected implied contract theory, it is defective in failing to explain why a contract to make reasonable payment or to repay is imputed. Jaffey purports to explain this by what he terms 'a reliance theory of contract', the heart of which is that contracts do not entail promises of performance but promises to be responsible for another's reliance. A more convincing explanation is that the requirement to make reasonable payment or to repay is triggered by the court's concern to reverse the defendant's unjust enrichment.

(e) Hedley's critique

Steve Hedley has been the most consistent, and fiercest, critic of the modern unjust enrichment school of thought. For over fifteen years, he has written articles[9] and, more recently, books[10] arguing that to

---

8   (2000). For a helpful review, see Barker [2001] RLR 232.
9   See, eg, Hedley, 'Unjust Enrichment as the Basis of Restitution – An Overworked Concept' (1985) 5 Legal Studies 56; 'Unjust Enrichment' [1995] CLJ 578; 'Restitution: Contract's Twin?' in *Failure of Contracts* (ed Rose, 1997), pp 247–274.
10 *Restitution: Its Division and Ordering* (2001). See also *A Critical Introduction to Restitution* (2001).

regard the law of restitution as underpinned by a principle against unjust enrichment is misguided and leads to undesirable results. While he has concentrated his attacks on exposing what he considers to be the flaws of the unjust enrichment approach, he has more recently turned from a 'deconstructionist' stance to sketching out an alternative thesis for at least some of the law of restitution. He suggests that the law that is called the law of restitution is residual and falls just outside the established categories of contract, tort and property. His tentative proposal is that most of that law can, and should, be returned to those categories.[11] He writes, '[R]ather than searching for a new principle outside "property", "contract" and "tort", we need to expand our understandings of those concepts to accommodate the neglected areas'.[12] So, for example, he argues that a properly-understood law of contract would absorb consensual transfers of value that are, at present, treated as triggering non-contractual liability (such as restitution in respect of anticipated or informal contracts).[13] Tracing and proprietary remedies should be seen simply as part of the law of property.[14] And he is sceptical about the merits, and scope for, 'restitutionary damages', rather than compensatory (or punitive) damages for torts and breach of contract.[15] In addition, Hedley offers particular alternative explanations for particular pockets of law, such as payment of another's debt and subrogation.[16]

Much of Hedley's work is thought-provoking, interesting and valuable, particularly his latest book, *A Critical Introduction to Restitution*,[17] in which he describes and analyses, applying various approaches, the main areas within what has traditionally been called the law of restitution. But it is arguable that some of his work adopts an approach to law that appears to reject, or to downplay, the importance of principles and principled reasoning. By so doing, it undermines the importance of like cases being treated alike.[18] Coherence in the law is lost if categories and ideas are unprincipled and if particular areas are analysed separately without the discipline of referring to underlying and wide-ranging principles that link different areas together. For

---

11 *Restitution: Its Division and Ordering* p vii, chapter 9.
12 Ibid at p 224.
13 Ibid, chs 1–3. See also *A Critical Introduction to Restitution*, chs 2–5, 8.
14 Ibid, chs 1–3. See also *A Critical Introduction to Restitution*, ch 9.
15 Ibid, chs 1–3. See also *A Critical Introduction to Restitution*, ch 10.
16 Ibid, chs 1–3. See also *A Critical Introduction to Restitution*, ch 11.
17 See similarly Hedley, 'Unjust Enrichment – A Middle Course?' (2002) 2 OUCLJ (forthcoming); Hedley, 'Restitution and Unjust Enrichment' in *The Law of Restitution* (eds Hedley and Halliwell, 2002), ch 1.
18 For my criticism of Hedley's view that the recognition of the principle against unjust enrichment serves no useful goal see Burrows, *Understanding the Law of Obligations* (1998), pp 99–108.

example, one would have thought that it was incumbent on Hedley to try to explain precisely what principles underpin the existing categories of contract, tort and property if their expansion is being seriously put forward as a preferable development to recognising a law of restitution based on unjust enrichment. It should also be observed that, whatever the position when Hedley's attacks on the unjust enrichment school of thought first started, the judicial tide of opinion has turned in favour of explicitly applying the unjust enrichment principle.

2. THE UNJUST ENRICHMENT PRINCIPLE AND ITS FOUR ESSENTIAL ELEMENTS

Stripping the unjust enrichment principle down into its component parts, there are four questions to be answered:[19]

(1)   has the defendant been *benefited* (ie enriched)?
(2)   was the enrichment *at the claimant's expense?*
(3)   was the enrichment *unjust?*
(4)   are there any *defences?*

If the first three questions are answered affirmatively and the fourth negatively the claimant will be entitled to restitution.

The law of restitution is therefore built around the four concepts of 'benefit', 'at the claimant's expense', 'unjust factors',[20] and 'defences'. Each of these fundamental building blocks in the theoretical structure of restitution will now be examined in turn with the aim of providing easy steps from the underlying principle of unjust enrichment to the black letter law. The restitutionary remedies by which the unjust enrichment is reversed will be considered later in this chapter.

---

19   That these are the four questions to be answered in a restitutionary claim was expressly approved by Lord Steyn in *Banque Financière de la Cité v Parc (Battersea Ltd)* [1999] 1 AC 221, 227. Similarly, albeit not identically, Lord Hoffmann, at 234, spoke of there being three questions: 'first, whether the defendant would be enriched at the plaintiff's expense; secondly, whether such enrichment would be unjust; and thirdly, whether there are nevertheless reasons of policy for denying a remedy'. In *Portman Building Society v Hamlyn Taylor Neck* [1998] 4 All ER 202, 206, Millett LJ referred to the first three questions but did not go on to mention defences. Writing extra-judicially, Sir Peter (now Lord) Millett has added a fifth question, 'What remedies are available to the plaintiff?': see, 'Restitution and Constructive Trusts' (1998) 114 LQR 399, 408.

20   This term coined by Birks may be inelegant but saves repeating the long-winded formulation that the question at issue is whether the enrichment at the claimant's expense is *unjust.* One could alternatively and more elegantly refer to 'the ground for restitution': but that phrase has to be used with care if one is not to confuse it with the general ground for restitution being unjust enrichment at the claimant's expense. In *Kleinwort Benson Ltd v Lincoln City Council* [1999] 2 AC 349 Lord Hope used the terminology of 'unjust factor'. See p 49 below.

(1) Benefit

Where the claimant seeks restitution of property retained by the defendant, establishing the latter's benefit is straightforward. There is no valuation involved. The benefit is established simply by showing that the defendant has the particular property claimed: the defendant cannot validly refuse to give up the property on the ground that it is of no value to him.

However, most of the law of restitution is concerned with the defendant having received monetary value. The valuation required means that the benefit issue is far from straightforward because, even if the defendant has been objectively benefited (ie a reasonable man could regard himself as benefited by what has occurred or, put another way, the claimant's 'performance' has a market value) he may validly argue that that benefit has been of no value to him. Birks has labelled this the argument of 'subjective devaluation'.[1]

In clarifying how to establish benefit, in the sense of value received, we shall first examine the notion of an objective benefit before going on to consider answers to the subjective devaluation objection.

(a) Objective benefit

Benefits may be positive or negative. The notion of an objective positive benefit is uncontroversial: a defendant is benefited positively and objectively where it receives something tangible – an end product – that can be realised in money. The receipt of money, land, or chattels or improvements to one's land or chattels are examples of positive objective benefits.

Benefits may also be negative. It may be their reluctance to accept this point that explains why some scholars have turned to the 'unjust sacrifice' view. A defendant is benefited negatively and objectively where saved an expense that it could reasonably have incurred. The receipt of services, the use of another's land or chattels, or the discharge by another of one's legal obligations are examples of negative objective benefits. Although these do not constitute realisable gains, they are equally valuable. To save someone an expense of £100 is as valuable to him as the receipt of a realisable gain of £100.

As it has been the subject of so much controversy, it is worth explaining in a little more detail that the crucial test for whether services are objectively beneficial is whether the services have been

---

1   Birks, pp 109–110. Birks' terminology was used by Hoffmann LJ in *Ministry of Defence v Ashman* (1993) 66 P & CR 195, 201.

received.[2] Prior to receipt no-one could reasonably consider services beneficial. No rational person would pay (after the event) for services that he (or a third party) did not receive.

So where the services comprise the cutting of hair or the removal of waste or the giving of a rock concert or the writing of a book or the building of a house the defendant can be said to be objectively benefited when, respectively, and subject to a *de minimis* threshold, locks of his hair are cut, items of waste are removed, the rock concert commences, the first part of the book is received and the first part of the building is erected.

This approach contrasts with that of both Birks and Beatson.

Birks appears to regard services as beneficial from the time when performance commences, irrespective of receipt, on the ground that the defendant has the benefit of the claimant's time and labour.[3] The making of a made-to-measure suit for the defendant would therefore be regarded as beneficial even if the defendant never receives the suit or any part of it. And in *Planché v Colburn*,[4] where the claimant was contracted to write a book for the defendant but had tendered no part of the book before the contract was terminated for the defendant's breach, Birks' approach means that the claimant's remedy can be viewed as restitutionary reversing an unjust *enrichment* conferred by him. This seems an unrealistic and overinclusive notion of benefit.

At the other end of the spectrum Beatson dismisses *pure* services – services that do not produce an end product – as non-beneficial.[5] In effect he recognises only positive benefits subject to the arguably irreconcilable exception of saving another's necessary expense. On this argument the inevitable but startling conclusion appears to be that having one's car cleaned or hair permed or attending a rock concert cannot be beneficial. Moreover, where services do produce end products (eg, the building of a house) Beatson must logically be concerned, as a matter of enrichment, only with the realisable value of the end product rather than valuing the services that have gone into producing that end product. One can agree with Beatson that the building of a house is beneficial only when the construction starts: but, with respect, the true explanation for this is that it is only then that the services are received, not that only positive benefits count. Another way of expressing this is to say that the distinction between

---

2   Cf Barker, 'Riddles, Remedies and Restitution: Quantifying Gain in Unjust Enrichment Law' [2001] CLP 255, 265–266.

3   Birks, pp 126–127, 129, 232, and 'In Defence of Free Acceptance' in *Essays on the Law of Restitution* (ed Burrows, 1991), pp 105, 140–141. See similarly Maddaugh and McCamus, *The Law of Restitution* (1990), pp 39, 411, 429–430.

4   (1831) 8 Bing 14.

5   *The Use and Abuse of Restitution* (1991), pp 21–44.

pure services and services producing an end product is helpful not because only an end product constitutes a benefit but rather because it assists in pinpointing when services are received and are hence objectively beneficial. Pure services are received when performance starts. Services designed to produce an end product are received when part of the end product is transferred.

(b) Subjective devaluation

It is not enough simply to establish objectively that the defendant has been benefited whether positively or negatively. For the law must be concerned with the issue of benefit in relation to the particular defendant. Just as when compensating loss in tort the law is concerned with whether, and to what extent, the particular claimant has suffered loss, so what is ultimately important in restitution is whether the particular defendant has been benefited. It is to cater for this individuality of value – to overcome subjective devaluation – that Birks[6] and Goff and Jones[7] have identified two main tests of benefit: (i) incontrovertible benefit and (ii) free acceptance.

(i) Incontrovertible benefit

The concept of an incontrovertible benefit has received the explicit approval of the judiciary in the cases of *BP Exploration Co (Libya) Ltd v Hunt (No 2)*,[8] per Robert Goff J, and *Proctor & Gamble Philippine Manufacturing Corpn v Peter Cremer GmbH*,[9] per Hirst J. The concept is easy to grasp. One is seeking to isolate objective benefits that are so obviously beneficial that any subjective devaluation argument by the defendant can be dismissed out of hand. Put another way, no reasonable man could seriously deny that he has been benefited. The receipt of money is the most obvious example of an incontrovertible benefit.

More problematic is the application of this concept other than to the receipt of money. It allows a narrower or wider approach depending on how far subjectivity is to be tolerated. Birks takes a narrow view so that, as regards positive benefits, only those that have

6   Birks, pp 114–124.
7   Goff and Jones, paras 1-017 to 1-032. See also Virgo, *The Principles of the Law of Restitution* (1999), pp 70–86.
8   [1979] 1 WLR 783. 'Incontrovertible benefit' was discussed at some length by the Supreme Court of Canada in *Peel (Regional Municipality) v Canada* (1993) 98 DLR (4th) 140 in dismissing a restitutionary claim where the claimant's payments had neither discharged a legal liability of the defendant nor saved it any inevitable or likely expense.
9   [1988] 3 All ER 843. Hirst J held that the buyers' payment of additional freight to the shipowners was not an incontrovertible benefit to the sellers. Although not discussed, there was in any event surely no unjust factor: the buyers chose to pay the additional freight in their own interests.

been *realised* – converted into money – are incontrovertibly beneficial.[10] In contrast Goff and Jones include *realisable* benefits so that the receipt of, or improvements to, chattels are treated as incontrovertibly beneficial even though the defendant has not sold them.[11] The receipt of, or improvement to, land is distinguished as not being realisable: ie, it cannot be sold so quickly and easily.

A problem with the narrow Birks view is that the date of trial is made crucial. Realisation of the benefit after trial is ignored and wily defendants may therefore be encouraged simply to wait before realising the benefit. Goff and Jones' view avoids this problem but has its own weakness because what is realisable cannot depend just on whether it is land or a chattel that is improved. The circumstances of the individual are also relevant. An improvement to a car is not realisable to the person who cannot afford to sell it and buy a suitable replacement. An improvement to land may be realisable to an owner who does not live on the land. In any event if it is clear that the defendant will not realise the benefit can it be said that he is so obviously benefited just because he *could* easily realise it? The best approach seems to be to take Birks' realised test but to add that the defendant will also be regarded as incontrovertibly benefited where the court regards it as reasonably certain that he will realise the positive benefit. Assessment of the defendant's future conduct is necessarily speculative but the courts commonly have to predict future conduct in assessing damages for loss, precisely to avoid the nonsense of rigidly cutting off loss at the date of trial.

Turning to negative benefits, the saving of legally or factually necessary expense is incontrovertibly beneficial. The defendant would inevitably have had to incur such expense and therefore cannot reasonably deny that it has been benefited by not having to do so. Discharging another's legal liability is therefore incontrovertibly beneficial,[12] as are services performed for a company which the company would have had to engage someone to carry out if the claimant had not done so.[13] Successful services performed by a necessitous intervener (at least if the defendant did not refuse consent) also fall within this test.[14]

A difficult question is whether even an incontrovertible benefit, whether positive or negative, can be subjectively devalued. Say, for example, the defendant's car is mistakenly improved by the claimant

---

10   Birks, pp 121–124.
11   Goff and Jones, para 1-023. For criticism of Goff and Jones' wider approach to 'incontrovertible benefit', see Spence, 'In Defence of Subjective Devaluation' (1998) 43 McGill LJ 889.
12   See, eg, most of the cases in chapter 8.
13   As in *Craven-Ellis v Canons Ltd* [1936] 2 KB 403.
14   Below, chapter 9.

and the improvements are realised to the tune of £1,000. The defendant would otherwise have made the same improvements to the car at a cost of £600. Can the defendant validly argue that he would in any event have made a profit of £400 so that the benefit to him of the claimant's work is merely the £600 saved expense and not the £1,000? Or say the claimant has discharged the defendant's liability but a relative of the defendant was about to discharge it gratuitously. Can the defendant validly argue that the claimant has conferred no benefit on him? Or say the claimant pays £1,000 to the defendant by mistake. As a result, a third party does not pay the defendant the £1,000 that she would otherwise have paid him. Is the claimant entitled to restitution of £1,000 from the defendant or can the defendant validly argue that he has not been enriched because he would have been £1,000 better off in any event?

In principle, there is much to be said for the view that the defendants in these situations should be able to devalue subjectively the incontrovertible benefits. To do so, would be to take full account of the particular defendant's own position.[15] Indeed, subjective devaluation can here be said to accord with a causal enquiry as to the defendant's own circumstances. However, the majority of the House of Lords in *Foskett v McKeown*[16] rejected the view that the claimants' proprietary rights following tracing should be limited because the defendant would have been so enriched irrespective of the enrichment traceably coming from the claimants' wealth. On the facts, the early premiums legitimately paid were sufficient to ensure the upkeep of the life insurance policy, under which the defendants were paid £1 million. Nevertheless, the claimants were held entitled to a share of the £1 million proportionate to the later premiums which, in breach of trust, had been paid using the claimants' trust money. Their Lordships, with respect erroneously, saw the issue in terms of the continuation of proprietary rights rather than unjust enrichment. But the important point here is that the decision may be interpreted as rejecting the (in principle, attractive) view that an incontrovertible benefit can be subjectively devalued.

(ii) Free acceptance

Goff and Jones, who coined the term 'free acceptance', explain the idea as follows: '... the defendant will not usually be regarded as having been benefited by the receipt of services or goods unless he has

---

15   For a possible example, see *Ministry of Defence v Ashman* (1993) 66 P & CR 195 (in an action for restitutionary damages for trespass, the benefit to the defendant was not the market rental value of the actual property but the expense saved of suitable local authority housing had any been available).

16   [2001] 1 AC 102.

accepted them (or, in the case of goods, retained them) with an opportunity of rejection and with actual or presumed knowledge that they were to be paid for. For convenience we shall refer to a person who has so acted as having *freely accepted* the services or goods in question.'[17] In Birks' words, 'A free acceptance occurs where a recipient knows that a benefit is being offered to him non-gratuitously and where he, having the opportunity to reject, elects to accept'.[18]

According to Birks' structure in *An Introduction to the Law of Restitution*, free acceptance is unique in showing both that there is an enrichment and that it is unjust. Confining ourselves here to its role as a test for enrichment[19] its crucial importance is that it is regarded as overcoming subjective devaluation.

In 'Free Acceptance and the Law of Restitution'[20] I argued that free acceptance was not clearly established by authority and was unwarranted in principle. As regards establishing benefit, free acceptance undermines respect for the individuality of values because it is a rational indication of nothing more than indifference to the objective benefit being rendered. Instead the most important test, outside incontrovertible benefit, is whether the defendant *bargained for* the objective benefit thereby manifesting a positive desire, and willingness to pay, for it. Moreover, once the defendant has bargained for services or goods, there is a rebuttable presumption that receipt of even a part of those services or goods is not merely objectively beneficial but is beneficial to the defendant. It was further argued that the authorities relied on by Birks and Goff and Jones are explicable on grounds other than free acceptance, usually failure of consideration as the unjust factor combined with the bargained-for principle of benefit.

This critical attack was taken even further by Garner.[1] He rejects not only free acceptance but also the presumption of benefit where the defendant receives part of what he bargained for. It would appear that for Garner only full requested performance or a subsequent completion by the defendant of a partly performed contract are sufficient indications of subjective benefit. Garner's view is that in deferring to freedom of choice one is trying to establish 'a willingness to pay for [a] benefit as a present priority',[2] and he firmly rejects any idea that subjective devaluation 'is to be disallowed on the grounds of moral obliquity'.[3]

---

17 Goff and Jones (1st edn, 1966), pp 30–31. See similarly Goff and Jones (6th edn, 2002), paras 1-019, 1-028.

18 Birks, p 265.

19 For criticism of free acceptance as an unjust factor, see below, pp 402–407.

20 (1988) 104 LQR 576.

1   'The Role of Subjective Benefit in the Law of Unjust Enrichment' (1990) 10 OJLS 42.

2   Ibid p 65.

3   Ibid p 50.

Beatson, too, rejects free acceptance but as part of his more fundamental objection, examined above, to regarding pure services as (even objectively) beneficial.

In his essay 'In Defence of Free Acceptance'[4] Birks responded to those criticisms. His central defence on the enrichment side is in fact a clarification of the way in which he sees free acceptance as working. He stresses that it was never intended that free acceptance should be taken to indicate that the recipient values the thing in question. Rather free acceptance is unconscientious conduct which debars the defendant from exercising his usual right to appeal to the subjective devaluation argument.[5] Birks also argues that free acceptance is clearly supported by several cases, most obviously statements by Brett MR in *Leigh v Dickeson*[6] and Bowen LJ in *Falcke v Scottish Imperial Insurance Co.*[7]

Two comments should be made on this defence. First, Birks' clarification tends to merge the 'injustice' and 'enrichment' sides of free acceptance with both ultimately resting on the same supposed injustice – the 'unconscientiousness' – of the free acceptor's conduct. Having said that one can, presumably, adopt free acceptance as an argument for enrichment while rejecting it as an unjust factor because two different roles are assigned to the unconscientiousness. On the one hand, as an unjust factor, it is seen as outweighing the risk-taking by the claimant. On the other hand, going to enrichment, it is seen as outweighing the defendant's normal right to appeal to subjective devaluation. It would seem that the balance of policies in the two roles need not be the same. Nevertheless my own intuitive inclination, that free acceptance is stronger as an argument for enrichment than as an unjust factor, may be more difficult to accommodate within Birks' clarified reasoning.

Secondly, while statements in the cases referred to by Birks[8] do support free acceptance their reasoning is not clearly directed to the benefit issue as opposed to the unjust factor. In any event, in most of them there was no difficulty in establishing the defendant's

---

4   In *Essays on the Law of Restitution* (ed Burrows, 1991), pp 105–146.
5   Virgo, *The Principles of the Law of Restitution* (1999), p 86 suggests that free acceptance, in relation to the issue of benefit, is a form of estoppel. 'By freely accepting the benefit the defendant is estopped from asserting that he or she did not value it.' The weakness of this suggestion, as Virgo himself goes on to recognise, is that estoppel requires a representation and reliance and with free acceptance there is no such positive conduct by the defendant.
6   (1884) 15 QBD 60, 64–65.
7   (1886) 34 Ch D 234, 249.
8   *Lamb v Bunce* (1815) 4 M & S 275; *Weatherby v Banham* (1832) 5 C & P 228; *Paynter v Williams* (1833) 1 Cr & M 810; *Alexander v Vane* (1836) 1 M & W 511; *Leigh v Dickeson* (1884) 15 QBD 60; *Falcke v Scottish Imperial Insurance Co* (1886) 34 Ch D 234; *Re Cleadon Trust Ltd* [1939] Ch 286. *Weatherby v Banham* is Birks' strongest case on the benefit issue but even that is susceptible to several explanations other than free acceptance.

benefit as the claimant had discharged the defendant's liability, which was to render an incontrovertible benefit. It is true that the clear statements in *Leigh v Dickeson* and *Falcke v Scottish Imperial Insurance Co* were in the context, respectively, of repairs to, and saving, another's property, which may not be incontrovertibly beneficial. But in both cases a restitutionary remedy was ultimately denied.

My opinion remains that, contrary to the views of Birks and Goff and Jones, free acceptance does not have a place in the law of restitution, albeit that the subjective benefit test of 'reprehensible seeking-out', suggested below, comes close to it as an argument for enrichment. On the other hand, Garner goes too far to the other extreme: that is, he advocates too subjective an approach so that a defendant's argument of subjective devaluation is given wider scope than seems justified. It is submitted that the best approach is to recognise that outside incontrovertible benefit, the most important test is the 'bargained-for' test. Beyond that there is at least[9] one further test – which can be accurately, if inelegantly, labelled the 'reprehensible seeking-out' test – which ought to be recognised in principle albeit that it cannot be said to be necessitated by the existing case law.

(iii) The 'bargained-for' test

A defendant can be regarded as negatively benefited where the claimant performs what the defendant bargained for. The reasoning behind this is that where the defendant has 'promised' to pay for a particular performance the outward appearance is that it regards that performance as beneficial or, put in an alternative way, that it has been saved expense that it would otherwise have been willing to incur. One could alternatively label this the 'promissory' or 'request' principle of benefit although, arguably, the last label does not as accurately indicate the defendant's willingness to pay as the term 'bargain'. On the other hand, the term 'contracted-for' would be too narrow in that the bargained-for test is intended to apply not only to discharged contracts but also to void, unenforceable, incomplete or anticipated contracts.

By similar reasoning, even if the defendant receives only part of what it bargained for, it can be rebuttably presumed that it regards itself as benefited by what it has received and that it has been saved part of the expense that it would otherwise have incurred. As has been mentioned above, Garner rejects this rebuttable presumption

---

9   This recognises that there may be other tests, not yet supported by authority, which can be argued for in terms of principle.

in part performance cases: he sees it as based 'on a fallacious jump in reasoning'.[10] But it is intended to reflect nothing more than the factual truth that in general – but clearly not always – a defendant who has bargained for a performance considers itself to be benefited by each part of that performance even if it has only agreed to pay on completion. For example, a three-quarters built house is generally a benefit to the owner who agreed to pay only on completion. The presumption is most obviously rebutted where the cost of completing performance would now be as much as the whole of the original bargain price for full performance.

While this bargained-for test of benefit has not received express unequivocal support in the cases it provides a ready explanation of the benefit in many decisions awarding restitution.[11]

It should not be thought that the contractual overtones of the 'bargained-for' terminology mean that the test confuses contract and restitution. Contractual remedies (ie, remedies for breach of contract) normally protect the claimant's expectation (or reliance) interest and are not geared simply to a benefit received from the claimant albeit that, in some situations (eg, where a claimant has fully performed his side of a contract) protection of the expectation interest and restitution may yield the same measure.

In principle the bargained-for test could be used irrespective of an objective benefit. Instead of overcoming the subjective *devaluation* argument it could be used to *overvalue* subjectively something that has no (or a lower) objective value.[12] But this idea of subjective overvaluation has not been applied in the case law. The outer parameters of the law of restitution have been fixed by the notion of an objective benefit qualified by downward subjectivity only.

(iv) The 'reprehensible seeking-out' test

The bargained-for test shows not only that the defendant wants the thing in question but also that he is willing to pay for it so that one can say that he has been saved an expense that he would otherwise have incurred. What about the defendant who has sought out the benefit, thereby clearly showing that he wants it, and yet his conduct shows equally clearly that he is unwilling to pay for it? Say, for example, services

---

10 'The Role of Subjective Benefit in the Law of Unjust Enrichment' (1990) 10 OJLS 42, 53, note 54.

11 See, eg, many of the cases discussed in chapter 10.

12 Cf Burrows, 'Free Acceptance and the Law of Restitution' (1988) 104 LQR 576, 587 note 47, 589 note 62, 590 note 68. See also Garner, 'The Role of Subjective Benefit in the Law of Unjust Enrichment' (1990) 10 OJLS 42, 43 and Virgo, *The Principles of the Law of Restitution* (1999) pp 86–88 who talk of 'subjective revaluation'.

are demanded by duress. If a man holds a pistol to a doctor's head and demands medical treatment, it is clear that he values that medical treatment and equally clear that he is unwilling to pay for it. Other obvious examples are stealing goods or intentionally using another's land without permission.

Although there are no authorities specifically on this point, the defendant in such situations must be regarded as benefited (by the objective value of the subject matter). He cannot rationally say that he was indifferent to receiving the thing: and he cannot be allowed to raise the argument 'I was not willing to pay' because his reprehensible conduct shows a disregard for the bargaining process (ie, the market system).[13]

Clearly this test runs close to free acceptance. But it is crucially distinct because in requiring a 'seeking-out' of the benefit rather than a 'standing-by' it overcomes the indifference argument. Moreover this test is a test of benefit only. It is not intended to establish that the enrichment is unjust.

(c) Separation of the benefit and injustice enquiries

The benefit issue can be and, for the sake of clarity, should be, cleanly isolated from the question of whether the enrichment is unjust. That is, the tests of benefit set out above are designed to fit with various unjust factors. One possible exception is the incontrovertible benefit of discharging another's debt which has traditionally been linked solely to the unjust factor of legal compulsion (and possibly necessity) on the basis that only such a compulsory payment automatically effects a discharge. That traditional picture is criticised in chapter 8, where it is argued that any payment made to discharge another's debt and accepted by the payee as so doing should operate to discharge it automatically irrespective of the debtor's consent. Payments made by, for example, mistake or duress should therefore trigger restitution from the discharged debtor just as much as legal compulsion (or necessity).

(2) At the expense of the claimant

(a) Two meanings: 'subtraction from' and 'wrong to'

It was *the* major theme of Birks' earlier work that 'at the expense of the claimant' ambiguously conceals two different ideas in the law of

---

13 It is arguable that the 'seeking-out' alone is sufficient to outweigh the subjective devaluation objection. But as the argument for this test is one of principle, without direct support from the case law, it has been considered preferable to focus on the stronger case where the conduct is also reprehensible.

restitution.[14] The first, and most natural meaning, is that the defendant's gain has come from the claimant's wealth: in Birks' terminology there has been a 'subtraction from' the claimant. The second, and less obvious meaning, is that the defendant's gain has been acquired by committing a wrong against the claimant.[15] These two meanings of 'at the expense of' mark an important divide in the law of restitution between unjust enrichment by subtraction (or autonomous unjust enrichment), where no wrong has to be established, and unjust enrichment by wrongdoing (or dependent unjust enrichment), where the defendant's wrong has to be established and restitution is merely one of several possible remedial responses to that wrong (alongside, for example, compensation or injunctive relief). Put another way, the divide is between, on the one hand, where unjust enrichment is the cause of action or event to which restitution responds and, on the other hand, where a wrong is the cause of action or event to which restitution responds.

As we have seen,[16] in Birks' later work he has gone on to argue that the above divide is so fundamental that the two sides should be seen as two separate subjects rather than as two parts of one subject. Unjust enrichment and restitution do not quadrate. The law of unjust enrichment is about the law on the cause of action of unjust enrichment; restitution for wrongs belongs with the law of wrongs. This book, however, adheres to the quadration approach so that the law of restitution is seen as embracing both restitution for the cause of action of unjust enrichment and restitution for wrongs.

What then is the exact importance of the division between unjust enrichment by subtraction and restitution for wrongs? Naturally as a matter of classification and exposition it is helpful to separate those cases where restitution is given for a wrong from those where restitution is given even though no wrong is established. But is this any more important than collecting in one chapter all cases concerned with restitution for mistake and in another restitution for duress and in another restitution for failure of consideration? In other words, are there particular features of restitution for wrongs, apart from the fact that the wrong is the cause of action with the consequence that non-restitutionary remedies can flow, that differentiate it from the rest of unjust enrichment?

First, Birks has argued that bars to actions for the wrong will extend to barring actions for restitution for the wrong but not necessarily to

---

14 Birks, pp 23–24, 40–44, 313–315.
15 This distinction was recognised, and Birks' terminology utilised, by the Court of Appeal in *Halifax Building Society v Thomas* [1996] Ch 217.
16 See above, pp 5–6.

bar actions for unjust enrichment by subtraction.[17] But this argument requires qualification. It is undoubtedly true that some legal rules are expressed as applying to particular wrongs. Present day examples are limitation periods, procedural rules for serving a claim form out of the jurisdiction under the Civil Procedure Rules, Rule 6.20, choice of law rules in the conflict of laws, and immunities against some tort actions in trade disputes. Important historical examples were the *actio personalis* bar to torts, Crown immunity for tort actions, and the inability to prove for unliquidated tort claims on bankruptcy. As is clear from this list, the different rules primarily concern bars to an action but not exclusively so and, to that extent, Birks' sole concentration on bars is too narrow. However the crucial point is that, applying a purposive construction, it is not necessarily the case that the rules (even though expressed as applying to wrongs) are applicable to *all* remedies, including restitution, for the particular wrong. For example, while it is indisputable that all the rules expressed as applying to a tort action are meant to apply to actions for compensatory damages for a tort, it is not clear – and must be a question for the policy of the rule – whether the language of tort actions is meant to include restitution for a tort. As one would in any event want to examine whether particular rules expressed as applying to wrongs ought, as a matter of policy, to be extended to particular claims in unjust enrichment by subtraction,[18] the difference here between restitution for wrongs and unjust enrichment by subtraction may be marginal. Having said that, there is obviously a difference in starting points and this may lead to a difference in result: unless the policies are clear the courts are unlikely to be moved by pleas to disapply to restitution for a wrong a rule expressed as applying to a wrong or to extend to unjust enrichment by subtraction a rule expressed as applying to a wrong.

A second argument for regarding restitution for wrongs as significantly different from unjust enrichment by subtraction concerns the measure of restitution.[19] In relation to restitution for wrongs it is clear that the claimant can recover more than his or her loss. In many cases, this will be the primary reason why the claimant seeks restitution rather than the standard remedy of compensation. Indeed the claimant may have suffered no loss at all. In contrast, in unjust enrichment by subtraction the claimant must establish that the defendant's gain has

---

17 Birks, pp 346–351. See similarly Virgo, *The Principles of the Law of Restitution* (1998), pp 447–448.
18 Birks, pp 350–351.
19 Birks, pp 351–355. See similarly Lionel Smith's influential view that there are two different measures which he labels 'restitution' (where there is a need for subtraction from the claimant) and 'disgorgement' (where there is no such requirement): 'The Province of the Law of Restitution' [1992] CBR 672.

come from the claimant's wealth. And normally there will be an equivalence or correspondence between the gain to the defendant and the loss to the claimant; that is, there will be an equivalent or corresponding plus and minus.

However, this argument again requires qualification. This is because it has now become clear that it is not a necessary requirement of unjust enrichment by subtraction that there is an equivalence or correspondence of loss and gain, albeit that that will normally be the case.[20] For example, through the operation of tracing, it appears that the claimant may have a personal restitutionary remedy reversing the value received by a defendant (eg, the value of shares) even though that value exceeds the loss of money (used to buy the shares) which the claimant initially suffered as a result of a third party's breach of fiduciary duty of which the claimant had no knowledge. Similarly, in respect of restitution for services the valuation of the defendant's enrichment recoverable by a *quantum meruit* may exceed any loss suffered by the claimant; for example, where the defendant who mistakenly carries out repairs to the claimant's car is not a professional car-repairer and, during the time carrying out the repairs, would not otherwise have been gainfully employed. The same may be said in respect of a defendant who, in the absence of the claimant, uses the claimant's bicycle for a week and then returns it undamaged: the defendant's enrichment, recoverable by a *quantum valebat,* may exceed any loss suffered by the claimant. Again, in an action for money had and received to recover a mistaken payment, the interest payable representing the defendant's use of the money may exceed any loss of use of the money that the claimant would have had. Furthermore, in rejecting a 'passing on' defence, the Court of Appeal in *Kleinwort Benson Ltd v Birmingham City Council*[1] rejected the argument that in reversing an unjust enrichment one was to an extent compensating for loss so that there would be no claim where, subsequent to the receipt of the enrichment, the loss had been avoided or passed on. This decision again indicates that an equivalence or correspondence of loss and gain is not required. Indeed, in the light of these examples, one can go further to argue that one does not need *any loss* to the claimant, to establish the

---

20   This is to be contrasted with the position in Canada where, in the classic formulation of unjust enrichment, the courts have insisted on a corresponding deprivation to the claimant: see, eg *Pettkus v Becker* (1980) 117 DLR (3d) 257. For a principled argument that the claimant should not be able to recover more than his or her loss, see McInnes, '"At the Plaintiff's Expense": Quantifying Restitutionary Relief' [1998] CLJ 472.

1   [1997] QB 380. See also *Commissioner of State Revenue v Royal Insurance Australia Ltd* (1994) 126 ALR 1, High Ct of Australia. See below pp 591–596.

cause of action in unjust enrichment provided that the defendant's enrichment came from (and in that weak sense was 'subtracted from') the claimant's wealth.[2]

A further reason for caution in treating the measure of restitution as a distinguishing feature of restitution for wrongs is that one can anticipate that, in deciding on how much profit should be taken from a wrongdoer, through an account of profits or restitutionary damages, a relevant consideration may be how far this exceeds the loss to the claimant. That is, it is possible that the courts may feel most comfortable stripping gains from a wrong where they are not out of all proportion to the claimant's loss.

There is a third distinguishing feature in cases where another's conduct, for example, misrepresentation, duress, or undue influence, induces the claimant to render a benefit. Irrespective of agency, restitution in unjust enrichment by subtraction may be available against the party who receives the benefit, even if not the person whose conduct induced it, whereas restitution for a wrong is available only against the wrongdoer himself. For example, if X induces C to give money to D by a fraudulent misrepresentation or duress, it appears that D will be prima facie liable in unjust enrichment by subtraction.[3] But there can be no restitution awarded against D for a wrong: the only action for a wrong (the tort of deceit or intimidation) lies against X, the wrongdoer, who has not been enriched.

The conclusion to be reached is that the force of the division between unjust enrichment by subtraction and restitution for wrongs essentially rests on the fact that different causes of action are involved. In other words, the root significance rests on the difference between not-wrongs and wrongs. In many cases – but not all – a further distinguishing feature will be the measure of restitution; and in a few cases there will be distinguishing features in terms of the operation of bars (or particular rules), and against whom restitution can be claimed.

At a deeper level, the distinction between unjust enrichment by subtraction and restitution for wrongs reflects different moral ideas underpinning the law of restitution.[4] Restitution for wrongs rests on the notion that 'no man shall profit from his own wrong'. Unjust

---

2 One might even argue that the minimum requirement is that the enrichment came from the claimant. But this seems misleading because if C transfers X's property to D, D is surely enriched at X's expense not C's expense. The enrichment, while coming from C, came from X's, not C's, wealth.

3 See Friedmann, 'Valid, Voidable, Qualified, and Non-Existing Obligations: An Alterntaive Perspective on the Law of Restitution' in *Essays on the Law of Restitution* (ed Burrows), p 277; and below, p 251, n 16.

4 Cf Barker, 'Unjust Enrichment: Containing the Beast' (1995) OLJS 457, 468–474; Weinrib, 'Restitutionary Damages as Corrective Justice' (2000) 1 Theoretical Inquiries in Law 1.

enrichment by subtraction principally reflects the idea of restoring the status quo for both claimant and defendant to the extent that the claimant's loss has unjustifiably become the defendant's gain. The moral force of this was neatly explained, albeit in the different context of damages for breach of contract, by Fuller and Perdue in their classic article 'The Reliance Interest in Contract Damages'.[5] 'If, following Aristotle, we regard the purpose of justice as the maintenance of an equilibrium of goods among members of society, the restitution interest presents twice as strong a claim to judicial intervention as the reliance interest, since if A not only causes B to lose one unit but appropriates that unit to himself, the resulting discrepancy between A and B is not one unit but two.'

But it is important to appreciate that there is a different, more controversial, underpinning of unjust enrichment by subtraction where, in the less common case, there is no correlation between the claimant's loss and the defendant's gain. Here the notion underpinning unjust enrichment appears to be that the owner of wealth is entitled to the product of that wealth.

Finally, while the division of the subject in line with Birks' two meanings of 'at the expense of' has won widespread acceptance and underpins this book, it has not won the full support of several leading commentators.[6] For example, Jack Beatson, in an important essay entitled 'The Nature of Waiver of Tort', raises several objections.[7] His principal argument is that, while he regards the 'waiver of tort' cases as involving the wrongful acquisition of a benefit, he treats that as an independent, rather than a parasitic, ground of restitution. On his view it is therefore incorrect to describe any 'waiver of tort' case as awarding restitution for a tort. In other words, wrongdoing in a tort context is seen as inherent in, but not synonymous with, the tort. The main difficulty with this is that no definition of wrongdoing

5   (1936–37) 46 Yale LJ 52, 56. See also McInnes, '"At the Plaintiff's Expense": Quantifying Restitutionary Relief' [1998] CLJ 472; 'Unjust enrichment: A Reply to Professor Weinrib' [2000] RLR 29.

6   In addition to the commentators referred to below, see Cane, 'Exceptional Measures of Damages: A Search for Principles' in *Wrongs and Remedies in the Twenty-First Century* (ed Birks, 1996), pp 301, 312–323.

7   *The Use and Abuse of Unjust Enrichment* (1991), pp 206–243, esp 208–210, 230–235, 242–243. For explanation of the term 'waiver of tort', see below, chapter 14. See similarly Friedmann, 'Restitution of Benefits Obtained Through the Appropriation of Property or the Commission of a Wrong' (1980) 80 Col LR 504; and, particularly importantly, 'Restitution for Wrongs: The Basis of Liability' in *Restitution: Past, Present and Future* (ed Cornish et al, 1998). In the latter, Friedmann argues not merely that restitution for a wrong can commonly be alternatively analysed as (autonomous) unjust enrichment – which this book accepts – but also that, even where the wrong is the basis for the restitution, the restitutionary claim is independent and not parasitic. See also Hedley, 'The Myth of Waiver of Tort' (1984) 100 LQR 653.

is offered. It is not clear what is meant by a wrong in tort cases if it is not the tort itself. If what is meant is reprehensible conduct it may be doubted whether a grouping of restitutionary cases based on that idea would aid clarity or understanding.

A possible alternative interpretation of Beatson's argument is that he is saying that every example of restitution for wrongs can in fact be analysed as an example of unjust enrichment by subtraction. Hence there is never a need to rely on the idea of restitution for wrongs. This is particularly attractive once one accepts (as this book does)[8] Beatson's view that 'subtraction' does not require a correlation of loss and gain but includes taking, selling or using the claimant's property. But this interpretation conflicts with Beatson's emphasis on wrongdoing; and in any event there are several cases on restitution for wrongs[9] where there is no realistic alternative analysis in terms of unjust enrichment by subtraction.

(b) Benefits conferred by third parties

Can a claimant (C) be entitled to restitution where the benefit has been rendered on the defendant (D) by a third party (X)?[10] One might say that this is a question of whether there is a privity element built into the unjust enrichment principle although, in order to avoid any conceivable confusion with the contractual doctrine of privity, it seems preferable to ask whether only the *direct provider* of a benefit is entitled to restitution.[11] In terms of the essential elements of the unjust enrichment principle, the issue is whether the defendant's benefit can be *at the claimant's expense* where rendered by a third party. It should be stressed that we are not here analysing defences, in particular the bona fide purchase defence. Our concern is with the prior issue of prima facie liability.

It is immediately apparent that restitution for wrongs is not so restricted. Gains wrongfully made by the defendant that are required to be disgorged (for example, unauthorised gains made in breach of

---

8   See above, pp 28–29.
9   Eg, *Reading v A-G* [1951] AC 507; *A-G v Blake* [2001] 1 AC 268.
10 Goff and Jones, paras 1-046 to 1-049; Birks, pp 133–139; Palmer, *The Law of Restitution* (1978), vol IV chapter 21; Virgo, *The Principles of the Law of Restitution* (1999), pp 106–113.
11 This can also be looked at from the recipient's perspective so that the question is whether only a *direct recipient* is liable to restitution. Birks and Mitchell, 'Unjust Enrichment' in *English Private Law* (ed Birks, 2000), paras 15.22–15.35 (and see also Birks, '"At the Expense of the Claimant" : Direct and Indirect Enrichment in English Law' in *Unjustified Enrichment: Key Issues in Comparative Perspective* (eds Johnston and Zimmermann, 2002), pp 37–75) phrase the question as being whether the claimant can 'leapfrog' the immediate enrichee. It should be noted that they include within their discussion the rather different question of whether a party to a contract may claim restitution from the third party beneficiary of the contract: see below, pp 347–350.

fiduciary duty) are commonly conferred by a third party. It is the wrong that creates the necessary link between C and D: ie, the wrong to C establishes that D's gain was at C's expense. The third party issue therefore relates purely to unjust enrichment by subtraction.

Central examples of the question being asked are therefore as follows. Say C confers a benefit on X who, as a consequence, transfers a benefit (for example, a gift) to D: there is an autonomous unjust factor operating between C and X (for example, mistake, duress, or failure of consideration): does C have a restitutionary remedy against D? Or say X mistakenly pays D when he intended to pay C (to whom, for example, he owes money or on whom he intended to confer a gift): is C entitled to restitution from D?

As a matter of language one could say that D has been unjustly enriched at the expense of C. There is a causal link between the unjust factor and D's gain; and D's gain has been subtracted from C (ie, D's gain is caused by the subtraction from C).

But as a general rule, subject to wide-ranging exceptions, the claimant is not entitled to the restitution of benefits conferred by a third party rather than by himself. In the above examples D's benefit is generally regarded as being at the expense of X not C.

Before looking at the exceptions, we should ask whether the general rule – restricting restitution (for unjust enrichment by subtraction) to the direct provider of a benefit – is justified. There are several arguments to consider.

First, it might be thought that otherwise D would be exposed to double liability in restitution. That is, if his gain is treated as being at the expense of both C and X, he might be bound to pay twice over subject, of course, to both C and X being able to establish the other necessary criteria for restitution, especially the unjust factor. However, that problem could perhaps be solved by a rule barring double liability, without going to the lengths of denying C a remedy altogether.[12] Such a rule would presumably favour the party (C or X) who first obtained judgment or reached settlement with D. In any event one can strongly argue that the denial of double liability is already catered for on the grounds that D's repayment to either X or C would entitle him to a change of position defence (construing that defence broadly) against a restitutionary claim by the other party. It is only if one gives change of position a narrow meaning, requiring detrimental reliance by D on the benefit being his to keep, that it would not cover D satisfying a restitutionary claim by X or C.

---

12 For such a solution to the analogous problem of contractual claims by both the promisee and a third party, see Contracts (Rights of Third Parties) Act 1999, s 5.

Secondly, it might be argued that it is theoretically impossible for D's gain to be at the expense of *both* C and X. If D's gain is £100, C and X cannot be said to have suffered separate subtractions of £100 because that would produce an overall loss of £200 whereas D's gain is only £100. As Lionel Smith writes, '... subtraction is a "zero-sum game". The sum of losses and gains must be zero. If somebody has been enriched by subtraction in the amount of £100, then there must be one or more people who have suffered expenses which total £100; not a penny more, not a penny less'.[13] From that starting point it would then follow that normally only X could sue D because, of the two competing claims of C and X to be the single loss-sufferer, it is self-evidently usually X, as the loss-sufferer most closely connected to D's gain, that should win.

However it seems that that approach is not an inevitable theoretical consequence of the 'at the expense of' concept. Certainly C and X, in the above example, cannot both have restitution of £100. But there is no theoretical reason why they cannot each be regarded as suffering *the same subtraction* of £100 with any competition between them being determined if and when it arises. Most obviously there would be no conceivable restitutionary competition if only C could establish an unjust factor.

Thirdly, it can be argued that the causal link between the subtraction from C and D's gain is too indirect where X has conferred the benefit on D. Indeed where X has first received the benefit and then transferred it to D, one can very naturally say that X has broken the chain of causation between C and D. As against that it can be said that legal causation is ultimately a malleable policy concept and may represent more of a legal conclusion than an explanation.

Fourthly, it may be thought that C's obvious legal claim lies against X and not D: and if C has no legal claim against X for his loss that is for good reason. But this may be more of an assertion than a rational explanation. Why should C not have actions against both X and D, given that his action against X may fail and that double recovery may be directly prevented in other ways (for example, by requiring C to account to X or D for any double recovery)? After all, even if C has a good legal claim against X, X may have disappeared or become insolvent.

Finally, it may be argued that restricting restitution to the direct provider prevents too much restitution. Clearly any new expansion of the ambit of restitution increases the number of claims and renders

---

13 'Three-Party Restitution: A Critique of Birks' Theory of Interceptive Subtraction' (1991) OJLS 481, 483.

the receipts of benefits less secure than under the previous law. But especially now that change of position has been recognised as a defence it seems that the fear of too much restitution is already adequately guarded against without the need to restrict restitution to direct providers only.

Putting on one side the last argument, the above arguments for and against restricting restitution in unjust enrichment by subtraction to direct providers are finely balanced. The only obvious conclusion to be reached is that there is no overwhelming case against that restriction and that one can readily understand the courts' preference for developing exceptions rather than departing from the general restriction. However, as is explained below, the present range of exceptions does depend on the drawing of some fine distinctions and this may be thought unsatisfactory.[14]

Turning now to the exceptions to restitution in unjust enrichment by subtraction being confined to direct providers, there appear to be seven main exceptions or possible exceptions. To do justice to Birks' theory of 'interceptive subtraction'[15] and to Lionel Smith's attack on that theory in his article 'Three-Party Restitution: A Critique of Birks' Theory of Interceptive Subtraction'[16] it is necessary to deal with several of these exceptions in some depth.

(i) Title and tracing

A defendant's enrichment is at the claimant's expense where it was the claimant's property, or its traceable substitute, that was transferred by the third party to the defendant.

Where C, not X, owned[17] the property prior to D's receipt, the rationale for this 'exception' is obvious. Only C can establish that D's gain was subtracted from his (C's) wealth. So if X has taken C's money and paid it to D, D's enrichment is at C's expense not at X's expense. This also explains part of the decision in *Rowland v Divall*.[18] The defendant sold the claimant a car that belonged to someone else. The claimant used the car for several months. The claimant was able to terminate the contract and recover the purchase money paid on

---

14 Andrew Tettenborn has interestingly argued that a principled approach to this issue is that there should be no restitution where a defendant has lawfully received the benefit from a third party: 'Lawful Receipt – A Justifying Factor' [1997] RLR 1. But in going beyond the bona fide purchase defence (see chapter 15 below) this idea seems to go too far; and it is not clear that it can explain several of the cases including, eg, *Lipkin Gorman v Karpnale Ltd* [1991] 2 AC 548.

15 Birks, pp 133–139.

16 (1991) OJLS 481.

17 Ownership includes legal title (which itself may include those who have possessory title, eg, a bailee) and equitable title.

18 [1923] 2 KB 500.

the ground of total failure of consideration without allowing the defendant counter-restitution for the use of the car that he had enjoyed. This aspect of the decision is justified because the enrichment comprising use of the car was not at the expense of the defendant but rather at the expense of the car's true owner.

More complex is where the claimant's property has been substituted by other property. Here the tracing rules (along with the rules of title) operate to enable the claimant to establish that the property received by the defendant came, by transactional links, from the claimant's property: that is, that the gain to the defendant is at the claimant's expense. We examine tracing in chapter 2 below. The important point to emphasise here is that it is a process that goes to the 'at the claimant's expense' inquiry and may enable a claimant to establish unjust enrichment by subtraction even though the defendant's enrichment was transferred by a third party.

(ii) Agency

If X is the agent of D in receiving a benefit from C, C may be able to recover from D. This is because the agency relationship between X and D means that X's gain is treated as D's gain. Similarly, if X is C's agent in rendering a benefit to D, C may be able to recover from D. Agency is fully considered in chapter 16.

(iii) Some subrogation rights

It will be seen in the next chapter that subrogation rights of indemnity insurers and the subrogation rights of creditors of a business carried on by trustees are exceptions to restitution being confined to direct providers only.

(iv) 'Usurpation of office' and related cases

When the claimant is entitled to certain fees or rents from a third party but the defendant, by usurping the claimant's office or position, collects the fees or rents from the third party for his own benefit, the claimant has for long been held entitled to an action for money had and received against the defendant.[19]

---

19 See, eg, *Arris and Arris v Stukely* (1677) 2 Mod Rep 260; *Jacob v Allen* (1703) 1 Salk 27; *Asher v Wallis* (1707) 11 Mod Rep 146; *Boyter v Dodsworth* (1796) 6 Term Rep 681; *King v Alston* (1848) 12 QB 971. Probably analogous are those rare situations where a claimant, who has recovered damages (or another monetary remedy), is bound to account to a person who has a better entitlement to some or all of that money: eg, *The Winkfield* [1902] P 42, 55; *Hepburn v A Tomlinson (Hauliers) Ltd* [1966] AC 451; *The Albazero* [1977] AC 774, 846. See McMeel, 'Complex Entitlements: The *Albazero* Principle and Restitution' [1999] RLR 21. For discussion of the unjust factor, see below, p 206.

One might think that the obvious explanation for this 'exception' is that the usurpation constitutes a wrong so that the defendant's gain is at the claimant's expense in the sense that he has committed a wrong against the claimant. This is supported by the Irish case of *Lawlor v Alton*.[20] The defendant had usurped the office of surgeon to a county infirmary. Eleven months later he was successfully ousted from the office by his rival candidate for the job on the grounds that he had been unqualified for it. The claimant was held entitled to compensatory damages for the salary he should have had as surgeon during those 11 months.

The difficulty is that usurpation of office has not traditionally been classified as a tort in English law and the emphasis has been on the action for money had and received, restricting the claimant to the defendant's gain,[1] not compensatory damages. Certainly this emphasis cannot be explained on the ground that usurpation of office is a 'restitution-yielding wrong' for it is clear that the claimant is not entitled to restitution in excess of his loss. For example, in *Boyter v Dodsworth*[2] the defendant had usurped the claimant's office of sexton of Salisbury Cathedral and had received tips from showing people round the church. The claimant's action for money had and received failed because it was not established that the fees received by the defendant constituted a loss to the claimant. Lawrence J said, 'The argument in support of the rule proceeds on a supposition that the plaintiff would have received the money that the defendant has received: but it depends entirely on the behaviour and civility of the person showing the church, and *non constat* that anything would have been paid to the plaintiff, if he had shown it.'[3]

Is there, therefore, an alternative analysis in unjust enrichment by subtraction whereby D's gain can be said to be at C's expense even though the fees or rent have been paid by X and even though none of the above three exceptions is in play?

For Birks, this area is a prime example of 'interceptive subtraction'. What he means by that concept is that, even though conferred by a third party, a claimant loses by the defendant's gain where 'the wealth in question would certainly have arrived in the claimant if it had not been intercepted by the defendant en route from the third party'.[4] And in the usurpation cases Birks argues that one can be sure that the claimant would have received the money if the defendant had not

---

20   (1873) IR 8 CL 160.
1   See esp *King v Alston* (1848) 12 QB 971.
2   (1796) 6 Term Rep 681.
3   Ibid at 683.
4   Birks, pp 133–134.

done so because 'the plaintiff had a claim for it against the third party'.[5]

Lionel Smith has subjected Birks' 'interceptive subtraction' theory to a wide-ranging attack on the grounds that it is not necessitated by the authorities and produces what he sees as the theoretical impossibility of a single gain being at the expense of more than one claimant. Nevertheless, on his view, the usurpation of office and similar cases are justified because they happen to be exceptional cases where X's liability to C is discharged by X's payment to D. Smith writes, 'The acts of a de facto holder of an office are binding on the true holder.'[6] C, but not X, is worse off by X's payment. D's gain is therefore at C's expense and not X's expense.

Although there seems no necessity to accept Smith's 'only one possible claimant' thesis,[7] his preference for examining the effect of X's payment on the pre-existing legal liability owed by X to C is an appealing one. And there appears to be no authority to contradict his view that X's debt to C is automatically discharged by payment to the usurper (D).

A closely linked alternative approach to Smith's, that is equally open on the authorities, is to say that C has the choice whether to treat the debt as discharged or not. That choice is exercised by C electing to sue either X in contract for the original debt (in which case X's debt to C is not discharged) or D in restitution (in which case X's debt to C is discharged). The explanation for giving C that option – and hence why exceptionally X's payment to the wrong party may discharge his debt to the right party – could then be that it saves the need for two actions: that is, C suing X in contract and X suing D in restitution (for mistaken payment). This derives support from dicta in *Official Custodian for Charities v Mackey (No 2)*,[8] a case in which, although rent had been received by an alleged 'usurper', the usurpation of office principle was held inapplicable because it had not been clearly established that X had a legal obligation to pay C the precise sum paid to D. But in examining the rationale for the action for money had and received in this context Nourse J said, 'It would be a waste of time and money if the plaintiff had to sue the third party and the latter had to sue the defendant. The suit for money had and received avoids circuity of action.'

Either of the above two alternatives seems a more satisfying explanation of the usurpation of office and related cases than does the

---

5   Birks, p 134.
6   (1991) OJLS 481, 494.
7   Above, p 33.
8   [1985] 1 WLR 1308, 1315.

idea of interceptive subtraction. In this context, the latter idea is strained because it relies not on the factual certainty of the claimant otherwise receiving the money but simply on his legal entitlement to it.

(v) The Ministry of Health v Simpson *line of authority*

The House of Lords' decision in *Ministry of Health v Simpson*[9] may be explained as illustrating a fifth exception. The case established that a beneficiary (C) who is entitled to a share of a deceased's estate, has an equitable personal remedy to recover money from D mistakenly paid to D by the personal representative (X) acting in breach of his fiduciary duty to C. D cannot escape liability although he is innocent: ie strict liability is imposed. Subsequent cases suggest that the same principle applies outside the realm of the administration of estates.[10]

One explanation for this line of authority is that it falls straightforwardly within the title and tracing exception considered above. So on the facts of *Ministry of Health v Simpson* the defendant charities received money that belonged in equity to the claimant beneficiaries. But there are two possible difficulties with that explanation. The first is that the strict liability imposed is inconsistent with the vast majority of cases on the transfer by X to D of C's equitable property which have imposed personal restitutionary liability only where the defendant was a 'knowing recipient'.[11] Secondly, the House of Lords in *Ministry of Health v Simpson* insisted, as have the cases following it, that C's entitlement to sue D is conditional on C first having failed to obtain full satisfaction in a claim against X for breach of fiduciary duty. Applying the title and tracing explanation it is hard to see the justification for that restriction.

An alternative interpretation suggested by Smith,[12] which avoids those two difficulties, is that while the charities' gain was primarily at the expense of the personal representative and not the beneficiaries – because 'legally' the beneficiaries were no worse off by the personal representative's mistake of law in that they were still entitled to sue him for breach of fiduciary duty – the beneficiaires would be factually worse off to the extent that the personal representative, by having irrevocably paid away the money *by mistake of law*, was unable fully to compensate the beneficiaries for their wrongfully caused loss. *To the extent to which the claimants*

---

9 [1951] AC 251 (sub nom *Re Diplock*).

10 Eg *Baker Ltd v Medway Building and Supplies Ltd* [1958] 2 All ER 532; on appeal [1958] 3 All ER 540, CA; *Butler v Broadhead* [1975] Ch 97; *Re J Leslie Engineers Ltd* [1976] 1 WLR 292.

11 Below, chapter 4.

12 (1991) OJLS 481, 497–500.

could not have their claim against the third party satisfied, the defendants' gain would be at the claimants' expense. The beauty of this interpretation is that the condition imposed by the House of Lords, and insisted on in all following cases, of the beneficiaries first claiming against the personal representative, is not only rendered intelligible but vital. In Smith's words, 'Some authors have criticised the pre-conditions which *Re Diplock* laid down for the recovery by the beneficiary from the defendant. The foregoing analysis shows that those pre-conditions are necessary to support a conclusion that the defendant was enriched at the plaintiff's expense.'[13]

If one agrees with Smith's interpretation (although there is no need to accept his 'one claimant only' thesis) *Ministry of Health v Simpson* establishes an exception distinct from title and tracing.

(vi) Rectification of a gift to the wrong person

Another possible exception is suggested by dicta of Lord Romilly MR in *Lister v Hodgson*[14] to the effect that a deed of gift, which the donor (X) has mistakenly drawn up in favour of D rather than C, may be rectified in favour of C if X died before realising his mistake. It was not spelt out that the action for rectification can be brought by C rather than X's representatives but it can readily be assumed that this was what was meant. Lord Romilly MR's contrast with the denial of such an action where X died after discovering the mistake can be justified on the ground that where X is still alive but chooses not to have the deed rectified or rescinded, the obvious inference is that he was not truly mistaken.

If this exception exists – there is no English authority on the point[15] – the 'at the expense of the claimant' requirement could only be satisfied by Birks' notion of 'interceptive subtraction'. The defendant's benefit is at the claimant's expense in the sense that, but for the mistake, the claimant and not the defendant would certainly (as a matter of fact) have been the donee.

Smith argues that there is no such exception. The defendant's benefit is at the expense of the donor, or, after his death, his personal representatives, and therefore, applying his 'only one claimant' thesis, the benefit cannot also be at the claimant's expense. 'If the donor

---

13 (1991) OJLS 481, 500.
14 (1867) LR 4 Eq 30, 34.
15 But see the Irish case of *M'Mechan v Warburton* [1896] 1 IR 435, 441. Cf the limited power of the court to rectify a will under s 20, Administration of Justice Act 1982. In *Walker v Geo H Medlicott & Son* [1999] 1 All ER 685 it was decided that a disappointed beneficiary suing his solicitor in the tort of negligence should mitigate his loss by first seeking rectification of the will under s 20. See, generally, O'Dell, 'Restitution, Rectification and Mitigation: Negligent Solicitors and Wills, Again' (2002) 65 MLR 360.

(or, later, his next of kin) has been impoverished by subtraction, then it is logically impossible that anyone else (such as the intended donee) has been impoverished by the subtraction of the same wealth.'[16] It has been argued above, however, that Smith's thesis is not a necessary theoretical consequence of the 'at the expense of' notion.

Nevertheless, it is true that, if this exception were permitted, D's gain would have to be recognised as being at the expense of both X and C. Moreover it seems clear that X during his lifetime, and hence his personal representative on his death, would be able to rescind the gift for mistake so that there would be a potential conflict between the interests of the residuary beneficiaries (wanting rescission) and C (wanting rectification). Commonly, however, the conflict would be more apparent than real because the residuary beneficiaries are often as keen as the claimant to ensure that the deceased's true intentions are fulfilled.

Two other features support recognising this exception. First, there is no obvious break in the chain of causation. C's loss becomes D's gain at one and the same time: the benefit does not first go to X from C and then on from X to D. And secondly, C has no possible claim against X (although he may have a negligence claim against X's solicitors by analogy to *White v Jones*).[17]

(vii) Khan v Permeyer *: avoiding circuity of action?*

Khan v Permeyer[18] constitutes another exception although its precise rationale is unclear. Here X paid money to D in purported discharge of C's debt to D. C reimbursed X. C and X were acting in the mistaken belief that C had an outstanding debt to D but in fact that debt had already been discharged (by a voluntary arrangement). The Court of Appeal decided that C had a restitutionary remedy against D to reverse D's unjust enrichment. Morritt LJ said, '[A] payment made by a third party under a mistaken belief which gives rise to unjust enrichment of the defendant may be recoverable by the person at whose ultimate expense it was paid if that person is also acting under the same mistake as the third party.'[19] Although Morritt LJ purported to find support in subrogation for this departure from the 'direct providers only' general rule, it is hard to see how the facts could have been regarded as an example of subrogation given that prior to X's payment there was no relevant debt owed by C to D. The better explanation is that allowing

16 (1991) OJLS 481, 518.
17 [1995] 2 AC 207.
18 [2001] BPIR 95.
19 Ibid at 104.

a direct claim by C against D avoided circuity of action.[20] That is, C was entitled to restitution from X for mistake (if necessary so to argue, the reimbursement contract between them was void for common mistake) and X was entitled to restitution from D for mistake (if necessary so to argue, the contract between them was void or voidable for common or unilateral mistake). Allowing C restitution direct from D therefore achieved in one action what would otherwise have required two actions.

(viii) Conclusion

Whether one would want to add further exceptions to the above seven or, more radically, would advocate departing altogether from restitution in unjust enrichment by subtraction being confined to direct providers, largely depends on one's view of the finely-balanced arguments for and against the restriction considered above. Those who argue against reform must face the fact, however, that the present law draws fine distinctions in allowing the claimant restitution of benefits conferred by third parties in some cases and not others.

Take the following three examples:

(i) C under a fundamental mistake (so that property does not pass) pays £100 to X who gives the same £100 to D as a gift.
(ii) C under a fundamental mistake pays £100 to X who, as a consequence of believing he has extra money, gives a different £100 to D as a gift.
(iii) C under a restitution-yielding but non-fundamental mistake pays £100 to X who, as a consequence of believing he has extra money, gives the same £100 to D as a gift.

Only in the first of those examples (assuming no agency relationship) is C entitled, under the present law, to restitution from D (in an action for money had and received). This is because it is only in the first example that an exception to the 'direct provider only' restriction (the 'title and tracing' exception) can be made out. And yet in the second and third examples (and ironically the same is not necessarily true of the first) C will not even have an action against X because X will have a change of position defence.

(3) Unjust factors

If the defendant is enriched at the claimant's expense restitutionary analysis turns to what is generally regarded as the crucial question – is

20   See above, p 37.

that enrichment unjust? The factors which the law regards as rendering the enrichment unjust – the 'unjust factors' – can be regarded as the grounds for restitution roughly analogous to the different torts in the law of tort. And to reiterate what was said at the start of this chapter, the question of what is unjust is not to be answered by a vague appeal to individual morality: it is a reference to what the decided cases show to be legally unjust.

In accordance with the two meanings of 'at the expense of' discussed above the unjust factors are conveniently divided according to whether the enrichment has been acquired by a wrong or not.

(a) Unjust enrichment by subtraction

Here one is asking, what are the factors (which one can label the 'autonomous unjust factors') that render a defendant's enrichment unjust where the enrichment has been subtracted from the claimant? Put another way, what are the grounds for restitution independent of a wrong?

Although the list should not be regarded as closed, examination of the case law reveals that the main autonomous unjust factors can be listed as follows:[1] mistake, ignorance, duress, undue influence, exploitation of weakness, legal compulsion, necessity, failure of consideration, illegality, incapacity, and ultra vires demands by public authorities.

It would be possible to subdivide those factors. For example, Birks principally structures unjust enrichment by subtraction according to 'factors negativing voluntariness' and 'policy-motivated restitution' and the former is itself divided into 'factors vitiating voluntariness' and 'factors qualifying voluntariness'.[2] But those divisions are not free from difficulty. 'Policy-motivated restitution' is not a happy subdividing label given that in one sense all the law can be regarded as policy-motivated: and while mistake is indisputably a 'factor negativing voluntariness' it arguably begs the controversial question of to what exactly the law is responding to regard duress, undue influence, exploitation of weakness, legal compulsion and necessity as resting on non-voluntariness. In this book, therefore, it has been thought preferable not to sub-categorise the autonomous unjust factors and instead to discuss possible linking themes in considering each one.

To isolate the main autonomous unjust factors is merely the start of the investigation. Only detailed examination of the case law will

---

1   In addition to this list, powerlessness should in principle be recognised as an unjust factor alongside ignorance: see below chapter 4. For other possible unjust factors see below, pp 110–111, 206, and p 313, n 16.

2   Birks, chapters 6–7 and 9.

reveal, for example, what is legally meant by duress or undue influence or which types of mistake trigger restitution. Indeed in some areas the law is best explained as responding to policy constraints on the pure principle of unjust enrichment. The scheme of autonomous unjust factors therefore operates at a general guiding level and does not itself specifically answer what the law regards as *unjust* enrichment. It is the task of chapters 3–13 to supply that answer at a detailed level.

Identification of the grounds for restitution is not intended to deny that those hitherto recognised can be added to and expanded. The categories of unjust enrichment are no more closed than the categories of tort.[3] But recognition of new unjust factors requires careful analysis of principle and policy and, if through the common law, is likely to be brought about by gradual incremental development.

Maddaugh and McCamus have argued that the principle uniting the grounds for restitution is that a claimant is entitled to restitution where he has *unofficiously* conferred a benefit other than through a contract or gift or other disposition of law.[4] And they have suggested that a person acts officiously if he acts maliciously, or frivolously, or '[without a request] for the exclusive purpose of attempting to exploit the profit needs of the other'.[5]

There are two central objections to this thesis. The first is that it obscures the role that many unjust factors have in invalidating gifts and contracts. For example, the reason why a mistaken payment to a charity may be recoverable in restitution is because the claimant's mistake vitiates his intention to benefit the charity. Entitlement to restitution clearly cannot be based on the payor being unofficious because that is true whether the gift is valid or not.

Secondly, the non-officious principle is too wide-ranging and is inconsistent with the limits to restitution mapped out in the case law. Most obviously, a person who indirectly confers a benefit on another while acting freely in his own self-interest is not (and should not be) entitled to restitution albeit that he is acting non-officiously.[6] In dicta in *Ruabon Steamship Co v The London Assurance*[7] Lord Halsbury thought it plainly unarguable that a person, who cut down trees on his own land for his own benefit and thereby gave his neighbour the advantage of a better view, could recover contribution from his neighbour. And

---

3   This is supported by the obiter dicta of Sir Donald Nicholls V-C in *CTN Cash and Carry Ltd v Gallaher Ltd* [1994] 4 All ER 714, 720: '[T]he categories of unjust enrichment are not closed'.
4   *The Law of Restitution* (1st edn, 1990), pp 31, 45–49.
5   Ibid p 48.
6   Goff and Jones, paras 1-078 to 1-079. Cf Maddaugh and McCamus, *The Law of Restitution* (1st edn, 1990), pp 742–744.
7   [1900] AC 6, 10.

in the well-known United States case of *Ulmer v Farnsworth*[8] restitution was denied to the owner of a quarry who had pumped it dry thereby draining, and rendering profitable, his neighbour's quarry.

(b) Restitution for wrongs

In contrast to unjust enrichment by subtraction this heading indicates at a general level what the unjust factor is, namely a wrong to the claimant (ie, a civil wrong). Reference to a wrong is not an appeal to an individual's view of wrongdoing nor even to what the law regards as reprehensible conduct. It is a reference to what the law regards as a wrong to the claimant, which may be committed without fault let alone dishonesty. Examples of wrongs are torts, breach of contract, breach of fiduciary duty and breach of confidence. In the area of restitution for wrongs it is irrelevant whether the defendant's gain has been subtracted from the claimant. The claimant may have suffered no loss at all. The question at issue is rather one of when it is that a defendant who has made a gain by committing a wrong against the claimant is bound to make restitution of that gain to the claimant. In other words, when is it that enrichment by wrongdoing is considered unjust? It is the aim of chapter 14 to answer that question. It will there be seen that restitution for wrongs remains a comparative rarity as against compensation for wrongs.

(c) Causation

Whether the unjust factor is autonomous or a wrong it only has relevance if it is causally linked to the 'enrichment at the claimant's expense'. Indeed that causal link can be regarded as an inherent element of each of the unjust factors. The general test in the law for factual causation is the 'but for' test. The difficult question is the extent to which in the law of restitution an unjust factor counts even though the enrichment at the claimant's expense would have occurred irrespective of the unjust factor (that is, even though the but for test is not satisfied).

Judicial discussion of this question has in fact been sparse. However, the position appears to be as follows:

(i) The relevant unjust factor generally only has to be *a* cause of the defendant's gain. It does not have to be the sole or predominant cause. For example, in *Edgington v Fitzmaurice*[9] the claimant was induced to lend money to the defendant company by fraudulent

8   15 A 65 (1888).
9   (1885) 29 Ch D 459.

misrepresentations as to the objects for which the money would be used and also by his mistaken belief that lenders would be given a charge over the company's assets. It was held that the claimant was entitled to damages for deceit (and the same approach to causation must apply, by analogy, to rescission for misrepresentation) even though he would not have lent the money but for his own non-induced mistake. In other words, it was sufficient that the misrepresentation was a cause of his entering into the contract even though his own non-induced mistake was also a cause. And in *Barton v Armstrong*,[10] a physical duress case, Lords Wilberforce and Simon, albeit dissenting on their interpretation of the facts, agreed with the majority of the Privy Council that the question at issue was whether 'the illegitimate means used was *a* reason (not *the* reason, nor the *predominant* reason, nor the *clinching* reason) why the complainant acted as he did'.[11]

(ii) The general test for establishing that the unjust factor was a cause of the defendant's gain is the but for test, which it is for the claimant to satisfy. For example, in *Holt v Markham*[12] the claimants, on the demobilisation of the RAF, paid the defendant officer too much given that he had merely been an officer on the Emergency List. Their claim for restitution on the grounds of payment under a mistake of fact failed because, inter alia, they would have paid the money even if they had known his name was on the Emergency List. This was because they were also making a mistake of law and, at that time,[13] mistakes of law did not trigger restitution. Scrutton LJ, in a clear application of the but for test said, '... if they had known that he was on that list that would in my opinion have made no difference, for I am satisfied that at that time no one appreciated what the effect was of an officer being on that list'.[14] And more recent cases, on mistaken payments, have treated the relevant test for restitution of payments made by mistake, whether of fact or law, as being the 'but for' test.[15]

(iii) In terms of principle, and by analogy to factual causation in tort compensation cases,[16] the 'but for' test must be displaced where more

---

10 [1976] AC 104.
11 Ibid p 121. See also *Crescendo Management Pty Ltd v Westpac Banking Corpn* (1989) 19 NSWLR 40.
12 [1923] 1 KB 504. See also *Home and Colonial Insurance Co Ltd v London Guarantee Accident Co Ltd* (1928) 45 TLR 134 (mistake); *Bank of Credit and Commerce International SA v Aboody* [1990] 1 QB 923, 971 (actual undue influence). The 'but for' test also underpins the decisions on the amount of profits to be disgorged where the defendant is required to account for profits made from a wrong: see below, p 466, n 1.
13 Prior to *Kleinwort Benson Ltd v Lincoln City Council* [1999] 2 AC 349, HL: see below, ch 3.
14 [1923] 1 KB 504, 515.
15 See below, p 136. For economic duress cases supporting the 'but for' test, see below, pp 48, 228.
16 Burrows, *Remedies for Torts and Breach of Contract* (2nd edn, 1994), pp 26–30.

than one unjust factor is a sufficient cause and there are no other sufficient causes. For example, it would clearly be unacceptable to deny restitution of a mistaken payment induced by an illegitimate threat on the grounds that the payment would have been made irrespective of the mistake because of the duress and irrespective of the duress because of the mistake. Similarly a defendant cannot keep gains made by a wrong by arguing that those gains would in any event have accrued from a second wrong committed by him. In this rare sort of case causation should be satisfied by establishing that the particular unjust factor was a sufficient rather than a necessary cause: that is, that if the second unjust factor had not been present the gain would still have been made because of the first unjust factor.

(iv) In physical duress and fraudulent misrepresentation cases the courts have applied a more pro-claimant approach than the 'but for' test in deciding whether the unjust factor was a cause of the claimant's entering a contract (and hence rendering benefits). The leading case is *Barton v Armstrong*.[17] The question at issue was whether the defendant's physical threats had induced the claimant to enter into a contract. The majority of the New South Wales Court of Appeal had thought that the claimant must prove that but for the threats he would not have entered the contract. The Privy Council unanimously disagreed and favoured Jacobs JA's dissenting judgment favouring a less stringent test. Lord Cross, giving the majority's opinion, said, '... if Armstrong's threats were "a" reason for Barton's executing the deed he is entitled to relief even though he might well have entered into the contract if Armstrong had uttered no threats to induce him to do so'.[18] And in the words of Lords Wilberforce and Simon, '... a decisive answer is not obtainable by asking the question whether the contract would have been made even if there had been no threats ...'.[19] Their Lordships saw this as consistent with the test for fraudulent misrepresentation.[20] Unfortunately the preferred less stringent test was not clearly spelt out. Three possibilities may be suggested.

First, the minority said that the duress had to be a 'conscious reason'.[1] This is consistent with Bowen LJ's view in *Edgington v Fitzmaurice*[2] that 'such misstatement was material if it was actively present to his mind when he decided to advance the money'. One interpretation therefore is that the less stringent test is whether the threat or misrepresentation was present in the claimant's mind at the time of rendering the benefit.

---

17   [1976] AC 104.
18   Ibid, p 119.
19   Ibid, p 121.
20   Reliance was placed especially on *Reynell v Sprye* (1852) 1 De GM & G 660.
1   [1976] AC 104, 122.
2   (1885) 29 Ch D 459, 483.

Secondly, it may be that the less stringent approach is that the courts will be satisfied if the physical duress or fraudulent misrepresentation was a sufficient rather than a necessary cause. That is, causation is satisfied if the claimant shows that the duress or fraud alone would have induced the rendering of the benefit even though, on the facts, he rendered the benefit irrespective of the duress or fraud.

Thirdly, it may be that the more pro-claimant test is simply a shifting of the burden of proof of the 'but for' test from the claimant to the defendant. That is, there is a presumption of causation which the defendant can negate by proving that the claimant would have rendered the benefit irrespective of the threat or misrepresentation. This derives support from the majority's judgment in *Barton* given by Lord Cross:

> 'If Barton had to establish that he would not have made the agreement but for Armstrong's threats, then their Lordships would not dissent from the view that he had not made out his case. But no such onus lay on him. On the contrary it was for Armstrong to establish, if he could, that the threats which he was making and the unlawful pressure which he was exerting for the purpose of inducing Barton to sign the agreement and which Barton knew were being made and exerted for this purpose in fact contributed nothing to Barton's decision to sign.'[3]

Of these three possibilities, the third should probably be supported. 'Presence in the mind' is a somewhat uncertain and elusive idea and, as between the second and third possibilites, the third alone has judicial support.

(v) Does the more pro-claimant test extend beyond physical duress and fraudulent misrepresentation? One might argue that it should extend to all cases within unjust enrichment by subtraction where the defendant's conduct is reprehensible; for example, to all forms of duress, undue influence and to exploitation of weakness.[4] Although there is no authority on the point one would certainly expect that for presumed undue influence the presumption would carry through to causation so that the burden of proof would be on the defendant. In contrast the courts in some cases of economic duress can be interpreted as having gone to the opposite extreme so that the claimant needs to establish that the threat was the predominant cause, rather than a cause, of his payment.[5]

---

3   [1976] AC 104, 120. See also *Crescendo Management Pty Ltd v Westpac Banking Corpn* (1988) 19 NSWLR 40 (duress); *Barton v County Natwest Ltd* [1999] Lloyd's Rep Bank 408 (fraudulent misrepresentation); Treitel, *The Law of Contract* (10th edn), pp 316, 378.
4   This may be thought to derive some support from *UCB Corporate Services Ltd v Williams* [2002] EWCA Civ 555 which concerned actual undue influence and fraudulent misrepresentation.
5   Below, pp 226–228.

In principle, the natural starting point, consistent with the approach to (factual) causation in the rest of the law of obligations, is that the general causation test is the 'but for' test and that this is for the claimant to prove. Any departure from that needs careful justification. Probably the best conclusion therefore is that it is only where there is highly reprehensible conduct within unjust enrichment by subtraction – physical duress and fraudulent misrepresentation – or where there is a presumed unjust factor – presumed undue influence – that the onus of disproving but for causation falls on the defendant.[6] Certainly the predominant cause approach suggested by some economic duress cases is unappealing.

(d) An alternative approach: 'unjust unless ...'

It can be argued that using the unjust enrichment principle as an organising tool linking together a mass of law does not go far enough. A significant feature of the second and third editions of Goff and Jones' work[7] was their call for recognition of a generalised right to restitution. They wrote, 'In our view the case law is now sufficiently mature for the courts to recognise a generalised right to restitution.'[8] It is not entirely clear what this meant and in later editions all reference to a generalised right to restitution has been abandoned.

What might have been meant was that the courts should discard past decisions in favour of referring directly to the principle of unjust enrichment. But this would represent an abandonment of the traditional incremental deductive approach of the common law and unacceptably would leave the question of what constitutes an unjust enrichment to a judge's unfettered discretion. On this interpretation the call for a generalised right provides ammunition for those who criticise unjust enrichment as leading to palm tree justice.

Alternatively, and it would seem what Goff and Jones had in mind,[9] is the idea that, instead of the onus lying on the claimant to establish an unjust factor, it should be for the defendant – once his enrichment at the claimant's expense is made out – to establish a good reason for denying restitution. The investigation of the unjust element would, on this view, be a matter of clarifying reasons against a presumption of

---

6   This is supported by recent economic duress cases, especially *Huyton SA v Peter Cremer GmbH* [1999] 1 Lloyd's Rep 620, 636, which have explicitly approved the 'but for' test provable by the claimant: see below, pp 227–228. But in *Crescendo Management Pty Ltd v Westpac Banking Corpn* (1988) 19 NSWLR 40 the burden of disproving causation was put on the defendant even though that was an economic duress case. See also *Mathias v Yetts* (1882) 46 LT 497, 502 (misrepresentation).

7   (2nd edn, 1978), pp 23–25; (3rd edn, 1993), pp 15, 29–30.

8   Goff and Jones, (3rd edn), p 15.

9   Ibid, pp 29–51.

restitution. This approach has been adopted in Canada where, once the defendant has been enriched at the claimant's expense, restitution will follow in the 'absence of any juristic reason ... for the enrichment'.[10] It also appears to be more in line with the tradition in civil law countries.[11]

In a rational system it may be doubted whether this negative approach would reach different results than the positive approach: and it is hard to see why preference for a negative approach should be necessarily linked to the particular state of development of the law of restitution as Goff and Jones implied. Even if no practical consequences were to turn on the choice, the positive approach of the claimant needing to identify unjust factors is preferred in this book for four reasons.

First, the very fact that it is the claimant who seeks the remedy (and has the burden of proof in establishing the defendant's enrichment at his expense) puts the natural onus on him of proving the injustice.

Secondly, the approach of the English courts is to look for a good reason to regard an enrichment as unjust rather than for reasons why it should not be considered unjust. This was most clearly adverted to by Lord Hope in *Kleinwort Benson Ltd v Lincoln City Council*.[12] He said:

> '[C]ivil law looks for the absence of a legal justification for the enrichment ... If the payer paid in the mistaken belief that he was under a duty to pay, it is prima facie unjust that the payee should be allowed to retain what he received. But the burden of proving that the payer knew that there was no duty, and was not mistaken, is on the recipient ... The approach of the common law is to look for an unjust factor, something which makes it unjust to allow the payee to retain the benefit ... The common law accepts that the payee is enriched where the sum was not due to be paid to him, but it requires the payer to show that this was unjust. Whereas in civilian systems proof of knowledge that there was no legal obligation to pay is a defence which may be invoked by the payee, under the common law it is for the payer to show that he paid under a mistake.'[13]

---

10   *Rathwell v Rathwell* (1978) 83 DLR (3d) 289, 306; *Pettkus v Becker* (1980) 117 DLR (3d) 257. See Maddaugh and McCamus, *The Law of Restitution* (1st edn, 1990) pp 27, 38, 45–48. Lionel Smith, 'The Mystery of "Juristic Reason"' (2000) 12 Supreme Court LR 211 examines the Canadian position in detail arguing that it is still open to the Canadian courts to adopt the preferable 'English' approach of looking for 'reasons for plaintiffs to have restitution' rather than 'reasons for defendants to keep enrichments'.

11   See, eg, Meier and Zimmermann, 'Judicial Development of the Law, Error Iuris, and the Law of Unjustified Enrichment – A View from Germany' (1999) 115 LQR 556; Krebs, *Restitution at the Crossroads: a Comparative Study* (2001); Meier, 'Unjust Factors and Legal Grounds' in *Unjustified Enrichment: Key Issues in Comparative Perspective* (eds Johnston and Zimmermann, 2002), pp 37–75. See also the passage cited below from Lord Hope's speech in *Kleinwort Benson Ltd v Lincoln City Council* [1999] 2 AC 349, 408–409.

12   [1999] 2 AC 349.

13   Ibid at pp 408–409.

Thirdly, the present law of restitution – with its sometimes questionable restrictions – seems easier to describe, understand and assess through the positive approach. Birks has made a similar point when comparing the English approach to that of the civil law. He argues that the need to identify unjust factors makes the law of restitution understandable to non-lawyers. The ideas behind the unjust factors can be expressed very simply: for example 'I did not mean you to have it'. But the civil system, concerned to identify why there should be no restitution, has to rely on a complex legal framework (for example, governing the nullity of contracts and gifts) which is not readily understandable by laymen. Compared to the automatic restitution that is consequent on nullity in the civil law, Birks writes, 'The common law's traditional approach has been to regard the consequences of nullity as flexible and to ask instead for a more down-to-earth reason for restitution, intelligible to, and likely to convince, the passengers on the Clapham omnibus.'[14]

Fourthly, the use of a presumption to enable a claimant to establish such a core element of a cause of action is rare. The rejection by the House of Lords in, eg, *Murphy v Brentwood District Council*[15] of the two stage test for establishing the duty of care for the tort of negligence in *Anns v Merton London Borough Council*[16] can be explained precisely because, whatever the theoretical merits of the test, it was interpreted in practice as putting the burden of the duty of care enquiry on the defendant instead of the claimant.

For these reasons, a generalised right to restitution or a presumption that enrichments are unjust unless there are reasons to the contrary should be rejected. Similarly one should not accept suggestions made in some recent English cases that restitution should be given because there has been an 'absence of consideration' or because the money paid 'was not due'.[17] These grounds for restitution slide from identifying positive reasons for restitution to looking for reasons to deny restitution. If accepted they would mark an unwelcome move away from the traditional common law approach to that favoured in civil law. Certainly it would be dangerous to make such a move without being clear that that is what one is doing, not

---

14 Birks, 'Mistakes of Law' [2000] CLP 205, 236. For a defence of the 'unjust factors' approach, see also Chen-Wishart, 'Unjust Factors and the Restitutionary Response' (2000) 20 OJLS 557.
15 [1991] 1 AC 398.
16 [1978] AC 728.
17 See, eg, *Woolwich Equitable Building Society v IRC* [1993] AC 70; *Westdeutsche Landesbank Girozentrale v Islington London Borough Council* [1994] 4 All ER 890, per Hobhouse J. For rejection of this approach, see below, pp 386–388, 441–442.

least because civil law systems may have ways of limiting the restitution that would flow from a presumption of restitution that are alien to the common law (for example, in German law gifts are characterised as contracts).[18] In Krebs' words, 'The danger is not so much the adoption of the German model by English law but a combination of the two approaches. If English law chooses to adopt the civilian "legal ground" model, it should do so consciously and openly. Only then will it be able to reap the benefits.'[19]

(4) Defences

Even though a claimant has established that the defendant has been (i) unjustly (ii) enriched (iii) at its expense, its restitutionary claim may still be defeated by (iv) a restitutionary defence. Examination of the case law reveals that there are eight main established defences in the law of restitution: change of position, estoppel, counter-restitution, limitation, 'dispute resolved', incapacity, illegality, and bona fide purchase. Along with passing on (which is controversial but, to the extent that valid, goes to the 'at the claimant's expense' issue), they are considered in detail in chapter 15.

The first two of those (and possibly the third) go, at least primarily, to the question of the defendant's enrichment. Although the defendant has received a benefit, its subsequent loss of that benefit may render it unacceptable to order restitution. Change of position was accepted for the first time by the House of Lords in *Lipkin Gorman v Karpnale Ltd.*[20] It has a pivotal role to play in protecting defendants. Now that it has been accepted the expansion of the ambit of the grounds for restitution can continue apace. Indeed the extension of restitution-yielding mistakes to include mistakes of law[1] can be regarded as a clear example of the courts' willingness to expand the grounds for restitution now that, and because, the defence of change of position is in place.

In contrast, the other established defences (including possibly counter-restitution) go to the injustice of an enrichment. They are the defendant's weapons against the prima facie force of an established unjust factor.

---

18 Krebs, *Restitution at the Crossroads: a Comparative Study* (2001), pp 60–66.
19 Ibid, at 310.
20 [1991] 2 AC 548.
1   *Kleinwort Benson Ltd v Lincoln City Council* [1999] 2 AC 349; see below, ch 3.

3. RESTITUTIONARY REMEDIES

(1) Generally

Restitutionary remedies are those concerned to *reverse* the defendant's unjust enrichment at the claimant's expense. There are four general comments to make on them.

(i) Most remedies reversing unjust enrichment are judicial rather than self-help: the claimant needs to come to court to obtain the remedy. An exception is rescission of a contract which, while it can be effected by a court, is most simply brought about by informing the other party of one's intention to wipe away the contract.

(ii) Judicial remedies reversing unjust enrichment are primarily coercive (ie court orders) but they may also be constitutive (ie altering the position of the parties).[2] Examples of the former are an award of money had and received, an account of profits, and contribution. An example of the latter is rescission of a contract under which the ownership of goods or land has been transferred.

(iii) Remedies reversing unjust enrichment may be personal or proprietary. Personal restitutionary remedies respond to value having been received by the defendant irrespective of whether it still retains particular property. They are not dependent on the existence of particular property and do not afford priority on the defendant's insolvency.[3] In contrast, proprietary restitutionary remedies afford priority on the defendant's insolvency and are dependent on the defendant's retention of particular property.

Examples of personal restitutionary remedies are restitutionary damages, money had and received to the claimant's use, money paid to the defendant's use,[4] *quantum meruit, quantum valebat,*[5] (which are

---

2 For this distinction see Lawson, *Remedies of English Law* (2nd edn, 1980), pp 12–13. A declaration, eg, that the claimant is entitled to a restitutionary remedy or that a self-help restitutionary remedy has been validly effected can also be regarded as concerned with the reversal of unjust enrichment and, therefore, as a restitutionary remedy.

3 A liquidator may be liable to a personal restitutionary remedy: see, eg, *Scott v Surman* (1742) Willes 400. See generally Scott, 'The Right to "Trace" at Common Law' (1965–1966) 7 WALR 480–483, Goff and Jones, para 2-025, note 39. As the liquidator receives the benefit from a third party the major hurdle for the claimant in unjust enrichment by subtraction lies in establishing title and tracing: above, pp 34–35.

4 This and the following common law remedies listed are not *necessarily* restitutionary. They could be given as remedies for a breach of contract (assuming, as regards the action for money paid, that attornment is a contractual doctrine).

5 *Quantum meruit* values services. *Quantum valebat* values goods. The former is often used to cover both: there is, eg, no mention of *quantum valebat* in *Atkins Court Forms* (2nd edn) esp Vol 12(2) (2001 Issue) and see Treitel, *The Law of Contract* (10th edn), p 988 et seq.

all common law remedies); and an account of profits, and rescission in so far as concerned with restitution of money or services (which are primarily[6] equitable remedies).

Examples of proprietary restitutionary remedies are an equitable lien, some constructive and resulting trusts, rescission in so far as concerned with revesting goods or land, and the conferment of secured rights by (non-contractual) subrogation.

(iv) The bulk of the law of restitution is concerned with personal remedies. As a matter of principle, rather than history, there is no good reason why there should be several different remedies to effect the same restitution and one could instead simply talk of restitution of value received or personal restitution.[7] Certainly 'money had and received, or paid, to another's use' can mean little to many lawyers let alone members of the public. But it is very difficult for a textbook to move to the simplified and principled position while judges and practitioners still use the jargon bequeathed by the forms of action. That is, although the nineteenth century abolition of the forms of action means that it is not necessary to fit one's facts within a particular form of words in order to succeed, the legacy of the old forms of action lives on to the extent that personal restitutionary remedies are described and pleaded using a variety of labels. Differently described remedies are applicable to different situations of unjust enrichment. Moreover the occasional statutory provision distinguishes, with consequences, between debts or liquidated claims and other claims.[8] It follows that, at the present time, a single label is inappropriate. It is therefore both for ease of exposition and because of the possible practical consequences that this book continues to refer to the several different (or differently described) remedies.

(2) Awards of interest

A court has the power to add interest to at least most restitutionary remedies under either s 35A of the Supreme Court Act 1981, where

---

6 Rescission for fraudulent misrepresentation and duress can be a common law remedy. The difference between common law and equitable rescission turns on the more flexible approach of the latter to the bar of *restitutio in integrum* being impossible. That that bar does not generally apply to duress explains why, in practice, common law rescission is restricted to duress. See generally Meagher, Gummow and Lehane, *Equity Doctrines and Remedies* (3rd edn, 1992), ch 24; Cartwright, *Unequal Bargaining* (1991), pp 69–71, 169, note 67.

7 In the narrower context of restitution for wrongs, the Law Commission has recommended that the personal remedy labelled 'restitutionary damages' should alone be used: *Aggravated, Exemplary and Restitutionary Damages*, Law Com No 247 (1997), paras 3.82–3.84.

8 Eg, Limitation Act 1980, s 29(5)(a) (acknowledgement or part payment).

the remedy constitutes the recovery of a debt or damages, or under its inherent jurisdiction where the remedy is equitable. Under the statute simple interest only can be awarded whereas in cases of breach of fiduciary duty or fraud compound interest has been given.[9] In *Westdeutsche Landesbank Girozentrale v Islington London Borough Council*[10] the House of Lords had the opportunity to develop the law by awarding compound interest on a common law restitutionary claim for money paid under a void interest rate swap transaction. By a bare majority (Lords Goff and Woolf dissenting) their Lordships refused to do so. To develop the equitable jurisdiction to award compound interest beyond its two recognised categories (fraud or breach of fiduciary duty) was felt to be unacceptable as outflanking the Legislature's decision to allow simple interest only under the Supreme Court Act 1981 (and before that under s 3(1) of the Law Reform (Miscellaneous Provisions) Act 1934). Lord Lloyd also argued that to allow the award of compound interest might cause uncertainty and consequent litigation, for example as to the rate to be awarded. In contrast, Lords Goff and Woolf saw the award of compound interest, in the instant case, as essential in order to achieve full and proper restitution; and there was thought to be no countervailing good reason for refusing to extend the equitable jurisdiction. They cited with approval Hobhouse J's statement at first instance: 'Anyone who lends or borrows money on a commercial basis receives or pays interest periodically and if that interest is not paid it is compounded ... I see no reason why I should deny the plaintiff a complete remedy or allow the defendant arbitrarily to retain part of the enrichment which it has unjustly enjoyed.'[11]

In *BP Exploration Co (Libya) Ltd v Hunt (No 2)*[12] Robert Goff J held that for the purposes of statutory interest a *quantum meruit*, and hence an award under s 1(3) of the Law Reform (Frustrated Contracts) Act 1943, constituted the recovery of a debt. This was confirmed by the

9   *Wallersteiner v Moir (No 2)* [1975] QB 373; *President of India v La Pintada Compania* [1985] AC 104; *Westdeutsche Landesbank Girozentrale v Islington London Borough Council* [1996] AC 669; *Kuwait Oil Tanker Co SAK v Al Bader* [2000] 2 All ER (Comm) 271, 339-344. In the *Westdeutsche* case, Lords Goff and Woolf, albeit dissenting, clarified that *Re Diplock* [1948] Ch 465, 517, 557-558, should not be interpreted as drawing any distinction for the purposes of interest (whether in relation to compound or simple interest) between equitable proprietary, and personal, remedies.

10   [1996] AC 669.

11   [1994] 4 All ER 890, 955. An added reason for enabling the courts to award compound interest is that arbitrators can now award such interest under s 49 of the Arbitration Act 1996. The Law Commission in *Compound Interest* Consultation Paper No 167 (2002) has provisionally recommended that s 35A of the Supreme Court Act 1981 should be amended to state that any interest awarded shall be compound unless there are good reasons to the contrary. See also *Bank of America Canada v Mutual Trust Co* (2002) SCC 43 (compound interest can be awarded as damages for breach of contract).

12   [1979] 1 WLR 783, 835–837.

House of Lords. Lord Brandon said, 'In my opinion the words "any debt or damages", in the context in which they occur, are very wide so that they cover any sum of money which is recoverable by one party from another, either at common law or in equity or under a statute of the kind here concerned.'[13] Under the statute the accrual of the cause of action is the earliest date from which interest can be awarded.[14]

In deciding whether to award interest and, if so, at what rate, the courts' approach tends to be a rough-and-ready one in the sense that the actual position of the parties is usually not scrutinised. Staughton J's general dictum on interest in *La Pintada Cia Navegacion SA v The President of India*[15] is apposite. 'In the ordinary case, not involving any fiduciary or breach of trust, I do not think that one should enquire what the defendant has in fact done with the money or what the plaintiff would in fact have done with it.' The practice in modern cases is to award interest at a rate of 1% above the clearing bank's average base rate.

Having said that, the explanation for adding interest to restitutionary remedies does merit brief consideration not only because it is important that the practice does not drift from its theoretical underpinnings but also because it can help in deciding the date from which interest is payable. Three situations can serve as illustrations. The first two fall within unjust enrichment by subtraction. The last concerns restitution for wrongs.

(i) Where the claimant pays money to the defendant, interest in an action for money had and received represents the claimant's loss of use of the payment and the defendant's use of it.[16] Ordinarily the interest

---

13 [1983] 2 AC 352, 373.
14 This perhaps produces an anomaly for claims based on failure of consideration where the failure occurs after the payment of money and yet one might have thought that, in general, interest should run from the date of receipt of the payment. In *BP Exploration Co (Libya) Ltd v Hunt (No 2)* [1983] 2 AC 352, 373-374 the House of Lords held that the cause of action accrued, for interest purposes, from the date when the contract was frustrated; and in *Guardian Ocean Cargoes v Banco de Brasil* [1994] 2 Lloyd's Rep 152 the cause of action was held to accrue, for interest purposes, from the date when the condition for the payment failed. Cf *Westdeutsche Landesbank Girozentrale v Islington London Borough Council* [1996] AC 669, where all of their Lordships agreed that interest should run from the date of the receipt of the payment in a case in which, on one possible analysis (but, perhaps, for this reason not the best analysis) the unjust factor was a (subsequent) failure of consideration. For the argument that, in principle, interest should, at the earliest, be payable from the date of payment even though the restitutionary cause of action accrues later, see Mason and Carter, *Restitution Law in Australia* (1995), pp 952-955. See also below, pp 332–333, 546.
15 [1983] 1 Lloyd's Rep 37, 43. See also *BP Exploration Co (Libya) Ltd v Hunt (No 2)* [1979] 1 WLR 783, 847 (per Robert Goff J).
16 Mason and Carter, *Restitution in Australia* (1995), ch 28, argue that, irrespective of the underlying claim, the justification for the award of interest is the reversal of unjust enrichment. See also *Heydon v NRMA Ltd (No 2)* (2001) 53 NSWLR 600.

should run from the accrual of the cause of action.[17] Although Lord Goff was arguing for compound, rather than merely simple, interest to be awarded, his Lordship's reasoning in the *Westdeutsche* case explains clearly that interest on a restitutionary remedy for money paid is awarded because the defendant has had the additional benefit of the use of the money (and the claimant has lost that use). Lord Goff said, 'It is plain on the evidence that, if [the council] had not had the use of the bank's money, it would (if free to do so) have borrowed the money elsewhere at compound interest. It has to that extent profited from the use of the bank's money. Moreover, if the bank had not advanced the money to the council, it would itself have employed the money on similar terms in its business.'[18]

(ii) Where the claimant has performed services for the defendant and seeks a *quantum meruit* the position is less staightforward. The claimant has not lost an income-producing asset and the defendant may, or may not, have gained an income-producing asset. It is therefore probably preferable to regard the relevant enrichment by subtraction for interest purposes as being the defendant's non-payment of the sum due (ie, the *quantum meruit*). And correspondingly interest should usually run here not from the accrual of the cause of action but from when the writ was served or from any earlier date when the defendant knew of the claimant's intention to make a claim. That was the approach taken by Robert Goff J in *BP Exploration Co (Libya) Ltd v Hunt (No 2)*[19] and his exercise of discretion was upheld by the House of Lords.

(iii) Where the defendant makes a profit in breach of fiduciary duty, interest on an account of profits represents the defendant's use of the profits. It in effect amounts to another tier of profit not reflected in the principal sum awarded. As Lord Denning said in *Wallersteiner v Moir (No 2)*,[20] 'The reason [for interest] is because a person in a fiduciary position is not allowed to make a profit out of his trust.' In general the interest should run from the accrual of the cause of action.

(3) When is rescission a restitutionary remedy?

Rescission (or, as it is sometimes called, 'setting aside') is one of the commonest remedies in the law of restitution. It is also one of the

---

17   But the date from when interest was payable on mistaken payments was postponed beyond the date of the accrual of the cause of action in *Nurdin & Peacock plc v DB Ramsden & Co Ltd* [1999] 1 All ER 941, 966–968.

18   [1996] AC 669, 691. See also Lord Woolf at 723.

19   [1979] 1 WLR 783, 845–850.

20   [1975] QB 373, 388. The remedy awarded was equitable compensation not restitution.

most difficult to analyse.[1] It seems as well to set out here, therefore, the preferred approach to the question of precisely when rescission is a restitutionary remedy. Our primary focus will be on rescission of a contract although it must be remembered that a deed of gift (or other voluntary settlement) may also be rescinded. Three introductory points should be made.

First, the principal effect of rescission is to wipe away a contract (or deed of gift) *ab initio*. In this it differs from the self-help remedy of termination of a contract for breach which merely wipes away future obligations.

Secondly, rescission of a contract is peculiar in that it can be both a self-help and a judicial remedy.[2] To effect self-help rescission the claimant must give notice to the other party that it is wiping away the contract although it was held in *Car and Universal Finance Co Ltd v Caldwell*[3] that, as the other party could not be traced, notification to the police or AA asking for help in recovering the car transferred was sufficient to effect rescission. Where the claimant seeks judicial rescission[4] (which it may wish to do to avoid arguments over its right to rescind or to recover, for example, money or goods) the rescission is backdated to when the legal proceedings were commenced.[5]

Thirdly, rescission is normally subject to four bars: lapse of time, affirmation, third party rights, and *restitutio in integrum* being impossible. The last of these is the most significant from a restitutionary perspective: it is bound up with the other party's possible counterclaim for restitution (in Birks' terminology 'counter-restitution').[6]

In examining the role of rescission, four situations are usefully distinguished:

(i) A contract to perform work is rescinded before any work has been commenced or price been paid: ie the contract is executory. Rescission

---

1 See also Nahan, 'Rescission: A Case for Rejecting the Classical Model?' (1997) 27 UW Aus LR 66; Watts, 'Rescission of Guarantees for Misrepresentation and Actionable Non-Disclosure' [2002] CLJ 301; Worthington, 'The Proprietary Consequences of Rescission' [2002] RLR 28.

2 *Contra* O 'Sullivan, 'Rescission as a Self-Help Remedy: A Critical Analysis' [2000] CLJ 509.

3 [1965] 1 QB 525. In *TSB Bank plc v Camfield* [1995] 1 All ER 951 Roch LJ gave as a reason for deciding that rescission was all or nothing, and could not be on terms, that the remedy was a self-help remedy. With respect, this seems a non sequitur.

4 Cf a declaration that a contract or deed of gift has been validly rescinded by the claimant.

5 *Reese River Silver Mining Co v Smith* (1869) LR 4 HL 64. The reason for this is unclear: does it follow that a defendant cannot give good title to a bona fide purchaser for value without notice in the period between commencement of the action and judgment? Of course this in no sense denies that, where validly rescinded, title to property transferred is retrospectively revested in the claimant as if he had never lost it.

6 Birks, pp 415, 421–423. The term was adopted by Steyn LJ in *Securities and Investments Board v Pantell SA (No 2)* [1992] 3 WLR 896. See below, pp 538–542.

here is non-restitutionary.[7] No benefit has been conferred under the contract and hence none can be returned. The importance of rescission is simply in allowing the parties to escape from their contractual obligations. The wiping away of the contract *ab initio* here has the same practical effect as wiping away the contract *in futuro* by termination for breach or frustration which is similarly not a restitutionary remedy.

(ii) Where a contract to perform work is rescinded after work has been commenced and after part of the price has been paid: ie, the contract is partly (or fully) executed. Rescission can here be regarded as a personal restitutionary remedy. In wiping away the contract *ab initio* it gives the claimant restitution of the value of benefits conferred and the defendant counter-restitution of the value of benefits conferred on the claimant. From the defendant's perspective the key to the entitlement to counter-restitution is the bar to rescission of *restitutio in integrum* being impossible. This bar is clearly posited on the basis that the claimant cannot have its restitution unless it gives counter-restitution of gains made at the defendant's expense. The unjust factor triggering counter-restitution can be viewed as total failure of consideration: the claimant's rescission and restitution mean that the defendant is left with nothing of what it bargained for. It is possible to separate the setting aside of the contract from consequential personal restitution (which may include judicial orders for, for example, the recovery of money or an indemnity). But rescission is generally taken to describe the whole process including restitution and certainly a claimant that is primarily interested in escaping from its contractual obligations (because, for example, it made a bad bargain) has to be able to make counter-restitution.

(iii) A contract to transfer proprietary rights to goods or land (or a deed of gift of goods or land) is rescinded before the intended proprietary rights have been transferred and before any price has been paid. Rescission here is non-restitutionary. The situation is analogous to (i) above.

(iv) A contract to transfer proprietary rights to goods or land (or a deed of gift of goods or land) is rescinded after the intended proprietary rights have been transferred and after any price has been paid. This is analogous to (ii) above except that here there is a proprietary angle to consider. The rescission carries with it the entitlement to restitution (or counter-restitution) of the money paid and to that extent it is a personal restitutionary remedy.[8] But rescission

---

7   See *Manifest Shipping Co Ltd v Uni-Polaris Insurance Co Ltd, The Star Sea* [2001] 1 Lloyd's Rep 389, 400 (*per* Lord Hobhouse). *Contra* is Birks, p 163.

8   For examples of the restitution of money paid, where a contract for proprietary rights over land has been rescinded, see *Erlanger v New Sombrero Phosphate Co* (1878) 3 App Cas 1218 (purchase of a mine); *Redgrave v Hurd* (1881) 20 Ch D 1 (purchase of a house); *Whittington v Seale-Hayne* (1900) 82 LT 49 (lease of a farm).

also revests the proprietary rights to the goods or land and, in that respect, it is a proprietary restitutionary (or counter-restitutionary) remedy.[9] That revesting may be a prelude to other claims, eg, for the tort of conversion. But it is the revesting of the proprietary rights that is itself restitutionary.[10]

The conclusion is that while rescission of a contract is always a contractual remedy – in the sense that it wipes away, and allows escape from, a contract – it is also often a personal and/or proprietary restitutionary remedy. It follows that, while at common law one can normally sharply distinguish contractual issues (eg termination of a contract,[11] factors rendering a contract void) from restitutionary issues (eg coercive remedies for the repayment of money) it is unattractive and difficult to do so where rescission is in play.[12] This explains why the sections of this book concerned with rescission cover similar ground to equivalent chapters in contract books albeit that the material is here being examined from an unjust enrichment perspective.

A final nuance is that rescission of a contract is sometimes given *on terms*. Sometimes the terms do no more than ensure full counter-restitution to the defendant.[13] But in other situations the terms imposed have been that the claimant enter into a new contract on

---

9   See, eg, the undue influence cases of *Tate v Williamson* (1866) 2 Ch App 55 (sale of land); *Goldsworthy v Brickell* [1987] Ch 378 (lease of land) and *Crédit Lyonnais Bank Nederland NV v Burch* [1997] 1 All ER 144 (charge over land): and the misrepresentation cases of *Car and Universal Finance Co Ltd v Caldwell* [1965] 1 QB 525 (sale of car) and *Barclays Bank plc v O'Brien* [1994] 1 AC 180 (charge over land). For examples of proprietary counter-restitution, see the cases in the previous note. Proprietary counter-restitution is probably best viewed as an exception to the normal rule that a total failure of consideration does not invalidate the passing of title. That rescission gives priority on a misrepresentor's insolvency as against unsecured creditors is established by *Load v Green* (1846) 15 M & W 216; *Re Eastgate* [1905] 1 KB 465; *Tilley v Bowman Ltd* [1910] 1 KB 745. See, generally, Worthington, 'The Proprietary Consequences of Rescission' [2002] RLR 28.

10 Analogously, albeit rarely, rectification of a document or the register for mistake can be a proprietary restitutionary remedy in revesting proprietary rights: eg where the wrong area of land is conveyed as in *Beale v Kyte* [1907] 1 Ch 564 and *Blacklocks v JB Developments (Godalming) Ltd* [1982] Ch 183.

11 Even where the contract terminated involves the temporary transfer of proprietary rights, termination itself is most naturally viewed as non-restitutionary: the defendant's proprietary rights cease for the future and the claimant's original proprietary rights take effect once more. This seems more natural than saying that by termination the claimant reacquires, eg, a lessee's or a hirer's proprietary rights as if the proprietary rights vested in an owner can be viewed as an amalgam of different temporary rights.

12 Rescission therefore poses difficult problems in applying s 2(2) of the Contracts (Applicable Law) Act 1990: below, p 620.

13 See, eg, *The Medina* (1876) 1 PD 272; affd 2 PD 5; *The Port Caledonia and The Anna* [1903] P 184 (extortionate salvage agreements); *Earl of Aylesford v Morris* (1873) 8 Ch App 484 (catching bargain with expectant heir); *Cooper v Phibbs* (1867) LR 2 HL 149 (mistake).

terms considered fair by the court.[14] Rescission on the terms of agreeing
to a new contract might be thought to be a restitutionary remedy in
that the claimant is able to recover benefits transferred including
having proprietary rights revested in him. But at least in the usual
case it is perhaps best regarded as non-restitutionary because the overall
aim is to set up a new contractual relationship: benefits that the law
restored to the claimant are partly required to be given back through
the new contract.[15]

4. PROPRIETARY RESTITUTION

(1) Introduction

We have explained above that remedies reversing unjust enrichment
may be personal or proprietary; that proprietary restitutionary remedies
afford priority on the defendant's insolvency and are dependent on
the defendant's retention of particular property; that examples of
proprietary restitutionary remedies are an equitable lien, some
constructive and resulting trusts, rescission in so far as concerned with
re-vesting title to goods or land, and the conferment of secured rights
by (non-contractual) subrogation; and that most restitution is effected
by personal, not proprietary, remedies. This section expands on these
ideas particularly by seeking to clarify the answer to the question, when
is, or should, restitution reversing an unjust enrichment be proprietary
rather than personal?

Before seeking to answer that question, which is probably the most
difficult of all those raised by the law of restitution, it may first be

---

14 See *Solle v Butcher* [1950] 1 KB 671; *Grist v Bailey* [1967] Ch 532: but note that these cases
    have been overruled, in granting rescission for common mistake, by *Great Peace Shipping
    Ltd v Tsavliris (International) Ltd* [2002] EWCA Civ 1407. In *TSB Bank plc v Camfield* [1995]
    1 All ER 951 the Court of Appeal controversially held that rescission for misrepresentation or
    undue influence is all or nothing and cannot be granted on the terms of the claimant
    entering into a new contract. A wife had granted a charge over the matrimonial home
    securing the bank against her husband's partnership's liabilities without limit. She was
    misled into believing that the maximum liability secured was £15,000. It was held that she
    was entitled to rescind totally for misrepresentation and that a court had no power to require
    the rescission to be on the terms that there was a valid security for £15,000. *Camfield* was
    distinguished in *Barclays Bank plc v Caplan* [1998] 1 FLR 532 where it was decided, in
    relation to undue influence, that severance of the unobjectionable part of the contract
    from the objectionable is possible. *Camfield* was applied by Colman J in *De Molestina v Ponton*
    [2002] 1 Lloyd's Rep 271. Cf *Vadasz v Pioneer Concrete (SA) Pty Ltd* (1995) 184 CLR 102, High
    Court of Australia, which is compared with *Camfield* by Proksch, 'Rescission on Terms' [1996]
    RLR 71. In *Far Eastern Shipping Co Public Ltd v Scales Trading Ltd* [2001] 1 All ER (Comm) 319
    a guarantor was held entitled to rescind a guarantee for non-disclosure without having to
    enter into a different guarantee: the Privy Council expressly said that it was unnecessary for
    it to decide whether *Vadasz* was to be preferred to *Camfield*.
15 Cf Birks, p 163.

helpful to explain that the approach offered in this second edition departs significantly from that put forward in the first edition.

In the first edition, it was primarily argued that, apart from rescission of a contract which revests title and subrogation to secured rights, proprietary restitutionary remedies are triggered by the retention of property belonging to the claimant without his consent. In other words, the basic model adopted was that proprietary restitution, including remedies after tracing, is concerned to restore property belonging to the claimant. It was envisaged that proprietary restitution essentially rests on the claimant being able to assert, 'That's mine and I want it back'. This was seen as based on the unjust enrichment principle by arguing that there was an unjust factor of 'retention of the claimant's property without consent'.

In retrospect, that was an artificial and unhelpful approach. Where the claimant is asserting that the property in the defendant's hands is and was the claimant's property, the claim is not one based on the unjust enrichment of the defendant. On the contrary, the assertion is that, viewed in terms of proprietary rights, the defendant has never been enriched. The property has never been the defendant's. The return of the property to the claimant simply rests on pre-existing ownership. It follows, for example, that one never looks at the value of the defendant's enrichment and it would seem that change of position can never be a defence. I now accept what Nick Segal[16] wrote about my approach to this question: 'Both in relation to the question of benefit to and enrichment by the defendant and the characterisation of the relevant unjust factor, it has to be said that Professor Burrows' approach in *The Law of Restitution* seems somewhat artificial and strained.'

I first put forward a different approach in the following passage of *Cases and Materials on the Law of Restitution:*[17]

'One of us has in the past argued that the law of restitution includes cases where a proprietary remedy is given because the plaintiff owned particular property before and after it was received by the defendant and that the law is best understood as resting on an unjust factor of "the retention of property belonging to the plaintiff". Although some have found that analysis helpful, it seems preferable to draw a clear distinction between that case (which Goff and Jones ... call a "pure proprietary claim") and other cases where the

16 'Cross-border Security Enforcement, Restitution and Priorities' in *Restitution and Banking Law* (ed Rose, 1998), p 109.
17 (1998), p 724 (co-authored with Ewan McKendrick). See also Burrows, *Understanding the Law of Obligations* (1998), pp 115–117. It follows from this approach that, because they respond to pre-existing title, the remedies of delivery up for wrongful interference with goods or recovery of land are not directly covered in this book. In any event, the availability of delivery up is linked to compensation not restitution: see 1st edn of this book, pp 396–397.

proprietary remedy is given because the law is creating new proprietary rights in response to the defendant's unjust enrichment at the plaintiff's expense (which Goff and Jones call a "restitutionary proprietary claim"). To regard the latter type of case as resting on "retention of property belonging to the plaintiff" obscures the distinction between the two types of case ... In [the law of restitution] we confine our attention to the latter type of case (the "restitutionary proprietary claim").'

It is submitted, therefore, that, contrary to my earlier doubts, the conventional picture of the relationship between the law of restitution and property law, adhered to by Goff and Jones (at one time) and Birks, is correct.[18] *The law of restitution, being concerned with the principle against unjust enrichment, includes that part of the law of property in which proprietary remedies respond to (or, as one might otherwise express it, proprietary rights are created in response to) unjust enrichment.*

In the first edition of this book[19] an attempt was also made to understand – and to translate into the English context – the grand theory put forward in the United States of America by the late Professor Austin Scott that the constructive trust bears the same fictional relationship to the express trust as quasi-contract does to contract.[20] Consideration was also given to the fashionable, but equally difficult, idea that the constructive trust is viewed as a substantive institution in England in contrast to being viewed as a remedy to reverse unjust enrichment in the United States.[1]

My conclusions were as follows:

---

18 Goff and Jones, *The Law of Restitution* (3rd edn, 1986), at p 60, wrote: 'In this book, it would not be appropriate to discuss every situation in which a proprietary claim can be asserted by a claimant. For that reason we do not discuss a claim that the plaintiff has never been divested of his property in money or chattels (pure proprietary claims). In contrast, those proprietary claims which seek to revest title in the plaintiff are manifestly restitutionary.' (Cf 6th edn, 2002, para 1-011). Birks, at p 70, writes: 'The principle is that passive preservation of existing title is not restitution but that active creation of interests to reverse enrichment is.' See also at pp 15–17, 25, 49–73, 87–93.

19 Burrows, *The Law of Restitution* (1st edn, 1993), pp 35–40.

20 Scott, 'Constructive Trusts' (1955) LQR 39, 41; *Scott on Trusts* (4th edn, 1989), vol V, para 462–1. See also Palmer, *The Law of Restitution* (1978), vol 1, p 12; Maddaugh and McCamus, *The Law of Restitution* (1st edn, 1990), pp 13–21, 78–100.

1   The substantive institution as against remedy distinction is used by, eg, Pound, 'The Progress of the Law' (1920) 33 Harv LR 420; Maudsley, 'Proprietary Remedies for the Recovery of Money' (1959) 75 LQR 234; Hanbury and Martin, *Modern Equity* (16th edn, 2001), pp 301–304; Waters, *The Constructive Trust* (1964); Oakley, *Constructive Trusts* (3rd edn, 1997), pp 19–28; Maddaugh and McCamus, *The Law of Restitution* (1st edn, 1990), pp 78–100; Goode, 'Property and Unjust Enrichment' in *Essays on the Law of Restitution* (ed Burrows, 1991); Wright, *The Remedial Constructive Trust* (1998). The distinction is most carefully analysed by Elias, *Explaining Constructive Trusts* (1990), pp 159–163; Rotherham, *Proprietary Remedies in Context* (2002), ch 1 and pp 57–63; and Birks, 'Proprietary Rights as Remedies' in *The Frontiers of Liability* (ed Birks, 1994), pp 214–223. See also below, pp 73–74.

(1) Scott's theory seems unhelpful at least from an English perspective. (2) In contrast to the equitable lien or the 'proportionate share'[2] chosen or imposed following tracing, it is difficult to describe constructive and resulting trusts as remedies. This is because the trusts arise irrespective of a choice exercised by the claimant or the court. They pre-date a court order or the issue of proceedings or a claimant's election.[3]

(3) Even if one puts to one side the difficulty in describing a constructive or a resulting trust as a remedy, there is an objection to justifying them as reversing unjust enrichment by subtraction. This is because the gain reversed can exceed the claimant's loss. Moreover the resulting or constructive trust cases on cohabitees are concerned to uphold the parties' intentions or to protect the claimant's expectations or to effect a social policy of co-ownership between cohabitees rather than being concerned merely to reverse an unjust enrichment.[4]

Developments since the first edition have, however, made clear that unjust enrichment by subtraction does not require a correspondence between gain and loss so that, even outside restitution for wrongs, the measure of restitution may exceed the claimant's loss.[5] This removes the main objection, in the third conclusionary point above, to seeing some resulting and constructive trusts as restitutionary remedies. Furthermore, while it remains true that there is some

---

2   This was the term coined by Hanbury and Maudsley, *Modern Equity* (13th edn, 1989), pp 639–640 (but not used in later editions). See also *Foskett v McKeown* [2001] 1 AC 102. It is more simply labelled a trust (whether resulting or constructive): see *Scott on Trusts* (1989), vol V, paras 507–529; Dawson, *Unjust Enrichment* (1952), pp 26–35. But unlike most other trusts, it does not impose fiduciary duties (eg, of investment) on the defendant. Rather the defendant's sole duty is to transfer to the claimant the property in which the claimant has a beneficial interest. Some commentators (eg, Palmer, *The Law of Restitution* (1978), vol 1 paras 1.3–1.4) appear to argue that in imposing a constructive trust to reverse unjust enrichment a court orders the transfer of specific property. This not only contradicts English law but logically requires abandoning all reference to a trust. What is in reality being advocated is a novel use of a mandatory enforcing injunction as a direct restitutionary proprietary remedy.

3   For consideration of the time when constructive trusts arise, including following tracing, see eg, *Rawluk v Rawluk* (1990) 65 DLR (4th) 161; *Scott on Trusts* (4th edn, 1989), vol V, para 462–4; Sherwin, 'Constructive Trusts in Bankruptcy' (1989) University of Illinois LR 297, esp 310–313; Birks, 'Proprietary Rights as Remedies' in *The Frontiers of Liability* (ed Birks, 1994), pp 214, 218.

4   This is despite judicial statements viewing constructive trusts in this context as restitutionary remedies in, eg, *Hussey v Palmer* [1972] 1 WLR 1286; *Pettkus v Becker* (1981) 117 DLR (3d) 257; *Sorochan v Sorochan* (1986) 29 DLR (4th) 1; *Rawluk v Rawluk* (1990) 65 DLR (4th) 161. Cf *Muchinski v Dodds* (1985) 160 CLR 583 (per Deane J). See also the constructive trust imposed in the joint venture case of *Banner Homes plc v Luff Developments Ltd* [2000] Ch 372 which protected the claimant's expectation interest albeit that there was no concluded contract between the parties.

5   See above, pp 28–29.

descriptive difficulty in describing constructive and resulting trusts as remedies, the same descriptive problem can be said to apply even to equitable liens. The explanation for this descriptive difficulty is that normally one cannot cleanly separate proprietary remedies from the proprietary rights which they protect. It is submitted that the preferable approach is not to be waylaid by such descriptive difficulties but to see the central question raised as being the following: when, if ever, are proprietary rights (or the power to choose to have proprietary rights) created to reverse the defendant's unjust enrichment at the claimant's expense (rather than being created by, for example, consent or in response to miscellaneous other events)? Or, more succinctly, when is (or should) proprietary restitution (be) given, rather than personal restitution, to reverse an unjust enrichment? We can now turn to that question.

(2) When is (or should) proprietary restitution (be) given, rather than personal restitution, to reverse unjust enrichment?

According to some commentators, most notably Graham Virgo,[6] proprietary restitution can never be awarded to reverse unjust enrichment. Rather proprietary restitution (and personal restitution awarded against indirect recipients) is based on the principle of vindicating property rights with which the defendant has interfered. Tracing is concerned with the continuation and vindication of proprietary rights in substitute property and not with the principle against unjust enrichment.

With respect, this is to adopt too narrow a view of the principle against unjust enrichment. It ignores numerous examples of proprietary rights created to reverse unjust enrichment. In respect of tracing, it relies on a fiction in asserting that tracing involves the continuation of proprietary rights into substitute property. In reality, new proprietary rights are created in the substitute property to reverse the defendant's unjust enrichment at the claimant's expense.

Unfortunately, the majority of the House of Lords in *Foskett v McKeown*[7] has taken a similar approach to tracing to that adopted by Virgo and has argued that a remedy imposed following tracing is purely a matter of property law and is not concerned to reverse the defendant's unjust enrichment. Lord Millett, giving the leading speech, said:

6   *The Principles of the Law of Restitution* (1999), pp 8, 11–16. See also, eg Grantham and Rickett, 'Property and Unjust Enrichment: Categorical Truths or Unnecessary Complexity' [1997] NZL Rev 668; *Enrichment and Restitution in New Zealand* (2000), ch 3; 'Tracing and Property Rights: the Categorical Truth' (2000) 63 MLR 905.
7   [2001] 1 AC 102.

'The transmission of a claimant's property rights from one asset to its traceable proceeds is part of our law of property, not of the law of unjust enrichment ... The claimant succeeds if at all by virtue of his own title, not to reverse unjust enrichment ...'[8]

He later continued:

'As I have already pointed out, the purchasers seek to vindicate their property rights, not to reverse unjust enrichment... A plaintiff who brings an action in unjust enrichment must show that the defendant has been enriched at the plaintiff's expense, for he cannot have been unjustly enriched if he has not been enriched at all. But the plaintiff is not concerned to show that the defendant is in receipt of property belonging beneficially to the plaintiff or its traceable proceeds. The fact that the beneficial ownership of the property has passed to the defendant provides no defence; indeed, it is usually the very fact which founds the claim... Furthermore, a claim in unjust enrichment is subject to a change of position defence, which usually operates by reducing or extinguishing the element of enrichment. An action like the present is subject to the bona fide purchaser for value defence, which operates to clear the defendant's title.'[9]

Lord Browne-Wilkinson said:

'The contrary view appears to be based primarily on the ground that to give the purchasers a rateable share of the policy moneys is not to reverse an unjust enrichment but to give the purchasers a wholly unwarranted windfall.... But this windfall is enjoyed because of the rights which the purchasers enjoy under the law of property. A man under whose land oil is discovered enjoys a very valuable windfall but no-one suggests that he, as owner of the property, is not entitled to the windfall which goes with his property by right. We are not dealing with a claim in unjust enrichment.'[10]

In Lord Hoffmann's words:

'This [claim] is not based upon unjust enrichment except in the most trivial sense of that expression. It is ... a vindication of proprietary right.'[11]

While this reasoning is, with respect, flawed and relies on the fiction that tracing involves the continuation of proprietary rights into substitute property,[12] the actual decision in *Foskett v McKeown* may have

---

8   Ibid, at 127.
9   Ibid, at 129.
10 Ibid, at 110.
11 Ibid, at 115.
12 Burrows, 'Proprietary Restitution: Unmasking Unjust Enrichment' (2001) 117 LQR 412. See also Birks, 'Property, Unjust Enrichment and Tracing' (2001) 54 CLP 231. As regards fictions in this context, see the wide-ranging article by Rotherham, 'The Metaphysics of Tracing: Substituted Title and Property Rhetoric' (1996) 34 Osgoode Hall LJ 321; and Rotherham, *Proprietary Remedies in Context* (2002), chs 2 and 5.

been justified and could have been satisfactorily reached applying an unjust enrichment analysis.[13] It follows that, while *Foskett* has made acceptance of the approach to proprietary restitution in this book more difficult, *Foskett* cannot and must not be regarded as the last word on the relationship in English law between the law of property and the principle against unjust enrichment.

It is submitted, therefore, that unjust enrichment may trigger both personal and proprietary restitution. Contrary to the views of Virgo and others, it is false to say that unjust enrichment triggers only personal restitution. Indeed, although the law is open to more than one interpretation, one can say that the following are all examples of proprietary restitution reversing unjust enrichment: the trust imposed on the mistaken payment in *Chase Manhattan Bank NA v Israel-British Bank (London) Ltd*;[14] equitable liens imposed over mistakenly improved land;[15] rescission of an executed contract, for misrepresentation or duress or undue influence, which revests the proprietary rights to goods or land transferred under the contract;[16] the equitable lien or trust imposed following tracing;[17] non-contractual subrogation entitling the subrogating person to take over proprietary rights;[18] and constructive trusts imposed

---

13   See above, p 20 and below, pp 101–102, 208–209.

14   [1981] Ch 105. But in *Westdeutsche Landesbank Girozentrale v Islington London Borough Council* [1996] AC 669 Lord Browne-Wilkinson, giving the leading speech of the majority, regarded the reasoning of Goulding J in the *Chase Manhattan* case as wrong albeit that the actual decision might be correct on the basis that the defendant knew of the mistake within two days of the receipt of the payment. Birks, 'Restitution and Resulting Trust' in *Equity and Contemporary Legal Developments* (ed Goldstein, 1992) and Chambers, *Resulting Trusts* (1997) label the trust in the *Chase Manhattan* case a resulting, rather than a constructive, trust. Cf Swadling, 'A New Role for Resulting Trusts?' (1996) 16 Legal Studies 110 who argues that presumed resulting trusts must be consistent with there being an intention to create a trust and that cannot be so where the payor did not intend to benefit the payee. Lord Browne-Wilkinson in the *Westdeutsche* case appeared to prefer Swadling's terminology: cf *Air Jamaica Ltd v Charlton* [1999] 1 WLR 1399.

15   Eg, *Cooper v Phibbs* (1867) LR 2 HL 149.

16   Eg, *Car and Universal Finance Ltd v Caldwell* [1965] 1 QB 525. See above p 59, n 9. In relation to rescission, the *creation* of proprietary rights in response to unjust enrichment is constituted by the power to *revest* the claimant's proprietary rights in goods or land. Chambers, *Resulting Trusts* (1997), ch 7, argues that in the period before the contract is rescinded (or rectified), the property transferred is held on resulting trust by the transferee. This now derives support from *Collings v Lee* [2001] 2 All ER 332 (although the CA's reasoning can be interpreted as limiting this to where the transferee has committed a breach of fiduciary duty ie proprietary restitution for a wrong). See also, eg, *Blacklocks v JB Developments (Godalming) Ltd* [1982] Ch 183. But this appears to be inconsistent with the traditional view that the claimant has a mere equity of rescission and not an equitable interest: see, eg, *Lonrho plc v Fayed (No 2)* [1992] 1 WLR 1, 11–12 (*per* Millett J); *Ciro Citterio Menswear plc v Thakrar* [2002] EWHC 662 (Ch), [2002] 1 WLR 2217, paras 32–41 (*per* Anthony Mann QC).

17   Eg, *Re Hallett's Estate* (1880) 13 Ch D 696; *Re Diplock* [1948] Ch 465, CA; *Foskett v McKeown* [2001] 1 AC 102.

18   Eg, s 5 of the Mercantile Law Amendment Act 1856: *Lord Napier and Ettrick v Hunter* [1993] AC 713; *Boscawen v Bajwa* [1996] 1 WLR 328; *Banque Financière de la Cité v Parc Battersea Ltd* [1999] 1 AC 221.

on gains made by equitable wrongs.[19] While most restitution is personal, these and other examples of proprietary restitution will be discussed at various stages in this book under the particular unjust factor in play.

Given that the above examples of proprietary restitution in the present law do not seem to rest on an obvious principle distinguishing them from situations where only personal restitution is given (ie, the present law as to when proprietary, rather than personal, restitution will be granted appears to lack coherence), the following question arises. Assuming that the claimant can establish that the defendant has been unjustly enriched at the expense of the claimant, and that the defendant retains the enrichment (whether in the same form or, by the rules of tracing, in a substitution),[20] what *should* determine whether the claimant is entitled to proprietary, rather than merely personal, restitution to reverse the enrichment?

One approach to this question would be to adopt the starting point that wherever an unjust enrichment at the claimant's expense triggers personal restitution so it should prima facie trigger proprietary restitution provided the enrichment exists in an asset to which the proprietary right can attach.[1] The main thrust of this approach is that the factors negativing voluntariness that account for most personal restitution also justify proprietary restitution. Applying this approach, mistake, duress, undue influence and ignorance, within autonomous unjust enrichment, should all, for example, trigger proprietary rights in the asset that comprises the defendant's unjust enrichment.[2]

19 Eg, *Boardman v Phipps* [1967] 2 AC 46; *A-G for Hong Kong v Reid* [1994] 1 AC 324.
20 Theoretically just as one can create *consensual* security over any (or even all) of the defendant's assets, it would be possible to give a proprietary remedy (eg a lien) over some or all of the defendant's assets to secure restitution of value received by the defendant. This possibility appears to underpin the 'swollen assets' theory on which see, eg, Oesterle, 'Deficiencies of the Restitutionary Right to Trace Misappropriated Property in Equity and in UCC 9–306' (1983) 68 Cornell LR 172; Lionel Smith, *The Law of Tracing* (1997), pp 270–274, 310–320; Evans, 'Rethinking Tracing and the Law of Restitution' (1999) 115 LQR 469. Lord Templeman's dicta in *Space Investments Ltd v Canadian Imperial Bank of Commerce Trust Co (Bahamas) Ltd* [1986] 1 WLR 1072, 1074 may be interpreted as supporting that theory. But under the present law (see, especially, *Bishopsgate Investment Management Ltd v Homan* [1995] Ch 211; *Re Goldcorp Exchange Ltd* [1995] 1 AC 74) – and for the same reasons as justify the requirement of a chain of substitutions in order to trace (see below, p 80) – a proprietary remedy is given only over the specific property retained by the defendant which, if necessary by applying tracing rules, comprises or contains the enrichment subtracted from the claimant.
1 Burrows and McKendrick, *Cases and Materials on the Law of Restitution* (1st edn, 1997), pp 765–766; Chambers, *Resulting Trusts* (1997).
2 Hence the decision in *Chase Manhattan Bank NA Ltd v Israel-British Bank (London) Ltd* [1981] Ch 105. But where the mistake is fundamental or one is concerned with absence of consent (eg ignorance), the claimant retains legal title to the original asset. The claimant's proprietary claim to that asset is therefore a pure proprietary, rather than a restitutionary proprietary, claim. But if the claimant chooses to assert an equitable proprietary interest in the original asset to reverse the defendant's unjust enrichment this presumably has the consequence that legal title in the original asset is regarded as having passed to the defendant. See analogously below, p 76.

However, a difficulty with this approach is that it contradicts the present law in that the factor negativing voluntariness comprising 'failure of consideration' does not normally generate a proprietary right even if the defendant retains the same asset transferred by the claimant. If a debtor fails to repay a loan to its creditor, the creditor is not entitled to proprietary restitution for failure of consideration even if the debtor retains the loaned money (or its traceable substitute). A plausible explanation for the 'failure of consideration' exception would then be to say that while 'vitiation of consent' counts, 'qualification of consent' normally does not, because a period of time during which the defendant was perfectly entitled to the enrichment – ie, the injustice is only subsequent – nullifies any prospect of a proprietary right being created over the enrichment.[3] In Robert Chambers' words (speaking of when a restitutionary resulting trust may arise following a failure of consideration):

> 'Where the provider of property to another had only a qualified intention to benefit the recipient in circumstances which have failed to arise or continue as expected, the transfer becomes non-voluntary on that failure and a resulting trust may arise, so long as the property remains identifiable and the recipient has not obtained the unfettered beneficial ownership of the property. If the recipient does obtain the unrestricted use of the property before the right to restitution arises ... the provider will only be entitled to a personal claim for restitution, if any.'[4]

And in a very clear summary of his approach in his excellent article, 'Constructive Trusts in Canada',[5] Chambers writes:

> 'The law has had difficulty working out precisely why and when an unjust enrichment will generate a trust ... [A] trust should arise only where (a) the unjust enrichment is an asset capable of being the subject matter of a trust; (b) the defendant did not

---

3   On this approach, the House of Lords' denial of the resulting trust in *Westdeutsche Landesbank Girozentrale v Islington London Borough Council* [1996] AC 669 is to be explained by saying that the unjust factor was a (subsequent) failure of consideration: see Chambers, *Resulting Trusts* (1997), p 162.

4   Chambers, *Resulting Trusts* (1997), p 169. See also Burrows and McKendrick, *Cases and Materials on the Law of Restitution*, p 766. Applying this approach, Chambers, *Resulting Trusts* (1997), pp 148–149, argues that *Barclays Bank Ltd v Quistclose Investments Ltd* [1970] AC 567 is an example of an unjust enrichment resulting trust where, although the unjust factor was failure of consideration, proprietary restitution was justified because the payee never obtained the unrestricted use of the money before the failure of consideration. An alternative analysis (for full discussion, see Chambers, *Resulting Trusts* (1997), ch 3) is that a *Quistclose* resulting trust is merely an unusual example (because the express trust is a purpose trust) of the common situation of a validly-created express trust subsequently failing. For a detailed judicial analysis of the *Quistclose* trust, see Lord Millett's (dissenting) speech in *Twinsectra Ltd v Yardley* [2002] UKHL 12, [2002] 2 AC 164.

5   (1999) 37 Alberta LR 173. See also Chambers, 'Resulting Trusts in Canada' (2000) 38 Alberta LR 378.

acquire the full beneficial ownership of that asset before the plaintiff's right to restitution arose; and (c) the enrichment is unjust because the plaintiff did not intend the defendant to have the benefit of the asset in the circumstances.'[6]

An alternative approach (which reaches similar, but not identical, conclusions) is to focus on the principal consequence of creating proprietary rights and to consider whether that consequence is merited in relation to the unjust enrichment in question. That is, the principal effect of giving the claimant proprietary restitution is that this will give priority on the defendant's insolvency. Although it is clear that creating proprietary rights has wider consequences than affording priority on insolvency (not least in relation to the criminal law of theft)[7] the law should only create proprietary rights if the claimant should be entitled to priority in the event of the defendant's insolvency. In other words, short of there being untoward consequences in other respects, it seems acceptable to work out whether the law should create proprietary rights by considering the position in the event of the defendant's insolvency.[8] Applying this approach, one can deduce a central principle or policy as follows. The law should not create proprietary rights where, analogously to an unsecured creditor, the unjust enrichment claimant has taken the risk of the defendant's insolvency. In contrast, the law should give priority where, analogously to a secured creditor, the unjust enrichment claimant has not taken the risk of the defendant's insolvency.

Another way of explaining this alternative approach is to say that proprietary restitution should not undermine the present law on insolvency. A central tenet of insolvency law is the distinction between secured and unsecured creditors. Proprietary restitution should therefore only be granted where there is an analogy between the restitution – claimant's position and that of a secured, rather than an unsecured, creditor.

---

6 Ibid at 219. Chambers points out that a trust arising in this situation has traditionally been labelled resulting rather than constructive. He argues that constructive trusts have traditionally been imposed to effect proprietary restitution for wrongs and, outside the law of restitution, to perfect intentions to benefit others (eg in contracts of sale, secret trusts, mutual wills, incomplete gifts, and the division of family property on the breakdown of a marriage or similar relationship). For a similar view that constructive trusts are often intention-based and not restitutionary, see Elias, *Explaining Constructive Trusts* (1990); Gardner, *An Introduction to the Law of Trusts* (1990), pp 233–234. In contrast Waters, *The Constructive Trust* (1964) argued that nearly all constructive trusts are restitutionary remedies.

7 Another consequence is that an interim preservation order under CPR 25.1(1)(c) can be granted in respect of a proprietary claim and this appears to be easier to obtain than a freezing (*Mareva*) injunction: see *Polly Peck International plc v Nadir (No 2)* [1992] 4 All ER 769.

8 Burrows, 'Proprietary Restitution: Unmasking Unjust Enrichment' (2001) 117 LQR 412; Finch and Worthington, 'The *Pari Passu* Principle and Ranking Restitutionary Rights' in *Restitution and Insolvency* (ed Rose, 2000) pp 1–20, esp p 17. *Contra* Birks, 'The Law of Restitution at the End of an Epoch' (1999) 28 U W Aus LR 13, 55–56.

Although several commentators[9] and judges,[10] analysing proprietary restitution, have relied on this principle or policy of 'taking the risk of insolvency', it needs 'fleshing out' to appreciate its full force and to see that the leading cases[11] (other than on proprietary restitution for wrongs) are consistent with it. A suggested 'fleshing out' is as follows:

(i) A person who gives credit confers a benefit on another in return for the promise of later payment. A secured creditor is given consensually created rights over some or all of the debtor's property as security for the promised payment. By being given proprietary rights, the creditor can take out 'his' property from the defendant's assets in the event of the latter's insolvency. The consensual creation of proprietary rights thereby secures the creditor against the risk of insolvency. An unsecured creditor, who is not given rights over the debtor's property, takes the risk of the debtor's insolvency.

(ii) The conferring of an *enrichment* on the defendant *by subtraction* from the claimant equates to the *giving of credit* by a creditor.

(iii) In some situations of subtractive unjust enrichment, the claimant has taken the risk of the defendant's insolvency. He is, or is in an analogous position to, an unsecured creditor. He should not therefore be granted proprietary restitution. The most obvious example is where the claimant is an actual unsecured creditor who, having conferred credit without security, seeks to obtain priority 'by the back door' by discharging the contract for breach and claiming proprietary restitution of the credit on the basis of failure of consideration.[12] The same applies wherever the claimant seeks restitution of benefits for failure of consideration conferred

9   Goff and Jones, *The Law of Restitution* (4th edn, 1993), p 94; (5th edn, 1998), p 90; Maddaugh and McCamus, *The Law of Restitution* (1st edn, 1990), pp 95–96, 137–139; Tettenborn, *The Law of Restitution in England and Ireland* (3rd edn, 2002), pp 129–130; Sherwin, 'Constructive Trusts in Bankruptcy' (1989) University of Illinois LR 297; Paciocco, 'The Remedial Constructive Trust: A Principled Basis for Priorities over Creditors' (1989) 68 Can BR 315; Friedmann, 'Payment under Mistake – Tracing and Subrogation' (1999) 115 LQR 195, 198; Rotherham, 'Tracing and Justice in Bankruptcy' in *Restitution and Insolvency* (ed Rose, 2000), pp 113–133, esp pp 126–130; Rotherham, *Proprietary Remedies in Context* (2002) esp chapters 4, 6, 9, 11 and 12.

10 Eg Lord Goff in the *Westdeutsche Landesbank Girozentrale v Islington London Borough Council* [1996] AC 669, 684: Lord Templeman in *Lord Napier and Ettrick v Hunter* [1993] AC 713, 737.

11 In particular, *Chase Manhattan Bank NA Ltd v Israel-British Bank (London) Ltd* [1981] Ch 105; *Re Goldcorp Exchange Ltd* [1995] 1 AC 74; *Westdeutsche Landesbank Girozentrale v Islington London Borough Council* [1996] AC 669; *Banque Financière de la Cité v Parc Battersea Ltd* [1999] 1 AC 221; *Foskett v McKeown* [2001] 1 AC 102. See notes 12–16 below.

12 This can explain why in *Re Goldcorp Exchange Ltd* [1995] 1 AC 74 the unallocated claimants were not entitled to proprietary restitution even if the defendant still retained the purchase money or its traceable proceeds. The claimants were basing their claim on failure of consideration and were unsecured creditors. (They had not elected to rescind the contracts for misrepresentation or mistake so as to revest title in the purchase money but rescission was, in any event, barred because the money did not now exist and third parties would have been prejudiced.)

under a discharged, unenforceable, void or incomplete or anticipated contract and there was no security created, or purportedly created, in the 'contract'.[13] The position would be different if security for the claimant had been created or purportedly created in the 'contract'.[14] One could not then say that the claimant was – or was analogous to – an unsecured creditor who had taken the risk of the defendant's insolvency. Rather he is, or is analogous to, a secured creditor.

(iv) Where the unjust factor is not failure of consideration (which constitutes a qualification of intention) but rather constitutes a vitiation of consent (eg mistake, duress, or undue influence) or an absence of consent (eg ignorance), the claimant's position will normally be analogous to that of a secured creditor: that is, he has not taken the risk of the creditor's insolvency because he did not mean the defendant to be enriched at all. Generally, therefore, proprietary restitution should be available.[15] However, it is tentatively suggested that, even in relation to such unjust factors, the particular circumstances may exceptionally mean that, although the claimant did not intend the defendant to be enriched, it nevertheless took the risk of the defendant's insolvency. A possible example is where a claimant has made a payment to the defendant by reason of a mistake of law in believing that a purported contract, under which it was to confer credit without security, was valid whereas, as a matter of law, it was void. The invalidity of the contract does not itself rest on the claimant's mistake. Although the claimant has a personal action for the recovery of the money paid by mistake of law, it is arguable that that mistake does not hide the risk taken by the claimant as to the defendant's insolvency. If so, the mistake of law should not trigger proprietary restitution so as to confer priority on the defendant's insolvency.[16]

13 This can explain why no proprietary restitution was granted in *Westdeutsche Landesbank Girozentrale v Islington London Borough Council* [1996] AC 669 where the claim for money paid under a void interest rate swap transaction rested on a failure of consideration. It can also explain why *Sinclair v Brougham* [1914] AC 398 was correctly overruled in the *Westdeutsche* case.

14 Similarly, applying this approach, the trust imposed in *Barclays Bank Ltd v Quistclose Investments Ltd* [1970] AC 567 can be justified because, despite the (subsequent) failure of consideration, the claimant had not taken the risk of the payee's insolvency given that it had expressly specified the exclusive purpose for which the money was to be held and used. The same can be said of resulting trusts imposed following the (subsequent) failure of express trusts.

15 It follows that, on this approach, cases such as *Chase Manhattan Bank NA Ltd v Israel-British Bank (London) Ltd* [1981] Ch 105 (mistake) and *Foskett v McKeown* [2001] 1 AC 102 (ignorance) were correct to grant or recognise proprietary restitution.

16 Hence, applying this approach, the same result would have followed in the *Westdeutsche* case even if the claim had been based on mistake of law rather than failure of consideration (as it would have to have been if the void swap had been fully performed as in *Kleinwort Benson Ltd v Lincoln City Council* [1999] 2 AC 349). For another excellent illustration see *Banque Financière de la Cité v Parc (Battersea) Ltd* [1999] 1 AC 221 (below, pp 117–120): the subrogation gave 'personal' security by which the defendant's charge ranked after repayment to the claimant and was designed precisely to match the risk of insolvency taken, and that not taken, by the claimant.

(v) The analogy between subtractive enrichment and the giving of credit exposes the important difference between unjust enrichment by subtraction and compensation for wrongs. The latter does not normally, if ever, rest on a benefit having been conferred on the defendant. There is therefore no analogy to credit. And even if in the context of breach of contract compensation for non-performance of a promise to repay credit can be regarded as resting on the credit conferred, the promisee will have had adequate opportunity to provide for security in the contract. If the creditor has failed to do so, he has taken the risk of the debtor's insolvency and there is no justification for the law imposing 'proprietary' compensation (eg, a charge over the defendant's assets securing compensation).

(vi) Although in respect of restitution for wrongs, the defendant acquires a gain, this normally differs fundamentally from the giving of credit because the gain is not acquired by subtraction from the claimant. This suggests that there is normally no good reason to give proprietary restitution for wrongs. Moreover, given that compensation for wrongs does not justify an imposed secured remedy, it would be odd to impose such security in respect of restitution, which is a more controversial and less obvious measure of recovery for a wrong than compensation.[17]

(vii) In summary, therefore, the key principle or policy in determining whether unjust enrichment should trigger a proprietary, rather than a merely personal, remedy is whether the claimant is, or is analogous to, a secured creditor who has not taken the risk of the defendant's insolvency. In general, where the unjust factor is failure of consideration, the remedy should be personal only. In general, for other unjust factors within unjust enrichment by subtraction the remedy can be proprietary as well as personal. But proprietary restitution for wrongs is unwarranted.[18]

---

17   Applying this approach, it follows that cases giving proprietary restitution for wrongs, such as *Boardman v Phipps* [1967] 2 AC 46 and *A-G for Hong Kong v Reid* [1994] 1 AC 324 should be regarded as wrongly decided; and *Lister & Co v Stubbs* (1890) 45 Ch D 1 as correctly decided.

18   Birks' 'proprietary base' theory, first put forward in his *Introduction to the Law of Restitution* (revised edn, 1989), pp 386–389, is that proprietary restitution should be given only where there has been a subtraction from the claimant's ownership. Normally restitution for wrongs should not therefore trigger proprietary restitution; nor should unjust enrichment by subtraction where the subtraction is not of property owned by the claimant (eg, 'interceptive subtraction' or the indirect subtraction in a case like *Lord Napier and Ettrick v Hunter* [1993] AC 713). But while it may reach similar conclusions to those in this text (eg, that proprietary restitution should not normally be awarded for wrongs) the justificatory force of the 'proprietary base' theory is unclear. If the idea is that the claimant should not end up in a better position than it started off from one might ask 'why not, if this is the best way to ensure restitution of an unjust enrichment?' Moreover, the 'proprietary base' theory offers no explanation for why failure of consideration does not in general trigger proprietary restitution. For criticism of Birks' approach, see also Rotherham, *Proprietary Remedies in Context* (2002), ch 15.

It should be emphasised that the above alternative approach is not intended to suggest that the question of whether proprietary, rather than merely personal, restitution should be given to reverse an unjust enrichment is to be decided by the discretionary decision of a court. On the contrary, proprietary rights should not be discretionary but should depend on clear and certain principles. What has been set out above is an attempt to give such clarity and certainty to the 'taking the risk of insolvency' approach.

In *Westdeutsche Landesbank Girozentrale v Islington London Borough Council*[19] Lord Browne-Wilkinson, giving the leading speech of their Lordships, suggested two approaches to proprietary restitution that, with respect, are difficult to accept (although the decision rejecting proprietary restitution in that case was correct).[20] Concerned that proprietary restitution would give unwarranted priority on insolvency, his Lordship first reasoned that a trust should only be imposed where the defendant's conscience is affected. This was presented as if it were an underpinning principle of all trusts. But an express trustee is surely a trustee from the moment property is transferred into his name irrespective of the trustee's own knowledge. Again, if an aunt puts shares in the name of her niece and the niece knows nothing of what she has done, there is a resulting trust irrespective of when the niece acquires the requisite knowledge. Moreover, applying the conscience test to decide whether there should be proprietary restitution seems not only inconsistent with the reasoning in most past cases[1] but also lacks justification in terms of principle or policy. If one is concerned to protect the defendant's unsecured creditors, one will not necessarily do so by insisting that the defendant knows of the unjust factor: applying that test unsecured creditors may, or may not, be able to share in a mistaken payment depending on whether the defendant knew, or did not know, of the mistake before the insolvency. The law on proprietary restitution would also be rendered unacceptably uncertain (and out of line with personal restitution) if it were dependent on the claimant always establishing, perhaps at a particular moment in time, the defendant's state of mind.

Secondly, Lord Browne-Wilkinson suggested that the English law of restitution might be developed by embracing the notion of

---

19 [1996] AC 669. See Birks, 'Trusts Raised to Reverse Unjust Enrichment: The *Westdeutsche* Case' [1996] RLR 1; Rotherham, *Proprietary Remedies in Context* (2002), pp 136–140.

20 See below, pp 409–410.

1 Eg, *Cooper v Phibbs* (1867) LR 2 HL 149; *Re Diplock* [1948] Ch 465; *Chase Manhattan Bank NA Ltd v Israel-British Bank (London) Ltd* [1981] Ch 105. An exception is *Neste Oy v Lloyds Bank plc* [1983] 2 Lloyd's Rep 658 in which Bingham J held that the final payment was held on constructive trust because the payee then knew that there would inevitably be a failure of consideration: see also *Triffit Nurseries v Salads Etcetera Ltd* [2000] 1 All ER (Comm) 737.

a remedial constructive trust.[2] It is not entirely clear what his
Lordship meant by this. He seemed to have in mind that proprietary
restitution might be decided upon not by rules of law but at the
discretion of the judges who could, for example, protect third
parties against the retrospective operation of the proprietary rights
granted. However, certainty, not discretion, should underpin
proprietary, as well as personal, restitution. And the law of restitution
already recognises defences, namely change of position and bona
fide purchase which, it may be thought, can adequately protect
third parties without the need to rely on a wide-ranging judicial
discretion.[3] The frosty reception given to Lord Browne-Wilkinson's
suggestion by the Court of Appeal in *Re Polly Peck (No 2)*[4] is therefore
understandable. It was there held that there was no seriously
arguable case for (retrospectively) granting a remedial constructive
trust, stripping gains made by an insolvent trespasser, because to
do so would undermine the *pari passu* insolvency regime. In
Mummery LJ's memorable phrase, 'The insolvency road is blocked
off to remedial constructive trusts, at least when judge driven in a
vehicle of discretion.'[5] And Nourse LJ clarified that the objection
to the remedial constructive trust was that it gave the courts 'a
discretion to vary proprietary rights'.[6]

It should be noted, finally, that in some Canadian cases difficulty in
assessing the quantum of personal restitution appears to have influenced
the decision to impose a constructive trust.[7] It is hard to accept that this
is a good justification for imposing proprietary rather than personal
restitution. While specific performance of a contract to transfer property

---

2   [1996] AC 669, 716. For this terminology, see also above, p 62.
3   Lord Browne-Wilkinson was particularly concerned that the restitution-claimant should
    not have priority over a *secured* creditor (eg, a fixed or floating charge-holder). But this
    would not be a problem if either the bona fide purchase defence were modified to say
    that a bona fide purchaser of an equitable (as well as a legal) interest took priority over
    prior equitable interests; or if one regarded a secured creditor as being able to rely on a
    change of position defence. That is certainly the position in relation to rescission where
    the bar of 'third party rights' and the notion that equitable interests have priority over
    mere equities means that the secured creditor would take priority (as Lord Mustill
    recognised in *Re Goldcorp Exchange Ltd* [1995] 1 AC 74).
4   [1998] 3 All ER 812. See also *Fortex Group Ltd v MacIntosh* [1998] 3 NZLR 171. On these
    cases, see Birks, 'The End of the Remedial Constructive Trust' (1998) 12 Trusts L
    International 202; Wright, 'Professor Birks and the Demise of the Remedial Constructive
    Trust' [1999] RLR 128. For earlier judicial discussion of the 'remedial constructive trust'
    see, eg, *Re Sharpe* [1980] 1 WLR 219, 225 (per Browne-Wilkinson J); *Chase Manhattan
    Bank NA v Israel-British Bank (London) Ltd* [1981] Ch 105; *Metall und Rohstoff v Donaldson
    Lufkin & Jenrette Inc* [1990] 1 QB 391, 473–478.
5   Ibid at 827.
6   Ibid at 831.
7   Eg, *LAC Minerals v International Corona Resources Ltd* (1989) 61 DLR (4th) 14. See below,
    pp 504–505.

may be ordered because damages for breach of contract are difficult to assess, the creation of proprietary rights as the enforcement of a contract rests, relatively uncontroversially, on the consent underpinning the contract. In contrast, the reversal of an unjust enrichment is imposed by law and is not based on intentions; the creation of proprietary rights to effect that reversal is therefore much more problematic. Moreover, in the context of restitution for wrongs (which is what the Canadian cases were concerned with) fairness to the defendant demands that restitution for a wrong should be limited in some way so that the defendant is not made liable to disgorge all gains factually caused by his wrong however far removed from it. The case for such a 'remoteness' restriction is even more pressing than in respect of compensation for loss because restitution for a wrong represents a windfall to the claimant. What the cut-off point should be is a matter of judicial policy. But to impose a constructive trust where the quantum of the gains to be disgorged is unclear would be to ignore remoteness altogether.

5. DOES RETENTION OF TITLE PRECLUDE RESTITUTION?

In the last section, we explored some aspects of the difficult relationship between the law of property and the principle against unjust enrichment. But there is a further aspect of that relationship that we have not so far touched on (because it does not concern proprietary restitution as such). It is sometimes argued that where the claimant retains legal (or possibly even equitable title) in property transferred – for example where the payment of money was made under a fundamental mistake – the claimant has no personal claim in (autonomous) unjust enrichment in relation to that property.

According to William Swadling,[8] this follows inevitably because the claimant has suffered no loss so that any gain to the defendant is not at the claimant's expense. He or she still has legal title. In similar vein, one might perhaps equally well suggest that the defendant has not been enriched. Similarly Grantham and Rickett[9] argue that a claim

---

8 Swadling, 'A Claim in Restitution' [1996] LMCLQ 63, 65. He relies on Brennan J's dicta in the Australian criminal case of *Ilich v R* (1987) 162 CLR 110, 140–141: 'the incurring of the [restitutionary] debt is the consequence of acquiring ownership of the money; the payee would not owe the debt if he had not become the owner of the money with which the overpayment was made.'

9 Grantham and Rickett, 'Restitution, Property and Ignorance – a Reply to Mr Swadling' [1996] LMCLQ 463; 'Property and Unjust Enrichment: Categorical Truths or Unnecessary Complexity' [1997] NZL Rev 668; 'Restitution, Property and Mistaken Payments' [1997] RLR 83; *Enrichment and Restitution in New Zealand* (2000), ch 3; 'On the Subsidiarity of Unjust Enrichment' (2001) 117 LQR 273, 282–284.

for interference with property is different from, and trumps, a claim for unjust enrichment so as to avoid needless duplication. The common feature of these arguments is that unjust enrichment only comes into play once the claimant's property rights have run out.

An answer to Swadling[10] is that losses and gains can plainly be established factually irrespective of legal entitlement. The claimant's retention of legal title may be relevant to the assessment of the loss or gain but it should not preclude a personal claim to reverse the defendant's unjust enrichment. Indeed if that were so, it would appear that one could never have personal restitution in respect of the use of another's property.

But, in any event, these arguments are contrary to the reasoning of the English courts. It has made no difference to an analysis of an action for money had and received in respect of mistaken payments whether the mistake was so fundamental as to stop property passing or not. Similarly, an action for money had and received – best analysed as a personal claim for restitution of an unjust enrichment – has been granted in cases where legal title in the money was retained by the claimant because he did not consent to the transfer.[11] The approach of Swadling and Grantham and Rickett would also seem to rule out the possibility of concurrent personal and proprietary restitutionary claims reversing unjust enrichment; and yet that possibility has plainly been accepted in the reasoning in cases which have grappled with whether merely personal restitution, or also proprietary, restitution should be granted.[12]

There does remain a question, however, as to what happens to legal title, where it does not initially pass to the transferee, once the claimant has elected (and had satisfaction of) a personal claim to reverse the defendant's (autonomous) unjust enrichment. It is submitted that, on satisfaction of the personal claim for the whole value of the property received, legal title passes to the defendant. A useful analogy can be drawn with the tort of conversion. The fact that the claimant owns the property in the defendant's hands does not prevent, and on the contrary is usually a condition of, the claimant being able to recover compensatory damages; and, on satisfaction of the claim for damages, the defendant acquires legal title.[13]

10 See for similar views refuting Swadling and others, Birks, 'Property and Unjust Enrichment: Categorical Truths [1997] NZL Rev 623, 654–656; Virgo, *The Principles of the Law of Restitution* (1999), pp 132–133.
11 See chapter 4 below.
12 Eg *Chase Manhattan Bank NA v Israel-British Bank (London) Ltd* [1981] Ch 105; *Westdeutsche Landesbank Girozentrale v Islington London Borough Council* [1996] AC 669.
13 Torts (Interference with Goods) Act 1977, s 5; Smith *The Law of Tracing* (1997), pp 291–292. Yet on Swadling's analysis, the claimant has suffered no loss.

6. THE STRUCTURE OF THE BOOK

Having in this chapter considered in general and theoretical terms the principle of reversing the defendant's unjust enrichment at the claimant's expense, the detailed examination of the application of that principle in the rest of this book is primarily structured according to the different unjust factors. The next chapter, however, looks at two difficult restitutionary techniques: tracing and subrogation. Chapters 3–13 then consider unjust enrichment by subtraction and chapter 14 restitution for wrongs. Chapter 15 examines defences and the final chapter looks at two miscellaneous issues, agency and the conflict of laws.

Finally, it may be helpful to clarify that, where applicable, both money and non-money benefits (which can alternatively be called 'benefits in kind') are considered under each of the chapters on the unjust factors and, while most restitution is effected by personal remedies, proprietary restitutionary remedies (eg, rescission revesting proprietary rights, equitable liens and some trusts) will also be considered, where applicable, under each of the chapters.

Chapter 2

Tracing and subrogation

It is not easy to describe what tracing and subrogation are. They are plainly not grounds for restitution and, although commonly thought of as remedies, they are more accurately described as a means of getting to particular remedies rather than being remedies themselves.[1] One can talk of a right to trace or a right to subrogation but it is not obvious what one then calls the actual tracing and subrogation. Neutral labels such as 'technique', 'process' or 'doctrine' are perhaps most apt.

However, the reason tracing and subrogation have been afforded a separate chapter is not to do with the above difficulty. Rather it is because they are 'techniques' which arise in various areas of restitution while being difficult to understand unless considered as a coherent whole.

As will become apparent, tracing and subrogation deal with very different aspects of the law.[2] Their treatment together is in no sense intended to suggest that they inter-relate.

1. TRACING[3]

(1) Introduction

Tracing is concerned with the substitution of one property for another. Where the claimant's property (that is, property to which the claimant had title) has been replaced by other property (whether through the actions of the defendant or a third party) the rules of tracing lay down whether the 'replacement' property counts in law as a substitute for the claimant's original property.

---

1 See, eg, as regards tracing, *Cowan de Groot Properties Ltd v Eagle Trust plc* [1992] 4 All ER 700, 767 (per Knox J); *Foskett v McKeown* [2001] 1 AC 102, 128 (per Lord Millett). Cf *Boscawen v Bajwa* [1996] 1 WLR 328 in which Millett LJ referred to tracing as a process but subrogation as a remedy.
2 But on particular facts, both may be relevant: see *Boscawen v Bajwa* [1996] 1 WLR 328, below pp 116–117.
3 For a useful succinct analysis of the law on tracing, see Rotherham, 'Tracing' in *The Law of Restitution* (eds Hedley and Halliwell, 2002), ch 4.

The importance of tracing in the law of restitution is that it enables a claimant to establish that property retained or received by the defendant is a substitute for – and therefore came from – the claimant's property. Hence tracing goes to establish that the defendant's receipt or retention of property was *at the expense of the claimant* in the subtractive sense.

It is an important linked point that for the traceable substitute to be at the claimant's expense, rather than at the expense of the person who has effected the substitution (whether the defendant or a third party) the claimant must establish that it had (legal or equitable) title to the property in the substituting person's hands immediately prior to the substitution.[4] Say, for example, C transfers £1,000 to D by a mistake which is not a sufficient mistake to prevent legal title in the £1,000 passing to D.[5] D obtains a car worth £5,000 in exchange for the £1,000. Even if the tracing rules are satisfied, C has no restitutionary claim to the car, or its value, against D (or against a third party to whom D has given the car). The reason is that the substitute property (the car) was not gained at the expense of C. This is because C did not have title to the £1,000 in D's hands immediately prior to its substitution by the car. If the mistake was sufficiently fundamental to prevent legal title to the £1,000 passing to D, the position would be different. Then, if the tracing rules are satisfied, C would prima facie have a restitutionary claim to the car, or its value, against D. The car would have been retained, or received, at C's expense.

Once one realises that the tracing rules go merely to the 'at the expense of the claimant' enquiry, it should be obvious that they do not in themselves determine whether the claimant has a valid restitutionary claim against the defendant. Other elements (for example, the 'unjust factor', the defendant's enrichment, and the non-applicability of defences such as change of position and bona fide purchase) must also be satisfied. This explains why their Lordships in *Foskett v McKeown*[6] were correct to observe that the tracing rules tell us nothing about the rights to the assets traced. There is a difference between tracing and claiming.[7]

---

4   Where, unusually, as illustrated by the facts of *Lipkin Gorman v Karpnale Ltd* [1991] 2 AC 548 (see below, pp 89–92), the substitution is effected by a person at the same time as he first receives the property, this requirement cannot be directly applied. Instead it should be read as requiring that the claimant must establish that it had title to the substituted property in the substituting person's hands when that person received that property.

5   Assume also that C had no equitable title to the £1,000: cf *Chase Manhattan Bank NA Ltd v Israel–British Bank (London) Ltd* [1981] Ch 105.

6   [2001] 1 AC 102 at pp 113 (Lord Steyn), 128–129 (Lord Millett). See also Millett, 'Restitution and Constructive Trusts' (1998) 114 LQR 399, 409.

7   See, eg, Birks, 'Mixing and Tracing: Property and Restitution' (1992) 45 CLP 69; Birks, 'On Taking Seriously the Difference Between Tracing and Claiming' (1997) 11 Trust Law International 2; Lionel Smith, 'Tracing into the Payment of a Debt' [1995] CLJ 290; *Law of Tracing* (1997).

Within the law of restitution, tracing is normally invoked by a claimant with a view to obtaining proprietary restitution (whether by an equitable lien or a trust) in respect of substitute property retained by the defendant. This is the motive most commonly focused on and explains why tracing and proprietary restitution are often, if inaccurately, viewed as two sides of the same coin. But tracing may also be invoked with the aim of obtaining personal restitution (through, for example, an award of money had and received or an equitable accounting). There are two main possible situations where this may be so. First, the claimant may be seeking personal restitution from an indirect recipient who has received substitute property.[8] Secondly, the claimant may be seeking a higher quantum of personal restitution from a direct recipient than would be granted without tracing. Say, for example, the claimant by a fundamental mistake paid £5,000 to the defendant, who provided no consideration. Using that money and no other the defendant bought shares or a diamond ring which he then sold for £7,500. It appears that, provided the claimant had title to the £5,000 prior to its substitution by the £7,500, he could trace to the £7,500 and recover £7,500 in an action for money had and received.[9] Were tracing not possible his quantum of restitution would presumably be restricted to £5,000.

It should be stressed that it is insufficient for tracing that D has gained property as a factual consequence of D (or X) having acquired the claimant's (C's) property. For example, if C's watch is stolen by X and X, as a consequence of having the watch, makes a gift of his own clock to D, C cannot trace to the clock. Tracing is therefore not explicable in terms of factual causation. Rather it requires a series of transactional links so that the property received by D is a substitute (or a successive substitute) for the claimant's property. One can explain this need for a chain of substitutions back to the claimant's property on the grounds that it not only avoids difficult factual causation enquiries but also avoids stretching the ambit of unjust enrichment liability too far.[10]

Our understanding of tracing has been considerably advanced by the work of Lionel Smith and Peter Birks.[11] Apart from clarifying the distinction between tracing and claiming highlighted above, they have

---

8   See above, pp 34–35. *Lipkin Gorman v Karpnale Ltd* [1991] 2 AC 548 is an example.
9   See, eg, *Jones & Sons (a firm)(Trustees) v Jones* [1997] Ch 159; *Foskett v McKeown* [2001] 1 AC 102. This would be irrespective of establishing the tort of conversion and irrespective of whether the £7,500 is retained by the defendant.
10 Cf Evans, 'Rethinking Tracing and the Law of Restitution' (1999) 115 LQR 469.
11 See above, n 7. Two earlier influential articles were Scott, 'The Right to "Trace" at Common Law' (1965–6) 7 W Aus LR 463; Goode, 'The Right to Trace and its Impact on Commercial Transactions' (1976) 92 LQR 360, 528.

also emphasised that tracing is different from following.[12] Traditionally no such clear line has been drawn. But the difference is crucial. It marks the important divide between, on the one hand, following one's property into different hands, where one is asserting a pure proprietary claim ('That property is mine'), which belongs outside the law of restitution. And, on the other hand, tracing where one is seeking the creation of new proprietary rights (or a personal remedy) to reverse the defendant's unjust enrichment in respect of property substituted for the claimant's original property. That lies within the law of restitution.[13] Analogously, it is misleading to regard tracing as being concerned with 'the vindication of proprietary rights'. That is, it is fictional to say that a claimant is given ownership of traced property because his or her ownership of the original property continues through to the substitute property. The truth is that the claimant may be given a new title to the traced property to reverse the defendant's unjust enrichment at the claimant's expense. Unfortunately the House of Lords in *Foskett v McKeown* has recently invoked that fiction.[14]

There are three final introductory points.

First, in this chapter we shall be primarily examining the tracing rules, that is the rules which lay down whether 'replacement' property counts in law as a substitute for the claimant's original property. Tracing is to be distinguished from the claims (or remedies) that may be brought (or sought) in respect of the traceable property. But it is worth clarifying here that more work needs to be done in clarifying the 'unjust factor' involved in the tracing cases. In principle, any unjust factor could be in play. As it is concerned with the 'at the expense of the claimant' enquiry, tracing is not tied to any particular unjust factor. However, in most of the cases, it is submitted that the ground for restitution is the claimant's ignorance (or, analogously, powerlessness) in that he or she does not know about (or is powerless to prevent) his or her property being substituted.[15]

---

12 While following into mixtures is possible, an accession, fixture or specification puts an end to following: Smith, *The Law of Tracing*, pp 104–119. See generally, Bell, *Modern Law of Personal Property* (1989), pp 69–73; *Borden (UK) Ltd v Scottish Timber Products Ltd* [1981] Ch 25; *Hendy Lennox (Industrial Engines) Ltd v Grahame Puttick Ltd* [1984] 1 WLR 485; *Indian Oil Corpn v Greenstone Shipping SA* [1988] QB 345; *Glencore International AG v Metro Trading Inc* [2001] 1 All ER (Comm) 103. In contrast to tracing, it is hard to see how the property rights created in the newly-created property or the property to which there has been an attachment can be explained by a desire to prevent the unjust enrichment of a defendant at the claimant's expense (eg, if my car is painted, without my consent, the reason why I own the paint is because the paint has been added to the primary asset which I own).

13 See above, pp 60–64.

14 For criticism of this, see Burrows, 'Proprietary Restitution: Unmasking Unjust Enrichment' (2001) 117 LQR 412. See, similarly, Birks, 'Property, Unjust Enrichment and Tracing' (2001) 54 CLP 231. See above, pp 64–66.

15 See below ch 4, esp pp 188–193, 207–210.

Secondly, in discussing tracing, Birks in *An Introduction to the Law of Restitution*[16] drew a fundamental distinction between two measures of restitution: value received and value surviving. That idea was criticised in the first edition of this book[17] and I continue to believe that it is an unnecessary, and potentially misleading, complication. The better approach is to recognise that tracing may be relevant to both personal and proprietary restitution; that personal restitution responds to value received by the defendant, while proprietary restitution responds to property retained by the defendant;[18] that change of position can be a defence to both personal and proprietary restitution;[19] and that, while one can perhaps say that tracing enables one to identify value surviving in substitute property, that must not be confused with value surviving in the different sense of the measure of personal restitution being value received minus, where operative, change of position.[20]

Thirdly, if one accepts that the tracing rules go to whether an enrichment was at the claimant's expense, and deal with whether property stands as substitute for other property, there can be no rational reason for having different tracing rules at common law and in equity. That there should be fused rules of tracing, enabling equity's more generous tracing rules to be applied in a common law claim, is now widely accepted by commentators.[1] It has been given a further boost by obiter dicta of Lords Steyn and Millett in *Foskett v McKeown*.[2] Unfortunately, we cannot yet say that the historical differences between tracing at common law and equity have been authoritatively abolished, although the courts seem very close to doing so. For the present therefore, this chapter continues to find it necessary to distinguish between tracing rules at common law and those in equity.

---

16 Birks, ch 11.

17 Burrows, *The Law of Restitution* (1st edn, 1993), pp 373–375. See also Barker, 'Riddles, Remedies and Restitution: Quantifying Gain in Unjust Enrichment Law' [2001] CLP 255, 275–278.

18 See above, pp 52, 60

19 See below, ch 15.

20 Birks now distinguishes these two different notions of value surviving by the terms 'traceably surviving enrichment' and 'abstractly surviving enrichment' : see Birks, 'Overview: Tracing, Claiming and Defences' in *Laundering and Tracing* (ed Birks, 1995), pp 289, 320–322.

1 Goff and Jones, *The Law of Restitution*, paras 2-031 to 2-033; Babafemi, 'Tracing Assets: A Case for the Fusion of Common Law and Equity in English Law' (1971) 34 MLR 12; Birks, 'The Necessity of a Unitary Law of Tracing' in *Making Commercial Law* (ed Cranston, 1997), p 239.

2 [2001] 1 AC 102, 113, 128–129.

(2) Tracing at common law

(a) The basic rules

The property being traced is normally money or its direct equivalent (such as a cheque) although it can, of course, be a chattel.[3] At common law the traditional approach has been that tracing to a substitute is possible provided there has been a 'clean substitution'.[4] However, where there has been no clean substitution, in particular where money being traced has been mixed with other money, tracing at common law has traditionally been thought to fail. So if, for example, the defendant steals £1,000 from the claimant and uses that same £1,000 to buy a car, the claimant can trace his money to the car. That is, he can treat the car as a substitute for the money and can thereby establish that the car is an unjust enrichment to the defendant at the claimant's expense (in the subtractive sense). But if the defendant having stolen the £1,000 then mixes it with £200 of his own money and uses £1,000 from the mixture to buy a car, the claimant, according to the traditional view, cannot trace his money at common law to the car.

The leading case from which this traditional view of common law tracing has been derived is *Taylor v Plumer*.[5] Sir Thomas Plumer, the defendant gave his broker, Walsh, a bank draft for £22,200 for the express purpose of buying Exchequer bills. Walsh bought some Exchequer bills for the defendant but used most to buy United States securities and bullion. He was apprehended just prior to boarding a ship to the United States and the defendant seized the securities and bullion. Walsh's assignees in bankruptcy claimed that the securities and bullion belonged to Walsh, and hence to them, and not to the defendant. They argued that it would only have been if Walsh had retained property of the defendant that was 'identically the same'[6] or if Walsh had been acting with authority that the defendant could trace through to property in Walsh's hands. Lord Ellenborough thought otherwise and held that the defendant could trace to, and claim ownership of, the securities and bullion. He said:

---

3   As in *Scott v Surman* (1742) Willes 400 in which it was held that an action for money had and received lay against assignees in bankruptcy who received the proceeds of sale of the claimant's chattel.

4   Lionel Smith, *The Law of Tracing* (1997), esp chs 4 and 5, distinguishes between 'clean substitutions' and 'mixed substitutions'. 'Clean substitution' means that 'all of the value which went into the substitution was the value being traced' (ibid, at p 133). 'Mixed substitution' means that 'the value being traced contributed only part of the value used to acquire an asset' (ibid, at p 160).

5   (1815) 3 M & S 562.

6   Ibid at p 568.

'The property of a principal entrusted by him to his factor for any special purpose belongs to the principal, notwithstanding any change which that property may have undergone in point of form, so long as such property is capable of being identified and distinguished from all other property ... it makes no difference in reason or law into what other form, different from the original, the change may have been made, whether it be into that of promissory notes for the security of the money which was produced by the sale of the goods of the principal, as in *Scott v Surman*[7] ... or into other merchandise, as in *Whitecomb v Jacob*[8] ... for the product of or substitute for the original thing still follows the nature of the thing itself, so long as it can be ascertained to be such, and the right only ceases when the means of ascertainment fail, which is the case when the subject is turned into money, and mixed and confounded in a general mass of the same description.'[9]

The traditional interpretation of Lord Ellenborough's judgement is that it established that, while one can trace at common law into substitute property – and that that is what the defendant was, on the facts, able to do – one cannot trace at common law into or through a mixed fund. This is to be contrasted with equitable tracing where numerous cases show that the mixing of money does not defeat tracing.

However, as some commentators, notably Lionel Smith,[10] have pointed out, the decision in *Taylor v Plumer*, although given by a common law court, was actually based on the defendant's successful assertion of *equitable* proprietary rights. Lord Ellenborough was therefore not concerned with tracing at common law as distinct from tracing in equity.

This error in the traditional interpretation of *Taylor v Plumer* has now been recognised by Millett LJ in *Jones & Son v Jones*.[11] He further emphasised that, while recognition of the error supports the case for having fused tracing rules, it does not cast doubt on tracing being possible at common law.[12]

But, however unsound the historical basis for the difference between common law and equitable tracing may have been exposed to be, it does not follow that we now have fused tracing rules. Too much water has passed under the bridge since – including, relatively recently, the Court of Appeal in *Agip (Africa) Ltd v Jackson*[13] and the

7   (1742) Willes 400.
8   (1710) 1 Salk 160.
9   (1815) 3 M & S 562, 575.
10 'Tracing in *Taylor v Plumer*: Equity in the Court of King's Bench' [1995] LMCLQ 240. See also Fox, 'Common Law Claims to Substituted Assets' [1999] RLR 55.
11 [1997] Ch 159.
12 The contrary view – that recognising the error indicates that one cannot trace at common law – was put forward by Khurshid and Matthews, 'Tracing Confusion' (1979) 95 LQR 78.
13 [1991] Ch 547.

House of Lords in *Lipkin Gorman v Karpnale Ltd*[14] – for one to be able to assert that the most accurate interpretation of the law is that there is no such difference. Typical are Lord Greene MR's words in *Re Diplock*:[15]

> 'The common law approached [tracing] in a strictly materialistic way. It could only appreciate what might almost be called the "physical" identity of one thing with another. It could treat a person's money as identifiable so long as it had not become mixed with other money. It could treat as identifiable with the money other kinds of property acquired by means of it, provided that there was no admixture of other money.'

Despite obiter dicta of Lord Millett in several cases, most importantly in *Foskett v McKeown*[16] where he was joined on this issue by Lord Steyn, one still awaits an authoritative decision that overturns the traditional approach and fuses common law and equitable tracing rules. For the moment, the traditional view that one cannot trace at common law into or through a mixed fund continues, unfortunately, to be the law.

Trustee of the Property of FC Jones & Sons v Jones,[17] in which, as we have seen, Millett LJ exposed the flaw in the traditional interpretation of *Taylor v Plumer*, is a particularly important case in recognising that one can trace at common law to a substitute even though of greater value than one's original property. One of the partners in a potato-growing firm, after its bankruptcy, drew £11,700 from the partnership account. He paid that money to his wife, the defendant, who used it to trade on the potato futures market at a profit of £50,760 which she paid into a deposit account. From that account £900 had been withdrawn leaving a balance of £49,860. It was held that the trustee in bankruptcy (on behalf of the firm) could trace at common law from the £11,700 to the £49,860. The defendant, who was assumed to be an innocent donee, was held personally liable at common law for £49,860.

(b) Tracing at common law into and through a bank account

In *Banque Belge pour l'Etranger v Hambrouck*[18] Hambrouck forged a number of cheques so that £6,000 was debited from his employer's account at the claimant bank and credited to his own account at Farrow's Bank. From that account Hambrouck drew sums which he paid to his mistress, Mlle Spanoghe, the second defendant, who

14 [1991] 2 AC 548.
15 [1948] Ch 465, 518, CA.
16 [2001] 1 AC 102, 113, 128–129.
17 [1997] Ch 159.
18 [1921] 1 KB 321.

provided no valuable consideration for them. She paid that money into her deposit account at the London Joint City and Midland Bank. At the time of the action £315 stood to her credit in that account. Having avoided the transaction with Hambrouck for fraud the claimant bank sought to trace its money through to the £315. The Court of Appeal held that its claim should succeed. Although the reasoning of the three judges differed, at least two of them (Bankes and Atkin LJJ) based their decision on common law as opposed to equitable tracing. Both emphasised that, on the facts, no money other than the proceeds of the fraud had been deposited in either Hambrouck's or Mlle Spanoghe's account.

In analysing that decision, a key point (as made clear by Lord Goff's reasoning in *Lipkin Gorman v Karpnale Ltd*,[19] the facts of which are set out in the next subsection) is that, if money is to be traced through a bank account, a chose in action (ie, the debt owed by the bank to its customer) must form part of the tracing chain. This is not only because separate accounts are not operated using separate cash but also because the money in the account is indisputably the property of the bank. The money paid in is replaced by the chose in action.

The best analysis of *Banque Belge* appears to be that the claimant bank was able to trace its money (property in the money in the employer's account belonging to the bank) through to the chose in action underpinning Hambrouck's account with Farrow's Bank (ie, the debt owed by Farrow's Bank to Hambrouck). And because no other money was paid into that account, it was then entitled to trace through that chose in action into its product, namely the withdrawn money handed by Hambrouck to Mlle Spanoghe and subsequently paid by Mlle Spanoghe to the London Joint City and Midland Bank. As we shall see in chapter 4, that tracing chain meant that Mlle Spanoghe (and her bank) were liable in an action for money had and received, subject to defences, for the sums received irrespective of the lower sum still retained in her account. It should therefore have been irrelevant that no other sums had been paid into Mlle Spanoghe's account.

It is submitted that that analysis shows that the majority in *Banque Belge* was correct in regarding it as possible to trace into and through bank accounts without infringing the traditional restriction that one cannot trace at common law into a mixed fund.

Birks offers a different interpretation of *Banque Belge*.[20] For him it is the judgments of Scrutton and Atkin LJJ that are crucial. Both expressed

19 [1991] 2 AC 548.
20 Birks at pp 361–362.

the view that even if money had been mixed in Hambrouck's account tracing would not have been defeated. According to Scrutton LJ this was because, while common law tracing would be defeated, the claimant could rely on the equitable tracing rules. And Atkin LJ said that in tracing at common law one could invoke the more liberal rules of equity. Birks therefore construes *Banque Belge* as authority for the idea that the tracing identification rules at common law and in equity are fused. This is a very attractive argument in principle. Unfortunately Atkin LJ ultimately based his decision on traditional common law tracing without invoking any assistance from equity so that it is hard to regard Birks' interpretation as the ratio of the case. Moreover the fusion of identification rules is directly contradicted by the authorities in which it has been held or accepted that the common law tracing rules are more restrictive in not allowing tracing into a mixed fund. For example, Fox LJ giving the leading judgment of the Court of Appeal in *Agip (Africa) Ltd v Jackson*,[1] continued to rely on the traditional distinction that at common law one cannot trace into a mixed fund. And he said of the radical approach (which he associated with only Atkin LJ's judgment in *Banque Belge*):

'[It] amounts virtually to saying that there is now no difference between the common law and equitable remedies. Indeed, the common law remedy might be wider because of the absence of any requirement of a fiduciary relationship. There may be a good deal to be said for that view but it goes well beyond any other case and well beyond the views of Bankes and Scrutton LJJ. And in the 70 years since the *Banque Belge* decision it has not been applied.'[2]

In *Agip (Africa) Ltd v Jackson*[3] common law tracing through bank accounts was, on the facts, held not to be possible and *Banque Belge* was distinguished. Zdiri, an employee of the claimant, fraudulently altered the name of the payee, to Baker Oil Services Ltd, on a payment order of some $518,000 from the claimant. The $518,000 was transferred from the claimant's account with the Banque du Sud in Tunisia to Baker Oil's account with Lloyds Bank in London. Baker Oil was a puppet company that had been set up and was controlled by the defendants, who were chartered accountants. Throughout they were acting on the instructions of clients. The $518,000 (which was the only sum in Baker Oil's account) was transferred to accounts of the defendants' accountancy firm and all but $43,000 of it was paid on to unknown parties. Although the

---

1 [1991] Ch 547. See also, eg, *Re Diplock* [1948] Ch 465; *Lipkin Gorman v Karpnale Ltd* [1991] 2 AC 548.
2 Ibid at p 566.
3 Noted by McKendrick, 'Tracing Misdirected Funds' [1991] LMCLQ 378.

claimant was successful in claiming equitable ownership of the $43,000 retained and in establishing the personal compensatory liability of the defendants for intermeddling by knowing assistance, it failed in its alternative claims based on the defendants' receipt of the money (both at common law and equity).

A difference to *Banque Belge* is that in *Agip* the claimant, suing as the victim of the employee's fraud, was the employer (Agip) and not the bank (Banque du Sud).[4] Discussed in the judgment under the heading of 'the right to sue' – although better described as the issue of whether the defendants' gain was 'at the claimant's expense' – the Court of Appeal decided that, whether legally entitled to or not, the Banque du Sud had debited Agip's account. Analysed correctly, Agip had therefore suffered a loss of its property (a decrease in the value of its chose of action with the bank) whereas the Banque du Sud had suffered no loss. Certainly it is difficult to dispute that Agip had suffered a loss when, as Fox LJ stressed, Agip's earlier action against the Banque du Sud to have its account re-credited had failed. The position would have been different if that earlier action had gone the other way. The defendant's gain would then have been at the expense of the Banque du Sud not Agip.

Agip's common law action for money had and received failed on the grounds that at common law money could not be traced into a mixed fund and in this case, in contrast to *Banque Belge*, the claimant's money had been mixed (in the New York clearing system).[5] The reasoning appears to be that, while in *Banque Belge*, one could simply regard the credit in respect of the fraudulent cheque as passing from the employer's account to Hambrouck's account (and then to Mlle Spanoghe's account), this was not possible in *Agip* because Lloyds Bank in London had credited the money to Baker Oil's account, on directions from Banque du Sud, *in advance* of being put in funds (by its correspondent bank in New York).

It is hard to understand why the advance crediting was thought to defeat common law tracing. On the contrary one might have thought that this established a clear link to the debiting of the employer's account *without* involving the clearing system. In any event in *Banque Belge* no one suggested that the clearing system posed any difficulty for tracing at common law. As McKendrick writes, '... in *Banque Belge* there was no enquiry as to whether Farrow's Bank had allowed Hambrouck to draw against the cheques before they collected them. The matter was treated

---

4   *Agip* is in this respect analogous to *Lipkin Gorman v Karpnale Ltd*, discussed below, in which no question was raised as to the bank, rather than the firm of solicitors, being the appropriate claimant.
5   See similarly *Bank of America v Arnell* [1999] Lloyd's Rep Bank 399.

as being irrelevant and, if it was irrelevant in *Banque Belge*, it is not at all clear why it should be a relevant factor in *Agip*.'[6]

Mention was also made by the Court of Appeal of Millett J's controversial primary reasoning at first instance,[7] namely that tracing at common law was not possible because the payment from Banque du Sud to Lloyds Bank was by telegraphic transfer so that only 'a stream of electrons' and no physical asset passed between the banks. Fox LJ appeared to disapprove of this: 'The inquiry which has to be made is whether the money paid ... "was the product of, or substitute for, the original thing". In answering that question I do not think that it matters that the order was not a cheque. It was a direction by the account holder to the bank.'[8]

It would appear that tracing at common law should have been possible in *Agip*. The analysis would be that Agip was able to follow the decrease in value of its chose in action underpinning its account with the Banque du Sud through to the chose in action of Baker Oil underpinning its account with Lloyds Bank. In the same way the decrease in value of that chose in action could then be followed into the increase in value of the chose in action underpinning the account of the defendants. It seems irrelevant that there was advance crediting or that money was transmitted by telegraphic transfer.

(c) *Lipkin Gorman v Karpnale Ltd* [9]

We have pointed out above that for the traceable substitute to be at the claimant's expense, rather than at the expense of the person who has effected the substitution, the claimant must establish that it had title to the property in the substituting person's hands immediately prior to the substitution.[10] We have also noted that where, unusually, the substitution is effected by a person at the same time as he first receives the property, that requirement cannot be directly applied.[11] Instead it should be read as requiring that the claimant must establish that it had title to the substituted property in the substituting person's hands when that person received that property. The latter situation is illustrated by *Lipkin Gorman v Karpnale Ltd* where the need for the claimant to establish proprietary rights to the substitute property when received by the substituting person led to a careful analysis of tracing and title in the context of common law tracing.

---

6   'Tracing Misdirected Funds' [1991] LMCLQ 378, 384.
7   [1990] Ch 265. His theory is set out in more detail in 'Tracing the Proceeds of Fraud' (1991) 107 LQR 71, 73–74.
8   [1991] Ch 547, 565.
9   [1991] 2 AC 548.
10   See above, p 79.
11   See above, p 79, n 4.

Cass, a partner in a firm of solicitors, had, without the firm's consent, drawn on its account (he was an authorised signatory) to subsidise his gambling. An action for money had and received was brought by the firm against the gambling club where Cass had spent the money. The basis of the claim (the unjust factor) was apparently treated as being that the club had received money that, at the time of receipt, was the property of the firm. In principle, this is better expressed by saying that, *without its knowledge*, the firm's money had been paid by Cass to the club.[12] Their Lordships held that the club provided no consideration for the money paid over by Cass (ie, it was not a bona fide purchaser for value without notice). It was also conceded that Cass had not mixed the money drawn from the bank with any other money in his hands. There was, nevertheless, an apparent serious obstacle to the firm's claim. Two decisions of the Privy Council[13] had long-established that a partner who appears to a bank to have his firm's authority and thereby obtains a banker's cheque or, *a fortiori*, cash, takes good title to that cheque or money even though in reality the partner does not have that authority. On the face of it, therefore, the firm could not establish that the money paid to the club enriched the club at the expense of the claimant firm of solicitors rather than at the expense of Cass. The money withdrawn from the account by Cass was owned by Cass not by the firm of solicitors.

Not surprisingly, counsel for the firm called upon the Lords to overrule those Privy Council decisions. Lord Goff declined to do so but interpreted the law in such a way as not to defeat the firm's claim. His Lordship's essential reasoning was that to describe Cass as having legal title to the money was consistent with recognising that, *if the money was traceable from the firm's property*, the firm could have claimed against Cass a proprietary right to that traceable property. To that extent, Cass' title to the money was defeasible: that is, it was vulnerable to being defeated by the firm's (restitutionary) proprietary rights to the traced money.[14] And that defeasibility was sufficient for the claimant firm to establish that traceable money paid over to the

---

12   Below, chapter 4.

13   *Union Bank of Australia Ltd v McClintock & Co* [1922] 1 AC 240; *Commercial Banking Co of Sydney Ltd v Mann* [1961] AC 1.

14   A very loose analogy may be drawn with ratification by a principal of an agent's unauthorised substitution of his original property by asserting ownership of the substitute. A closer analogy can be drawn with a voidable title where, for example, a contract of sale has been induced by misrepresentation. Like a voidable title, the title of the owner of the substitute property is not absolute and is liable to be vested in the original owner at the latter's election. Birks, 'The English recognition of unjust enrichment' [1991] LMCLQ 473, esp 478–479, has described the claimant as having a power, triggered by the defendant's unjust enrichment at the claimant's expense, to vest in himself title to the traced property.

club by Cass was at the firm's expense rather than at the expense of Cass. It did not matter that the firm had not actually asserted its (restitutionary) proprietary rights to the money while it was in Cass' hands.

Lord Goff further explained that the money in Cass' hands was indeed traceable from the firm's property. This was because the original property that had been substituted by other property by Cass was not money but was rather the chose in action underpinning the firm's bank account. In other words, the firm had owned the chose in action underpinning its bank account; the very act of drawing out the money constituted the substitution (and indeed destruction) of the firm's chose in action; and money drawn out from that account by Cass was therefore the traceable substitute for property belonging to the firm.

In Lord Goff's words:

'On this aspect of the case ... the only question is whether the solicitors can establish legal title to the money when received by Cass from the bank by drawing cheques on the client account without authority ... "Tracing" or "following" property into its product involves a decision by the owner of the original property to assert his title to the product in place of his original property ... Before Cass drew upon the solicitors' client account at the bank, there was of course no question of the solicitors having any legal property in any cash lying at the bank. The relationship of the bank with the solicitors was essentially that of debtor and creditor; and, since the client account was at all material times in credit, the bank was the debtor and the solicitors were its creditors. Such a debt constitutes a chose in action, which is a species of property; and, since the debt was enforceable at common law, the chose in action was legal property belonging to the solicitors at common law. There is, in my opinion, no reason why the solicitors should not be able to trace their property at common law in that chose in action, or in any part of it, into its product, ie cash drawn by Cass from their client account at the bank. Such a claim is consistent with their assertion that the money so obtained by Cass was their property at common law.'[15]

If this was correct, why could not the claimant firms in the two Privy Council cases have elected to assert title to the bank cheques so as to render the bank, which had received those cheques from the fraudulent partner, liable for conversion?

The answer, according to Lord Goff, is that tracing into a substitute 'cannot be relied upon so as to render an innocent recipient a wrongdoer'.[16] As the claims in those two cases were founded on the

15 [1991] 2 AC 548, 574.
16 [1991] 2 AC 548, 573.

tort of conversion and, as the banks were innocent, tracing could not assist the claimants. In contrast the claim for restitution of the money in *Lipkin Gorman* did not rest on establishing that the gaming club was a wrongdoer: it was a claim based on the cause of action of unjust enrichment.

(d) Tracing and the claimant's original property

Although after tracing at common law, the common law proprietary remedy of delivery up will rarely be awarded and one is, in practice, concerned with personal remedies only, the question still arises as to the relationship between the tracing claim and the claimant's legal title to the original property. There is an obvious objection to the claimant being treated as owner of both the original property and the substitute property. Birks has called this the problem of a 'geometric multiplication of the plaintiff's property'.[17] If D1 steals £1,000 from C and uses that same £1,000 to buy a car from D2 and D2 knows that the money is stolen (ie, he is not a bona fide purchaser for value without notice), C owns the £1,000 in D2's hands and can trace to the car in D1's hands. But he surely cannot claim to own both the £1,000 and the car.

This is a particular problem for those who argue that tracing is concerned with vindicating one's existing proprietary rights and that one's pre-existing ownership of the original property continues through to give ownership of the substitute. Applying that approach it is indeed hard to see how one can rationally avoid a geometric multiplication of property. If the owner of a tree owns both the tree and its fruits and the owner of land owns both the land and the oil underneath it and the owner of a pig owns both the pig and her piglets the owner of the original property should, applying the continuing ownership theory, own both the original property and its substitute product.

In contrast, there is an obvious solution if one accepts that tracing is different from following; and that, in truth, one is concerned with a restitutionary claim (whether personal or proprietary) that rests on the defendant's unjust enrichment constituted by the receipt or retention of the traced property. Just as where in a standard two-party non-tracing case, for example where C pays D money under a fundamental mistake, C can seek a personal restitutionary remedy even though he may continue to own the property transferred to the defendant, so here the solution lies in election.[18] In electing to make a restitutionary claim after tracing, the claimant should be taken to

17 Birks, at p 394.
18 See above, p 76.

have elected for title in the original property to pass to the transferee
(on condition that the claim succeeds and is satisfied).

(3) Tracing in equity[19]

(a) Introduction

We are concerned here with the extent to which replacement
property counts as a substitute for other property (normally money)
that was owned in equity by the claimant. We are, in other words,
dealing with the equitable rules of tracing and not with whether the
claimant had equitable title to the original property.

Nevertheless it is worth stressing, at the outset, that the traditional
difference drawn between common law and equitable tracing rules is
posited on the notion that only a claimant with equitable title to the
original property (or, as it has sometimes been expressed, the claimant
was someone to whom a fiduciary duty was owed in respect of the property)
can invoke equity's tracing rules. For example, Lord Greene MR in *Re
Diplock*[20] said that it was a 'right of property recognised by equity' that
triggered equity's tracing rules. He said, 'Lord Parker and Viscount
Haldane [in *Sinclair v Brougham*[1]] both predicate the existence of a
right of property recognised by equity which depends on there having
existed at some stage a fiduciary relationship of some kind (though
not necessarily a positive duty of trusteeship) sufficient to give rise to
the equitable right of property. Exactly what relationships are sufficient
to bring such an equitable right into existence for the purposes of the
rule which we are considering is a matter which has not been precisely
laid down. Certain relationships are clearly included, eg, trustee (actual
or constructive) and *cestui que trust*, and "fiduciary" relationships such
as that of principal and agent.' So the conventional view has been
that, while the rules of tracing in equity are less restrictive than those
at common law, there is an initial requirement that is inapplicable at
common law; namely, that the claimant had an equitable proprietary
right in the original property.[2] The call for fused rules of tracing is in

---

19 See generally Hayton, 'Equity's Identification Rules' in *Laundering and Tracing* (ed Birks,
   1995), pp 1–21.
20 [1948] Ch 465, 540. See also, eg, *Agip (Africa) Ltd v Jackson* [1991] Ch 547, 566; *El Ajou v
   Dollar Land Holdings plc* [1993] 3 All ER 717, 733–734 (rvsd on a different point [1994] 2
   All ER 685); *Boscawen v Bajwa* [1996] 1 WLR 328, 335.
1 [1914] AC 398.
2 The absurdity of this requirement is highlighted by theft. A thief acquires no legal title to
   stolen property so that, on the face of it, equitable tracing is not possible. Cf *Westdeutsche
   Landesbank Girozentrale v Islington London Borough Council* [1996] AC 669, 716 in which
   Lord Browne-Wilkinson accepted that a thief should be treated as a (constructive) trustee
   for the purposes of tracing.

essence a call for equity's less restrictive tracing rules to be applied irrespective of whether the claimant's proprietary right to the original property was legal or equitable.

It should also be re-emphasised that equitable tracing goes merely to establish that the traced property is an enrichment to the defendant *at the claimant's expense*, and that the other elements of an unjust enrichment claim must also be satisfied before restitution will be granted. Very often the unjust factor in play will be ignorance (or powerlessness). Where the traced property, following tracing, is retained by the defendant, the restitutionary claim will usually be proprietary, not least because, in contrast to the position at common law, there are *proprietary* restitutionary remedies in equity. These are the conferring of beneficial ownership through a trust or the conferring of a security interest through an equitable lien. But equitable tracing may also be relevant to establishing, for the purposes of a personal restitutionary claim, that property received (even if no longer retained) by the defendant was received at the claimant's expense.

(b) The basic rules

As at common law, where the money owned in equity by the claimant has not been mixed but has been used to buy substitute property (that is, there has been a clean substitution), the claimant can trace through to the substitute property.[3]

But the great difference from the traditional common law approach is that equity indisputably allows money to be traced into mixed funds and the product of mixed funds. As Fox LJ said in *Agip (Africa) Ltd v Jackson*,[4] 'Both common law and equity accepted the right of the true owner to trace his property into the hands of others while it was in an identifiable form. The common law treated property as identified if it had not been mixed with other property. Equity, on the other hand, will follow money into a mixed fund ...'.

The crucial question is, what part of a mixed fund, or a product bought with a mixed fund, counts as a substitute for money owned in equity by the claimant?

The law differs according to whether the claimant's money has been mixed with an innocent party's money or has been mixed by a fiduciary with his own money. In the latter case, where the contest is between the claimant and a wrongdoing fiduciary, the courts have, not surprisingly, felt able to adopt tracing rules that favour the claimant.

---

3   *Re Hallett's Estate* (1880) 13 Ch D 696, 709, per Sir George Jessel MR.
4   [1991] Ch 547, 566. See also *Re Diplock* [1948] Ch 465, 520 (per Lord Greene MR).

(i)   Where the mixed fund comprises the money of two innocent parties (for example, two beneficiaries or a beneficiary and an innocent volunteer) the general equitable tracing rule is 'proportionate sharing' subject sometimes to 'first in, first out'

Here the prima facie rule is that the two parties can trace to shares of the mixed fund proportionate to the money put into it.[5] So if £1,000 of the claimant's money was mixed with £2,000 of X's money, the claimant can trace through to a third of the mixed fund and X to two thirds. How much that one third or two thirds share will be worth depends on whether the fund has declined in value (for example, by dissipation of money from it) or has increased in value (for example, by the profitable investment of the fund in a substitute product). So if half the mixed fund has been dissipated and it has therefore declined to a value of £1,500, C will be entitled to trace to £500 of the fund and X to £1,000. If the fund has doubled in value (for example, by the purchase of shares which have been sold) C will be entitled to trace to £2,000 of the fund and X to £4,000.[6]

In contrast, where the mixed fund is held in a bank account, the exceptional 'first in, first out' rule of *Clayton's Case*[7] has traditionally been applied. So if the claimant's £1,000 was paid into a current account before X's £1,000, and £600 is withdrawn, that £600 is assumed to represent the claimant's money (and X will be able to trace to £1,000 of the fund). Although, as we shall discuss below, this rule has been criticised as arbitrary and unjust it is even-handed in one sense, namely that each party stands equally to gain or lose. Whether in the particular case the rule turns out to work to a party's advantage or disadvantage will turn on whether the withdrawn money has been dissipated or used for profitable substitute products.

The above rules were applied in *Sinclair v Brougham*[8] and *Re Diplock*.[9] In the former, a building society, which had been carrying on an ultra vires banking business was ordered to be wound up. The House of Lords decided (although this has subsequently been overruled without casting doubt on the 'proportionate sharing'

---

5   *Sinclair v Brougham* [1914] AC 398; *Re Diplock* [1948] Ch 465; *Barlow Clowes International Ltd v Vaughan* [1992] 4 All ER 22.

6   There appears to be no direct authority applying proportionate sharing where a mixed fund of two innocent parties has increased in value. But proportionate sharing is in principle correct; and is supported by common law tracing to a substitute of increased value in, eg, *Jones & Sons (a firm)(Trustees) v Jones* [1997] Ch 159: see above, p 85 and below, p 193. That proportionate sharing applies where a mixed fund, comprising a beneficiary's and a trustee's moneys, has increased in value was established in *Foskett v McKeown* [2001] 1 AC 102: see below, pp 101–102.

7   (1816) 1 Mer 572. See also *Re Hallett's Estate* (1880) 13 Ch D 696.

8   [1914] AC 398.

9   [1948] Ch 465.

tracing rule applied)[10] that, while the depositors had no personal restitutionary action for money had and received for total failure of consideration, they had a right to trace in equity into the mixed fund held by the society as the society held their money in a fiduciary capacity. The mixed fund comprised money of the depositors and money of the society's shareholders (both innocent) and so it was held that their claims to the mixed fund should be treated rateably in proportion to their contributions.

In *Re Diplock* executors, in breach of their fiduciary duty to the next of kin and by a mistake of law, had distributed the deceased's estate to various charities rather than to the next of kin. In addition to being held entitled to a personal equitable action against the charities, subject to exhausting their remedies against the executors, the next of kin were held entitled to an equitable proprietary remedy in respect of money traced to mixed funds held by the charities.[11] The mixed funds comprised money traced from that belonging in equity to the next of kin and money of the charities who were innocent volunteers. It was laid down that dissipation of the mixed funds not held in current accounts (eg the funds of the Royal Sailors Orphan Girls' School and Home) should be borne proportionately by the next of kin and the charities, whereas *Clayton's Case* applied as regards withdrawals from mixed funds held in current accounts (eg the funds of Dr Barnardo's Homes).

It is also of importance that in *Re Diplock*[12] it was held that money from mixed funds used by some of the charities to improve or erect new buildings could not be traced. Two main reasons for this were given. First, that the building work might not have objectively improved the value of the real property. That is, the money may have been dissipated by the building work. Secondly, that it would be inequitable for there to be an equitable charge, following tracing, over the land and buildings when the money had not been used to acquire the land which already belonged to the charities.

It is submitted that these reasons are insufficient to reject the possibility, in principle, of tracing into improved buildings. The first reason is accurate as far as it goes. Where a building has not been objectively improved, there is no traceable product and the money should instead be treated as dissipated. However, this provides no good

---

10   *Sinclair v Brougham* was overruled in *Westdeutsche Landesbank Girozentrale v Islington London Borough Council* [1996] AC 669 both as regards its rejection of the personal claim for money had and received and its obscure finding (as a prerequisite for equitable tracing) of an equitable proprietary interest/fiduciary relationship. See above, p 8 and below, pp 409–410, 568.

11   Without deciding the point, the Court of Appeal thought that the condition of first exhausting remedies against the executors also applied to the equitable proprietary remedy.

12   [1948] Ch 465, 545–548.

reason to reject tracing where the property has objectively been improved (that is, the market value has increased).[13] The traceable substitute is the improved value of the building retained by the building owner. The second reason (which goes to the connected issue of the remedy to be imposed after tracing, rather than to the tracing process itself) fails to explain precisely why an equitable charge over the land and buildings to secure restitution of the traced value would have been inequitable. What may have been in mind is what we would now term the change of position defence.[14] The charities would have been in a worse position to repay the money than if they had never received it and, in particular, it would be unacceptable to require them to sell off the land and buildings in order to make the repayment. But again this is not a reason to reject the principle of tracing into improvements to buildings. Rather it is to accept that, after tracing, the remedy to be imposed, whether personal or proprietary, must be subject to a change of position defence. Where, for example, the improved land was an investment property that the defendant was, in any event, intending to sell, forcing a sale may cause no significant inconvenience so that the defence of change of position could not be made out.

If one is applying the prima facie proportionate share approach the question of how much of each party's money is in the mixed fund ought logically to be judged as at the time of each mixing, applying the 'lowest intermediate balance' rule.[15] If a trustee had £200 of the claimant's money but dissipated half of it before mixing it with £200 of X's money the relevant shares are one third and two thirds, not half and half. Similarly if a trustee had £200 of the claimant's money, mixed it with £200 of X's money, dissipated half of it and then added £200 of X's money, the relevant shares are one quarter and three quarters. But where there are many payments in and out of a mixed fund this strictly logical approach can produce excessive complexity and, where so, practicality may override strict logic. In *Sinclair v Brougham*, for example, no attempt was made to apply the 'intermediate balance' rule.

These rules were the subject of a careful review by the Court of Appeal in *Barlow Clowes International Ltd v Vaughan*.[16] On the liquidation of an investment company the question arose as to how the surviving assets should be distributed among the many thousands of defrauded

13 This is supported by Lionel Smith, *The Law of Tracing* (1997), pp 241–242.
14 See Goff and Jones, paras 2-042 to 2-043; Hanbury and Martin, *Modern Equity* (16th edn, 2001), p 701. In *Boscawen v Bajwa* [1996] 1 WLR 328, 340–341, Millett LJ rationalised the similar rejection of subrogation against the Leaf Homeopathic Hospital in *Re Diplock* [1948] Ch 465, 549–550 as nowadays turning on the change of position defence.
15 See below, pp 102–104.
16 [1992] 4 All ER 22.

investors. It was held that while *Clayton's Case* should normally be applied to decide the tracing rights of multi-beneficiaries in respect of a mixed fund in a current bank account, the rule was inapplicable where, as here, the fund was intended to be held as a common investment fund. An analogy was drawn with resulting trust cases on the distribution of surplus funds of non-charitable purpose trusts where *Clayton's Case* has been rejected, or ignored, in favour of *pari passu* distribution.[17] Furthermore while in strict logic a proportionate share approach should have been combined with the 'intermediate balance' rule, so that withdrawals were treated as being 'in the same proportions as the different interests in the account bear to each other at the moment before the withdrawal is made',[18] the Court of Appeal felt that the disproportionate expense of that made it an unrealistic option even if technically possible. The approach laid down, therefore, was *pari passu* distribution in the rough-and-ready sense that the surviving assets would be shared 'on a proportionate basis among all the investors who could be said to have contributed to the acquisition of those assets, ignoring the dates on which they made their investment'.[19]

Woolf LJ went further than Dillon and Leggatt LJJ in suggesting that, whether the fund was a common investment fund or not, *Clayton's Case* should not be applied. Relying on the dicta of Learned Hand J in *Re Walter J Schmidt & Co*[20] criticising *Clayton's Case* as a fiction productive of injustice, Woolf LJ relegated the rule to being one that *could* be applied depending on the intentions of the parties and the justice of the case. On the facts it could produce arbitrary results; eg, it might enable a small group of investors to take particular assets just because they happened to invest on one day of the week rather than another. Where, as on the facts, thousands of investors were the victims of a 'common misfortune' *pari passu* distribution accorded more with their intentions and with what was just:

> 'While the rule in *Clayton's Case* is prima facie available to determine the interests of investors in a fund into which their investments have been paid, the use of the rule is a matter of convenience and if its application in particular circumstances would be impracticable or result in injustice between the investors it will not be applied if there is a preferable alternative.'[1]

---

17 Eg *Re British Red Cross Balkan Fund* [1914] 2 Ch 419; *Re Hobourn Aero Components Ltd's Distress Fund* [1946] Ch 86, 194; Hanbury and Maudsley, *Modern Equity* (16th edn, 2001), pp 246–247. *Clayton's Case* was also held inapplicable in *Re Eastern Capital Futures Ltd* [1989] BCLC 371.
18 [1992] 4 All ER 22, 35, per Woolf LJ. This was unhelpfully labelled the 'North American' solution.
19 Ibid at p 36, per Woolf LJ.
20 298 F 314, 316 (1923).
1   [1992] 4 All ER 22, 42.

Woolf LJ's views on *Clayton's Case* should be accepted. They are in line with numerous academic writings[2] and with, eg, the influential decision of the Court of Appeal of Ontario in *Re Ontario Securities Commission and Greymac Credit Corpn*.[3]

(ii) Where the mixed fund comprises the money of a beneficiary and a fiduciary, who has acted in breach of duty in mixing the moneys, the general equitable tracing rule is proportionate sharing subject to loss to the mixed fund first being borne by the fiduciary.

In this situation the principle of even-handedness is qualified, because of the fiduciary's breach of duty, by the principle that losses to the mixed fund should first be borne by the fiduciary. So *Clayton's Case* has no application and the proportionate sharing rule is modified to the extent that, where the fiduciary dissipates money from the mixed fund, it will be assumed that he was acting honestly and drawing out only his own money.[4] For example, if the mixed fund is worth £3,000 made up of £1,000 of the claimant beneficiary's money and £2,000 of X's (the fiduciary's) money, and X dissipates £900 so that the value of the fund falls to £2,100, the claimant can trace through to £1,000 (the appropriate remedy being an equitable lien over the fund to secure the £1,000) rather than being confined to a proportionate share (one third) of the £2,100.

The leading case is *Re Hallett's Estate* in which a solicitor holding bonds for his client wrongfully sold the bonds for £2,145 and paid that money into his current account where it was mixed with his own money. He subsequently made withdrawals from, and repayments into, the account so that at the date of his death the account stood at £3,000. Had the 'first in, first out' rule of *Clayton's Case* been applied it was clear that a large portion of the trust money would have been paid out. But the majority of the Court of Appeal (Thesiger LJ dissenting) refused to apply *Clayton's Case* holding rather that the withdrawals were of the trustee's own money on the presumption that he was

---

2   See, eg, McConville, 'Tracing and the Rule in *Clayton's Case*' (1963) 79 LQR 388; Higgins, 'Re Diplock – A Reappraisal' (1965) 6 WALR 428; Goff and Jones, para 2-040; Birks, p 364. See also the Law Reform Commission of British Columbia 'Report on Competing Rights to Mingled Property' (1983) proposing the abolition of the rule in *Clayton's Case* for tracing purposes.

3   (1986) 30 DLR (4th) 1; affd (1989) 52 DLR (4th) 767. In a more controversial decision in *Law Society of Upper Canada v Toronto-Dominion Bank* (1999) 169 DLR (4th) 353 the Court of Appeal of Ontario went beyond rejecting *Clayton's Case* to rejecting the intermediate balance rule. While the decision can be understood as applying proportionate sharing because of the complexity of the intermediate balance rule, the reasoning goes beyond that. For strong criticism see Lionel Smith, 'Tracing in Bank Accounts: The Lowest Intermediate Balance Rule on Trial' (2000) 33 Can Bus LJ 75.

4   *Re Hallett's Estate* (1880) 13 Ch D 696.

acting honestly. The client was therefore held entitled to trace through to £2,145 in the account (the appropriate remedy being an equitable lien of £2,145 over the fund).

That the modifying principle is that the fiduciary should first bear losses, rather than that money first withdrawn is taken to be the fiduciary's, is clearly shown by *Re Oatway*.[5] A trustee mixed £3,000 of the beneficiary's money with £4,000 of his own. After using £2,137 from the fund to buy shares he dissipated the rest. It was held that the beneficiary could trace through to (and have an equitable lien for £3,000 over) the proceeds of sale of the shares. As the sale proceeds amounted to only £2,475 the beneficiary was entitled to take that whole sum.

Where the mixed fund has increased in value (eg by the defaulting fiduciary's prudent investment) there was until recently some doubt as to whether proportionate sharing applied so as to enable the innocent party to trace to (and claim a proprietary remedy in respect of) a substitute of higher value than the value of its original property.

A major reason for the doubt was Sir George Jessel MR's classic dictum in *Re Hallett's Estate*[6] on the tracing rules governing purchases made by a trustee using a beneficiary's money. He said:

> '[Where the beneficiary's money has not been mixed] the beneficial owner has a right to elect either to take the property purchased, or to hold it as a security for the amount of the trust money laid out in the purchase: or, as we generally express it, he is entitled at his election either to take the property, or to have a charge on the property for the amount of the trust money. But ... where a trustee has mixed the money with his own there is this distinction, that the ... beneficial owner ... can no longer elect to take the property because it is no longer bought with the trust money simply and purely but with a mixed fund. He is, however, still entitled to a charge on the property for the amount of the trust money laid out in the purchase.'

It is submitted that that dictum need not be read as ruling out proportionate sharing in respect of part of the property bought with a mixed fund. The major point of the dictum, that the claimant should not be entitled to *the whole* of a substitute product of a mixed fund is, of course, perfectly valid.

Although Ungoed-Thomas J in *Re Tilley's Will Trusts*[7] firmly supported the view that one can trace to (and claim) a proportionate share of a higher value fund, his comments were unfortunately only *obiter dicta*. In that case, Mrs Tilley received £2,237 on trust for her

5   [1903] 2 Ch 356. See also, eg, *Boscawen v Bajwa* [1996] 1 WLR 328.
6   (1879) 13 Ch D 696, 709. See also Lord Parker in *Sinclair v Brougham* [1914] AC 398, 442.
7   [1967] Ch 1179.

daughter and son. In breach of trust she mixed it with her private funds and used the mixed fund to purchase houses so that at her death the fund stood at £94,000. The question at issue (in an action by the personal representative of her deceased daughter) was whether the daughter and son were entitled to a proportionate share of the higher mixed fund or were limited to the £2,237. Ungoed-Thomas J held that normally a beneficiary would be entitled to a proportionate share even in the case of a mixed fund which has increased in value but that, on the facts, this was displaced by the trustee's intention to use only her own money or overdraft facilities to make the (profitable) purchases. The daughter was therefore merely entitled to a charge on Mrs Tilley's bank account for half of £2,237 (plus interest).

In the first edition of this book, it was argued that, in line with the *obiter dicta* in *Re Tilley's Will Trusts*, there should be no doubt about being able to trace to (and claim) a proportionate share of a mixed fund that has increased in value. On the contrary, this must follow logically once one accepts, as English law does, that (i) a claimant can trace in equity into a mixed fund and (ii) a claimant can trace unmixed money into a substitute property and can require the transfer of that property whatever its value.[8]

This argument was expressly approved by Lord Millett (with whom Lords Browne-Wilkinson and Hoffmann agreed on this point) in *Foskett v McKeown*.[9] A fraudulent trustee had taken money from a trust fund held by him for the claimants, mixed it with his own in bank accounts, and used it to pay premiums on a life insurance policy on his life. When he later committed suicide, the defendants (his children) were paid out £1 million under the insurance policy. The claimants argued that they were entitled to a share of the £1 million proportionate to the premiums that, in breach of trust, had been paid using the trust money. Their claim succeeded before the House of Lords by a three to two majority.

It can be seen from the facts that this was a case of tracing into a mixed fund and subsequently into a profitable investment made from that mixed fund. To the argument that the claimants should be restricted to an equitable lien over the insurance pay-out, Lord Millett said the following: '[T]he time has come to state unequivocally that English law has no ... rule [that in the case of a mixed substitution the beneficiary is confined to a lien] ... I agree with Burrows that the beneficiary's right to elect to have a proportionate share of a mixed substitution necessarily follows once one accepts, as English law does, (i) that a claimant can trace in equity into a mixed fund and (ii) that

8   Burrows, *The Law of Restitution* (1st edn, 1993), p 367.
9   [2001] 1 AC 102.

he can trace unmixed money into its proceeds and assert ownership of the proceeds.'[10]

It is important to add that the claim in *Foskett v McKeown* was being brought not against the defaulting trustee (or his estate) but against innocent donees. The claim was, in other words, not one for restitution for a wrong but was rather one for the cause of action of unjust enrichment by subtraction (albeit that their Lordships, with respect incorrectly, saw the claim as being a pure proprietary claim vindicating pre-existing ownership rather than being one within the law of restitution reversing unjust enrichment). Although the mixed fund comprised money of the trustee and the innocent beneficiaries, the justification for being able to trace to, and claim, a proportionate share of the higher value substitute was therefore no stronger than if the higher value substitute had been bought from a mixed fund comprising the moneys of two innocent parties.[11] Ultimately that justification rests on tracing and title satisfying the 'at the expense of' requirement of unjust enrichment by subtraction which does not necessitate an equivalence of loss and gain but rather merely insists that the defendant's gain came from the claimant's wealth.[12]

(iii) The 'lowest intermediate balance' (or 'exhaustion of the fund') rule

One cannot trace where there is no substitute property. So tracing stops where money being traced has been 'dissipated'. In relation to mixed funds, this means that one cannot trace into a mixed fund after the mixed fund has been exhausted. Analogously (and leaving aside profitable investment) where a fiduciary's own money or a non-claimant's money is being added to a fund, the tracing claimant cannot trace to a higher amount than the lowest intermediate balance in the fund. Money coming into the fund above that amount cannot be traced back to the claimant's money.

However, it should be noted at the outset that, as we have seen above,[13] where there have been many payments in and out of a mixed fund comprising the money of many innocent parties, the courts have been willing, on grounds of practicality, to side-step the strictly logical lowest intermediate balance rule in favour of proportionate sharing of the surviving fund.

10 Ibid at 131.
11 See above, p 95, n 6.
12 See above, pp 28–29, 34–35, 78–80.
13 See especially *Barlow Clowes International Ltd v Vaughan* [1992] 4 All ER 22: above, pp 97–98. Woolf LJ expressly recognised, at p 42, that exhaustion of the fund ruled out tracing by prior investors into a subsequently replenished fund; nevertheless he did not apply proportionate sharing to each intermediate balance in the fund because of the complexity of so doing.

A simple application of the lowest intermediate balance rule is to be seen in *Roscoe (Bolton) Ltd v Winder*.[14] The defendant misappropriated £455 of the claimant company's money – which he was under a fiduciary duty to collect and pay over – and paid it into his own account. He then dissipated all but £25 of it before mixing his own money so that at his death the balance in the account stood at £358. It was held that the claimant could trace through to only £25.

In *Re Goldcorp Exchange Ltd*,[15] the Privy Council was concerned with the claims of two separate sets of investors to gold bullion that was held by the defendant insolvent company. The 'non-allocated claimants' failed because they could establish no initial proprietary interest in the gold or the purchase money; but in any event the Privy Council considered it hard to understand how the purchase money could have been traced because it had been 'paid into an overdrawn account and thereupon ceased to exist'.[16] As regards the 'Walker and Hall claimants', applying *Roscoe v Winder*, tracing was allowed to the lowest intermediate balance of the (mixed fund of) gold held by the company. An equitable lien in respect of other general assets of the company was rejected because that would have been inequitable. A preferable explanation for that last part of the decision was that there could be no proprietary remedy where there was no traceably surviving enrichment.

Another important decision here is *Bishopsgate Investment Management Ltd v Homan*.[17] Money from pension funds belonging to the claimant was wrongly transferred by Robert Maxwell into Maxwell Communication Corporation Plc (MCC). The claimant sought an equitable charge over all MCC's assets for the amount of the moneys transferred which would give it priority over MCC's unsecured creditors. The Court of Appeal rejected the claim because the claimant could not trace from the misappropriated money to the present assets of MCC. The misappropriated money had been paid into an account of MCC that, at the time of payment, was overdrawn or subsequently became so. The mixed fund at that point was exhausted. *Roscoe v Winder* was cited with approval.

Dillon LJ suggested in obiter dicta that it might be possible to trace money paid into an exhausted fund to property previously purchased from that fund. He termed this 'backward tracing'.[18] The apparent justification for recognising such a concept is the clear causal link

14   [1915] 1 Ch 62.
15   [1995] 1 AC 74.
16   Ibid at 105.
17   [1995] Ch 211.
18   Ibid at 216–217.

between the payment of the money into the fund and the purchase of the property, even though the latter, unusually, has occurred prior to the former. Leggatt LJ appeared to reject this.[19] However, Lionel Smith has argued that the idea of tracing to assets acquired before the receipt of the money in question is not only possible but should not be regarded as unusual because this is how one should view tracing into the discharge of a debt.[20] Rather than regarding such a discharge as a dissipation and as ending tracing, the correct view is that, '[W]hen money is used to pay a debt, it is traceable into what was acquired in exchange for the incurring of the debt.'[1] Lionel Smith gives the example of a thief who buys a car on credit and the next day uses stolen money to pay off the debt. He persuasively argues that the owner of the money can trace it into the car even though the car was acquired before the thief stole the money.

(4) Conclusion

The rules of tracing may, at first sight, seem baffling. It is hoped that the above account may help to show that, subject to the malign influence of the divide between common law and equity, the rules are largely coherent and logical. Wholesale rejection of the present tracing rules therefore seems unnecessary. Where there is a need for reform is in making equity's more flexible rules on tracing into mixed funds available in respect of common law claims.

2.   SUBROGATION

(1) Introduction

The law on subrogation allows one party (C) to step into the shoes of another party (X) so as to have the benefit of X's present or former rights and remedies against another party (D). Put another way, subrogation allows one party, without an assignment, to take over another's present or former rights and remedies.

The right of one contracting party to be subrogated to the rights and remedies of another contracting party may be provided for in the contract between them. Such contractual subrogation rests on the parties' agreement and is a matter of contract law not the law of

---

19   Ibid at 222.
20   'Tracing into the Payment of a Debt' [1995] CLJ 290; *The Law of Tracing* (1997), pp 146–152, 353–356.
1   [1995] CLJ 290, 293.

restitution. But on close analysis it transpires that non-contractual subrogation rests on the principle against unjust enrichment. It is the primary purpose of this section to examine and explain this restitutionary analysis of (non-contractual) subrogation. In doing so the five main examples of (non-contractual) subrogation will be considered: (1) indemnity insurers' subrogation rights; (2) subrogation rights of business creditors dealing with trustees; (3) sureties' subrogation rights; (4) lenders' subrogation rights; and (5) bankers' subrogation rights.[2]

A restitutionary view of subrogation has been argued for by several commentators, led by Goff and Jones.[3] Outside contractual subrogation, this has now been approved by the House of Lords in *Banque Financière de la Cité v Parc (Battersea) Ltd.*[4] Lord Hoffmann, giving the leading speech, said:

'[T]he subject of subrogation is bedevilled by problems of terminology and classification which are calculated to cause confusion … [T]he doctrine of subrogation in insurance rests upon the common intention of the parties and gives effect to the principle of indemnity embodied in the contract … Subrogation in this sense is a contractual arrangement for the transfer of rights against third parties and is founded upon the common intention of the parties. But the term is also used to describe an equitable remedy to reverse or prevent unjust enrichment which is not based upon any agreement or common intention of the party enriched and the party deprived. The fact that contractual subrogation and subrogation to prevent unjust enrichment both involve transfers of rights or something resembling transfers of rights should not be allowed to obscure the fact that one is dealing with radically different institutions. One is part of the law of contract and the other part of the law of restitution. Unless this distinction is borne clearly in mind, there is a danger that the contractual requirement of mutual consent will be imported into the conditions for the grant of the restitutionary remedy or that the absence of such a requirement will be disguised by references to a presumed intention which is wholly fictitious. There is an obvious parallel with the confusion caused by classifying certain restitutionary remedies as quasi-contractual and importing into them features of the law of contract.'[5]

And in Lord Steyn's words in the same case, '[D]istinguished writers have shown that the place of subrogation on the map of the law of

---

2 See also Bills of Exchange Act 1882, s 68(5): below, p 305, n 12. A further probable example is where a tenant for life pays off a charge over settled property: see below, pp 279–280.
3 Goff and Jones, ch 3.
4 [1999] 1 AC 221.
5 Ibid at 231–232.

obligations is by and large within the new sizeable corner marked out for restitution ...'.[6]

Charles Mitchell, the foremost expert on the English law of subrogation, draws an important distinction, which has been adopted in this book and underpins the structure of this section, between two forms of subrogation.[7] The rarer form of subrogation, which he labels 'simple subrogation' is where a person takes over another's 'live' rights and remedies against a third party.[8] It is most obviously illustrated by an indemnity insurer's right to take over the assured's live rights against a wrongdoer. The commoner form, which Mitchell labels 'reviving subrogation', is where a person has discharged (or his money has been used to discharge) another's liability to a third party and takes over the third party's *former* rights and remedies against that other party (ie, the discharged liability is revived). For example, where money has been borrowed by D from C and D has used it to discharge its liability to a third party (X), reviving subrogation may entitle C to take over X's former rights and remedies, including secured rights, against D.

There are four further introductory points. First, it will be seen that one key to unlocking the mysteries of restitutionary subrogation is to recognise that it is triggered by a range of unjust factors. In principle, therefore, it ought to be dispersed into the chapters on those unjust factors. However at the present time, when subrogation has only recently begun to be properly understood, it is too hard, as a matter of exposition, to go straight to that advanced position.

Secondly, subrogation may entitle the claimant to take over proprietary, as well as personal, rights and remedies. In this respect, subrogation is of central importance to the continuing debate and controversy over the extent of, and justification for, proprietary restitution.

Thirdly, where subrogation does rest on the principle against unjust enrichment, there is sometimes a question as to whether it is a necessary technique or whether restitution could be more straightforwardly effected without relying on subrogation.[9] In this respect, it is significant that, in the *Banque Financière* case, Lord Steyn (in contrast to Lord Hoffmann who gave the leading speech) reached the same decision

---

6   Ibid at 228.

7   Mitchell, *The Law of Subrogation* (1994). For a summary of his approach, see Mitchell, 'The Law of Subrogation' [1992] LMCLQ 483.

8   This explains why one cannot simply say that one linking principle of subrogation is that it concerns an enrichment by the discharging of D's liability to X.

9   Birks, pp 93–98 argues 'that within the law of restitution [subrogation] adds nothing to the number of techniques already identified. It is in the nature of a metaphor which can be done without'.

as their other Lordships by direct application of the principles of unjust enrichment. It was only at the end of his speech that he said that, if it were necessary to do so, he would reach the same conclusion by applying subrogation.

Finally, it was pointed out in the first edition of this book that subrogation is sometimes concerned to prevent, rather than to reverse, an unjust enrichment; and that, where so, subrogation, on an extreme view, would belong outside the law of restitution. But there is no good reason to take that extreme view.[10] While the law of restitution is normally concerned to reverse an accrued unjust enrichment, there is no reason to regard a right to restitution created to prevent an unjust enrichment as outside this area of the law. Certainly Lord Hoffmann, in the passage set out above from the *Banque Financière* case, spoke of reversing or preventing unjust enrichment.

(2) Simple subrogation

(a) Indemnity insurers' subrogation rights[11]

An indemnity insurer has two distinct types of subrogation right.[12] First, in what is, arguably, the classic example of subrogation, it is entitled to take over the remedies of the assured (X) against another party (D) in order to recover the sum paid out by it to the assured and by which the assured would otherwise be overcompensated.[13] For example, if C insures X against damage to his property and D tortiously damages X's property and C pays out for the loss in accordance with the insurance policy, C is subrogated to X's remedies (in tort) against D.[14]

Secondly, the insurer is entitled to recover from the assured (X), up to the amount it paid X, money that X has already received or subsequently receives from another party (D) and by which X is overcompensated.[15] In this respect, subrogation operates to allow the

---

10 Cf Williams, 'Preventing Unjust Enrichment' [2000] RLR 492.

11 The same principles apply to a contract of indemnity even if not an insurance contract: *Esso Petroleum Ltd v Hall, Russell & Co Ltd and Shetland Islands Council, The Esso Bernicia* [1989] AC 643.

12 Cf MacGillivray and Parkington, *Insurance Law* (9th edn, 1997), para 22-2.

13 Eg *Mason v Sainsbury* (1782) 3 Doug KB 61; *Morris v Ford Motor Co* [1973] QB 792. In principle the insurer should be able to recover the sum paid *plus interest.*

14 In *Caledonia North Sea Ltd v Norton (No 2) Ltd* [2002] UKHL 4, [2002] 1 Lloyd's Rep 553 the House of Lords clarified that an indemnity insurer may be subrogated even to X's rights to a contractual indemnity from D.

15 *Castellain v Preston* (1883) 11 QBD 380; *Assicurazioni Generali de Trieste v Empress Assurance Corpn Ltd* [1907] 2 KB 814; *Re Miller, Gibb & Co Ltd* [1957] 1 WLR 703; *Yorkshire Insurance Co Ltd v Nisbet Shipping Co Ltd* [1962] 2 QB 330.

insurer to take over the fruits of X's rights and remedies.[16] It has sometimes been said that the assured holds any overcompensation received from D as trustee for the insurer.[17] But in *Lord Napier & Ettrick v Hunter*[18] the House of Lords held that, while the insurer is not confined to a personal remedy, the appropriate proprietary 'remedy' is an equitable lien over the damages recovered by X from D not a constructive trust. It was also controversially held that in working out the overcompensation to which the insurer is entitled the assured cannot first recover the whole of his uninsured loss and must instead bear the excess agreed.

Are these subrogation rights restitutionary?

Commonly the subrogation rights are the subject of an express or clear implied agreement between the parties. Moreover, as was pointed out in *Lord Napier and Ettrick v Hunter*, it is customary for the assured, on payment of the loss by the insurer, to provide the insurer with what is called 'a letter of subrogation' which effectively constitutes an express assignment to the insurer of the assured's rights of recovery against a third party. Clearly all this belongs within the law of contract not the law of restitution.

But where there is no agreement, express or implied, between the parties as to the transfer of rights, subrogation arises by operation of law.[19] Unfortunately, in several cases the courts have arguably obscured this by seeing the rights as stemming from implied terms of the insurance contract. For example, in *Yorkshire Insurance Co Ltd v Nisbet Shipping Co Ltd*,[20] Diplock J said:

> 'The expression "subrogation" in relation to a contract of marine insurance is thus no more than a convenient way of referring to those terms which are to be implied in the contract between the assured and the insurer to give business efficacy to an agreement whereby the assured in the case of a loss against which the policy has been made shall be fully indemnified, and never more than fully indemnified.'

In *Lord Napier and Ettrick v Hunter*,[1] Lord Goff rejected Diplock J's view that an indemnity insurer's right of subrogation always arises from the contract. Rather he clarified that, as shown in equity cases, it can arise by operation of law outside the contract albeit that the contractual

---

16   Mitchell, *The Law of Subrogation* (1994), pp 67–86 argues that this is not subrogation.
17   Eg *Re Miller, Gibb & Co Ltd* [1957] 1 WLR 703, MacGillivray and Parkington, *Insurance Law* (9th edn, 1997) para 22-23.
18   [1993] AC 713. See also below, p 112. An equitable lien was also granted in the early case of *White v Dobinson* (1844) 14 Sim 273.
19   This is supported by the judgments in, eg, *Castellain v Preston* (1883) 11 QBD 380 and *Morris v Ford Motor Co Ltd* [1973] QB 792.
20   [1962] 2 QB 330, 339–340. See also *Orakpo v Manson Investments Ltd* [1978] AC 95, 104 where Lord Diplock said that subrogation rights in insurance contracts are contractual.
1   [1993] AC 713.

context is important because the underlying principle is that the insurer is to be indemnified but no more than indemnified. He said:

'[I]t is proper to start with the contract of insurance, and to see how the common law courts have worked out the mutual rights and obligations of the parties in contractual terms with recourse to implied terms where appropriate. But, with all respect, I am unable to agree with Diplock J that subrogation is in this context concerned *solely* with the mutual rights and obligations of the parties under the contract ... I cannot derive from Diplock J's judgment any justification for sweeping the line of equity cases under the carpet as though it did not exist. In my opinion, this line of authority must be recognised ... Even so, an important feature of these cases is that the principle of subrogation in the law of insurance arises in a contractual context. ... it has been regarded, both at law and in equity, as giving effect to the underlying nature of a contract of insurance, which is that it is intended to provide an indemnity but no more than an indemnity.'[2]

Lord Hoffmann in *Banque Financière de la Cité v Parc (Battersea) Ltd*[3] purported to support this but unfortunately his comments[4] are most naturally interpreted as indicating that, in contrast to subrogation designed to prevent or reverse unjust enrichment, subrogation in indemnity insurance rests on the common intention of the parties and is contractual.

If one were to put a contractual analysis to one side – on the basis that, as Lord Goff said, it is not always applicable – can unjust enrichment explain an indemnity insurer's (non-contractual) subrogation rights?

On an unjust enrichment analysis, the relevant *enrichment* would be the assured's (X's): it cannot be D's because, even with the first type of subrogation right, D's liability to X is not discharged by C's payment, but remains alive to be enforced in X's name by C.

This was emphasised in *Esso Petroleum Ltd v Hall, Russell & Co Ltd.*[5] Esso (C) had indemnified Scottish crofters (X) under a tanker owners' oil pollution agreement (TOVALOP) – analogous to an indemnity insurance contract – for oil damage caused by the negligence of Hall Russell (D). It was held that C's rights of subrogation did not entitle it to bring an action in its own name: its payment to X did not discharge D's liability to X so that C's action, through subrogation, had to be brought in X's name. In an important passage, Lord Goff said:

'If ... a payment were made under a contract of indemnity between Esso and the crofters, there can be no doubt that Esso would upon payment be subrogated to the crofters' claims against Hall Russell. This would enable Esso

---

2   Ibid at 743–744.
3   [1999] 1 AC 221, 231–232.
4   Set out above at p 105.
5   [1989] AC 643. See also, eg, *Mason v Sainsbury* (1782) 3 Doug KB 61.

to proceed against Hall Russell in the names of the crofters; but it would not enable Esso to proceed, without more, to enforce the crofters' claims by an action in its own name against Hall Russell. The reason for this is plain. It is that Esso's payment to the crofters does not have the effect of discharging Hall Russell's liability to them ... There can, of course, be no direct claim by Esso against Hall Russell in restitution, if only because Esso has not by its payment discharged the liability of Hall Russell, and so has not enriched Hall Russell; if anybody has been enriched, it is the crofters, to the extent that they have been indemnified by Esso and yet continue to have vested in them rights of action against Hall Russell in respect of the loss or damage which was the subject matter of Esso's payment to them. All that is left is the fact that the crofters' rights of action against Hall Russell continued to exist ... and that it might have been inequitable to deny Esso the opportunity to take advantage of them – which is the classic basis of subrogation in the case of contracts of indemnity.'[6]

Can X's enrichment be said to be *at C's expense* (within unjust enrichment by subtraction)? The difficulty is that it is D's payment or liability to pay that appears to be regarded as the direct source of the entitlement. Nevertheless that money paid or payable by D is only relevant in overcompensating X because of the payment by the insurer. The enrichment can therefore be said to have been subtracted from the insurer albeit that, strictly speaking, this should be seen as an exception to the normal rule (of restitution being confined to direct providers only) in that the benefit is being rendered by someone (D) other than the claimant.

The unjust factor is most obviously explained on the basis of there being a general policy that a claimant should be fully but not overcompensated through an indemnity insurance policy.[7] So in *Castellain v Preston*,[8] Brett LJ said:

'... the contract of insurance contained in a marine or fire policy is a contract of indemnity and of indemnity only, and ... this contract means that the assured, in the case of a loss against which the policy has been made, shall be fully indemnified, but shall never be more than fully indemnified. That is the fundamental principle of insurance, and if ever a proposition is brought forward which is at variance with it, that is to say, which either will prevent the assured from obtaining a full indemnity, or which will give to the assured more than a full indemnity, that proposition must certainly be wrong.'

6   Ibid at 662–663.
7   See similarly Degeling, 'A New Reason for Restitution: The Policy Against Accumulation' (2002) 22 OJLS 435, esp 454–460. But Williams, 'Preventing Unjust Enrichment' [2000] RLR 492 argues that simple subrogation is not explicable as restitutionary reversing or preventing unjust enrichment: the concern is to provide the insurer with an indemnity not to prevent the insurer being over-indemnified.
8   (1883) 11 QBD 380, 386.

Similarly in *Lord Napier and Ettrick v Hunter* Lord Goff said that the purpose of subrogation in this context was to give 'effect to the underlying nature of a contract of insurance, which is that it is intended to provide an indemnity but no more than an indemnity'.[9] And in Lord Hoffmann's words in *Banque Financière de la Cité v Parc (Battersea) Ltd*, 'the doctrine of subrogation in insurance ... gives effect to the principle of indemnity embodied in the contract'.[10]

Alternatively (and in an attempt to break any circularity in reasoning stemming from subrogation rights being so well-established) the second subrogation right could be seen as based on either a mistake of fact, where unknown to the insurer the loss has already been recouped from D prior to the insurer's payment, or failure of consideration (in the sense of an unpromised future event)[11] where, contrary to the basis for the insurer's payment as understood by the assured, the loss is subsequently recouped from D. Indeed invocation of those standard restitutionary grounds raises a puzzling question. Why has the law gone to the lengths of involving subrogation, and hence rights to recover money *paid by D* to the insured, if there is, as there appears to be, a straightforward claim available to the insurer for restitution of the money *it has paid* to the insured either for mistake of fact or failure of consideration?

Certainly in the early case of *Darrell v Tibbitts*,[12] where an insurance company had paid out for fire damage to a house before the loss was recouped by the owner from the tortfeasor, the ordinary restitutionary action was clearly seen as one route to recovery in the judgments of Brett and Thesiger LJJ. The latter said:

> 'It appears to me that this suit may be supported upon one of two grounds: it may be maintained either as an action at common law for money had and received to recover the sum which they paid upon the ground that that money was paid upon the conditions, that the person to whom it was paid had sustained a loss, that in point of fact no loss had been sustained, and therefore that the money paid by the company ought in justice to be returned to them. It is also maintainable as a kind of suit in equity founded upon the following grounds; the assured having been indemnified against the loss sustained by him through the payment by the insurance company, the latter have a right to be subrogated into the place of the assured.'[13]

Yet in subsequent cases, with the exception of Diplock J in *Yorkshire Insurance Co Ltd v Nisbet Shipping Co Ltd*,[14] an insurer's direct restitutionary

---

9   [1993] AC 713, 744.
10 [1999] 1 AC 221, 231.
11 Below, p 326.
12 (1880) 5 QBD 560.
13 Ibid at p 568. See also Brett LJ at pp 562–563.
14 [1962] 2 QB 330, 341–342.

claim disappeared from judicial view. The fact remains that the difference between that claim and the insurer's subrogation rights to take the benefit of money paid by the third party is paper-thin and, as the direct claim is indisputably restitutionary, so must be the latter.

A final question is, were their Lordships correct in *Lord Napier and Ettrick v Hunter* to award proprietary, rather than personal, restitution to the indemnity insurer by granting an equitable lien? Or is the view of Stirling LJ in *Stearns v Village Main Reef Mining Co*,[15] that the insurer should be confined to a personal remedy, to be preferred? It is submitted that the latter view is indeed preferable.[16] This is because the indemnity insurer is, in two respects, in a significantly different position than a secured creditor and should therefore be regarded as having taken the risk of the assured's insolvency. First, because the money paid to the insured did not belong to the insurer prior to its payment there is no strong analogy between the insurer's position and that of a creditor conferring credit on a debtor. Secondly, and perhaps more importantly, the indemnity insurer is in a contractual relationship with the assured in which provision could be made for the consequences of subsequent payment by a third party to the assured, including security over that payment in favour of the insurer. Where the insurer has failed to include such a provision, it has taken the risk of the assured's insolvency and it is very hard to see why it should be afforded preferential status to other unsecured creditors on the assured's insolvency.

(b) Subrogation rights of creditors of a business carried on by trustees

A trustee who properly carries on a deceased's business for the benefit of the beneficiaries is generally entitled to be indemnified by the beneficiaries for personal loss incurred and has a lien over the trust assets to secure compensation. If the trustee (X) fails to pay creditors (C), who he has dealt with in running the business, they are entitled to be subrogated to those personal and proprietary remedies of the trustee against the beneficiaries (D).[17]

On an unjust enrichment analysis the relevant enrichment could be viewed as the trustee's in failing to pay the creditors. However it is probably better seen as the beneficiaries' in that the carrying on of the business is ultimately for their benefit so that they will have had the realised benefit of the creditors' goods (or other consideration) without

15 (1905) 10 Com Cas 89. Interestingly Stirling LJ drew an analogy with *Lister & Co v Stubbs* (1890) 45 Ch D 1, discussed below pp 497–500.
16 See also Mitchell, *The Law of Subrogation* (1994), pp 82–84.
17 *Re Johnson* (1880) 15 Ch D 548, 552; *Re Oxley* [1914] 1 Ch 604.

payment. So in *Yonge v Reynell*[18] Sir GJ Turner V-C drew an analogy between this type of subrogation and a surety's subrogation rights; and the only obvious parallel in the two situations is between the enrichment of the debtor and the enrichment of the beneficiaries. And in *Re Johnson*,[19] Sir George Jessel MR explained the rationale behind the business creditors' subrogation rights as follows: 'The trust assets having been devoted to carrying on the trade, it would not be right that the *cestui que trust* should get the benefit of the trade without paying the liabilities.' This is an exception to the normal rule of restitution being confined to direct providers only: here the enrichment is conferred by the trustee not the claimant.

The most obvious unjust factor is failure of consideration in that the creditors have carried out their side of the contracts with the trustee without the contracted-for return. This would require, however, that the creditors terminate the contracts before being entitled to exercise their subrogation rights. It also requires one to accept that failure of consideration can trigger restitution from a third party beneficiary of a contract.[20]

As with indemnity insurers' subrogation rights, the law can be criticised for allowing the creditors to take over not only the trustee's personal remedies against the beneficiaries but also his lien over the trust assets.

(3) Reviving subrogation

(a) Sureties' subrogation rights

The authorities establish that a surety (C) who has paid off another's (D's) debt is subrogated to the creditor's (X's) (former) remedies against the debtor to recover the sum paid.[1] This right of subrogation is statutorily enshrined in the Mercantile Law Amendment Act 1856, s 5.[2] This is straightforwardly explicable on unjust enrichment reasoning. The unjust factor is the legal compulsion on the surety and the enrichment is the discharge of the debtor's liability to his creditor.

As far as personal remedies are concerned, subrogation seems superfluous. On a restitutionary analysis C, irrespective of subrogation, should be entitled to a claim against D in an action for money paid to D's

---

18 (1852) 9 Hare 809, 819.
19 (1880) 15 Ch D 548, 552.
20 Below, pp 347–350.
1   Eg *Forbes v Jackson* (1882) 19 Ch D 615. See analogously *Duncan, Fox & Co v North and South Wales Bank* (1880) 6 App Cas 1 (indorser on bill of exchange entitled to subrogation).
2   For application of the Act, see *Re Parker* [1894] 3 Ch 400; *Re Lamplugh Iron Ore Co Ltd* [1927] 1 Ch 308.

use or contribution.[3] Admittedly *Owen v Tate*[4] stands in the way of giving a voluntary surety the former direct restitutionary remedy. But it is argued in chapter 8 that the decision is wrong. Indeed it is hard to see how it can stand in the face of s 5 of the 1856 Act (which was not mentioned in the case). Goff and Jones argue that *Owen v Tate* was wrongly decided because the claimant should have been entitled to subrogation.[5] It can be more obviously criticised on its own terms and the switch of terminology to subrogation ought, on a restitutionary analysis, to change nothing.

The importance of subrogation, however (as reflected in the cases), is that the surety on payment is also subrogated to a creditor's security (eg a lien) so as to recover the sum paid. This is not easy to justify. One initial problem is that it is normally a pre-requisite for proprietary restitution that the enrichment is retained by the defendant in an asset to which the proprietary restitution can attach. This requirement is not straightforwardly satisfied in relation to a discharged liability. But this can probably be regarded as satisfied if the discharged liability was directly related to property retained by the defendant (ie where the debt discharged was secured over property retained by the defendant, restitution may be secured over that property). The more significant difficulty is that the surety could have contracted with the debtor for security to protect itself against the insolvency of the debtor; and, where it has not done so, one can argue that it has taken the risk of that insolvency and should be confined to personal restitution. In Mitchell's view, 'It must be concluded that there is no valid reason why, for example, a surety who pays a creditor should be entitled as a general rule to be subrogated to securities formerly held by the creditor against the principal debtor.'[6] Similarly, Goff and Jones think that 'arguably' a surety's subrogation to securities that he did not know about and which came into existence after the contract of guarantee place him 'in too favourable a position'.[7] Birks seeks to justify the present law on the basis that the surety traces his money through the discharge of the debt to the securities and that an analogy can be drawn to there being an undestroyed 'proprietary base'.[8] There is no authority to support that novel view of tracing and it has been persuasively criticised by Lionel Smith.[9] In any event, it is hard to see the justificatory force in Birks' 'proprietary base' theory.[10]

3   Below, chapter 8.
4   [1976] QB 402.
5   Goff and Jones at para 3-017. See also Watts, 'Guarantees undertaken without the Request of the Debtor' [1989] LMCLQ 7.
6   *The Law of Subrogation* (1994), p 53.
7   Goff and Jones at para 3-027.
8   Birks at pp 93–98, 372–375, 389–393, 397–399.
9   'Tracing into the Payment of a Debt' [1995] CLJ 290; *The Law of Tracing*, pp 149–154.
10   See above, p 72, n 18.

(b) Lenders' subrogation rights

Although the leading cases of *Boscawen v Bajwa*[11] and *Banque Financière de la Cité v Parc (Battersea) Ltd*[12] involved added complexity, the standard situation in mind here is that of a lender (C) lending money to a borrower (D), which D uses to pay off his debt to a third party (X) (or C may pay the money directly to X discharging D's debt).

C is subrogated to X's (former) remedies against D to the extent of the debt discharged. In analysing whether this type of subrogation is explicable by unjust enrichment reasoning, it is helpful to distinguish between valid and invalid loans.

(i) Valid loans

In the standard situation just referred to, where the loan is a valid one, C already has his personal contractual rights against D to recover the money loaned (or a personal restitutionary claim for total failure of consideration). In general, therefore, subrogation to X's *personal* rights is of no advantage to C especially as it will only entitle him to the amount of the debt discharged which may be less than the money lent. But subrogation may be advantageous where D is insolvent for it sometimes allows an unsecured lender to take over X's secured rights against D for the debt discharged. It is for this reason that the main cases on lenders' subrogation rights following valid loans have concerned proprietary subrogation[13] (or, in the leading case of *Banque Financière de la Cité v Parc (Battersea) Ltd*,[14] a personal right which gave priority as against another creditor of an insolvent debtor).

In the standard situation, one can explain lenders' subrogation rights by unjust enrichment reasoning as follows. The enrichment is the discharge of D's debt to X. D's enrichment is at C's expense where C can establish, if necessary by application of the tracing rules, that the loaned money was used to discharge the debt to X. And while the unjust factor cannot usually be legal compulsion, because C was generally under no legal obligation to pay X and has simply performed his binding contractual obligation to pay the money loaned to D, C will generally be able to rely on the unjust factor of failure of consideration in not being repaid the loan by D. Alternatively, another unjust factor, such as mistake, may be present on particular facts.

---

11 [1996] 1 WLR 328
12 [1999] 1 AC 221.
13 Eg, *Butler v Rice* [1910] 2 Ch 277; *Wylie v Carlyon* [1922] 1 Ch 51; *Ghana Commercial Bank v Chandiram* [1960] AC 732; *Paul v Speirway Ltd* [1976] Ch 220; *Boscawen v Bajwa* [1996] 1 WLR 328; *Halifax plc v Omar* [2002] EWCA Civ 121, [2002] 2 P & CR 377.
14 [1999] 1 AC 221.

So, for example, in *Butler v Rice*[15] the claimant lent £450 to Mr Rice so as to enable him to pay off a banker's charge over a house in Bristol. The money was lent on the express understanding that Mr Rice would give the claimant a charge over the house to secure repayment of the £450. In fact Mr Rice was unable to do this as his wife owned the house and she refused to create a charge. It was held that the claimant was entitled to take over the bank's charge. Although Warrington J saw the relevant test as one of whether the claimant must be presumed to have intended to keep the charge alive in his own favour – an approach which has been disapproved by the House of Lords in *Banque Financière de la Cité v Parc (Battersea) Ltd*[16] – the result is straightforwardly explicable as an example of proprietary restitution reversing an unjust enrichment. Mr Rice was enriched by discharge of his debt to the bank. That enrichment was at the claimant's expense because the money used to pay off the debt had come from the claimant. And the unjust factor was the failure of consideration in that the claimant had not been repaid the money by Mr Rice. *Furthermore, proprietary, as opposed to personal, restitution was justified because the claimant had bargained for security and had therefore not taken the risk of the defendant's insolvency.*

The facts of the important case of *Boscawen v Bajwa*[17] were slightly more complex than the standard situation referred to above because the discharge of D's (Bajwa's) debt to X (the Halifax Building Society) at the expense of the claimant lender (Abbey National) involved several intermediate parties and transactions. Mr Bajwa was the owner of a house. The Halifax Building Society had a charge over the house. Bajwa contracted to sell the house to purchasers who were to obtain a mortgage from the Abbey National. Abbey National paid the purchase money to the purchasers' solicitors pending completion of the sale. They in turn paid the money by cheque to Bajwa's solicitors (Hill Lawson) who then paid off the Halifax Building Society's charge over the property. Hill Lawson had acted with undue haste in paying off the Halifax because the purchasers' solicitors' cheque was dishonoured and the only equity partner was insolvent. The sale then fell through. Judgment creditors of Bajwa with a charging order on the house brought a claim to enforce the charging order and the house was sold for £105,312 net. Abbey National counter-claimed that it was entitled to an equitable charge over the house (and hence the proceeds of sale) on the basis that it was subrogated to the charge of the Halifax Building Society which had been paid off with the Abbey National's money. The Court of Appeal

15 [1910] 2 Ch 277. See also *Ghana Commercial Bank v Chandiram* [1960] AC 732.
16 [1999] 1 AC 221.
17 [1996] 1 WLR 328. See Mitchell, 'Subrogation, Tracing, and the *Quistclose* Principle' [1995] LMCLQ 451.

held that that counterclaim succeeded and that Abbey National was subrogated to the Halifax Building Society's charge.

In an enlightened judgment, Millett LJ (with whom Waite and Stuart-Smith LJJ agreed) dismissed an argument that one could not combine tracing and subrogation. On the contrary, subrogation came into play on these facts once it had been established, by tracing, that the discharge of the debt to the Halifax had been at the Abbey National's expense. Millett LJ said, 'There was nothing illegitimate in the deputy judge's invocation of the two doctrines of tracing and subrogation in the same case. They arose at different stages of the proceedings. Tracing was the process by which the Abbey National sought to establish that its money was applied in the discharge of the Halifax's charge; subrogation was the remedy which it sought in order to deprive Mr Bajwa (through whom the appellants claim) of the unjust enrichment which he would thereby otherwise obtain at the Abbey National's expense.'[18]

Millett LJ also clarified that the principle examined by Oliver J in *Paul v Speirway Ltd*,[19] that proprietary subrogation should not be granted if it would give the claimant more than he bargained for, did not arise because, 'The Abbey National did not intend to be an unsecured creditor of anyone. It intended to retain the beneficial interest in its money unless and until that interest was replaced by a first legal mortgage on the property.'[20]

Although the unjust factor was not specifically identified by Millett LJ, it was most obviously failure of consideration (in the non-promissory sense).[1] Abbey National paid the purchasers' solicitors on the condition that the money would be used to finance the purchase of the house and that Abbey National would take a charge over the house when purchased. Once the sale did not go ahead the basis for the payment totally failed.

The leading case on non-contractual subrogation – and indeed one of the most important in the whole law of restitution – is *Banque Financière de la Cité v Parc (Battersea) Ltd*.[2] As we have seen, this authoritatively established that the principle against unjust enrichment underpins non-contractual subrogation. The case concerned a lender's subrogation rights in respect of a valid loan but it was significantly more complex than the standard situation referred to above in two main respects. First, the relevant enrichment in issue was not that of D (the borrower), to whom the money had been loaned by C, but a

---

18 Ibid at 335.
19 [1976] Ch 220.
20 [1996] 1 WLR 328, 339.
1 See below, chapter 10.
2 [1999] 1 AC 221. See Mitchell, 'Subrogation, Unjust Enrichment and Remedial Flexibility' [1998] RLR 144. The decision is strongly criticised in a difficult article by Bridge, 'Failed Contracts, Subrogation and Unjust Enrichment' [1998] JBL 323.

subsequent lender to D who was benefited by the discharge of D's debt to X using C's loan. Secondly, the reason for seeking restitution was to obtain security not against D the borrower but against the subsequent lender to D; and this priority would be achieved by personal, rather than full proprietary, subrogation.

The facts were as follows. The claimants, a Swiss bank (BFC) loaned DM30 million to Parc who used it to pay off a loan to another bank (RTB). RTB's loan had been secured by a first charge over Parc's development land at Battersea. The defendant (OOL) had a second charge over that property securing a loan made by it to Parc. The claimants obtained no security for their loan to Parc but had been promised in a 'postponement letter' that other companies in the group to which Parc belonged, which included the defendant, would not demand repayment of their loan until the claimants had been paid. But that promise was made without the authority of the defendant and was therefore not binding on the defendant. The claimants did not know this and therefore mistakenly believed that they had priority as against the defendant (albeit not against RTB). On Parc's insolvency, the claimants claimed to be subrogated to the rights of the first chargee (RTB) so that they had priority against the defendant.

Their Lordships, with the leading speech being given by Lord Hoffmann, held that the claimants were indeed entitled, as against the defendant, to be subrogated to the right of the first chargee so that they had priority against the defendant. This was justified on the basis that it reversed, or prevented, the defendant's unjust enrichment at the expense of the claimants. More specifically, it was explained that, first, the defendant had been enriched because the repayment of Parc's loan to RTB pro tanto improved the defendant's position as chargee. In Lord Hoffmann's words, 'The result of the transaction is that BFC's DM30m has been used to reduce the debt secured by RTB's first charge and that this reduction will, by reason of OOL's second charge, enure wholly to the latter's advantage.'[3] Secondly, that enrichment was at the expense of the claimants because it came from the money loaned to Parc by the claimants. According to Lord Hoffmann, '[T]here is no difficulty in tracing BFC's money into the discharge of the debt due to RTB: the payment to RTB was direct.'[4] And thirdly, the claimants would not have made the loan but for their mistaken belief that it had priority over any intra-group indebtedness. As Lord Hoffmann said, 'The bank advanced the DM30m upon the mistaken assumption that it was obtaining a postponement letter

3   Ibid, at 235.
4   Ibid.

which would be effective to give it priority over any intra-group indebtedness. It would not otherwise have done so.'[5]

On the face of it, a difficulty in applying subrogation to these facts, so that the claimants were subrogated to the rights of RTB, was that this would give the claimants the benefit of a first charge (which RTB had). Yet this would put them in a better position than they had bargained for. The claimants had never thought that they had a charge against Parc. Their Lordships overcame this difficulty by simply accepting that subrogation can be tailored to fit the circumstances. More specifically, there was no need to regard it as transferring rights that would go beyond what was necessary to prevent or reverse the defendant's unjust enrichment at the claimant's expense. Here subrogation as against the defendant was all that was justified and was all that was being claimed. In Lord Hoffmann's words, '[S]ubrogation as against OOL, which is all that BFC claims in the action, would not give it greater rights than it bargained for. All that would happen is that OOL would be prevented from being able to enrich itself to the extent that BFC's money paid off the RTB charge.'[6] The initial apparent difficulty in applying subrogation no doubt explains why Lord Steyn considered that it would be more straightforward to deal directly with a restitutionary remedy for unjust enrichment rather than relying on subrogation. But if necessary to do so, he too would have reached the same conclusion in terms of the principles of subrogation. He said, 'It would admittedly not be the usual case of subrogation to security rights in rem and in personam. The purpose of the relief would be dictated by the particular form of security, involving rights in personam against companies in the group, which BFC mistakenly thought that it was obtaining ... [T]here can be no conceptual impediment to the remedy of subrogation being allowed not in respect of both rights in rem and rights in personam but only in respect of rights in personam.'[7]

Lord Hoffmann emphasised that non-contractual subrogation is concerned to reverse or prevent the defendant's unjust enrichment at the claimant's expense and is not dependent on there being a common intention between the parties. The fact that there was no common intention between the claimants and the defendant in this case did not therefore mean that subrogation was inapplicable. His Lordship said, '[I]t is a mistake to regard the availability of subrogation as a remedy to prevent unjust enrichment as turning entirely upon the question of intention, whether common or unilateral. Such an

5 Ibid at 234. This looks like a mistake of law not fact but, although prior to *Kleinwort Benson Ltd v Lincoln City Council* [1999] 2 AC 349, this problem was not mentioned by their Lordships.
6 Ibid at 237.
7 Ibid at 228.

analysis has inevitably to be propped up by presumptions which can verge upon outright fictions, more appropriate to a less developed legal system than we now have. I would venture to suggest that the reason why intention has played so prominent a part in the earlier cases is because of the influence of cases on contractual subrogation.'[8]

However, while the basis of non-contractual subrogation was rightly seen as the principle against unjust enrichment, their Lordships did regard intention as relevant in a weaker sense; namely that, in deciding on the extent to which the rights transferred by subrogation should be proprietary (or, if not proprietary, personal but conferring a form of security) rather than merely personal, the claimant should not be given better rights than would have been conferred had the postponement letter been binding. In other words, the award of restitution should not override the risk of the defendant's insolvency that the claimant, albeit mistaken, had taken. Put another way still, the claimant should not be given greater rights than it bargained for. This was the principle which Lord Hoffmann regarded as having been applied by Oliver J in *Paul v Speirway Ltd*[9] and was to be distinguished from the incorrect and fictional 'common intention as the basis of subrogation' approach also found in that case and in several others.[10] In *Paul v Speirway Ltd* the claimant had lent £55,000 to a company which used it to complete an existing contract to buy land. On the company's liquidation, the claimant claimed to be subrogated to the lien of the vendor which had sold the land to the company (ie to an unpaid vendor's lien). Oliver J, in talking about subrogation to secured rights, said, '… where a court … comes to the conclusion that what was intended between parties was really an unsecured borrowing … there is no room for the doctrine of subrogation … to apply the doctrine of subrogation in such a case would in fact be putting the lender in a better position than he is bargaining to be put in when he advances the money.'[11]

(ii) Invalid loans

Where the loan is an invalid one (eg because it is made to an *incapax* or to an unauthorised agent or because made by a company ultra vires)[12] an additional issue must be added to the usual unjust enrichment analysis of subrogation. This is that subrogation should be denied where it contradicts the policy rendering the loan invalid.

---

8   Ibid at 234.
9   [1976] Ch 220.
10 Eg *Chetwynd v Allen* [1899] 1 Ch 353; *Butler v Rice* [1910] 2 Ch 277; *Ghana Commercial Bank v Chandiram* [1960] AC 732.
11 [1976] Ch 220, 233.
12 The ultra vires doctrine has been abolished for non-charitable companies; below, p 419.

An additional reason for treating a lender's subrogation rights in respect of an invalid loan separately from those in respect of a valid loan is because subrogation to personal rights has here been as centrally important as subrogation to proprietary rights.[13] As we have seen, this has not generally been so in valid loan cases.[14] The explanation for this is that the lender's personal contractual rights to recover the money loaned are unenforceable. Moreover, it was also the traditional view, laid down in *Sinclair v Brougham*[15] before being overruled in *Westdeutsche Landesbank Girozentrale v Islington London Borough Council*,[16] that the lender could not recover the money in an action for money had and received for total failure of consideration because this would indirectly undermine the contractual bar. In contrast to most valid loan cases on subrogation therefore, C's personal subrogation rights (ie to take over X's personal remedies against D) will be advantageous to him even though he will only be entitled to recover the amount of the debt discharged which may be less than the money lent.

An important restriction on restitution in this context, which reflects the need to avoid undermining the policy rendering the loan invalid, is that the debt discharged must be one which the borrower could validly undertake; subrogation would otherwise represent too much of a contradiction of contractual rules. So Goff and Jones write, 'The invalid loan ... [is] validated *pro tanto* because it has been used to discharge the borrower's *valid* liability to the third person.'[17] Thus in the case of invalid loans to infants and the insane subrogation rights apply if, for example, the loan was used to discharge debts in purchasing necessaries, a contract for necessaries being the main type of contract binding on an *incapax*.[18]

As with valid loans, restitutionary reasoning can explain subrogation in most invalid loan cases on the basis that failure of consideration is the

---

13 See, eg, *Re Cork and Youghal Rly* (1869) 4 Ch App 748; *Blackburn Benefit Building Society v Cunliffe Brooks & Co* (1882) 22 Ch D 61; *Baroness Wenlock v River Dee Co* (1887) 19 QBD 155; *Re Wrexham, Mold and Connah's Quay Rly* [1899] 1 Ch 440 (all concerning a company borrowing ultra vires); *Marlow v Pitfield* (1719) 1 P Wms 558; *Lewis v Alleyne* (1888) 4 TLR 560, *Thurstan v Nottingham Permanent Benefit Building Society* [1902] 1 Ch 1 (borrowing by minor); *Bannatyne v D & C MacIver* [1906] 1 KB 103; *Reversion Fund and Insurance Co Ltd v Maison Cosway Ltd* [1913] 1 KB 364 (borrowing by unauthorised agent); *Re Beaven* [1912] 1 Ch 196 (borrowing by insane person); *Orakpo v Manson Investments Ltd* [1978] AC 95 (lending contrary to the Moneylenders Act 1927). Arguably analogous is *Jenner v Morris* (1861) 3 De GF & J 45 (lender subrogated to creditors' rights against husband for his wife's purchase of necessities).
14 See above, p 115.
15 [1914] AC 398.
16 [1996] AC 669. See below, p 568.
17 Goff and Jones, para 3-056. For criticism of the language of 'validating' the loan, see Maddaugh and McCamus, *The Law of Restitution* (1st edn, 1990), pp 179–180.
18 Eg *Lewis v Alleyne* (1888) 4 TLR 560; *Re Beaven* [1912] 1 Ch 196.

unjust factor and the discharge of the debt is the enrichment. Even prior to the authoritative application of unjust enrichment reasoning to non-contractual subrogation in the *Banque Financière* case, the restitutionary analysis of subrogation in the context of invalid loans derived support from dicta of Lord Diplock in *Orakpo v Manson Investments Ltd*:[19]

> 'Some rights of subrogation ... such as the right of an innocent lender to recover from a company moneys borrowed ultra vires to the extent that these have been expended on discharging the company's lawful debts, are in no way based on contract and appear to defeat classification except as an empirical remedy to prevent a particular kind of unjust enrichment.'

As with valid loans, it is important as regards proprietary subrogation to recognise the principle in *Paul v Speirway Ltd* and not to give the lender a security which it had not bargained for.

For example, in *Re Wrexham, Mold and Connah's Quay Rly Co*[20] it was held that a bank – that had made an unsecured loan to a company, borrowing ultra vires, which the company had used to pay debts to its debenture-holders – was not entitled to be subrogated to the secured interests of the debenture-holders. Rigby LJ said:

> 'I do not think that any right of subrogation to the securities or priorities of creditors paid off out of moneys borrowed in excess of borrowing power has ever been allowed or can be justified in principle ... I see no reason why the parties to an illegal lending should have anything more than bare justice dealt out to them; and this they get if they are allowed, as they have hitherto been allowed, to have that portion of the advance actually expended in payment of debts of the company treated as a valid advance. If the advance had been within the borrowing powers of the company, the bank could have had no right to the securities or priorities of the creditors paid off. It seems to me that it would be unjust to other creditors that a fiction should be invented for the purpose of making an invalid loan more valuable than a valid one.'[1]

In contrast a few years later, the House of Lords in *Nottingham Permanent Benefit Building Society v Thurstan*[2] confirmed, without discussion, the Court of Appeal's decision[3] that a building society, that had paid money on behalf of an infant to purchase land, was subrogated to the unpaid vendor's lien over the land. No clear justification for this was given by the Court of Appeal and the *Wrexham* case was not referred to. Nevertheless, like the *Wrexham* case, the

19　[1978] AC 95, 104.
20　[1899] 1 Ch 440.
1　Ibid at pp 449, 455. See also *Reversion Fund and Insurance Co Ltd v Maison Conway Ltd* [1913] 1 KB 364, 377.
2　[1903] AC 6.
3　[1902] 1 Ch 1.

decision is consistent with the *Paul v Speirway* principle in that an express mortgage over the land to secure all the money loaned to the infant had been concluded but was held void for infancy.

Although it was distinguished rather than overruled – and indeed said by Lord Salmon to have been 'decided correctly'[4] – doubt has been cast on *Thurstan* by the House of Lords' reasoning in *Orakpo v Manson Investments Ltd.* A borrower loaned money from registered moneylenders to complete the purchase of two houses and to pay off equitable charges over another six houses. It was expressly agreed that the loans were to be secured by a first mortgage on each of the houses. Those loans and mortgages were unenforceable under s 6 of the Moneylenders Act 1927 because, inadvertently, the written memorandum of the contract did not contain all its terms. The moneylender claimed, instead, to be subrogated to the unpaid vendor's lien or to the equitable charges discharged by the loan. This was rejected (irrespective of a limitation bar). The reasoning was that this type of subrogation rests on contract and is dependent on there being a term of the contract between the lender and the borrower that the loan should be used to pay off the particular debt discharged. Even if on the facts that contractual term was established it was unenforceable, and the subrogated security rights with it, because of the failure to comply with s 6 of the 1927 Act. Indeed that term itself would need to have been set out in the memorandum. The relevant statutory provisions could not therefore be outflanked by subrogation.[5] In contrast it was thought that such outflanking could have been justified in *Thurstan* because it was dealing with a different statute and one which made the contract of loan void rather than unenforceable.

This is excessively restrictive reasoning. Given the unjust enrichment of a borrower and the intention of the parties that the loan should be secured there seems no sound reason to limit proprietary restitution through subrogation to where there is a contractual term that the debt should be paid off. The distinguishing of *Thurstan* was particularly unconvincing. As contracts with infants were void under the Infants Relief Act 1874 the contractual term, necessary for subrogation acccording to the Lords' reasoning, should also have been void, thereby ruling out subrogation. And it surely cannot be sensibly maintained that a different type of subrogation to secured rights arises where, pursuant to the purported contract with the borrower, the lender pays off the creditor directly rather than paying the money to the borrower for the borrower to pay the creditor.

4 [1978] AC 95, 110.
5 The House of Lords overruled *Congresbury Motors Ltd v Anglo-Belge Finance Co Ltd* [1971] Ch 81 which, on very similar facts to *Orakpo*, had relied on *Thurstan* to give a lien by subrogation.

Moreover the result is odd in terms of policy because the Infants Relief Act 1874 was more protective of the class in issue than is s 6 of the Moneylenders Act 1927. Yet, according to *Orakpo*, the more protective Act could be outflanked by proprietary subrogation; the less protective Act could not be.[6] Although Lord Hoffmann in the *Banque Financière* case referred to *Orakpo* as an example of a case where restitutionary subrogation was denied for reasons of policy, it is submitted that that reference should not be interpreted as indicating that Lord Hoffmann agreed with the actual decision in that case.

(c) Bankers' subrogation rights

Where a bank (C), acting on what it erroneously believes to be the valid mandate of its customer (D), pays money to X which discharges D's liability to X, C is subrogated to X's former remedies against D to the extent of the debt discharged.

A leading case is *B Liggett (Liverpool) Ltd v Barclays Bank Ltd.*[7] A bank (C) in good faith, but negligently, honoured cheques apparently drawn by its customer (D), a company, in favour of its creditors (X). In fact the cheques were unauthorised by D as one of the two signatories had not been properly appointed as a director. In the company's action against the bank to recover the money paid, the bank, by its defence, successfully claimed to be subrogated to X's former remedies against D. Although the company's account may have been in credit, Wright J relied on the invalid loan subrogation cases and pointed out that, if the company's account had been overdrawn – so that the money paid was being loaned by the bank to the company – those cases would have been on all fours with the instant case. He said:

> 'I think that the equity I have been referred to ought to be extended even in the case where the cheque which was paid was paid out of the credit balance, and was not paid by way of overdraft, so that the banker will be entitled to the benefit of that payment if he can show that that payment went to discharge a legal liability of the customer. The customer in such a case is really no worse off because the legal liability which has to be discharged is discharged ...'[8]

This decision is readily explicable on restitutionary reasoning. The unjust factor was the mistake of fact of the bank. The enrichment was

6   Goff and Jones, at para 1-090 make the same point.
7   [1928] 1 KB 48. See Ellinger and Lee, 'The "Liggett" Defence: a banker's last resort' [1984] LMCLQ 459. *Liggett* was distinguished (Sir Wilfred Greene dissenting) in *Re Cleadon Trust Ltd* [1939] Ch 286. The majority of the Court of Appeal surely misinterpreted *Liggett* in regarding the one true director who signed as having the authority of the company to discharge its debts. Any distinction between the cases should have turned on whether there was an unjust factor in *Re Cleadon*.
8   Ibid, at p 64.

D's in having its legal liabilities to X discharged. What is more puzzling is why, as proprietary rights were not in issue, it was thought necessary to go beyond a direct restitutionary remedy for money paid to D's use. The answer is presumably that, in accordance with the traditional dogma, it is only where an unrequested payment is made under legal compulsion or necessity that a debt is automatically discharged so as to give the payor an action for money paid to D's use. This dogma underpins the decision on similar facts in *Barclays Bank Ltd v WJ Simms, Son and Cooke (Southern) Ltd*[9] to the effect that the customer's debt to the payee was not discharged. If it is accepted, as is argued in chapter 8, that the dogma is incorrect it becomes plain that the subrogation reasoning in *Liggett* is an unnecessary complication; the bank should have been entitled to set off a direct restitutionary remedy against D for money mistakenly paid to D's use.

Liggett was distinguished by the Court of Appeal in *Crantrave Ltd v Lloyds Bank plc.*[10] A bank (C), following a garnishee order nisi but not absolute, paid £13,497 to two judgment creditors (X) of its customer (D). The bank had then debited the customer's account for that amount. The customer's liquidator successfully sought repayment of that amount. The money had been paid by the bank without the customer's authority. *Liggett* was distinguished because the bank had not established that the payment had discharged the customer's debt to X. In so doing, the Court of Appeal applied the traditional dogma that the unauthorised payment of another's debt does not discharge that debt. May LJ said that it could not be the law that a bank could 'unilaterally choose to pay money to a creditor of the customer and then reduce the credit balance in the customer's account by debiting the amount of the payment'.[11] And in Pill LJ's words, '[A] contrary principle would place the bank in a position to act as debt collector for creditors of the customer ... The bank could decide in what priority the claims of creditors were to be met out of the sums in the account, without the customer having recourse against the bank.'[12] These statements have great force but only where there is no unjust factor in play. But on the facts of the case, there was an unjust factor. Although in contrast to the *Liggett* case, the bank did not mistakenly believe that it had the customer's authority to pay X, it did mistakenly believe – and would not otherwise have paid the money – that it was entitled to pay and debit the customer's account.

A controversial case – in which one would have expected the *Liggett* principle to have been discussed, yet it was not even cited – was *Re*

---

9   [1980] QB 677. Below, chapter 8.
10 [2000] 3 WLR 877. *Re Cleadon Trust Ltd* [1939] Ch 286 was applied: see above, note 7 and below, p 301.
11 Ibid, at 883–884.
12 Ibid, at 883.

Byfield.[13] A bankrupt (D), after notice of her bankruptcy had been gazetted, instructed her bank (C) to transfer £19,500 to her mother's account at another bank. C did so. The mother used £12,356 of the money to pay off some of D's creditors (X). After C had complied with the demand of D's trustee in bankrupcy to be paid the £12,356 (that he could not recover from the mother), C sought to be subrogated to X's rights against D. Goulding J refused this claim primarily on the ground that it would conflict with the scheme of the Bankruptcy (Amendment) Act 1926, s 4, whereby the cut-off point for the protection of those transferring a bankrupt's money was fixed at when the receiving order had been gazetted. He also argued that the case was significantly different from one (like *Liggett*) where the bank itself knowingly paid off the creditors: '... there was no immediate compelling nexus between those payments [by the mother to the creditors] and the bank's acts.'[14]

However, even if the chain of causation was longer than in, for example, *Liggett,* the mother had indisputably used the money from C to pay off D's creditors: that is, the enrichment of D at C's expense could be made out. And as in *Liggett* there was an obvious unjust factor, namely the bank's factual mistake in not realising that its customer was bankrupt. Moreover, it is far from clear that the 1926 Act intended to rule out personal restitutionary claims against the bankrupt. Perhaps, therefore, Goulding J ought not to have stopped his ears 'to the siren song of unjust enrichment'.[15]

(4) Conclusion

Subrogation is a difficult technique to pin down to underlying principle. Our examination has shown that, as first argued by Goff and Jones and clarified subsequently by Charles Mitchell – and as now accepted for non-contractual subrogation by the House of Lords in the *Banque Financière* case – non-contractual subrogation belongs within the law of restitution as being concerned to reverse, or prevent, unjust enrichment. Some central points are as follows:

(i) It is helpful to distinguish between simple subrogation, where a person takes over another's live rights and remedies against a third party; and reviving subrogation, where a person has discharged (or his money has been used to discharge) another's liability to a third party and takes over the third party's former rights and remedies against that other

---

13   [1982] Ch 267.
14   Ibid at p 276.
15   [1982] Ch 267, 276. The decision is also criticised by Goff and Jones at paras 1-090 to 1-091, 5-013. A bank is now protected by ss 284(5) and 307(4) of the Insolvency Act 1986.

party. Subrogation is normally reviving subrogation; but examples of simple subrogation are the subrogation rights of an indemnity insurer and of the creditors of a business carried on by trustees.

(ii) With reviving subrogation, there is an incontrovertible enrichment of D (at C's expense) by the discharge of D's liability to X. With an insurer's subrogation rights, the enrichment is the assured's (X's); and in relation to the subrogation rights of the creditors of a business carried on by trustees the enrichment is D's (the beneficiary's).

(iii) There are several types of unjust factor in play in the subrogation situations; for example, legal compulsion (sureties' subrogation), failure of consideration (some subrogation rights of an insurer, lenders' subrogation, subrogation rights of creditors of a business carried on by trustees), and mistake of fact (some subrogation rights of an insurer, bankers' subrogation rights).

(iv) Occasionally (for example, sureties' and bankers' subrogation rights) personal subrogation is an unnecessary complication and a direct restitutionary remedy should be recognised instead.

(v) In some situations (for example, indemnity insurers' subrogation rights, the subrogation rights of creditors of a business carried on by trustees) subrogation acts as an exception to the normal 'direct providers only' restriction in unjust enrichment by subtraction in that the enriched party (whether X or D) is enriched not directly by C but by another party.

(vi) Sureties, creditors of a business, and lenders have been held entitled to be subrogated to securities. Similarly, an insurer (C) is entitled to an equitable lien (albeit not a constructive trust) to secure restitution of overcompensation recovered by an assured (X) from another party (D). These examples of proprietary restitution are, in general, difficult to justify because the claimant has taken the risk of the defendant's (or X's) insolvency and therefore does not appear to merit priority over unsecured creditors. The major exception is precisely where the claimant has not taken that risk (and applying the *Paul v Speirway* principle is not therefore being given more than it bargained for) as illustrated by the cases on a lender's subrogation rights.

In the first edition of this book, it was suggested that comprehensible consolidation of the law on subrogation was a more appropriate ideal than calls for subrogation to be developed as a general remedy to accomplish the goals of the law of restitution. However, now that the *Banque Financière* case has firmly anchored non-contractual subrogation in the law of restitution, one can indeed look forward to new categories and examples of subrogation being developed to reverse or prevent unjust enrichment.

Chapter 3

Mistake

Helpful categorisation of the law on restitution for benefits conferred under mistake is surprisingly difficult. The approach taken in this chapter is to divide between mistaken payments, benefits in kind rendered by mistake, and rescission of an executed contract entered into by mistake. Cases falling within the third category are excluded from the first two categories.

What makes categorisation difficult here is that, in the sphere of mistake, it is sometimes difficult to draw the line between restitution and contract. A helpful underlying theme is that, where there is a valid contractual obligation to render the benefit, restitution of the benefit would almost always[1] contradict that contractual obligation and is therefore unwarranted. It follows that the rules on restitution for mistake are almost always applicable only where any purported contract (or contract term) requiring the rendering of the benefit is void, or unenforceable, or has been discharged, or is voidable and the claimant has chosen to rescind. As Millett LJ said in *Portman Building Society v Hamlyn Taylor Neck*, 'It is fundamental that, where money is paid under a legally effective transaction, neither misrepresentation nor mistake vitiates consent or gives rise by itself to an obligation to make restitution.'[2] *Kleinwort Benson Ltd v Lincoln City Council*[3] is an example of restitution of money paid by mistake (of law) under a contract that was void (because outside the powers of the local authority); and the leading Australian case of *David Securities Pty Ltd v Commonwealth Bank of Australia*[4] illustrates the restitution of money paid by mistake (of law) under a contractual clause void for illegality.

The claimant's attack on the contract – establishing the invalidity of the contract – can normally be regarded as purely a matter of contract law and does not involve the law of restitution. But the remedy of rescission of a contract makes no clean divide between attacking

---

1 An exception would be where C mistakenly enters into a contract with X whereby he discharges D's debt to X and C seeks restitution from D for that discharge. See *County of Carleton v City of Ottawa* (1965) 52 DLR (2d) 220; below, pp 167–168.
2 [1998] 4 All ER 202, 208.
3 [1999] 2 AC 349.
4 (1992) 175 CLR 353.

the contract (the law of contract) and reversing benefits rendered under it (the law of restitution). It has therefore been considered convenient to treat rescission of an executed contract entered into by mistake separately in the third section of this chapter.

Where a purported contract is void or unenforceable, the claimant seeking restitution will commonly have alternative grounds for restitution, namely mistake and failure of consideration (the latter being concerned with the non-performance of the defendant's promise which was the basis of the claimant's rendering of the benefit to the defendant).[5] Examples of the courts referring to both these grounds for restitution are *Rover International Ltd v Cannon Film Sales Ltd (No 3)*[6] where the contract was void because the claimant company was not incorporated; and *Strickland v Turner*[7] and *Pritchard v Merchant's and Tradesman's Mutual Life-Assurance Society*[8] where, on similar facts involving a common mistaken belief (rendering the contract void) that a person was alive when he was in fact dead, different courts relied on total failure of consideration and mistake (of fact) respectively to ground restitution of money paid.

However, given that the scope of restitution-yielding mistakes has been expanded to include mistakes of law, and that it is still a formal requirement that a failure of consideration be total, it is hard to see when it could ever be advantageous (if both are available on the facts) to base one's restitutionary claim on failure of consideration rather than mistake. In particular, it would seem that there is no objection to a claimant being awarded restitution for mistake even though a claim for failure of consideration would fail (eg, because there has been no such failure or because the failure has been only partial rather than total). Take *Bell v Lever Bros.*[9] The claimant employees had given up their employment rights in return for severance pay: had the contract been held void for common mistake, which it was not, it would seem that the employers could not have recovered their money on the grounds of failure of consideration. The employers had got all they had bargained for. But the employers would have been entitled to restitution, if the contract had been void, on the ground of mistake (subject to a restitutionary counterclaim by the employees).[10] Similarly

5   See below, chapter 10.
6   [1989] 1 WLR 912.
7   (1852) 7 Exch 208.
8   (1858) 3 CBNS 622.
9   [1932] AC 161.
10 Contra is Birks, 'Restitution after Ineffective Contracts: Issues for the 1990's' (1990) JCL 227, 236. He argues that a mistake claim cannot circumvent the insistence that failure of consideration must be total. It is submitted that *National Mutual Life Association of Australia Ltd v Walsh* (1987) 8 NSWLR 585, referred to by Birks, was wrongly decided: the claim for mistake should have been allowed subject to recognising the defendant's entitlement to a restitutionary counterclaim for mistake.

in *Kleinwort Benson Ltd v Lincoln City Council*,[11] where the interest rate swap was a closed one (that is, fully executed), the claimant was held entitled to restitution of the payments it had made under a mistake of law (subject to giving counter-restitution of the payments received). This was so even though the claimant had been paid all that it had bargained for so that there was no failure of consideration.

1. MISTAKEN PAYMENTS

This is generally regarded as the central area in the law of restitution. This is because the issues are clear-cut, mistaken payments are very common, and the case law is voluminous.

Mistaken payments are easy to analyse according to the unjust enrichment principle. The unjust factor is the mistake of the payor; more specifically, the mistake negatives the voluntariness with which the claimant paid the money. The enrichment is the sum of money received, and because it is money and not a benefit in kind, there are no problems over subjective devaluation. And the enrichment is at the claimant's expense in the sense that it is a subtraction from the claimant. In terms of pure principle therefore and, subject to defences, unjust enrichment should dictate that mistaken payments are readily recoverable.

However, English law traditionally took a narrow view of recovery, which restricted the types of mistakes allowing restitution in two main ways. First, payments made under a mistake of fact were recoverable only if the mistake was as to a liability to make the payment: the so-called 'supposed liability' test. And secondly, payments made under a mistake of law, as opposed to fact, were irrecoverable. In exciting recent developments, both these restrictions have been judicially removed and the English law on mistaken payments has thereby been brought into line with the pure principle against unjust enrichment.

(1) Mistakes of fact: demise of the 'supposed liability' test

(a) The traditional 'supposed liability' test

The traditional approach was that money was recoverable in an action for money had and received if the payor paid in the false belief that

---

11 [1999] 2 AC 349. The House of Lords unanimously specifically rejected Birks' argument, in 'No Consideration: Restitution after Void Contracts' (1993) 23 UWALR 195, 230 n 137, that one could not have restitution for mistake of law where the void contract had been fully performed so that there was no failure of consideration. See also Burrows, 'Swaps and the Friction between Common Law and Equity' [1995] RLR 15, 18-19.

the facts were such that he was under a legal liability to the payee to make the payment. The classic authorities for this supposed liability test were *Kelly v Solari*[12] and Bramwell B's judgment in *Aiken v Short*.[13]

In the former, the claimant insurance company paid over money on a life insurance policy, apparently not realising that the policy had lapsed because the deceased had failed to pay a premium. A new trial was ordered to ascertain whether the claimant had indeed made a mistake but, if it had, the money was held to be recoverable. Parke B said, 'I think that where money is paid to another under the influence of a mistake, that is, upon the supposition that a specific fact is true, *which would entitle the other to the money* but which fact is untrue, and the money would not have been paid if it had been known to the payor that the fact was untrue, an action will lie to recover it back, and it is against conscience to retain it.'[14]

In *Aiken v Short*, the claimant bank, believing that it had acquired certain property from X, subject to a charge in favour of the defendant securing a debt owed to her by X, paid off the defendant's charge so as to make the property more saleable. It transpired that the property had been inherited by someone other than X so that the claimant had no valid title to it and the defendant had had no charge over it. The claimant's action to recover the money from the defendant failed. The majority's reasoning was in effect that this was a payment under a valid contract under which the consideration for the claimant's payment was the discharge of X's debt to the defendant.[15] On that reasoning therefore, any restitutionary claim by the claimant lay against X and not against the defendant.[16] But Bramwell B's reasoning was simply that the claimant could not recover because the mistake of fact it had made in paying was not one of supposed liability. He said, 'In order to entitle a person to recover back money paid under a mistake of fact, the mistake must be as to a fact which, if true, would make the person paying liable to pay the money; not where, if true, it would merely make it desirable that he should pay the money.'[17]

Even on this traditional view a payor needed to establish that the mistake (as to liability) caused him to make the payment. *Holt v Markham*[18] provides a good illustration of a claim failing because a supposed liability mistake of fact did not cause the payment. On the

---

12   (1841) 9 M & W 54.
13   (1856) 1 H & N 210.
14   (1841) 9 M & W 54, 58 (author's italics).
15   An alternative explanation now would be that, because of the discharge of X's debt to the defendant, the defendant had the defence of change of position.
16   Below, chapter 8. See also below, p 137.
17   (1856) 1 H & N 210, 215.
18   [1923] 1 KB 504.

demobilisation of the RAF the claimants, in accordance with regulations, paid gratuities to officers. The defendant was paid the full amount even though he was merely an officer on the Emergency List and, according to the regulations, should therefore have been paid a lesser sum. The claimants sought to recover the overpayment but failed. They argued that they had paid the money in the mistaken belief that the defendant was not on the Emergency List and that they were therefore bound to pay it. The Court of Appeal decided, inter alia, that the claimants would still have paid even if they had known that the defendant was on the Emergency List. Applying the 'but for' test, that factual mistake did not cause the payment, which was rather caused by the claimants' supposed liability mistake *of law* in misunderstanding the regulations.

Similarly in *Home and Colonial Insurance Co Ltd v London Guarantee and Accident Co Ltd*[19] a liquidator of an insurance company paid money to the defendant not realising that he was not legally bound to do so because policies had not been issued. Restitution was denied because the liquidator would still have made the payment even if he had known that no policies had been issued: the payment was caused by a mistake of law not fact. In the words of Wright J, '[T]he more important aspect … was the ignorance or mistake as to the law … If he had been told there were no policies he would still have done what he actually did.'[20]

Both these decisions would now be decided differently given that it is no longer good law that a mistake of law cannot ground restitution.[1]

It is important to add that the fact that the payor has been negligent in making the mistake has not been considered a relevant criterion for determining the prima facie right to restitution. In *Kelly v Solari*, for example, the claimant insurance company ought to have known that the policy had lapsed. But as Parke B said, '… [if money] is paid under the impression of the truth of a fact which is untrue, it may, generally speaking, be recovered back, however careless the party paying it may have been, in omitting to use due diligence to enquire into the fact'.[2] Numerous subsequent cases have confirmed this by ignoring the payor's negligence including the landmark decision in *Barclays Bank Ltd v WJ Simms Son and Cooke (Southern) Ltd*[3] in which the claimant bank overlooked a customer's stop instruction in paying out on a cheque.

19 (1928) 32 Ll L Rep 267.
20 Ibid at p 270.
1   *Kleinwort Benson Ltd v Lincoln City Council* [1999] 2 AC 349.
2   (1841) 9 M & W 54, 59.
3   [1980] QB 677. See also, eg, *Anglo-Scottish Beet Sugar Corpn v Spalding UDC* [1937] 2 KB 607; *Saronic Shipping Co v Huron Liberian Co* [1979] 1 Lloyd's Rep 341, 363; affd [1980] 2 Lloyd's Rep 26; *Kleinwort Benson Ltd v Lincoln City Council* [1999] 2 AC 349, 399 (per Lord Hoffmann); *Scottish Equitable plc v Derby* [2001] EWCA Civ 369, [2001] 3 All ER 818.

(b) Exceptions to the traditional test

In the vast majority of the reported cases on mistaken payments – no doubt reflecting the position in everyday life – the mistake in question has been one as to supposed liability. But even before *Barclays Bank Ltd v WJ Simms*, there were a few cases which cannot be explained according to the traditional supposed liability rule. Those exceptional cases fall into two main groups: first, cases which can be justified on an extended meaning of supposed liability; and secondly, cases which cannot be so justified.

The most obvious cases within the former group are those in which the claimant paid the money to the defendant under the mistaken belief that he was bound to do so under a legal liability *to a third party*. In *RE Jones Ltd v Waring and Gillow Ltd*,[4] for example, a rogue had fraudulently induced the claimants to draw up a cheque for £5,000 payable to the defendants. The claimants were able to recover the £5,000 as money had and received by the defendants even though the claimants' mistake was in believing that they were under a legal liability to pay the company that the rogue purported to be representing (the defendants being that company's nominees).

Also within the first group is *Larner v LCC*.[5] The claimants had promised their employees, who joined the services during the war, that they would make up the difference between their service pay and their civil pay. This promise was not legally binding being unsupported by consideration. The claimants overpaid the defendant and it was held that they could recover the overpayment on the ground of mistake even though they had paid under a supposed moral, and not a legal, obligation to the payee.

In contrast, the House of Lords' decision in *Kerrison v Glyn, Mills, Currie & Co*[6] is probably not one that can be justified on any meaning of supposed liability. The claimant had a standing arrangement with a New York bank, whereby the New York bank agreed to honour drafts drawn by the manager of a Mexican mine in return for the claimant reimbursing the bank by putting money into its account at the defendant bank. At a time when, unknown to the claimant, the New York bank had gone bankrupt, the claimant paid £500 into the defendant bank in anticipation of future liabilities to the New York bank. It was held that the claimant could recover the £500, the reasoning being that the claimant had paid the money under a mistake as to the credit-worthiness of the New York bank. Although at first

---

4   [1926] AC 670. See also *Kleinwort Sons & Co v Dunlop Rubber Co* (1907) 97 LT 263.
5   [1949] 2 KB 683.
6   (1911) 81 LJKB 465.

sight it may seem equally plausible to argue that there was a liability mistake, in the sense that the payor made the payment mistakenly believing that he would be liable in the future to the New York bank, Birks is surely correct to argue that one cannot have a mistake as to the future.[7] By definition mistake refers to the present, and in so far as one uses a liability analysis for *Kerrison*, the claimant had mispredicted, not mistaken, his future liability.[8]

In *Morgan v Ashcroft*[9] the claimant bookmaker mistakenly paid the defendant twice on a bet. The Court of Appeal held that he could not recover the overpayment. Much of the reasoning and the decision are firmly in line with the traditional restriction to supposed liability mistakes. There was no legal liability in question here because the betting contract was void under the Gaming Act 1845. However, in important dicta Sir Wilfred Greene MR said, 'If A makes a voluntary payment of money to B under the mistaken belief that he is C, it may well be that A can recover it'.[10] In other words, mistake as to the identity of the recipient of a gratuitous payment was recognised as a possible ground for recovery and clearly this cannot be justified on any extended meaning of supposed liability.

In addition, the rescission of formal gifts[11] on the grounds of mistake has traditionally required merely that the mistake of fact be a serious one and not one of a supposed liability.[12] Indeed, applying the traditional supposed liability rule, gifts made by mistake would never be recoverable. Although rescission is a different remedy from the action for money had and received normally at issue in mistaken payment cases, there seems no reason in principle why the tests for mistake should differ.

A recognition that there have been cases that do not fit the traditional supposed liability rule[13] paves the way for an analysis of the path-breaking decision in *Barclays Bank Ltd v WJ Simms, Son and Cooke (Southern) Ltd.*[14]

7   Birks at p 147.
8   For judicial acceptance that a misprediction, as opposed to a mistake, does not ground restitution, see *Dextra Bank & Trust Co Ltd v Bank of Jamaica* [2002] 1 All ER (Comm) 193, discussed below, p 519.
9   [1938] 1 KB 49.
10   Ibid at p 66.
11   The gift has usually been of money but this paragraph applies equally to gifts of other property (which fall within the second of the major categories in this chapter).
12   Eg *Ogilvie v Littleboy* (1897) 13 TLR 399, CA; affd (1899) 15 TLR 294; *Lady Hood of Avalon v Mackinnon* [1909] 1 Ch 476.
13   An analogy can also be drawn with *Greenwood v Bennett* [1973] QB 195, discussed in the second main section of this chapter. One would expect a further exception to be where a non-liability mistake is induced by a misrepresentation: see Birks at p 168. But as regards a non-contractual payment there appears to be no example of this.
14   [1980] QB 677.

(c) Acceptance of a prima facie causation test

Through a scholarly and comprehensive review of the authorities Robert Goff J took the opportunity in this case to launch a full-scale attack on the traditional supposed liability rule and attempted to move the law to a new prima facie causation test for mistakes of fact. His approach has since been authoritatively approved by the Court of Appeal in *Lloyds Bank plc v Independent Insurance Co Ltd*,[15] a mistake of fact case. A but for causation test for mistaken payments (whether of fact or law) was also approved in the reasoning of the majority of the House of Lords (albeit not directly mentioning the *Simms* case) in *Kleinwort Benson Ltd v Lincoln City Council*;[16] and in *Nurdin & Peacock plc v DB Ramsden & Co Ltd*[17] Neuberger J applied *Barclays Bank v WJ Simms* in explicitly rejecting a supposed liability test for restitution of payments made by mistake of law and favouring a prima facie but for causation test for all mistakes, whether of fact or law. It is therefore now clear that Robert Goff J's approach constitutes good law.

In *Barclays Bank Ltd v WJ Simms Ltd*, the claimant bank had overlooked a stop instruction on a cheque for £24,000 drawn by its customer, X, in favour of the defendant company for building work done. The claimant sought to recover the £24,000 from the defendant as money paid under a mistake of fact. On the traditional supposed liability rule the claim would have failed. The claimant's supposed legal obligation was owed to X, its customer, and not to the defendant. But Robert Goff J, relying on the exceptional cases considered above, and arguing that Parke B's words in *Kelly v Solari* had to be read in the context of supposed liability being present on the facts, and dismissing Bramwell B's judgment in *Aiken v Short* as obiter dicta, held that the money was recoverable because it was caused by the claimant's mistake of fact. He set out the central principles as follows:

'1. If a person pays money to another under a mistake of fact which causes him to make the payment, he is prima facie entitled to recover it as money paid under a mistake of fact. 2. His claim may however fail if: (a) the payor intends that the payee shall have the money at all events whether the fact be true or false, or is

---

15 [1999] 2 WLR 986. At p 1002, Peter Gibson LJ referred to the approach in *Barclays Bank v Simms* as 'Robert Goff J's celebrated formulation'. See also Dillon LJ's dicta in *Rover International Ltd v Cannon Film Sales Ltd (No 3)* [1989] 1 WLR 912, 933 that he found Robert Goff J's judgment a 'very valuable explanation of the cases'.
16 [1999] 2 AC 349. See at p 372 (per Lord Goff), at p 399 (per Lord Hoffmann), at pp 407–408 (per Lord Hope).
17 [1999] 1 All ER 941. Without enthusiasm Neuberger J thought it possible that the but for test would need to be 'coupled with a requirement for a close and direct connection between the mistake and the payment and/or a requirement that the mistake impinges on the relationship between the payer and payee': see at pp 963–964.

deemed in law so to intend; or (b) the payment is made for good consideration, in particular if the money is paid to discharge, and does discharge, a debt owed to the payee (or a principal on whose behalf he is authorised to receive the payment) by the payor or by a third party by whom he is authorised to discharge the debt; or (c) the payee has changed his position in good faith, or is deemed to have done so.'[18]

On Robert Goff J's approach, therefore, the type of factual mistake does not matter. It is purely its effect on the payor that counts.

There are seven additional points on Robert Goff J's judgment that are worth emphasising.

(i) As with the first group of exceptional cases considered above, *Barclays Bank Ltd v WJ Simms, Son and Cooke (Southern) Ltd* could have been decided by simply extending the meaning of supposed liability. That is, the claimant bank paid the money to the defendant under the mistaken belief that it was bound to do so under a legal liability to its customer. This 'formalistic' explanation was not adopted by Robert Goff J and it is easy to understand why. Not only would it fail to explain all the important cases (for example, *Kerrison v Glyn, Mills, Currie & Co*) but it would not be as true to the underlying principle of unjust enrichment.

(ii) Robert Goff J gave several helpful examples illustrating how unacceptable the non-recovery dictated by the supposed liability test would be. To take just one, 'A man, forgetting that he has already paid his subscription to the National Trust, pays it a second time.'[19]

(iii) Robert Goff J did not attempt to articulate any test for causation. However, as with the cases supporting the supposed liability approach, the decision is clearly explicable on the 'but for' test which, as has been argued in chapter 1, should be the primary basis for adjudging causation throughout the law of restitution. Moreover, the reasoning of the majority of the House of Lords in *Kleinwort Benson Ltd v Lincoln City Council*[20] and Neuberger J's judgment in *Nurdin & Peacock plc v DB Ramsden & Co Ltd*[21] expressly support a 'but for' test for causation in mistaken payment cases.[1]

(iv) As with supposed liability, the negligence of the payor is irrelevant to prima facie responsibility under Robert Goff J's approach, although it may have relevance under an estoppel or change of position defence.

(v) Robert Goff J's second qualification 2(b) was applied in *Lloyds Bank plc v Independent Insurance Co Ltd*.[2] W Ltd owed the defendant

---

18   [1980] QB 677, 695.
19   [1980] QB 677, 697.
20   [1999] 2 AC 349.
21   [1999] 1 All ER 941.
1   See above, p 135.
2   [1999] 2 WLR 986.

insurance company £162,388 (comprising premiums it had collected for the defendant). W Ltd requested its bank, the claimant, to pay that sum to the defendant's account. In the mistaken belief that three cheques for £172,132 in total payable to W Ltd had been cleared, the claimant bank made a credit transfer of £162,388 to the defendant's account. In fact one of the three cheques which was for £168,000 had not been cleared so that W Ltd's account was substantially overdrawn. The claimant bank sought restitution from the defendant of £107,388 (which was the £162,388 paid minus £55,000 which was subsequently paid into W Ltd's account). The Court of Appeal refused restitution on the ground that the claimant bank's payment to the defendant, albeit made by a mistake of fact, had discharged a debt owed by W Ltd to the defendant. It was therefore paid for good consideration and Robert Goff J's qualification 2(b) applied (as did *Aiken v Short*)[3] to rule out restitution. In contrast to the facts of *Barclays Bank v WJ Simms*, the payment by the claimant's bank was authorised by W Ltd and did operate to discharge W Ltd's debt to the defendant.

What is the basis of this second qualification and hence of the decision in the *Lloyds Bank* case? One possibility, referred to by Peter Gibson LJ,[4] is that one is here concerned with Lord Hope's proposition, put forward in obiter dicta in *Kleinwort Benson Ltd v Lincoln City Council*,[5] that a mistaken payor cannot have restitution – because there is no unjust enrichment – where the payee was entitled to receive the sum paid to him. But it is far from clear that Lord Hope's novel proposition is correct in so far as it goes beyond being an application of the 'but for' causation test. In particular, it does not appear to provide a sound justification where, as on the facts of *Lloyds Bank*, the payee has no legal entitlement *against the payor* to be paid.

A second possibility is that one is here concerned with an aspect of the bona fide purchase defence.[6] However, that defence normally applies where the defendant is an indirect recipient who receives the enrichment from a third party; and in *Lloyds Bank* the claimant bank paid the money direct to the defendant who was therefore a direct, and not an indirect, recipient.

A third possibility is that qualification 2(b) illustrates that there can be no restitution where this would be inconsistent with the terms of a valid contract. The contract in mind is one between the payor (C) and the creditor/payee (D) whereby, in return for the payment from C, D promises to discharge the debt owed to it by X. D thereby provides

---

3   (1856) 25 LJ Ex 321. See above, p 131.
4   [1999] 2 WLR 986, 1005.
5   [1999] 2 AC 349, 407–408.
6   See below, chapter 15.

good consideration for C's payment; and in accordance with normal principle it would be insufficient to render that contract void or voidable that the payor made a unilateral mistake not shared or known about or induced by the payee. This explanation is in line with Robert Goff J's words to the effect that the payment must discharge the debt and must be paid *to discharge* the debt. Applying this explanation to the facts of *Simms,* one can argue (although Robert Goff J himself decided that there was no discharge of a debt) that the bank made the payment to D to discharge the debt owed by X to D *on the cheque.* But there is greater difficulty where, as in the *Lloyds Bank* case, the only conceivable debt in question is that on the underlying contract between X and D. It is hard to see that the claimant bank (C) made the credit transfer in favour of D in order to discharge X's debt to D. The bank may have known nothing of X's debt to D. In these circumstances, it is hard to see that there was a valid contract between C and D.

A final possibility[7] is that qualification 2(b) should now be regarded as an example of the change of position defence.[8] This would appear to have been the preferred explanation of Waller LJ, giving the leading judgment, in the *Lloyds Bank* case. The discharge of a debt means that the defendant creditor would be worse off if the payment now had to be repaid. This would only not be so if the debt could be revived by repayment of the mistaken payment. However, revival of a debt is a controversial idea and, even if ever possible, it might not be allowed where the debtor has adopted the discharge.[9] But while change of position may be the best explanation of the *Lloyds Bank* case, it would appear, as Peter Gibson LJ pointed out, that this is not what Robert Goff J had in mind by his qualification 2(b). This is not only because, as we have just seen, he required an intention to discharge the debt rather than just its discharge but also because change of position was his separate qualification (2)(c).

(vi) It is not entirely clear what Robert Goff J meant by his first qualification 2(a), which he based on a dictum of Parke B in *Kelly v Solari,*[10] to the effect that a claim may fail if 'the payor intends that the payee shall have the money at all events whether the fact be true or false ...'. What appears to be in mind is what Goff and Jones call 'a submission to an honest claim'.[11] They treat this as *analogous* to a

---

7   A further possible explanation of the decision in the *Lloyds Bank* case – but not one that ties in with qualification 2(b) or the Court of Appeal's reasoning – is that to allow restitution from the payee would undermine the valid contract between the bank and its customer. See analogously below, pp 347–350.

8   This appears to be the explanation favoured by Goff and Jones, para 4-043.

9   See below, p 296.

10   (1841) 9 M & W 54, 59.

11   Goff and Jones at paras 1-070 to 1-071, 4-030 to 4-032.

compromise (or settlement) which is a binding contract whereby the payor pays part or all of a sum claimed by the payee in return for the payee's promise not to bring or continue a legal action in relation to the claim. A compromise falls within Robert Goff J's second qualification – 'the payment is made for good consideration' – so that recovery is ruled out unless the more stringent contractual rules invalidating a contract are satisfied. The difficulty is that the concept of a *non-contractual* submission to an honest claim raises more problems than it solves.[12] For example, should the central case of *Kelly v Solari* be regarded as involving a submission to an honest claim and, if not, why not? Does the concept require that an express threat of legal action has been made by the payee and, if so, why should this be necessary? And why should one want to differentiate the payor who pays without any demand for payment (believing that it is bound to pay and that a claim will, or may, ultimately be made) from the payor who is responding to a demand? Without a contractual settlement the payor is not receiving anything for its payment (that is, there is no promise not to sue) and prima facie it should be sufficient to unwind the payment for the payor to establish a causal mistake.

However, Goff and Jones' discussion of a submission to an honest claim also refers to the payor having 'assumed the risk of his mistake'.[13] This seems a more fruitful line of enquiry than looking for a non-contractual submission to an honest claim. Indeed it can be regarded as raising the important question of whether the payor's realisation when paying that it may be mistaken bars recovery. Peculiarly, there has been little discussion by English judges as to the effect of doubt and suspicion on recovery for mistake. But in *Maskell v Horner*[14] it was held, inter alia, that the claimant who paid market tolls 'in doubt as to his liability to pay'[15] but wishing to avoid litigation was not making a

---

12 See generally Andrews, 'Mistaken Settlements of Disputable Claims' [1989] LMCLQ 431; Arrowsmith, 'Mistake and the Role of "Submission to an Honest Claim"' in *Essays on the Law of Restitution* (ed Burrows, 1991) pp 17–38; Law Commission Report No 227, *Restitution: Mistakes of Law and Ultra Vires Public Authority Receipts and Payments* (1994), paras 2.25–2.38. This is not to deny that the policy of finality in litigation (embodied in, for example, the defence of 'dispute resolved', see below, pp 556–559) means that money mistakenly paid under court judgments or even following the issue of proceedings is generally irrecoverable: *Hamlet v Richardson* (1833) 9 Bing 644; *Moore v Vestry of Fulham* [1895] 1 QB 399. As with a compromise it seems that *the payee* is also here prevented from reopening the claim (eg, he cannot sue for more money on the same cause of action).

13 Goff and Jones at paras 1-070 to 1-071, 4-030 to 4-032.

14 [1915] 3 KB 106.

15 Ibid at p 117 (per Lord Reading CJ). See also at p 123 (per Buckley LJ) and at p 126 (per Pickford LJ). Cf *Woolwich Building Society v IRC (No 2)* [1991] 4 All ER 577, 626 (per Ralph Gibson LJ); Goff and Jones, para 4-030 note 56. In the *Woolwich* litigation, which went to the Lords [1993] AC 70, none of the nine judges involved thought that the claimant was mistaken as to the law: its actions in challenging the ultra vires demand showed that it had no (serious) doubt as to the correct law.

mistake, let alone a mistake of fact as opposed to law. And in *Kleinwort Benson Ltd v Lincoln City Council,* in which the mistake of law bar was removed, Lord Hope said, 'Cases where the payer was aware that there was an issue of law which was relevant but, being in doubt as to what the law was, paid without waiting to resolve that doubt may be left on one side. A state of doubt is different from that of mistake. A person who pays when in doubt takes the risk that he may be wrong – and that is so whether the issue is one of fact or one of law.'[16]

It is submitted that the fact that the payor had some doubt as to the facts (or law) is not necessarily incompatible with a mistake claim. Hence the United States Restatement of Restitution, s 10(1) reads, 'A transferor is not precluded from restitution for mistake because, at the time of the transfer, he had some doubt as to the facts.' The difficult question is what degree of doubt is compatible with a mistake claim. Clearly at one extreme if the payor knows the true facts he is not mistaken at all and cannot recover. At the other extreme is the payor who has no suspicion that the facts may be other than he believes them to be: he should be able to recover. In between are payors with varying degrees of suspicion and doubt. It would be unduly restrictive if Robert Goff J's first qualification were to be interpreted as ruling out restitution for all such in-between payors on the ground that they were not mistaken or had taken the risk of being mistaken. McKendrick suggests that this can simply be resolved by causation.[17] But if one allows restitution whenever the claimant (who had doubts as to the facts) would not have paid had it known the truth, this would allow restitution despite a very high degree of doubt by the payor. Virgo goes to the opposite extreme and would rule out restitution whenever the payor was aware that there was a possibility that he or she was mistaken.[18] It is submitted that the best approach, in principle and policy, is to take a mid-position by applying a balance of probabilities test. If the payor pays believing that the facts are *probably* what they in truth are he cannot recover for mistake: his belief precludes restitution for mistake either on the grounds that he was not mistaken or that he took the risk of his mistake.

There may also be extreme cases where the claimant, while mistaken, so recklessly chooses not to investigate the true facts that he should be regarded as taking the risk of his mistake.

(vii) Although not affecting his formidable assessment of the principles governing restitution for mistakes of fact, in applying those principles

---

16   [1999] 2 AC 349, 410.

17   'Mistake of Law – Time for a Change?' in *The Limits of Restitutionary Claims : A Comparative Analysis* (ed Swadling, 1997), pp 212, 232–233.

18   *The Principles of the Law of Restitution* (1999), p 161.

to the facts, Robert Goff J controversially took the view that the bank's payment on the countermanded cheque did not discharge the customer's liability to the defendant building company. There was therefore no consideration for the bank's payment (nor change of position by the payee) and hence qualification 2(b) (and 2(c)) did not operate to disallow restitution. With respect, this aspect of the decision can be criticised. A payment made to discharge another's debt and accepted as so doing by the payee creditor should be regarded as discharging the debt irrespective of the consent of the debtor. The bank's restitutionary claim should therefore have been against its customer. This is explained in detail in chapter 8.[19]

(d) Why is the causation test better than the supposed liability test?

In terms of the pure unjust enrichment principle, any type of mistake causing the payment should trigger restitution (subject to defences), the injustice being that, as he was mistaken, the payor did not mean the payee to have the money. Any restriction on that principle can only be justified on policy grounds. Two major policy justifications, both aspects of the 'too much restitution' argument, can be offered in support of the supposed liability test.

The first is that the causation approach will lead to too much restitution in the 'floodgates' sense of clogging the courts with restitutionary claims. But supposed liability already covers the commonest cases of factually mistaken payments and it is difficult to believe that the move to causation will produce a significant, let alone overwhelming, increase in claims. In any event, the House of Lords in *Lipkin Gorman v Karpnale Ltd*[20] has accepted a change of position defence to restitutionary claims. The consequence will be that some claims will fail that on the previous law would have succeeded. One can also add that the floodgates argument, while heavily influential throughout the common law, is an easy objection put to many reforms and yet its own apparent rationale, limiting justice for the sake of cost, is highly controversial.

A second policy justification is that supposed liability prevents too much restitution in the sense of the undermining of the security of payments. That is, the more limited the scope for recovery, the more the payee can count on the money being his. However, bearing in mind that we are not here considering the scope of the rules allowing

19 Goode, 'The Bank's Right to Recover Money Paid on a Stopped Cheque' (1981) LQR 254 argues that, applying normal agency principles, the debt should have been regarded as discharged because the bank had the customer's apparent authority to pay. This is strongly refuted by Goff and Jones, paras 4-037 to 4-038.

20 [1991] 2 AC 548.

escape from a contract for mistake, the supposed liability test already widely infringes the security of receipts and it is to be doubted whether the move to causation will make much difference. In any event, the payee who in good faith detrimentally relied on the money being his has a change of position defence. If the payee has not changed his position, it is difficult to see the force of the security argument.

The conclusion is that neither of these possible arguments is strong enough to justify retaining a supposed liability test in preference to the pure unjust enrichment approach of causation. The recent authoritative acceptance of causation as the prima facie test for the restitution of payments made by mistake of fact (or law) is therefore to be warmly welcomed.

(e) Alternative approaches

The discussion so far has centred on whether the new causation approach is preferable to the traditional supposed liability test. For the purposes of completeness we must finally consider, albeit to reject, three alternative approaches that have been advocated in this area: (i) fundamental mistake; (ii) failure of consideration; and (iii) no legal ground.

(i) Fundamental mistake

The English courts have occasionally insisted that the mistake must be fundamental in order to allow recovery of money paid. The classic example is *Norwich Union Fire Insurance Society Ltd v WH Price Ltd.*[1] The claimant insurance company paid up on a policy insuring lemons in the mistaken belief that the lemons had been damaged by an insured event, whereas in fact the lemons had started to ripen because of a delay in transit which was not covered by the policy. This was a clear example of a supposed liability mistake but, in allowing restitution, Lord Wright, giving the judgment of the Privy Council, thought that what was important was that the mistake was fundamental. In a judgment which runs together the approach to mistake for contracts, passing of title in property, and restitution of money, Lord Wright said:

> 'The mistake being of the character that it was, prevented there being that intention which the common law regards as essential to the making of an agreement or the transfer of money or property ... [Proof] of mistake affirmatively excludes intention. It is, however, essential that the mistake relied on should be of such a nature that it

---

1   [1934] AC 455. See also *Morgan v Ashcroft* [1938] 1 KB 49. For the rejection of this approach in Australia see *David Securities Pty Ltd v Commonwealth Bank of Australia* (1992) 109 ALR 57. Cf the earlier cases of *Porter v Latec Finance (Queensland) Pty Ltd* (1964) 111 CLR 177; *Australia and New Zealand Banking Group Ltd v Westpac Banking Corpn* (1988) 78 ALR 157, 160–161.

can be properly described as a mistake in respect of the underlying assumption of the contract or transaction or as being fundamental or basic.'[2]

Two main criticisms can be made of this approach. First, it provides in itself a vague and uncertain test. It could mean the same as supposed liability or, at the other extreme, the same as causation. Or it could cover in-between types of mistakes, such as mistakes as to identity. In short, without further clarification as to what the courts regard as fundamental, this test tells one nothing. Moreover, it is ambiguous as to whether it is focusing on the type of mistake in question or on the effect of a mistake on the payor's mind: for example, one could be referring to a strict causation test, stricter than the usual but for test, by which the mistake, of whatever type, would have to be *the* predominant reason for making the payment. The same criticism of vagueness can be levelled at the use of the fundamental test for mistakes in contract and in relation to title in property.

Secondly, although not a direct criticism of the test itself, Lord Wright's vision in *Norwich Union* (which may well be shared by other judges applying the fundamental test) of there being the same approach to mistake in contract, restitution and in relation to the passing of title in property seems misconceived.

A contract generally constitutes a bargain between at least two parties; and one of the purposes of contract law is to allow the binding allocation of risks. It follows that the courts should not be as willing to allow an escape from a contract, thereby disappointing bargained-for expectations, as they are to allow the restitution of money paid. That is borne out by the present law on mistake in contract. Although that area of the law is not straightforward, it is clear that it bears no obvious relation to either a supposed liability or a causation test. It is hard to believe that the courts would move to a position whereby a party could escape from a contract, in the sense of a legally binding bargain, simply by establishing that it had made a mistake but for which it would not have entered the contract. As Waller J said in dicta in *Midland Bank plc v Brown Shipley & Co Ltd*:[3]

'The type of mistake necessary to give rise to a right to recover under the restitutionary remedy of money paid under a mistake of fact need not necessarily be of the same fundamental character that makes a contract totally void. Thus to point to a case where the plaintiff has succeeded on a restitutionary remedy would not establish that the plaintiff would also have established a mistake fundamental enough to avoid any contract altogether.'

2   Ibid at pp 462–463.
3   [1991] 2 All ER 690, 700–701. See also *Portman Building Society v Hamlyn Taylor Neck* [1998] 4 All ER 202: above, p 128.

The relationship between mistake in restitution and mistake in relation to the passing of title in property is problematic. Certainly there is no obvious way of reconciling the law, on whether mistake does or does not prevent title passing,[4] with either a supposed liability or a causation test. In terms of theory, the potentially detrimental effect on transferees of the claimant retaining title in particular property suggests that mistake ought to have a narrower scope in relation to whether title passes than in restitution. This is supported by dicta of Robert Goff J in *Barclays Bank Ltd v Simms*: 'The kind of mistake that will ground recovery [in restitution] is far wider than the kind of mistake which would vitiate intention to transfer property.'[5]

Similar to one interpretation of what is meant by fundamental mistake is Andrew Tettenborn's suggestion that, even in the law of restitution, one needs a more serious mistake than merely a but for causative mistake. He writes, 'Assume I give £1,000 to my niece as a birthday present, not realising that she has just married a man I privately detest. It seems instinctively odd that a footling or idiosyncratic error like that should entitle me to repent of my generosity and recover my money, even if I can prove by impeccable evidence that had I known the relevant facts, I would not have made the gift in the first place.'[6] He then advocates a test of whether a reasonable person would have regarded the mistake as immaterial or not. 'If such a person, knowing the facts behind the rendering of the benefit, but not the individual characteristics of the parties, would have regarded the mistake as immaterial, then restitution is not available: otherwise, prima facie, it ought to be.'[7] But, with respect, the supposed distinction between facts behind the rendering of the benefit and the individual characteristics of the parties is unworkable and unprincipled. If a person, who loves dogs and hates cats, pays £1,000 to a charity for the care of cats mistakenly believing that it is a charity for the care of dogs, that is surely a serious mistake that should ground restitution. Yet applying Tettenborn's test, the reasonable person will not be told that the payor loves dogs but hates cats and will therefore be unable to appreciate the seriousness of the mistake. In any event, Tettenborn's general concerns seem unfounded. If in his example of the gift to

4   See, eg, several theft cases such as *R v Gilks* [1972] 1 WLR 1341; *A-G's Reference (No 1 of 1983)* [1985] QB 182; *Ilich v R* (1987) 162 CLR 110; *R v Shadrokh-Cigari* [1988] Crim LR 465; *R v Davis* [1988] Crim LR 762; *R v Hinks* [2000] 4 All ER 833. For an excellent discussion see Virgo, *The Principles of the Law of Restitution* (1999), pp 607–610. See generally Smith, *The Law of Theft* (8th edn, 1997), paras 2-81 to 3-86.
5   [1980] QB 677, 689.
6   Tettenborn, *The Law of Restitution in England and Ireland* (3rd edn, 2002), p 76.
7   Ibid at p 77.

the niece, the payor can establish that, had he known that the niece had married X, he would not have made the payment, there seems no good reason to deny restitution of the £1,000. In practice, of course, the payor would have a difficult burden in proving 'but for' causation on such facts.

(ii) Failure of consideration

A few commentators have suggested that there is no need to have recourse to a doctrine of mistake of fact and that the cases from *Kelly v Solari* to *Barclays Bank v Simms* are preferably explained on the standard restitutionary ground of failure of consideration.[8] For example, Butler writes, 'The basal principle which founds recovery for payments mistakenly made is not mistake but a failure of consideration.'[9] However, it is difficult to see the alleged substantive importance of opting for a failure of consideration approach and the debate appears to boil down to a matter of semantics: to the question of what is precisely meant by failure of consideration.

In this book failure of consideration is *primarily* taken to correlate to the meaning of consideration used in relation to the formation of a contract: that is, it basically means that the defendant has failed, partially or totally, to perform his promise to the claimant where that performance was the basis for the claimant rendering a benefit to the defendant.[10]

Nevertheless the term can be, and has been, used in a wider sense as meaning the failure of a condition as to the future which was the basis for the claimant rendering a benefit to the defendant: and that condition need not be a promised performance by the defendant so that failure of consideration can operate outside the contractual (or promissory) sphere. Birks, for example, writes, 'Failure of consideration ... means that the state of affairs contemplated as the basis or reason for the payment has failed to materialise or, if it did exist, has failed to sustain itself.'[11]

It may not seem a long step from Birks' definition to the anti-mistake view that whenever a claimant mistakenly renders a benefit to a defendant there has been a failure of the consideration which was the claimant's basis for rendering the benefit. The main difference

---

8   Eg, Matthews, 'Money Paid under Mistake of Fact' (1980) NLJ 587; 'Stopped Cheques and Restitution' [1982] JBL 281; Butler, 'Mistaken Payments, Change of Position and Restitution' in *Essays on Restitution* (ed Finn, 1990), pp 87–137.
9   Ibid at p 123.
10 See below, chapter 10.
11 Birks at p 223. Cf Birks and Mitchell, 'Unjust Enrichment' in *English Private Law* (ed Birks, 2000), paras 15.95–15.100, 15.103.

is that the condition referred to is a condition relating to an existing state of affairs rather than a condition relating to a future state of affairs.

It is submitted therefore that, as a matter of terminology, one *could* indeed use the language of failure of consideration in a wide sense to incorporate mistake. But the law treats differently and, as a matter of policy, arguably should treat differently, the situation where it is a mistaken view of an existing state of affairs rather than the defendant's promised performance or a future event that forms the basis for the claimant's rendering of the benefit. For example, there is no requirement in the mistake cases directly correlating to the traditional insistence that the failure of consideration be total. And given that such a distinction has to be made, even if merely for the purposes of exposition, it seems most helpful to adopt the different, and arguably more natural, labels to describe the two different situations. It should also be emphasised that the anti-mistake school are fighting against the language used by the courts themselves. This argument mirrors the more famous, long-standing, and analogously semantic, debate as to whether a *contractual* doctrine of mistake is a myth.[12]

(iii) No legal ground

Meier and Zimmermann have argued that the unacceptable width of the causative mistake approach shows the merits of the civilian 'no legal ground' approach to restitution.[13] An important feature of their preferred approach is that while 'supposed liability' mistakes would ground restitution (because the legal ground which was the basis for the payment did not exist), a mistake in making a gift would generally not trigger restitution (unless, according to the law on gifts, the gift is invalid). They give two examples. First, a charterer, to maintain the goodwill of the shipowner where the currency of payment has depreciated, increases his monthly hire payments. He then finds out that the shipowner is an enemy of a close relative of his. He would not have paid had he known this. Secondly, a Lloyd's syndicate makes payments to another syndicate, which is in financial difficulties, in order to maintain the reputation of Lloyd's. The

---

12   See, eg, Slade, 'The Myth of Mistake in the English Law of Contract' (1954) 70 LQR 385.

13   'Judicial Development of the Law, Error Iuris, and the Law of Unjustified Enrichment – A View from Germany' (1999) 115 LQR 556. See also Meier, 'Unjust Factors and Legal Grounds' in *Unjustified Enrichment: Key Issues in Comparative Perspective* (eds Johnston and Zimmermann, 2002), pp 37–75. Krebs, *Restitution at the Crossroads* (2001), pp 77–81 points out that, in work published only in German, Meier has focused on two additional examples: a man makes a donation to the Red Cross in the mistaken belief that the mayor and vicar have made donations too; a man gives money to Friends of the Earth, not knowing that they are opposed to an additional runway at Heathrow, which he supports.

syndicate then finds out that it has overestimated its own financial position. It would not have paid had it known the truth. In these examples, Meier and Zimmermann suggest that, despite satisfying the 'but for' causation test, it would not be reasonable to grant restitution. Rather restitution should only be granted if the law would invalidate the gift for the mistake and, in their view, a mere causative mistake would not do this under German law and should not do so under English law.

Similarly, in a section of his book that rejects restitution of mistaken gifts, Hedley writes, 'It is ... hard to accept that the law as proposed in *Barclays Bank Ltd v WJ Simms and Cooke (Southern) Ltd* is reasonable, at least without the introduction of defences going far beyond those currently envisaged ... A straightforward "bright line" rule, based on the externals of the transaction rather than on anyone's mental state, seems to fit the bill. And so the rule that payers can recover only if they did not get what they paid for has much to commend it.'[14]

These criticisms are puzzling. As with Tettenborn's gift example considered above,[15] it is hard to see why it is thought unreasonable for there to be restitution in the examples given by Meier and Zimmermann. The claimant in each example did not mean the defendant to have the money in the sense that, had the claimant known the truth, the payment would not have been made. And the change of position defence will ensure that the defendant will be no worse off than if he or she had not received the payment. Moreover, their approach merely shifts to the so-called law on gifts the need to answer the question, to which the causation test provides a straightforward answer, of when it is that gifts are invalidated for mistake.[16]

(2) Mistakes of law

(a) The old law barring restitution

The old general rule of English law, taken to be laid down in *Bilbie v Lumley*,[17] and applied many times since,[18] is that payments made under

---

14 *A Critical Introduction to Restitution* (2001), pp 106–107.
15 Above, p 144.
16 For a robust defence, from a comparative perspective, of the English 'causation' test against such criticisms, see Krebs, *Restitution at the Crossroads* (2001), pp 77–81.
17 (1802) 2 East 469.
18 Eg *Brisbane v Dacres* (1813) 5 Taunt 143; *Rogers v Ingham* (1876) 3 Ch D 351; *Henderson v Folkestone Waterworks Co* (1885) 1 TLR 329; *William Whiteley v R* (1909) 101 LT 741; *Re Hatch* [1919] 1 Ch 351; *Holt v Markham* [1923] 1 KB 504; *National Pari-Mutuel Association Ltd v R* (1930) 47 TLR 110; *Sawyer and Vincent v Window Brace Ltd* [1943] 1 KB 32; *Avon County Council v Howlett* [1983] 1 WLR 605.

a mistake of law, as opposed to fact, are not recoverable. In that case, the claimant underwriter had paid £100 under an insurance policy not realising that he was not liable to pay because of a non-disclosure of a material fact (the time of sailing of a particular ship) by the assured. It was held that the claimant had paid under a mistake of law and that such a mistake did not ground recovery.[19] In Lord Ellenborough's words, 'Every man must be taken to be cognisant of the law; otherwise there is no saying to what extent the excuse of ignorance might not be carried.'[20]

However, the general rule was subject to a number of exceptions.[1] So, for example, mistakes of law did ground restitution where payments were made to,[2] or by,[3] an officer of the court; or where money was overpaid by fiduciaries to their beneficiaries;[4] or where rescission of a deed of gift was in issue;[5] or where the payor was *non in pari delicto* with the payee.[6] Furthermore, in several cases,[7] the courts treated what was more obviously a mistake of law as a mistake of fact thereby circumventing the bar on recovery.

This state of the law, and in particular the general rule barring restitution for mistakes of law, was heavily criticised by numerous commentators.[8] McCamus went so far as to say that, 'It would be difficult to identify another private law doctrine which has been so universally condemned or another reform which enjoys such widespread support.'[9]

---

19 Presumably the claimant could not rescind the contract for non-disclosure of a material fact because he had affirmed the contract by paying knowing of all the facts.

20 (1802) 2 East 469, 472.

1   For details, see the 1st edition of this book, pp 111–116.

2   *Re Condon, ex p James* (1874) 9 Ch App 609; *Re Carnac, ex p Simmonds* (1885) 16 QBD 308; *Re Byfield* [1982] Ch 267.

3   *Re Birkbeck Permanent Benefit Building Society* [1915] 1 Ch 91.

4   *Dibbs v Goren* (1849) 11 Beav 483; *Re Musgrave* [1916] 2 Ch 417. The exception was limited to allowing fiduciaries to set-off sums overpaid from future sums payable to the overpaid beneficiary.

5   *Gibbon v Mitchell* [1990] 1 WLR 1304.

6   *Kiriri Cotton Co Ltd v Dewani* [1960] AC 192. See also *Hughes v Liverpool Victoria Legal Friendly Society* [1916] 2 KB 482; *Eadie v Township of Brantford* (1967) 63 DLR (2d) 561; *Shelley v Paddock* [1980] QB 348.

7   *Cooper v Phibbs* (1867) LR 2 HL 149; *Solle v Butcher* [1950] 1 KB 671; *George (Porky) Jacobs Enterprises Ltd v City of Regina* (1964) 44 DLR (2d) 179. Note also that traditionally a mistake of foreign law has been artificially treated as a mistake of fact: *Lazard Bros & Co v Midland Bank Ltd* [1933] AC 289.

8   Eg, the first edition of this book, pp 116–118; Goff and Jones (5th edn, 1998), ch 5; Maddaugh and McCamus, *The Law of Restitution* (1st edn, 1990), ch 11; Needham, 'Mistaken Payments: A New Look at an Old Theme' (1978) 12 UBCLR 159; Knutson, 'Mistake of Law Payments in Canada: A Mistaken Principle?' (1979) 10 Man LJ 23. For criticism of the rule in the United States see Palmer, *The Law of Restitution* (1978) vol III, pp 336–357.

9   'Restitutionary Recovery of Moneys Paid to a Public Authority under a Mistake of Law: *Ignorantia Iuris* in the Supreme Court of Canada' (1983) 17 UBCLR 233, 236.

The mistake of law rule was removed by legislation in New Zealand in 1958,[10] and judicially abrogated in Canada in 1989,[11] in Australia in 1992,[12] in South Africa in 1992,[13] and in Scotland in 1995.[14] Its statutory reform in England was recommended by the Law Commission in 1994.[15]

So the scene was set for the decision of the House of Lords removing the mistake of law rule in *Kleinwort Benson Ltd v Lincoln City Council.*[16]

(b) Removal of the mistake of law bar

In *Kleinwort Benson Ltd v Lincoln City Council* the claimant bank had made payments to defendant councils under interest rate swap agreements. The agreements had been fully performed by both parties (ie, the swaps were 'closed'). Then it was decided by the House of Lords in *Hazell v Hammersmith and Fulham Borough Council*[17] that interest rate swap agreements were void as being outside the powers of local authorities. Kleinwort Benson had made net payments to the local authorities of £811,208. The local authorities were willing to pay back the £388,114 which had been paid to them within six years of the date of the issue of the writ. But they were not willing to pay back the £423,094 that had been paid prior to the six years, arguing that a claim for such repayment was statute-barred. The claimant bank sought restitution of the £423,094 on the basis that it had paid under a mistake of law and that, therefore, under s 32(1) of the Limitation Act 1980 the six year limitation period did not start to run until the claimant discovered, or could with reasonable diligence have discovered, the mistake. And that mistake of law was not discoverable until the decision of the House of Lords in *Hazell v Hammersmith and Fulham Borough Council.*

A majority of the House of Lords in *Kleinwort Benson* (Lords Goff, Hoffmann and Hope; Lords Browne-Wilkinson and Lloyd dissenting) held that there should be restitution of the money paid because it was paid by a mistake of law. The rule denying restitution for mistakes of law was abrogated; and the claim was not time-barred because s 32 of the Limitation Act 1980 applied.

10 New Zealand Judicature Amendment Act 1958, ss 94A–94B. See also the Western Australian Property Law Act 1969, ss 124–125.
11 *Air Canada v British Columbia* (1989) 59 DLR (4d) 161.
12 *David Securities Pty Ltd v Commonwealth Bank of Australia* (1992) 109 ALR 57.
13 *Willis Faber Enthoven Pty Ltd v Receiver of Revenue* 1992 (4) SA 202 (A).
14 *Morgan Guaranty Trust Co of New York v Lothian Regional Council* 1995 SLT 299.
15 *Restitution: Mistakes of Law and Ultra Vires Public Authority Receipts and Payments* (1994), Law Com No 227.
16 [1999] 2 AC 349. See, generally, L Smith, 'Restitution for Mistake of Law' [1999] RLR 148.
17 [1992] 2 AC 1.

Lord Goff, giving the leading speech for the majority, first of all examined how the mistake of law rule became established through cases such as *Bilbie v Lumley*[18] and *Brisbane v Dacres*.[19] He then referred to three main criticisms of the rule.[20] First, it was contrary to justice in that it allowed the payee to retain a payment which would not have been made but for the payor's mistake. Secondly, it produced capricious distinctions both between mistakes of fact and mistakes of law and between the main rule barring recovery and the exceptions to it. Thirdly, the rule was uncertain and unpredictable in its application because judges manipulated the distinction between fact and law in order to achieve practical justice. Lord Goff further pointed to the removal of the rule in Commonwealth countries. Finally, and perhaps most importantly, he considered that developments in the law of restitution, including the recognition of the change of position defence, made clear 'that the policy underlying the rule can best be achieved, consistently with justice, by the recognition of a right of recovery subject to specified defences to cater for the fears which formerly appeared to require a blanket exclusion of recovery'.[1]

However, the difficult question raised by the case was not so much whether the mistake of law rule should be departed from – even the defendant councils conceded that the rule could not stand – but was how one should deal with changes in the law.[2] Say the payor pays money in reliance on an Act of Parliament that is subsequently repealed or a judicial decision that is subsequently reversed or overruled. Can it recover the money on the grounds of mistake of law?

The answer is easy in respect of repealing legislation assuming that it is not given retrospective effect. The payor should not be entitled to restitution because at the time that it paid the money (which must be the correct time to consider whether it was mistaken) it was not mistaken. The difficulty comes with the common law where the jurisprudential tradition is that 'changes' are retrospective. A decision simply declares what the law is and has always been. To reverse or overrule a past decision is to correct an earlier error rather than to alter the law. On this retrospective view the payor did make a mistake of law at the time it made the payment and, in accordance with the abolition of the mistake of law bar, it would be prima facie entitled to restitution.

---

18   (1802) 2 East 469.

19   (1813) 5 Taunt 143.

20   See also the first edition of this book, pp 116–118.

1   [1999] 2 AC 349, 372.

2   See also the first edition of this book, pp 118–120. Prior to the *Kleinwort Benson* case, this was an issue specifically mentioned in, eg, *Henderson v Folkestone Waterworks Co* (1885) 1 TLR 329.

This question in turn raised the issue of whether reform of the mistake of law rule was best brought about judicially or should be left to legislation. The Law Commission in its 1994 Report had recommended legislation abolishing the mistake of law rule while including a clause denying restitution where payments had been made in accordance with a settled view of the law. The recommended clause was as follows: 'An act done in accordance with a settled view of the law shall not be regarded as founding a mistake claim by reason only that a subsequent decision of a court or tribunal departs from that view.'[3] This was influenced by a somewhat similar section in the New Zealand Judicature Amendment Act 1958. After laying down in s 94A(1) that payments made under mistake of law should be equated to those made under mistake of fact, s 94A(2) of the 1958 Act continues as follows: 'Nothing in this section shall enable relief to be given in respect of any payment made at a time when the law requires or allows, or is commonly understood to require or allow, the payment to be made or enforced, by reason only that the law is subsequently changed or shown not to have been as it was commonly understood to be at the time of payment.'[4]

The facts of *Kleinwort Benson Ltd v Lincoln City Council* raised this 'change in the law' question because the House of Lords in *Hazell v Hammersmith and Fulham London Borough Council*[5] had reversed the Court of Appeal's decision[6] which had held that interest rate swap transactions might not be outside the powers of local authorities and could be valid contracts. Moreover, prior to the first instance decision in that litigation in 1989,[7] it is arguable that the settled view of the law was to the effect that such transactions were valid.[8]

Lord Goff's approach to this question was as follows. He accepted the declaratory theory of judicial decision-making and with it the consequence that judicial 'changes' to the law are retrospective. This was not to accept the fiction that the law is unchanging and that judges merely discover the fixed and true law. Rather Lord Goff accepted that judges plainly do develop the law but they do so restrained by precedent and principle and it is in that respect that the development must be viewed as retrospective. It followed that the claimant banks were making a mistake of law when they paid money to local authorities

---

3   *Restitution: Mistakes of Law and Ultra Vires Public Authority Receipts and Payments,* Law Commission No 227 (1994), Draft Bill, cl 3(1).
4   In Western Australia the identical provision is s 124(2) of the Property Law Act 1969.
5   [1992] 2 AC 1.
6   [1990] 2 QB 697.
7   Ibid.
8   For the fullest analysis of the background to the *Kleinwort Benson* case, see Lord Hope's speech [1999] 2 AC 349, 403–405.

under interest rate swap transactions which they believed to be valid but were, in truth, void. It further followed that, in so far as the 'settled view of the law' defence was being put forward on the basis that it revealed that the banks had made no mistake, it must be rejected. Moreover, while there might be special policy grounds for denying restitution of overpaid taxes where the tax was paid in accordance with a settled understanding of the law – because of the public interest involved and the large number of taxpayers affected – there were no such special policy grounds for denying restitution under private law transactions. Rather standard restitutionary defences, such as change of position and compromise, would be sufficient to protect the stability of receipts. In any event, the concept of a 'settled view of the law' was a difficult one to apply in practice – as shown if one tried to apply it to the circumstances of the *Kleinwort Benson* case – and, if accepted, would give rise to much scope for argument. In Lord Goff's view, therefore, the banks were entitled to restitution of the payments which they had made under a mistake of law.

Lords Hoffmann and Hope agreed with Lord Goff. In Lord Hoffmann's view, it made no difference that the payor paid in accordance with a settled view of the law because that did not alter the essential injustice involved, namely that if the payor had known the true state of affairs he would not have paid. And if there were a need for a 'settled view' rule on grounds of policy that was for the Legislature not the courts. According to Lord Hope, a subsequent change to, or clarification of, the law was no different than a subsequent discovery of true facts. It did not alter the point that the claimant was, at the time of payment, making a mistake.

> '[I]t is the state of mind of the payer at the time of payment which will determine whether he paid under a mistake. But there seems to me to be no reason in principle why the law of unjust enrichment should insist that that mistake must be capable of being demonstrated at the same time as the time when the payment was made. A mistake of fact may take some time to discover. If there is a dispute about this, the question whether there was a mistake may remain in doubt until the issue has been resolved by a judge. Why should this not be so where the mistake is one of law?'[9]

The two minority judges, Lords Browne-Wilkinson and Lloyd, dissented because, while agreeing with the majority that the mistake of law bar should be removed, they considered that there should be no restitution where there was a change in the law or a departure from the settled view of the law. In their view, in these situations the

9   [1999] 2 AC 349, 411.

claimants could not be said to have been mistaken. The declaratory theory of judicial decision-making was a 'fairy tale'[10] because judges plainly make and change the law. If the law is changed retrospectively, whether judicially or, exceptionally, by statute, that does not alter the payor's state of mind: the payor, at the time of payment, was not mistaken. To abrogate the mistake of law rule, without denying restitution where the law has been changed, would be unacceptable. Lord Browne-Wilkinson and Lord Lloyd (who had the other Lords agreed with him would have introduced the 'settled view of the law' provision judicially) therefore preferred legislative, not judicial, abolition of the mistake of law rule.

What, then, should be said about this momentous and fascinating decision? First, and most obviously and uncontroversially, the removal of the mistake of law bar is to be warmly welcomed. Lord Ellenborough in *Bilbie v Lumley* based the mistake of law bar on the presumption that everyone knows the law. This is clearly untrue as an observation of fact and, in contrast to where the defendant seeks to argue that he is not responsible for a crime or a civil wrong because he did not know that his conduct was wrongful, there is no justification for such a fiction in respect of mistaken payments. This is because the mistaken party is not seeking to excuse wrongful conduct but is rather seeking to reverse an unjust enrichment, that is, to undo the consequences of the mistake. Moreover, as Lord Goff emphasised, the policy, which lies behind the mistake of law bar, of avoiding too much restitution in the sense of clogging the courts and undermining payees' security of receipt, is more appropriately dealt with by allowing restitution for all types of mistake subject to defences that specifically cater for such fears, such as change of position. And, irrespective of one's views on the 'too much restitution' objection, the former law was also unacceptable, as Lord Goff again pointed out, because the exceptions to the general rule lacked coherence, and the very distinction between mistakes of law and fact was imprecise and subject to manipulation by the courts.

Secondly, albeit more controversially, it is submitted that the majority was probably correct to say that a claimant is still entitled to restitution for mistake of law where the law, or a settled view of the law, has been changed by judicial decision. Prior to the decision of their Lordships, this was a hotly-debated topic, and different views had been taken by the Scottish and English Law Commissions. In favour of the majority's view, there are two main groups of arguments. First, on the retrospectivity point, it can be argued that legislative and common law 'changes' are distinct precisely because the latter are always

10   Ibid, at 358, 362, 394.

retrospective; that the retrospective effect of common law decisions logically entails that the payor relying on a subsequently-reversed or overruled decision did pay under a mistake of law; and that to deny restitution is to accept a form of prospective overruling which has traditionally been denied. Secondly, it can be said that the restrictions on restitution laid down for mistakes of fact, and equally applicable to mistakes of law, will adequately control the ambit of restitution and prevent too much restitution. A payor who is aware of the probability that the judicial decision on which he relies may be reversed or overruled (that is, that the decision is probably wrong) will be ruled out from restitution either because he is not mistaken or because he assumes the risk of his mistake. Contractual compromises will not be disrupted unless the more stringent contractual rules allowing escape are satisfied.[11] And the change of position defence will apply.

Given those restrictions, it would seem that the minority judges, Lords Browne-Wilkinson and Lloyd, painted too alarmist a picture of the consequences of the majority's view. Lord Browne-Wilkinson said, 'On every occasion in which a higher court changed the law by judicial decision, all those who had made payments on the basis that the old law was correct (however long ago such payments were made) would have six years in which to bring a claim to recover money paid under a mistake of law.'[12] And according to Lord Lloyd, 'One consequence is that in all those cases where the House of Lords has overruled a previous decision of the Court of Appeal it would be open to those who have entered into transactions in reliance on the previous decision to seek to re-open their transactions.'[13] But this is to ignore the defence of 'dispute resolved':[14] a payment made, albeit mistakenly, in response to the good faith initiation of legal proceedings is irrecoverable and payments made under contractual compromises cannot be recovered, unless – as with all contractual payments – the contract is invalid. This means that, in most cases, payments made on the basis of the law that has subsequently been changed cannot be recovered. And in so far as there is a need for reform of limitation periods, so as to ensure that s 32 does not postpone indefinitely the running of time for the restitution of mistaken payments, that is a reform requiring legislation and is as much needed for payments made by mistake of fact as for mistake of law. Indeed, although not referred to by their Lordships, the Law Commission had already provisionally recommended reform (which would introduce a ten-year long-stop

11   See, eg, *Derrick v Williams* [1939] 2 All ER 559.
12   [1999] 2 AC 349, 364.
13   Ibid, at 397–398.
14   See below, pp 556–559.

from the date of payment where the starting date for the running of time is discoverability) that would meet their Lordships' concerns.[15] Certainly the experience since the decision in *Kleinwort Benson* – and borne out by the position in other countries, such as Scotland, which have similarly abolished the mistake of law bar without introducing a 'settled view of the law' restriction – is that there has been no noticeable, let alone unacceptable, surge of claims for restitution of money paid under law that has subsequently been changed.

What about the minority's view that, where the law has been changed judicially, the claimant who has paid on the basis of the old law has simply made no mistake? At the time when it paid the money, it was not mistaken. Peter Birks[16] supports the minority's view of this arguing that in such a situation the payor is not relevantly mistaken. Mistakes grounding restitution must be ones where the payor pays on the basis of data that can be verified as true or false at the time the payment is made. Other mistakes – which Birks suggests are more accurately labelled 'mispredictions' – cannot be demonstrated to be true or false at the time of payment. Rather it is only with the benefit of hindsight that they can be shown to be such. Some mistakes of law therefore ground restitution because, at the time of payment, they can be demonstrated to be false (eg the payor thought a statute said X but in truth it said Y). But 'mistakes of law' do not ground restitution where the 'mistake' is only revealed to be such by a subsequent decision. The best that the payor can say is that he made a misprediction as to what the law would turn out to be. The reason why the difference between mistakes and mispredictions is so crucial is that, in relation to mispredictions, one is exercising an element of choice or judgment which is significantly different from the impairment of will necessary to ground restitution. In Birks' words, 'There is ... [a] crucial difference between decisions which are made on data which are false at the time they are made and decisions which are made on data which cannot be falsified at the time, but which are falsified later. The crucial difference consists in the fact that in the latter case there is no impairment of the decision.'[17] A further policy merit of this

---

15 Law Commission Consultation Paper No 151, *Limitation of Actions* (1998), paras 13.77–13.83. See now Law Commission Report No 270, *Limitation of Actions* (2001), paras 4.76–4.79.

16 Birks, 'Mistakes of Law' [2000] CLP 205. Meier and Zimmermann, 'Judicial Development of the Law, Error Iuris, and the Law of Unjustified Enrichment – a View from Germany' (1999) 115 LQR 556 argue that there was no mistake but that restitution was required because, following the German approach, there was no legal ground for the payment because the contract was void. See similarly Hedley, *A Critical Introduction to Restitution* (2001), p 105.

17 Ibid at 224.

approach is that it obviates the fear of there being too much restitution, and achieves the same result as in the New Zealand legislation and as recommended by the Law Commission, without the difficulty of a 'settled view of the law' formulation.

Nevertheless, it is submitted that Birks' view – and that of the minority – is flawed.[18] It is false to equate questions of common law to mispredictions. Mispredictions relate to future events and it is certainly true that one cannot verify, in advance, future events (what the weather will be like, what X will do, what market movements will be). Although the claimant may be able to say that it would not have paid had it known how matters would turn out, it should not be entitled to restitution on the basis of its misprediction alone because it has plainly taken the risk of being wrong. To ground restitution for a misprediction it would need to establish, for example, that the defendant promised to do something so that there is a failure of consideration if the promise is unfulfilled. However, it is incorrect to say that the line between mistakes and mispredictions turns on whether data can be verified as true or false at the time the payment is made. Rather the line is between a false belief as to the present state of affairs (where we are in the realm of mistake) and a false belief as to a future state of affairs (where we are in the realm of misprediction). Just as the verification of facts may be complex and indeed, at the time, impossible (eg, because scientific techniques, like DNA testing, have not yet been developed) so the verification of the law may be complex and indeed, at the time, impossible. But, as Lord Hope most clearly emphasised,[19] this does not mean that a person who pays on the basis of what are later proved to be incorrect facts, or is later proved to be incorrect law, has not made a mistake of fact or law respectively. Rather he did make a mistake of fact or law even though the proof of that mistake was only possible subsequently. His will has been impaired – wrong data has been fed into his decision-making – even though we can only see this subsequently and not at the time of the payment.

Three questions remain outstanding following *Kleinwort Benson Ltd v Lincoln City Council*. First, what is the position with retrospective

---

18 Sheehan, 'What is a mistake?' (2000) 4 Legal Studies 538 also disagrees with Birks' conclusion on the *Kleinwort Benson* case. In his view *Kleinwort Benson* was mistaken because, applying a Dworkinian approach to judicial decision-making, 'Hercules' can prove what the correct common law position is. But in contrast to the view I here put forward Sheehan agrees with Birks that 'a mistake can be seen as a belief in something that can, at the time at which it is acted upon, be proven not to be correct' (at 539): and he further agrees with Birks, contrary to my view, that retrospective legislation cannot make a payor mistaken. For the view that the minority was incorrect in denying that the payor made a mistake of law, see also Finnis, 'The Fairy Tale's Moral' (1999) 115 LQR 170.

19 See the passage from his speech set out above, p 152.

legislation? Is it to be treated in the same way as retrospective judicial law-making, so that a person who pays on the basis of the previous law that has been retrospectively changed, is entitled to restitution as a mistaken payor? This provoked disagreement between the three Lords in the majority. Lord Goff did not accept that retrospective legislation (which is, of course, unusual) should necessarily be treated in the same way as judicial development of the law. He said, '[E]ven where it is retrospective, it has the effect that as from the date of the legislation a new legal provision will apply retrospectively in place of that previously applicable. It follows that retrospective change in the law does not necessarily have the effect that a previous payment was, as a result of the change in the law, made under a mistake of law at the time of payment.'[20] Lord Hope went further and firmly stated that if the law is changed retrospectively by statute, so that a payment which was legally due when it was paid has now become undue, the correct analysis is that there was no mistake.[1] In contrast, Lord Hoffmann thought that, in this situation, the payor would be deemed to have been mistaken.[2]

It is submitted that the best view is that taken by Lord Hoffmann and that the claimant is entitled to restitution on the basis of mistake. Any concern that we may have that this seems unpalatable stems from our general antipathy to retrospective legislation. In so far as this produces an undesirable result the Legislature would, of course, be free to qualify the full effect of retrospectivity by denying restitution in the relevant statute.

Secondly, should there be a 'settled view of the law' policy restriction in respect of taxes demanded ultra vires which, as we have seen, was a question which Lord Goff specifically left open? It is submitted that, for reasons discussed in chapter 13 below in relation to the similar idea of a special defence of 'extreme disruption of public funds',[3] the answer in principle and policy should be 'no'. But most tax statutes dealing with restitution do contain provisions denying restitution where the tax was paid in line with 'settled practice'. Just as the 'passing on' defence embodied in several tax statutes is objectionable, in allowing the State to retain unlawfully-demanded taxes, so the same can be said of 'settled practice' provisions.

Thirdly, and most importantly, is the law on restitution of payments made by mistake of law identical to the law on restitution of payments made by mistake of fact? Lord Goff, with whom Lords Hoffmann and

---

20   [1999] 2 AC 349, 381.

1   Ibid, at 410.

2   Ibid, at 400. Lord Hoffmann here relied for support on the view of Mason CJ in *Commissioner of State Revenue v Royal Assurance Australia Ltd* (1994) 182 CLR 51.

3   See below, pp 451–454.

Hope agreed, summarised the position by saying that 'the mistake of law rule should no longer be maintained as part of English law and … English law should now recognise that there is a general right to recover money paid under a mistake of fact or law, subject to the defences available in the law of restitution'.[4] And, while there was no express mention of the leading restitution case on mistake of fact, namely Robert Goff J's decision in *Barclays Bank v WJ Simms*, a 'but for' causation test for mistaken payments, whether of fact or law, was approved in the reasoning of each of the speeches of the majority.[5] It seems clear therefore that, while the conceivable possibility of a special defence (or defences) being developed for mistakes of law was left open, prima facie liability in restitution for mistaken payments rests on exactly the same criteria whether the mistake is one of fact or law.

Finally, it is noteworthy that, subsequent to *Kleinwort Benson*, a 'logical paradox' was raised in *Nurdin & Peacock plc v D B Ramsden & Co Ltd*[6] that is unique to restitution for some mistakes of law. This paradox was not touched on in *Kleinwort Benson*. Nor had it been discussed in the academic literature.

On the facts of *Nurdin*, the defendant landlord increased the rent owing by the claimant tenant in respect of business premises. Although acting in good faith, the landlord was not entitled to do this because there had been no rent review. Nevertheless the claimant tenant paid the first five instalments demanded ('the first five overpayments') without complaint because it had overlooked or forgotten about the need for a rent review. It then received advice that, because there had been no rent review, it was not bound to pay the extra rent. Nevertheless it paid five more instalments ('the last five overpayments') at the higher rate because it had been legally advised that, if overpaying, it would be entitled to restitution of the overpayment.

Neuberger J held that all ten overpayments were recoverable as paid by mistake. The first five were straightforward after *Kleinwort Benson*; they had been paid by mistake of fact or law. More difficult were the last five overpayments[7] because the relevant mistake – the tenant incorrectly believed that it was entitled to restitution of those overpayments even though it knew that they were not owing – was one of law which raised the 'logical paradox'. That is, to allow restitution would logically contradict the alleged mistake which was posited on the truth being that one was *not* entitled to restitution.

---

4   [1999] 2 AC 349, 375.
5   See above, p 135.
6   [1999] 1 All ER 941.
7   Although as regards four of these, Neuberger J held that there was a contractual right to repayment. The resolution of the 'logical paradox' was therefore necessary only in relation to one of those overpayments.

But Neuberger J simply said that one must 'cut the vicious circle' and that this type of mistake of law – as to the recoverability of a payment – grounded restitution just as much as the more standard mistake of law as to the liability to make a payment. In Neuberger J's words:

'It may ... be said that my conclusion involves wrong advice turning out to be right, a logical paradox of the type illustrated by the fictional Cretan who said that all Cretans were liars. [I]t seems to me that the right point at which to cut the vicious circle is at the point where one concludes that Nurdin made the ... overpayment under a mistake of law. In other words, while I accept that the particular nature of the mistake in the present case does present an unusual logical problem in relation to the payer's claim for repayments, I do not think it should stand in the way of the conclusion I have reached.'[8]

(3) Proprietary restitution in respect of mistaken payments

The above discussion of restitution for mistaken payments has been dealing with the usual situation where the claimant seeks *personal* restitution. But if, by reason of the mistaken payment, an unjust enrichment at the claimant's expense is established and the defendant retains the payment (whether in the same form or, by the rules of tracing, in a substitute), is the claimant entitled to *proprietary* restitution?[9] This will be of vital importance if the defendant has become insolvent because proprietary restitution gives priority on the defendant's insolvency.

This question, which remains unresolved in English law, has mainly been posed in terms of whether the payee is, or should be, a trustee (whether resulting or constructive) of the mistaken payment.

The main decision on this point is that of Goulding J in *Chase Manhattan Bank NA v Israel-British Bank (London) Ltd.*[10] On 3 July 1974 by a clerical error the claimant, a New York bank, mistakenly made

---

8   [1999] 1 All ER 941, 964–965. For criticism of this decision, see Virgo, 'Recent Developments in Restitution of Mistaken Payments' [1999] CLJ 478. Hedley, *A Critical Introduction to Restitution* (2001) pp 104–105 argues that the decision was correct but that it cannot be justified on the ground of mistake.

9   For general discussion see, eg, Goff and Jones, paras 4-033 to 4-036; Maddaugh and McCamus, *The Law of Restitution* (1990), pp 95–96, 239–240; Chambers, *Resulting Trusts* (1997), pp 125–132; Birks, 'Restitution and Resulting Trusts' in *Equity and Contemporary Legal Developments* (ed Goldstein, 1992), pp 335–373.

10 [1981] Ch 105. The constructive trust imposed in respect of the sixth payment in *Neste Oy v Lloyds Bank plc* [1983] 2 Lloyd's Rep 658 may also be best justified as an example of proprietary restitution for a mistaken payment: but leave to amend to allege mistake had been refused (ibid at 665) and Bingham J instead based his decision on the payee's knowledge that the consideration would be bound to fail. For whether the trust in *Chase Manhattan* should be labelled constructive or resulting, see above p 66, n 14.

two payments of some $2 million, instead of one, to another New York bank, for the account of the defendant, an English bank. On 5 July 1974 the defendant knew, or should have known, of the mistake. Shortly afterwards the defendant became insolvent. The claimant sought a declaration that the defendant became a trustee of the second $2 million payment on receipt of it on 3 July 1974. Goulding J granted that declaration. This meant that the claimant would have priority if, which did not fall to be decided by Goulding J, the claimant could show, by the rules of tracing, that the defendant retained the mistaken payment or its traceable substitute. In reaching this decision, Goulding J thought that English law was in line with that in the United States; and he cited with approval a leading American case of *Re Berry*[11] in which a trust of a mistaken payment had been imposed. It is also significant that Goulding J regarded the defendant's knowledge of the mistake as irrelevant.[12]

While this decision is controversial,[13] it is submitted that it can be justified applying either of the two approaches to proprietary restitution discussed in chapter 1.[14] On one approach, this followed because mistake vitiates, rather than qualifies, consent so that there was never a time when the defendant was entitled to the enrichment; on an alternative approach, the mistake meant that the claimant had not taken the risk of the defendant's insolvency.

That *Chase Manhattan* was correctly decided is further supported if one extends one's examination of proprietary restitution for mistaken payments beyond trusts.[15] For example, rescission can be a proprietary remedy in so far as it revests title to property in the claimant.[16] Examples of proprietary rescission of a contract (for misrepresentation) are examined later in this chapter[17] and we have already referred to examples of formal gifts being rescinded because

---

11   147 F 208 (1906), Circuit Court of Appeals, Second Circuit. Several other cases in the USA have taken a similar approach. *Contra* is *Re Dow Corning Corp* 192 Bankruptcy R 428 (1996), US Bankruptcy Court for the Eastern District of Michigan. For an excellent general discussion of the position in the USA, see Kull, 'Restitution in Bankruptcy' (1998) 72 Am Bankruptcy LJ 265.

12   [1981] Ch 105, 114.

13   See, eg, Tettenborn, 'Remedies for the Recovery of Money Paid by Mistake' [1980] CLJ 272.

14   See above, pp 67–73.

15   Within the realm of trusts, one can also regard some examples of resulting trusts imposed where an express trust has initially failed as illustrating proprietary restitution for mistake (usually of law); eg, *Morice v Bishop of Durham* (1805) 9 Ves 399 (express trust for objects of benevolence and liberality held to be void and resulting trust imposed); *Air Jamaica Ltd v Charlton* [1999] 1 WLR 1399 (pension scheme void for perpetuity and resulting trust imposed).

16   See also rectification of a document or the register for mistake where the wrong area of land has been conveyed: above, p 59, n 10.

17   See below, pp 173–174.

of mistake.[18] Analogously, an equitable lien can be imposed for the mistaken improvement of land;[19] and, perhaps most importantly, as we have seen in chapter 2, subrogation giving priority as against a subsequent lender (albeit not against all creditors) was granted by the House of Lords in *Banque Financière de la Cité v Parc (Battersea) Ltd*[20] in which the claimant had mistakenly made a loan which benefited the subsequent lender. Daniel Friedmann has written:

'[T]he plaintiff's mistake in the case of *Chase Manhattan* was more severe than that of the plaintiff in *Banque Financière* ... . In *Banque Financière* the plaintiff intended to make a loan, which he did. The mistake merely related to a condition, albeit an important one, of that loan. If priority over creditors was granted in *Banque Financière*, it is *a fortiori* justified in *Chase Manhattan*. Thus, although *Chase Manhattan* was not mentioned in *Banque Financière*, the inescapable conclusion is that the decision of the House of Lords in *Banque Financière* must be taken to have dispelled the clouds that surrounded the decision in *Chase Manhattan*.'[1]

Unfortunately those doubts about the status of *Chase Manhattan* were created explicitly by the House of Lords itself in *Westdeutsche Landesbank Girozentrale v Islington London Borough Council*.[2] This was one of the void interest rate swap cases. The House of Lords, quite rightly, decided that the money paid by the bank under the partly-completed swap was not held on trust by the defendant local authority (this being regarded as important in deciding whether the bank was entitled to compound, rather than merely simple, interest on the repayment). Prior to the abolition of the mistake of law bar, the unjust factor was most obviously failure of consideration. Proprietary restitution was not justified because, applying one approach, the claimant's consent was qualified, rather than vitiated, and prior to the failure of consideration the defendant was free to deal with the money as its own.[3] On an alternative approach, one can say that the bank was analogous to an unsecured creditor and therefore did not merit the secured protection of a trust.[4] But the important point here is that in discussing proprietary restitution and trusts, Lord Browne-Wilkinson, giving the leading speech of the majority, said that he thought the reasoning in

---

18 See above, p 134.
19 *Cooper v Phibbs* (1867) LR 2 HL 149. Another possible example is *Unity Joint-Stock Mutual Banking Association v King* (1858) 25 Beav 72. Such a lien was refused on the facts in *Lee-Parker v Izzet (No 2)* [1972] 1 WLR 775.
20 [1999] 1 AC 221. See above, pp 117–120.
1 'Payment Under Mistake – Tracing and Subrogation' (1999) 115 LQR 195, 198.
2 [1996] AC 669. See also *Eldan Services Ltd v Chandag Motors Ltd* [1990] 3 All ER 459; *Bank of America v Arnell* [1999] Lloyd's Rep Bank 399.
3 Chambers, *Resulting Trusts* (1997), p 162. See above pp 67–69.
4 See above, pp 70–71.

Chase Manhattan was incorrect. For a trust to have arisen the conscience of the payee had to have been affected. That would only have been so once the payee knew of the payor's mistake. So while the decision might have been correct – because the payee bank knew of the payor's mistake two days after the payment and before the payee's insolvency – Goulding J's reasoning imposing a trust from the date of receipt was not. With respect, these obiter dicta should be put to one side[5] and *Chase Manhattan* should be regarded as good law.

2.   BENEFITS IN KIND RENDERED BY MISTAKE

The mistaken rendering of benefits in kind (ie benefits other than payments to the defendant) is clearly less commonplace than mistakenly making payments to the defendant. This is reflected in the paucity of the case law (other than on rescission of an executed contract, entered into by mistake, which is dealt with in the next main section).

(1) Mistaken improvement of goods

The leading case is *Greenwood v Bennett*.[6] Harper had repaired a car that he had bought thinking that he had acquired good title to it. In fact the car belonged to the owners of a garage managed by Bennett. In interpleader proceedings taken out by the police to determine the parties' rights, Harper claimed that he ought to be paid £226 for the cost of the improvements he had made to the car. The Court of Appeal allowed his claim.

The reasoning of Phillimore and Cairns LJJ goes no further than accepting that a mistaken improver has a passive claim: that is, Bennett here was in the same position as if he had been seeking a court order for repossession of the car in a detinue action and, as such, the county court judge had had the power, which he should have exercised, to make it a condition of repossession that Harper was reimbursed. Cairns LJ expressly rejected any active claim: 'If the car had, before any proceedings were brought, reached the hands of

---

5   See above, pp 67–75, esp 67, 70–71.
6   [1973] QB 195. Matthews, 'Freedom, Unrequested Improvements and Lord Denning' [1981] CLJ 340; McKendrick, 'Restitution and the Misuse of Chattels – the Need for a Principled Approach' in *Interests in Goods* (eds Palmer and McKendrick, 2nd edn, 1998), pp 600–611. For a wide-ranging discussion of mistaken improvement (of land as well as goods) see Sutton, 'What Should be Done for Mistaken Improvers?' in *Essays on Restitution* (ed Finn, 1990), pp 241–296.

Mr Bennett, it is difficult to see that Mr Harper could have had any claim against him for the expenditure that he was put to in making the repairs to it.'[7]

In contrast, the reasoning of Lord Denning was that a mistaken improver has an active claim for the value of his work based on unjust enrichment. He said:

'There is a principle at hand to meet the case. It derives from the law of restitution. The plaintiffs should not be allowed unjustly to enrich themselves at his expense. The court will order the plaintiffs, if they recover the car, or its improved value, to recompense the innocent purchaser for the work he has done on it. No matter whether the plaintiffs recover it with the aid of the courts, or without it, the innocent purchaser will recover the value of the improvements he has done to it.'[8]

Although he did not explain how the unjust enrichment principle was made out on the facts, Lord Denning's judgment should be supported. The unjust factor was the improver's mistake in believing that he had good title to the car which negatived the voluntariness with which he carried out the repairs (and it is significant, in supporting the modern rejection of the supposed liability test for mistaken payments, that there was no question in this case of the non-liability mistake not counting).

The defendant had been negatively benefited by being saved the repair expense.[9] This can be explained in one of two ways. Either the cost of repair was a commercially necessary expense so that the defendant had been incontrovertibly negatively benefited. Or the defendant had been incontrovertibly positively benefited in that, as a business, the defendant was highly likely to realise the improved value of the car (and indeed had done so after the trial and before the appeal hearing): but the defendant could, nonetheless, validly subjectively devalue that resale profit down to the expense saved because it would itself have carried out the repairs and reaped the profit.[10]

And the benefit was conferred at the claimant's expense in the subtractive sense. The defendant's benefit came from the claimant's wealth (which includes labour).

Section 6(1) of the Torts (Interference with Goods) Act 1977 statutorily recognises a passive claim by an improver who mistakenly believed that he had good title to goods:[11]

---

7 Ibid at p 203.
8 Ibid at p 202.
9 Cf Birks at p 124, Goff and Jones at para 6-011.
10 Above, pp 19–20.
11 See similarly the tortious mining cases where the expense of making the goods saleable was deducted from the damages: *McGregor on Damages* (16th edn, 1997), paras 1399–1410.

'If in proceedings for wrongful interference against a person (the improver) who has improved goods, it is shown that the improver acted in the mistaken but honest belief that he had a good title to them, an allowance shall be made for the extent to which, at the time as at which the goods fall to be valued in assessing damages, the value of the goods is attributable to the improvement.'

So, for example, where the mistaken improver improves the goods and then commits a fresh act of conversion by selling them, and the true owner sues the improver for damages for that later conversion, the improver is entitled to an allowance.

However, s 6(1) only applies where the owner is suing for damages. It does not recognise an active claim by the improver. Nor is the improver entitled to a passive claim where the owner recaptures the goods or is given delivery up without damages (although by s 3(7) the court *may* make it a condition for delivery up that the mistaken improver is given an allowance). Section 6(1) would therefore have had no application in *Greenwood v Bennett.* The strongest argument in favour of that statutory restriction is that, as one is concerned purely with the assessment of damages, the improvement has been realised in money and is therefore incontrovertibly beneficial.[12] But an incontrovertible benefit can be established in other ways (as, for example, in *Greenwood v Bennett*). So viewed in terms of unjust enrichment the statute is unnecessarily restrictive: indeed, it is illogical to accept a passive but not an active claim.

Section 6(2) makes the same provision for an allowance in favour of a bona fide purchaser of the goods from the improver (or down a chain of purchasers from the improver). This is to ensure that the true owner is not unjustly enriched *at the expense of the bona fide purchaser* where, through the purchase price, the purchaser has paid the mistaken improver for the improvement. But by s 6(3), if the bona fide purchaser recovers the purchase price from the mistaken improver in an action for failure of consideration – so that the true owner's enrichment is again at the mistaken improver's expense – the mistaken improver is again entitled, where appropriate, to the allowance.

(2) Mistaken improvement of land

Goff and Jones, in a chapter called 'Restitution in Respect of Services Rendered under a Mistake', regard the equitable doctrine of acquiescence or proprietary estoppel as illustrating restitution for

12 Birks at pp 122–123.

mistaken improvements to land.[13] They therefore deal in depth with well-known cases like *Ramsden v Dyson*,[14] *Willmott v Barber*,[15] and *Taylor Fashions Ltd v Liverpool Victoria Trustees Co*,[16] and rely on them to argue that, in contrast to the mistaken improvement of chattels, where the benefit is incontrovertible, one needs acquiescence or free acceptance by the owner to establish that a mistaken improvement of land is beneficial. While it can readily be conceded that the classic statements of the equitable doctrine in *Ramsden v Dyson* and *Willmot v Barber* tended to mix restitution for mistaken improvement with the protection of expectations engendered, there have been hardly any English cases in which an application of the equitable doctrine has resulted in a restitutionary remedy being awarded for a mistaken improvement to land.[17] For example, no remedy at all was ordered in *Ramsden v Dyson* or *Willmot v Barber* principally on the ground that the owner did not know of the improver's mistake. And in the numerous cases where a remedy has been awarded on the basis of acquiescence or proprietary estoppel it would seem that the courts have almost invariably been concerned to protect the claimant's expectation (or, more rarely, reliance) interest and not his restitution interest.[18] With respect, it therefore seems inaccurate to rely on the acquiescence doctrine as if it underpinned a rich seam of cases awarding restitution for mistaken land improvement.

Nor can it be taken that in a mistake case the acquiescence is important in establishing that the owner was benefited. It seems rather that the courts have been concerned to restrict the types of relevant mistake so that, as with the notion of a unilateral mistake in contract law, only a mistake by the improver known about by the owner counts. Indeed one probably has to face the fact that, as shown by land improvement cases awarding restitution outside the acquiescence doctrine (including those not based on a mistake),[19] the courts have been content to ignore the subjective devaluation argument in respect

---

13 Goff and Jones at paras 6-001 to 6-006.
14 (1866) LR 1 HL 129.
15 (1880) 15 Ch D 96.
16 [1982] QB 133n. See also, eg, *Plimmer v Wellington Corpn* (1884) 9 App Cas 699; *Inwards v Baker* [1965] 2 QB 29; *Crabb v Arun District Council* [1976] Ch 179; *A-G of Hong Kong v Humphreys Estate (Queen's Garden)* [1987] AC 114.
17 A possible example is *Unity Joint Stock Mutual Banking Association v King* (1858) 25 Beav 72, where an equitable lien was granted.
18 Moriarty, 'Licences and Land Law: Legal Principles and Public Policies' (1984) 100 LQR 376; Cooke, 'Estoppel and the Protection of Expectations' (1997) 17 Legal Studies 258. See below, p 492, n 16.
19 Eg *Cooper v Phibbs* (1867) LR 2 HL 149 (see the third main section of this chapter); *Pulbrook v Lawes* (1876) 1 QBD 284 (where the unjust factor was failure of consideration); *Rowley v Ginnever* [1897] 2 Ch 503 (passive claim for mistaken land improvement allowed).

of improvements to land and have been satisfied as to the defendant's enrichment simply by there being an objective positive benefit to the defendant.

(3) Other mistakenly rendered benefits in kind

Some of the cases on reviving subrogation considered in chapter 2 – most importantly, *B Liggett (Liverpool) Ltd v Barclays Bank Ltd* [20] and *Banque Financière de la Cité v Parc (Battersea) Ltd* [1] – are best analysed as examples of restitution for the mistaken rendering of benefits in kind through the discharge of the defendant's (or another's) [2] liability. Leaving aside subrogation, there are very few other cases to consider here.

In *Rover International Ltd v Cannon Film Sales Ltd (No 3)*, [3] the facts of which are set out in chapter 10 below, [4] Kerr LJ, but peculiarly not Dillon LJ, considered not only Rover's claim for money had and received but also its claim for a *quantum meruit* for the dubbing and distribution work carried out. On appeal, Cannon had conceded that Rover was entitled to a *quantum meruit* and Kerr LJ regarded that concession as correctly made. On an unjust enrichment analysis that was plainly right. As with the money claim the unjust factor was either mistake of fact [5] or failure of consideration. Cannon was benefited because it had bargained for and received the work. And that benefit was at Rover's expense in the subtractive sense.

In view of the concession Kerr LJ's judgment was principally concerned with the outstanding issue of whether the *quantum meruit* should be limited by the contract terms. That is examined in chapter 10.

One further English case that merits discussion here, although on the face of it not involving restitution, is *Upton-on-Severn RDC v Powell.* [6] The defendant, whose farm had caught fire, phoned the police to ask for the fire brigade to be sent. The Upton Fire Brigade was sent and attended the fire. It transpired that, unknown to the Upton Fire Brigade, the farm was in the Pershore Fire District, so that while the defendant would have been entitled without charge to the services of

---

20   [1928] 1 KB 48. But contrast *Crantrave Ltd v Lloyds Bank plc* [2000] 3 WLR 877. See above, p 125.

1   [1999] 1 AC 221. See above, pp 117–120.

2   In the *Banque Financière* case, the enrichment was not of the discharged debtor but of a second creditor of that debtor.

3   [1989] 1 WLR 912. See also *Cotronic (UK) Ltd v Dezonie* [1991] BCC 200: below, p 396.

4   See below, pp 393–394.

5   For the Court of Appeal's view that the mistake was one of fact not law, see below, p 393.

6   [1942] 1 All ER 220.

the Pershore Fire Brigade, the Upton Fire Brigade was entitled to contract for payment. They claimed payment from the defendant.

The Court of Appeal held that there was a valid contract between the parties entitling the Upton Fire Brigade to payment for their services. However, this contractual reasoning seems fictional because both parties assumed that the services were being rendered gratuitously. It has therefore been suggested that the decision may be better explained on the basis of unjust enrichment.[7] The claimants were mistaken in believing that the farm lay within their district (unjust factor) and the services rendered were necessitous so that the defendant was saved inevitable expense (enrichment). However, while necessitous services are generally incontrovertibly beneficial, this was surely not so on these peculiar facts: as the defendant was entitled to fire services free from the Pershore Fire Brigade, the Upton Fire Brigade had not saved the defendant inevitable expense. Nor was any other test of benefit satisfied. At first sight an alternative solution would have been to recognise that the Upton Fire Brigade had a restitutionary claim, not against the defendant, but against the Pershore Fire Brigade in that it had mistakenly (unjust factor) discharged Pershore Fire Brigade's statutory duty to render free fire services to those within its area (enrichment). The difficulty is that the Pershore Fire Brigade probably had no statutory duty until it knew that there was a fire within its area and, on the facts, it appears that that was not known until several hours after the Upton Fire Brigade had been attending the fire. It is doubtful, therefore, whether any remedy should have been awarded to the claimant on the facts of *Upton*.

The suggestion of a restitutionary claim for mistaken discharge of another's statutory duty leads conveniently and finally to the well-known Canadian case of *County of Carleton v City of Ottawa*.[8] Carleton was under a statutory duty to provide care for its residents who were insane. Not having its own home, it sent them to Lanark and paid Lanark for providing for them. When Ottawa annexed part of Carleton, Ottawa should have taken over payment to Lanark for Norah Baker, who was an insane resident of one of the annexed areas. By an oversight her name was missed off the list of those for whom Ottawa would be responsible, and Carleton mistakenly carried on paying for her. When Carleton discovered its mistake, it sought reimbursement from Ottawa of the payments it had made to Lanark for Norah Baker's care. The Supreme Court of Canada held that it was so entitled on the grounds of unjust enrichment.

---

7   Birks at p 120; Treitel *The Law of Contract* (10th edn, 1999) at p 34.
8   (1965) 52 DLR (2d) 220.

Unfortunately it was not made clear exactly why there was thought to be an unjust enrichment. Although the unjust factor was obvious – the claimant had made a mistake of fact – the establishment of the benefit is more problematic. The most straightforward view is that Ottawa was under a statutory duty to provide for Norah Baker so that it was incontrovertibly benefited by having that duty fulfilled by Carleton. But the Ontario Court of Appeal had specifically rejected the trial judge's view that Ottawa had such a statutory duty.[9] Ottawa's duty may therefore have been a contractual one owed to Lanark. If so the Supreme Court should at least have made reference to the unclear state of the law on whether the mistaken payment of another's debt does automatically discharge that debt.[10]

(4) Conclusion

The difficulty in the area of mistakenly rendered benefits in kind, in contrast to mistaken payments, lies in establishing that the defendant has been benefited so that there is an enrichment to go with the unjust factor of mistake. In principle, provided there is a benefit that is incontrovertible or bargained-for or reprehensibly sought-out, restitution (in an action for *quantum meruit, quantum valebat,* or money paid to the defendant's use) should be granted as it is for a mistaken payment.[11] Lord Denning's judgment in *Greenwood v Bennett* comes closest to a clear acceptance of this.

3.   RESCISSION OF AN EXECUTED CONTRACT ENTERED INTO BY MISTAKE

The remedy of rescission of a contract is one of the most difficult remedies to analyse.[12] While it is always a contractual remedy (because it wipes away and allows escape from a contract) it is also a restitutionary remedy where a contract has been wholly or partly executed and where the effect of the rescission is therefore to restore benefits to the contracting parties. The rescission may effect personal restitution (for example, by entitling the payor to the repayment of a purchase

---

9   (1964) 46 DLR (2d) 432, CA; (1963) 39 DLR (2d) 11, 14–15 (Grant J).

10   Below, chapter 8.

11   Although in *Kleinwort Benson Ltd v Lincoln City Council* [1999] 2 AC 349, above, pp 149–159, their Lordships were concerned only with payments made by mistake of law, their reasoning is equally applicable to all mistakenly rendered benefits. In so far as it was ever applied to benefits in kind, the traditional mistake of law bar therefore no longer applies to mistakenly rendered benefits in kind any more than it does to mistaken payments.

12   See above, pp 56–60.

price or by requiring payment for the value of work done); but it is also commonly a proprietary restitutionary remedy in that it revests the proprietary rights to goods or land transferred under the contract. It is because rescission makes no clean divide between contract and restitution that it has been considered convenient to treat it separately in this third section of this chapter. However, it should be emphasised that the approach to restitution through rescission should be consistent with the restitution through other restitutionary remedies that we have so far examined in this chapter. The usual categorisation, which we shall here follow, distinguishes between rescission for mistake; rescission for misrepresentation (where the mistake is induced by a false representation); and rescission for non-disclosure (where there is a duty on the non-mistaken party to disclose the true facts to the mistaken party). Whichever type of rescission is in issue, it appears that there are four main bars to rescission: *restitutio in integrum* being impossible; affirmation; lapse of time; and third party rights. Of these bars, the most significant from a restitutionary perspective is the first.

(1) Mistake[12a]

There has been a long-running controversy as to whether there is a contractual doctrine of mistake. One view, which is most clearly supported by Steyn J's analysis of common mistake (where both parties make the same mistake) in *Associated Japanese Bank (International) Ltd v Credit Du Nord*[13] is that there is a contractual doctrine of mistake. However, it is narrower in scope at common law than in equity while having a more drastic effect (rendering the contract void as opposed to voidable).[14]

In equity a wider approach to common mistake than at common law – albeit with less drastic consequences – was adopted by the Court of Appeal in *Solle v Butcher.*[15] Lord Denning used a test of fundamental

---

12a This subsection must now be read subject to (and indeed has largely been erased by) the very bold decision of the Court of Appeal in *Great Peace Shipping Ltd v Tsavliris (International) Ltd* [2002] EWCA Civ 1407. This has overruled *Solle v Butcher* [1950] 1 KB 671 and cases following it as being inconsistent with *Bell v Lever Bros* [1932] AC 161. It has laid down that there is no equitable jurisdiction to rescind a contract for common mistake. Unfortunately the decision came too late to be incorporated into the text.

13 [1989] 1 WLR 255.

14 Restitution where a contract is void for mistake at common law (including under the doctrine of *non est factum*) falls within the first two sections of this chapter. See esp pp 128–129 above. See also pp 388–390 below.

15 [1950] 1 KB 671. In *Clarion Ltd v National Provident Institution* [2000] 1 WLR 1888 Rimer J thought that the relevant mistake in equity had to be one as to the terms of the contract or its subject matter. It was held that a mistake as to the commercial advantage of the contract did not trigger rescission for that would simply be to give relief for having made a bad bargain.

mistake to decide when a contract would be rescinded. Although it can be taken that respect for the sanctity of contract means that this test requires a more serious shared mistake of fact than merely saying that neither party would have entered the contract but for the mistake, it would seem clear that it is wider than the test, however formulated, for when common mistake makes the contract void at common law. *Solle v Butcher*, while controversial, has been followed and rescission granted in several subsequent decisions.[16]

Rescission for mistake in equity is presumably subject to its usual bars of affirmation, lapse of time, third party rights, and *restitutio in integrum* being impossible.[17]

In support of his approach in equity Lord Denning relied on *Cooper v Phibbs*,[18] which is a particularly interesting case from a restitutionary perspective because, as a term of granting the rescission, the House of Lords ensured that the successors of a mistaken improver of land were given counter-restitution for the value of improvements he had made. The claimant had contracted with the defendants to take a lease of a fishery, neither party realising that it already belonged to the claimant (as tenant in tail under a settlement). Rescission was granted because of that common mistake, their Lordships holding that a mistake as to a private right of ownership was one of fact not law. This was a classic illustration of the courts' manipulation of the distinction between mistakes of law and fact prior to *Kleinwort Benson Ltd v Lincoln City Council.* But the important point for us here is that the rescission was accompanied by a declaration that the defendants should have a lien over the fishery securing the value of the improvements to it made by their deceased father (who had mistakenly believed that he was the owner). No obvious test of benefit, to overcome the subjective devaluation argument, was satisfied here. The land improvement was not an incontrovertible benefit. Nevertheless, the decision was consistent with the general judicial approach to restitution for land improvement by which the courts seem content to ignore subjective devaluation and to treat the objective positive benefit as sufficient. And proprietary restitution – through the grant of the

---

16   Eg *Grist v Bailey* [1967] Ch 532; *Magee v Pennine Insurance Co Ltd* [1969] 2 QB 507; *Laurence v Lexcourt Holdings Ltd* [1978] 1 WLR 1128. In none of these decisions was the rescission a personal or proprietary restitutionary remedy.

17   Treitel (10th edn, 1999), p 285, Goff and Jones, para 9-055. Lapse of time and *restitutio in integrum* being impossible were mentioned in dicta of Lord Denning in *Campbell v Edwards* [1976] 1 WLR 403, 407. Affirmation was discussed and held not to be made out on the facts in *Laurence v Lexcourt Holdings Ltd* [1978] 1 WLR 1128. Exceptionally rectification of a contract for mistake can also be a restitutionary remedy (and the same bars apply): above, p 59, n 10.

18   (1867) LR 2 HL 149.

equitable lien – can be said to be justified on either of the approaches discussed in chapter 1.[19] That is, the enrichment existed in an asset to which the proprietary right could attach; and either the improver's consent was vitiated by the mistake so that there was never a time when the other party was entitled to treat the improvement as its own; or the mistake meant that the improver was not analogous to an unsecured creditor and had not taken the risk of the other party becoming insolvent.

In *Solle v Butcher* itself, and in the occasional subsequent case,[20] rescission was granted *on the terms of entering a new contract.* As has been explained in chapter 1,[1] this is non-restitutionary in that the overall aim is to set up a new contract: benefits restored by the law to the claimant are partly required to be given back through the new contract.

Lord Denning in *Solle v Butcher* may have intended to widen the approach not only to common mistake but also to unilateral mistake (mistake of one party known to the other) from that narrowly adopted at common law but there has been no clear acceptance of this in subsequent rescission cases.[2]

(2) Misrepresentation

A misrepresentation is basically an untrue statement of fact[3] or, presumably, after *Kleinwort Benson Ltd v Lincoln City Council,*[4] of law (but not of opinion or intention). Leaving aside liability in tort for deceit or negligence or under the Misrepresentation Act 1967, s 2(1), if the misrepresentation is relied on by the claimant in entering into a contract with the misrepresentor (or with a third party who has notice) the contract is rendered voidable (ie, liable to be rescinded).[5]

---

19 See above, pp 67–73.
20 Eg *Grist v Bailey* [1967] Ch 532.
1   Above, pp 59–60.
2   Cf *Riverlate Properties Ltd v Paul* [1975] Ch 133; *Clarion Ltd v National Provident Institution* [2000] 1 WLR 1888.
3   A failure to correct a statement in the light of subsequent changes or a partial disclosure of true facts can also constitute misrepresentation: see, eg, *With v O'Flanagan* [1936] Ch 575.
4   [1999] 2 AC 349. Although their Lordships were concerned only with restitution for mistaken payments and not rescission of a contract, or damages, for misrepresentation, their reasoning is equally applicable to the fact/law distinction in relation to misrepresentation. See McKendrick, *Contract Law* (4th edn, 2000), p 268. Note however that the Misrepresentation Act 1967 is formulated on the assumption that one is concerned with misrepresentation of fact: see s 2(1).
5   For the details of what constitutes an actionable misrepresentation, see Treitel, *The Law of Contract* (10th edn, 1999), pp 305–317.

(a) Examples of restitutionary rescission

A straightforward example of rescission operating as a restitutionary remedy for misrepresentation is provided by *Redgrave v Hurd*.[6] The claimant contracted to buy a house attached to a solicitor's business on the faith of false non-fraudulent representations as to the profitability of the business. The Court of Appeal held that the claimant was entitled to rescission of the purchase contract and the return of the £100 deposit paid. In contrast he was held not entitled to compensation for the loss and trouble incurred in giving up his existing practice and moving because no tort had been made out.

In two well-known cases, the personal restitutionary consequences of rescission were complex. In *Newbigging v Adam*,[7] the claimant had been induced to enter into a contract of partnership by non-fraudulent misrepresentations. After holding that the contract should be rescinded the Court of Appeal decided that the claimant was entitled to the return of the £9,700 which he put into the business plus £324 that he had paid to discharge debts of the partnership (minus £745 that he had received from the partnership). It was also held that he was entitled to an indemnity against all outstanding debts or liabilities of the partnership that he was, or would be, liable to pay. Such an indemnity was a restitutionary remedy in that it envisaged the claimant discharging the partners' debts or liabilities which would be a benefit to them. The indemnity was therefore distinct from compensatory damages which would have been concerned purely with the claimant's loss.

Bowen LJ explained the approach to restitution following rescission as follows:

> '[There must be] the giving back by the party who makes the misrepresentation of the advantages he obtained by the contract. Now those advantages may be of two kinds. He may get an advantage in the shape of an actual benefit, as when he receives money: he may also get an advantage if the party with whom he contracts assumed some burden in consideration of the contract. In such a case, it seems to me, that complete rescission would not be effective unless the misrepresenting party not only hands back the benefits which he has himself received – but also re-assumes the burden which under the contract the injured person has taken upon himself.'[8]

---

6   (1881) 20 Ch D 1. See also, eg, *Lindsay Petroleum Co v Hurd* (1874) LR 5 PC 221.

7   (1886) 34 Ch D 582. An appeal to the House of Lords, *Adam v Newbigging* (1888) 13 App Cas 308, was dismissed albeit that there was some variation of the order made at first instance to reflect concessions made by the claimant. In particular, the payment of the £324 by the claimant to discharge liabilities of the partnership was no longer in dispute; and there was no need for their Lordships to consider the validity of the general indemnity ordered because it was accepted by the claimant that the firm had no outstanding general liabilities.

8   Ibid at p 594.

And later he stressed that there should be 'a giving back and a taking back on both sides'.[9]

There may have been a difference of opinion between Bowen LJ and Cotton LJ as to the scope of an indemnity. For while Bowen LJ emphasised that the claimant must have contracted to discharge the partnership's debts it is possible to interpret Cotton LJ as saying that it was sufficient that the claimant had discharged, or would discharge, those debts as a result of the contract. If there was that difference (and the third judge, Fry LJ, thought so) Bowen LJ's narrow view seems more in line with the nature of rescission which is concerned to wipe away contractual obligations.

In *Whittington v Seale-Hayne*[10] the claimant was induced to take a lease of a farm by the defendant's non-fraudulent misrepresentation that the premises were in a thoroughly sanitary condition. The claimant had been using the premises for his poultry-breeding business and as a consequence of the water supply being poisoned his manager became seriously ill and the poultry either died or became valueless for breeding. The claimant was granted rescission of the lease including repayment of the rent paid. Additionally he was given an indemnity for the rates paid and the repairs that had been carried out in conformity with a local authority order. Those were expenses which the defendant would himself have legally had to incur had the contract not been made and the payment of them was therefore of benefit to the defendant. Farwell J expressed preference for Bowen LJ's view in *Newbigging v Adam*: on that view, it was crucial that the claimant had been legally obliged to incur those expenses by a covenant in the lease. In contrast the claimant could not recover for the loss of the poultry and for the consequent loss of profit and costs, nor for removal and medical expenses. Those were losses to the claimant without any corresponding benefit to the defendant and therefore could only have been recovered had there been a possible tort claim for compensatory damages.

The well-known case of *Car and Universal Finance Co Ltd v Caldwell*[11] provides a good example of rescission effecting proprietary restitution. That is, the rescission revested in the defendant (Caldwell) the proprietary rights to a Jaguar car that had been transferred to a fraudster (Norris) and thence to the claimant. In interpleader proceedings to determine whether the claimant or the defendant owned the car, the central question at issue was whether the defendant had validly rescinded the contract, by informing the police and the Automobile

9   Ibid at p 595.
10   (1900) 82 LT 49.
11   [1965] 1 QB 525.

Association of the fraud, before the car had been acquired by the claimant who was a bona fide purchaser for value without notice. The Court of Appeal held that there had been a valid rescission so that the car belonged to the defendant. The proprietary effect of the rescission was particularly clearly summarised by Lord Denning MR, sitting at first instance. He said:

'[W]here a seller of goods has a right to avoid a contract for fraud, he sufficiently exercises his election if he at once, on discovering the fraud, takes all possible steps to regain the goods even though he cannot find the rogue or communicate with him. That is what Caldwell did here by going to the police and asking them to get back the car. I, therefore, hold that on January 13 the contract of sale to these rogues was avoided and Caldwell then became the owner of the car again. It was only after he avoided it (so that it was once again his property), that these rogues purported to sell it to Motobella and Motobella purported to sell it to G & C Finance. Those sales were ineffective to pass the property because it had already been revested in Caldwell.'[12]

The equally well-known case of *Barclays Bank plc v O'Brien*,[13] which is a leading authority on rescission for the misrepresentation (or undue influence) of a third party that induces the claimant to enter into a contract with the defendant, also illustrates proprietary restitution. Here the proprietary restitution constituted the removal of a charge in favour of the defendant bank (securing a loan to the claimant husband's company) over the claimant's matrimonial home (ie title, unencumbered by that charge, was re-vested in the claimant). The claimant had been induced to enter into the guarantee with the bank, secured by a charge over the house, by her husband's misrepresentation that the charge was limited to £60,000 and that its duration was short. The defendant bank was held to have had constructive notice of that misrepresentation.

The misrepresentation cases are consistent with the approach to restitution in the simple mistaken payment cases considered in the first main section of this chapter. A factual misrepresentation inducing a contract means that the payment made by the misrepresentee falls under not only the causation test but also the traditional supposed liability test. And as regards the link between the mistake and the benefit conferred, the misrepresentation case of *Edgington v Fitzmaurice*[14] was relied on in chapter 1 in arguing that, while a 'but for' test provable by the claimant is the basic causation test, in cases

---

12 [1965] 1 QB 525, 532.
13 [1994] 1 AC 180. See below p 249.
14 (1885) 29 Ch D 459.

involving highly reprehensible conduct, such as fraudulent misrepresentation, the burden of proof is reversed.

(b) Bars to rescission

There is a good deal of case law on bars to rescission for misrepresentation. As usual there are four such bars:[15] *restitutio in integrum* being impossible, affirmation, lapse of time,[16] and third party rights.[17] The last two of these link in to the general restitutionary defences of, respectively, limitation and bona fide purchase and are discussed in chapter 15.

To establish affirmation, it appears that the misrepresentor must prove two essential elements. First, that the claimant knew that the representation was false.[18] And, secondly, that by his words or conduct the claimant showed unequivocally, but not necessarily by communication to the misrepresentor,[19] that he had decided not to exercise his right of rescission.[20] So, most obviously, a person who is induced by misrepresentation to buy goods cannot rescind if, after discovering the truth, he uses them.[1] Lapse of time can be evidence of affirmation.[2]

Some doubt was cast on these requirements by the Court of Appeal in *Peyman v Lanjani*.[3] It was there held that, at least for 'rescission' for breach of a contract, affirmation requires that the claimant knows of his *legal right* to rescind unless his conduct has caused prejudice to the defendant. One of the judges, Stephenson LJ, suggested that the same approach applies to affirmation in respect of rescission for fraudulent misrepresentation.[4] This controversial suggestion does not appear to have been the subject of subsequent judicial comment and commentators disagree in the importance they attach to it.[5] Whatever its attraction in principle, the suggestion does fall foul of the usual judicial refusal to afford significance to a party's ignorance of the law.[6]

---

15 See generally Treitel, *The Law of Contract* (10th edn, 1999), pp 350–357.
16 Eg, *Lindsay Petroleum Co v Hurd* (1874) LR 5 PC 221; *Leaf v International Galleries* [1950] 2 KB 86.
17 Eg, *Cundy v Lindsay* (1878) 3 App Cas 459, 463–464.
18 *Car and Universal Finance Co Ltd v Caldwell* [1965] 1 QB 525, 550.
19 Ibid.
20 *Clough v London and North Western Rly Co* (1871) LR 7 Exch 26, 34.
1 Eg, *United Shoe Machinery Co of Canada v Brunet* [1909] AC 330.
2 *Clough v London and North Western Rly Co* (1871) LR 7 Exch 26, 35.
3 [1985] Ch 457.
4 Ibid at p 489.
5 Contrast the approach of Treitel, *The Law of Contract* (10th edn, 1999) who does not discuss the decision in his misrepresentation chapter (chapter 9), with Cartwright, *Unequal Bargaining* (1991) at pp 95–96.
6 It seems unlikely that this has been altered by *Kleinwort Benson Ltd v Lincoln City Council* [1999] 2 AC 349.

From a restitutionary perspective the bar of *restitutio in integrum* being impossible is particularly interesting and important. What is primarily in mind is that for the claimant to be allowed rescission and consequent restitution, the claimant must himself be able to restore any benefits transferred by the defendant under the contract.[7] The importance of recognising that counter-restitution is that, without it, the claimant would end up unjustly enriched at the defendant's expense. As Lord Wright said in *Spence v Crawford*,[8] in which the claimant misrepresentee was held able to rescind a contract for the sale of shares on repayment of the purchase price received (plus an agreed sum of compensation):

> '... if a plaintiff who has been defrauded seeks to have the contract annulled and his money or property returned to him, it would be inequitable if he did not also restore what he had got under the contract from the defendant. Though the defendant has been fraudulent, he must not be robbed, nor must the plaintiff be unjustly enriched, as he would be if he both got back what he had parted with and kept what he had received in return.'

The unjust factor triggering counter-restitution is most obviously a total failure of consideration in the sense that the effect of the claimant's rescission and consequent restitution would be to remove the claimant's promised performance which was the defendant's basis for rendering the benefit to the claimant.

What is more difficult to rationalise is why recognition of the need for counter-restitution should have been transformed into a bar. It is, strictly speaking, a nonsense to talk of restitution being impossible given that, assuming solvency, it is always possible for the claimant to pay the defendant a sum of money for the value of the benefit received.

The case law shows that the bar has been successfully invoked where the claimant has consumed or disposed of property received.[9] That is, the bar applies where the counter-restitution involves valuing non-money benefits. This suggests that the explanation for the bar is that, where valuing the claimant's non-money benefits would be required, so that precision is impossible, the courts prefer to abide by the rough-and-ready justice of leaving matters as they stand and hence deny rescission. On this explanation the bar can be regarded as consistent with the insistence that a failure of consideration must be *total* before money can be recovered.[10] In principle neither restriction seems

---

7   Above, p 58; below, pp 538–542.
8   [1939] 3 All ER 271, 288–289.
9   Eg *Vigers v Pike* (1842) 8 Cl & Fin 562; *Clarke v Dickson* (1858) EB & E 148; *Ladywell Mining Co v Brookes* (1887) 35 Ch D 400. Cf *Compagnie des Chemin de Fer Paris-Orleans v Leeston Shipping Co Ltd* (1919) 36 TLR 68, 69: substantial use of a ship did not bar rescission.
10   Below, chapter 10.

necessary or desirable. The courts should not favour rough-and-ready justice over the finely tuned justice attainable by valuing non-money benefits.[11]

Indeed, in the leading case of *Erlanger v New Sombrero Phosphate Co*[12] (a non-disclosure case) the House of Lords watered down the bar by rejecting the need for there to be precise counter-restitution and supporting a more flexible approach whereby benefits in kind may be valued to some extent. A company had bought and worked a phosphate mine. It was held entitled to rescind for non-disclosure on the terms of returning the mine and accounting for the profits of working it. Lord Blackburn said, '... the practice has always been for a court of equity to give relief whenever, by the use of its powers, it can do what is practically just, though it cannot restore the parties precisely to the state they were in before the contract'.[13]

Despite that lead over a century ago, the courts cannot yet be said to have abandoned the bar.[14] It is submitted that they should do so. All that should be required is counter-restitution by a monetary equivalent. This is strongly supported (outside the mistake context) by the undue influence case of *O'Sullivan v Management Agency and Music Ltd*.[15]

It is important to stress that the bar is generally not concerned merely with avoiding detriment to the misrepresentor. So a decline or deterioration in value of property (not connected with value taken from it by the claimant) generally does not bar rescission. For example, in *Armstrong v Jackson*[16] a broker purported to buy shares for his client but in fact sold the client his own shares. Nearly six years later, when the shares had fallen in value from nearly £3 to 5s, the client was held able to rescind, thereby recovering the purchase money paid and returning to the broker the shares plus dividends received. Similarly in *MacKenzie v Royal Bank of Canada*[17] a wife was induced by a misrepresentation by the defendant bank to deposit share certificates with the bank as security for a loan to her husband's company. She was held entitled to rescind the contract and to recover the share certificates, subject to paying back the dividends received. The fact

---

11 Non-valuation also contrasts glaringly with the approach to, eg, the remedy of delivery up of goods for the tort of conversion where damages are generally considered adequate.

12 (1878) 3 App Cas 1218.

13 Ibid at p 1278.

14 There are suggestions in *Spence v Crawford* [1939] 3 All ER 271, 280–282, 288 that greater flexibility may be shown where the misrepresentation is fraudulent rather than innocent.

15 [1985] QB 428. Below, pp 245–246. See also dicta of Lord Goff in *Guinness plc v Saunders* [1990] 2 AC 663, 697–698 (non-disclosure); and of Lord Browne-Wilkinson in *Smith New Court Securities Ltd v Scrimgeour Vickers (Asset) Management Ltd* [1997] AC 254, 262 (fraudulent misrepresentation).

16 [1917] 2 KB 822.

17 [1934] AC 468.

that the bank had advanced money on the faith of the security was not a bar. As Treitel writes, 'It is sometimes said that the object of rescission is to restore the parties to the situation in which they would have been if the contract had never been made, but in the light of *MacKenzie's* case such statements are not quite accurate. The essential point is that the representee should not be unjustly enriched at the representor's expense; that the representor should not be prejudiced is a secondary consideration.'[18]

However, there may be exceptional situations in which the bar can only be explained as concerned to prevent loss to the defendant. The most obvious are where the misrepresentee has detrimentally changed the condition of the property received.[19] Say, for example, the claimant has crashed a car bought in reliance on the defendant's misrepresentation. The concern behind the insistence that *restitutio in integrum* is possible may be not so much that the claimant would be unjustly enriched if he kept the car and recovered the purchase price but rather that the misrepresentor's recovery of the car in return for repaying the purchase price would leave him worse off than if no contract had been made. This is supported by Lord Blackburn's recognition in the *Erlanger* case[20] that rescission may be accompanied not only by an award of an account of profits but also by an allowance for deterioration. Given this power to award equitable compensation there is again no need (viewed now from a loss perspective) to bar rescission on the grounds of *restitutio in integrum* being impossible: as with the reversal of benefits, so with loss, monetary remedies can produce finely tuned justice.

It is important to add that the concern with the misrepresentor's loss may now be best rationalised as recognising a change of position defence.[1] That defence was not authoritatively accepted in English law until *Lipkin Gorman v Karpnale Ltd.*[2] However, some of the rescission cases which have been concerned with the misrepresentor's loss may be best understood as recognising the same idea. Moreover, in a case like *MacKenzie*, one must now consider whether the change of position defence would make a difference. To invoke change of position, the defendant must have acted in good faith so that this would not assist a

<hr>

18 Treitel, *The Law of Contract* (10th edn, 1999) at p 352.
19 Ibid, pp 350–351.
20 (1878) 3 App Cas 1218, 1278–1279. See also *Lagunas Nitrate Co v Lagunas Syndicate* [1899] 2 Ch 392, 456. In *Spence v Crawford* [1939] 3 All ER 271 compensation, for stock sold at a loss by the misrepresentor as a result of the contract, was agreed between the parties.
1   See also below, pp 246–247 (undue influence). To the extent that the concern with loss cannot be rationalised in terms of the change of position defence, the law is operating outside a restitutionary framework. Cf the arguments concerning 'loss apportionment' and 'unjust sacrifice' in respect of frustrated and anticipated contracts in chapter 10.
2   [1991] 2 AC 548. See below, ch 15.

fraudulent misrepresentor. But in the *MacKenzie* case the bank's misrepresentation was non-fraudulent and, on the face of it, it would therefore now be able to invoke its change of position, constituted by the loan paid to the company, as a partial or total defence to the wife's claim to recover the share certificates.

An unconventional use was made of the *restitutio in integrum* bar in the Scottish case of *Boyd and Forest v Glasgow and South West Railway*.[3] The claimant building contractors had been induced to enter into a contract to build a railway by alleged misrepresentations as to the strata. After the railway had been built, they sought to rescind the contract in an attempt to recover a *quantum meruit* higher than the contract price. This was rejected, inter alia, on the ground that a misrepresentee cannot rescind to recover the value of services rendered because *restitutio in integrum* is impossible. This is the reverse of the normal situation where the bar operates to prevent the restitution of money because of services received. Nevertheless, if the explanation for the bar is the courts' reluctance to value benefits in kind, the reasoning is consistent with the usual application of the bar. This is not to say that it is justified. Contrary to *Boyd* a misrepresentee should be able to rescind a contract and gain restitution of the value of benefits in kind. But on the facts of the case, where the alleged misrepresentations were innocent, the claimant could probably only have established that the defendant was benefited by the 'bargained-for' test so that a *quantum meruit* ought, in any event, to have been limited by the contract price.[4]

Apart from the usual four bars, rescission for non-fraudulent misrepresentation may be denied by the courts exercising their discretion under s 2(2) of the Misrepresentation Act 1967 to award damages in lieu of rescission.[5] In exercising that discretion – which, as clarified in *Government of Zanzibar v British Aerospace (Lancaster House) Ltd*,[6] is dependent on rescission otherwise being available and not being barred by one of the four standard bars – the closing words of the subsection require the courts to consider the nature of the misrepresentation, the loss to the misrepresentee, and the loss that rescission would cause to the misrepresentor. The purpose of the

3   1915 SC (HL) 20.
4   Below, p 346.
5   See generally, Treitel, *The Law of Contract* (10th edn, 1999), pp 330, 339, 350; Cartwright, *Unequal Bargaining* (1991), pp 99–101; *Atlantic Lines and Navigation Co Inc v Hallam Ltd, The Lucy* [1983] 1 Lloyd's Rep 188, 201–202; *Highlands Insurance Co v Continental Insurance Co* [1987] 1 Lloyd's Rep 109n, 117–118.
6   [2000] 1 WLR 2333 rejecting Jacob J's obiter dicta in *Thomas Witter Ltd v TBP Industries* [1996] 2 All ER 573 that damages in lieu of rescission could be awarded even though rescission was barred because *restitutio in integrum* was not possible. This rejection is correct because the purpose of s 2(2) is not to add to the misrepresentee's remedies.

subsection is to give the courts a discretion to cut back the misrepresentee's remedy of rescission where the misrepresentation has been trivial and rescission would cause undue hardship to the misrepresentor. The measure of damages under s 2(2) is presumably compensatory and concerned to protect, even if only partially, the misrepresentee's reliance loss.[7] It would be irrational to award a more favourable measure of damages than is given for the torts of deceit or negligent misrepresentation or under s 2(1) of the Act.

(3) Non-disclosure

Where a defendant has failed in a duty to disclose material facts to the claimant prior to the conclusion of a contract (eg where the contract is one of insurance or is made between a fiduciary and his beneficiary)[8] the claimant is entitled to rescind the contract and recover benefits conferred under it, subject to the usual four bars of lapse of time, affirmation, third party rights, and *restitutio in integrum* being impossible.[9]

An example of restitutionary rescission is provided by *Cornhill Insurance Co Ltd v L & B Assenheim.*[10] An insurer was held able to rescind a contract of insurance for non-disclosure and to recover money paid out on claims subject to giving counter-restitution of premiums.[11] MacKinnon J said, 'Avoidance of the policy, of course, results in it being set aside *ab initio*, the repayment of any losses, and the return of any premiums paid under it ...'[12] And in *Sybron Corpn v Rochem Ltd*,[13] where the claimants had entered into a contract whereby their defendant employee had taken early retirement in return for, inter alia, a payment of £13,000, it was held that the claimants were able to rescind the contract and recover the £13,000 because of the

---

7   Cf *William Sindall plc v Cambridgeshire County Council* [1994] 1 WLR 1016.

8   For details see, eg, Treitel, *The Law of Contract* (10th edn, 1999), pp 361–372.

9   The leading case on the last bar, *Erlanger v New Sombrero Phosphate Co* (1878) 3 App Cas 1218, as discussed in the previous sub-section, was a non-disclosure case. See also above, p 177, n 15.

10 (1937) 58 Ll L Rep 27. Where the insured rescinds for the insurer's non-disclosure, he is entitled to recover the premiums: see dicta of Lord Templeman in *Banque Financiere de la Cite SA v Westgate Insurance Co Ltd* [1991] 2 AC 249, 280. For an example of restitutionary rescission where a beneficiary rescinds for a fiduciary's non-disclosure, see the interesting Australian case of *Maguire v Makaronis* (1997) 188 CLR 449, noted by Moriarty, 'Fiduciaries and Discretion' (1998) 114 LQR 9.

11 The unjust factor triggering the counter-restitution is most obviously failure of consideration. This is statutorily embodied in s 84(3)(a) of the Marine Insurance Act 1906. See also *Anderson v Thornton* (1853) 8 Exch 425; MacGillivray and Parkington, *Insurance Law* (9th edn, 1997), para 17-29.

12 (1937) 58 Ll L Rep 27, 31.

13 [1984] Ch 112.

defendant's failure to disclose the fraudulent misconduct of his subordinate employees. As with misrepresentation, the restitution in these cases is consistent with not only the causation test but also the traditional supposed liability test for simple mistaken payments considered in the first main section of this chapter.

Chapter 4

Ignorance

1. THE ARGUMENT FOR RECOGNISING IGNORANCE

The courts have never expressly recognised ignorance as a ground for restitution. However, it is the best explanation of numerous decisions.[1] To deny it is to reject illogically the simple point that ignorance is analogous to mistake.

Take the following four examples:

(i) C pays D £100 by a mistake of fact.
(ii) C's computer, because of a malfunction, pays D, without C's knowledge, £100 twice over.
(iii) C loses £100 which is picked up by D.
(iv) D steals £100 from C without C's knowledge.

As the law is willing to give a personal restitutionary remedy in the first example it must be willing to do so in the second, third and fourth examples, where C does not make a mistake. In each C does not mean D to have the £100: consent is vitiated or absent. And in each it is clear that D's gain is at the expense of C in the subtractive sense.

There have been very few cases on ignorance involving just two parties. The great practical importance of recognising ignorance is revealed if one modifies the fourth example by saying that it is X who steals £100 from C without his knowledge and passes that £100 to D. This is the three party scenario that has featured so prominently in the case law and literature.

In principle the unjust factor should not change just because the benefit has been conferred by a third party rather than by the claimant. There are, however, two difficulties in bringing a claim against an *indirect recipient* (ie, against someone who has received the benefit from

---

1 See Birks at pp 140–146; Birks, 'Misdirected Funds: Restitution from the Recipient' [1989] LMCLQ 296; Birks, 'The English Recognition of Unjust Enrichment' [1991] LMCLQ 473; Birks, 'Trusts in the Recovery of Misapplied Assets: Tracing, Trusts and Restitution' in *Commercial Aspects of Trusts and Fiduciary Obligations* (ed McKendrick, 1992), pp 149, esp 159–161. See also below, p 202, n 13.

a third party rather than from the claimant) that do not arise in a standard two party case.[2]

First, as the benefit has been rendered by a third party, the claimant encounters the difficulty of showing that the defendant's gain was at his expense rather than at the third party's expense. This has been discussed in chapter 1. Of the exceptions to the general rule that only a direct provider of a benefit is entitled to restitution the obvious one in play in most three party ignorance cases is 'title and tracing'. To establish this exception, the claimant must show, through title and tracing rules, that the property transferred by the third party to the defendant was the claimant's legal or equitable property or its substitute.[3] If so the defendant's gain was at the claimant's expense.

Secondly, an indirect recipient often has a defence to a restitutionary claim if he is a bona fide purchaser for value without notice. Viewed from a restitutionary perspective, the idea behind this defence, as explained in chapter 15, is that the courts are not prepared to unwind a contract to which the claimant is not a party where the indirect recipient had no notice of the claimant's restitutionary rights to the benefit transferred under the contract. The bona fide purchase defence is consistent with the courts' greater reluctance in two party cases, as shown in the sphere of mistake,[4] to unwind contracts than simply to allow restitution of non-contractual benefits rendered.

In principle, therefore, the correct analysis where money is stolen by X from C without his knowledge and paid by X to D is that the unjust factor is C's ignorance and that, subject to general defences, C has a personal restitutionary claim against D provided two conditions are satisfied: first, that C can establish through title and tracing rules that D's gain is at C's expense; and, secondly, that D is not a bona fide purchaser for value without notice.

The same position would apply if C mistakenly paid £100 to X which X then transferred to D. C would only be entitled to restitution of £100 from D (whether one views the unjust factor as mistake or ignorance) if he could establish, by title and tracing rules, that D's gain was at C's expense and that D was not a bona fide purchaser for value without notice.

---

2   Some commentators suggest that the differences between the claims against direct and indirect recipients are so fundamental that the latter, unlike the former, should be viewed as based on vindication of proprietary rights not reversing unjust enrichment: see, eg, Virgo, *The Principles of the Law of Restitution* (1999), pp 6–17, 108; Lionel Smith, 'Restitution: The Heart of Corrective Justice' (2001) 79 Texas LR 2115, 2155–2175. A major difficulty for that approach is in explaining why the change of position defence was applied in *Lipkin Gorman v Karpnale Ltd* [1991] 2 AC 548.

3   Above, pp 34–35. See also the 'important linked point' made above at p 79.

4   Above, p 143.

The courts have not analysed the three party cases in this way. If one focuses on the main situation of a third party transferring the claimant's property to the defendant, they have tended to regard the unjust factor, at least in the common law cases, as being the defendant's interference with the claimant's ownership. In other words, in line with Stoljar's proprietary theory of restitution,[5] they appear to have considered the injustice as being that, without the claimant's consent, the defendant received property that at the time of receipt belonged to the claimant.

Although there may be no major practical significance in viewing the unjust factor as ignorance rather than interference with ownership there are several reasons for preferring the former.[6]

(i) Ignorance clearly belongs to the same series as the well-recognised unjust factors triggering personal restitution, such as mistake, duress and failure of consideration. Interference with ownership is a different animal in that it does not identify facts relevant to the claimant's reasoning process.

(ii) Logic necessitates that if one is willing to recognise an unjust factor of mistake one must be willing to recognise ignorance.

(iii) To recognise interference with ownership means that in principle one ought to back-track over the ground covered by the standard unjust factors so as to recognise an alternative restitutionary claim wherever title in the property transferred did not pass to the defendant. For example, if C pays D £100 by a fundamental mistake of fact, one would need to recognise two unjust factors triggering an action for money had and received: mistake and receipt of property that, at the time of receipt, belonged to the claimant.

(iv) In practice there is no indication that the courts have reasoned in terms of interference with ownership in standard two party personal restitution cases, such as those dealing with mistake or duress. And in other cases interference with ownership clearly cannot have any relevance. For example, title to money passes to the defendant despite a total failure of consideration: and restitution for services rendered plainly cannot rest on the claimant owning the benefit when received by the defendant.

(v) Where tracing into substitute property is involved in establishing that D's gain was at C's expense, it is misleading to say that D received substitute property that, at the time of receipt, legally belonged to the claimant. On the better view, tracing does not involve the continuation

---

5   Above, p 9.

6   See also McKendrick 'Restitution, Misdirected Funds and Change of Position' (1992) 55 MLR 377, 380–382. The contrary view is taken by, eg, Virgo, *The Principles of the Law of Restitution* (1999), pp 11, 14, 601, 656, as part of his wider argument that vindication of proprietary rights not reversing unjust enrichment is here in play: see above, p 183, n 2.

of pre-existing proprietary rights into substitute property.[7] Rather personal restitution is given in respect of the substitute property to reverse the defendant's unjust enrichment. The fact that the defendant has good legal title to the substitute property does not undermine the claim that the defendant is unjustly enriched by that substitute property. It must be the case, therefore, that the unjust factor here is something other than interference with (legal) ownership.

One minor problem with ignorance is that it does not itself sweep up all situations of personal restitution that are left outside the well-established unjust factors. Interference with ownership, with its stress on the owner not having consented, has the merit of indicating that, even if the claimant knows that his property is being transferred, he is entitled to personal restitution where he does not consent. However, there does not appear to have been any clear example, in the reported cases, of known non-consensual enrichment falling outside the well-established unjust factors like mistake and duress. And in principle, as Birks has stressed,[8] the way to deal with this is to recognise that, alongside ignorance, 'powerlessness' is a further unjust factor.[9] It is on this ground that the claimant who is, for example, too terrified to stop the defendant stealing his money would be entitled to restitution in unjust enrichment by subtraction.

Having put the argument for recognising ignorance as a ground for restitution the rest of this chapter is devoted to an examination of the relevant case law. This is divided into first, two party cases; secondly, and most importantly, the standard three party cases where a third party transfers the claimant's property or its traceable substitute to the defendant; and, thirdly, other three party cases.

Although in the great majority of the cases the benefit in question has comprised money, ignorance can also ground restitution for benefits in kind provided the usual tests for overcoming subjective devaluation are satisfied; as, eg, where a chattel has been reprehensibly sought out or is reasonably certain to be sold or has been sold.[10]

2. TWO PARTY CASES

There is very little authority on personal restitutionary claims in unjust enrichment by subtraction against the direct recipient of a benefit

---

7   See above, p 81.
8   Birks at p 174.
9   Ignorance and powerlessness may not entirely cover the residual examples of 'lack of consent'. A possible example is the claimant who knows of his loss and has the power to prevent it but is too busy or lazy to do so.
10 See, eg, *Re Montagu's Settlement Trusts* [1987] Ch 264: below, pp 197–198.

that has been received, or taken, from the claimant without his knowledge. The explanation is that a claimant in this situation will normally choose to sue for a wrong seeking compensation or, less commonly, restitution for the wrong: ie he will normally sue for the tort of conversion or trespass to goods or land or the equitable wrong of breach of fiduciary duty.

Two rare apparent examples of unjust enrichment by subtraction are *Holiday v Sigil*[11] and *Neate v Harding*.[12] In the former, the defendant found a £500 note that had been dropped and lost by the claimant. He was held liable for £500 in an action for money had and received. In the latter the defendants stole the claimant's money from his mother's house. The claimant successfully brought an action for money had and received.

In each case the claimant's ignorance of his loss is the best explanation of the unjust factor: and it is clear that the defendant's gain was at the claimant's expense in the subtractive sense.

3. STANDARD THREE PARTY CASES: X TRANSFERS C'S PROPERTY, OR ITS SUBSTITUTE, TO D

There have been many cases of this type, especially in equity. For the purposes of exposition it is helpful to distinguish the common law and equity cases for a unique feature of the equitable restitutionary regime is that the defendant – the indirect recipient – has only been held personally liable if he had knowledge (the level of relevant knowledge being a matter of intense controversy) that the property he received was transferred to him without the knowledge (or otherwise without the authority) of the equitable owner. And given this emphasis on the defendant's knowledge for equitable liability there has been no scope left in equity, as opposed to at common law (where the liability is strict), for the application of the bona fide purchase defence. The restitutionary remedies awarded at common law and equity also differ. At common law the relevant remedy is the award of money had and received whereas the appropriate personal equitable remedy is accounting for money (or the value of other property) received.

Of course an owner commonly consents to a trustee or agent dealing with his property without requiring to be informed of specific transactions. However the claimant clearly cannot be taken to have consented to a transferring away of his property in breach of a trustee's

11 (1826) 2 C & P 176.
12 (1851) 6 Exch 349.

or agent's duty. It is for this reason that ignorance as an unjust factor often constitutes the reverse side of the coin from a breach of duty by the third party.

This leads on to a further point of some importance. Although it is believed that the three party cases involving X transferring C's property to D are nearly all susceptible to an ignorance analysis, there is arguably a difficulty in deciding whether ignorance or powerlessness is truly in issue. This is particularly so where directors of a company act in breach of fiduciary duty in transferring the company's property, where the root of the problem stems from the difficulty of distinguishing a company's knowledge from that of its directors.[13] In line with the judicial language often used one may prefer, therefore, at some sacrifice to precision, to describe the ground for restitution as being that the claimant's property has been transferred away *without authority*.

(1) Common law

The reasoning in the common law cases has tended to focus on the idea that money received by the defendant belonged, at the time of receipt, to the claimant: ie 'interference with ownership'. However, all the decisions are equally consistent with the unjust factor being the claimant's ignorance (with the title and tracing reasoning going to establish that the indirect recipient's gain was at the claimant's expense) and, for the reasons explored earlier, this is a preferable approach.

Eight main cases merit close examination.[14]

In *Clarke v Shee and Johnson*[15] the claimant's clerk received money (and negotiable notes) from the claimant's customers in the ordinary course of the claimant's trade as a brewer. The clerk, without the claimant's knowledge, used £460 from the money received to buy lottery tickets from the defendants. Lotteries were illegal so that the defendants gave no valid consideration for the money. The claimant was held able to recover that money from the defendants in an action for money had and received. Lord Mansfield said:

> '...the plaintiff does not sue as standing in the place of Wood his clerk: for the money and notes which Wood paid to the defendants are the identical notes and

---

13 For a general consideration of this issue see, eg, *El Ajou v Dollar Land Holdings plc* [1994] 2 All ER 685; *Meridian Global Funds Management Asia Ltd v Securities Commission* [1995] 2 AC 500; *Trustor AB v Smallbone (No 2)* [2001] 1 WLR 1177.

14 Apart from the cases considered below, see those additionally mentioned in Goff and Jones at para 2-026, note 44. See also *Moffatt v Kazana* [1969] 2 QB 152 where the actual remedy was not clarified. See generally, Fox, 'Legal Title as a Ground of Restitutionary Liability' [2000] RLR 465.

15 (1774) 1 Cowp 197.

money of the plaintiff. Where money or notes are paid bona fide, and upon a valuable consideration, they never shall be brought back by the true owner: but where they come mala fide into a person's hands, they are in the nature of specific property; and if their identity can be traced and ascertained, the party has a right to recover ... Here the plaintiff sues for his identified property, which has come to the hands of the defendant iniquitously and illegally, in breach of the Act of Parliament ... and consequently the plaintiff is well entitled to recover.'[16]

In *Marsh v Keating*[17] a partner in the defendant firm fraudulently drew up a power of attorney by which, without her knowledge, the claimant's stock (standing to her credit in the Bank of England) was sold and the proceeds of sale paid to the defendants. The opinion of the judges, on a request by the House of Lords, was that the claimant was entitled to restitution from the defendants in an action for money had and received. Park J, giving the judges' opinion, formulated the central question at issue, to which an affirmative answer was given, as follows: '... is [the plaintiff] at liberty to abandon all further concern with her stock and to consider the price which was paid by the purchaser for that which was her stock to be her money and to follow it into the hands of the present defendants ...?'[18]

Calland v Loyd[19] shows the same 'interference with ownership' reasoning. The claimant gave some money to his wife to keep safe. Without his knowledge she paid £50 of it into the defendant bank in the name of her infant son. The claimant was held entitled to recover the £50 from the defendant bank as money had and received. Lord Abinger CB said, 'The question is whether the bankers, when the claimant has given them notice that it is his money, have a right to set up the *ius tertii*: it is admitted that the money is the claimant's and the defendants are merely setting up an unlawful title in answer.'[20]

The facts of *Banque Belge pour l'Etranger v Hambrouck*[1] were considered in chapter 2. We saw there that the claimant bank was held able to trace its money through the bank account of the fraudster, Hambrouck, and into the £315 in the bank account of Mlle Spanoghe. The remedy given against Mlle Spanoghe was restitution of £315 in an action for money had and received. This is perfectly explicable on the ground that the money received by Mlle Spanoghe from

16 Ibid at pp 199–201. The last sentence was not intended to indicate that the defendant retained the money. The remedy in issue was personal not proprietary.
17 (1834) 1 Bing NC 198.
18 Ibid at p 215. Peculiarly, in that the common law approach has conventionally imposed strict liability, Park J, at p 220, seemed to regard it as important that the defendants were negligent.
19 (1840) 6 M & W 26.
20 Ibid at p 31.
1   [1921] 1 KB 321. Above, pp 85–87.

Hambrouck traceably belonged to the claimant bank so that her gain was at the claimant's expense. The unjust factor may be regarded as either mistake, in that the claimant was factually mistaken in paying out money to Hambrouck, or ignorance in that it did not know that its traceable money was being paid to Mlle Spanoghe. A difficulty is that the remedy was limited to the lower amount retained in the defendant's account rather than the higher amount received by her. Prima facie as the claim was for personal restitution she should have been liable for the higher amount received. But as the claimant only ever sought restitution of £315 it is understandable that there was no discussion in the judgments of its prima facie entitlement to a higher amount. After *Lipkin Gorman v Karpnale Ltd*[2] it could be argued that, in any event, and assuming she did not know of the fraud, the defence of change of position meant that the claimant was not entitled to more than £315; that is, the claimant's prima facie entitlement to the higher amount was overridden by Mlle Spanoghe's good faith detrimental reliance – to the extent represented by the money spent – on the money being hers.

Also of great interest is Denning J's judgment in *Nelson v Larholt*.[3] Although glossing over significant differences between the common law and equitable approaches in this area the judgment is visionary in its attempt to articulate a fused underlying principle. An executor had fraudulently drawn cheques, on the estate's account (without the knowledge of the deceased's beneficiaries), in favour of his turf accountant (the defendant). An action by the beneficiaries against the defendant to recover the money either in equity or as money had and received succeeded. In typically clear and forthright language Denning J said:

'A man's money is property which is protected by law. It may exist in various forms, such as coins, treasury notes, cash at bank, or cheques, or bills of exchange of which he is "the holder" but, whatever its form, it is protected according to one uniform principle. If it is taken from the rightful owner, or indeed, from the beneficial owner, without his authority, he can recover the amount from any person into whose hands it can be traced, unless and until it reaches one who receives it in good faith and for value and without notice of the want of authority ... This principle has been evolved by the courts of law and equity side by side. In equity it took the form of an action to follow moneys impressed with an express trust or with a constructive trust owing to a fiduciary relationship. In law it took the form of an action for money had and received or damages for conversion of a cheque. It is no longer appropriate, however, to draw a distinction between law

2   [1991] 2 AC 548.
3   [1948] 1 KB 339.

and equity .... The right here is not peculiar to equity or contract or tort but falls
naturally within the important category of cases where the court orders restitution
if the justice of the case so requires.'[4]

More recently in *Agip (Africa) Ltd v Jackson*[5] – the facts of which
were set out in chapter 2 – the Court of Appeal confusingly took the
view that the claim at common law (although, inconsistently, there
was no mention of this in equity) was for mistake of fact. This was
incorrect. Agip, the claimant, had made no mistake. It had simply
been defrauded of its money without its knowledge. And the mistaken
party – Banque du Sud – was not Agip's agent in paying the money to
Baker Oil because the payment instruction was fraudulent so that the
bank was acting without Agip's authority.

The action for money had and received failed on the ground,
examined and criticised in chapter 2, that Agip could not trace into
the money received by the defendants. Although not mentioned in
the Court of Appeal, Millett J at first instance suggested two further
reasons why that action should fail. The first was that the defendants
were agents and had the defence of 'payment over' to their principal.[6]
The second was that, assuming they were not agents, the defendants
were 'subsequent recipients' and the action for money had and
received lies only against 'immediate recipients' (ie, here against Baker
Oil).

With respect, the latter cannot be supported. Contrary to the
general 'direct providers only' rule, a claimant who can establish that
he owned the money traceably transferred to the indirect recipient
can successfully recover. The defendant's gain is regarded as being at
the claimant's expense rather than at the expense of the third party
transferor. Whatever one's views on whether 'direct providers only' is
justified as a general rule, once the 'title and tracing' exception is
made out there is no sense in restricting liability to the first indirect
recipient rather than subsequent indirect recipients. The necessary
link between the claimant and defendant is forged by establishing
that the recipient (wherever in the chain) received property that
traceably belonged to the claimant. Millett J suggested that only *Banque
Belge* was an authority against his proposition. But if that was a
subsequent recipient case so were all those where the fraudulent party
first received the money and then passed it on, such as *Clarke v Shee*,
Calland v Loyd and (subsequent to *Agip*) *Lipkin Gorman v Karpnale Ltd*.
Writing extra-judicially Millett J has since accepted that Mlle Spanoghe

4   Ibid at pp 342–343.
5   [1991] Ch 547. Above, pp 87–89.
6   Below, p 604.

in *Banque Belge* was an immediate and not a subsequent recipient:[7] and he has clarified that, on his scheme, subsequent recipients are those who do not receive from the fraudulent or defrauded party. Admittedly there appears to be no authority allowing an action for money had and received against a subsequent recipient as so defined. Nevertheless the restriction is inconsistent not only with cases imposing personal restitutionary liability in equity (for example, *Belmont Finance Corpn Ltd v Williams Furniture Ltd (No 2)*)[8] but also with the tort of conversion where liability follows the chain of recipients however long. One might try to defend the restriction by the general arguments for the 'direct providers only' rule considered in chapter 1. But that rule is already indisputably breached in this area by allowing restitution, as Millett J accepts, from those who receive from the fraudulent party rather than from the claimant and it is hard to see how one can rationally depart from that rule to that extent only to erect a wider cut-off point.

As regards the leading case of *Lipkin Gorman v Karpnale Ltd,*[9] we have examined the facts – and Lord Goff's approach to tracing into a substitute product – in chapter 2. The actual decision was that the claimant firm of solicitors was entitled by an action for money had and received to restitution of money that 'belonged' to it (in the sense that it could have asserted restitutionary proprietary rights to the money in Cass's hands) at the time when paid by Cass, without its knowledge, to the defendant gaming club, subject to a reduction for the club's change of position.[10] The House of Lords recognised that, as personal restitution was sought here from an indirect recipient, it was necessary to show that the money paid by the third party (Cass) was the claimant's. This is in accordance with the 'title and tracing' exception to the 'direct providers only' rule and goes to whether the gain was at the claimant's expense. However their Lordships appeared to go on to see the unjust factor as itself being that the defendant had received property that, at the time of receipt, belonged to the claimant.

Lord Goff said:

---

7   'Tracing the Proceeds of Fraud' (1991) 107 LQR 71, 77–79.

8   [1980] 1 All ER 393.

9   [1991] 2 AC 548. Above, pp 89–92. See McKendrick, 'Restitution, Misdirected Funds and Change of Position' (1992) 55 MLR 377.

10   In the *Lipkin Gorman* case, there was a separate tort of conversion claim by the solicitors against the club in respect of a banker's draft for £3,735 which Cass had procured to be issued in favour of the solicitors. Despite Cass having legal title to that draft, the solicitors had an immediate right of possession, sufficient to found an action for conversion, because the draft was made payable to them. And the club was not a holder in due course because it provided no valuable consideration for the draft.

'It is to be observed that the present action, like the action in *Clarke v Shee and Johnson*,[11] is concerned with a common law claim to money, where the money in question has not been paid by the appellant directly to the respondents – as is usually the case where money is, for example, recoverable as having been paid under a mistake of fact, or for a consideration which has failed. On the contrary, here the money had been paid to the respondents by a third party, Cass; and in such a case the appellant has to establish a basis on which he is entitled to the money. This (at least, as a general rule) he does by showing that the money is his legal property, as appears from Lord Mansfield's judgment in *Clarke v Shee and Johnson*. If he can do so, he may be entitled to succeed in a claim against the third party for money had and received to his use, though not if the third party has received the money in good faith and for a valuable consideration. The cases in which such a claim has succeeded are, I believe, very rare (see the cases, including *Clarke v Shee and Johnson*, collected in Goff and Jones, *The Law of Restitution* (3rd edn, 1986) p 64, note 29). This is probably because, at common law, property in money, like other fungibles, is lost as such when it is mixed with other money. Furthermore, it appears that in these cases the action for money had and received is not usually founded upon any wrong by the third party, such as conversion; nor is it said to be a case of waiver of tort. It is founded simply on the fact that, as Lord Mansfield said, the third party cannot in conscience retain the money – or, as we say nowadays, for the third party to retain the money would result in his unjust enrichment at the expense of the owner of the money.

So, in the present case, the solicitors seek to show that the money in question was their property at common law. But their claim in the present case for money had and received is nevertheless a personal claim; it is not a proprietary claim, advanced on the basis that money remaining in the hands of the respondents is their property.'[12]

It was also fundamental in the House of Lords' reasoning that the club did not provide consideration for the money paid by Cass. It was therefore not a bona fide purchaser for value without notice so as to have an absolute defence to restitution. Any suggestion that bona fide purchase is merely a sub-category of the general 'change of position' defence[13] was firmly rejected by the House of Lords. Each of the two defences was treated separately and it was held that, while the former was not made out, the latter was (as a partial defence). Had the club provided valuable consideration, and hence been a bona fide

---

11   (1774) 1 Cowp 197.
12   [1991] 2 AC 548, 572. The last sentence clarifies that the remedy sought was personal, responding to the receipt of money, not proprietary responding to the retention of money. Cf Lord Templeman's speech.
13   For this suggestion see Birks, 'The English Recognition of Unjust Enrichment' (1991) LMCLQ 473; Millett, 'Tracing the Proceeds of Fraud' (1991) 107 LQR 71, 82. Birks (1991) LMCLQ 473, 487, note 67, concedes that his earlier attempt to subsume bona fide purchase in 'counter-restitution essential' was flawed.

purchaser *for value*, it is clear that it would have had a full defence and there would have been no point in examining change of position. In Lord Goff's words, 'The defence of change of position is akin to the defence of bona fide purchase: but we cannot simply say that bona fide purchase is a species of change of position.'[14]

Finally, there is the somewhat unusual case of *Trustee of the Property of F C Jones and Sons v Jones*,[15] which we have also examined in chapter 2. The partners in a potato-growing firm became bankrupt. After the act of bankruptcy, one of the partners (FWJ Jones) drew three cheques totalling £11,700 on the partnership account. He paid that money to his wife (Mrs Jones) who used it to trade on the potato futures market, making a profit of £50,760. She paid that profit into a deposit account at Raphaels & Sons plc. Mr FWJ Jones withdrew £900 from the account leaving a balance of £49,860. Raphaels were informed of the trustee in bankruptcy's claim to the money. They interpleaded and paid the money into court. The rival claimants to the £49,860 were the trustee in bankruptcy (the claimant) and Mrs Jones (the defendant). The Court of Appeal upheld the decision in favour of the claimant. That is, the defendant (who was assumed to be an innocent donee) was held personally liable at common law for the £49,860.

The reasoning of the Court of Appeal was that Mrs Jones had no title, whether legal or equitable, to the money. From the date of the bankruptcy the money belonged to the trustee in bankruptcy. The trustee was able to trace at common law the £11,700 to the £49,860. Although this reasoning was therefore in terms of the money belonging to the claimant in the defendant's hands, the facts are consistent with an ignorance analysis. The money had been paid to Mrs Jones without the knowledge or consent of the other partners or the trustee in bankruptcy.

The picture at common law, therefore, is that, subject to defences (especially bona fide purchase) the courts impose strict restitutionary personal liability on indirect recipients of money that belonged to the claimant, not the third party transferor, and was transferred without the claimant's knowledge. Although the judges' reasoning has tended to focus on the money belonging to the claimant in the defendant's hands (ie, 'interference with ownership') the decisions are equally consistent with the preferable view that the unjust factor is ignorance.

---

14 [1991] 2 AC 548, 580. The differences between the two defences are discussed further below, pp 587–588.
15 [1997] Ch 159.

(2) Equity: knowing receipt

(a) Introduction

The unique feature of the restitutionary regime here is that the indirect recipient will only be held personally liable if he had knowledge that the benefit received was being transferred in breach of fiduciary duty (ie, without the knowledge of the equitable owner). In the time-honoured phrase there must be 'intermeddling by knowing receipt and dealing'.[16]

What traditionally contributed to the undoubted difficulty of this area of the law was that it was not seen as part of, or as analogous to other parts of, the law of restitution. Until very recently, despite an increased realisation by the judiciary that, in the words of Lord Nicholls, 'recipient liability is restitution-based ...',[17] Goff and Jones devoted relatively little attention to it.[18] As was said in the first edition of this book, in a sentence approved extra-judicially by Lord Nicholls,[19] 'Nothing is more important for the future rational development of "knowing receipt" than that its role within restitution is fully appreciated and examined by the judiciary'.

Before proceeding any further, it is necessary to clarify that, traditionally, 'knowing receipt' has been linked with a different form of equitable liability which, in short-hand, has been referred to as 'knowing assistance' and more fully 'intermeddling by knowing assistance in a fraudulent and dishonest scheme'. The leading case on this latter form of liability is now *Royal Brunei Airlines Sdn Bhd v Tan*.[20] In a brilliant judgment of the Privy Council, delivered by Lord Nicholls, three main points were laid down. First, contrary to earlier authority,[1] it is not necessary for the scheme assisted to be fraudulent and dishonest. It is sufficient that what is assisted, with the required state of mind, is a breach of fiduciary duty. Secondly, the required state of mind for this form of liability is dishonesty. One is centrally

---

16 See generally Harpum, 'The Stranger as Constructive Trustee' (1986) 102 LQR 267; Gardner, 'Knowing Assistance and Knowing Receipt: Taking Stock' (1996) 112 LQR 56.
17 *Royal Brunei Airlines Sdn Bhd v Tan* [1995] 2 AC 378, 386.
18 Goff and Jones, *The Law of Restitution* (5th edn, 1998), pp 742–746. Cf Goff and Jones (6th edn, 2002), paras 33-027 to 33-033.
19 Lord Nicholls, 'Knowing Receipt: The Need for a New Landmark' in *Restitution, Past, Present and Future* (eds Cornish, Nolan, O'Sullivan and Virgo, 1998), pp 231, 234–235.
20 [1995] 2 AC 378. Although only of persuasive authority, being a decision of the Privy Council, *Tan* was said to be 'the leading authority on knowing assistance' by the Court of Appeal in *BCCI Ltd v Akindele* [2001] Ch 437, 455; and it was approved by the House of Lords in *Twinsectra Ltd v Yardley* [2002] UKHL 12, [2002] 2 AC 164. See generally Mitchell, 'Assistance' in *Breach of Trust* (eds Birks and Pretto, 2002), pp 139–212.
1 *Barnes v Addy* (1874) LR 9 Ch App 244; *Belmont Finance Corp v Williams Furniture Ltd (No 2)* [1980] 1 All ER 393.

concerned with 'accessory liability' for dishonestly assisting a breach of fiduciary duty. Thirdly, the range of conduct extends beyond assistance to include procuring a breach of fiduciary duty.[2]

Prior to the *Tan* case, controversy had raged in the 'knowing assistance' cases, as well as in the 'knowing receipt' cases, as to whether the standard of liability included negligence (ie constructive knowledge) as well as dishonesty. It had become commonplace to refer to this as the question of whether the relevant knowledge encompassed more than the first three points on the scale adopted in *Baden, Delvaux and Lecuit v Société Generale*[3] (a 'knowing assistance' case). Peter Gibson J said:

> '...knowledge can comprise any one of five different mental states ...; (i) actual knowledge; (ii) wilfully shutting one's eyes to the obvious; (iii) wilfully and recklessly failing to make such inquiries as an honest and reasonable man would make; (iv) knowledge of circumstances which would indicate the facts to an honest and reasonable man; (v) knowledge of circumstances which would put an honest and reasonable man on inquiry.'[4]

Tan made it clear beyond doubt that the dishonesty standard was correct for the 'assistance' cases. In so doing Lord Nicholls said that in this context 'the *Baden* scale of knowledge is best forgotten'.[5] In *Twinsectra Ltd v Yardley*[6] the House of Lords clarified (Lord Millett dissenting) that dishonesty involves a subjective and objective element. In Lord Hoffmann's words, there must be 'consciousness that one is transgressing ordinary standards of honest behaviour'.[7] And in Lord Hutton's words, 'dishonesty requires knowledge by the defendant that what he is doing would be regarded as dishonest by honest people'.[8]

By emphasising 'accessory liability', Lord Nicholls in *Tan* also indicated that 'dishonest assistance' is a type of wrong, triggering principally compensation, which is analogous to the economic torts. He said, '[D]ishonesty is a necessary ingredient of accessory liability. It is also a sufficient ingredient. A liability in equity to make good resulting loss attaches to a person who dishonestly procures or assists in a breach of trust or fiduciary obligation.'[9] Within this book, therefore,

---

2   Extra-judicially, Lord Nicholls has referred to the liability as 'dishonest participation' in a breach of fiduciary duty, see Lord Nicholls, 'Knowing Receipt: The Need for a New Landmark' in *Restitution: Past, Present and Future* (eds Cornish, Nolan, O'Sullivan and Virgo, 1998), pp 231, 243.
3   [1983] BCLC 325.
4   Ibid at p 407.
5   [1995] 2 AC 378, 392. But in *BCCI Ltd v Akindele* [2001] Ch 437, 455 Nourse LJ thought that the *Baden* classification was still helpful in 'knowing assistance' cases.
6   [2002] UKHL 12, [2002] 2 AC 164.
7   Ibid at para 20.
8   Ibid at para 36.
9   [1995] 2 AC 378 at 392.

'dishonest assistance' is of relatively little importance. It falls within chapter 14 (restitution for wrongs) and then only to the extent that restitution, rather than the more usual compensatory award, is triggered by that wrong.

Tan did not seek to clarify what the law is in relation to 'knowing receipt'. All that Lord Nicholls said as regards knowing receipt was that different considerations apply to the two heads of liability because 'Recipient liability is restitution-based, accessory liability is not'.[10]

This section is principally concerned with the 'knowing receipt' cases. Analysis of these cases is bedevilled with difficulty. Until recently the main controversy (as with 'knowing assistance') was whether the standard of liability includes negligence as well as dishonesty. But in *BCCI (Overseas) Ltd v Akindele*,[11] the Court of Appeal has laid down, with respect unhelpfully, that the relevant test (which, depending on the particular facts, may encompass more than dishonesty) is whether the recipient's state of knowledge renders it unconscionable for him to retain the benefit of the receipt. In contrast, and with the exception of what the Court of Appeal termed a footnote in the *Akindele* case, the courts have not considered, let alone accepted, an argument that, in line with the position at common law, the 'knowing receipt' cases should have recognised strict restitutionary liability subject to the standard defences of change of position and bona fide purchase.

A final introductory point is that it is normally said that knowing receipt and dealing makes the defendant liable *as a constructive trustee*. This may have practical significance in construing, for example, Rule 6.20(14) of the Civil Procedure Rules dealing with service of a claim form outside the jurisdiction.[12] But there is no question of the defendant holding property for the benefit of the claimant or of a proprietary remedy being imposed because it is irrelevant whether the defendant retains the property received or not. It follows that the terminology of constructive trusteeship ought, in this context, to be excised as meaningless and superfluous.[13] It should add nothing to

---

10   Ibid at 386.

11   [2001] Ch 437.

12   A further consequence is that compound rather than simple interest can be awarded for breach of a constructive trustee's duty: above, p 54. On interpreting constructive trusteeship for the purposes of the Limitation Act 1980, s 21, see *Paragon Finance plc v DB Thakerar & Co* [1999] 1 All ER 400: below, p 555.

13   This point is forcibly made by Birks, 'Trusts in the Recovery of Misapplied Assets: Tracing, Trusts and Restitution' in *Commercial Aspects of Trusts and Fiduciary Obligations* (ed McKendrick, 1992), pp 149, 153–156; and by Lord Nicholls, 'Knowing Receipt: The Need for a New Landmark' in *Restitution: Past, Present and Future* (eds Cornish and others, 1998), pp 231, 243-244. See especially at p 244 where Lord Nicholls writes, 'The law is perhaps now sufficiently mature to dispense with an ill-fitting deemed trusteeship as the source of liability.' See generally Lionel Smith, 'Constructive Trusts and Constructive Trustees' [1999] CLJ 294.

saying that the defendant is subject to a personal restitutionary remedy. The practical significance attached to that language must be regarded as irrational. Hanbury and Martin's view that, strictly speaking, liability for dishonest *assistance* does not involve a constructive trust applies equally to knowing *receipt*.[14]

(b) Dishonesty or negligence?

The majority of English cases have favoured a dishonesty standard – the first three points on the *Baden* scale – for knowing receipt. The first in the line is *Carl-Zeiss Stiftung v Herbert Smith & Co (No 2).*[15] The Carl Zeiss company based in East Germany claimed to be equitable owners of the assets of the Carl Zeiss company based in West Germany. In this action the claimant East German company sought to establish that the solicitors acting for the West German company were personally liable to account, as constructive trustees, to the claimant for the legal fees, allegedly belonging to the claimant, received from the West German company. The action failed because the solicitors did not know, nor had they wilfully shut their eyes to the fact, that the property of the West German company was held on trust for the claimant. Edmund Davies LJ stressed that what was needed for liability was 'want of probity'.[16]

This was followed in *Competitive Insurance Co Ltd v Davies Investments Ltd*[17] in which, in breach of fiduciary duty, two directors of the claimant company had transferred shares in the company to another company which, in turn, transferred those shares to the defendant company, whose liquidator sold them off. The claimant company sought to make the liquidator personally liable as a constructive trustee for receipt of the proceeds of sale of the shares. Goff J held that the liquidator was not liable because, at most, he had been negligent not dishonest.

Carl Zeiss (No 2) was also applied in *Re Montagu's Settlement Trusts.*[18] In breach of trust, trustees transferred a number of settled chattels to the tenth Duke of Manchester, who disposed of several of them. After his death, the eleventh duke sought to make the tenth duke's executor liable, inter alia, for the tenth duke's personal liability as a constructive trustee for the value of the chattels he had received and sold off. Sir Robert Megarry VC, in an influential judgment, held that the tenth Duke had not been personally liable because he had not even been

---

14 Hanbury and Martin, *Modern Equity* (16th edn, 2001) at 206. The argument is arguably more obvious for dishonest assistance because it is irrelevant whether the defendant receives property.
15 [1969] 2 Ch 276.
16 [1969] 2 Ch 276, 302.
17 [1975] 1 WLR 1240.
18 [1987] Ch 264.

shown to be negligent let alone wanting in probity or reckless as to the breach of trust: and he considered that that higher standard was what was required for knowing receipt, which was what was in issue, as well as for knowing assistance, which was not in issue. Additionally Megarry VC sharply, and rightly, distinguished equitable proprietary remedies for retention of the claimant's equitable property from the equitable personal remedy, in issue in the case, for receipt of property that belonged to the claimant. Unfortunately he saw 'tracing' as confined to the former whereas it also has a role vis-à-vis the latter in establishing that, where the property was transferred by a third party, it was 'at the claimant's expense' and not the third party's.

In *Eagle Trust plc v SBC Securities Ltd*[19] the dishonesty theme of the above cases was apparently maintained but with an emphasis on the commercial nature of the transaction. A director of the claimant company, allegedly misappropriated £13.5 million of the claimant's money to honour his own sub-underwriting obligations to the defendants. Vinelott J in striking out the action appeared to favour the dishonesty standard on the ground that this was a commercial transaction, although his use of the concept of 'inferred knowledge' could be interpreted as going beyond the first three points on the *Baden* scale. The implication that a different standard might be applied as between commercial and non-commercial transactions is hard to support. The distinction is reminiscent of the difference between a bona fide purchaser for value and an innocent volunteer but that difference is clearly irrelevant where even the widest standard of liability being discussed requires constructive knowledge.

In similar vein Knox J in *Cowan de Groot Properties Ltd v Eagle Trust plc*[20] considered that in a commercial transaction categories (i) to (iii) of the *Baden* classification needed to be satisfied for knowing receipt albeit that he cast some doubt on the appropriateness of that

---

19 [1993] 1 WLR 484.
20 [1992] 4 All ER 700. The case would now appear to fall within s 322A of the Companies Act 1985. A peculiarity of Knox J's judgment is that the legal analysis differed in respect of the two types of breach of fiduciary duty alleged. Knowing receipt principles were applied in respect of the land having been sold to Pinepad plc at a gross undervalue. But as regards the directors having failed to disclose an interest the issue was treated as one of whether or not the vendor company could rescind the contracts of sale (for non-disclosure). This appears to be inconsistent. If the sale contracts bound the company, subject only to rescission, knowing receipt principles should have been irrelevant. (Although not suggested in the reasoning knowing receipt principles would have been applicable if the relevant property of the vendor company received by Pinepad was treated as the unauthorised profit made by the directors in breach of their fiduciary duty and held by them on constructive trust.) Unless the company could and did rescind, the contracts should have governed. This coincides with the fact that an ignorance analysis seems inapplicable (and the case was in reality a two party one) because the board of the vendor company had officially ratified the sale of the properties. The unjust factor in play is better viewed as mistake.

classification. Pinepad plc, through its director Samuelson, was therefore held not liable for having bought land (which it had subsequently sold) from the vendor company owing to a breach of fiduciary duty by the vendor's directors.

In *Polly Peck International plc v Nadir (No 2)*[1] the degree of requisite knowledge required was left open by the Court of Appeal albeit that Scott LJ, giving the leading judgment, said that he had some doubts whether for knowing receipt one could go beyond the third point on the *Baden* scale. On the facts it was held unlikely that even constructive knowledge could be made out against the defendant bank, which in exchange for currency had received £45 million of misapplied funds belonging to the claimant company.[2] A freezing injunction against the bank was therefore discharged.

A dishonesty standard – the first three points on the *Baden* scale – was also preferred by Arden J in the trial of the action in *Eagle Trust plc v SBS Securities Ltd (No 2)*.[3]

Knox J applied *Carl-Zeiss* and *Re Montagu* in *Hillsdown Holdings plc v Pensions Ombudsman*.[4] Although the defendants in that case did not realise that what they were instigating constituted a breach of trust, they had full knowledge of it and took a very active part in it. Knox J was therefore able to conclude that they were less innocent than the defendants in the *Carl-Zeiss* and *Re Montagu* cases. The Pensions Ombudsman was therefore correct to have regarded them as liable for knowing receipt.

On the other side of the line from the above cases and favouring a negligence standard for knowing receipt – all five points on the *Baden* scale – is *Belmont Finance Corpn v Williams Furniture Ltd (No 2)*.[5] All the

1   [1992] 4 All ER 769.
2   The likely finding of no constructive knowledge was also taken to mean that the bank was probably a bona fide purchaser for value so that an alternative claim for a restitutionary proprietary tracing remedy to recover the funds still held (£8.9 million) would also probably fail: an interlocutory injunction preserving that subject matter was therefore refused (although a very limited form of injunction was granted).
3   [1996] 1 BCLC 121.
4   [1997] 1 All ER 862. In *Dubai Aluminium Co Ltd v Salaam* [1999] 1 Lloyd's Rep 415, 453 (which was primarily a dishonest assistance case) Rix J said that he thought the test for knowing receipt and dishonest assistance was likely to be the same and that was the dishonesty test laid down in *Royal Brunei Airlines Sdn Bhd v Tan* [1995] 2 AC 378.
5   [1980] 1 All ER 393. There were official board resolutions authorising the directors' activities. The Court of Appeal made clear, at pp 406, 411, that the innocent directors were told what to do. On these facts the unjust factor seems better viewed as duress or powerlessness rather than ignorance. The negligence standard was applied in *Westpac Banking Corpn v Savin* [1985] 2 NZLR 41; *Powell v Thompson* [1991] 1 NZLR 597, 607–610; *Equiticorp Industries Group Ltd v Hawkins* [1991] 3 NZLR 700; *Ninety Five Pty Ltd v Banque Nationale de Paris* [1988] WAR 132, 176; *Citadel General Assurance Co v Lloyds Bank Canada* (1997) 152 DLR (4th) 411. It is also supported by dicta of Millett J in *Agip (Africa) Ltd v Jackson* [1990] Ch 265 (although writing extra-judicially, 'Tracing the Proceeds of Fraud' (1991) LQR 71, 81–82, he appears to favour strict liability).

shares in Belmont were owned by City Industrial Finance Ltd. In breach of fiduciary duty, and contrary to the statutory prohibition against a company providing financial assistance for the purchase of its own shares, the directors of Belmont paid £500,000 of Belmont's money under a scheme to help a company called Maximum buy the shares in Belmont from City. City ultimately traceably received £489,000 of that money. It was held that City was personally liable as a constructive trustee for £489,000 because, through its agents and directors, it knew or ought to have known – constructive knowledge being sufficient – that the £489,000 it received was transferred in breach of trust.[6]

The view that mere negligence is sufficient was also taken in *International Sales and Agencies Ltd v Marcus*,[7] although on the facts the defendant moneylender knew that Marcus, a director and shareholder of the claimant company, was using the claimant company's money, in breach of his fiduciary duty, to repay the defendant a loan he had made to a friend of Marcus. In a very clear statement Lawson J said:

> '...the knowing recipient of trust property for his own purposes will become a constructive trustee of what he receives if either he was in fact aware at the time that his receipt was affected by a breach of trust or if he deliberately shut his eyes to the real nature of the transfer to him (this could be called "imputed notice") or if an ordinary reasonable man in his position and with his attributes ought to have known of the relevant breach. This I equate with constructive notice. Such a position would arise where such a person would have been put on inquiry as to the possibility of a breach of trust. I am satisfied that in respect of actual recipients of trust property to be used for their own purposes the law does not require proof of knowing participation in a fraudulent transaction or want of probity, in the sense of dishonesty, on the part of the recipient. That is a test which relates, not to knowing recipients of trust property for their own use, but to those who knowingly participate by assisting in a breach of trust.'[8]

This debate as to whether liability for knowing receipt should rest on dishonesty or negligence has recently been recast by the Court of Appeal in *BCCI (Overseas) Ltd v Akindele*.[9] The defendant, A, entered into an agreement with I Ltd, a company owned by the BCCI group, for the purchase of shares in the BCCI group's holding company. The agreement guaranteed the defendant a return of 15% per annum

6   The reasoning that there was no liability for the wrong of 'knowing assistance in a dishonest and fraudulent scheme' because there had been no dishonest scheme on the part of the directors of Belmont (who genuinely believed that the scheme was a sound and bona fide commercial one) was rejected by the Privy Council in *Royal Brunei Airlines Sdn Bhd v Tan* [1995] 2 AC 378. See above, p 194.
7   [1982] 3 All ER 551.
8   Ibid at 558.
9   [2001] Ch 437.

on his investment of $US10 million. Unknown to A, this agreement was part of a fraudulent scheme by officers of the BCCI group enabling the holding company to buy its own shares. In line with the agreement, BCCI Overseas Ltd paid the defendant $16,679 million. The liquidator of BCCI Overseas Ltd, the claimant, sought to hold the defendant liable to account for the $16,679 million as a constructive trustee for knowing receipt (and knowing assistance). The Court of Appeal held that the defendant was not liable. In so doing, Nourse LJ, giving the leading judgment, said that while *Belmont Finance Corpn v Williams Furniture Ltd (No 2)* showed that dishonesty is not a necessary ingredient for knowing receipt, that did not necessarily mean that constructive knowledge was sufficient. The relevant test was not one of a particular knowledge but was rather one of whether it was unconscionable for the recipient to retain the benefit of the receipt. The implication of this was that the state of knowledge required would vary according to the context; and that the apparently conflicting past decisions could be reconciled. In the words of Nourse LJ:

'[T]here is no need for categorisation. All that is necessary is that the recipient's state of knowledge should be such as to make it unconscionable for him to retain the benefit of the receipt … just as there is now a single test of dishonesty for knowing assistance, so ought there to be a single test of knowledge for knowing receipt. The recipient's state of knowledge must be such as to make it unconscionable for him to retain the benefit of the receipt. A test in that form, though it cannot, any more than any other, avoid difficulties of application, ought to avoid those of definition and allocation to which the previous categorisations have led. Moreover, it should better enable the courts to give common sense decisions in the commercial context in which claims in knowing receipt are now frequently made … .'[10]

While Nourse LJ should be commended for a valiant attempt to reconcile past cases, the truth of the matter, with respect, is that unconscionability is of no assistance. It is a vague and malleable concept that, at least in this context, will merely serve to obscure the policy choice (between dishonesty and negligence) that the courts are making. The reasoning of the Court of Appeal goes on to make clear that the defendant was not liable because he had no actual or constructive knowledge of the breach of fiduciary duty. He neither knew nor ought to have known of the breach. And the Court of Appeal was thereby implicitly accepting that negligence was sufficient to trigger liability for knowing receipt. The reference to unconscionability only served to hide that crucial reasoning.

10 Ibid at 455.

(c) Strict liability?

(i) *The analogy to common law*

Peter Birks[11] has for many years argued that, in line with the position at common law, the 'knowing receipt' cases should have recognised strict restitutionary liability, subject to the standard defences of change of position and bona fide purchase. The facts of the cases reveal that the defendant has received property, which was transferred without the equitable owner's knowledge or consent. That is, the unjust factor is ignorance (or powerlessness) and the defendant's enrichment was at the claimant's expense as satisfied by tracing and title rules. The defendant should, prima facie therefore, be strictly liable for that unjust enrichment. To insist on *knowing* receipt produces an irrational clash with *Lipkin Gorman v Karpnale Ltd* [12] and, indeed, with restitution for mistaken payments.

Birks' thesis has been accepted, albeit with an important refinement, by Lord Nicholls writing extra-judicially.[13] The refinement is that, where the receipt has been dishonest, Lord Nicholls argues that this is itself an equitable accessory wrong. It belongs alongside 'knowing assistance' (or, in the full modern terminology, 'dishonestly assisting or procuring a breach of fiduciary duty') as an aspect of what Lord Nicholls refers to as the general equitable wrong of dishonest participation in a breach of fiduciary duty. In short, Lord Nicholls argues that underpinning the knowing receipt cases are two separate grounds of liability: first, strict liability based on reversing an (autonomous)

---

11 See above, p 182, n 1.

12 [1991] 2 AC 548. It also appears to clash with *Ministry of Health v Simpson* [1951] AC 521, see below, pp 203–206; and with the long-accepted position that an innocent volunteer is liable to an equitable proprietary remedy (for traceable property retained), see below, pp 207–210.

13 Lords Nicholls, 'Knowing Receipt: The Need for a New Landmark' in *Restitution: Past, Present and Future* (1998), pp 230–245. For approval, see Harpum in his response to Lord Nicholls' essay, ibid, pp 247–250; Creighton and Bant, 'Recipient Liability in Western Australia' (2000) 29 UWALR 205; Birks, 'The Role of Fault in the Law of Unjust Enrichment' in *The Search for Principle* (eds Jones and Swadling, 2000) pp 235, 268–271; Burrows, *Fusing Common Law and Equity: Remedies, Restitution and Reform* (Hochelaga Lecture 2001), pp 26–44; Birks, 'Receipt' in *Breach of Trust* (eds Birks and Pretto, 2002), pp 213–240. Strict liability has also been supported by Sir Peter (now Lord) Millett, writing extra-judicially, 'Tracing the Proceeds of Fraud' (1991) 107 LQR 71, 81–82 and in *Twinsectra Ltd v Yardley* [2002] 2 AC 164, para 105, his Lordship said of 'knowing receipt', 'There is no basis for requiring actual knowledge of the breach of trust, let alone dishonesty, as a condition of liability. Constructive notice is sufficient, and may not even be necessary. There is powerful academic support for the proposition that the liability of the recipient is the same as in other cases of restitution, that is to say strict but subject to a change of position defence.' There is also strong judicial support in *Koorootang Nominees Pty Ltd v Australia and New Zealand Banking Group* [1998] 3 VR 16, 100–105. Cf Lionel Smith, 'Unjust Enrichment, Property and the Structure of Trusts' (2000) 116 LQR 412; Thomas, '"Goodbye" Knowing Receipt, "Hello" Unconscientious Receipt' (2001) 21 OJLS 239.

unjust enrichment; and, secondly, liability for the equitable wrong of dishonest participation in a breach of fiduciary duty which, like other equitable wrongs, may trigger compensation or restitution.

Unfortunately the Court of Appeal in the *Akindele* case, while mentioning Lord Nicholls' article in what it termed a footnote, tentatively regarded it as unattractive both as a matter of authority and principle. Nourse LJ said:

> 'No argument before us was based on the suggestions made in Lord Nicholls' essay. Indeed, at this level of decision, it would have been a fruitless exercise. We must continue to do our best with the accepted formulation of the liability in knowing receipt, seeking to simplify and improve it where we may. While in general it may be possible to sympathise with a tendency to subsume a further part of our law of restitution under the principles of unjust enrichment, I beg leave to doubt whether strict liability coupled with a change of position defence would be preferable to fault-based liability in many commercial transactions, for example where, as here, the receipt is of a company's funds which have been misapplied by its directors. Without having heard argument it is unwise to be dogmatic, but in such a case it would appear to be commercially unworkable ... that, simply on proof of an internal misapplication of the company's funds, the burden should shift to the recipient to defend the receipt either by a change of position or perhaps in some other way.'[14]

With respect, Nourse LJ's fears of commercial unworkability are unfounded. The standard restitutionary defences serve to protect defendants. For example, on the facts of the *Akindele* case itself, the defendant would not have been liable in restitution, even applying strict liability, because he was a bona fide purchaser for value. And if strict liability were commercially unworkable, this would mean that the whole of the common law on restitution was also unworkable. No-one has ever suggested that.

(ii) Ministry of Health v Simpson[15]

A further argument in favour of strict liability, relied on by Peter Birks and Lord Nicholls, is that even in equity there is a line of cases imposing strict personal restitutionary liability. In *Ministry of Health v Simpson* it was laid down that a beneficiary (C), who is entitled to a share of a deceased's estate, has an equitable personal remedy against an innocent volunteer (D) to recover money mistakenly paid to D by the personal representative (X) acting in breach of his fiduciary duty to C. While not referring to the apparent conflict with the usual

---

14   [2001] Ch 437, 456.
15   [1951] AC 521 (sub nom *Re Diplock*).

insistence on 'knowing receipt', other cases suggest that *Ministry of Health v Simpson* can apply outside the realm of the administration of estates to claims by any beneficiary where his fiduciary has wrongly paid out his money to an innocent volunteer.[16]

On the face of it, *Ministry of Health v Simpson* is a rare example of the courts imposing strict personal restitutionary liability in equity for ignorance (or 'interference with equitable ownership') albeit that restitution is somewhat peculiarly pushed into second place by an insistence that the beneficiaries first exhaust their remedies against the personal representatives.[17] There therefore appears to be an inconsistency between the *Ministry of Health v Simpson* approach and the many cases of knowing receipt. That decision, albeit by the House of Lords, has had no influence on those cases – indeed it has rarely been cited - and the conventional view is that it belongs to a specialised pocket of law principally concerned with the administration of estates. To hive the decision off in this way does nothing to resolve the inconsistency. Furthermore it can be argued that *Ministry of Health v Simpson* is consistent with the strict personal restitutionary liability of indirect recipients imposed at common law and epitomised by *Lipkin Gorman v Karpnale Ltd.*[18]

If there is this inconsistency, the best way for the law to develop would be for *Ministry of Health v Simpson* to lose its fringe identity and to become the lead player obviating the need for knowing receipt. The condition concerning the exhaustion of remedies would also probably have to be removed and change of position would need to be accepted as a defence. This is precisely the strategy espoused extra-judicially by Lord Nicholls. He writes:

> 'The *Diplock* principle is at hand and available to be reshaped, by being extended to all trusts but in a form modified to take proper account of the subsequent decision of the House of Lords in *Lipkin Gorman v Karpnale*. The modification would make the *Diplock* principle more acceptable, by softening its rigour with the defence arising from change of position. At the same time the opportunity should be taken to decide that this form of relief is no longer subject to a pre-condition that a plaintiff must first exhaust his remedy against the trustees.'[19]

---

16 Most importantly, *Baker Ltd v Medway Building and Supplies Ltd* [1958] 2 All ER 532 (Danckwerts J), [1958] 3 All ER 540, CA, where an auditor fraudulently transferred to a third party money held for the claimant company. See also dicta in *Butler v Broadhead* [1975] Ch 97, 105–111; *Re J Leslie Engineers Ltd* [1976] 1 WLR 292, 299–300.

17 [1951] AC 251, 266–267. The supporting dicta in *Butler v Broadhead* [1975] Ch 97 and *Re J Leslie Engineers Ltd* [1976] 1 WLR 292 also insisted on this restriction.

18 [1991] 2 AC 548.

19 'Knowing Receipt: The Need for a New Landmark' in *Restitution, Past, Present and Future* (eds Cornish, Nolan, O'Sullivan and Virgo), pp 231, 241. See also Birks, 'Misdirected Funds: Restitution from the Recipient' [1989] LMCLQ 296.

An alternative strategy is to deny the inconsistency by arguing that *Ministry of Health v Simpson* is significantly different from the knowing receipt cases in not being based on the 'title and tracing' exception to the 'direct providers only' rule. For example, at first blush it might be thought that C was given a direct remedy against D merely to avoid circuity of action: that is, as C could sue X for breach of fiduciary duty and as X could sue D for restitution of the money transferred by mistake, giving C a remedy against D cut out the need for two claims. But this reasoning cannot stand up to close scrutiny for at least two reasons. First, it appears that the mistake of law rule would have barred X's claim against D;[20] and secondly, the beneficiaries' direct personal claims were made conditional on the prior exhaustion of their remedies against the personal representatives. Rather than avoiding double action, double action was expressly contemplated and, to an extent, insisted on.

A much more convincing alternative explanation of the exception to the 'direct providers only' rule is proferred by Lionel Smith.[1] As we have seen in chapter 1, he argues that the decision in *Ministry of Health v Simpson* represents a justifiable exception to that normal restriction on restitution because, although the claimant next of kin were legally no worse off by X's mistake of law, in that they were still entitled to sue X for breach of fiduciary duty, they would be factually worse off to the extent that X, by having irrecoverably paid away the money by mistake of law, would be unable fully to compensate them for their wrongfully caused loss. In that factual sense the defendants' gain would be at the claimants' expense. The great merit of this theory is that it provides a convincing explanation for the insistence that the claimants first exhausted their claim against X.

If the decision can be explained in that way it differs from the other three party equity cases considered in this subsection because the indirect recipient's gain was *at the claimants' expense* irrespective of the claimants establishing the 'title and tracing' exception to the 'direct providers only' rule.[2] And in the light of this significant distinction the apparent conflict in the equity cases between the House of Lords' strict liability approach and the usual insistence on knowing receipt would melt away.

It should be added that, if Smith's explanation of *Ministry of Health v Simpson* is correct, it provides powerful support for ignorance being recognised as an unjust factor. The importance of his explanation is

20 [1951] AC 251, 270.
1 'Three-Party Restitution: A Critique of Birks' Theory of Interceptive Subtraction' (1991) 4 OJLS 481. Above, pp 38–39.
2 Cf *Baker Ltd v Medway Building Supplies Ltd* [1958] 2 All ER 532, 534–535 in which Danckwerts J at first instance regarded *Ministry of Health v Simpson* as based on title and tracing. See also [1958] 3 All ER 540, 543, CA.

that it obviates the need to rely on title and tracing reasoning and it would be irrelevant whether or not the defendant could be said to have received property that at the date of receipt belonged in equity to the claimant. Stripped of ownership reasoning *Ministry of Health v Simpson* most obviously rests on the defendants' gain having been subtracted from the claimants, without their knowledge.

4.   OTHER THREE PARTY CASES

There are two situations other than where X transfers C's property (or its substitute) to D where an indirect recipient may be personally liable in restitution. Both have been examined as constituting exceptions to the 'direct providers only' rule (ie, as exceptions to the standard approach to 'at the claimant's expense' within unjust enrichment by subtraction) in chapter 1. Reference will here be made to them from the perspective of their resting on the unjust factor of ignorance.

First, and most important, are the usurpation of office and related cases. It has long been established that, where a defendant usurps a claimant's office or position to receive from a third party fees or rents owed by the third party to the claimant, the claimant has an action for money had and received against the defendant to recover those fees or rents.[3] As neither the courts nor textbook writers have traditionally treated 'usurpation' as a tort triggering compensatory damages, the cases may be better viewed as belonging within unjust enrichment by subtraction.

If so, what is the unjust factor? If the payment to the usurper discharges the third party's debt to the claimant, the obvious unjust factor is the claimant's ignorance. Quite simply, the claimant did not know of his loss: the debt was discharged without his knowledge. The unjust factor cannot be 'interference with ownership' because the claimant never owned the fees or rents received by the defendant. Nor can it be the claimant's mistake because he was not mistaken.

If, in contrast, the better view is that the third party's debt is only discharged when the claimant elects to treat it as such, the ground for restitution should be seen more loosely as resting on the policy of avoiding circuity of action.[4]

Secondly, if Lord Romilly MR's dicta in *Lister v Hodgson*[5] – that a deed of gift mistakenly drawn up in favour of the defendant rather than the claimant can be rectified by the claimant – is good law, the obvious unjust

---

3   Above, p 35.
4   Above, p 37.
5   (1867) LR 4 Eq 30. Above, p 39.

factor affecting the claimant is ignorance. He did not know that he was suffering a loss in the sense of not receiving the gift that the third party wanted him to have. The unjust factor cannot be interference with ownership because the claimant never owned the gift.

Finally mention should be made of where a claimant is able to rescind a contract (or deed of gift) with X (eg for misrepresentation or undue influence by X) so as to revest proprietary rights in property that has subsequently been transferred to D (D not being a bona fide purchaser for value without notice).[6] This may again be best explained as an example of ignorance. Although the unjust factor affecting C was initially the mistake or undue influence, the unjust factor affecting C in relation to the transfer of the property by X to D is more obviously that C did not know of that transfer (or was powerless to prevent it).

5. PROPRIETARY RESTITUTION IN RESPECT OF PROPERTY TRANSFERRED WITHOUT THE OWNER'S KNOWLEDGE

The above discussion of ignorance has largely[7] been dealing with where the claimant seeks *personal* restitution. But if, by reason of the transfer without the claimant's knowledge, the defendant's unjust enrichment at the claimant's expense is established and the defendant retains the property (whether in the same form or, by the rules of tracing, in a substitute), is the claimant entitled to *proprietary* restitution?[8] This will be of vital importance if the defendant has become insolvent because proprietary restitution gives priority on the defendant's insolvency.

Where the property is in the same form, a restitutionary proprietary claim, as opposed to a pure proprietary claim, will in this context rarely, if ever, be in issue. This is because the owner's absence of consent means that legal title in the property will simply not pass to the defendant.

In contrast where, by the rules of tracing, the property is retained in a substitute, the reversal of the defendant's unjust enrichment by proprietary, rather than personal, restitution, has in this context been commonplace. Indeed all of the leading cases on the doctrine of equitable tracing that have been examined in chapter 2 exemplify proprietary restitution awarded where the unjust factor is best viewed as ignorance (or powerlessness). In other words, if one disentangles claiming from tracing, most claims following tracing are for proprietary

---

6 Eg *Cundy v Lindsay* (1878) 3 App Cas 459, 463–464; *Morley v Loughnan* [1893] 1 Ch 736.
7 A minor exception is the discussion of ignorance and rescission in the previous paragraph.
8 For general discussion, see Chambers, *Resulting Trusts* (1997), pp 116–118.

restitution where the unjust factor is ignorance. The proprietary restitution may take the form of either an equitable lien or a trust over the traced property. An equitable lien is a charge imposed by law over the traced property to secure a certain sum of money. A trust is a beneficial interest imposed by law in the traced property: that interest may be a sole interest or an interest proportionate to the sum of money used, along with other moneys, to acquire the traced property. Hence the trust imposed following tracing is sometimes termed the 'proportionate share' remedy.[9]

So, equitable liens were imposed over traced property which unjustly enriched the defendant at the claimant's expense and where the unjust factor is best viewed as ignorance (or powerlessness) in, for example, *Re Hallett's Estate*,[10] *Re Oatway*,[11] *James Roscoe (Bolton) Ltd v Winder*,[12] *Re Diplock* (in respect of funds to which *Clayton's Case* applied),[13] and *Re Tilley's Will Trusts*.[14]

Proportionate share trusts were imposed over traced property which unjustly enriched the defendant at the claimant's expense and where the unjust factor is best viewed as ignorance (or powerlessness) in, for example, *Re Diplock* (in respect of funds to which *Clayton's Case* was inapplicable), *Barlow Clowes International Ltd v Vaughan*[15] and *Foskett v McKeown*.[16]

All those leading cases have been fully discussed in chapter 2.

Proprietary restitution where the unjust factor is ignorance (or powerlessness) can be justified applying either of the two approaches to proprietary restitution discussed in chapter 1.[17] On one approach this is because the claimant's consent is absent, rather than qualified, so that there was never a time when the defendant was entitled to the enrichment; on an alternative approach the absence of consent means that the claimant has not taken the risk of the defendant's insolvency.

The above analysis – which treats an equitable lien or a trust imposed over traced property as a proprietary restitutionary remedy to reverse the defendant's unjust enrichment at the claimant's expense with the unjust factor being ignorance – is not one that has been expressly accepted by the courts. On the contrary, as we have seen in our discussion of proprietary restitution in chapter 1,[18] the majority of

---

9   See above, pp 63, 101.
10   (1880) 13 Ch D 696.
11   [1903] 2 Ch 356.
12   [1915] 1 Ch 62.
13   [1948] Ch 465, CA.
14   [1967] Ch 1179.
15   [1992] 4 All ER 22.
16   [2001] 1 AC 102.
17   See above, pp 67–73.
18   See above, pp 64–66.

the House of Lords in *Foskett v McKeown*[19] has argued that a remedy imposed following tracing is purely a matter of property law and is not concerned to reverse the defendant's unjust enrichment. But, with respect, that approach is flawed in ignoring the wider picture of numerous examples of proprietary rights being created to reverse unjust enrichment and in relying on the fiction that tracing involves the continuation of proprietary rights into substitute property.

On the other hand, *Foskett v McKeown* is to be welcomed, as we have seen in our discussion of the case in chapter 2 on tracing,[20] in making clear that, after tracing into a mixed fund that has increased in value, a claimant is not restricted to an equitable lien to secure a sum initially paid into the fund but may elect to have a proportionate share (ie, a beneficial interest under a trust) of the mixed fund. A claimant entitled to proprietary restitution of traced property is therefore free to choose between an equitable lien or a trust depending on which will render him or her the higher sum.

An unjust enrichment analysis of proprietary restitution after tracing brings welcome consistency with personal restitution. This can be illustrated by comparing the personal and proprietary claims in *Re Diplock*.[1] As we have seen,[2] money was mistakenly paid by personal representatives of a deceased to certain charities rather than to the next-of-kin of the deceased. The House of Lords held that the next-of-kin had an equitable personal remedy against the charities to recover the sums received by them, subject to a (controversial) condition that they first exhausted their remedies against the personal representatives. In the Court of Appeal it had also been held that the next-of-kin could trace the money to various assets retained by some of the charities and, depending on the property and the charity in question, were entitled to an equitable lien over, or a proportionate share of, the traced property. It is submitted that, just as the best analysis of the personal claim is that this exemplified personal restitution, on a strict liability basis, to reverse the charities' unjust enrichment with the unjust factor being the next-of-kin's ignorance, so the same should be said of the proprietary claim. On this analysis, the basis of both claims is the same. The essential advantage of being able to trace through to property still retained by the defendant and claiming proprietary restitution would be to give priority on the defendant's insolvency. After *Lipkin Gorman v Karpnale Ltd*[3] both personal and

---

19 [2001] 1 AC 102.
20 See above, pp 101–102.
1   [1948] Ch 465, CA; sub nom *Ministry of Health v Simpson* [1951] AC 251, HL.
2   Above, pp 96–97, 203–204.
3   [1991] 2 AC 548.

proprietary claims should now be subject to a change of position defence. The pleasing picture that emerges on this unjust enrichment analysis, therefore, is one of consistency between personal and proprietary restitution, as there should be where the same set of facts is in issue.

6. CONCLUSION

Ignorance is the most difficult of the unjust factors. Not only have the courts not explicitly recognised it but also most of the relevant case law involves benefits conferred by third parties. Three party cases in restitution are notoriously complex and there is a temptation to see them as raising self-contained issues outside the usual restitutionary scheme. This temptation should be resisted because the issue in question primarily centres on the standard enquiry of whether the defendant's gain, albeit conferred by a third party, can be said to be *at the claimant's expense.* Of the exceptions to the normal 'direct providers only' restriction (that the defendant's gain is not at the claimant's expense where conferred by a third party rather than the claimant) 'title and tracing' is here the most important. However even when that exception is combined with the bona fide purchase defence there is no need to elevate it to an unjust factor focusing on the claimant's ownership of the property at the time when received by the defendant. Normally the true ground for restitution, belonging in the familiar series comprising mistake, failure of consideration, and duress, is ignorance. Even if that is accepted, coverage of all the forms of non-consent requires that not only ignorance but also powerlessness must be added to the list of unjust factors.

Chapter 5

Duress

1. INTRODUCTION

(1) The nature of duress: illegitimate threats and causation

In this chapter we are concerned with the claimant being pressurised into conferring a benefit on the defendant by the latter's illegitimate threats.[1] It is that core feature of illegitimate threats that distinguishes duress from other autonomous unjust factors that, to a greater or lesser extent, also deal with compulsion, such as legal compulsion and necessity.

Duress is intended to encompass, and to be convenient shorthand for, not only the common law doctrine of duress but also that aspect of the equitable doctrine of actual undue influence concerned with illegitimate threats (almost always illegitimate threats to prosecute, sue or publish information). In the modern law the historical divide between common law and equity should not be allowed to drive a wedge through uniting principle.

The leading cases on duress are the House of Lords' decisions in *Universe Tankships Inc of Monrovia v International Transport Workers' Federation, The Universe Sentinel*[2] and *Dimskal Shipping Co SA v International Transport Workers' Federation, The Evia Luck (No 2)*.[3] These cases indicate that there is a two stage test for restitution:[4] first, that the pressure (ie threat) was illegitimate and, secondly, that the payment (or rendering of a benefit in kind) was caused by that threat. The first of these, which goes to the *quality* of the threat, is an objective inquiry and will take up most of this chapter. The second, which goes to the *quantum* of the threat, is a subjective investigation into the claimant's state of

1 Although there appears to be no case directly in point, restitution can in principle also be sought from the recipient of a benefit conferred by the claimant because of the duress exerted by a third party: above, p 29. See also pp 248–251 (undue influence).
2 [1983] 1 AC 366.
3 [1992] 2 AC 152.
4 See also *Barton v Armstrong* [1976] AC 104 (per Lords Wilberforce and Simon dissenting on the facts); *Crescendo Management Pty Ltd v Westpac Banking Corpn* (1988) 19 NSWLR 40,46; Birks, pp 174–185.

mind. Both go to make up the duress which, along with the payment or other enrichment received by the defendant from the claimant, constitutes the unjust enrichment.

It has sometimes been suggested that it is a defence to restitution for duress that the claimant paid 'in submission to an honest claim' or 'to close the transaction'.[5] Those are vague and confusing notions.[6] In this context they appear to add nothing and are probably best viewed as synonymous with saying that causation has not been satisfied or that a threat to sue is not illegitimate.

Birks regards duress as belonging alongside mistake (and other grounds for restitution like legal compulsion and necessity) as a factor vitiating voluntariness.[7] Certainly it is acceptable to describe duress in this way. The claimant does not freely intend the defendant to have the money. However, in contrast to the approach to mistake, duress focuses on the conduct of the person exerting the duress as well as the effect on the claimant. It should also be noted that, as has been pointed out by several commentators and judges,[8] the effect of duress is not to overbear the will in the mistake sense of the claimant not meaning the defendant to have the money. In the circumstances the claimant does intend the defendant to have the money in order to avert the threatened evil. The objection is rather that the claimant does not reach that decision freely but rather under illegitimate pressure.

This chapter is purely concerned with the subtractive sense of 'at the claimant's expense'. In *The Universe Sentinel*[9] Lord Scarman said that 'duress, if proved, not only renders voidable a transaction into which a person has entered into under its compulsion but is actionable as a tort if it causes damages or loss'. This overstates the case.[10] The threat (causing loss) *may* itself constitute a tort, most obviously intimidation. But the scope of the tort of two party intimidation is unclear and it may not yet have been expanded to cover threats to break a contract[11] (let alone *colore officii* demands or illegitimate threats to prosecute or sue).[12] Lord Diplock summarised the position more accurately when he said:

---

5   Eg *Maskell v Horner* [1915] 3 KB 106; *Woolwich Equitable Building Society v IRC* [1993] AC 70; Goff and Jones, paras 10-052 to 10-058.
6   Contrast the defence of 'dispute resolved': below, pp 556–559.
7   Birks at pp 140, 173–174.
8   Below, pp 226–227.
9   [1983] 1 AC 366, 400.
10 See Carty and Evans, 'Economic Duress' [1983] JBL 218, 224.
11 *Winfield & Jolowicz on Tort* (16th edn, 2002), pp 645–646.
12 As these are not normally unlawful, duress, if a tort, would be out of line with the general insistence on unlawful means for the economic torts.

'The use of economic duress to induce another person to part with property or money is not a tort per se; the form that duress takes may, or may not, be tortious ... Where the particular form taken by the economic duress used is itself a tort, the restitutional remedy for money had and received by the defendant to the plaintiff's use is one which the plaintiff is entitled to pursue as an alternative remedy to an action for damages in tort.'[13]

That passage was cited with approval by Lord Goff in *The Evia Luck*[14] who went on to say, '...conduct does not have to be tortious to constitute duress for the purpose of English law; this is so even at common law, and still more so if one has regard to the equitable doctrine of undue influence as an extended form of duress'.[15]

It should be stressed however that this debate has no direct implications for the place of duress within the law of restitution. Even if duress were itself a tort, one would still need to recognise that benefits conferred because of illegitimate pressure could be recovered in unjust enrichment by subtraction[16] albeit that in practice a claimant would then almost always choose to sue in tort for compensatory damages.[17] It would be a wholly separate question whether a tort of duress would be a restitution-yielding tort.[18]

A layman may describe duress as blackmail. But blackmail is a crime and it can be misleading to reason from one to the other, as the ambit of duress in civil law should be, and is, wider than criminal blackmail. Having said that, it is interesting that the actus reus of blackmail can clearly include threats to carry out acts that are not crimes or civil wrongs (for example, reporting a crime to the police or disclosing an adulterous relationship to the press).[19] In the light of this it is not at all surprising that, as we shall see, the ambit of illegitimate threats in civil duress is not confined to threats to carry out unlawful acts.[20]

That there is no necessary correlation between, on the one hand, threats of lawful and unlawful acts and, on the other hand, legitimate and illegitimate pressure is further shown by the converse fact that threats to break a contract, albeit unlawful, may not be illegitimate.[1]

13 [1983] 1 AC 366, 385.
14 [1992] 2 AC 152, 166.
15 Ibid at 169.
16 See *The Evia Luck* [1992] 2 AC 152, 165 (per Lord Goff).
17 Cf the relationship between the tort of deceit and restitution for mistake.
18 See generally chapter 14.
19 Smith, *Law of Theft* (8th edn, 1997), paras 10-29 to 10-32.
20 See especially Steyn LJ in *CTN Cash and Carry Ltd v Gallaher* [1994] 4 All ER 714, 718: '[T]he fact that the defendants have used lawful means does not by itself remove the case from the scope of the doctrine of economic duress.' But acceptance of this does mean that a person has a way of stopping threatened lawful activity by giving in to the demand and then seeking restitution.
1 Below, pp 230–234. Contra is dicta of Lord Scarman in *The Universe Sentinel* [1983] 1 AC 366, 401.

In the body of this chapter we shall examine the two aspects of duress – illegitimacy of threat and causation – under each of the main heads of illegitimate pressure recognised in the case law. While accepting, as Lord Goff has stressed, that the categories of compulsion are not closed,[2] there can at present be said to be five main heads: (i) duress of the person; (ii) duress of goods; (iii) illegitimate threats (other than by a public authority ultra vires) made to support a demand for payment above what is statutorily permitted; (iv) economic duress; (v) illegitimate threats to prosecute or sue or publish information. A sixth head, illegitimate threats by public authorities made to support ultra vires demands, is omitted here and dealt with in chapter 13. That is because it has been swallowed up by the acceptance in *Woolwich Equitable Building Society v IRC*[3] that an ultra vires payment demand by a public authority is itself a ground for restitution of the payment.

Our focus is on money received as the relevant benefit, not least because there have been no reported English duress cases on the restitution of benefits in kind.[4] The same approach to benefit should apply whatever the benefit. And establishing that the defendant is benefited by a benefit in kind should not present a problem because even where the incontrovertible benefit test is not satisfied, the illegitimate demand by the defendant is sufficient to displace subjective devaluation under the 'reprehensible seeking-out' test. The defendant who holds a gun to the head of the claimant and demands work shows that he wants the work and cannot be allowed to argue that he was not willing to pay for it.

There remains an important introductory point to make on both illegitimate threats and causation. As regards the former, it must be emphasised that in principle an implied threat ought to count as duress: that is, if the demand for payment is reasonably construed as carrying with it a threat of particular consequences if the payment is not made it should be treated in the same way as if that accompanying threat was expressly spelt out. In Lord Goff's words in the *Woolwich* case, 'In cases of compulsion, a threat which constitutes the compulsion may be expressed or implied...'.[5] So, for example, if the defendant has wrongfully seized the claimant's goods and demands payment for their release, there is, and should be legally recognised as being, an

---

2   *Woolwich Equitable Building Society v IRC* [1993] AC 70, 165.
3   [1993] AC 70.
4   Cf *Peter Kiewit Sons' Co of Canada and Raymond International Co Ltd v Eakins Construction Ltd* [1960] SCR 361.
5   [1993] AC 70, 165.

illegitimate implied threat that without payment the goods will not be released. This perhaps obvious point is supported by several cases.[6] It follows that the terms 'illegitimate pressure' and 'illegitimate threats' are treated here as synonymous: pressure carries with it at least an implied threat.

Turning to causation, the view put forward in chapter 1 is that, in line with *Barton v Armstrong*[7] and *Edgington v Fitzmaurice*,[8] the general approach to causation throughout the law of restitution is that the unjust factor must be *a* cause of the benefit being conferred or an enrichment being wrongfully acquired. The 'but for' test, to be proved by the claimant, generally determines this (although the burden of proof is reversed where there is highly reprehensible conduct by the defendant, for example, physical duress or deceit). This approach to causation has now been supported for economic duress by Mance J in *Huyton SA v Peter Cremer GmbH*.[9] But traditionally this approach to causation ran into formidable obstacles in the economic duress cases where the emphasis on coercion of the will easily led to the argument that the claimant alleging economic duress had to prove that it was the predominant, rather than a, cause of his actions.[10]

(2) Contracts entered into by duress

It is unhelpful to treat separately payments made under contracts entered into under duress. There are three main reasons for this:

(i) For some categories of duress (eg economic duress) there are few cases dealing with the restitution of non-contractual as opposed to contractual payments.

(ii) The line between contractual and non-contractual payments, which (leaving aside deeds) turns on whether there is consideration for the payment, can be problematic where one is paying to remove a threat, especially a threat to break a contract.[11] Traditionally the 'pre-existing duty rule' established in *Stilk v Myrick*[12] meant that the threatener's promise to perform, or performance of, what it was already

---

6   See eg, *B & S Contracts and Design Ltd v Victor Green Publications Ltd* [1984] ICR 419, where the concept of a 'veiled threat' was recognised, and *The Alev* [1989] 1 Lloyd's Rep 138, 142, 145.

7   [1976] AC 104.

8   (1885) 29 Ch D 459.

9   [1999] 1 Lloyd's Rep 620. See below, p 228.

10 See below, p 227.

11 Eg Mocatta J had great difficulty in deciding whether there was consideration in *North Ocean Shipping Co Ltd v Hyundai Construction Co Ltd* [1979] QB 705.

12 (1809) 2 Camp 317.

contractually bound to do did not count as consideration for the other contracting party's promise of more money. But the Court of Appeal's decision in *Williams v Roffey Bros and Nicholls (Contractors) Ltd*[13] comes close to overruling *Stilk v Myrick*. Indeed, one can regard the pre-existing duty rule as an early but blunt method of allowing escape from a contract for economic duress, which has been rendered obsolete by the modern development of an economic duress doctrine. As Purchas LJ said in the *Roffey* case, 'The modern cases tend to depend more on the defence of duress in a commercial context rather than lack of consideration for the second agreement ... the court is more ready in the presence of this [duress] defence being available in the commercial context to look for mutual advantages which would amount to sufficient consideration to support the second agreement under which the extra money is paid.'[14]

It was held in *Roffey* that there was consideration to support a promise by head contractors to pay more to their sub-contracting carpenter for him to carry out his existing contractual duties. The head contractors would be factually benefited by that performance because, for example, they would avoid paying liquidated damages for late completion under the head contract. And there was no question of the new contract being voidable for duress because the carpenter had made no threat to break the original contract. On the contrary the initiative to pay more had come from the head contractors who knew that the original contract price had been too low and were anxious, for their own purposes, to reduce the carpenter's financial difficulties.

(iii) It may be that there is no difference between the scope of duress for contractual and non-contractual payments. In *Skeate v Beale*[15] it was held that, while duress of goods might well be a ground of restitution for non-contractual payments, it was not a ground for invalidating a contract and recovering payments made under it: duress of the person was needed for that. However, that restriction was abandoned in *The Siboen and The Sibotre*[16] and *North Ocean Shipping Co Ltd v Hyundai Construction Co Ltd*.[17] More controversially in those and subsequent cases (most importantly *The Evia Luck*)[18] the courts have not sought to distinguish in any way the ambit of duress for contractual and non-contractual payments,

13 [1991] 1 QB 1.
14 Ibid at p 21.
15 (1841) 11 Ad & El 983.
16 [1976] 1 Lloyd's Rep 293. Over a century earlier the restriction had been ignored in
    Tamvaco v Simpson (1866) LR 1 CP 363.
17 [1979] QB 705.
18 [1992] 2 AC 152.

although admittedly there has been virtually no direct judicial discussion of whether there should be any difference.[19]

That there should be no such distinction is supported by Goff and Jones[20] and Beatson.[1] If correct, this would represent a marked difference between restitution for duress and for mistake; because for mistake it is clear that a more stringent test has to be satisfied before a contractual, as opposed to a non-contractual payment, can be recovered.[2] And certainly, one can strongly argue that a contract (supported by consideration), as a bargain in which both parties stand to gain or lose, should be less willingly wiped away for pressure than a simple payment.

Although for the above three reasons contractual payments will not be afforded separate treatment in this chapter it should be realised that, strictly speaking, the restitutionary remedies in play are different. Where no contract has to be wiped away, the claimant's restitutionary remedy is an action for money had and received. In contrast, where the payment was rendered under a contract which consequently has to be wiped away (on the assumption that duress renders the contract voidable not void)[3] the claimant's remedy is rescission with a consequential order for repayment of the money.[4]

In the context of duress it may be doubted how sharply distinct those remedies are. Of the usual four bars to rescission, affirmation[5]

---

19 A possible exception is Steyn LJ's judgment in *CTN Cash and Carry Ltd v Gallaher* [1994] 4 All ER 714, 717: 'It seems to me not to matter whether the correct analysis of the facts is that an agreement was made that the plaintiffs would pay the sum in question or whether payment is to be regarded simply as a unilateral act of the plaintiffs. In either event the claim must succeed if the case of duress is made out; if that case is not made out, the claim must fail.'

20 Goff and Jones at paras 10-013 to 10-014.

1   *The Use and Abuse of Unjust Enrichment* (1991), pp 106–108.

2   Above, p 143.

3   *The Evia Luck* [1992] 2 AC 152; Trietel, *The Law of Contract* (10th edn, 1999), p 375.

4   In *North Ocean Shipping Co Ltd v Hyundai Construction Co Ltd* [1979] QB 705, 714, Mocatta J talked of both rescission and the award of money had and received; see also *The Olib* [1991] 2 Lloyd's Rep 108. This contrasts with the normal approach to rescission whereby the consequential order to repay the money is not separated out as a separate claim for money had and received and is regarded as part of the process of rescission: see above, p 58. There are two linked explanations for this tendency in duress cases: first, there is generally no bar of *restitutio in integrum* being impossible; secondly, rescission for duress is normally a *common law* remedy (see above, p 53, n 6). In dicta in *The Evia Luck* [1992] 2 AC 152, 165 Lord Goff suggested that, once the contract had been set aside, the restitution of money could possibly be grounded on failure of consideration as an alternative to duress. The success of that alternative would depend, however, on the claimant establishing that the defendant was not ready, able and willing to perform; below, chapter 10. Certainly it is difficult to see any practical advantage that failure of consideration would offer the claimant.

5   Affirmation was the reason for the denial of rescission in *North Ocean Shipping Co Ltd v Hyundai Construction Co Ltd* [1979] QB 705; and was an alternative reason in *DSND Subsea Ltd v Petroleum Geo-Services ASA* [2000] BLR 530. See also *Mutual Finance Ltd v John Wetton & Sons Ltd* [1937] 2 KB 389, 397.

and the third party rights bar no doubt apply in the usual way.[6] In contrast, there appears to be no case in which it has been accepted that lapse of time is a relevant bar to rescission for duress (although this may simply reflect the fact that there is generally no clear division between affirmation and lapse of time). Most importantly, it appears that the bar that *restitutio in integrum* is impossible generally does not apply to rescission for duress.

The explanation for that is that it would generally contradict the basis for the claimant's restitution to recognise a counter-claim by the defendant: if it was illegitimate for the defendant to demand a sum of money for a particular consideration, for example, carrying out work, it would be inconsistent then to award the defendant counter-restitution for that work. Care must be exercised, however, where the duress relates to only part of the consideration paid overall. Most obviously if a contract is varied as a result of duress by threatened breach of contract, the defendant is still entitled to be paid for the work done in accordance with the terms of the original contract. For example, in *North Ocean Shipping Co Ltd v Hyundai Construction Co Ltd*[7] the shipbuilders were indisputably entitled to payment for the ship built according to the terms of the original contract irrespective of whether they were entitled to the varied price. One explanation for that is to say that, while the varied contract is rescinded, the defendant is entitled to counter-restitution evaluated according to the terms of the original contract. Alternatively one can say that there are two separate contracts and that it is only the second that is rescinded for duress (without any need for counter-restitution).

It should be noted that for rescission the relevant time for assessing whether there was duress is when the contract was entered into, whereas for money had and received it is when the payment was made. Hence in *North Ocean Shipping* Mocatta J held that the contract was voidable for economic duress but that by affirming the contract by paying when the pressure was off the right to rescind had been lost. If the payment had been non-contractual it would have been irrecoverable simply because there was no duress causing the payment.

(3) Proprietary restitution in respect of payments made under duress

The discussion of restitution of payments made under duress in the rest of this chapter deals with where the claimant seeks *personal*

---

6   See Cartwright, *Unequal Bargaining* (1991), p 169.
7   [1979] QB 705. Below, p 225.

restitution. But if, by reason of the payment under duress, an unjust enrichment at the claimant's expense is established and the defendant retains the payment (whether in the same form or, by the rules of tracing, in a substitute), is the claimant entitled to *proprietary* restitution? This will be of vital importance if the defendant has become insolvent because proprietary restitution gives priority on the defendant's insolvency.

In contrast to where the payment was made by mistake, there appears to have been no consideration of this by the English courts.[8] But one would expect the answer to be decided in the same way for duress as in respect of mistaken payments; if, as has been argued above,[9] *Chase Manhattan Bank NA v Israel-British Bank (London) Ltd*[10] was correctly decided in imposing a trust of the payment, the same should apply in relation to a payment made under duress. This is supported by the fact that rescission can be a proprietary remedy in so far as it revests title to property in the claimant; and if property, other than money, were transferred under a contract induced by duress, proprietary rescission would surely be available.

Indeed, if contrary to the view taken in this book,[11] one regards Lord Browne-Wilkinson's conscience test in *Westdeutsche Landesbank Girozentrale v Islington London Borough Council*[12] as being an appropriate one for determining whether restitution should be proprietary rather than merely personal, the case for imposing a trust in duress cases is even stronger than in relation to mistake. A defendant who induces payment by duress knows of the duress whereas a recipient of a mistaken payment may not know of the other's mistake.

2. DURESS OF THE PERSON

The classic example of duress of the person is where the defendant threatens physical violence to the claimant or the claimant's family. In *Barton v Armstrong*[13] there was a bitter struggle for the control of Landmark Corporation Ltd between the defendant, who was chairman of the company, and the claimant, its managing director. Ultimately the claimant contracted to buy out the defendant's interest in the company. The claimant sought a declaration that the contract, which

---

8   For discussion by commentators, see Goff and Jones, *The Law of Restitution* (5th edn, 1998), pp 354–355; Chambers, *Resulting Trusts* (1997) pp 133–135; Maddaugh and McCamus, *The Law of Restitution* (1990), p 96.
9   See above, pp 159–162.
10   [1981] Ch 105.
11   See above, p 73.
12   [1996] AC 669.
13   [1976] AC 104.

had been executed, was 'void'[14] on the ground that it had been induced by the defendant threatening the claimant with murder. The Privy Council (Lords Wilberforce and Simon dissenting on the facts) granted the declaration because the defendant's threats of violence had been a reason for the claimant making the contract.

Lords Wilberforce and Simon said, '... the first step required of the plaintiff is to show that some illegitimate means of persuasion was used. That there were threats to Barton's life was found by the judge ... The next necessary step would be to establish the relationship between the illegitimate means and the action taken.'[15] This is to recognise the two-step approach which underpins this chapter and which was accepted by the House of Lords in *The Universe Sentinel*[16] and *The Evia Luck.*[17]

On causation Lord Cross, giving the majority's judgment, said the following: '... if Armstrong's threats were "a" reason for Barton's executing the deed he is entitled to relief even though he might well have entered into the contract if Armstrong had uttered no threats to induce him to do so.'[18] And in the words of Lords Wilberforce and Simon:

> 'For the purposes of the present case ... we are prepared to accept, as the formula most favourable to the appellant the test proposed by the majority, namely that the illegitimate means was *a* reason (not *the* reason, nor the *predominant* reason, nor the *clinching* reason) why the complainant acted as he did. We are also prepared to accept that a decisive question is not obtainable by asking the question whether the contract would have been made even if there had been no threats ...'[19]

Those passages constitute an important recognition of a general feature of causation in the law of restitution, namely that the unjust factor need be only a cause and not the predominant cause of the benefit. The Privy Council's rejection of the 'but for' test, provable by the claimant, for determining whether the threats were a cause is best viewed as an exception to the usual application of that test. The exception is justified because of the highly reprehensible conduct in issue in a physical duress case.

What then is the causation test for physical duress? Lords Wilberforce and Simon chose to express it in terms of whether the illegitimate means were 'a conscious reason'[20] for the claimant's actions.

---

14 As duress renders a contract voidable not void, the claimant was in reality seeking rescission by the court or a declaration that he had validly rescinded the contract.
15 [1976] AC 104, 121.
16 [1983] 1 AC 366.
17 [1992] 2 AC 152.
18 [1976] AC 104, 119.
19 Ibid at p 121.
20 Ibid at p 122.

Probably to be preferred was the majority's mode of expression whereby the burden of proving 'but for' causation was reversed.[1]

Duress of the person can be regarded as also including an improper threat to detain (or continue detention of) a person. For example, in *Duke de Cadaval v Collins*[2] the Duke was arrested by Collins on the false basis that he owed Collins money. The Duke paid £500 to be released. It was held that he could recover the money in an action for money had and received. The arrest had been wrongful and the money had been paid 'under the arrest to get rid of the pressure'.[3] It is not surprising that examples of restitution for duress of the person are rare. The claimant can generally alternatively sue for compensatory damages for the tort of trespass to the person and thereby recover the loss of the money paid; and nowadays it would seem that he will always have an alternative claim for the tort of two party intimidation.[4]

3. DURESS OF GOODS

Where the defendant improperly threatens not to return the claimant's goods, or to seize them, unless the claimant pays him money, the claimant can recover that money, assuming causation, in an action for money had and received.

A leading case is *Astley v Reynolds*[5] where the claimant pawned plate for £20 to the defendant who, at the end of the three year period, refused to return the plate unless the claimant paid £10 interest which was far above the legally permitted amount. The claimant initially refused to pay but a few months later did so. It was held that the claimant was entitled to recover the £10 minus the legally permitted interest. The threats here were clearly illegitimate and the defendant's conduct constituted what would now be the tort of conversion. The primary focus in the reasoning was therefore on whether the claimant had freely chosen to pay, Holt CJ stressing that the fact that the claimant had an alternative remedy in trover did not rule out recovery for duress. 'The plaintiff might have such an immediate want of his goods that an action of trover would not do his business.'[6] On the facts 'but for' causation was clearly established.

---

1   The relevant passage from Lord Cross' judgment is set out above, p 47.
2   (1836) 4 Ad & El 858. See also *Pitt v Coomes* (1835) 2 Ad & El 459; *Clark v Woods* (1848) 2 Exch 395.
3   Ibid at p 864 (per Lord Denman CJ).
4   *Winfield & Jolowicz on Tort* (16th edn, 2002), p 645. The tort of intimidation was first developed in *Rookes v Barnard* [1964] AC 1129.
5   (1731) 2 Stra 915. See also *Somes v British Empire Shipping Co* (1860) 8 HL Cas 338; *Spanish Government v North of England Steamship Co Ltd* (1938) 54 TLR 852.
6   Ibid at p 916.

In *Maskell v Horner*[7] the defendant, the owner of Spitalfields Market, demanded tolls from the claimant, and many others, who carried on business from stalls near to the market. The claimant initially refused to pay and his goods were seized by the defendant. For several years thereafter the claimant paid under protest in the face of the defendant's threat to seize, or actual seizure of, his goods. It then transpired that the defendant was not entitled to the tolls and the claimant sought to recover them in an action for money had and received. His claim was successful, in respect of tolls paid during the six years prior to the claim, on the ground that they had been paid under improper threats to seize or continue detention of the claimant's goods. In Lord Reading CJ's words, 'If a person pays money which he is not bound to pay, under the compulsion of ... seizure, actual or threatened, of his goods he can recover it as money had and received.'[8] 'But for' causation was again clearly made out on the facts although Lord Reading CJ used language akin to that of the minority in *Barton v Armstrong*.[9] 'The pressure of seizure was always present to his mind and never ceased to operate on it whenever demand for tolls was made.'[10]

As mentioned in the introduction to this chapter, *Skeate v Beale*[11] laid down that a contract was not voidable, so that contractual payments could not be recovered, for duress of goods as opposed to duress of the person. This distinction was explicitly rejected by Kerr J in *The Siboen and The Sibotre*[12] and by Mocatta J in *North Ocean Shipping v Hyundai*[13] and is plainly inconsistent with the doctrine of economic duress. In *The Alev*[14] a contract was set aside for economic duress *or duress of goods* where the claimants had refused to deliver the defendants' cargo, as they were contractually bound to do, until the defendants entered into a contract to pay certain expenses and to refrain from arresting the carrying ship. That decision shows that economic duress can be regarded as encompassing duress of goods[15]

---

7   [1915] 3 KB 106.
8   Ibid at p 118. While a seizure of goods in support of an invalid claim has long been tortious (whether trespass to goods or conversion) it appears that a threatened seizure, as was principally in issue in the case, has only been tortious since the development of two party intimidation.
9   [1976] AC 104. See also *Edgington v Fitzmaurice* (1885) 29 Ch D 459, 483 (per Bowen LJ).
10   Ibid at p 121.
11   (1841) 11 Ad & El 983.
12   [1976] 1 Lloyd's Rep 293.
13   [1979] QB 705.
14   [1989] 1 Lloyd's Rep 138.
15   This is supported by *The Olib* [1991] 2 Lloyd's Rep 108 where a threat to sell the claimants' goods to preserve the defendants' lien was discussed using purely the language of economic duress. See also *Alf Vaughan & Co Ltd v Royscot Trust plc* [1999] 1 All ER (Comm) 856 where a case that was most obviously raising economic duress was pleaded as one concerning duress of goods.

although, given the law's historical development, the distinction is useful for the purposes of exposition.

4. ILLEGITIMATE THREATS (OTHER THAN BY A PUBLIC AUTHORITY ULTRA VIRES) MADE TO SUPPORT A DEMAND FOR PAYMENT IN EXCESS OF WHAT IS PERMITTED BY STATUTE

This category cannot be regarded as well-established. The only obvious illustrations of it are nineteenth century cases concerning money demanded by railway companies for carrying goods. The most important is *Great Western Rly v Sutton.*[16]

The claimant, who was in business as a carrier of goods, was charged more for carriage of goods by the defendant railway company than the defendant was charging other customers. The claimant successfully sought restitution of the overpayment in an action for money had and received. The relevant statute required railway companies to charge all like customers on the same basis, one purpose being to allow fair competition by rival carriers wishing to carry goods by rail. Blackburn J described the claim as follows:

'The defendants being bound by the statute to carry for the plaintiff at a rate not exceeding what they charged to others, for goods of the like description under the like circumstances, refused to do so unless the plaintiff paid them a larger sum, which the plaintiff under protest was compelled to pay in order to procure them to perform their duty, whereby an action had accrued to him to recover back the excess thus extorted from him.'[17]

Willes J, in a well-known dictum, explained the governing principle in wide terms: 'When a man pays more than he is bound to do by law for the performance of a duty which the law says is owed to him for nothing, or for less than he has paid, there is compulsion or concussion in respect of which he is entitled to recover the excess by *conditio indebiti*, or action for money had and received.'[18]

Until *Woolwich Equitable Building Society v IRC*[19] this category arguably merited merely a footnote reference. However in that case Lord Goff specifically isolated it as an established category of compulsion similar to, but distinct from, *colore officii* cases. The recognition in *Woolwich* that a public authority's ultra vires demand is itself an unjust factor means that

16 (1869) LR 4 HL 226.
17 Ibid, p 246. See also p 263 (per Lord Chelmsford).
18 (1869) LR 4 HL 226, 249.
19 [1993] AC 70.

the *colore officii* group of duress cases no longer merit separate treatment. But the *Woolwich* decision applies only to public authorities: ie to where the public law ultra vires doctrine applies. In contrast the category of duress with which we are dealing here applies to private bodies. It may therefore be suggested that Lord Goff deemed this category worthy of mention for two particular reasons. First, it may assume greater importance given the modern governmental policy of denationalisation. Secondly, it highlights that the restitutionary consequences of making the notoriously difficult divide between public and private bodies (or functions) may not be as significant as might have been thought following the recognition in *Woolwich* of a special public law ground for restitution.

It is open for debate whether Lord Goff was correct to treat a case like *Great Western Rly v Sutton* as an example of duress (or, in his words, compulsion). A duress analysis would rest on there having been a causative implied threat by the railway company not to carry the goods unless the sum demanded was paid. That implied threat would be illegitimate because the money demanded was contrary to statute. Mirroring the debate about the *colore officii* cases,[20] it can be argued that the presence of a threat should be unnecessary to ground restitution. On that view it would be sufficient simply that, on a purposive construction, the statute intended to protect the claimant by banning the excessive charge demanded. This category would then effectively be subsumed within the restitutionary ground of 'illegality designed to protect a vulnerable class from exploitation'.[1] On that view the analogy between this category and the *Woolwich* ultra vires ground for restitution would be exact.

5. ECONOMIC DURESS[2]

The doctrine of economic duress ranks as one of the most exciting modern developments in English civil law. Starting as late as 1976, and spawning numerous cases since, the scope of the doctrine is unsettled. While principally concerned with threatened breach of contract, the doctrine can extend to any form of economic pressure, for example the blacking of the ships in the leading cases of *The Universe Sentinel* and *The Evia Luck*.

---

20 Below, chapter 13.
1   Below, pp 269–271.
2   Beatson, *The Use and Abuse of Unjust Enrichment* (1991), pp 95–136; Macdonald, 'Duress by Threatened Breach of Contract' [1989] JBL 460; Birks, 'The Travails of Duress' [1990] LMCLQ 342; Halson, 'Opportunism, Economic Duress and Contractual Modifications' (1991) 107 LQR 649; Bigwood, 'Coercion in Contract: The Theoretical Constructs of Duress' (1996) 46 U Tor LJ 201; Stephen Smith, 'Contracting Under Pressure: A Theory of Duress' [1997] CLJ 343.

(1) Threats to break a contract

(a) The decisions

By far the most important question raised by the new doctrine is, when does a threat to break a contract constitute economic duress?

It is sensible to begin by summarising the main English decisions on this point. Although there were two early Australian cases[3] accepting that a threat to break a contract could and, on the facts, did constitute economic duress and, although the Court of Appeal's decision in *D & C Builders Ltd v Rees*[4] showed acceptance of this so as to negate promissory estoppel, the doctrine was first clearly accepted in England, albeit not made out on the facts, in *The Siboen and The Sibotre*.[5] The threat in question was one made by the charterers of two ships to break their charterparties by not paying the agreed charter rate unless that rate was lowered. This was followed and economic duress found, although the threatened party's affirmation of the contract ruled out rescission, in *North Ocean Shipping Co Ltd v Hyundai Construction Co Ltd*,[6] where the builders of a ship being paid in dollars demanded an extra 10% payment when the dollar was devalued by 10%. In *Pao On v Lau Yiu Long*[7] the claimants refused to complete a purchase of shares from the defendants unless a subsidiary agreement, by which the defendants were to buy back the shares at the end of the year at $2.50 a share, was replaced by the claimants being guaranteed, by way of an indemnity, the price of $2.50 (which left the claimants free at the end of the year to sell back at a higher price): the Privy Council held that there was no economic duress on the facts.

Since then there have been four threatened breach of contract cases in which a plea of economic duress has succeeded: the Court of Appeal's decision in *B & S Contracts and Design Ltd v Victor Green Publications Ltd*,[8] in which a firm (itself under a strike threat from its employees) impliedly threatened not to perform its contractual obligations to erect exhibition stands unless paid an extra £4,500; the first instance decisions in *Atlas Express Ltd v Kafco Ltd*[9] and *The Alev*[10] in which carriers of goods, by land and sea respectively, refused to carry out their contractual obligations unless paid more money; and the decision of Dyson J in *Carillion*

3　*Nixon v Furphy* (1925) 25 NSW (SR) 151; *Sundell (TA) & Sons Pty Ltd v Emm Yannoulatos (Overseas) Pty Ltd* (1956) 56 SR NSW 323.
4　[1966] 2 QB 617.
5　[1976] 1 Lloyd's Rep 293.
6　[1979] QB 705.
7　[1980] AC 614.
8　[1984] ICR 419.
9　[1989] QB 833.
10　[1989] 1 Lloyd's Rep 138.

Construction Ltd v Felix (UK) Ltd[11] where a sub-contractor threatened not to supply cladding units in accordance with the sub-contract unless a final account sum of £3.2 million was agreed by the head-contractor which was £500,000 more than the head-contractor thought the sub-contractor would be entitled to.

Although of no significance for analysing the approach to economic duress it should be noted that, of the reported cases on a threatened breach of contract, only *North Ocean Shipping v Hyundai* and *B & S Contracts v Green* concerned restitution as such rather than rescission of a contract without personal or proprietary restitutionary consequences.

(b) The overborne will approach

On one view, and it is the view that dominated the reasoning in the early cases, a threat to break a contract constitutes economic duress whenever the will of the threatened party is overborne. In other words, *a threatened breach of contract is always regarded as illegitimate* because it is a threatened wrong and the important focus switches to the effect of the illegitimate threat. The classic statement of this approach is the Privy Council's judgment, given by Lord Scarman, in *Pao On v Lau Yiu Long*.[12] He said:

> '... in a contractual situation commercial pressure is not enough. There must be some factor "which could in law be regarded as a coercion of his will so as to vitiate his consent"[13] ... In determining whether there was a coercion of will and that there was no true consent, it is material to inquire whether the person alleged to have been coerced did or did not protest; whether, at the time he was allegedly coerced into making the contract, he did or did not have an alternative course open to him such as an adequate legal remedy; whether he was independently advised; and whether after entering the contract he took steps to avoid it. All these matters are ... relevant in determining whether he acted voluntarily or not.'

As has been pointed out in the introduction to this chapter, the language of an overborne will and non-voluntariness can be criticised as obscuring the fact that in contrast to, for example, mistake, a coerced claimant does in the circumstances intend the defendant to have the money; he chooses to pay (or to contract to pay) in order to avert the threatened evil. As Atiyah writes, 'A victim of duress does normally know what he is doing, does choose to submit and does intend to do

---

11   [2001] BLR 1.
12   [1980] AC 614, 635.
13   Citing Kerr J in *The Siboen and The Sibotre* [1976] 1 Lloyd's Rep 293, 336.

so.'[14] In McHugh JA's words in *Crescendo Management Pty Ltd v Westpac Banking Corpn*,[15] 'The overbearing of the will theory of duress should be rejected. A person who is the subject of duress usually knows only too well what he is doing. But he chooses to submit to the demand or pressure rather than take an alternative course of action.' In dicta in *The Evia Luck*[16] Lord Goff said, 'I myself, like McHugh JA, doubt whether it is helpful in this context to speak of the plaintiff's will having been coerced.' And in Lord Diplock's words in *The Universe Sentinel*:[17]

> 'The rationale of this development of the common law ... is not that the party seeking to avoid the contract which he has entered into with another party, or to recover money that he has paid to another party in response to a demand, did not know the nature or the precise terms of the contract at the time when he entered into it or did not understand the purpose for which the payment was demanded.'

As the overbearing of the will is, on its face, plainly a nonsense in the context of duress, what do the courts mean when they use such language? There appear to be two major possible interpretations.

The first is that the courts are here rejecting the usual 'a reason' approach to causation in favour of a more stringent test whereby the threat must be the overwhelming or predominant cause of the claimant's conduct. Assuming this is a correct interpretation, Birks condemns it as involving 'an impossible and inscrutable inquiry into the metaphysics of the will'.[18] But it is hard to see why any test of causation is not open to the same criticism. On the other hand, the more stringent test of causation can be validly criticised simply for being inconsistent with the approach to causation in relation to other areas of duress and, indeed, in relation to the rest of restitution.[19] If all that the courts look for in a mistake case is that the mistake was a cause of the payment there can be no justification for a predominant cause approach for economic duress. Even if one has a vision of a sliding scale, whereby the stringency of causation is increased as the illegitimacy of the threat weakens, the causation standard should not be more stringent than requiring the duress to be a cause of the benefit. In contrast there is probably no good reason to go to the reverse extreme of equating totally the causation test for economic duress with that for physical duress. As has been suggested in chapter 1, the better view is that the normal 'but for' test, to be proved by

14 'Economic Duress and the "Overborne Will"' (1982) 98 LQR 197, 200.
15 (1988) 19 NSWLR 40, 45–46.
16 [1992] 2 AC 152, 166.
17 [1983] 1 AC 366, 384. See also Lord Scarman at 400.
18 Birks at p 183.
19 Above, pp 44–48.

the claimant, should apply to economic duress. This is supported by Mance J in *Huyton SA v Peter Cremer GmbH*.[20] He said, '[The] relaxed view of causation in the special context of duress to the person cannot prevail in the less serious context of economic duress. The minimum basic test of subjective causation in economic duress ought, it appears to me, to be a "but for" test.'[1] He later went on to say that the legal onus of proving causation in economic duress cases was on the claimant.[2] On the facts of the case Mance J held that, even if there had been an illegitimate threat (which, in his view, there was not), economic duress was not made out because causation (between the pressure and the making of the agreement) was not satisfied.[3]

Whatever the theoretical defects of the predominant cause test the practical effects of adopting a more or less stringent test are unlikely to be very significant. In so far as a threatened breach of contract has been a cause of a claimant paying money or entering into a new contract, one can nearly always say that the claimant has been predominantly motivated by the desire to avoid the evil consequences of the contract not being performed. True, a claimant may pay primarily because he feels sorry for the threatener or because he wants to maintain good relations for the future. Those would be highly exceptional situations.

A second interpretation of the overborne will language used by the courts is that duress is only made out where the claimant did not have a free choice in giving in to the illegitimate threatened breach of contract. If the claimant had *a reasonable alternative* he cannot successfully raise duress even though causation is satisfied. In other words, this is a third requirement in addition to the illegitimacy of the threat and causation.

This idea has been mentioned as important in several cases. It was the second of Lord Scarman's more specific criteria in *Pao On v Lau Yiu Long*[4] and by the time of *The Universe Sentinel*[5] he had taken it out as a more fundamental point: 'The classic case of duress is not the lack of will to submit but the victim's intentional submission arising from the realisation that there is no other practical choice open to him.' In *B & S Contracts and Design Ltd v*

---

20   [1999] 1 Lloyd's Rep 620, 636.
1   A 'but for' test of causation was applied to economic duress/duress of goods in *Alf Vaughan & Co Ltd v Royscot Trust plc* [1999] 1 All ER (Comm) 856, 860.
2   [1999] 1 Lloyd's Rep 620, 639. Contra is *Crescendo Management Pty Ltd v Westpac Banking Corpn* (1988) 19 NSWLR 40 where the burden of disproving causation was put on the defendant even though that was an economic duress case.
3   Causation was also held not to be satisfied in *DSND Subsea Ltd v Petroleum Geo-Services ASA* [2000] BLR 530.
4   [1980] AC 614.
5   [1983] 1 AC 366, 400.

Victor Green Publications Ltd,[6] Griffiths LJ said, '[The organiser] was over a barrel, he had no alternative but to pay: he had no chance of going to any other source of labour to erect the stands.' And in probably the most important statement on this notion, Kerr LJ in the same case said the following: '... a threat to break a contract when money is paid by the other party can, but by no means always will, constitute duress. It appears from the authorities that it will only constitute duress if the consequences of a refusal would be serious and immediate so that there is no reasonable alternative open, such as by legal redress, obtaining an injunction, etc.'[7] This concept was further regarded as important in *The Alev*[8] where Hobhouse J decided that there was 'no reasonable alternative open' to the victim of the duress. And in *Huyton SA v Peter Cremer GmbH & Co,*[9] Mance J said, '[I]t seems ... self-evident that relief may not be appropriate if an innocent party decides, as a matter of choice, not to pursue an alternative remedy which any and possibly some other reasonable persons in his circumstances would have pursued.'

Moreover, in a recent construction case Dyson J has expressly elevated the 'no practical alternative' element to be a third requirement alongside illegitimacy and causation. In *DSND Subsea Ltd v Petroleum Geo-Services ASA*[10] he said, 'The ingredients of actionable duress are that there must be pressure, (a) whose practical effect is that there is compulsion on, or a lack of practical choice for, the victim, (b) which is illegitimate, and (c) which is a significant cause inducing the claimant to enter into the contract...'

There are, however, several objections to this approach. First, the fact that the claimant did not opt for an alternative is a strong indication that there was no reasonable alternative open to him. Secondly, even if one is convinced that there was a reasonable alternative open to the claimant, is it not objectionable in this context to rule out restitution on the ground that the claimant was weak or foolish to have given in? As Goff and Jones have written, 'Such a rule can only be justified on the ground that a person of reasonable courage would not be coerced by such duress. This justification is hardly tenable ...'[11] Thirdly, the

---

6   [1984] ICR 419, 426.
7   [1984] ICR 419, 428.
8   [1989] 1 Lloyd's Rep 138, 146–147. See also *Hennessy v Craigmyle & Co Ltd* [1986] ICR 461 where the Court of Appeal controversially held that economic duress was not made out because the claimant had a real, even if unattractive, alternative. The decision seems wrong because the recognised unattractiveness of the alternative (complaining to an industrial tribunal and drawing social security) meant that it was not a reasonable alternative.
9   [1999] 1 Lloyd's Rep 620, 638. See also at 636. For an interesting note on this case, see Nolan, 'Economic Duress and the Availability of a Reasonable Alternative' [2000] RLR 105.
10   [2000] BLR 530, 545. See also *Carillion Construction Ltd v Felix (UK) Ltd* [2001] BLR 1.
11   Goff and Jones (5th edn, 1998), at p 244. Cf (6th edn, 2002), paras 10-032 to 10-034. See also *Silsbee v Webber* 50 NE 555 (1898).

importance placed on this factor in economic duress cases is inconsistent with other areas of duress. For example, in *Astley v Reynolds*[12] the fact that the claimant could alternatively have sued for trover to recover his pawned plate was dismissed as unworthy of serious investigation because the claimant 'might' have had such an immediate want of his goods that trover would not do his business.

In any event, it may again be doubted whether acceptance of this requirement would have any major practical significance. Where a threatened party has succumbed, there will rarely have been any reasonable alternative open, especially given the cost, delay and uncertainty of litigation. Certainly in none of the reported cases on threatened breach of contract would there appear to have been a reasonable alternative open to the claimant.

There are therefore several theoretical problems with the 'predominant cause' and 'no reasonable alternative' interpretations of the overborne will language. Nor should it be thought that those ideas are consistent with the decisions in all the cases: in *The Siboen and The Sibotre* and, most importantly, *Pao On v Lau Yiu Long* the courts held that there was no economic duress even though, on the facts, there was a threatened breach of contract and it would appear that the predominant cause and no reasonable alternative criteria were both satisfied.

The conclusion is that, despite much of their reasoning, the courts should not decide whether a threatened breach of contract constitutes economic duress without analysing whether the particular threatened breach of contract is or is not illegitimate. It would be a misleading and flawed strategy to treat all such threats as illegitimate.[13]

(c) How does one decide whether the threatened breach of contract is illegitimate?

Three tests, which may interrelate, can be suggested for deciding whether a threatened breach of contract is or is not illegitimate.

A first test, and the one favoured by Birks, is whether the threat was made in bad faith, by which Birks means that the threat was 'intended to exploit the plaintiff's weakness rather than to solve financial or other problems of the defendant'.[14] Goff and Jones also refer to the possible relevance of the threatener not believing that the threat, if carried out, would be a breach of contract.[15] A difficulty

---

12   (1731) 2 Stra 915, 916.
13   For a contrary view, see Virgo, *The Principles of the Law of Restitution* (1999), pp 200–218.
14   Birks at p 183.
15   Goff and Jones at para 10-028.

with either approach is that it is hard to tell what motivates a threatening party. Peculiarly, Goff and Jones' approach also seems to require that the threatener is mistaken as to the law. Birks' test is more appealing but reverses traditional contract values in that bad faith in breaking a contract has traditionally been afforded no importance (eg, it does not affect the measure of damages) precisely because the self-interested pursuit of profit is regarded as acceptable provided the innocent party is compensated for loss.

One decision that clearly does fit the bad faith test is *D & C Builders Ltd v Rees.*[16] The claimants, builders and decorators, had carried out work for the defendants who refused to pay the £482 still owed. The claimants ultimately agreed to accept £300 in satisfaction of the whole. Lord Denning and Danckwerts LJ held that the defendants could not rely on the doctrine of promissory estoppel to enforce the claimants' promise to accept the lesser sum because the defendants had acted inequitably in intimidating the claimants; although able to pay (at least on account) the defendants, knowing of the claimants' need of the money to stave off bankruptcy, had threatened to pay nothing unless the claimants promised to accept £300 in full satisfaction. In Danckwerts LJ's words, 'The Rees really behaved very badly. They knew of the plaintiffs' financial difficulties and used their awkward situation to intimidate them.'[17]

Albeit less clear-cut, *B & S Contracts and Design Ltd v Victor Green Publications Ltd*[18] can also be justified on the bad faith test. Although the threatening party was ostensibly reacting to difficulties caused by their own employees they had no good reason (other than personal gain) to demand that the organiser pay half of what their employees were demanding: the employees' demands had no direct relation to the contract in hand but were rather a consequence of the employees having been made redundant from their main jobs.

In contrast other decisions are inconsistent with the bad faith test. For example, there was no obvious bad faith in *North Ocean Shipping Co Ltd v Hyundai Construction Co Ltd*[19] or *Atlas Express Ltd v Kafco (Importers and Distributors) Ltd*[20] and yet duress was made out.

16 [1966] 2 QB 617. In *Huyton SA v Peter Cremer GmbH* [1999] 1 Lloyd's Rep 620, 637, Mance J, while not expressing enthusiasm for the bad faith test in threatened breach of contract cases, said that it was 'better not to exclude the possibility that the state of mind of the person applying such pressure may in some circumstances be significant'. In *DSND Subsea Ltd v Petroleum Geo-Services ASA* [2000] BLR 530, 545–546 Dyson J considered that it was a relevant factor in determining the illegitimacy of an actual or threatened breach of contract whether the person exerting the pressure was acting in good or bad faith.
17 Ibid at p 626.
18 [1984] ICR 419.
19 [1979] QB 705.
20 [1989] QB 833.

A second test suggested by Birks is to ask whether the defendant is threatening a breach of contract of his own making or is merely warning the claimant that the circumstances are such that he may be unable to perform as agreed.[1] There are two notions in mind here. One is a purported distinction between a threat and a warning; but, given that an implied threat counts, it is hard to make that distinction stick. The other notion is the distinction between threats dictated by outside events (legitimate) and threats of the defendant's own making (illegitimate).

Although the idea of a change of circumstances analogous to, but not as extreme as, that needed to frustrate a contract may be helpful in determining that a threat is *legitimate*, it is hard to see that just because a defendant's threat is not a reaction to outside events it should be classed as illegitimate. For example, in *Pao On v Lau Yiu Long* the purchasers were not reacting to outside events but rather to their own 'mistake' in fixing an initial bad bargain. Yet economic duress was held not to be made out and, although one can criticise the 'overborne will' language, the decision seems correct.

A third approach is to consider the substantive fairness of the terms proposed by the 'threatener'. On this view the procedural unfairness of threatening to break a contract must be supplemented by the substantive unfairness of the terms in order to justify judicial intervention. This is to borrow from the approach taken to presumed undue influence and exploitation of weakness as considered in the next two chapters.[2]

Naturally one difficulty with this approach is in deciding whether the new terms are fair and this is a task that the courts have traditionally steered well clear of. Nevertheless, particularly with the use of expert evidence, it should be possible to ascertain the range of fair market prices for particular contractual performances. A more serious problem is that this test would be likely to produce an extremely narrow doctrine of economic duress for it will be rare for terms proposed by a party threatening a breach of contract to fall outside the possible bounds of fairness. So in nearly all the reported cases, whether duress was held to be made out or not, the terms demanded were fair.

However, even if in general a test of substantive unfairness seems unhelpful, one aspect of it is of use. If the threatener is merely seeking to correct what was always a clearly bad bargain his threat should be

1   Birks at p 183.
2   See below, pp 256–258, 260.

regarded as legitimate. One can regard a threatened breach of contract as significantly different from other threatened wrongs precisely because it is dependent on the parties' own initial fixing of terms, which may have been badly weighted against one of them. To threaten breach to obtain a correction is to threaten a wrong but barely so. In line with this, in *Pao On v Lau Yiu Long* and *Williams v Roffey*, in neither of which was economic duress made out, the courts drew attention to the fact that the initial contract had been a bad one for the purchasers and carpenter respectively.

Of the above tests the most appealing is that focusing on bad faith. A threatened breach of contract should be regarded as illegitimate if concerned to exploit the claimant's weakness rather than solving financial or other problems of the defendant. To this can be added two supplementary or clarificatory ideas (derived from aspects of the other two tests considered). First, a threat should not be considered illegitimate (made in bad faith) if the threat is a reaction to circumstances that almost constitute frustration. And, secondly, a threat should not be considered illegitimate (made in bad faith) if it merely corrects what was always clearly a bad bargain.[3]

Underlying the question of the appropriate test is a crucial and difficult policy choice which the courts have hitherto signally failed to address, be it under the old 'consideration or no consideration' approach or through the modern, supposedly more transparent, economic duress doctrine. Should the law lean in favour of protecting *the original bargain* or *the renegotiated bargain*?

Protecting the original bargain encourages parties to be disciplined in their initial contractual negotiations. It can be argued that a party who tenders too low ought to have great difficulty in renegotiating out of the consequences of its initial poor judgment.

A preference for protecting the renegotiated bargain is, in contrast, based on the idea that, applying a laissez-faire philosophy of keeping legal intervention to a minimum, the parties' last bargain should, on the face of it, stand. Genuine renegotiations must not be disrupted.

Although the courts should be responsive to both these policies it seems that a preference for one or the other is required. Of the two the latter is more appealing. On any view drawing the parameters of illegitimacy is difficult and there is therefore good sense in opting for an approach of lesser, rather than greater, intervention. It is believed that, in accordance with this policy, the approach advocated above ('bad faith' supplemented by the 'near frustration' and 'bad bargain

---

3   In *Huyton SA v Peter Cremer GmbH* [1999] 1 Lloyd's Rep 620, 637, Mance J referred to the approach suggested in this paragraph as 'by no means uncontentious'.

correction' ideas) would produce a sufficiently wide and sensitive doctrine of economic duress.[4]

It has to be accepted, however, that no test can reconcile all the English cases which are thereby revealed to be inconsistent. On the suggested approach *North Ocean Shipping v Hyundai* and *Atlas Express v Kafco* do seem to have gone too far in protecting the threatened party.

There is one final point. An argument can be made[5] that, on an analogy with mistake, the courts should adopt a wider doctrine of economic duress where no contract has to be wiped away (ie in simple payment cases like *B & S Contracts v Green*) than where a contract has to be wiped away. However, given the contractual context of the payments here (whether technically there is consideration or not) it is perhaps unwise to make such a differentiation and there is no hint of it in the cases.

(2) Other forms of economic duress

Both the leading cases on economic duress,[6] *The Universe Sentinel*[7] and *The Evia Luck*,[8] concerned the blacking of ships sailing under flags of convenience by the International Transport Workers' Federation. In the former the blacking comprised procuring tugmen at Milford Haven to refuse, in breach of their contracts of employment with the Harbour Authority, to operate their tugs. In order to lift the blacking the claimants, inter alia, agreed to pay and paid $6,480 into the ITF's seamen's welfare fund. Having sailed from Milford Haven the claimants sought to recover the payment on the ground that it was money had and received paid under economic duress. The action succeeded (Lords Scarman and Brandon dissenting). It was clear that what the defendants were threatening, that is, the continuation of the blacking, was a tort against the claimants (whether the tort of indirect interference with a contract or three party intimidation) unless the defendants were protected by the trade dispute defence under ss 13 and 29 of the Trade Union and Labour Relations Act 1974 (now ss 219 and 244 of the Trade Union and Labour Relations (Consolidation) Act 1992). Moreover, it was conceded by the defendants that, subject to that trade dispute defence, the claimants were entitled to the

---

4   This is irrespective of whether one insists, contrary to what has been argued above, that the threat be the predominant cause and/or that the threatened party has no reasonable alternative.

5   For this general argument, see above, p 217.

6   The cases could have been, but were not, treated as unusual examples of duress of goods.

7   [1983] 1 AC 366.

8   [1992] 2 AC 152.

recovery of the money on the grounds of economic duress: and it was conceded by the claimants that, if the trade dispute defence was made out on the facts, the claimants could not recover the money. Therefore the sole issue between the parties in the House of Lords was whether on the facts the trade dispute defence was made out. The majority held that it was not.

The crucial factual difference in *The Evia Luck* was that the blacking occurred in Sweden. The primary focus in the case was on the conflict of laws point as to whether the illegitimacy of the pressure should be judged by English law (whereby the pressure was considered to be illegitimate, statutory reform since *The Universe Sentinel* having removed any possible trade dispute defence) or by Swedish law, whereby the pressure was lawful. That issue is considered in chapter 16. A further difference in the focus of the two cases is that in *The Evia Luck* it was common ground between the parties that the $140,000 paid (comprising, for example, the backdated wages to the Filipino seamen, and the ITF entrance fees, membership fees and welfare fund contributions) was paid under a contract. The clear issue was whether economic duress entitled the owners to avoid the contract and hence to recover their money. In contrast in *The Universe Sentinel* it was left unclear whether there was a contract to pay the money and hence whether a contract had to be avoided in order to get to restitution.

In the light of the concessions made in both cases, and the primary conflict of laws point in issue in *The Evia Luck*, their importance for the law on economic duress lies not in the decisions reached but in the approach taken in the leading speeches of, respectively, Lords Diplock and Goff. They are important in three main respects.

First, Lords Diplock and Goff recognised the two aspects of duress that have been the cornerstone of the discussion in this chapter: the illegitimacy of the pressure and the effect on the threatened party. In Lord Goff's words, '... it is now accepted that economic pressure may be sufficient to amount to duress ... provided at least that the economic pressure may be characterised as illegitimate and has constituted a significant cause inducing the plaintiff to enter into the relevant contract'.[9] Neither of their Lordships clarified the precise effect on the threatened party that is required. This has been fully discussed in the previous sub-section. It is sufficient to recap here by saying that there is no justification for the normal 'a cause' approach to be ousted by a predominant cause test nor, despite Lord Scarman's judgment in *The Universe Sentinel*, is there any good reason for an additional requirement that the claimant had 'no reasonable alternative' to submission.

9   [1992] 2 AC 152, 165. See also Lord Diplock in *The Universe Sentinel* [1983] 1 AC 366, 384; and Lord Scarman at pp 400–401.

Secondly, both their Lordships stressed, as we have seen in the introduction to this chapter, that economic duress is not a tort per se.

Thirdly, it was accepted that the statutory trade dispute defence, albeit expressed as applying to torts, could and should be extended, as a matter of policy, to a claim for duress made in unjust enrichment by subtraction. In Lord Diplock's words:

> 'The immunities from liability in tort provided by ss 13 and 14 [of the Trade Union and Labour Relations Act 1974] are not directly applicable to the ship owners' cause of action for money had and received. Nevertheless, these sections, together with the definition of trade dispute in s 29, afford an indication, which all your Lordships should respect, of where public policy requires that the line should be drawn between what kind of commercial pressure by a trade union upon an employer in the field of industrial relations ought to be treated as legitimised despite the fact that the will of the employer is thereby coerced and what kind of commercial pressure in that field does amount to economic duress that entitles the employer victim to restitutionary remedies.'[10]

In *The Evia Luck* that passage was cited with approval by Lord Goff who thought that an analogy might be drawn with the search for the inferred legislative purpose in respect of the tort of breach of statutory duty.

Turning aside from those two leading cases and from pressure through industrial action, another major question under economic duress is whether a threat not to enter into a contract with the claimant can constitute illegitimate pressure.[11] This is not to threaten the claimant with a tort or other wrong and, although the lawful/unlawful distinction is not decisive, a threat not to enter into a contract is likely to be regarded as legitimate pressure in a commercial world. The well-known Australian case of *Smith v Charlick (William) Ltd*[12] held against duress. The Wheat Harvest Board refused to supply wheat to the claimant miller unless he paid a surcharge for wheat that had been delivered in the past. His action for restitution of the money paid on the grounds that it was paid under duress was dismissed. Although the claimant would not have been able to acquire wheat from any other source it was held, perhaps controversially, that the Wheat Board was acting within its powers, was not bound to sell wheat to the claimant, and was not threatening to infringe any other right. The facts are strong because the defendant was a public authority in a

---

10 [1983] 1 AC 366, 385. See also Lord Cross at p 391 and Lord Scarman at p 401.

11 A further interesting question is whether a threat lawfully to terminate a contract can ever be illegitimate: see, eg, the notice to the employee given in *Bank of Baroda v Shah* [1988] 3 All ER 24 although that was in the context of a relationship of presumed undue influence; below, p 252, n 19.

12 (1924) 34 CLR 38.

monopolistic position. The position of a private contractor is *a fortiori.*

Duress was also held not to have been made out in the main relevant English case of *CTN Cash and Carry Ltd v Gallaher Ltd.*[13] The defendants delivered cigarettes to the claimants. Unfortunately they were mistakenly delivered to the claimants' Burnley warehouse rather than their Preston warehouse. The cigarettes were then stolen. Believing mistakenly that the risk had passed to the claimants, the defendants demanded the £17,000 contract price and made clear that they would withdraw the claimants' credit facilities on future contracts if they failed to pay. The claimants paid the £17,000 and later sought repayment on the ground that they had paid under duress. The Court of Appeal held that the claim failed. It was stressed that the defendants were entitled to refuse to enter into any future contacts with the claimants and that, *a fortiori*, it was lawful for them to insist that they would no longer grant credit. Although it was accepted that duress can be constituted by lawful acts, it was thought that this would rarely be so between commercial parties. That was so even though the defendants were the sole distributors of popular brands of cigarettes and in a sense, therefore, were in a monopoly position. Of particular importance on these facts was that the defendants were acting in good faith in making the demand: albeit mistakenly, they thought that the goods were at the risk of the claimants and that they were therefore legally entitled to payment. Steyn LJ said, 'Outside the field of protected relationships, and in a purely commercial context, it might be a relatively rare case in which "lawful act duress" can be established. And it might be particularly difficult to establish duress if the defendant bona fide considered that his demand was valid.'[14]

Another form of alleged economic duress, although pleaded as an example of duress of goods, was in issue in *Alf Vaughan & Co Ltd v Royscot Trust plc.*[15] On the administrative receivership of the claimants, the defendants became contractually entitled to re-take possession of vehicles that the claimants had leased, or taken on hire-purchase, from them. So as to be able to sell the business as a group concern, the receivers offered to buy the vehicles by paying off the balance owing on the hire and hire-purchase agreements (which totalled about £34,000). The defendants threatened to re-take possession of the vehicles unless they were paid £82,000. The receivers reluctantly paid that sum but then sought to avoid the contract and to recover the difference between the two figures (about £48,000) on the ground

13 [1994] 4 All ER 714. For a useful note on this case, see Carter and Tolhurst, 'Restitution for Duress' (1996) 9 JCL 220. See also *Deemcope Pty Ltd v Cantown Pty Ltd* [1995] 2 VR 44.
14 Ibid, at 719.
15 [1999] 1 All ER (Comm) 856.

of duress. Some of the argument turned on whether the fact that the claimants would be likely to have succeeded in seeking relief against forfeiture gave it an interest in the goods so that the case fell within duress of goods. Judge Rich QC thought not. But his essential reasoning was that the defendants' threat to re-possess their goods was not illegitimate applying the language of Lord Goff in *The Evia Luck*. Unfortunately he did not spell out precisely why it was not illegitimate beyond recognising that, prior to any relief against forfeiture being applied for, let alone granted, the defendants were acting lawfully. Certainly one would have thought that, by analogy to the discussion of threatened breach of contract above, this was a situation where the defendants were acting in bad faith and were concerned to exploit the claimants' weakness rather than solving their own financial problems. On the other hand, bad faith should perhaps be largely irrelevant where what is threatened is perfectly lawful.

6. ILLEGITIMATE THREATS TO PROSECUTE OR SUE OR PUBLISH INFORMATION

There is a long-standing line of cases under which contracts for payments induced by *threats to prosecute* the claimant or, more usually, a relative of the claimant have been held invalid for duress or actual undue influence.

For example, in *Williams v Bayley*[16] a father agreed to pay promissory notes in favour of a bank (secured by a charge over his property) in order to avert the bank's implied threat to prosecute his son for forging his signature on the notes. It was held that the contract was invalid as it had been procured by undue influence.

In *Kaufman v Gerson*,[17] Kaufman threatened Gerson that he would institute criminal proceedings against her husband unless she contracted to pay him a considerable sum of money. The contract was held unenforceable for undue influence or duress even though according to the law of France, which was where the contract was made and the parties were domiciled, the contract was valid. Collins MR said:

'The judge seems to admit that, if the agreement had been obtained by the threat of physical violence, for example, by threatening the defendant with a pistol, or something of that kind, the case would be brought within a general

---

16 (1866) LR 1 HL 200. The alternative ground for the decision was that the contract was unenforceable because illegal. For an example of the claimant himself being threatened with prosecution see *Société des Hotels Reunis v Hawker* (1913) 29 TLR 578.

17 [1904] 1 KB 591. The conflict of laws point in the case is considered in chapter 16.

principle, upon which the court would be entitled to refuse to enforce the contract, whatever might be the law of any other country on the subject ... But, if so, what does it matter what particular form of coercion is used so long as the will is coerced? Some persons would be more easily coerced by moral pressure, such as was exercised here, than by the threat of physical violence. It seems to me impossible to say that it is not coercion to threaten a wife with dishonour of her husband and children.'[18]

And in *Mutual Finance Ltd v John Wetton and Sons Ltd*[19] a guarantee of payment to the claimant company was signed by Percy Wetton on behalf of the defendant company in order to avert the claimant company's implied threat to prosecute Joseph Wetton (Percy's brother) for forgery in acquiring a lorry on hire purchase. Percy Wetton signed the agreement for fear that prosecution of his brother would kill their father who was very ill. Porter J distinguished duress at common law, which he thought was confined to duress of the person, but held that the contract here was voidable for undue influence.

Although none of the above cases dealt with restitutionary consequences, it is clear that repayment of any money paid would be required on rescission;[20] and it is *a fortiori* that restitution of *non-contractual* payments will be ordered where induced by a threat to prosecute.

To threaten to prosecute unless money is paid (which, by analogy, one can extend to include informing the police of a crime unless money is paid)[1] is, generally,[2] not to threaten anything unlawful.[3] The illegitimacy rests with it being contrary to the public interest for criminal proceedings to be stifled for the sake of personal gain. Indeed it seems that contracts entered into to avert threats of criminal prosecution are illegal.[4] If so, restitution of money paid is explicable on the basis that illegality is no defence to the claim based on duress: ie, on the traditional approach to illegality the payor was *non in pari delicto*.

Threats to sue unless money is paid are almost always regarded as legitimate. It was for this reason that duress was held not to be made

---

18 Ibid at p 597.
19 [1937] 2 KB 389.
20 See, eg, *Davies v London and Provincial Marine Insurance Co* (1878) 8 Ch D 469.
1   Lord Scarman gave this as an example of a lawful but illegitimate threat in *The Universe Sentinel* [1983] 1 AC 366, 401.
2   If the threatener has no reasonable and probable cause he may be threatening the tort of malicious prosecution. Even with such a cause he may be regarded as threatening the tort of abuse of legal process: *Speed Seal Products v Paddington* [1985] 1 WLR 1327; *Metall und Rohstoff v Donaldson Lufkin & Jenrette Inc* [1990] 1 QB 391.
3   This is not to deny that the threatener, by accepting money not to disclose information concerning an arrestable offence, may be guilty of a criminal offence: see, eg, Criminal Law Act 1967, s 5.
4   *Williams v Bayley* (1866) LR 1 HL 200; *Davies v London and Provincial Marine Insurance Co* (1878) 8 Ch D 469.

out in *William Whiteley Ltd v R*[5] and *Woolwich Equitable Building Society v IRC*,[6] which concerned mere threats to sue by the Inland Revenue to recover unpaid tax (demanded ultra vires) and penalties. In the latter Lord Goff said, '... where money has been paid under pressure of actual or threatened legal proceedings for its recovery, the payor cannot say that for that reason the money has been paid under compulsion and is therefore recoverable by him'.[7] And as Windeyer J said in *Mason v New South Wales*,[8] 'A threat of proceedings for a pecuniary penalty does not make a payment made thereafter involuntary: for the payor might have defended the proceedings and relied upon the unlawfulness of the demand.'

Indeed if it is correct that the ambit of duress is not to be drawn differently for contractual and non-contractual payments, one detrimental consequence of treating threats to sue as illegitimate would be that out of court settlements would be seriously undermined.

There have been rare exceptions. For example, in *Smith v Cuff*[9] a creditor who had entered into a composition agreement, while demanding extra money from the debtor, was held bound to repay that extra money as paid by oppression. That is, it was paid under an implied illegitimate threat of suing for the full debt, where the threat was clearly illegitimate because the payment demanded was an illegal fraud on the creditors (and illegality afforded the creditor no defence because the duress meant that the debtor was *non in pari delicto*).[10]

Closely related to threats to prosecute – in that again a person's reputation may be at stake and what is threatened is generally not unlawful – is where a defendant *threatens to publish information* detrimental to the claimant or a relative of the claimant unless the claimant pays him money. Surprisingly there appears to be no direct English authority on this, although obiter dicta in *Norreys v Zeffert*[11] is

---

5   (1909) 101 LT 741.
6   [1993] AC 70.
7   Ibid, p 165. See also p 161 (per Lord Keith), p 184 (per Lord Jauncey); and [1989] 1 WLR 137, 144 (per Nolan J). Similarly the restitution of money paid under reversed judgments cannot be explained as grounded on duress: McFarlane, 'The Recovery of Money Paid Under Judgments Later Reversed' [2001] RLR 1 argues that restitution (and compensation) is here best explained as 'policy-based' and concerned to balance upholding the finality of judgments with the protection of litigants from judicial mistakes.
8   (1959) 102 CLR 108, 144.
9   (1817) 6 M & S 160. See similarly *Smith v Bromley* (1760) 2 Doug KB 696n. A further exception is *Unwin v Leaper* (1840) 1 Man & G 747 (threat of civil proceedings used to induce the claimant to settle a separate dispute with the defendant held to constitute duress allowing the restitution of money paid). A threat is also likely to be considered illegitimate where what is threatened constitutes the tort of maliciously instituting proceedings or abuse of legal process: above, p 239, n 2.
10   Below, pp 577–578.
11   [1939] 2 All ER 187. See *Silsbee v Webber* 50 NE 555 (1898): threat to inform a father, who was ill, of his son's thieving unless the mother assigned property.

in point. The defendant 'punter' had defaulted on various horse racing bets including one with the claimant bookmaker. Acting through the secretary of the National Turf Protection Society the claimant induced the defendant to agree to pay the bet owed by threatening to tell of his betting defaults to Tattersalls, to the trade protection societies, and to the defendant's social club. The threats, except to inform Tattersalls, were held to be illegitimate so that the alleged contract, if made, would have been voidable. Atkinson J said that the dividing line in issue was:

> '... between legitimate business threats and threats which are not legitimate ... In my opinion, the threat to report to Tattersalls was a threat which the plaintiff ... was entitled to make ... Such a step is one primarily aimed at protecting and furthering the interests of bookmakers, but threats that the National Turf Protection Society would notify members of a social club and the trade protection societies are, in my view, threats to defame, which are threats to injure and seem to me to come within that class of threats which ... the creditor is not entitled to make.'[12]

As regards causation the case law does not suggest that the threat to prosecute or sue or publish information need be anything more than *a* cause of the claimant rendering the benefit to the defendant, to be established by the claimant according to the usual 'but for' test. In particular, use has rarely been made of 'overborne will' language.

---

12 Ibid at pp 189–190.

Chapter 6

Undue influence

1. INTRODUCTION

(1) Unjust enrichment at the claimant's expense

In order to understand properly the law on undue influence, it is submitted that one should first put to one side those cases of actual undue influence that are concerned with illegitimate threats or pressure. Their true place is within the law on duress and they have therefore been included in the last chapter.[1]

Examination of the remainder – which is the bulk – of the law on undue influence reveals that one is concerned with where, as a result of the relationship between them, one party is in a position to exercise undue influence over the other. Where the other party enters into a particular transaction as a result of the undue influence of the other, the influenced party fails to apply a full and free independent judgement in relation to that transaction and the transaction is, therefore, voidable at the instance of the influenced party.

What is less clear is what precisely is meant by *undue* influence. One view is that the courts are solely concerned with the extent of the influence – the degree of impairment of the claimant's will – so that 'undue' means 'excessive'.[2] The better view is that, like duress, undue influence focuses on the conduct of the person exerting the influence as well as the effect on the claimant.[3] 'Undue' means 'unacceptable' and in deciding what is unacceptable influence the courts may take into account not only the effect on the claimant but also the substantive fairness of the transaction and the state of mind of the defendant. Unacceptable or undue influence occurs where the

---

1 · See above, pp 211, 238–241. In speaking of actual undue influence, Lord Nicholls in *Royal Bank of Scotland v Etridge (No 2)* [2001] UKHL 44, [2001] 3 WLR 1021, para 8 said, 'Today there is much overlap with the principle of duress. …'

2 See Birks and Chin, 'On the Nature of Undue Influence' in *Good Faith and Fault in Contract* (eds Beatson and Friedmann, 1995), 57–97.

3 Bigwood, 'Undue Influence: "Impaired Consent" or "Wicked Exploitation"' (1996) 16 OJLS 503.

'influencing' party has taken unfair advantage of his or her position of influence. He or she has abused the influence arising from the parties' relationship.

In Lord Nicholls' words in *Royal Bank of Scotland v Etridge (No 2):*[4]

> 'The objective is to ensure that the influence of one person over another is not abused ... If the intention [to enter into the transaction] was produced by an unacceptable means, the law will not permit the transaction to stand. The means used is regarded as an exercise of improper or "undue" influence, and hence unacceptable, whenever the consent thus procured ought not fairly to be treated as the expression of a person's free will.'

However, this does not necessarily mean that the defendant must have acted in bad faith dishonestly knowing that he or she is taking advantage of his or her position of influence. For example, in *Cheese v Thomas*[5] the Court of Appeal, while setting aside a transaction for undue influence, expressly recognised that the defendant had not acted in a morally reprehensible way.

Ever since *Allcard v Skinner*[6] the law has been divided into two categories of undue influence: actual and presumed. In the case itself, the claimant's deed of gift transferring stock to her spiritual adviser (to be used for the purposes of the religious charity with which they were both involved) would have been set aside for presumed undue influence but for laches. In a famous passage Cotton LJ said:

> 'The decisions [on undue influence] may be divided into two classes. First, where the court has been satisfied that the gift was the result of influence expressly used by the donee for the purpose; second, where the relations between donor and donee have at or shortly before the execution of the gift been such as to raise a presumption that the donee had influence over the donor. In such a case the court sets aside the voluntary gift, unless it is proved that in fact the gift was the spontaneous act of the donor acting under circumstances which enabled him to exercise an independent will and which justified the court in holding that the gift was the result of a free exercise of the donor's will.'[7]

In *Royal Bank of Scotland v Etridge (No 2)*[8] the House of Lords has clarified that the difference between the two categories is not as marked as has sometimes been thought. The difference between them is that, in the category of presumed undue influence, the claimant

---

4   [2001] UKHL 44, [2001] 3 WLR 1021, paras 6–7.
5   [1994] 1 WLR 129, 138. See also *Allcard v Skinner* (1887) 36 Ch D 145; *Hammond v Osborn*, [2002] 34 LS Gaz R 29.
6   (1887) 36 Ch D 145.
7   Ibid, at p 171.
8   [2001] UKHL 44, [2001] 3 WLR 1021.

has the benefit of a rebuttable evidential presumption of undue influence. One could manage without the two categories (although for ease of exposition this book continues to use them) by simply saying that it is for the person alleging it (the claimant) to prove that a transaction was entered into as a result of undue influence; and that in some situations the claimant is assisted by a rebuttable evidential presumption of undue influence which shifts the evidential burden of proof to the other party.

It follows from this that it would be inconsistent for a judge to conclude that there was no actual undue influence while at the same time deciding that the claimant succeeds by reason of a presumption of undue influence.[9] To avoid inaccuracy, what a judge should be saying in that situation is that it is only with the benefit of a presumption of undue influence that the claimant succeeds in proving undue influence.

What causal link must there be between the undue influence and the rendering of the benefit? It was explained in chapter 1 that the normal test for causation is that the ground for restitution must be shown by the claimant to be a cause of the benefit applying the 'but for' test. This is supported in relation to undue influence by *Bank of Credit and Commerce International SA v Aboody*,[10] in which Slade LJ, giving the judgment of the Court of Appeal, took the view that a transaction should not be set aside for actual undue influence 'where the evidence establishes that on the balance of probabilities the complainant would have entered into the transaction in any event'. Slightly different are presumed undue influence cases in which it appears that there is a presumption of causation so that the evidential burden shifts to the defendant to prove that the claimant would have entered into the transaction anyway. As Cartwright says, 'In effect the rebutting of the presumption requires the party presumed to have exercised the influence to prove that he did not, by abuse of his position, cause the contract.'[11]

So much for the unjust factor. 'At the claimant's expense' here means by subtraction from the claimant. And the benefit in play in the cases has generally comprised either money or proprietary rights to goods, shares or land. A personal restitutionary remedy in respect of benefits in kind (services and the use of intellectual property rights) was in issue in only one leading case – *O'Sullivan v Management Agency & Music Ltd*[12] – and, although not discussed in the judgments, there

9 Ibid, at paras 210–228 (Lord Scott).
10 [1990] 1 QB 923, 971.
11 *Unequal Bargaining* (1991), p 187.
12 [1985] QB 428.

was on the facts no difficulty in overcoming subjective devaluation either on the ground that the 'benefits' were incontrovertibly beneficial (the defendants had realised profits) or because they were bargained for by the defendants in the contract or, perhaps, because the benefits had been reprehensibly sought out.

(2) Rescission

The restitutionary remedy for undue influence has invariably been rescission. As explained in chapter 1, this is a complex remedy which, depending on the context, may be non-restitutionary (but there have been no well-known cases of undue influence in which rescission has simply been concerned to allow escape from a transaction) or a personal or proprietary restitutionary remedy. Rescission is subject to its usual four bars:[13] lapse of time,[14] affirmation,[15] third party rights,[16] and *restitutio in integrum* being impossible.

The last bar is the most significant from a restitutionary perspective and is best viewed as recognising that the defendant could successfully counterclaim for failure of consideration where the basis for the defendant's rendering of the benefit has been removed by the claimant's rescission of the transaction.[17] *O'Sullivan v Management Agency & Music Ltd*[18] is directly in point. The claimant, a singer-songwriter, when young and unknown, had entered into a contract to be managed by one of the defendants and had thereafter made contracts with that defendant's publishing and recording companies by which the claimant, inter alia, assigned away his copyright in songs and tapes. After the agreements had been performed and had expired the claimant sought to have the contracts set aside on the grounds, inter alia, that they had been obtained by presumed undue influence. On appeal the issues principally centred on the appropriate remedy for undue influence. The Court of Appeal dismissed the defendants' arguments that the contracts could not now be set aside because it was impossible to achieve *restitutio in integrum*. All three judges cited as

---

13 See generally Treitel, *The Law of Contract* (10th edn, 1999) pp 386–389.

14 See, eg, *Allcard v Skinner* (1887) 36 Ch D 145, esp at 187 (Lindley LJ): rescission of a gift was barred by delay/affirmation.

15 See, eg, *Mitchell v Homfray* (1881) 8 QBD 587 (rescission of gift barred by affirmation). See also *Allcard v Skinner* (1887) 36 Ch D 145 and the useful discussion of this bar, albeit that it was rejected on the facts, in *Goldsworthy v Brickell* [1987] Ch 378.

16 Ie rescission is barred where a bona fide purchaser without notice has acquired the subject matter. See, eg, *Bridgeman v Green* (1757) Wilm 58; *Bainbrigge v Browne* (1881) 18 Ch D 188, 196–197; *Morley v Loughnan* [1893] 1 Ch 736, 757.

17 See below, pp 538–542.

18 [1985] QB 428.

the key test Lord Blackburn's words in *Erlanger v New Sombrero Phosphate Co*[19] (a non-disclosure case) to the effect that precise *restitutio in integrum* was unnecessary in equity and that what should be aimed for was what was 'practically just'. Dunn LJ said:

> 'Transactions may be set aside even though it is impossible to place the parties precisely in the position in which they were before, provided that the court can achieve practical justice between the parties by obliging the wrongdoer to give up his profits and advantages, while at the same time compensating him for any work that he has actually performed pursuant to the transaction'.[20]

And in Fox LJ's words, 'The question is not whether the parties can be restored to their original position; it is what does the justice of the case require?'[1]

The Court of Appeal therefore upheld the trial judge's setting aside of the contract and made the following consequential orders: an account of profits made by the defendants subject to an allowance for reasonable remuneration, including a profit element, for the work done in promoting and managing the claimant; reconveyance of the song copyrights; and delivery up of some of the master tapes. The first of these orders is analogous to the remedy awarded in *Boardman v Phipps*[2] but some of the reasoning of the Court of Appeal can be criticised for treating *O'Sullivan* as if it were a case of wrongdoing by making unauthorised profit in breach of a fiduciary duty rather than as a case of undue influence within unjust enrichment by subtraction. Despite this criticism, the decision in *O'Sullivan* is highly significant for one can strongly argue that, by its willingness to award complex mutual restitution, the Court of Appeal has effectively emptied the traditional '*restitutio in integrum* must be possible' bar of any content. What is required is that the rescinding claimant makes counter-restitution, whether specifically or by a monetary equivalent: counter-restitution may be difficult to assess but is never impossible.

Alongside counter-restitution, one must also now consider change of position. The leading case to be analysed in this context is *Cheese v Thomas*.[3] The claimant contributed £43,000 to the purchase of a house (for £83,000) by his great nephew (the defendant). The agreement between them was that the claimant was to be entitled to live in the property rent-free for the rest of his life. However, when the defendant failed to pay off the mortgage instalments, the claimant sought to set aside the transaction for presumed undue influence. This succeeded.

19   (1878) 3 App Cas 1218, 1278.
20   [1985] QB 428, 458.
1   Ibid at pp 466–467.
2   [1967] 2 AC 46. Below, pp 495–496.
3   [1994] 1 WLR 129.

The difficult issue was what restitution and counter-restitution required consequent on the setting aside of the transaction. At first blush, the claimant was entitled to repayment of £43,000 while being required to vacate the house. But this would have left the defendant considerably worse off than if the transaction had never been entered into because the house had plummeted in value and had been sold for only £55,400. The Court of Appeal decided that the loss in value of the house should be borne proportionately to the amounts contributed to the purchase. Hence the defendant should pay only £11,000, not £43,000, to the claimant. Nicholls LJ, giving the leading judgment, stressed that, in addition to restoring benefits, this 'sharing of the loss' was justified in the pursuit of 'practical justice for both parties'[4] because this was not a straightforward sale or gift. Rather the transaction involved both parties making a financial contribution to an asset from which both were intended to benefit. Moreover, he clarified that, although undue influence had been exercised, the defendant had not been acting in a morally reprehensible way.

This concern with the defendant's loss is probably best rationalised as an application of the defence of good faith change of position. As Mindy Chen-Wishart has written, '[C]hange of position explains the result in *Cheese* without invoking joint venture, an uncertain concept of uncertain significance, and without leaning so heavily on the elusive conscience of the court.'[5] She also helpfully points out that had rescission not been barred by laches or affirmation in the seminal case of *Allcard v Skinner*,[6] the novice nun would not have been granted restitution of the full gift paid but rather only that part that was left taking into account what her spiritual adviser had spent on religious purposes. This might be rationalised as an early recognition of the idea of change of position in a case where, again, the defendant was acting in good faith.

Separate from rescission and counter-restitution for undue influence is an award of equitable compensation for the equitable wrong of breach of fiduciary duty. This is analogous to an award of compensatory damages for the tort of deceit which may, of course, be awarded in addition to, or instead of, rescinding a contract for fraudulent misrepresentation. In *Mahoney v Purnell*,[7] May J decided

---

4 Ibid, at 136.
5 'Loss Sharing, Undue Influence and Manifest Disadvantage' (1994) 110 LQR 173, 178. See also Birks, 'Overview: Tracing, Claiming and Defences' in *Laundering and Tracing* (ed Birks, 1995), pp 289, 327–328; Chen-Wishart, 'Unjust Factors and the Restitutionary Response' (2000) 20 OJLS 557, 559–566. Cf McKendrick, 'Total Failure of Consideration and Counter-Restitution: Two Issues or One?' in *Laundering and Tracing* (ed Birks, 1995), pp 217, 238.
6 (1887) 36 Ch D 145.
7 [1996] 3 All ER 61.

that as precise restitution, unwinding a transfer of shares, was not possible because the company had been wound up so that the shares could not be returned, the fair and just remedy was instead to award compensation for the loss the claimant had suffered in entering into the contract. On the best interpretation of the case, the compensation was not being awarded for the undue influence as such. Undue influence is not an equitable wrong triggering compensation. Rather the compensation was for the equitable wrong of breach of fiduciary duty.[8]

(3) Non-contractual benefits

This chapter does not divide between the restitution of benefits conferred under contracts entered into under undue influence and the restitution of non-contractual benefits. This is not only because most of the cases are concerned with contractual benefits[9] but also because it is far from clear that the scope of undue influence differs whether the benefit is rendered under a contract or not. This is not to deny that, in principle and by analogy to mistake, a strong argument can be mounted for having a wider notion of undue influence where no escape from a contract is involved because that does not require reallocating agreed risks and undermining bargained for expectations. Dicta of Vaughan Williams LJ in *Wright v Carter*,[10] a case of presumed undue influence, support this: '... it is perfectly plain that in the case of a gift the rule applied by the Court of Equity [objecting to undue influence] is much more stringent, is more absolute, than the rule that is applied in the case of a bargain or a contract.'

(4) Three-party cases

In recent years, most of the reported undue influence cases have concerned contracts made not between the influencer (X) and the influenced party (C) but between the influenced party and another party (D). Probably the commonest example is where, under her husband's (X's) undue influence, a wife (C) guarantees to a bank

---

8   See Birks, 'Unjust Factors and Wrongs: Pecuniary Rescission for Undue Influence' [1997] RLR 72. For an argument that, in appropriate cases, undue influence should be seen as a wrong triggering compensation, see Lusina Ho, 'Undue Influence and Equitable Compensation' in *Restitution and Equity* (eds Birks and Rose, 2000), pp 193–210.

9   But, eg, *Mitchell v Homfray* (1881) 8 QBD 587; *Allcard v Skinner* (1887) 36 Ch D 145; *Inche Noriah v Shaik Allie Bin Omar* [1929] AC 127; and *Re Craig* [1971] Ch 95 all concerned gifts.

10   [1903] 1 Ch 27, 50.

(D), secured by a charge over the matrimonial home, the debts to the bank of her husband or her husband's company. Is the wife (C) entitled to rescind the contract with D, even though D did not induce the contract by undue influence (or duress or misrepresentation)?

In *Barclays Bank plc v O'Brien*[11] (which actually concerned misrepresentation by a third party) the House of Lords held that C can rescind where either X was acting as D's agent in procuring the contract (which will be very rare); or where D has actual or constructive notice of X's conduct inducing the contract. Lord Browne-Wilkinson, with whom the other Lords agreed, spelt out what constitutes constructive notice in this situation. There are three main elements: (i) D must be aware that C is in a relationship of trust and confidence with X so that there is a substantial risk of undue influence (or misrepresentation); (ii) the transaction on its face must not be to the financial advantage of C; (iii) D must have failed to take reasonable steps to be satisfied that the transaction was entered into by C freely and with knowledge of the full facts (as, for example, where D has failed to advise C to take independent legal advice). The first two elements go to putting D on inquiry, while the third element goes to what D, who has been put on inquiry, must do to avoid being fixed with constructive notice.

Unfortunately, while admirably clear, Lord Browne-Wilkinson's statement of principles spawned a mass of case law. This culminated in a re-examination of the issues by the House of Lords in *Royal Bank of Scotland v Etridge (No 2)*.[12] Their Lordships, while confirming the basic approach in *O'Brien*, were particularly concerned to lay down in a code of practice the reasonable steps that a bank, which is put on inquiry of a husband's undue influence over (or misrepresentation to) his wife, must take to avoid being fixed with constructive notice. If such steps are not taken, and the bank has been put on inquiry, a wife who can establish actual or presumed undue influence (or misrepresentation) will be able to rescind the contract (guaranteeing her husband's debts) with the bank.

The purpose of the reasonable steps is for the bank to try to ensure that the wife fully understands what she is doing. Their Lordships laid down that ordinarily there is no need for the bank to meet the wife, provided it has confirmation from the wife's solicitor that the solicitor has advised her appropriately. It is not a matter for the bank if the wife is improperly advised, unless the bank actually knows of this.

The practice banks should adopt is therefore as follows. First, the bank should communicate directly with the wife informing her that

---

11 [1994] 1 AC 180. See Cartwright, 'Taking Stock of *O'Brien*' [1999] RLR 1.
12 [2001] UKHL 44, [2001] 3 WLR 1021.

the bank requires written confirmation from a solicitor acting for her that she understands what she is doing. Secondly, the bank should forward to the wife directly, or to her solicitor, the financial circumstances regarding her husband's application for a loan (for example, his request and the amount of his existing indebtedness). Thirdly, the bank should not proceed unless it has received from the wife's solicitor a confirmation that the solicitor has advised her appropriately.

It can be seen, therefore, that while, irrespective of whether it suspects undue influence or not, a prudent bank would now always ensure that a wife is advised by a solicitor, the bank is protected once the solicitor has confirmed that appropriate advice has been given (unless the bank knows that that is false).

Analogously the House of Lords laid down a code of practice for solicitors. While a failure to comply with this code may be relevant to determining whether the wife was free from the exercise of undue influence (and, in particular, whether presumed undue influence has been rebutted) it will be most directly relevant to any claim by the wife against the solicitor for professional negligence. The practice laid down is that the solicitor should meet the wife face-to-face, in the absence of the husband, and should explain the purpose for which the solicitor has become involved, the nature of the documents, the seriousness of the risks involved and that she has a choice whether to proceed. The solicitor should also check whether she wishes to proceed. The solicitor for the wife may be the same solicitor as is acting for the husband (or the bank) but, if that is so, the solicitor must be careful to guard against any conflict of interest.

There are two additional important points that emerge from *Etridge.* First, in deciding when a bank is put on inquiry (ie when it should reasonably suspect undue influence or misrepresentation) their Lordships said that this would be so whenever a wife offers to stand as surety for her husband's debts or her husband's company's debts or the debts of a company jointly owned by the wife and her husband. But this would not be so where the loan is made jointly to a husband and wife unless the bank knows that the loan is only intended to be used for the husband's purposes. Towards the end of his speech, Lord Nicholls suggested that the underpinning wider principle is that a bank is put on inquiry wherever a person offers to stand as surety for the debts of another and the relationship between the surety and the debtor is non-commercial. This principle therefore extended to the facts of *Crédit Lyonnais Bank Nederland v Burch*[13] in which a junior

---

13   [1997] 1 All ER 144. Chen-Wishart, 'The *O'Brien* Principle and Substantive Unfairness' [1997] CLJ 60.

employee had entered into a mortgage transaction by which she secured, by a charge over her flat, all her employer company's debts to the bank. She was held able to rescind the guarantee as against the bank because of her employer's undue influence.

Secondly, prior to *Etridge*, doubts were raised as to whether reliance on the concept of notice in this situation was justified.[14] The decision of the House of Lords in *Barclays Bank plc v Boulter*[15] clarified that this is not an application of the bona fide purchase defence. Hence the burden of proof in relation to the bank's constructive notice is on C (the person seeking to set aside the transaction) not D (the bank). In *Etridge*, their Lordships confirmed that utilising the concept of notice is here appropriate albeit that this is an unconventional use of that concept. By invoking the idea of reasonableness, it enables the courts to deal appropriately with whether those who have not themselves exercised undue influence (and not made a misrepresentation) should be affected by it. In the specific context of wives and banks, it acts as a policy device for the reasonable protection of wives. However, Lord Nicholls was at pains to emphasise that his observations as to the appropriateness of the concept of notice were confined to contracts of guarantee. It may be that a different approach (perhaps requiring actual knowledge of the undue influence or misrepresentation) would apply if other types of contract are to be voidable as against a contracting party which has not itself exercised the undue influence (or has not itself made the misrepresentation). And certainly it appears that where a non-contractual payment or gift is made by the influenced party to the defendant as a result of the undue influence of a third party, the defendant's liability to make restitution applies irrespective of notice or actual knowledge.[16]

(5) Proprietary restitution in respect of payments made under undue influence

What has been said in the last chapter on proprietary restitution in respect of payments made under duress applies analogously in relation to whether there may be proprietary restitution in respect of payments made under undue influence.[17] Nothing would be gained by repeating

---

14 See, eg, O'Sullivan, 'Undue Influence and Misrepresentation after O'Brien: Making Security Secure' in *Restitution and Banking Law* (ed Rose, 1998), p 42, esp pp 43–48.
15 [1999] 4 All ER 513.
16 *Bridgeman v Green* (1757) Wilm 58; Friedmann, 'Valid, Voidable, Qualified, and Non-Existing Obligations: An Alternative Perspective on the Law of Restitution' in *Essays on the Law of Restitution* (ed Burrows, 1991), pp 246, 277.
17 See above, pp 218–219. For discussion by commentators, see Goff and Jones, para 11-015; Chambers, *Resulting Trusts* (1997), pp 135–137.

what has there been said. The only difference that should be noted is that, while no English case appears to have directly addressed the question whether money paid under undue influence is held on trust, there are more analogous examples of proprietary rescission of contracts or gifts for undue influence[18] than there are for duress.

2. ACTUAL UNDUE INFLUENCE

It is clear that some cases, while using the language of undue influence, are better treated under the heading of duress for they concern illegitimate threats.[19] This then leaves the category of actual undue influence – where the claimant has to prove (without the assistance of an evidential presumption of undue influence) that he or she entered the transaction as a result of undue influence – as virtually bereft of case examples: in almost all the leading cases claimants have succeeded on the sole basis of presumed undue influence. Not surprisingly, therefore, Goff and Jones' discussion of actual undue influence is very short.[20] A rare modern example of a claim succeeding on the basis of actual undue influence is *Re Craig*[1] in which Ungoed-Thomas J decided that gifts by the deceased to his housekeeper of shares and cash and land should be set aside either on the ground of presumed undue influence, built up on the facts, or actual undue influence.

In *CIBC Mortgages plc v Pitt*[2] the House of Lords decided that any requirement of showing that the transaction was 'manifestly disadvantageous' (which had been laid down as a requirement for presumed undue influence by the House of Lords in *National Westminster Bank plc v Morgan*)[3] did not apply to actual undue influence. This appeared to give claimants an incentive to establish actual undue influence thereby evading the requirement of 'manifest disadvantage'. But any such

18 See, eg, *Allcard v Skinner* (1887) 36 Ch D 145; *Royal Bank of Scotland v Etridge (No 2)* [2001] 3 WLR 1021.

19 See, eg, *Williams v Bayley* (1866) LR 1 HL 200; *Mutual Finance Ltd v John Wetton & Sons Ltd* [1937] 2 KB 389; discussed above, chapter 5. It is significant that there was no mention of *Williams v Bayley* in *Allcard v Skinner*. See also Lord Denning's division between undue influence (actual or presumed) and undue pressure in *Lloyds Bank Ltd v Bundy* [1975] QB 326. In *Bank of Baroda v Shah* [1988] 3 All ER 24 there were both threats (arguably illegitimate) and a presumed relationship of undue influence (and, no doubt, actual undue influence). The Court of Appeal solely used the language of undue influence and not duress. The actual decision was that the claimant bank was not 'infected' by the undue influence. In *Re Craig* [1971] Ch 95 Ungoed-Thomas J indicated that there were background threats: but these would not in themselves have been illegitimate and his judgment was solely based on undue influence.

20 Goff and Jones, para 11-003.

1   [1971] Ch 95. See also *UCB Corporate Services Ltd v Williams* [2002] EWCA Civ 555.

2   [1994] 1 AC 200.

3   [1985] AC 686.

incentive has been significantly reduced by their Lordships' view in *Royal Bank of Scotland v Etridge (No 2)*[4] that showing that a transaction is disadvantageous is a usual indicator of undue influence in all cases (including actual undue influence). In Lord Nicholls' words, giving the leading speech, 'In *CIBC Mortgages plc v Pitt* your Lordships' House decided that in cases of undue influence disadvantage is not a necessary ingredient of the cause of action ... However, in the nature of things, questions of undue influence will not usually arise and the exercise of undue influence is unlikely to occur, where the transaction is innocuous.'[5]

3. PRESUMED UNDUE INFLUENCE

There are two conditions for the presumption to arise. First, there must be a relationship in which the claimant is under the defendant's influence: ie a relationship of influence. And secondly, the transaction, be it gift or contract, must be disadvantageous to the claimant in the sense of not being readily explicable on ordinary motives. Once those two conditions are satisfied, the onus of proof switches to the defendant to rebut the presumption of undue influence, most obviously by showing that the claimant had independent advice.

In *Royal Bank of Scotland v Etridge (No 2)*,[6] the House of Lords clarified the nature of the presumption that applies when one talks of 'presumed undue influence'. What is meant is that there is a shift in the evidential burden of proof. Analogously to the principle of *res ipsa loquitur*, the presumption of undue influence is a rebuttable evidential presumption.[7] But as their Lordships pointed out, confusion can be, and has been, caused because, as we shall see, in establishing the relationship of influence (which is the first requirement for the evidential presumption) some categories of relationship are irrebuttably presumed, as a matter of law, to be ones in which one party had influence over the other.

(1) Establishing the presumption of undue influence

(a) The relationship of influence

This relationship is most easily made out by showing that the parties were within certain well-established categories of relationship

---

4   [2001] UKHL 44, [2001] 3 WLR 1021. The term 'manifest disadvantage' was also rejected: see below, pp 256–258.
5   Ibid, at para 12. Cf Lord Scott, ibid, at para 156.
6   [2001] UKHL 44, [2001] 3 WLR 1021.
7   Ibid, at para 16 (Lord Nicholls); paras 151–162 (Lord Scott). Cf Lord Hobhouse at paras 103–107 who said that this was not a presumption properly so-called.

which, by their very nature, involve influence by one over the other;[8] for example, parent over child,[9] spiritual adviser over follower,[10] solicitor over client,[11] trustee over beneficiary,[12] or doctor over patient.[13] However, a husband and wife relationship is not a relationship of this type (that is, it is not automatically a relationship of influence).[14]

It has sometimes been argued that a trustee and beneficiary relationship is not one of influence.[15] Certainly the traditional view is that a beneficiary can rescind a sale of trust property to the trustee on the grounds of breach of fiduciary duty irrespective of substantive unfairness.[16] But such a strict approach is not always imposed. For example, substantive unfairness is required where the sale is of the beneficial interest.[17] At least where that is so, it appears that the relevant principles are those of presumed undue influence and that the relationship is being treated as one of influence.

As an alternative to the fixed categories, the claimant may be able to establish that, on the facts, there was a relationship in which he was under the defendant's influence.[18] In *Tate v Williamson*,[19] for example, executors of the deceased, who had died from drink at the age of 24, successfully sought to set aside his sale of mines to the defendant. The defendant was distantly related to the deceased and had been put in touch with him to help sort out his debts. It was held that on the facts the defendant had put himself in a fiduciary position of influence over the deceased and had taken advantage of it by buying the mines at a price that he knew to be an undervalue. Lord Chelmsford LC said:

---

8   In *Barclays Bank plc v O'Brien* [1994] 1 AC 180 and several cases following it (eg, *Crédit Lyonnais Bank Nederland NV v Burch* [1997] 1 All ER 144, 154) the House of Lords referred to these relationships as within class 2A as distinct from where the relationship is built from the facts which was referred to as within class 2B. In *Royal Bank of Scotland v Etridge (No 2)* [2001] UKHL 44, [2001] 3 WLR 1021 Lord Hobhouse, at paras 103–107, and Lord Scott, at paras 151–162, in the course of criticising the class 2B classification for potentially leading judges to presume undue influence too readily, clarified that there is an irrebuttable legal presumption of a relationship of influence in class 2A but not class 2B.

9   Eg, *Lancashire Loans Ltd v Black* [1934] 1 KB 380.

10 Eg, *Allcard v Skinner* (1887) 36 Ch D 145.

11 Eg, *Wright v Carter* [1903] 1 Ch 27.

12 Eg, *Plowright v Lambert* (1885) 52 LT 646; *Tito v Waddell (No 2)* [1977] Ch 106, 241.

13 Eg, *Mitchell v Homfray* (1881) 8 QBD 587, although here the gift was affirmed.

14 *Barclays Bank plc v O'Brien* [1994] 1 AC 180; *Royal Bank of Scotland v Etridge (No 2)* [2001] UKHL 44, [2001] 3 WLR 1021.

15 Winder 'Undue Influence and Fiduciary Relationship' (1940) 4 Conv 274.

16 Below, p 493, n 5.

17 See the cases cited above in note 12.

18 In *Barclays Bank plc v O'Brien* [1994] 1 AC 180 this was referred to as class 2B presumed undue influence. But see above note 8.

19 (1866) 2 Ch App 55. For an earlier example, see *Huguenin v Baseley* (1807) 14 Ves 273.

'Wherever two persons stand in such a relation that, while it continues, confidence is necessarily reposed by one, and the influence which naturally grows out of that confidence is possessed by the other, and this confidence is abused, or the influence is exerted to obtain an advantage at the expense of the confiding party, the person so availing himself of his position will not be permitted to retain the advantage, although the transaction could not have been impeached if no such confidential relation had existed.'[20]

That decision was followed by the Court of Appeal in *Tufton v Sperni*[1] in setting aside a sale, at an overvalue, of a house which the vendor and purchaser intended to be used as a Moslem centre. On the facts the vendor had built up a relationship of influence over the purchaser. Sir Raymond Evershed MR stressed the law's recognition of such factual relationships commenting that it was wrong to suggest that 'to create the relationship of confidence, the person owing the duty must be found clothed in the recognisable garb of a guardian, trustee, solicitor, priest, doctor, manager or the like'.[2] And on a point confirmed later in *Goldsworthy v Brickell*[3] it was held that it was not necessary for the defendant to have 'dominated' the claimant: influence not domination was in issue.

In important modern cases a factual relationship of influence has been established between a husband and a wife,[4] between a housekeeper and her elderly charge,[5] between a bank and its elderly customer,[6] between a manager and his pop singer 'employer',[7] between a farm manager and an elderly farm owner,[8] and between an employer and a junior employee.[9]

As Lord Nicholls noted in *Royal Bank of Scotland v Etridge (No 2)*[10] the question that is here important is whether, on the facts, one party has reposed sufficient trust and confidence in the other rather than whether the relationship between the parties belongs to a particular type.

---

20 Ibid, at p 61.
1   [1952] 2 TLR 516.
2   Ibid, at p 522.
3   [1987] Ch 378.
4   *Barclays Bank plc v Coleman* [2000] 3 WLR 405, CA; affd *Royal Bank of Scotland v Etridge (No 2)* [2001] UKHL 44, [2001] 3 WLR 1021, HL. See also *Simpson v Simpson* [1992] 1 FLR 601 (presumed undue influence of wife over her ill husband).
5   *Re Craig* [1971] Ch 95.
6   *Lloyds Bank Ltd v Bundy* [1975] QB 326.
7   *O'Sullivan v Management Agency and Music Ltd* [1985] QB 428.
8   *Goldsworthy v Brickell* [1987] Ch 378.
9   *Crédit Lyonnais Bank Nederland v Burch* [1997] 1 All ER 144.
10 [2001] UKHL 44, [2001] 3 WLR 1021, para 10.

(b) The transaction must be disadvantageous (ie, not readily explicable on ordinary motives)

A leading case on this requirement is *National Westminster Bank Ltd v Morgan*,[11] in which a wife failed in her claim to set aside a charge which secured a bridging loan over her and her husband's home in favour of the claimant bank. The House of Lords held that there was no relationship of influence between the bank and the wife but that, in any event, and contrary to the view of the law taken by the Court of Appeal, the transaction would not be set aside because it had not been shown to be manifestly disadvantageous to her. Like Lindley LJ in *Allcard v Skinner*, Lord Scarman (with whom the other Law Lords agreed) thought that the principle underlying undue influence was 'the victimisation of one party by the other'.[12] And earlier he said:

> 'I know of no reported authority where the transaction set aside was not to the manifest disadvantage of the person influenced ... Whatever the legal character of the transaction, the authorities show that it must constitute a disadvantage sufficiently serious to require evidence to rebut the presumption that in the circumstances of the relationship between the parties it was procured by the exercise of undue influence.'[13]

As a test for manifest disadvantage, the House of Lords approved the words of Lindley LJ in *Allcard v Skinner* that the transaction must be one that is 'not to be reasonably accounted for on the ground of friendship, relationship, charity, or other ordinary motives on which ordinary men act ...'.[14] In the context of gifts Lindley LJ suggested that the dividing line was between small and large gifts. And in *Goldsworthy v Brickell*, in which the Court of Appeal set aside a tenancy agreement for the presumed undue influence of a farm manager over the elderly owner of the farm, Nourse LJ thought that the transaction should be 'so improvident as not to be reasonably accounted for by ordinary motives'.[15]

After Lord Browne-Wilkinson in *CIBC Mortgages plc v Pitt*[16] had expressed some doubt about manifest disadvantage being a

---

11 [1985] AC 686. In *Geffen v Goodman Estate* [1991] 2 SCR 353 it was laid down that a different approach applies in Canada whereby a relationship of dominance is required and, as regards gifts, 'manifest disadvantage' is not a necessary requirement (although, according to Wilson and Cory JJ, in commercial contracts there is a requirement of undue disadvantage to the claimant or undue benefit to the defendant).

12 Ibid, at p 705.

13 Ibid, at p 704.

14 (1887) 36 Ch D 145, 185.

15 [1987] Ch 378, 407. See also at p 416 (per Parker LJ).

16 [1994] 1 AC 200.

requirement even for presumed undue influence, the Court of Appeal in *Barclays Bank plc v Coleman*[17] strongly criticised that requirement and gave it a narrow meaning. But the House of Lords in *Royal Bank of Scotland v Etridge (No 2)*[18] has laid down that it is only the label 'manifest disadvantage' that should be discarded not the idea underlying it. The label is ambiguous and has given rise to difficulties. One should instead rely directly on the words of Lindley LJ in *Allcard v Skinner* which were approved by Lord Scarman in *National Westminster Bank v Morgan*. The requirement is therefore one of the transaction not being readily explicable on ordinary motives.

In Lord Nicholls' words, giving the leading speech:

'The need for this second prerequisite has recently been questioned ... [Counsel for the claimants] invited your Lordships to depart from the decision of the House on this point in *Morgan*'s case. My Lords, this is not an invitation I would accept. The second prerequisite, as expressed by Lindley LJ, is good sense. It is a necessary limitation upon the width of the first prerequisite [ie, a relationship of influence]. It would be absurd for the law to presume that every gift by a child to a parent, or every transaction between a client and his solicitor or between a patient and his doctor, was brought about by undue influence unless the contrary is affirmatively proved. Such a presumption would be too far-reaching. The law would be out of touch with everyday life if the presumption were to apply to every Christmas or birthday gift by a child to a parent, or to an agreement whereby a client or patient agrees to be responsible for the reasonable fees of his legal or medical advisor. The law would be rightly open to ridicule, for transactions such as these are unexceptionable. They do not suggest that something may be amiss. So something more is needed before the law reverses the burden of proof, something which calls for an explanation. ... Lord Scarman attached the label "manifest disadvantage" to this second ingredient necessary to raise the presumption. This label has been causing difficulty. ... In recent years judge after judge has grappled with the baffling question whether a wife's guarantee of her husband's bank overdraft, together with a charge on her share of the matrimonial home, was a transaction manifestly to her disadvantage. ... The answer lies in discarding a label which gives rise to this sort of ambiguity. The better approach is to adhere more directly to the test outlined by Lindley LJ in *Allcard v Skinner*, and adopted by Lord Scarman in *Morgan*'s case ...'[19]

---

17 [2000] 3 WLR 405; decision affirmed in *Royal Bank of Scotland v Etridge (No 2)* [2001] 3 WLR 1021.

18 [2001] UKHL 44, [2001] 3 WLR 1021.

19 Ibid, at paras 23–29. See also Lord Scott, ibid, at para 156.

So, for presumed undue influence, the second requirement validly serves to raise the suspicion, which requires rebuttal, that the transaction was not entered into as a matter of free will. The relationship alone, leading to, for example, a transaction at a fair market value, does not raise that suspicion. Put another way, one can say that where the procedural unfairness is clear (as with duress or actual undue influence) legal intervention is justified irrespective of substantive unfairness; but where the procedural unfairness is not so clear, it is the combination of procedural and substantive unfairness that justifies legal intervention.

(2) Rebutting the presumption of undue influence

Once a relationship of influence and disadvantage has been established, the onus of proof switches to the defendant to rebut the presumption of undue influence. The primary method of rebuttal is to show that the claimant obtained the fully informed and competent independent advice of a qualified person, most obviously a solicitor. This redresses the procedural imbalance. In the leading case of *Inche Noriah v Shaik Allie Bin Amar*[20] Lord Hailsham, giving the judgment of the Privy Council, said:

> 'It is necessary for the donee to prove that the gift was the result of the free exercise of independent will. The most obvious way to prove this is by establishing that the gift was made after the nature and effect of the transaction had been fully explained to the donor by some independent and qualified person so completely as to satisfy the court that the donor was acting independently of any influence from the donee and with the full appreciation of what he was doing ...'[1]

Even though the claimant had obtained the advice of an independent solicitor, her gift of land to her nephew was set aside for presumed undue influence because the solicitor was not aware of the full facts and, while acting in good faith, did not advise her competently. In other words, independent legal advice will only count if it is informed and competent.

Lord Hailsham also stressed that the Privy Council was not prepared to accept the view that independent legal advice was the only way in which the presumption could be rebutted.[2] But it is difficult to see ways by which the presumption can be rebutted other than by the claimant having obtained independent advice, albeit not necessarily

---

20   [1929] AC 127.
1   Ibid, at p 135.
2   Ibid, at 135. See also *Re Brocklehurst's Estate* [1978] Ch 14.

legal advice. Indeed in *Royal Bank of Scotland v Etridge (No 2)* Lord Nicholls, giving the leading speech, indicated that, even after receiving informed and competent advice, a person may still not be free from the exercise of undue influence. His Lordship said, 'Proof of outside advice does not, of itself, necessarily show that the subsequent completion of the transaction was free from the exercise of undue influence. Whether it will be proper to infer that outside advice had an emancipating effect, so that the transaction was not brought about by the exercise of undue influence, is a question of fact to be decided having regard to all the evidence in the case.'[3] Clearly, therefore, the onus of proof on the defendant is a heavy one.

---

3   [2001] UKHL 44, [2001] 3 WLR 1021, para 20.

Chapter 7

Exploitation of weakness

1. INTRODUCTION

This chapter primarily considers the equitable jurisdiction to set aside so-called 'unconscionable bargains' and the common law jurisdiction to set aside extortionate salvage agreements. While these categories of case are sometimes linked with duress and, even more commonly, with undue influence, they seem sufficiently distinct to merit separate treatment under the general heading of exploitation of weakness.[1] The courts are not here responding to either illegitimate threats, as in duress cases, or unacceptable influence, as in undue influence cases. Rather they seek to protect the claimant against a weakness (whether natural or circumstantial). On the other hand, the weakness is not so extreme as to constitute incapacity. In the absence of lies, threats or influence, and given that the claimant has capacity, it is not surprising that the courts have generally regarded the weakness alone – the claimant's lack of full and free choice in rendering the benefit – as insufficient to merit legal intervention. Rather the courts look for exploitation – taking advantage – of the claimant's weakness (his lack of full and free choice) as evidenced by the terms of the transaction being unfair to the claimant. The touchstone for intervention is a combination of procedural and substantive unfairness.

In an excellent examination of the English and Commonwealth authorities, Bamforth concludes that 'Unconscionability has now emerged as a distinct vitiating factor and four elements must be present for a transaction to be set aside – special or serious disadvantage, actual or constructive fraud, lack of independent advice, and disadvantageous terms.'[2] The second of these elements is perhaps the most problematic. It raises the question, unresolved in the case law, as to whether the defendant needs to have acted in bad faith, dishonestly knowing that he was taking advantage of the claimant.

---

1 For the contrary view, that unconscionability and undue influence are so similar that they should be merged into one (the former swallowing up the latter), see Capper, 'Undue Influence and Unconscionability: A Rationalisation' (1998) 114 LQR 479.
2 Bamforth, 'Unconscionability as a vitiating factor' [1995] LMCLQ 538, 559.

We also consider in this chapter an exception to the need for substantive unfairness, which is where the potential for exploitation of a weaker party in entering into a particular type of contract is so great that the law treats the contract as illegal. That is, the illegality protects the vulnerable class to which the claimant belongs even without the claimant having to show that, on the particular facts, there has been actual exploitation. The weaker party will be entitled to 'rescission' of the illegal contract and restitution of benefits conferred under it. Restitution here is conventionally viewed as an example of the *non in pari delicto* exception to the rule that illegality bars restitution.

As will by now be apparent, the term 'exploitation of weakness' is used in this book to describe the unjust factor.[3] Judges and commentators have alternatively used the terms 'inequality of bargaining power' or 'unconscionability'. Nothing of real significance should turn on one's chosen label but 'exploitation of weakness' does seem preferable. 'Inequality' can be misleading in that it is generally no reason in itself for restitution that the claimant was in a position of inequality with the defendant: it is the abuse of particular positions of strength that the law normally objects to. And 'unconscionability' is vague and wide-ranging and is a term used in several other areas of the law. To use it again here requires careful delineation and may be confusing.

What has been said in the undue influence chapter about the necessary causal link (between the unjust factor and the enrichment), at the claimant's expense, the establishing of benefit, the lack of distinction between contractual and non-contractual benefits, the remedy of rescission,[4] and proprietary restitution,[5] applies analogously to the unjust factor of exploitation of weakness.

2. EXPLOITATION OF THE CLAIMANT'S MENTAL WEAKNESS

Traditionally two main types of 'unconscionable bargain'[6] have here been in mind: 'catching bargains' with expectant heirs and transactions with the poor and ignorant. In recent years, the latter has been

---

3 For use by the judges of this terminology see, eg, *Alec Lobb (Garages) Ltd v Total Oil GB Ltd* [1983] 1 WLR 87, 94–95 Peter Millett QC; *Portman Building Society v Dusangh* [2000] 2 All ER (Comm) 221, 229 (per Simon Brown LJ).
4 In *Alec Lobb (Garages) Ltd v Total Oil GB Ltd* [1985] 1 WLR 173, even if the contract had been voidable because unconscionable, rescission would have been ruled out by lapse of time.
5 See Chambers, *Resulting Trusts* (1997), pp 137–138. Note that in *Louth v Diprose* (1992) 175 CLR 621 a trust was declared: see below, p 266.
6 Treitel, *The Law of Contract* (10th edn, 1999), pp 382–384.

expanded so that these two types of transaction are better viewed as illustrations of a wider principle protecting those with a mental weakness against exploitation.

(1) The traditional categories

(a) Expectant heirs

The leading case is *Earl of Aylesford v Morris*[7] where a 22 year-old, who stood to inherit his father's estates, took out a loan from the defendant moneylender at a rate of 60% interest in order to pay off his debts. He did so without independent advice. In setting aside the loan, on condition that the claimant repaid the principal plus 5% interest, Lord Selborne LC, citing the words of Lord Hardwicke in *Earl of Chesterfield v Janssen*,[8] said that a presumption of fraud arose where there was 'weakness on one side, usury on the other, or extortion or advantage taken of that weakness'. And he went on:

> 'Fraud does not here mean deceit or circumvention; it means an unconscientious use of the power arising out of these circumstances and conditions; and when the relative position of the parties is such as prima facie to raise this presumption, the transaction cannot stand unless the person claiming the benefit of it is able to repel the presumption by contrary evidence, proving it to have been in point of fact, fair, just and reasonable ... it is sufficient for the application of the principle if the parties meet under such circumstances, as in the particular transaction, to give the stronger party dominion over the weaker; and such power and influence are generally possessed, in every transaction of this kind, by those who trade upon the follies and vices of unprotected youth, inexperience and moral imbecility.'[9]

The approach is therefore similar to that for presumed undue influence. The vulnerability of a young expectant heir plus substantive unfairness – 'an inadequate price' as it was termed in *O'Rorke v Bolingbroke*[10] – gives rise to an evidential presumption of exploitation which it is then for the defendant to rebut, principally by establishing that independent advice was obtained.

Two further points, which are arguably not entirely settled by the case law, are noteworthy. First, the reasoning in *Earl of Aylesford v Morris* suggests that there is no requirement of poverty although on the facts the expectant heir was, at the time, financially hard-pressed. In contrast

---

7   (1873) 8 Ch App 484.
8   (1751) 2 Ves Sen 125, 157.
9   (1873) 8 Ch App 484, 490–491.
10   (1877) 2 App Cas 814, 835 (per Lord Blackburn).

to the 'poor and ignorant' category, it appears, therefore, that the weakness, against which the law is here offering protection from exploitation, is simply the claimant's mental immaturity. Secondly, the reasoning in *O'Rorke v Bolingbroke*, where a transaction at an undervalue with an expectant heir was not set aside, suggests that it may be important whether the defendant was acting in bad faith, knowing that he was striking a harsh bargain.

(b) The poor and ignorant: *Fry v Lane*

In *Fry v Lane*,[11] following on the earlier case of *Evans v Llewellin*,[12] sales of reversionary interests in land at considerable undervalue were set aside because the vendors were poor and ignorant. After referring to the expectant heir cases Kay J said:

> 'The result of the decisions is that where a purchase is made from a poor and ignorant man at a considerable undervalue, the vendor having no independent advice, a Court of Equity will set aside the transaction. This will be done even in the case of property in possession, and *a fortiori* if the interest be reversionary. The circumstances of poverty and ignorance of the vendor, and absence of independent advice, throw upon the purchaser, when the transaction is impeached, the onus of proving in Lord Selbourne's words [in *Aylesford v Morris*], that the purchase was "fair, just and reasonable".'[13]

Again, therefore, the approach is one of presuming exploitation subject to rebuttal by the defendant. Here, however, both mental inadequacy and poverty are important. It is not entirely clear why this should be so. Why is it that rich and ignorant people cannot have harsh transactions set aside? Presumably the answer is that poverty adds an element of desperation inducing rash judgments.

(c) Modern developments

The *Fry v Lane* principle had new life breathed into it in 1968 by Megarry J in *Cresswell v Potter*,[14] where a wife's release of her share in the matrimonial home for a small consideration, on divorce, was set aside. Although she had a job as a Post Office telephonist Megarry J took the view that she fell within the modern equivalent of 'poor and ignorant'. 'Eighty years ago, when *Fry v Lane* was decided, social conditions were very different from those which exist today. I do not, however, think that the principle has changed, even though the

---

11 (1888) 40 Ch D 312.
12 (1787) 1 Cox Eq Cas 333.
13 (1888) 40 Ch D 312, 322.
14 [1978] 1 WLR 255n.

euphemisms of the twentieth century may require the word "poor" to be replaced by "a member of the lower income group" or the like, and the word "ignorant" by "less highly educated".'[15] It may be doubted, however, whether this modern approach to 'poverty' corresponds with the 'desperation' rationale put forward above; and without that it is hard to understand the precise relevance of 'poverty'.

In *Crédit Lyonnais Bank Nederland v Burch*,[16] although the case was argued purely on the basis of undue influence, Nourse LJ thought that Miss Burch might well have had the legal charge set aside against the bank on the basis that the contract was an unconscionable bargain. He said that *Creswell v Potter* demonstrated that the jurisdiction to relieve against such transactions was 'in good heart and capable of adaptation to different transactions entered into in changing circumstances'.[17]

The limits of the doctrine were carefully analysed in *Portman Building Society v Dusangh*.[18] Here the defendant, a 72 year-old man who spoke English poorly and was on a low income, took out a mortgage from the claimant building society by which he was loaned £33,750 in return for granting a charge over his home. The repayment was guaranteed by the defendant's son to whom the defendant paid over the loan to enable him to buy a small supermarket. When the supermarket failed and the son was unable to repay the loan, the claimant sought to enforce its charge over the defendant's home. The same solicitor acted for the claimant, the defendant and his son. The Court of Appeal held that the mortgage should not be set aside as an unconscionable bargain. Although the defendant was the modern equivalent of poor and ignorant, and although the transaction was an unwise and risky one from the defendant's perspective, it was not an overreaching and oppressive one. Similarly one could not say that the claimant (or the son) had acted in a morally reprehensible way. In Simon Brown LJ's words, 'I simply cannot accept that building societies are required to police transactions of this nature to ensure that parents (even poor and ignorant ones) are wise in seeking to assist their children ... [The defendant's] situation was not exploited by the building society. The building society did not act in a morally reprehensible manner. The transaction, although improvident, was not "overreaching and oppressive." In short, the conscience of the court is not shocked.'[19]

15　Ibid, at p 257.
16　[1997] 1 All ER 144, CA. See above, pp 250–251, 255.
17　Ibid, at 151.
18　[2000] 2 All ER (Comm) 221. Although the primary argument in the case concerned direct exploitation by the building society, Ward LJ decided that the principles laid down for three-party cases of undue influence and misrepresentation in *Barclays Bank plc v O'Brien* [1994] 1 AC 180 also apply here. But, had there been exploitation by the son, the building society did not have actual or constructive notice of it.
19　Ibid, at 229.

It remains to be seen whether the 'expectant heir' category will also be adapted to the modern context. A major difficulty is that it seems unjustified to restrict the protection of the young and inexperienced to those who will be rich one day. If one excises the emphasis on potential wealth, it can be argued that the category could act as a valuable supplement to the rules on a minor's incapacity; for while the incapacity rules protect minors, without any requirement that the terms of a transaction are substantively unfair, a person in the early years of adulthood perhaps needs the more limited protection offered by the law on exploitation.

A similar argument could be made for extending the realm of exploitation – with its emphasis on substantive unfairness – to supplement the other forms of mental incapacity, namely insanity and drunkenness. This derives support from the New Zealand case of *Archer v Cutler*[20] where McMullin J, following, inter alia, *Aylesford v Morris* and *Fry v Lane*, set aside as an 'unconscionable bargain' a contract for the sale of land made by an old lady suffering from senile dementia (unknown to the purchaser) because of her mental weakness, the significant undervalue and her lack of independent advice. He also held the contract voidable for incapacity by reasoning that, where the contract is 'unfair', the incapacity rules do not require knowledge by the sane party of the other's insanity. But in *Hart v O'Connor*[1] the Privy Council overruled *Archer v Cutler*'s approach to the rules on incapacity by reason of insanity on the ground that the defendant must know of the claimant's insanity. And their Lordships similarly seemed to regard it as essential for unconscionability that the defendant should know of the claimant's mental inadequacy although, on the facts of *Hart*, the claimant had in any event been independently advised and there was no very clear 'contractual imbalance'.[2] As we have seen, such an emphasis on bad faith derives support from *O'Rorke v Bolingbroke*[3] but it did not explicitly feature in other 'expectant heir' or 'poor and ignorant' cases and it must remain open whether it is a necessary requirement of exploitation. Indeed in the New Zealand case of *Nichols v Jessup*,[4] in which *Hart v O'Connor* was carefully examined, it was

20 [1980] 1 NZLR 386.
1 [1985] AC 1000. Below, chapter 10.
2 This is Lord Brightman's phrase, ibid, at p 1018, which he contrasts with 'procedural unfairness'.
3 (1877) 2 App Cas 814.
4 [1986] 1 NZLR 226, NZCA. The defendant was ignorant about property matters and muddle-headed. She had entered into a disadvantageous agreement with her estate agent neighbour to have mutual rights of way over their respective driveways. Somers J said, at p 235, 'A party may be regarded as unconscientious not only when he knew at the time the bargain was entered into that the other suffered from a material disability or disadvantage and its effect on that other, but also when he ought to have known of that circumstance ...'

expressly said to be unnecessary, in order for a bargain to be set aside as unconscionable, for the defendant to know that he was taking unfair advantage of the claimant's weakness. It was enough that he ought to have known.

One may also want to extend the scope of exploitation to other forms of mental inadequacy that have no direct link to incapacity. In this respect dicta of Balcombe J in *Backhouse v Backhouse*[5] are of interest. A wife, on separation from her husband, had transferred to him for nothing her interest in the matrimonial home. Although she could not be classed as 'poor and ignorant', as she was an intelligent woman, Balcombe J suggested that the law might want to move to setting aside a transaction because of the 'great emotional strain'[6] that divorcing parties are under. Given the rather forced findings of poverty and ignorance in *Creswell v Potter*, 'exploitation of emotional strain' may provide a better explanation for that decision.

That argument for an extension of exploitation also derives strong support from Lord Denning's judgment – on the principle of 'inequality of bargaining power' – in *Lloyds Bank v Bundy*.[7] He said:

> 'English law gives relief to one who, without independent advice, enters into a contract upon terms which are very unfair or transfers property for a consideration which is grossly inadequate, when his bargaining power is grievously impaired by reason of his own needs or desires, *or by his own ignorance or infirmity*, coupled with undue influences or pressures brought to bear on him by or for the benefit of the other.'[8]

Reference can also be made to three radical decisions of the High Court of Australia.[9] In *Commercial Bank of Australia Ltd v Amadio*[10] a doctrine of 'unconscionable dealing' was accepted and applied in setting aside a mortgage and guarantee executed by an elderly and ignorant couple who were unfamiliar with written English and had received no independent advice. Again in *Louth v Diprose*[11] a gift of a house was set aside (ie, the house was declared to be held by the defendant on trust for the claimant) because of unconscionable dealing where the claimant had bought the house for a woman with whom he was infatuated. She had manipulated to her advantage his 'special disability' of which she

---

5　[1978] 1 WLR 243.
6　Ibid, at p 251.
7　[1975] QB 326. But for a contrary view see Lord Scarman's dicta in *National Westminster Bank v Morgan* [1985] AC 686, 708.
8　Ibid, at p 339 (author's italics).
9　See also Browne-Wilkinson J's dicta in *Multiservice Bookbinding Ltd v Marden* [1979] Ch 84, 110: 'I do not think the categories of unconscionable bargains are limited.'
10　(1983) 151 CLR 447.
11　(1992) 175 CLR 621.

was well aware. In the words of Deane J giving the leading judgment, 'The case was one in which the [defendant] deliberately used [the plaintiff's] love or infatuation and her own deceit to create a situation in which she could unconscientiously manipulate [the plaintiff] to part with a large proportion of his property. The intervention of equity is not merely to relieve the plaintiff from the consequences of his own foolishness. It is to prevent his victimisation.'[12] And in *Garcia v National Australia Bank Ltd*[13] the High Court of Australia saw itself as extending 'unconscionability' beyond *Amadio* in holding that a wife was not bound by guarantees given by her to a bank, secured over the matrimonial house, in respect of loans paid by the bank to her husband's businesses. She was not bound because enforcement of the guarantees would be unconscionable in the sense that she did not understand the effect of the guarantees and the bank had not taken steps to explain it to her or to find out that a stranger had explained it to her.

Finally, although the reasoning does not make clear precisely what the Privy Council objected to on the facts, *Boustany v Pigott*[14] may be regarded as an important case in focusing not so much on the 'poor and ignorant' category as on general criteria for the setting aside of contracts as 'unconscionable bargains'. Miss Pigott, the claimant, was an elderly landlady. As she had become 'quite slow' her affairs were managed by her cousin, George Pigott. One of her tenants, Mrs Boustany, persuaded the claimant, while George Pigott was away, to agree to a new lease being drawn up by an independent lawyer. The lease was for ten years at a monthly rent of $1,000 (the present rent being $833.35) renewable at the same rent at the tenant's option. The lawyer pointed out forcibly to Miss Pigott the disadvantages of the new lease but she insisted on going ahead with it. After her death, her estate sought to have it set aside as an unconscionable bargain and the Privy Council upheld the decision of the Court of Appeal of the Eastern Caribbean States that it should be so set aside. Lord Templeman agreed with counsel for the defendant that the essence of this area of the law was the morally reprehensible and unconscientious abuse of power that meant that, exceptionally, the strong should not be allowed to push the weak to the wall. It would appear that it was not thought necessary to treat the claimant as 'poor and ignorant.'[15]

---

12 Ibid, at 638.
13 (1998) 194 CLR 395.
14 (1993) 69 P & CR 298.
15 The lower court had relied directly on *Fry v Lane* (1888) 40 Ch D 312 and had said that, while not poor in the sense of being destitute or from a low family background, she was anxious to have a regular and steady income from the premises.

3. EXPLOITATION OF THE CLAIMANT'S CIRCUMSTANTIAL WEAKNESS (IE, DIFFICULT CIRCUMSTANCES)

There is little support in English law for setting aside transactions for this form of exploitation. So, for example, the desperation of poverty must be linked to the mental inadequacy of ignorance in the *Fry v Lane* line of cases.

Lord Denning's 'inequality of bargaining power' principle, which he expressed to include impairment of bargaining power by reason of one's 'own needs or desires', could be applied to include exploitation of the claimant's difficult circumstances. But the leading case, which emphasised the need for bad faith, is *Alec Lobb (Garages) Ltd v Total Oil (GB) Ltd*.[16] The claimants sought to have set aside a lease and lease-back agreement for their petrol station. While accepting that the claimants' financial difficulties and their relationship with the defendants were such that they had no practical choice but to enter the contract, the Court of Appeal did not consider that, absent the unconscientious use of power, the contract should be set aside even if its terms were unfair. On the facts, however, the claim was a weak one as the claimants had, in any event, obtained independent advice.

One major common law area where a claimant has traditionally been protected against exploitation of his difficult circumstances is that of extortionate salvage agreements. In *Akerblom v Price*,[17] Brett LJ said that, because salvage agreements are generally made as a matter of urgency so that the parties are not on equal terms, they would not be upheld if 'manifestly unfair and unjust'. Striking examples are provided by *The Medina*[18] and *The Port Caledonia and Anna*.[19] In the former, 550 pilgrims were shipwrecked on a rock. The salvor refused to rescue them unless the master of the shipwrecked ship agreed to pay £4,000, which he reluctantly agreed to do. The agreement was set aside and £1,800 was awarded instead as a fair sum for the salvage services rendered. In the latter case, the salvor refused to help a ship in distress unless he was paid £1,000. The agreement was set aside and £200 awarded instead.

There are also certain statutory provisions, which one can view as based on protecting a claimant against exploitation of his difficult

---

16 [1985] 1 WLR 173.
17 (1885) 7 QBD 129, 132–133.
18 (1876) 1 PD 272.
19 [1903] P 184. Treitel (10th edn, 1999), p 375, note 4 treats this case under duress. But this would require extending the notion of illegitimate threats to include threats of lawful omissions. Moreover, in contrast to duress, substantive unfairness here is crucial.

circumstances. For example, ss 137–139 of the Consumer Credit Act 1974 protect against exploitation of the claimant's need for credit by giving the courts a wide range of remedies to undo 'extortionate credit agreements'.[20]

4. ILLEGALITY DESIGNED TO PROTECT A VULNERABLE CLASS FROM EXPLOITATION

The reason why a particular contract is illegal may be to protect the claimant as a member of a vulnerable class. For the same reason the claimant may be entitled to 'rescission' of the illegal contract and restitution of benefits conferred under it. At first sight such class protection might appear to be nothing more than another standard example of exploitation of weakness. But actual exploitation requires that the terms of the contract are substantively unfair, whereas the protection here is more extensive. The illegality protects members of a class even if the terms are substantively fair. In other words, protection against possible, rather than actual, exploitation is in mind here.

Conventionally class protection has been regarded as an aspect of the *non in pari delicto* exception to illegality barring restitution.[1] In a classic dictum in *Browning v Morris*,[2] Lord Mansfield explained the position as follows:

> 'Where contracts or transactions are prohibited by positive statutes, for the sake of protecting one set of men from another set of men; the one, from their situation and condition, being liable to be oppressed or imposed upon by the other; there the parties are *non in pari delicto*; and in furtherance of these statutes, the person injured, after the transaction is finished and completed, may bring his action and defeat the contract.'

In *Lodge v National Union Investment Co Ltd*,[3] the claimant took out a loan of £1,075 from the defendants secured by bills of exchange and assignments of insurance policies. The contract was illegal because the defendants were not registered as moneylenders under the Moneylenders Act 1900. The claimant was held entitled to recover his securities from the defendants because the purpose of the statute

---

20 Outside the realm of restitution one can perhaps regard exploitation of the defendant's weaker bargaining position as the root principle behind certain contracts or contractual terms being held void or unenforceable: eg, forfeiture clauses, some contracts in restraint of trade, and unfair terms under the Unfair Contract Terms Act 1977 and the Unfair Terms in Consumer Contracts Regulations 1999.
1 Below, p 578. See generally on illegality as a defence, below, pp 570–584.
2 (1778) 2 Cowp 790, 792.
3 [1907] 1 Ch 300.

was to protect persons in the claimant's position. No reference was made in Parker J's reasoning to whether the claimant was mistaken or whether the contractual terms were unfair (ie neither mistake nor actual exploitation were in mind). He said:

> 'The usual rule is that in the case of a transaction void for illegality neither party can take any proceedings against the other party for the restoration of any property or for the repayment of any money which has been transferred or paid in the course of the illegal transaction. To this rule, however, there are exceptions, one of them being in favour of the person for whose protection the illegality of the contract had been created.'[4]

The major issue in the case was whether, as with normal rescission, the claimant was required to give counter-restitution of the £1,075. In holding that this was essential Parker J said:

> 'I do not think that it is either *aequum* or *bonum* that the plaintiff who has had the benefit of the £1,075, and who is relying on the illegality of the contract and the exception enabling him to sue notwithstanding such illegality, should have relief without being put on terms by which both parties may be restored to the positions they occupied before the transaction commenced.'[5]

This requirement of counter-restitution was not followed in *Kusumu v Babe-Egbe*,[6] another moneylending case, where the statutory illegality in question was that the moneylender had kept no record of the transaction as required by a Nigerian moneylending ordinance. The claimant was held entitled to recover possession of the land mortgaged – presumably on the basis of class protection – but without repaying any part of the loan. According to the Privy Council, to have insisted on repayment as a condition of recovery of the land would have indirectly infringed the policy of the Act, which rendered the loan unenforceable.

Consistency within the law may favour *Kusumu* as against *Lodge*. As is argued in chapter 15 below, one explanation of the requirement of counter-restitution is that it recognises a defendant's counterclaim.[7] Most obviously, such a counterclaim would here be for total failure of consideration; and therefore so long as illegality remains a defence to a claim for total failure of consideration, counter-restitution should not be required and it should be no bar that *restitutio in integrum* is impossible.[8]

---

4   [1907] 1 Ch 300, 306.
5   Ibid, at p 312.
6   [1956] AC 539. See also *Barclay v Prospect Mortgages Ltd* [1974] 1 WLR 837.
7   Below, pp 538–542.
8   This is supported by Birks, at p 423. See below, p 434, n 1 and pp 572–574.

One might also bring within this ground for restitution cases like *Kiriri Cotton Co Ltd v Dewani*,[9] *Re Cavalier Insurance Co Ltd*,[10] and *Hermann v Charlesworth*.[11] Certainly there was overt class protection reasoning in the former two cases but, ultimately, it seems central to the reasoning in both that the claimant was mistaken as to the law in making the payments. And in *Hermann*, where the claimant was held able to recover the money paid under a marriage brokage contract, the primary reasoning was based on a withdrawal during the *locus poenitentiae*.[12] If the class protection illegality ground were uncontroversial, there would be a case for including such cases within it and for marginalising their narrower 'alternative' grounds for restitution. But restitution based on protecting a class against potential, rather than actual, exploitation is arguably excessively protectionist and should not be given a wider ambit than absolutely necessary.

It follows that, perhaps contrary to *Lodge* and *Kusumu*, the courts should only intervene on the ground of class protection where there is a statute which indisputably requires them to do so. This is supported by *Green v Portsmouth Stadium Ltd*[13] where the Court of Appeal held that a bookmaker – on the assumption that he did not pay by mistake – could not recover course charges paid to the defendants which were in excess of what was permitted under the Betting and Lotteries Act 1934. The central reasoning was that the particular statute was not intended to protect bookmakers.

5. CONCLUSION

Judicial reluctance to tolerate enrichments rendered as a result of the exploitation of weakness has a long history and, while some of the equitable categories and principles have an archaic ring to them, recent developments have shown that they are capable of performing useful roles in the modern era. The principles are fluid and open-ended and raise in a sharp form the tension between reversing unjust enrichment on the one hand and respecting the security and sanctity of transactions on the other. Without Lord Denning, the judicial desire

---

9 [1960] AC 192. See below, p 575. See also, eg, *Great Western Rly Co v Sutton* (1869) LR 4 HL 226; above, pp 223–224.

10 [1989] 2 Lloyd's Rep 430. See below, pp 575–576.

11 [1905] 2 KB 123.

12 See below, p 434

13 [1953] 2 QB 190. Under the Financial Services and Markets Act 2000, ss 26–30 agreements made by unauthorised persons in relation to investment and related regulated activities are unenforceable against the other party but the courts are given a discretion to hold the contract enforceable and to deny restitution to the other party where 'just and equitable'.

to push forward the frontiers of legal protection on the grounds of exploitation has receded but the interventionist approach embodied in his principle of inequality of bargaining power,[14] while at present frowned upon, may yet prove to be the way of the future.

14 See above, p 266.

Chapter 8

Legal compulsion: compulsory discharge of another's legal liability

1. INTRODUCTION

Legal compulsion is shorthand for 'legitimate application of the legal process'.[1] Legal process refers to the procedures and remedies provided by the law to protect rights. Where legal process is applied improperly by the defendant's illegitimate threats to detain the claimant or to seize his goods or to prosecute or sue him, unless the claimant pays him money, restitution of that money falls within the ambit of duress (including actual undue influence). Legitimate application of the legal process – legal compulsion – which pressurises the claimant into paying the defendant gives rise to no right to restitution from the defendant because, even if threats are made by the defendant (eg to sue), they are by definition legitimate and cannot comprise duress. There is no unjust enrichment between the claimant and defendant.

On the other hand, where legal compulsion by X against C leads to C discharging a liability of D to X it would appear that very often D has been unjustly enriched at C's expense.[2] The enrichment comprises the discharge of D's liability which is an incontrovertible benefit to D. The precise injustice is more tricky to identify but in general terms can be said to be the pressure of the legal process which leaves C with no free choice but to discharge D's liability even though, as between C and D, responsibility for the payment ought to rest with D. In a sense the legal process has compelled the wrong party to pay or, at least, to pay too much. Causation, as usual, should primarily be determined by the 'but for' test. And D's gain is at C's expense in the subtractive sense.

Where responsibility between C and D ought to rest entirely on D, C is given restitution of the whole sum paid. This can be called

---

1 This is not intended to exclude the case of a claimant paying because he is legally liable to do so but without being requested to do so.
2 The initials C, D and X are used throughout this chapter to refer to, respectively, the person seeking restitution, the person whose liability has been discharged, and the third party to whom the liability was owed.

'recoupment' although the term 'reimbursement' is also often used. The actual remedies normally awarded are money paid to the defendant's use or an indemnity.[3] Where, on the other hand, both C and D are under a common liability to X, and C pays more than, as between C and D, he should be responsible for, C is given restitution of part of the sum paid. This is known as 'contribution', as is the actual remedy awarded.

That the injustice of legal compulsion can only lie between C and the party whose liability is discharged (D) explains why legal compulsion is automatically linked to the particular form of enrichment in the standard phrase used in this area – 'compulsory discharge of another's liability'.

In principle, however, the reverse proposition ought not to hold good. In principle there is no reason why the incontrovertible benefit of a discharge of D's liability to X should not allow C restitution from D where C has paid by, for example, mistake or under duress. The fact that in these situations C can alternatively claim restitution from X ought not to debar restitution from D provided C is not allowed double restitution. But in practice, this linking of other unjust factors to discharge of another's liability is hampered by the supposed rule that only compulsory payment of another's debt automatically discharges that debt.

The vexed question, going to enrichment, of when payment of another's debt discharges that debt is analysed in the final part of this chapter. Strictly speaking it properly belongs within the general discussion of benefit in chapter 1 of this book. However, given its complexity and, with the warning that it is relevant to grounds for restitution beyond legal compulsion, it has been considered best to discuss it here.

One should further note the close link between this chapter and 'reviving subrogation'. This type of subrogation has been examined in chapter 2 above.[4] The link is a close one because reviving subrogation rests on the claimant's (C's) money having been used to discharge a liability (including a debt) of D to X. C is then subrogated to the former rights and remedies of X against D (ie, they are revived) in order to reverse D's unjust enrichment at C's expense. Reviving subrogation is therefore analogous to an award of money paid to the defendant's use (or an indemnity), albeit that subrogation can be proprietary rather than merely personal and is also wider in including

---

3   In principle where the liability discharged is not a debt C might be awarded a *quantum meruit* for the value of his services in performing the act discharging the liability. But there appears to be no example in the case law of the award of that remedy in this context.

4   See above, pp 104–107, 113–126.

situations where the payment to the creditor (X) is by the debtor (D)[5] rather than directly by C. Certainly one should keep the law on reviving subrogation in mind throughout this chapter. As we shall see, a failure to do so led the Court of Appeal into error in *Owen v Tate*.[6]

The idea that legal compulsion is a useful and intelligible ground for restitution does not appeal to everyone. Stoljar rejected it and preferred the view that 'subject to the significant exception of C's actions constituting manifest officiousness, C can recover money paid by him to discharge D's debt or liability to X, even where C is technically a volunteer'.[7]

This chapter does not seek to deny that standard unjust factors other than legal compulsion, such as mistake, duress, and necessity, can trigger restitution for discharge of another's liability. But to depart from the standard unjust factors in favour of a control device of 'officiousness' is unhelpful.[8] For example, a person who discharges another's debt by way of a gift is not officious but plainly cannot claim restitution. And, although practical examples are not obvious,[9] a person who indirectly discharges another's legal liability while acting freely in his own self interest cannot claim restitution even though he is non-officious.

Is proprietary, rather than merely personal, restitution justified in relation to compulsory discharge of another's liability? This question has normally been discussed in the context of reviving subrogation.[10] We have seen in chapter 2 that, in a situation which is best analysed as resting on the unjust factor of legal compulsion, a surety is entitled to proprietary restitution. One problem justifying this is that it is normally a pre-requisite for proprietary restitution that the enrichment is retained by the defendant in an asset to which the proprietary right can attach. One might have thought that this requirement could not be met in relation to a discharged liability. However, this requirement can be regarded as satisfied if the discharged liability was directly related to property retained by the defendant. For example, where a debt discharged was secured over particular property retained by the defendant, restitution may be secured over that property. But it is not clear that, even then, the unjust factor of legal compulsion justifies proprietary, rather than merely, personal restitution. In particular, in

5   Eg, D using a loan, paid by the claimant C to D, to discharge D's debt.
6   [1976] QB 402: below, p 285.
7   *The Law of Quasi-Contract* (2nd edn, 1989), at p 173. See generally at pp 151–156, 170–174.
8   See above, pp 43–44.
9   A possible example would be where a tenant cleans up a yard thereby discharging his landlord's liability in nuisance to his neighbour.
10 See, eg, Mitchell, *The Law of Subrogation* (1994), esp pp 59–60.

most circumstances it appears that the legally compelled claimant is similar to other unsecured creditors and has taken the risk of the defendant's insolvency.

2. LEGAL COMPULSION: RESTITUTION BY RECOUPMENT

Birks' approach to this area is to regard C and D as being under a common liability to X with the injustice stemming from the fact that C's liability is clearly secondary to D's.[11] The difficulty with this analysis is that in some cases involving the seizure of C's property C was not under any liability to X in the sense of X having an action against C if C failed to pay or act. Birks explains such cases as involving a secondary 'proprietary' as opposed to personal liability. With respect this seems to distort the normal meaning of the word 'liability' and, although ultimately a matter of semantics, it seems preferable to recognise two main categories of legal compulsion giving rise to recoupment.[12] First, where C discharges D's liability to X in order to recover his (C's) property; and secondly, where C and D are under a common liability to X but C's liability is secondary to D's.[13] We shall examine each of these categories in turn before considering finally cases in which restitution has been denied because no liability of D's has been discharged: ie cases which fall within neither of the above two categories.

(1) C discharges D's liability to X in order to recover his (C's) property

The earliest cases of discharging another's liability under legal compulsion fall within this category. In *Exall v Partridge*[14] the claimant had left his carriage on the defendants' premises for repair. The defendants were tenants of the premises who had not paid their rent. The landlord (X) lawfully seized the claimant's carriage as distress for rent. The claimant therefore had to pay the rent due in order to

---

11 Birks at pp 186–188.
12 Clarity is impaired rather than enhanced by using the vague label 'practical compulsion' to describe the first category: contra is Maddaugh and McCamus, *The Law of Restitution* (1st edn, 1990) chapter 29.
13 Note that there can be no restitution where the liability C discharged is D's liability to C rather than D's liability to a third party, X. One explanation for this is that where the liability is owed to C, one cannot say that C's liability is secondary to D's. For example, C contracts with D for D to repair C's house. Before D starts, C, under threat of a penalty, carries out the repair work himself. While C can be said to have discharged D's liability, that liability was owed to C not to a third party. C plainly cannot claim restitution from D for having discharged D's liability to C.
14 (1799) 8 Term Rep 308.

recover his carriage. It was held that he could recover the money paid, discharging the defendants' debt, from the defendants. It was stressed in the judgments that while a voluntary payment benefiting another would not trigger a remedy for the payor the situation was different here where the claimant had paid by compulsion.

Again in *Johnson v Royal Mail Steam Packet Co*[15] the claimants were mortgagees of two ships which they called to be delivered up by the defendants. The defendants did deliver up but failed to pay the wages of the crew as they were legally bound to do under the contract of employment. The ships were seized by officers of the court as the crew had a maritime lien over them for their unpaid wages. As the defendants still refused to pay, the claimants paid the sum claimed by the crew in order to obtain possession of the ships. It was held that the claimants were able to recover the sums paid from the defendants as paid under compulsion.

In each of those cases the claimants had discharged the defendants' liabilities in order to recover their goods which had been seized by legitimate application of the legal process. The claimants were compelled in the sense that, if they wanted to recover their goods, they had to pay. And, as between the claimants and defendants, there can be no dispute that responsibility for the payment rested on the defendants because it was only the defendants who were legally liable to pay. As with duress one cannot say that the will of the claimants was overborne in the mistake sense that they did not mean to discharge the defendants' liability; in the circumstances the claimants did intend to benefit the defendants in order to avoid a worse evil but that choice was not a free one because it was induced, applying the usual restitutionary approach to causation, by legal process.

The modern case of *Kleinwort Benson Ltd v Vaughan*[16] is best analysed as analogous to *Johnson v Royal Mail Steam Packet Co*, which was the principal case relied on by counsel for the claimant. That is, recoupment was granted where the claimant had discharged another's debt in order to 'recover its property'. Here the claimant was entitled to sell off a house owned by defendants in order to recover money stolen from them by one of the defendants that had been traced into the purchase of the house. The claimants used some of the proceeds of the forced sale to pay off a legal charge of Nationwide Home Loans Ltd over the house. They successfully sought restitution from the defendants for the discharge of that legal charge. What made these facts different from an ordinary voluntary paying off of a prior legal charge was precisely that the paying off of that charge was part of the

15 (1867) LR 3 CP 38.
16 [1996] CLC 620.

process designed to enable the claimant to recover its stolen money. Nourse LJ said:

> '[T]he redemption of the charge by the plaintiff was not the simple case of a volunteer paying off another's debt. It was the debt of those whose charge had partially defeated the plaintiff's right, as against them, to claim the beneficial interest in the property. The defendants cannot deny the plaintiff's entitlement to perfect that right. If the plaintiff cannot recover [the amount of the debt discharged], the defendants will have been unjustly enriched by that amount.'[17]

One question that has arisen is whether legal compulsion is sufficient to justify restitution where C took the risk of his goods being seized. In other words does initial voluntariness, or, in Goff and Jones' terminology 'officiousness',[18] nullify the ultimate legal compulsion?

In *England v Marsden*[19] the claimant, under a bill of sale, seized the defendant's goods but allowed them to remain on the defendant's premises. They were later distrained for rent by the defendant's landlord and the claimant paid that rent in order to have his goods released. The claimant's restitutionary claim against the defendant for the money paid failed on the ground that the claimant had left his goods on the defendant's premises for his own advantage and without any request from the defendant and that that differentiated this case from *Exall v Partridge*. But this decision was held to be wrong by the Court of Appeal in *Edmunds v Wallingford*.[20] Here certain goods of the defendant's sons were lawfully seized from the defendant's shop and sold by the sheriff in execution of a judgment against the defendant by a creditor. The claimant, the trustee in bankruptcy for the sons, sought and was awarded an indemnity of the whole value of the goods sold. Although the sons had not actually paid off the defendant's debt in order to recover their goods, the situation was analogous to *Exall v Partridge* for their goods had been seized and sold to pay off the defendant's debt. The Court of Appeal said that *England v Marsden* ought not to be followed although it did appear to recognise that a restitutionary claim would fail if the goods were left by the claimant on the defendant's premises against the latter's will. There was no question of that on the facts of the instant case where the defendant had set his sons up in business in his shop.

It may be strongly doubted whether there should be any such general qualification to the restitutionary claim for legal compulsion. Of course if the legal compulsion did not cause the payment (eg,

17 Ibid, at 624.
18 Goff and Jones at paras 15-009 to 15-014.
19 (1866) LR 1 CP 529.
20 (1885) 14 QBD 811.

because C would have paid off D's debt irrespective of the application of the legal process) restitution fails. Otherwise it is hard to see why it should matter whether C was initially foolish or acting in his own interests or knew that there was a risk of his goods being seized or even that he was trespassing in leaving his goods on D's premises. The fact remains that he has ultimately been compelled – without any *free* choice – to discharge a liability that was solely D's.

How far can this category of legal compulsion be extended? In the leading cases the claimant's goods had already been seized under legal process. Presumably the claimant would also be entitled to restitution if he paid in order to avert X's threat to seize his goods under legal process. The claimant is denied a free choice whether the legal compulsion be exercised or threatened.

This then leads onto an old line of authority, largely forgotten until recently focused on by commentators,[21] whereby a tenant for life, who paid off a debt charged over the settled property, was held entitled to the charge over the property to secure restitution (from the remainderman) of the money paid.[1] This looks like an example of subrogation, albeit that that language has not generally been used in this context.[2] The important question, however, is whether this line of authority is explicable by the unjust factor of legal compulsion. One view would be that it is simply wrong by modern standards: that the claimant was not acting under legal compulsion and falls foul of the principle that restitution should be denied to the claimant who indirectly enriches another while acting freely in his own self interest.[3] Arguably the cases are also inconsistent with the predominant judicial view that a person with an interest under a life assurance policy, who pays premiums to prevent the policy lapsing, is not entitled to a lien over the assured deceased's estate.[4] The alternative view is that the line of authority can be justified on the ground that, albeit the threat was not immediate, the tenant for life was paying off the charge in

---

21 Eg, Maddaugh and McCamus, *The Law of Restitution* (1st edn, 1990), at pp 757–758; Sutton, 'Payment of Debts Charged Upon Property' in *Essays on the Law of Restitution* (ed Burrows, 1991), pp 71–104.

1 Eg, *Countess Shrewsbury v Earl of Shrewsbury* (1790) 1 Ves 227; *Burrell v Earl of Egremont* (1844) 7 Beav 205; *Harvey v Hobday* [1896] 1 Ch 137. Cf *Morley v Morley* (1855) 5 De GM & G 610 where the debt was not charged over the settled property.

2 But it was used by Oliver J in dicta in *Paul v Speirway Ltd* [1976] 1 Ch 220, 229.

3 Above, p 43–44.

4 Eg, *Re Leslie* (1883) 23 Ch D 552; *Falcke v Scottish Imperial Insurance Co* (1886) 34 Ch D 234. Cf *Burridge v Row* (1842) 1 Y & C Ch Cas 183. A trustee who pays insurance premiums is entitled to reimbursement and has a lien over the policy (*Re Smith's Estate* [1937] Ch 636; *Re Roberts* [1946] Ch 1). But this is merely one example of a trustee's right to be reimbursed (secured by a lien over the trust funds) for costs incurred in carrying out his duties: see Pettit, *Equity and the Law of Trusts* (9th edn, 2001), pp 473–480; *Snell's Equity* (30th edn, 1999), pp 291–293.

order to remove the potential threat of the property, in which he had a life interest, being sold off for non-payment of the debt. On this approach the payment was being made under legal compulsion and the cases are analogous to *Exall v Partridge*. Moreover an insistence on legal compulsion – paying to avoid the exercise of disadvantageous legal remedies – can explain why, irrespective of there being no charge to take over, that old line of cases was not extended to cover a tenant for life who carried out repairs or improvements to the settled property.[5]

(2) C and D are under a common liability to X but C's liability is secondary

(a) Illustrations of the general principle

In *Moule v Garrett*[6] the claimant was the tenant of certain premises. He assigned his lease to B who assigned it to the defendants. The lease contained a covenant to keep the property in repair. The landlord (X) recovered damages from the claimant for a breach of that covenant during a period when the defendants were in possession. The claimant successfully sought restitution of the damages paid from the defendants. Two points are crucial in understanding the decision. First, the defendants could have been sued by the landlord for the breach of covenant; the claimant had therefore discharged a liability of the defendants. Secondly, as the defendants were subsequent assignees, there was no privity of contract between the claimant and the defendants and hence the recoupment could not rest on contract. Cockburn CJ cited with approval,[7] as the root principle, the following passage from *Leake on Contracts*:[8] '... where the plaintiff has been compelled by law to pay, or being compellable by law, has paid money

---

5   Eg, *Caldecott v Brown* (1842) 2 Hare 144. Restitution was also refused to a co-tenant who repaired or improved jointly owned property; *Leigh v Dickeson* (1884) 15 QBD 60.

6   (1872) LR 7 Exch 101. See also *Selous Properties Ltd v Oronel Fabric Ltd* (1984) 270 Estates Gazette 643, *Becton Dickinson UK Ltd v Zwebner* [1989] QB 208 (lessee entitled to indemnity against surety of assignee of the lease); *Re Healing Research Trustee Co Ltd* [1992] 2 All ER 481; *Electricity Supply Nominees Ltd v Thorn EMI Retail Ltd* (1991) 63 P & CR 143. The 'common liability' in these cases will not arise in precisely the same form in relation to leases granted after 1995. This is because the Landlord and Tenant (Covenants) Act 1995, ss 3 and 5, has cut back privity of contract in this sphere so that the head-tenant is generally released from covenants after assignment. There will therefore generally be no common liability on a sub-tenant and head-tenant to keep leasehold property in repair. But by s 16 a head-tenant will still remain liable where he or she has entered into an 'authorised guarantee agreement' to guarantee compliance with the covenants by the assignee.

7   Ibid, at p 104.

8   1st edn at p 41.

which the defendant was ultimately liable to pay, so that the latter obtains the benefit of the payment by the discharge of his liability, under such circumstances the defendant is held indebted to the plaintiff in the amount.' The defendants were clearly primarily or 'ultimately' liable to pay because they were in possession of, and enjoying the land, at the time of the breach.

Moule v Garrett was applied, and the above passage relied on, by the Court of Appeal in *Brook's Wharf and Bull Wharf Ltd v Goodman Bros.*[9] The defendants, a firm of furriers, had imported squirrel skins and stored them in the claimant's bonded warehouse. Without any negligence on behalf of the claimants the skins were stolen from the warehouse. The defendants were liable to pay import duties on the skins but the customs (X), as they were statutorily entitled to do vis-à-vis goods removed from the warehouse, demanded payment of the import duties on the skins from the claimants. The claimants paid and successfully claimed the sum from the defendants as money paid to their use. Although the claimants and defendants were under a common liability to the customs to pay import duties it was clear that, as between the claimants and the defendants, the primary liability was on the claimants. They were the importers and the goods were theirs. In an excellent judgment Lord Wright MR said, '...the obligations so imposed on the plaintiffs as warehousemen are ancillary to and by way of security for the due payment to the customs'.[10] And he later went on:

> 'The essence of the rule is that there is a liability for the same debt resting on the plaintiff and the defendant and the plaintiff has been legally compelled to pay, but the defendant gets the benefit of the payment because his debt is discharged either entirely or *pro tanto*, whereas the defendant is primarily liable to pay as between himself and the plaintiff. The case is analogous to that of payment by a surety which has the effect of discharging the principal's debt and which, therefore, gives a right of indemnity against the principal... The defendants would be unjustly benefited at the cost of the plaintiffs if the latter ... should be left out of pocket by having to discharge what was the defendants' debt.'[11]

In the cases so far discussed in this chapter, D's liability to X discharged by C has comprised a debt owed to X. However, the liability may comprise the duty to perform an act other than paying money to X. In *Gebhardt v Saunders*,[12] for example, the claimant tenant of a house was served with a notice by the local sanitary authority addressed to

---

9   [1937] 1 KB 534.
10 Ibid, at p 543.
11 Ibid, at pp 544–545.
12 [1892] 2 QB 452. See also *Andrew v St Olaves' Board of Works* [1898] 1 QB 775; *Rhymney Iron Co v Gelligaer District Council* [1917] 1 KB 589.

'the owner or occupier' requiring the abatement of a nuisance arising from a defect or blockage in the drains. The claimant, who the court regarded as liable to a penalty if the notice was not complied with, carried out the necessary work. In the course of so doing he discovered that the problem with the drain was a structural one for which the owners were primarily responsible under the relevant statute. It was held that, whether by interpretation of the statute or at common law, the claimant was able to recover the costs and expenses incurred as money paid to the defendants' use. In Charles J's words, 'The plaintiff is entitled to recover from the defendants as having been legally compelled to incur expense in abating a nuisance which the defendants themselves ought to have abated'.[13] And Day J said, 'If two people are required to do certain work under a penalty in case of disobedience, and one does the work, and it turns out afterwards that the other ought to have done it, the expenses are properly money paid at the request of the person who was primarily liable, but who neglected to do the work'.[14]

Birks argues that the reasoning that the claimant would have been subject to a penalty for not abating the structural defect was 'forced and fragile' and that mistake would therefore have been a better basis for the restitution.[15] Certainly if there was no liability on the claimant, because the liability was on the owner only, mistake (of fact) would still justify the decision.

One final point to note is that where the claimant and defendant are liable to pay compensation for the same damage it is conceivable that a court might award restitution by a full indemnity – rather than the usual mere contribution – under the Civil Liability (Contribution) Act 1978. This power is expressly provided for in s 2(2): '... the court shall have power ... to direct that the contribution to be recovered from any person shall amount to a complete indemnity'. If it were to exercise this power a court would in effect be taking the view that C's liability was secondary to D's. By s 7(3) nothing in the 1978 Act affects any other right to an indemnity.

(b) The *Owen v Tate* controversy

Analogous to the controversy regarding *England v Marsden* considered above is whether C's voluntary or, in Goff and Jones' terminology, 'officious' incurring of the secondary liability bars restitution. In particular the question has arisen as to whether a 'voluntary' surety –

---

13 Ibid, at p 458.
14 Ibid, at p 457.
15 Birks, p 191. This argument is supported by *Hackett v Smith* [1917] 2 IR 508, 528–529 (per Sir James Campbell CJ). One might alternatively regard necessity as the unjust factor.

that is, one who has not been requested to act as surety by the debtor – can succeed in a restitutionary claim against the debtor for having discharged the debtor's liability to his creditor (X). *Owen v Tate*[16] is the difficult leading case.

The defendants had loaned £350 from a bank (the creditor) which was secured by a mortgage on the property of a Miss Lightfoot. Miss Lightfoot wanted to be released from this mortgage and to recover her title deeds. The claimant offered to help her and did so by guaranteeing the defendants' loan of £350 to the bank in consideration of the bank redeeming the mortgage. This was done without consulting the defendants and was contrary to the defendants' wishes who wanted to be secured by Miss Lightfoot's property. Over a year later the bank called on the claimant's guarantee to discharge the defendants' overdraft with it. The claimant subsequently sought an indemnity from the defendants for the debt paid. This was refused by the Court of Appeal on the ground that the claimant had voluntarily incurred the obligation to repay. Scarman LJ regarded the true principle as being as follows:

> 'If without an antecedent request a person assumes an obligation or makes a payment for the benefit of another the law will, as a general rule, refuse him a right of indemnity, but if he can show that in the particular circumstances of the case there was some necessity for the obligation to be assumed, then the law will grant him a right of reimbursement if in all the circumstances it is just and reasonable to do so.'[17]

This is a controversial decision. Goff and Jones argue that while the claimant's conduct was officious vis-à-vis the debtor it was not so vis-à-vis the creditor and that, for this reason, restitution (by subrogation) should have been awarded.[18] Birks also considers that restitution should have been granted but on the more difficult reasoning that, as the claimant was almost but not quite entitled to restitution on normal grounds and, as there was no policy objection to recovery – in that the creditor was not deceived into thinking that the claimant would not be seeking reimbursement from the debtor – restitution should have been allowed in order to avoid leaving the volunteer surety in 'an indefensibly isolated position of disadvantage'.[19]

One initial problem may be thought to be whether the debt was automatically discharged or not. The Court of Appeal clearly took the view that it was and in terms of principle, as we shall see in the last

16 [1976] QB 402.
17 Ibid, at pp 411–412.
18 Goff and Jones, paras 3-017, 15-011.
19 Birks, at pp 311–312.

main section of this chapter, this seems the preferable approach. It then appears that the key question produced by *Owen v Tate* relates simply to the unjust factor and is whether one can sensibly distinguish the person who voluntarily pays off another's debt straightaway (no unjust factor and hence no entitlement to restitution) from the voluntary surety.[20]

It seems that one generally can, albeit that the distinction is a thin one. A surety no doubt hopes that he will not be required to pay, a hope founded on the possibility that the debtor will not default and that, even if he does, the creditor will not enforce his rights against the surety. It follows that, if the surety is called upon, it will generally be the case that the legal compulsion of the contractual obligation is a cause of his payment. In contrast, legal compulsion is clearly irrelevant to the person who chooses to pay straightaway. The positions of the payors would only be indistinguishable in an unusual circumstance where the legal compulsion was not a cause of the voluntary surety's payment: ie where the surety would have paid irrespective of the legal obligation to do so (unless legal compulsion was a sufficient cause where there is another sufficiently causative unjust factor in play). Applying this approach to causation to *Owen v Tate*, restitution should have been awarded as legal compulsion was a cause of C paying off D's debt to the bank.

Alternatively if one believes that this distinction is too thin in its own right one may wish to argue that legal compulsion is supplemented here by a failure of consideration (in its rarer sense of the failure of an unpromised future event). A voluntary surety is not only contractually bound to pay but, subject to clear evidence to the contrary, does so on the well-understood assumption that he will be able to recover his payment from the principal debtor. When the debtor refuses to repay, the basis for the surety's payment fails and, while he cannot recover from the creditor (either because there is a valid contract between them or because of the creditor's change of position), he is permitted to have restitution from the debtor. So, for example, Birks and Beatson explain that when a creditor accepts a voluntary surety 'he must know, at least unless he has clear indication to the contrary, that he is dealing with a person who, if he ultimately pays the debt, will expect to be able to seek reimbursement from the debtor'.[1]

Above all, *Owen v Tate* is hard to reconcile with other strands of authority. For example, it appears to have been assumed that, as an

---

20 For a useful discussion see Maddaugh and McCamus, *The Law of Restitution* (1st edn, 1990), at pp 730–740.
1   'Unrequested Payment of Another's Debt' (1976) LQR 188, 211.

alternative to his straightforward contractual claim, a surety who has been requested to provide a guarantee by the debtor, is allowed restitution for discharging the debt under legal compulsion.[2] Yet on a restitutionary legal compulsion analysis the position of the requested and the voluntary surety cannot be distinguished.[3] Even more startlingly, the law on subrogation contradicts *Owen v Tate*: both common law authorities and s 5 of the Mercantile Law Amendment Act 1856 (which was not mentioned in the judgments) entitled the claimant to be subrogated to the bank's (former) rights against the defendants.[4] It is also inconsistent with restitution by contribution: a surety (C) is entitled to contribution from his co-surety (D) irrespective of whether D requested C to act as surety. Indeed there is authority to the effect that contribution should be denied if a surety becomes a surety at the request of his co-surety.[5] Although in all the cases dealing with contribution to a co-surety the surety was requested to act as surety by the principal debtor, the analogous restitutionary claim to that in *Owen v Tate* is between co-surety and co-surety and the principal debtor's request corresponds to the consent of the principal creditor in *Owen v Tate*.

Furthermore if a surety were not entitled to restitution on the grounds of legal compulsion it is not obvious why the leading case of *Moule v Garrett* was decided as it was, for clearly the claimant tenant *voluntarily* covenanted to keep the property in repair.

Clearly there can be exceptional circumstances (for example, where the surety is maliciously motivated, as is discussed below)[6] in which a voluntary surety should be denied restitution. But in general and provided causation is satisfied it should not be and, on the preponderance of authority, is not a bar to restitution for legal compulsion that the claimant voluntarily or officiously incurred the legal liability.[7]

If the above analysis were rejected and the view were taken that the voluntary incurring of a legal liability to pay and subsequent payment is always indistinguishable from a voluntary outright payment, the fact that the preponderance of case law (with the major exception of *Owen v Tate*) does allow restitution in the former situation would appear to lead to the inevitable conclusion that volunteers who discharge others'

2   *Re a Debtor (No 627 of 1936)* [1937] Ch 156; *Anson v Anson* [1953] 1 QB 636.
3   They would be distinguishable in restitution if the requested surety's restitutionary claim were instead viewed as being for failure of consideration in the sense of a failure of the promised return.
4   Above, pp 113–114.
5   *Turner v Davies* (1796) 2 Esp 478.
6   Below, pp 296–297.
7   In support of this see Goff and Jones' criticism, at paras 15-012 to 15-013, of *Jones v Broadhurst* (1850) 9 CB 173.

legal liabilities (restitution normally given) are treated more favourably than volunteers who confer other types of benefit (restitution normally denied). Such a conclusion would be very hard to defend in terms of principle or policy.

Owen v Tate has since been distinguished but its reasoning applied in *The Zuhal K.*[8] There the claimant sureties were granted restitution by indemnity for discharging the defendant shipowners' liability in damages to the owners of a cargo of grapefruits. Sheen J reasoned that the claimants were not voluntary sureties either on the ground that their guarantee was reasonably necessary in the defendants' interests (without it their ship would not be released from arrest by the cargo owners) or because the defendants, through their agent, had requested the claimants' guarantee.

(3) No restitution because no liability of D has been discharged

In *Bonner v Tottenham and Edmonton Permanent Investment Building Society*[9] the claimants were tenants of certain premises. They assigned their lease to Price who mortgaged it to the defendants. On Price's bankruptcy the defendant mortgagees took possession of the premises but in breach of their contract with Price they failed to pay any rent. The landlord (X) enforced the claimants' covenant to pay the rent and the claimants sought to recover the amount paid from the defendant mortgagees. The claim failed because, in contrast to *Moule v Garrett*, the claimants had not discharged any liability of the defendants to the landlord as the landlord could not sue the defendants for the rent.

Although this decision is tentatively criticised by Goff and Jones,[10] it seems correct. As the claimants' payment had not discharged any liability of the defendants it is hard to see how the claimants had benefited the defendants. In particular the defendants remained liable to pay rent to Price (and hence to his trustee in bankruptcy) and presumably they consequently remained vulnerable to forfeiture or distress.

In contrast there are decisions in which the courts may have adopted an over-technical approach to the issue of whether a liability of the defendant has been discharged. In *Re Nott and Cardiff Corpn*[11] the claimant building contractor was engaged by the defendant

---

8   [1987] 1 Lloyd's Rep 151.
9   [1899] 1 QB 161.
10 Goff and Jones, para 13-003.
11 [1918] 2 KB 146.

corporation to build a reservoir and, inter alia, the claimant was to 'take over' a railway and to put it in repair. The rating authority had placed the claimant in the rate book as the occupier of the railway and hence liable to pay the rates for it. The claimant paid the rates demanded but sought unsuccessfully to recover them from the defendant. Although the Court of Appeal was prepared to accept the arbitrator's finding that the claimant was not the occupier and had therefore been wrongly placed in the rate book, it held that the *Exall v Partridge* principle did not apply because no liability of the defendant had been discharged: the rate book, whether rightly or wrongly drawn up, determined who was liable. One can argue that this is an excessively technical approach. Although a technical approach has the merit of certainty – and avoids the acute difficulty of deciding when in substance, if not in form, a liability has been discharged – it does seem sufficiently clear that, because the rate book had been wrongly drawn up, the claimant had in reality discharged a liability of the defendant. More difficult should have been the issue of whether the claimant had discharged the liability *under legal compulsion* given that he could have successfully challenged the entry in the rate book. But the situation was arguably analogous to *Gebhardt v Saunders* where, as we have seen, the restitutionary claim was successful.

An equally technical approach to the issue of discharge has been taken on a question which is of great practical importance to the law on damages for personal injury. If a tortiously injured person (X) receives a 'collateral benefit' from C, who is legally bound to pay that benefit, which is taken account of in reducing the damages that X would otherwise be entitled to from the tortfeasor (D), can C obtain restitution from D? A negative answer was given in the leading case of *Metropolitan Police District Receiver v Croydon Corpn*,[12] where the claimant police authority had continued to pay a policeman's wages, as it was statutorily bound to do, despite his absence from work owing to an injury caused by the negligence of the defendants. The reasoning of the Court of Appeal was that the defendants had not been benefited by the claimant's payment because their liability had not been reduced. The defendants were only legally liable to pay the damages which a court would award and in assessing those damages a court would deduct the collateral benefit paid by the claimant. As Morris LJ said, 'I cannot see that there was any unjust benefit here received by the defendants when they have been held liable for all that they were in law liable to pay.'[13] One can argue that

---

12 [1957] 2 QB 154.
13 Ibid at p 168.

this is an over-technical approach and it is to be contrasted with the judgment of Slade J at first instance.[14] In reality the tortfeasors had been relieved of part of their liability.[15] Indeed the decision has arguably had the detrimental effect of encouraging over-compensatory awards of damages because the courts have been unnecessarily unwilling to deduct collateral benefits in assessing damages on the ground that deduction simply relieves tortfeasors.

The recoupment scheme for social security benefits contained in the Social Security (Recovery of Benefits) Act 1997[16] may be regarded as a rejection of the *Croydon Corpn* approach. This Act allows the state, which has paid social security benefits to an injured party thereby reducing the tortfeasor's liability to pay, to recoup (through the Compensation Recovery Unit) those payments from the tortfeasor. However, there is now to be no deduction of social security benefits from damages awarded for non-pecuniary loss.[17]

While the legislature's motivation in introducing these 'recoupment provisions' was, no doubt, purely financial (claiming back state money) the heart of them can be interpreted as resting on the principle of unjust enrichment: the state and the tortfeasor are under a common legal liability to pay the victim but, as between the tortfeasor and the state, the tortfeasor, as the party responsible for the injury, is primarily liable. However, unjust enrichment (ie, compulsory discharge of another's liability) cannot explain the tortfeasor's liability to pay to the state the value of social security benefits that are not deducted in assessing damages (so that no liability is discharged). The wider explanation for the scheme is, therefore, that the tortfeasor is, exceptionally, being held liable in tort for the pure economic loss caused to the state by the tort.

One can also apply an unjust enrichment analysis – according to which the NHS has compulsorily discharged a liability of the tortfeasor – to explain the NHS' right to recover from tortfeasors the costs of

---

14 [1956] 1 WLR 1113. The Law Commission provisionally preferred Slade J's view to that of the Court of Appeal. But even accepting that the tortfeasor is enriched, the Law Commission did not recommend a new statutory right for the provider of a deductible collateral benefit to recoup its value from the tortfeasor. See Law Com No 262, *Damages for Personal Injury: Medical, Nursing and Other Expenses; Collateral Benefits* (1999), paras 10.68–10.72, 12.28–12.32.

15 However, once one moves from the technical approach, there will be difficulties in deciding when another's liability is in reality discharged. Can one say, eg, that in providing free care to a tort victim, the National Health Service in reality discharges (by compulsion) a legal liability of the tortfeasor to pay private medical expenses? For the argument that one can, see Law Com No 262, paras 3.22–3.25.

16 See *Clerk and Lindsell on Torts* (18th edn, 2000), para 29–34.

17 By s 8 and Sch 2 of the 1997 Act, recoupment shall only be against compensation for loss of earnings, cost of care and loss of mobility, and then only 'like for like'.

treatment provided to victims of motor accidents under the Road Traffic (NHS Charges) Act 1999.[18] Alternatively, one may again see this as the state, exceptionally, being compensated for pure economic loss caused by a tort.

Metropolitan Police District Receiver v Croydon Corpn was distinguished in *Land Hessen v Gray & Gerrish.*[19] This case concerned a road traffic accident in which two German teachers were injured, one of them subsequently dying from her injuries. Land Hessen is a German state and employed the two teachers. It was required by German law to make various payments to them, and to the widower and children of the deceased. Land Hessen asserted a restitutionary right to recover the payments from those whose negligence had allegedly caused the accident. It was argued that all that needed to be shown was that the payments were compelled by law, that the claimant did not officiously expose itself to the liability to make the payments, and that the payments discharged a liability of the defendants. Sachs J accepted that all of these elements were present, and distinguished *Metropolitan Police District Receiver v Croydon Corpn* as follows:

> 'That decision only binds me to the extent of the Plaintiff's claim to emoluments. It does not bind me in relation to the other parts of the Plaintiff's claim not covered by the decision of the Court of Appeal and which the Plaintiff was liable to pay in consequence of this accident.'

Accordingly he found that the claimant had a restitutionary right to recover some of the payments made but left the decision about exactly which for a later hearing.

It is not clear precisely what is meant by the term 'emoluments' and thus the basis on which Sachs J distinguished the facts in *Land Hessen* from those in the *Croydon Corpn* case is obscure. The reasoning in the *Croydon Corpn* case excludes the recoupment of any benefit which is deductible from tort damages. It is therefore strongly arguable that the decision in *Land Hessen* is inconsistent with that of the Court of Appeal in *Croydon Corpn* and lends support to the view that Slade J's reasoning at first instance in the *Croydon Corpn*[20] case is to be preferred to that of the Court of Appeal.

It is also important to note the significance of Sachs J's view that the unjust factor of legal compulsion was made out in this case. It

---

18 See Law Com No 262, paras 3.19–3.43, esp 3.22–3.25, which examines the case for a wider scheme for the recoupment by the NHS from tortfeasors of the costs of treatment provided to tort victims.
19 (31 July 1998, unreported).
20 [1956] 1 WLR 1113.

is implicit in this analysis that there is an injustice in allowing the cost of wrongdoing to fall on the providers of collateral benefits. In other words, on this analysis, as between tortfeasors and those who provide collateral benefits under a valid contractual (or perhaps statutory) obligation, the tortfeasor's liability to the tort victim is primary.

The approach to indemnity insurance is altogether different from (other) collateral benefits. The law here is that no liability of the tortfeasor (D) to the victim (X) is discharged not because D is treated as having no liability after the insurer's (C's) payment but rather because D's liability is treated as still alive irrespective of C's payment under legal compulsion. So if an assured (X) insures himself against property damage with an insurer (C) and C pays out (by reason of its contractual obligation) when X's property is damaged by a tortfeasor (D), D's tortious liability to X is not discharged. C therefore has no restitutionary remedy against D for compulsory discharge of D's liability to X. As Lord Goff said in *Esso Petroleum Ltd v Hall, Russell & Co Ltd*,[1] where Esso (C) had indemnified Scottish crofters (X), under a tanker owners' oil pollution agreement, for oil damage caused by the negligence of Hall Russell (D), 'There can of course be no direct claim by Esso against Hall Russell in restitution, if only because Esso has not by its payment discharged the liability of Hall Russell, and so has not enriched Hall Russell ...' This is not to say that the assured is to be left unjustly enriched at the insurer's expense. On the contrary, the law has chosen a different line of reasoning whereby the insurer is subrogated (by 'simple subrogation') to the assured's remedies against the tortfeasor.[2]

3. LEGAL COMPULSION: RESTITUTION BY CONTRIBUTION

Where C and D are under a common liability to X – but one cannot say that C's liability is secondary to D's – and C, under legal compulsion, pays more than, as between C and D, he should be responsible for, C is entitled to restitution of that part of the sum paid that constitutes the over-payment. The restitutionary award is known as contribution. The law here is partly contained in statute, principally the Civil Liability (Contribution) Act 1978, and partly remains governed by the common law.

---

1   [1989] AC 643, 663.
2   See above, pp 107–112.

(1) Civil Liability (Contribution) Act 1978[3]

The Act applies where more than one person is liable to pay compensation in respect of the same damage to another person.[4] It does not matter what the basis of the legal liability is: it may be tort, breach of contract, breach of trust, or otherwise. By s 2(1), '... the amount of the contribution recoverable from any person shall be such as may be found by the court to be just and equitable having regard to the extent of that person's responsibility for the damage in question'. And by s 10(2)–(4) of the Limitation Act 1980, the right to recover contribution accrues when the person seeking contribution is held liable for the damage by a judgment or arbitration award or when he agrees (with the victim) to pay a certain amount of compensation.

Despite earlier judicial doubts vis-à-vis the identical forerunner to s 2(1),[5] it is clear that in exercising its discretion as to how much contribution to award (ie, the amount of the payment the co-obligor should be responsible for) a court should take account of both the relative culpability and causative potency of the co-obligors' conduct.[6]

(2) Common law

The 1978 Act does not affect the common law on contribution where there is a common liability to pay the same debt. The early case of *Deering v Earl of Winchelsea*[7] established that, irrespective of a contractual right to contribution and, arising from a general principle of equity, co-sureties of the same debt are entitled to contribution from each

---

3   The Merchant Shipping Act 1995, s 189 is a further statute allowing contribution claims. For a detailed examination of the 1978 Act, see Mitchell, 'The Civil Liability (Contribution) Act 1978' [1997] RLR 27.

4   In *Friends' Provident Life Office v Hillier Parker May & Rowden* [1997] QB 85 the Court of Appeal held that a liability to pay compensation for damage under the 1978 Act includes a liability to make restitution of a mistaken payment. This was a strained interpretation not least because restitution of money paid by mistake is most naturally viewed as a claim in debt and the 1978 Act does not cover contribution between co-debtors. It illustrates that, along with several other statutes, the 1978 Act needs updating to take account of restitutionary claims. In *Royal Brompton Hospital NHS Trust v Hammond* [2002] UKHL 14, [2002] 1 WLR 1397, the House of Lords expressly disapproved the wide interpretation of 'same damage' applied in the *Friends' Provident* case; and it was emphasised that those statutory words should be applied without any glosses, extensive or restrictive. For other recent decisions on the meaning of liability in respect of the same damage to the same person under the 1978 Act see, eg, *Birse Construction Ltd v Haiste Ltd* [1996] 1 WLR 675, CA; *Eastgate Group Ltd v Lindsey Morden Group Inc* [2001] EWCA Civ 1446, [2001] 2 All ER (Comm) 1050; *Co-operative Retail Services Ltd v Taylor Young Ltd* [2002] UKHL 17, [2002] 1 WLR 1419.

5   *Smith v Bray* (1939) 56 TLR 200; *Weaver v Commercial Press Co Ltd* (1947) 63 TLR 466.

6   *Madden v Quirk* [1989] 1 WLR 702.

7   (1787) 2 Bos & P 270.

other;[8] and that, while prima facie co-sureties are equally bound and therefore entitled to equal contribution, they can bind themselves as sureties for different amounts with a corresponding entitlement to proportionate contribution. This approach in *Deering* was particularly clearly summarised by Alderson B in *Pendelbury v Walker*:[9] '... where the same default of the principal renders all the co-sureties responsible, all are to contribute; and then the law superadds that which is not only the principle but the equitable mode of applying the principle, that they should all contribute equally, if each is a surety to an equal amount; and if not equally, then proportionately to the amount for which each is a surety.' A similar principle enables an insurer to recover contribution from a co-insurer[10] and a partner to recover contribution from a co-partner.[11] Similarly, albeit rare, a mortgagor can recover contribution from a co-mortgagor[12] and a contractor can recover contribution from a joint contractor.[13]

Where equality is the relevant basis for the contribution the sum to be awarded is easy to assess. For example, if C and D are sureties for a debt of £800 and C pays the £800, it is entitled to £400 contribution from D. If the creditor accepted £600 from C in discharge of the debt of £800, C would be entitled to £300 contribution from D.

More tricky is proportionate rather than equal contribution. If C was surety for a debt of £800 and D for merely half of that debt (£400) and C pays £800, C is clearly entitled to £266.66 contribution from D

---

8   It was stressed that the debt must be the same in *Coope v Twynam* (1823) Turn & R 426. For an analogous principle in insurance cases see *North British and Mercantile Insurance Co v London, Liverpool and Globe Insurance Co* (1876) 5 Ch D 569. See also *Craythorne v Swinburne* (1807) 14 Ves 160 and *Re Denton's Estate* [1904] 2 Ch 178: a surety cannot recover contribution from his surety. For the effect on sureties of the creditor releasing or giving time to the principal debtor, see Goff and Jones, paras 14-014 to 14-015. Where a co-surety is insolvent he is in effect treated for contribution purposes as no longer being a co-surety; *Ellesmere Brewery Co v Cooper* [1896] 1 QB 75, 80. As it is a condition of contribution from a co-surety that the surety cannot recoup from the principal debtor under the principle of *Moule v Garrett*, the principal debtor should be joined as a party to the action unless he is insolvent: *Hay v Carter* [1935] Ch 397.

9   (1841) 4 Y & C Ex 424, 441.

10   *North British and Mercantile Insurance Co v London, Liverpool and Globe Insurance Co* (1876) 5 Ch D 569; *Legal and General Assurance Society Ltd v Drake Insurance Co Ltd* [1992] QB 887 (co-insurer prima facie liable for contribution even though assured had not given in the required notice): but on the facts contribution was denied because the payment in respect of which contribution was sought had been voluntarily made in excess of the claimant insurer's liability to pay: see Friedmann, 'Double Insurance and Payment of Another's Debt' (1993) 109 LQR 51); *Eagle Star Insurance Co v Provincial Insurance plc* [1994] 1 AC 130.

11   *Re The Royal Bank of Australia, Robinson's Executors Case* (1856) 6 De GM & G 572. See generally *Lindley & Banks on Partnership* (17th edn, 1995) chapter 20.

12   *Re Mainwaring* [1937] Ch 96.

13   *Boulter v Peplow* (1850) 9 CB 493. See also *Spiers & Son Ltd v Troup* (1915) 84 LJKB 1986, 1992 which falls outside the well-established relationships and concerned not a debt as such but a common statutory liability to pay for building work.

(on a 2:1 ratio). But what if the creditors accepted £600 from C in discharge of the debt of £800? Two views as to how to work out the appropriate contribution ratio would here produce different results. On one view, the appropriate ratio correlates to the maximum sum each surety could have been liable for; on this view the 2:1 ratio is therefore appropriate despite the reduction of the debt to £600 and C would be entitled to £200 contribution from D. In the leading case of *Commercial Union Assurance Co Ltd v Hayden*[14] this was called the 'maximum liability' basis. An alternative view is that the appropriate ratio correlates to the sum each surety would have been liable for, independently of the other, on the particular facts. As the debt was reduced to £600 the ratio would be 3:2 (ie, C would independently have been liable for £600 and D for £400) and C would therefore be entitled to £240 from D. In the *Hayden* case this was referred to as the 'independent liability' basis.

The Court of Appeal in *Hayden* held that a 'rateable proportion clause' in a contract of liability insurance should be construed according to the 'independent liability' basis. But it was stressed that no analogy should necessarily be drawn with co-sureties or property co-insurers where the general assumption appears to be that the maximum liability basis is correct. Cairns LJ said, 'I am prepared to assume that as between co-sureties the basis of apportionment is the maximum liability basis, though there is no decision to that effect binding on this court, but I do not consider that there is any authority for the proposition that the proportion must be fixed in the same way between co-insurers as between co-sureties.'[15] However, it is hard to see why, if the independent liability basis is considered the best approach for liability insurance, the position should change where contribution between co-sureties or property co-insurers is in play.

4. WHEN DOES PAYMENT OF ANOTHER'S DEBT DISCHARGE THAT DEBT?

(1) The position in principle

The doctrine put forward as their analysis of the case law by Goff and Jones and, in particular detail, by Birks and Beatson[16] is that the unrequested (by the debtor) payment of another's debt only discharges that debt automatically (ie, without the debtor's acceptance) where

14 [1977] QB 804.
15 Ibid, at p 815.
16 'Unrequested payment of Another's Debt' (1976) 92 LQR 188.

it was paid under legal compulsion or, probably, by necessity. The only unjust factors that can be linked to the incontrovertible benefit of the discharge of a debt are therefore legal compulsion and probably necessity: otherwise, free acceptance by the debtor is required for a restitutionary claim to succeed against the debtor.

It is difficult to see the force of this doctrine. Why should the mind of the payor affect whether the debt is automatically or non-automatically discharged? The explanation advanced by Birks and Beatson[17] is that the debt ought not to be automatically discharged where the payor can recover directly from the creditor. The reason why payments under legal compulsion and probably necessity differ from payments by mistake or under duress is, so it is argued, that the former, unlike the latter, do not allow restitution from the creditor; and because they do not allow restitution from the creditor the debt should be regarded as automatically discharged.

But that supposed explanation seems circular in failing to go on to answer the crucial question of why it should matter that the payor can recover directly from the creditor provided he is not allowed double restitution.

The doctrine also seems misconceived in assuming that if the debt were discharged automatically by, eg, a mistaken payment, the payor could still recover his money directly from the creditor. As is discussed below,[18] such a claim against the creditor would generally fail.

Furthermore, the doctrine has the unfortunate consequence of requiring one to drive a wedge between discharging debts and discharging other legal liabilities. Most cases on the discharging of another's legal liability concern discharging debts. But this is not always so. An example is *Gebhardt v Saunders,*[19] where the liability discharged was repairing the drains of a house so as to abate a nuisance. Clearly the defendant's liability was automatically discharged by the claimant's abating the nuisance and there could be no question of that discharge turning on whether the act was done under legal compulsion or not. Indeed, as we have seen, it can be argued that mistake is a better explanation than legal compulsion of the unjust factor in *Gebhardt* and no one would suggest that such a switch in the unjust factor would lead to problems over the defendant's enrichment.

Another problem with the approach of Birks and Beatson is that it is geared to the view that a requirement of 'adoption' by the debtor for the debt to be discharged is reconcilable with restitutionary principles in that the adoption constitutes free acceptance by the

17 Ibid, at pp 201, 207.
18 Below, p 295.
19 [1892] 2 QB 452.

debtor. Hence the Court of Appeal in *Owen v Tate* is criticised for failing to consider a free acceptance analysis.[20] However, it is argued elsewhere in this book[1] that free acceptance is a misconceived concept; and, while *Owen v Tate* is a difficult case,[2] the difficulty is not to do with there having been no examination of free acceptance.

It is submitted therefore that, in principle, the doctrine espoused by the leading commentators is unsound. A payment made to discharge a debt owed to the creditor and accepted by the creditor as discharging that debt ought to discharge that debt automatically (ie without the debtor's acceptance).[3]

It follows that there is no reason why the unjust factors linked to the enrichment of the discharge of the debt should be confined to legal compulsion and necessity; any other autonomous unjust factor, for example mistake or duress, ought in principle to be capable of grounding a restitutionary claim against the debtor. This derives support from the mistake cases of *County of Carleton v City of Ottawa*,[4] although it is not clear that that case concerned the discharge of a debt as opposed to the fulfilment of a statutory duty, and *B Liggett (Liverpool) Ltd v Barclays Bank Ltd*[5] where a bank that had mistakenly honoured a cheque drawn without its customer's authority, but in favour of its customer's creditors, was held to be subrogated to the creditor's former personal remedies against the customer.

Adopting the preferred view, could C alternatively sue the creditor (X) to recover the money paid? The general position[6] would be that X, by accepting the payment from C as discharging D's debt, would be providing consideration for C's payment. If C wished to reclaim the money from X, as opposed to D, he would therefore need to establish the invalidity of the contract. Even if he could do so, the discharge of the debt (unless the debt was revived) would presumably give X a defence of change of position. Additionally if the contract were voidable (for, eg, mistake or undue influence) C might fall foul of the '*restitutio in integrum* is impossible' bar to rescission.

---

20   See also the criticism of *Re Cleadon Trust Ltd* [1939] Ch 286 in Birks, pp 288–290.
1   Below, chapter 10.
2   Above, pp 282–286.
3   This is supported by Friedmann, 'Payment of Another's Debt' (1983) 99 LQR 534; Stoljar, *The Law of Quasi-Contract* (2nd edn, 1989), p 166; Maddaugh and McCamus, *The Law of Restitution* (1st edn, 1990), pp 762–764; Virgo, *The Principles of the Law of Restitution* (1999), pp 225–230.
4   (1965) 52 DLR (2d) 220: above, pp 167–168. On the facts of *Aiken v Short* (1856) 1 H & N 210 – above, p 131 – a restitutionary claim for mistake against the debtor should have been possible.
5   [1928] 1 KB 48. See above, pp 124–125.
6   If there is no consideration there is no question of unwinding a contract: however, change of position would still be a defence to the creditor.

Even if it is felt that the application of standard principle would not adequately protect the creditor (X) from a restitutionary claim by C, one could add to the automatic discharge approach that, if C does recover his money from X, D's debt to X should be treated as having 'revived'. Once revived, C could not go on to sue D in restitution because D would not have been benefited, whereas X could recover from D on the revived debt. That a debt can revive is supported by Friedmann, who further argues that (so as to enable D to know exactly where he stands) D's adoption of C's payment stops the possibility of the debt reviving: ie, D can in effect stop C and X taking back the incontrovertible benefit by 'adopting' it.[7] Once adopted, C's restitutionary claim would be against D only and not against X.

One objection that might be raised to the automatic discharge theory is that the debtor has a new creditor (C) foisted on him without his consent. But this is also a problem with the traditional doctrine where the debt is paid under legal compulsion or necessity. In any event the objection loses force when it is realised that the creditor can make an assignment of his rights without the debtor's consent.

Alternatively it may possibly be thought that the traditional doctrine has the merit of protecting the interests of creditors who wish to shield their debtors from hostile interveners: that is, interveners who falsely present themselves as willing to pay off the debt without subsequent recourse against the debtor. Put another way, it may be argued that the traditional doctrine prevents an intervener being afforded a way round a creditor's desire not to assign his rights. In the American case of *Norton v Haggett*[8] the claimant, after a dispute with the defendant, found that the defendant was in debt to a bank (X). In order to have a hold over the defendant he offered X to pay off the defendant's debt and this was accepted by X. When the claimant found out that he had not 'bought' X's rights against the defendant (ie he had not been assigned X's rights) but had rather mistakenly discharged the defendant's debt to X, the claimant sought restitution from the defendant. His claim was refused. Blackmer J said, 'To give the plaintiff restitution from the Haggetts would be to substitute him for the bank as creditor of the Haggetts without the consent of either the bank or the Haggetts. No protection is deserved by one who intermeddles by paying another's debt either without reason or to secure rights against the debtor without the consent of the creditor.'[9]

7   'Payment of Another's Debt' (1983) LQR 534, esp at pp 542, 556. Unfortunately at p 542 Friedmann equates adoption with free acceptance. There is no need for free acceptance reasoning on his theory: the unjust factor is legal compulsion and the benefit is incontrovertible.

8   85 A 2d 571 (1952).

9   Ibid, at p 574.

This decision is perfectly explicable because there was no unjust factor. The claimant was not acting under legal compulsion and his mistake was one of law not fact (and at the time it would appear that, as in England, so in the United States, a mistake of law did not generally trigger restitution). In any event (ie even if he had paid under a legal obligation to do so, or even if one takes the preferable view, now accepted in England, that a mistake of law should count) one ought to carve out an exception to the normal restitutionary approach so that a ground for restitution is negatived where the intervener is shown to be motivated by maliciousness towards the debtor as on the facts of *Norton v Haggett.* The problem of the hostile intervener can therefore be dealt with satisfactorily at the stage of establishing the unjust factor. There is no need to see it as a reason for rejecting the automatic discharge theory.[10]

This is supported by *Norton v Haggett* itself for the court assumed that the debt had been automatically discharged by the bank's acceptance of the payment by the claimant. If the debt had not been automatically discharged the defendant's subsequent acceptance of the payment as discharging the debt ought, on the Birks and Beatson view, to have entitled the claimant to restitution based on the defendant's free acceptance.

Even if the hostile intervener problem were thought to be best dealt with by denying that the debt is automatically discharged, it is surely a difficulty that rarely arises and could merely justify a rare exception to the automatic discharge theory rather than a blanket rejection of it.

In the *Use and Abuse of Unjust Enrichment*[11] Beatson returned to this topic and offers three original and interesting arguments in support of a general 'no automatic discharge' rule.

First, he attacks the notion of a debt reviving. 'Revival of the debt is wrong in principle because it permits parties to impose a burden on a non-consenting third party.' But the original parties are not imposing a burden on the debtor, they are merely taking back a benefit. Moreover, the whole law of restitution is the antithesis of a principle that one should only have to give up, or pay for, benefits where one has consented to do so. Nor is it easy to see the force of Beatson's additional point that there would be a practical difficulty if the debtor paid the creditor after the intervention and the creditor took the payment. If the debt has already been discharged, the debtor could simply recover the money on the basis that it paid under a mistake of fact.

10 If the intervener does positively deceive the creditor, the creditor might be able to rescind the contract with the intervener for misrepresentation, although this might be barred by '*restitutio in integrum* being impossible'.

11 (1991), at pp 200–206.

Secondly, he argues that a 'no-discharge' rule deals more satisfactorily with where the debtor has a defence or, especially, a counterclaim against the creditor. However in principle this should go to the question of the extent to which the defendant has been benefited. If the debtor had a defence to the claim for the debt, he is plainly not benefited by its discharge. Similarly in the rare situation where the debtor would have resisted payment on the basis of having a counterclaim, so that discharge carries the disadvantage of requiring the debtor to instigate a separate legal action against the creditor, that disadvantage reduces the value of the discharge to the debtor and should reduce the quantum of restitution. In any event this objection applies with equal force to the Birks and Beatson doctrine: a debtor is just as likely to have a defence or counterclaim against the creditor when the debt is paid off by legal compulsion or necessity as where other unjust factors are involved.

Thirdly, Beatson argues that automatic discharge subverts the law on assignment of contractual rights. Restitution should not permit the intervener to side-step the rules of assignment (eg the requirement of giving notice to the third party). However in many situations, even outside legal compulsion and necessity, the claimant could not reasonably be expected to seek an assignment; for example, where he pays under duress or undue influence. And where the intervener can reasonably be expected to take an assignment there will generally be no unjust factor triggering restitution. The threat posed by restitution to the law on assignment is therefore minimal. In any event there is no good reason to think that the rules of assignment produce better justice than the law of restitution. Furthermore Beatson is happy to accept restitution by subrogation which equally outflanks the rules of assignment.

(2) The authorities

To argue that the automatic discharge theory is preferable in principle leaves untouched the root question of whether it can be supported on the authorities: or whether, on the contrary, the authorities force one to accept the traditional doctrine however unsatisfactory it appears to be.

It must be immediately conceded that there have been cases laying down or accepting that payment by a stranger does not automatically discharge a debt: rather there is a need for the debtor's acceptance. In the leading case of *Belshaw v Bush*[12] it was held that where D's debt

---

12 (1851) 11 CB 191.

to X – for the price of goods, sold and delivered – was voluntarily paid by C 'on account of the debt' *and adopted by* D, D had a good defence to X's action against him for payment of the debt. Again in *Simpson v Eggington*,[13] in an action brought by a corporation (D) to recover money paid to its former employee (X), X sought to set-off a year's salary as still owing to him by D. In fact the salary had been paid by C, D's treasurer, without prior authority. It was held that X was not entitled to the set-off because C's payment had been ratified by D so that D's salary debt to X was discharged. Parke B said, 'The general rule as to payment or satisfaction by a third person, not himself liable as a co-contractor or otherwise, has been fully considered in the cases ... and the result appears to be that it is not sufficient to discharge a debtor unless it is made by the third person, as agent, for and on account of the debtor, and with his prior authority or subsequent ratification.'[14] In the Australian case of *City Bank of Sydney v McLaughlin*,[15] in which a bank (C) successfully argued that it was entitled to be subrogated to X's rights against D (who was temporarily insane) in a situation where C had made payments to D's wife (under a void power of attorney) which were used to discharge D's debts to X, Isaacs J cited *Belshaw v Bush* with approval and said, 'Unless there is something in the nature of adoption, the attempted payment is not really a payment, for the debtor might refuse to accept it, and insist on paying his debts himself, leaving the first person to get back his money as best he could.'[16] In *Barclays Bank Ltd v W J Simms, Son and Cooke (Southern) Ltd*[17] Robert Goff J held that a bank's (C's) mistaken payment to its customer's (D's) creditor (X), on a cheque countermanded by D, did not discharge D's liability to X. C could therefore recover from X applying restitutionary principles of mistake. There was no change of position by X nor any need to upset a contract supported by consideration between C and X. Finally, in *Crantrave Ltd v Lloyds Bank plc*[18] it was accepted by the Court of Appeal, citing Goff and Jones[19] and *Barclays Bank v Simms*[20] that the unauthorised payment of another's debt does not discharge that debt. Pill LJ said, 'In the absence of evidence that the bank's payment has been made on the customer's behalf or

---

13 (1855) 10 Exch 845.
14 Ibid, at p 847.
15 (1909) 9 CLR 615.
16 Ibid, at p 633.
17 [1980] QB 677. Although there was a doubt as to whether D had a liability to X on the underlying transaction, D clearly had a liability to X on the cheque itself. See generally Goode, *Commercial Law* (2nd edn, 1995), pp 560–562.
18 [2000] QB 917. See above, p 125.
19 *The Law of Restitution* (5th edn, 1998), p 17. See now (6th edn, 2002), para 1-018.
20 Dicta of Fox LJ in *Electricity Supply Nominees Ltd v Thorn EMI Retail Ltd* (1991) 63 P & CR 143, 148 was also cited with approval.

subsequently ratified by him, the payment to the creditor will not of itself discharge the [customer's] liability to the creditor ...'[1] On the other hand, and on the face of it inconsistently, Pill LJ said, 'It is unnecessary in this appeal to decide general questions as to the circumstances in which another's debt may be discharged.'[2]

In contrast to those cases it seems clear that where C pays under legal compulsion the debt is automatically discharged and the debtor's adoption is irrelevant. So, for example, there was no mention of the debtor's adoption in cases like *Exall v Partridge, Moule v Garrett* or *Brook's Wharf v Goodman Bros.*

One may therefore be tempted to take the traditional reconciling view that legal compulsion (and necessity) does automatically discharge the debt, while otherwise the debtor's adoption is needed. Yet in, for example, *Belshaw v Bush,* there was certainly no indication that D's adoption would be unnecessary if C had paid under legal compulsion.

An alternative view, therefore, is that there is inconsistency in the authorities, that no neat reconciliation of all the authorities is possible, and that one must make a straightforward choice between either the 'automatic discharge' or the 'debtor's acceptance' theories. In the light of the preferred position in principle advocated above, it is submitted that this alternative view of the authorities should be favoured and that the choice should be exercised in favour of extending across the board the automatic discharge approach of the legal compulsion cases.

That no neat reconciliation of the authorities is possible is shown by several further cases in which C's payment of D's debt has been regarded as automatically discharging that debt, even though C's payment was unrequested (by the debtor) and not made under legal compulsion or necessity and indeed may not have been made by reason of any unjust factor.

In *Welby v Drake,*[3] for example, X agreed with C (D's father) that C's part payment of D's debt to X would satisfy the whole debt. It was held that X could not then sue D and no mention was made of any need for D's consent. In dicta in *Cook v Lister*[4] Willes J said:

'... if a stranger pays a part of a debt in discharge of the whole, the debt is gone because it would be a fraud on the stranger to proceed. So, in the case of a composition made with a body of creditors, the assent to receive the composition discharges the debt, because otherwise fraud would be committed against the

1   [2000] 3 WLR 877, 882.
2   Ibid.
3   (1825) 1 C & P 557. See also, on very similar facts, *Re Barnes* (1861) 4 LTNS 60.
4   (1863) 13 CBNS 543, 594–595.

rest of the creditors. And with respect to the necessity for showing the assent of the debtor, I apprehend that it is contrary to the well-known principle of law, by which a benefit conferred upon a man is presumed to be accepted by him, until the contrary is proved.'

Again, in *Hirachand Punamchand v Temple*[5] X applied to D's father (C) for payment of D's debt to X. C offered part payment by banker's draft in full satisfaction and, although X did not expressly agree to this, they cashed the draft and kept the proceeds. It was held that X could not enforce the debt against D and, although several grounds of reasoning were offered by the three judges, Fletcher Moulton LJ's preferred view was simply that the debt was extinguished by X's acceptance of the money offered by C. Furthermore *B Liggett (Liverpool) Ltd v Barclays Bank Ltd*[6] directly contradicts *Barclays Bank v WJ Simms* (although it was not referred to in Robert Goff J's judgment) in holding that a bank's mistaken honouring of an unauthorised cheque in favour of its customer's creditors discharged the customer's debts to those creditors. Finally in *Re Cleadon Trust Ltd*,[7] in which C, a director of a company (D), paid off D's obligations under a guarantee thinking that D would ratify his payments which it could not do (because with his vote disqualified, on the ground of his personal interest, the board was inquorate), the Court of Appeal appeared to take it for granted that D's liabilities *had been automatically discharged* by C's payments.[8] The majority's refusal to allow C a restitutionary claim against D (Sir Wilfred Green MR dissenting) is best interpreted as turning on the lack of any unjust factor. C was a volunteer: ie a risk-taker or mispredictor.[9]

Moreover, while Friedmann's view, that D's adoption is not a necessary requirement for the debt to be discharged but is instead simply designed to prevent C and X reviving the debt, does not appear to derive general support from the cases in which adoption has been stressed, there is one case, *Walter v James*,[10] which supports it. X claimed £63 17s 3d from D who paid £3 17s 3d into court and pleaded that C (Southall) had paid X the remaining debt of £60. Although C had

---

5   [1911] 2 KB 330.

6   [1928] 1 KB 48. See above, pp 124–125.

7   [1939] Ch 286. See also *Re National Motor Mail-Coach Co Ltd* [1908] 2 Ch 515 (no recovery as there was no unjust factor but it was apparently assumed that the debt was discharged); and *Norton v Haggett* which has been discussed above, pp 296–297.

8   At pp 298, 304–305 (per Sir Wilfred Greene MR) and at p 319 (per Clauson LJ).

9   But one could argue that C was mistaken in believing that he could vote so that the board would be quorate and that this caused his payment. Certainly that seems the best ground for supporting restitution on the facts.

10 (1871) LR 6 Exch 124. See Friedmann, 'Payment of Another's Debt' (1983) LQR 534, 541–542.

paid the £60 to X he had subsequently requested its return and this had been acceded to by X. It was held that X was entitled to recover the £60 from D on the ground that, until the payment by C had been adopted and ratified by D, C and X were free to unwind what they had done.

(3) Conclusion

The conclusion to be drawn is that, while the authorities are not consistent, there is sufficient support for the automatic discharge theory, which, in terms of principle, is eminently preferable to the view proposed by Birks and Beatson and Goff and Jones.

One final point of importance is that a recognition that, in some past cases, the courts have unfortunately thought D's adoption to be important (irrespective of stopping revival of the debt) is not to commit one to accepting that those courts have been applying 'free acceptance' reasoning. Other explanations of their insistence on adoption are possible. Most obviously, the courts may have been applying contractual agency reasoning:[11] by ratifying the payment D treats C as his agent for paying X so that C has a normal contractual entitlement to reimbursement (just as if D had requested him to pay X from the outset). Alternatively the courts may have been adhering to a very subjective theory of benefit by reasoning that even incontrovertible benefits do not count as benefits until D has consented to them.

---

11 See Birks and Beatson, 'Unrequested Payment of Another's Debt' (1976) LQR 188, 194–196.

Chapter 9

Necessity

A passer-by dives into a lake to save a drowning child. A neighbour repairs serious storm damage to the roof of the next-door house while the occupant is away. A carrier of goods pays for them to be warehoused when they are not collected at the place of delivery by the owner. Do these 'necessitous interveners' have a remedy (leaving aside any available in contract or tort)[1] against the person whose life or property has been saved?[2]

The picture traditionally painted is that, in contrast to the position in civil law systems, necessitous interveners have bleak prospects of recovery under English law. In reality, however, the contrast is not as sharp as is often thought. By pulling together

---

1 Where the necessity was created by the defendant's negligence, an injured intervener may be able to recover compensatory damages in tort: see, eg, *Haynes v Harwood* [1935] 1 KB 146; *Chadwick v British Railways Board* [1967] 1 WLR 912. The Road Traffic Act 1988, ss 158–159 in effect imposes strict liability on a vehicle user for loss caused to a doctor or a hospital in rendering emergency medical treatment to the victim of an accident arising out of the use of the vehicle. Note also that, as laid down in *Hunt v Severs* [1994] 2 AC 350, an injured victim has a claim for damages against a tortfeasor for necessary nursing and visiting 'services' rendered gratuitously by an intervener (whether friend or relative); and these damages are held on trust for the intervener (unless the intervener is the tortfeasor). Although the intervener has no direct claim against the tortfeasor, the damages appear to be viewed as a means of compensating the intervener for his or her loss caused by the tort. The damages have not been regarded as recognising a restitutionary claim of the intervener against the victim (based on necessity) or against the tortfeasor (based on necessitous discharge of the tortfeasor's liability to pay for commercial nursing care). See generally Law Commission Report No 262, *Damages for Personal Injury: Medical, Nursing and Other Expenses; Collateral Benefits* (1999) esp paras 3.44–3.100. Degeling, 'Carers' Claims: Unjust Enrichment and Tort' [2000] RLR 172 argues that the intervenor's entitlement to a share of the damages reverses the victim's unjust enrichment based on a policy against over-indemnity. See also Degeling, 'A New Reason for Restitution: The Policy Against Accumulation' (2002) 22 OJLS 435. In *Kars v Kars* (1997) 71 ALJR 107 the High Court of Australia rejected *Hunt v Severs* and preferred the former English approach in *Donnelly v Joyce* [1974] QB 454, whereby the victim was regarded (artificially) as recovering for his or her own loss, constituted by the need for nursing care, even though that care was provided gratuitously. In both *Hunt v Severs* and *Kars v Kars* the gratuitous care was rendered by the tortfeasor.

2 See generally Rose, 'Restitution for the Rescuer' (1989) 9 OJLS 167; Muir, 'Unjust Sacrifice and the Officious Intervener' in *Essays on Restitution* (ed Finn, 1990), p 29; Jones, *Restitution in Public and Private Law* (1991), ch 4; Dagan, 'In Defence of the Good Samaritan' (1999) 97 Michigan Law Review 1152.

cases from apparently disparate areas – for example, burial, salvage, and agency of necessity – one finds common law support for giving the necessitous intervener a remedy. Drawing together the authorities both for and against the necessitous intervener is one important exercise in this area. Another is to answer the central conceptual and policy questions that are raised: are the cases sensibly viewed as restitutionary and, if so, what precisely is the injustice in issue?; should one develop the law further in favour of necessitous interveners and on what principles?[3]

1. THE CASE LAW GRANTING A REMEDY TO THE NECESSITOUS INTERVENER

(1) Burial

In *Jenkins v Tucker*[4] a father paid for his married daughter's funeral. The daughter's husband, the defendant, had left her to go to live in Jamaica. It was held that the father could recover the money paid for the funeral from the defendant as money paid to his use. The father, who was a 'proper person to interfere ... in the absence of her husband',[5] had discharged what was at least a strong moral duty on the husband arising from 'common decency',[6] and was probably a legal duty, to pay for his wife's funeral. There was therefore an incontrovertible benefit to the husband and an analogy was drawn with *Exall v Partridge*,[7] the classic authority on restitution for discharge of another's debt under legal compulsion.

In *Rogers v Price*[8] it was the undertaker who had carried out the funeral who succeeded in recovering for his work and labour from the executor of the deceased. It was again stressed that, even if not a strict legal duty of burial, there was 'a duty which decency and the interests of society render incumbent upon the executor'.[9] On the facts the undertaker had been called in by the deceased's brother but without any agreement for payment between them: and the undertaker did not know at the time who the deceased's executor was. In dicta, which is more obviously applicable to those who pay for

---

3   It is perhaps worth pointing out that 'necessity' has another very different role to play as providing a defence to torts or crimes. See, eg, *Winfield and Jolowicz on Tort* (16th edn, 2002), pp 872–877.
4   (1788) 1 Hy Bl 90.
5   Ibid, at p 93 (per Lord Loughborough).
6   Ibid.
7   (1799) 8 Term Rep 308. Above, chapter 8.
8   (1829) 3 Y & J 28.
9   Ibid, at p 36 (per Hullock B).

funerals rather than to claims by those in the business of providing funerals, Garrow B said the following:

> 'Suppose a person to be killed by accident at a distance from his home; what, in such a case, ought to be done? The common principles of decency and humanity, the common impulses of our nature, would direct everyone, as a preliminary step, to provide a decent funeral, at the expense of the estate; and to do that which is immediately necessary upon the subject, in order to avoid what, if not provided against, may become an inconvenience to the public.'[10]

It should be noted that, alongside the common law, s 46(1) of the Public Health (Control of Disease) Act 1984 provides that local authorities have a duty to bury or cremate the body of any person found dead in their area, if it appears that no suitable arrangements for the disposal of the body are being made. By s 46(5) the expenses of the authority can be recovered from the estate of the deceased person.

(2) Agency of necessity

While the doctrine of 'agency of necessity' has long been recognised in the law, the exact scope and justification of the doctrine are unclear. Its origins lie in cases of carriage by sea in which the master of a ship in an emergency takes action to save the ship or its cargo. His actions may bind the shipowner or cargo owner to pay third parties and the master may himself be entitled to recover expenses incurred.[11] Another long-established application of the doctrine is the entitlement to reimbursement of a person who accepts a bill of exchange for the honour of the drawer (ie to preserve the credit of the drawer) after it has been protested for non-acceptance.[12]

In some nineteenth century cases[13] there was a reluctance to advance the doctrine beyond those two classic areas, but this conservative approach was rejected in two landmark decisions. In *Great Northern Rly Co v Swaffield*[14] the defendants sent a horse by the claimants' railway. On arrival at the station of destination there was no representative of the defendants to collect the horse. The station master therefore took it to a livery stable near the station. The defendants refused to pay the livery charges to release the horse and after it had been in the stable for over four months the claimants paid

10 Ibid, at p 34.
11 *Hawtayne v Bourne* (1841) 7 M & W 595, 599 (per Parke B); *Notara v Henderson* (1872) LR 7 QB 225, 233–235; *Brown v Gaudet* (1873) LR 5 PC 134.
12 Eg *Hawtayne v Bourne* (1841) 7 M & W 595, 599; Bills of Exchange Act 1882, s 68(5) which talks of the payor for honour being subrogated to the rights of the holder against the drawer.
13 *Hawtayne v Bourne* (1841) 7 M & W 595; *Gwilliam v Twist* [1895] 2 QB 84, esp 87.
14 (1874) LR 9 Exch 132.

the charges and delivered the horse to the defendants. The claimants were held entitled to recover the charges paid from the defendants. Although the phrase 'agency of necessity' was not employed by the judges, they reached their decision by drawing an analogy between the carriage by land involved on the facts of the case and the agency of necessity cases involving carriage by sea. Kelly CB said:

> 'It has been held that a shipowner who, through some accidental circumstance, finds it necessary for the safety of the cargo to incur expenditure, is justified in doing so, and can maintain a claim for reimbursement against the owner of the cargo. That is exactly the present case. The plaintiffs were put into much the same position as the shipowner occupies under the circumstances I have described. They have no choice, unless they would leave the horse at the station or in the high road to his own danger and the danger of other people, but to place him in the care of a livery stable keeper, and as they are bound by their implied contract with the livery stable keeper to satisfy his charges, a right arises in them against the defendant to be reimbursed those charges which they have incurred for his benefit.'[15]

In *Prager v Blatspiel, Stamp and Heacock Ltd*[16] McCardie J relied on *Swaffield* in expressly rejecting the conservative approach. 'Agency of necessity is not confined to shipmaster cases and to bills of exchange.'[17] The defendants had bought fur skins as agents for a Romanian claimant. War-time conditions had made delivery of the skins to the claimant difficult at first and then impossible. Two years later the defendants sold off the skins and were therefore unable to supply them to the claimant when he demanded them after the war ended. While accepting that an agency of necessity could in principle arise in such circumstances, it was held that the claimant's claim for damages for conversion succeeded and that the defence of agency of necessity failed. McCardie J laid down three essential requirements for an agency of necessity. First, the alleged agent cannot communicate with his principal.[18] Secondly, there is a commercial necessity for the act. And thirdly, the alleged agent is acting bona fide in the interests of the principal. On the facts the defendants failed on the second and third requirements.

This move away from the two classic situations, while perhaps to be welcomed, has left uncertain the parameters of agency of necessity.[19]

---

15 Ibid, at p 136.
16 [1924] 1 KB 566.
17 Ibid, at p 569.
18 See also *Surrey Breakdown Ltd v Knight* [1999] RTR 84, CA.
19 In *Surrey Breakdown Ltd v Knight* [1999] RTR 84, CA Sir Christopher Staughton said, at 88, 'The doctrine of agency of necessity is not wholly settled in English law. It is well established in maritime cases … whether the same is the case on land is not settled.' On the facts, a company requested by police to remove a stolen car from a pond and to store it could not recover the cost of so doing under the doctrine of agency of necessity because necessity did not compel them to remove the car without the owner's authority.

On a wide interpretation the *Prager* principles are capable of swallowing up all necessity cases (including, for example, the burial cases) and, within the terminology of agency of necessity, the common law would have taken a giant stride forward in favour of necessitous interveners.

A narrower interpretation appears to have been generally preferred. In dicta in *Jebara v Ottoman Bank*[20] Scrutton LJ stressed the importance of the pre-existing contractual agency existing in *Prager*:

> 'The expansion desired by McCardie J becomes less difficult when the agent of
> necessity develops from an original and subsisting agency, and only applies itself
> to unforeseen events not provided for in the original contract, which is usually
> the case where a shipmaster is agent of necessity. But the position seems quite
> different when there is no pre-existing agency, as in the case of a finder of
> perishable chattels or animals ...'

Goff and Jones similarly, albeit slightly wider, confine agency of necessity to where there is a 'contractual or other pre-existing legal relationship':[1] and, consistently with this, they treat the preservation of credit through bills of exchange as a distinct category outside agency of necessity.

In *Prager* itself, agency of necessity was being invoked as a *defence* to a claim for conversion. This shows that agency of necessity is not inevitably concerned with the subject matter of this chapter, namely whether a necessitous intervener is entitled to a remedy. Also outside the scope of this chapter are the contractual rights and liabilities that arise between the principal of the agent of necessity and the third party.[2] Lord Diplock giving the leading judgment in *China Pacific SA v Food Corpn of India, The Winson*[3] suggested that it would be 'an aid to clarity of legal thinking'[4] if the use of the expression 'agency of necessity' were confined to that latter context. And he thought that in a 'reimbursement' action by the intervener – which, on the facts, he saw as stemming from the pre-existing bailment relationship between the parties which imposed a duty of care on the claimants to pay for the storage of wheat that they had salved – the conditions necessary for a remedy (especially the need for communication) might not be as stringent as where a true agency of necessity was in issue. Reimbursement was therefore awarded even though communication with the owner of the wheat

20 [1927] 2 KB 254, 271.
1 Goff and Jones at para 17-002.
2 Whether there was a contract between the principal and the third party was the issue in,
   eg, *Hawtayne v Bourne* (1841) 7 M & W 595; *The Choko Star* [1990] 1 Lloyd's Rep 516,
   noted by Brown, 'Authority and Necessity in the Law of Agency' (1992) 55 MLR 414.
3 [1982] AC 939.
4 Ibid, at p 958.

was not impracticable: indeed the salvors had communicated with the owners but had failed to receive any instructions.[5]

Analytically, Lord Diplock is clearly correct to distinguish between necessity grounding a non-contractual remedy and necessity 'authorising' an agent to conclude a contract between its principal and a third party. However, for Lord Diplock's suggestion on terminology to gain acceptance would require a confusing fight against the traditional well-established usage: and it is significant that Lord Goff continued to use the phrase 'agency of necessity' in its traditional sense in *F v West Berkshire Health Authority*[6] (in which it was decided that a mentally handicapped woman could be lawfully sterilised without her consent). Moreover it is not at all obvious that the conditions required, before a necessitous intervener (eg, a shipmaster) can establish a valid contractual relationship between a principal and a third party, should be more stringent than where a necessitous intervener seeks reimbursement.[7] In particular if it is sufficient for reimbursement that, watering down McCardie J's first requirement, the 'agent' has communicated with his 'principal' but has failed to receive any instructions, it is hard to see why the same should be insufficient to establish a contract between the principal and the third party.

Lord Diplock's apparent vision of reimbursement as being largely correlative to a bailee's duty of care is an interesting one. He said:

> 'It is, of course, true that in English law a mere stranger cannot compel an owner of goods to pay for a benefit bestowed on him against his will; but this latter principle does not apply where there is a pre-existing relationship between the owner of the goods and the bestower of the benefit, such as that of bailor and bailee, which imposes on the bestower of the benefit a legal duty of care in respect of the preservation of the goods that is owed by him to their owner.'[8]

However that approach does raise several difficulties. First, there is an element of circularity in relying on a branch of the law that is notoriously complex and unclear. For example, the precise content of a bailee's *positive* duty of care is not well-settled. Secondly, bailment reasoning is too narrow in failing to explain, for example, 'agency of necessity' in relation to bills of exchange. Thirdly, and in contrast, the reasoning could lead one beyond the scope of this chapter for a bailee's duty of care to preserve goods may not be confined to situations of necessity. Finally, it is not clear whether Lord Diplock's emphasis on a

---

5   See also *Sims & Co v Midland Rly* [1913] 1 KB 103.
6   [1990] 2 AC 1. See also *Surrey Breakdown Ltd v Knight* [1999] RTR 84, CA.
7   For the contrary view, see *Bowstead & Reynolds on Agency* (17th edn, 2001), para 4-005.
8   [1982] AC 939, 961.

pre-existing legal relationship was intended to include gratuitous bailments arising from finding goods. In that context the need to preserve the goods and the duty of care arise at the same time so that it is far from obvious that one can talk of a pre-existing relationship. The conclusion to be reached is that, while the House of Lords' bailment reasoning could be used to expand significantly the scope of redress for necessitous interveners, it is unclear whether that was what was intended. And it must be doubted whether a focus on bailment offers real advantages over the well-established, albeit imprecise, idea of agency of necessity.

(3) Salvage

The law on salvage, most importantly maritime salvage, is voluminous and detailed and whole books are devoted to it.[9] No attempt will therefore be made here to expound the details of the law. Rather the aim is to provide a brief sketch which highlights the necessitous intervention theme of this chapter.[10] It should also be emphasised at the outset that the parties are free to, and in most cases do, regulate the rendering of salvage services by agreement so that the non-contractual principles described here are applicable in only a minority of cases.[11]

The law on salvage has its origins in the saving or recovery of ships and cargo on the high seas. But the law has been extended to include the saving of life,[12] and aircraft,[13] and consequential protection of the environment,[14] and also geographically to include United Kingdom tidal waters.[15] For the salvor to have a remedy it is essential that there was a situation of necessity: that is, a danger or a real threat of danger to property or life such that 'no reasonably prudent and skilful person in charge of the venture would refuse a salvor's help if it were offered

---

9 Eg, Kennedy and Rose, *The Law of Salvage* (6th edn, 2002); Brice, *Maritime Law of Salvage* (3rd edn, 1999).

10 For the view that the maritime doctrine of general average also reverses unjust enrichment with the ground for restitution being necessity, see Rose, 'General Average as Restitution' (1997) 113 LQR 569; Virgo, *The Principles of the Law of Restitution* (1999), pp 321–322.

11 The usual agreement is the Lloyd's Standard Form of Salvage Agreement (No Cure – No Pay).

12 Merchant Shipping Act 1995, s 224, Sch 11, Arts 10 and 16. Under Arts 13 and 14 the salvage award is payable by the owner of the vessel or property saved.

13 Civil Aviation Act 1982, s 87.

14 Merchant Shipping Act 1995, s 224, Sch 11, Arts 8, 13–14; *Semco Salvage and Marine Pte Ltd v Lancer Navigation Co Ltd, The Nagasaki Spirit* [1997] 1 All ER 502.

15 The claim in *The Goring* [1988] AC 831 failed because the boat was in non-tidal inland waters when saved. Cf Merchant Shipping Act 1995, s 224, Sch 11, Art 1(a).

to him upon the condition of his paying a salvor's reward'.[16] The salvor must also act 'voluntarily' in the sense that he must neither be acting within the scope of a pre-existing legal duty to the owner of the salved property nor must he be acting solely to save himself.[17] And the salvage must be a success in contributing to the saving of property or life or preventing or minimising damage to the environment.[18]

A salvage award includes an element of reward so as to encourage rescue. In *The Telemachus*[19] Willmer J said, 'I have to arrive at such an award as will fairly compensate the master and the crew of the salving vessel without injustice to the salved interests, and such an award as will, in the interests of public policy, encourage other mariners in like circumstances to perform like services.' This is consistent with numerous other judicial statements emphasising that the policy of the law is to encourage salvage.[20] And *professional* salvors have been held entitled to more generous awards than those who act on the spur of the moment.[1] The value of the property saved, the skill used, and the degree of danger involved are also important considerations in fixing the size of the award.[2] The award is payable by those interested in the property saved[3] and is apportioned among the salvors who have contributed to the successful salvage.[4] In order to satisfy the award, a salvor is entitled to a maritime lien over the salved property.[5]

(4) Miscellaneous cases

Outside the above three areas support for a remedy for a necessitous intervener is rather thin. Nevertheless there are odd cases or groups of cases that are pro-restitution.[6]

---

16   Kennedy and Rose, *Law of Salvage*, para 333, chapter 4. The effect of the owner refusing consent to the salvage is unclear but it probably debars an award: see Goff and Jones at para 18-014. Cf Merchant Shipping Act 1995, s 224, Sch 11, Art 19.

17   Kennedy and Rose, *Law of Salvage*, chapters 6 and 7; and see *The Lomonosoff* [1921] P 97.

18   Kennedy and Rose, *Law of Salvage*, chapter 8. By Merchant Shipping Act 1995, s 224, Sch 11, Art 2, 'Except as otherwise provided, no payment is due under this Convention if the salvage operations have had no useful result.'

19   [1957] P 47, 59.

20   Eg, *The St Blane* [1974] 1 Lloyd's Rep 557, 560. By Merchant Shipping Act 1995, s 224, Sch 11, Art 13, 'The reward shall be fixed with a view to encouraging salvage operations ...'

1   *The Queen Elizabeth* (1949) 82 Ll L Rep 803; Kennedy and Rose, *Law of Salvage*, paras 42–47.

2   Kennedy and Rose, *Law of Salvage* chapter 15. The award may be forfeited if the salvor has been guilty of serious misconduct; Kennedy and Rose, *Law of Salvage* chapter 11.

3   Kennedy and Rose, *Law of Salvage* chapter 16. Cf above, p 309, n 12.

4   Kennedy and Rose, *Law of Salvage* chapter 17.

5   Kennedy and Rose, *Law of Salvage* chapter 13.

6   Although the best explanation of the benefit in *Craven-Ellis v Canons Ltd* [1936] 2 KB 403 is that the services were factually necessary, the unjust factor was more obviously failure of consideration; below, pp 390–391.

(a) Necessaries supplied to an *incapax*

Although a matter of some controversy it seems that the liability of a minor or an insane person to pay a reasonable price for 'contracted for' necessaries can be satisfactorily analysed as contractual liability rather than being recast as restitutionary. The particular weakness of the restitutionary analysis of such liability is that even executory contracts appear to impose an obligation on the *incapax* to pay a reasonable price.[7]

However, if there is clearly no contract, an intervener who has supplied necessary goods or services to an *incapax* may nonetheless be entitled to a restitutionary remedy. The leading case is *Re Rhodes*[8] where, over a 25 year period, certain relatives of a woman of unsound mind paid part of the charges for her to be in a private asylum. On her death those relatives claimed repayment of the moneys so paid from her estate. The Court of Appeal accepted that in principle such a claim could lie but held that it would not lie on the facts because the relatives had not established that they intended to be repaid. That restriction, if strictly adhered to, means that the scope for recovery in this sphere is very narrow.

(b) Medical or nursing care provided for a pauper

Although obviously no longer of direct relevance, this category was important historically and is included here because one may want to draw a modern day analogy.

Under the old poor law parish officers were under a legal obligation to provide medical treatment to paupers who were injured or ill while in their parish. In *Simmons v Wilmott*[9] the claimant, who had looked after an injured pauper for ten days, including paying for nursing help, was held able to recover the expenses incurred from the parish officers. This is most obviously explained as an example of restitution for necessity. In the words of his counsel the claimant had afforded relief 'under the pressure of immediate want'.[10] Similarly in *Tomlinson v Bentall*[11] a surgeon who had been called in to look after an injured pauper at her home was held able to recover his fees from the parish where the accident occurred, the pauper having been improperly moved from that parish to her home.

---

7   Goff and Jones, at paras 25-001 to 25-003; Treitel, *The Law of Contract* (10th edn, 1999), pp 498–505. See also, s 3(2) of the Sale of Goods Act 1979.
8   (1890) 44 Ch D 94. See also, eg, *Re Clabbon* [1904] 2 Ch 465.
9   (1800) 3 Esp 91.
10 Ibid, at p 92.
11 (1826) 5 B & C 738. See also, eg, *Lamb v Bunce* (1815) 4 M & S 275.

(c) Necessitous payment of another's debt?

In dicta in *Owen v Tate*,[12] in which the Court of Appeal refused restitution to a voluntary surety who had paid off another's debt, Scarman LJ emphasised that the position would have been different if the surety had assumed the obligation out of necessity. This was applied in granting restitution in *The Zuhal K*,[13] where the necessity for the claimants' guarantee was held to be that, otherwise, the defendant could not secure a release of their ship. However, it should be stressed that the necessity in these cases is perhaps not being regarded as a ground for restitution in its own right but rather as an aspect of legal compulsion in a situation where the legal compulsion has, on the face of it, been voluntarily assumed.

(d) Necessitous services rendered by a liquidator

In *Re Berkeley Applegate (Investment Consultants) Ltd*[14] it was held that a liquidator (in a voluntary liquidation) could be reimbursed and remunerated not only out of the company's free assets (this was already statutorily authorised) but also out of the assets held by the company as trustee, on the grounds, inter alia, that his work was necessary for the beneficiaries' assets to be realised. Edward Nugee QC, sitting as a deputy High Court judge, said the following:

> 'His skill and labour may not have added directly to the value of the underlying assets in which the investors have equitable interests; but he has added to the estate in the sense of carrying out work which was necessary before the estate could be realised for the benefit of the investors ... [I]f the liquidator had not done this work, it is inevitable that the work, or at all events a great deal of it, would have had to be done by someone else, and on an application to the court, a receiver would have been appointed whose expenses and fees would necessarily have had to be borne by the trust assets.'[15]

That passage clearly emphasises the benefit to the investors of the liquidator's work. However, whether one can realistically regard a liquidator as a 'necessitous intervener' analogous to the other interveners considered in this chapter is debatable. This is primarily because the situation is at the outer limits of where one can sensibly say that the defendant's (person or) property would be harmed or lost unless someone intervened. But the judge did say, 'The situation which existed

---

12   [1976] QB 402. The relevant passage from Scarman LJ's judgment, at pp 411–412, is cited above, p 283.
13   [1987] 1 Lloyd's Rep 151.
14   [1989] Ch 32.
15   Ibid, at p 50. The judge relied especially on *Scott v Nesbitt* (1808) 14 Ves 438.

in the present case immediately before the commencement of the winding up could ... fairly be called an emergency.'[16]

2. AUTHORITIES HOSTILE TO THE NECESSITOUS INTERVENER

Despite the above authorities allowing a remedy to a necessitous intervener, the traditional view is that necessitous interveners are generally denied recovery.

The leading hostile authority is *Falcke v Scottish Imperial Insurance Co*[17] where the Court of Appeal refused a claim for a lien by a mortgagor of a life insurance policy who had paid premiums to keep the policy alive. Bowen LJ in a famous dictum said:

> 'The general principle is, beyond all question, that work and labour done or money expended by one man to preserve or benefit the property of another do not according to English law create any lien on the property saved or benefited, nor, even standing alone, create any obligation to repay the expenditure. Liabilities are not to be forced upon people behind their backs any more than you can confer a benefit upon a man against his will.'[18]

Bowen LJ went on to explain that maritime salvage was an exception to this but that salvage did not extend to goods lost upon land let alone keeping alive an insurance policy.

That approach is also supported by the eighteenth century case of *Nicholson v Chapman*[19] where it was held that the defendant, who had collected and kept safe a quantity of the claimant's timber that had been carried downstream, was liable in trover for his refusal to give up the timber unless the claimant paid him for his time and trouble. Eyre CJ held that the defendant had no lien over the property as this was not a case of maritime salvage; and although he left open whether the defendant might be entitled to a personal remedy he did suggest

---

16 Ibid, at p 52. The alternative analysis is that the liquidator's right is best treated alongside the general right of a trustee to be reimbursed, and sometimes remunerated, for costs incurred and work done in the proper discharge of his duties: see *Snell's Equity* (30th edn, 2000), pp 287–293, Pettit, *Equity and the Law of Trusts* (9th edn, 2001), pp 435–441, 473–481. The most important case examining this is *Re Duke of Norfolk's Settlement Trusts* [1982] Ch 61. See also, eg, *Foster v Spencer* [1996] 2 All ER 672. In so far as restitutionary the injustice in play is difficult to pinpoint (one possibility might be a policy goal of encouraging the good administration of trusts).

17 (1886) 34 Ch D 234. Apart from the cases mentioned in the text, one can also interpret *Shallcross v Wright* (1850) 12 Beav 558 (doctor's claim) and *Macclesfield Corpn v Great Central Rly Co* [1911] 2 KB 528 as being anti-restitution although in neither was necessitous intervention argued. See also the cases above, p 305, n 13.

18 Ibid, at p 248.

19 (1793) 2 Hy Bl 254.

that recompense should perhaps be a moral rather than a legal duty of the owner. 'Perhaps it is better for the public that these voluntary acts of benevolence from one man to another, which are charities and moral duties, but not legal duties, should depend altogether for their reward upon the moral duty of gratitude.'[20]

In the twentieth century there were dicta echoing the same sentiments. For example, in *Sorrell v Paget*[1] Bucknill LJ said, 'There is no doubt that ... salvage on land is not a recognised head of claim in the common law as it is by maritime law at sea.' And in *The Tojo Maru*,[2] which principally concerned a salvor's lability to pay damages for negligent damage to the property being saved, Lord Reid said, 'On land a person who interferes to save property is not in law entitled to any reward.'

Finally, in *The Goring*,[3] where there was a glorious opportunity for a wide-ranging judicial review of the authorities on necessity, the House of Lords contented itself with the narrow technical decision that maritime salvage did not extend to saving a boat on non-tidal inland waters. While recognising the force of Sir John Donaldson MR's dissenting judgment in the Court of Appeal – that confining salvage actions to tidal waters was irrational – the House of Lords thought that any extension of the law should be for the legislature.

3. AN UNJUST ENRICHMENT ANALYSIS

(1) The unjust factor

The authorities do not speak with one voice. It would certainly be possible to use the existing pockets of law allowing recovery to push for wider recovery for necessitous intervention. Whether this would be desirable turns, from a restitutionary perspective, on first clarifying the injustice in play.

In his *An Introduction to the Law of Restitution*, Birks equated necessity with 'moral compulsion' and separated out as 'policy-motivated restitution' the law on maritime salvage.[4] But the notion of moral compulsion is fraught with difficulty both as a matter of principle and authority. As a matter of principle, one can strongly argue that if it is

---

20 Ibid, at p 259.
1   [1950] 1 KB 252, 260.
2   [1972] AC 242, 268.
3   [1988] AC 831.
4   Birks at pp 193–202, 304–308. Cf Birks and Mitchell, 'Unjust Enrichment' in *English Private Law* (ed Birks, 2000), paras 15.156–15.160 which discuss under policy-based restitution all the examples of benefits conferred in an emergency.

moral compulsion that is driving the claimant he ought not to expect the law to intervene and should instead rely on the moral duty of the recipient for his reward. And applying this idea to a payment of money would produce the alarming conclusion that the law ought to allow restitution of charitable donations. Moreover, as a matter of authority, moral compulsion requires a fragmentation of the authorities supporting recovery for the necessitous intervener. For while it can explain some of the cases (for example, *Jenkins v Tucker*,[5] *Re Rhodes*,[6] and most of the agency of necessity cases) it certainly cannot explain them all, as is most obviously shown by the law on maritime salvage, where professional salvors are not merely entitled to a remedy but are given more generous awards than those who act on the spur of the moment. Even if mysteriously one were to hive off maritime salvage to a separate sphere, moral compulsion was not motivating the claimant in, for example, *Rogers v Price*[7] (professional undertaker) or *Re Berkeley Applegate (Investment Consultants) Ltd*[8] (liquidator) or *The Zuhal K*[9] (guarantor). In short, therefore, the law does not equate the claimant's intervention in a situation of necessity or 'out of necessity' with his being morally compelled. At best, moral compulsion is a sub-category of necessity.

If moral compulsion is rejected, the obvious alternative explanation is the policy-motivated desire of the law to encourage people to intervene to preserve the health or property of others. That this is the thinking behind salvage awards has been clearly stated on several occasions. The words of Willmer J on this point have already been cited.[10] In *Nicholson v Chapman*[11] Eyre CJ said of salvage, 'Principles of public policy dictate to civilised and commercial countries, not only the propriety, but even the absolute necessity, of establishing a liberal recompense for the encouragement of those who engage in so dangerous a service.' And in *The St Blane*[12] Brandon J regarded the courts' lenient approach to mistakes by salvors as explicable by this policy of encouragement: 'This principle of the lenient approach to mistakes is an important one. It derives from the basic policy of the law relating to salvage services, which is always to encourage rather than discourage the rendering of such services.' Although the courts in other pro-necessity cases have made no overt reference to a policy

5   (1788) 1 Hy Bl 90.
6   (1890) 44 Ch D 94.
7   (1829) 3 Y & J 28.
8   [1989] Ch 32.
9   [1987] 1 Lloyd's Rep 151.
10 Above, p 310.
11 (1793) 2 Hy Bl 254, 257.
12 [1974] 1 Lloyd's Rep 557, 560.

of encouraging 'rescue' this does provide a satisfactory explanation for the decisions.[13] It should also be noted that on this reasoning the refusal of the law to allow the reclaiming of charitable donations is perfectly explicable for to allow such restitution would hardly encourage people to make such donations.

As it stands, a policy of encouraging 'rescue' may seem too loose and open-ended to be a basis for a legal remedy. But the case law on necessity fleshes it out with specific principles and control devices. Three are particularly important.

First, the situation must be one in which it is essential for someone to intervene in order to protect the defendant or his property: that is, harm (to health or property) would be very likely to ensue if someone did not intervene. This is the crucial restriction which stops this area from spilling over into allowing a remedy simply because the intervener has carried out services benefiting another. It is helpful to think in terms of a core concept of an emergency although, as Lord Goff stressed in *F v West Berkshire Health Authority*,[14] this idea may be inapt for necessitous services rendered over a period of time (eg supplying necessaries to an *incapax*). It is an unusual use of language to talk of a 'permanent emergency'.

Secondly, the claimant must be a suitable person to intervene. In the law of salvage the courts clearly seek to encourage *professional* salvors. In classic agency of necessity cases there is a pre-existing contractual relationship between the parties. And it was relatives who intervened in *Jenkins v Tucker*[15] and *Re Rhodes*.[16] The law would clearly not want to encourage non-professionals to seek out emergency situations for their own gain. This was precisely the fear of Eyre CJ in *Nicholson v Chapman* when, in deciding against a remedy for the intervener who had rescued the claimant's timber, he said that to allow a remedy would encourage 'the wilful attempts of ill-designing people to turn ... floats and vessels adrift, in order that they might be paid for finding them'.[17]

Thirdly, as the law on salvage shows, an intervener who acts within his pre-existing legal duty should not be entitled to a remedy for necessitous intervention. A fireman (acting within the scope of his duty) should not be able to claim a remedy against the owner of a house that he has saved from destruction. The rationale for this is that the pre-existing duty already acts as a sufficient incentive for intervention.

---

13   In the burial cases it was generally the health of the public that was threatened rather than that of the defendant.
14   [1990] 2 AC 1, 75.
15   (1788) 1 Hy Bl 90.
16   (1890) 44 Ch D 94.
17   (1793) 2 Hy Bl 254, 259.

Other principles are much more problematic. For example, how crucial is it that the intervener attempts to seek the consent of the defendant?[18] Where necessitous services are rendered over a long period of time should it be a requirement that the claimant intended to charge for the services?[19] Is it ever a bar that the intervention was primarily motivated by the prospect of remuneration or reward?[20]

Apart from enabling one to clarify more specific principles, recognition that the encouragement of 'rescue' is the clear policy goal enables one to face squarely the central question of whether the law should build on the existing categories to give more widespread recovery for necessitous interveners. On the one hand, it can be argued that, given the availability of public services in the modern welfare state, there is no need for the judiciary to encourage private 'rescue': rather the law should be frozen at its existing position which, while perhaps not entirely rational, reflects the historical need for private intervention in certain spheres. Subject to the existing exceptions, altruism should remain its own reward.

Ranged against that – and more persuasive – is the view that, as the present categories do not even apply to all straightforward emergencies (eg saving a drowning child, or the repair of an absent neighbour's roof) and as there is no rational reason to distinguish the excluded situations from those where a remedy is now given, the law should be extended. Private 'rescue' should be encouraged because the public services cannot adequately deal with all situations in which another's health or property are in danger. The public services do not cover all types of emergency and, in any event, there may simply be inadequate time to call them out.

If the argument for extension of the law were accepted, then one area where there has been extensive recent litigation – the gratuitous provision of nursing care to those tortiously injured – might take on a fresh perspective.[1] For one can argue that the carer should have a direct restitutionary claim against the victim for the necessitous services rendered.[2]

---

18 Communication to the owner was the first of the conditions for agency of necessity laid down in *Prager v Blatspiel, Stamp and Heacock Ltd* [1924] 1 KB 566. Cf *China Pacific SA v Food Corpn of India, The Winson* [1982] AC 939. As regards salvage the effect of the owner refusing consent is unclear: see above, p 310, n 16. In *F v West Berkshire Health Authority* [1990] 2 AC 1, 76 Lord Goff thought that necessitous intervention was not justified 'when it is contrary to the known wishes of the assisted person to the extent that he is capable of rationally forming such a wish'.

19 This was insisted on in *Re Rhodes* (1890) 44 Ch D 94.

20 This is clearly not a bar to a salvage award. Cf *The Winson* [1982] AC 939, 965–966 (per Lord Simon).

1 See p 303, n 1 above.

2 For consideration of this possibility, see, eg, Law Commission Consultation Paper No 144, *Damages for Personal Injury: Medical, Nursing and Other Expenses* (1996), para 2.29.

The two sides of the debate are neatly reflected in the differing judicial approaches in *The Goring*.[3] Sheen J and Sir John Donaldson MR rejected as irrational the distinction between rescue on tidal waters, to which the law of salvage did apply, and rescue on non-tidal waters, where there was no salvage remedy; and in Sheen J's words, 'If a ship or her cargo is in danger in non-tidal waters it is highly desirable, as a matter of public policy, that other ships should be encouraged to go to her assistance without hesitation.'[4] In contrast the majority of the Court of Appeal and the House of Lords preferred to retain the restriction to tidal waters on the basis, inter alia, that the need for extension of the law on the ground of public policy had not been established.

It may be that this issue should be linked to the question, hotly debated by tort lawyers, as to the extent to which tort liability is, or should be, imposed for a failure to intervene to prevent another's injury or property damage.[5] By and large there is no such tort liability. An argument can be put forward that the law should not impose such liability unless it is also prepared to award the necessitous intervener a restitutionary or other remedy.[6] More controversially it can also be reasoned that, if the law were to award a remedy to a necessitous intervener, based on the policy of encouraging 'rescue', it ought to go further and to impose tort liability for failure to 'rescue'.

Before moving on, the views of Maddaugh and McCamus merit examination. They reject the idea that the law on necessitous intervention is primarily to be explained by the policy of encouraging intervention. 'The optimistic view that the granting of restitutionary relief might encourage altruism may provide additional support for the imposition of liability but the unjust enrichment principle is engaged merely by the existence of an unofficiously conferred windfall benefit.'[7]

But the fact that a necessitous intervener is non-officious cannot be the root explanation for regarding the enrichment conferred as unjust. An initial difficulty is what one means by non-officious. The

---

3   [1987] QB 687, CA; [1988] AC 831, HL.
4   Ibid, at p 693.
5   See, eg, *Smith v Littlewoods Organisation Ltd* [1987] AC 241 (esp per Lord Goff); *Stovin v Wise* [1996] AC 923, esp 949; *Capital and Counties plc v Hampshire County Council* [1997] QB 1004; *Winfield & Jolowicz on Tort* (16th edn, 2002), pp 134–145; McBride and Bagshaw, *Tort Law* (2001), pp 137–139, 150–158; Burrows, *Understanding the Law of Obligations* (1998), pp 34–40; Bowman and Bailey, 'Negligence in the Realms of Public Law – A Positive Obligation to Rescue?' (1984) PL 277; Markesinis, 'Negligence, Nuisance and Affirmative Duties of Action' (1989) 105 LQR 104.
6   Cf the emphasis on a correlation between reimbursement and a bailee's duty of care in *The Winson* [1982] AC 939: above, p 308.
7   *The Law of Restitution* (1st edn, 1990), at p 682.

United States Restatement of Restitution, s 2 vaguely defines the concept of officiousness as 'interference in the affairs of others not justified by the circumstances under which the interference takes place.' Much more helpful is Maddaugh and McCamus' suggestion that a person acts officiously if he acts maliciously or frivolously or 'confers unrequested benefits on another for the exclusive purpose of attempting to exploit for profit the needs of the other'.[8]

Using that as a working definition, it is plain that non-officiousness is too wide an idea to explain necessity. It encompasses not only restitutionary recovery under other standard grounds outside necessity (for example, mistaken payments) but also situations where the law does not award restitution. For example, all gifts and benefits conferred under contracts are non-officious, yet there is no prospect of restitution unless the contract or gift is invalidated in some way. Again if a person indirectly confers a benefit on another while freely acting in self-interest he is not entitled (and should not be entitled) to restitution albeit that he is acting non-officiously.[9]

With respect, therefore, while necessity is undoubtedly a fuzzy-edged concept, officiousness is of no assistance in understanding and clarifying its ambit.

(2) Benefit

In certain situations it is clear that necessitous services incontrovertibly benefit the defendant. For example, in the burial cases it may well have been that the defendant was under a legal, rather than merely a moral, duty to bury the dead so that the claimant's intervention had saved the defendant inevitable legal expense. In most other situations the very necessity – the need to take action to preserve the defendant's health or property – suggests that the intervention was an incontrovertible negative benefit, provided that it was successful[10] and provided, probably, that the recipient did not refuse consent to the intervention (refusal of consent proving subjective devaluation).[11] Certainly success is essential for a salvage award (irrespective of the benefit issue one can argue that on policy grounds there should be encouragement to press on and succeed rather than making half-

---

8   Ibid, at p 48.
9   Above, pp 43–44.
10 An unsuccessful attempt would not be incontrovertibly beneficial (ie, a reasonable man could say that he would only have been willing to pay for a result not an attempt): and no other relevant test of benefit (overcoming subjective devaluation) could be made out.
11 A further probable qualification is that services are only incontrovertibly beneficial to the extent that their price is not higher than the value of the property saved.

hearted attempts) and it is probably the case that the owner's refusal to consent also debars a salvage remedy.[12] And even outside salvage there has been no case in English law in which a remedy has been awarded to a necessitous intervener where these 'requirements' were not met.[13]

Of course this emphasis on benefit runs directly counter to the views of those scholars advocating an 'unjust sacrifice' approach which focuses solely on the claimant's loss in the necessitous services (and other) cases. That approach has been examined and rejected in chapter 1.[14]

(3) At the expense of the claimant

As there is no question in this context of restitution for wrongdoing, the requirement that the defendant's benefit is at the claimant's expense means that there must be a subtraction from the claimant's wealth. Normally this is satisfied without difficulty for the claimant will have incurred expense and/or, as a 'professional', will have lost the opportunity to sell his time and labour in the market. But it should be noted that in *The Goring*,[15] for example, the benefit to the defendant was arguably not at the claimants' expense in the subtractive sense. They had certainly incurred no expense and they had not suffered any obvious loss of earnings. Perhaps loosely it could be said that they had lost the opportunity to bargain with the defendant for their time and labour but as 'amateurs' it is arguably unrealistic to imagine that they would have sought such a bargain.[16] On the other hand, the gain had plainly come from the claimant's wealth in the sense that the services were rendered by the claimant.

(4) Does the remedy seek to reverse the enrichment?

Assuming that the defendant has been benefited at the expense of the necessitous intervener, the remedy will only be restitutionary if it seeks to reverse that enrichment. In this context, a division is often

---

12 Above, p 310, n 16.
13 Cf *Matheson v Smiley* [1932] 2 DLR 787 where neither of the two requirements was satisfied but a surgeon was held entitled to remuneration for his unsuccessful attempts to save the life of a suicide victim. This is probably best viewed as compensating the surgeon's loss and not reversing unjust enrichment.
14 Above, pp 10–11.
15 [1988] AC 831.
16 Cf the thesis of Sharpe and Waddams 'Damages for lost opportunity to bargain' (1982) 2 OJLS 290 on wrongful use of another's property: below, p 477.

drawn between reimbursement, remuneration and reward.[17] Given that the defendant has been benefited the first two of these are restitutionary measures and relate, on the one hand, to the claimant's expenses and, on the other, to his time and labour. In contrast it is hard to see that a reward is restitutionary unless one gives an artificially low remuneration leaving the reward to reflect the actual market value of the services. In principle, a reward, which is a standard remedy in salvage cases, is given over and above the remuneration and has as its aim the encouragement of rescue. The apparent thinking in salvage law is that there would be insufficient incentive to salvors if they were merely entitled to reimbursement and remuneration. It therefore seems that while the burial, agency of necessity, and miscellaneous cases are restitutionary (reversing unjust enrichment) because they only go so far as to give reimbursement and remuneration,[18] the salvage cases go beyond restitution. This inconsistency is surprising. If the argument above is accepted – that in all necessity cases the policy goal is the encouragement of 'rescue' – there probably ought to be consistency of remedy between the salvage and non-salvage cases.[19] Whether this should be achieved by limiting salvage awards to reimbursement and remuneration or by allowing all necessitous interveners a reward depends on whether one considers that remuneration is sufficient to encourage rescue.

4. CONCLUSION

Necessity differs from the grounds for restitution that have been considered in earlier chapters in that, stripping away the notion of 'moral compulsion', the claimant has freely rendered the benefit. A legal remedy is awarded not because of a defect in the claimant's

---

17 Goff and Jones at para 17-014; Rose 'Restitution for the Rescuer' (1989) 9 OJLS 167, 200. See also *Semco Salvage & Marine Pte Ltd v Lancer Navigation Co Ltd, The Nagasaki Spirit* [1997] 1 All ER 502 in which it was decided that, in applying Merchant Shipping Act 1995, s 224, Sch 11, Art 14, special compensation for consequential environmental protection was to be calculated as a multiple of expenses incurred, as distinct from remuneration or profit.

18 Of course to be restitutionary the reimbursement and remuneration must not exceed the defendant's benefit. For discussion of proprietary, rather than merely personal, restitution in respect of the unjust factor of necessity, see Mitchell, *The Law of Subrogation* (1994), pp 103–104. It is not easy to justify why necessitous intervenors should ever be entitled to proprietary, rather than merely personal, restitution. They have surely taken the risk of the defendant's insolvency. Cf the trust imposed in *Hunt v Severs* [1994] 2 AC 350, noted above at p 303, n 1. The maritime lien given to salvors is a common law possessory lien which is dependent on the salvor's possession of the defendant's property.

19 Cf *The Goring* [1987] QB 687, 708 (per Ralph Gibson LJ); Rose 'Restitution for the Rescuer' (1989) 9 OJLS 167, 201; Goff and Jones, at para 17-014.

reasoning process but to encourage intervention to preserve another's health or property. How far that policy goal justifies extension of the present narrow range of recovery for a necessitous intervener is open to argument, although it has been suggested in this chapter that the case for expansion is persuasive. Perhaps it is no coincidence that the resort to a policy goal is to be found in an area where the remedies awarded by the courts are not necessarily confined to reversing unjust enrichment and can include a non-restitutionary reward.

Chapter 10

Failure of consideration

If one were to rank the grounds for restitution in order of importance, failure of consideration would come second only to mistake. Indeed its true potential may not have yet been fully realised in four respects:

(i) It has conventionally been viewed as confined to the restitution of money. Symmetry dictates that it must also be an unjust factor for benefits in kind.

(ii) It has traditionally been insisted that the failure of consideration needs to be total. There is no good reason for this, a criticism which derives support from the reform of the common law by s 1(2) of the Law Reform (Frustrated Contracts) Act 1943.

(iii) While the very language of consideration may lead one to think that one is concerned here solely with failure of a contracted-for performance, this would be to adopt too narrow a definition of failure of consideration.

(iv) The idea that on rescission for, for example, misrepresentation a defendant is entitled to counter-restitution – shown by the insistence that a claimant is debarred from rescission if *restitutio in integrum* is not possible – appears to rest (as we shall see in chapter 15) on a covert recognition that a defendant would be entitled to a restitutionary counterclaim for failure of consideration.

On the other hand, the ambit of failure of consideration is rightly kept in check by the principle that, before a party can claim restitution for failure of consideration, he must establish that he has no contractual obligation to confer the relevant benefit on the defendant: any relevant contract must be ineffective.[1] This may be, for example,

---

1   Goff and Jones, at paras 1-063 to 1-067; Birks, at pp 47, 464; *Chitty on Contracts* (28th edn, 1999), para 30-050; Virgo, *The Principles of The Law of Restitution* (1999), p 329. This principle is not as explicitly spelt out in any case as one would have expected. But see, eg, *Goodman v Pocock* (1850) 15 QB 576; *Kwei Tek Chao v British Traders and Shippers Ltd* [1954] 2 QB 459; *The Olanda (1917)* [1919] 2 KB 728n; *Re Richmond Gate Property Co Ltd* [1965] 1 WLR 335. However, this principle has been attacked as a matter of policy and authority by Tettenborn, 'Subsisting Contracts and Failure of Consideration – A Little Scepticism' [2002] RLR 1. Moreover, it has been departed from in some cases: see, eg, *Miles v Wakefield District Council* [1987] AC 539, discussed by Mead, 'Restitution within contract?' (1991) 11 LS 172, esp 183–186; and, particularly importantly, by a majority of the High Court of Australia in *Roxborough v Rothmans of Pall Mall Australia Ltd* [2001] HCA 68. Beatson and

because an initially valid contract has been discharged for breach or frustration; or because the contract was void, unenforceable or incomplete. It is by this principle that an undermining of contract by restitution is avoided and restitution is made subservient to contract. It is only when the parties' own allocation of risk is ineffective that the imposed standards set by the law of restitution can step in.

This chapter looks at first, what is meant by failure of consideration; secondly, at how satisfactory the 'total failure' requirement is; thirdly, and constituting the core of this chapter, at the various areas of the law (ie ineffective, other than voidable, contracts) in which this unjust factor (in its primary sense of a failure of promised performance) has been, or can be, applied to justify the restitution of benefits conferred; fourthly, at whether it is necessary to supplement failure of consideration by an unjust factor of 'free acceptance'; fifthly, at failure of consideration as meaning the failure of an *unpromised* future event; and finally, at proprietary restitution in respect of payments made for a failed consideration.

1.   WHAT IS MEANT BY FAILURE OF CONSIDERATION?

(1) Failure of promised performance?

Clearly the meaning of failure of consideration that is primarily in mind (corresponding to the traditional 'reciprocity' view of consideration as a requirement of a valid contract) is that there has been a failure of what the claimant was promised (which can be taken to include what the claimant was reasonably led to expect) in return for rendering the benefit to the defendant. In short, a failure of the bargained-for counter-performance. And this constitutes an unjust factor precisely because the basis for the claimant's conferral of the benefit has been undermined. In Birks' terminology, while failure of consideration links alongside, eg, mistake, duress, and legal

---

Virgo, 'Contract, Unjust Enrichment and Unconscionability' (2002) 118 LQR 352 argue that the dissenting judgment of Kirby J in *Roxborough* is to be preferred: the contract between the claimant and the wholesale seller of the tobacco was valid so that restitution of part of the purchase price should not have been awarded. Cf Birks, 'Failure of Consideration and its Place on the Map' (2002) 2 Oxford University Commonwealth Law Journal 1 who argues that, exceptionally, restitution did not on the facts subvert the valid contract because the tax element of the price was fixed and not negotiated (and, analogously, he suggests at p 5 that *Orphanos v Queen Mary College* [1985] AC 761, HL, may have been wrongly decided). See, generally, on the relationship between contract and (autonomous) unjust enrichment, Beatson, 'The Temptation of Elegance: Concurrence of Restitutionary and Contractual Claims' in *The Search for Principle* (eds Swadling and Jones, 1999), pp 143–170; S Smith, 'Concurrent Liability in Contract and Unjust Enrichment: The Fundamental Breach Requirement' (1999) 115 LQR 245.

compulsion, as a factor negativing voluntariness, it differs in being concerned with qualification of the will as opposed to its vitiation.[2]

This meaning of failure of consideration was clearly spelt out in Viscount Simon LC's classic comment in *Fibrosa Spolka Akcyjna v Fairbairn Lawson Combe Barbour Ltd*[3] distinguishing consideration in the formation of a contract from restitutionary failure of consideration:

> 'In English law, an enforceable contract may be formed by an exchange of a promise for a promise, or by the exchange of a promise for an act ... and thus, in the law relating to the formation of a contract, the promise to do a thing may often be the consideration, but when one is considering the law of failure of consideration and of the quasi-contractual right to recover money on that ground, it is, generally speaking,[4] not the promise which is referred to as the consideration, but the performance of the promise. The money was paid to secure performance and, if performance fails the inducement which brought about the payment is not fulfilled.'

Unfortunately the Court of Appeal in *Guinness Mahon & Co Ltd v Kensington and Chelsea Royal London Borough Council,*[5] supported in this respect by obiter dicta of Lord Browne-Wilkinson in *Westdeutsche Landesbank Girozentrale v Islington London Borough Council,*[6] has more recently argued that there is always a total failure of consideration where a contract is void. This muddies the promise/performance distinction drawn by Viscount Simon LC. His Lordship's classic statement was said, by Morritt LJ in the *Guinness Mahon* case, not to be exhaustive – hence the qualification introduced by the words 'generally speaking' – and to have been made in the context of a case dealing with a valid contract, discharged for frustration, not a void contract.[7] It is submitted that the better view, in terms of authority and principle, is that Viscount Simon LC's statement is applicable to void as well as valid contracts; and that it is incorrect to say that a void contract automatically means that there has been a total failure of consideration.[8]

---

2 Birks, at p 219.
3 [1943] AC 32, 48. *Chandler v Webster* [1904] 1 KB 493, which was overruled, was regarded as having misunderstood the meaning of failure of consideration.
4 In some situations the performance and the promise cannot be clearly distinguished. Eg an insured cannot recover premiums paid on the ground of total failure of consideration by arguing that no insured against event has yet occurred. Treitel, *The Law of Contract* (10th edn, 1999), p 977 argues that this is an example of where there is a 'bargain for the promise itself'.
5 [1999] QB 215.
6 [1996] AC 669.
7 But Viscount Simon LC's statement was applied in the case of a void contract by Kerr LJ, with whom Nicholls LJ agreed, in *Rover International Ltd v Cannon Film Sales Ltd (No 3)* [1989] 1 WLR 912.
8 See further below, pp 386–388, 397–401.

What complicates matters further is that, while still conforming to an underlying idea of 'failure of basis' or 'qualification of the will', there is another main meaning of failure of consideration extending beyond the promissory realm. A claimant may transfer a benefit to a defendant on the basis of a future event without the defendant promising that that event will occur: that is, the basis may be a non-promissory contingent condition.[9] If that event does not happen (whether partially or totally) one can describe there as being a failure of consideration. For example, the claimant may pay £100 to the defendant because he is about to be married or the claimant may pay £100 to the defendant 'subject to contract' as an indication of good faith. If the defendant does not marry, or no contract is concluded between the parties, the defendant breaks no contract or promise but one can say, and the courts have said,[10] that the consideration for the claimant's payment has totally failed.

Birks has been keen to incorporate this secondary meaning and to break the link between failure of consideration and contract. He writes, 'In the law of restitution the word "consideration" should be given the meaning with which it first came into the common law. It means that the state of affairs contemplated as the basis or reason for payment has failed to materialise or, if it did exist, has failed to sustain itself.'[11] This seems right. Having said that, it is indisputable that the non-promissory meaning is much less familiar. It has rarely featured in the case law. To avoid needless confusion this book treats 'failure of consideration' and 'failure of promised performance'[12] as synonymous subject to rare instances where the contrary is stated. In this chapter the penultimate section looks specifically at restitution for the failure of an unpromised future event.

It should be added that, as has been explained in chapter 3,[13] the language of mistake is in this book preferred to using failure of consideration to refer to existing matters being different than the claimant believes them to be.

---

9   See Treitel, *The Law of Contract* (10th edn, 1999), pp 58–62; *Anson's Law of Contract* (28th edn, 2002), pp 135–138.

10   *Chillingworth v Esche* [1924] 1 Ch 97. Cf the resulting trust cases of *Essery v Cowlard* (1884) 26 Ch D 191; *Re Ames' Settlement* [1946] Ch 217.

11   Birks, at p 223. This was expressly approved by the High Court of Australia in *Roxborough v Rothmans of Pall Mall Australia Ltd* [2001] HCA 68.

12   Strictly speaking this encompasses the unusual situation where the promised performance is not in return for the benefit conferred, as in *Pulbrook v Lawes* (1876) 1 QBD 284. See Burrows, 'Free Acceptance and the Law of Restitution' (1988) 104 LQR 576 note 23. Unless the contrary is stated, it is assumed in this chapter that the promised performance is a bargained-for counter-performance.

13   Above, pp 145–146.

(2) Total and partial failure

In order to recover money – and it is for this form of benefit alone that the courts have expressly used the language of failure of consideration – it has been a traditional requirement that the failure of consideration be total. What is meant by total as against partial failure of consideration? In other words, what precisely is meant by saying that the defendant must have failed totally, rather than partially, to perform his promise to the claimant?

This turns on the nature of the contract in question and the courts' construction of what the claimant was paying for. If, for example, the contract was for the sale of goods, there will generally[14] be a total failure of consideration until property in the goods passes to the buyer[15] (or, on the better view, until the buyer has the use and enjoyment of the goods).[16] The fact that the seller has incurred expense in manufacturing the goods is irrelevant (ie it does not prevent there being a total failure of consideration) because that is not what the buyer is paying for. So, in *Fibrosa*[17] the claimants made an advance payment of £1,000 under a contract for the delivery of machines by the defendants. When the contract was frustrated by the outbreak of the Second World War the claimants were held able to recover the £1,000 in an action for money had and received on the ground that, because no machines had been delivered to them, there was a total failure of consideration. This was so despite the fact that the defendants had incurred significant expense in manufacturing the machines. In talking of total failure of consideration Lord Atkin said, '... the man who pays money in advance on a contract which is frustrated and receives nothing for his payment is entitled to recover it back'.[18] And Lord Wright said that recovery of money for total failure of consideration 'was based on the simple theory that a man who has paid in advance for something which he has never got ought to have his money back'.[19]

In contrast, where the contract is for work and materials there will generally be no total failure once the work has commenced. This is because the performance being paid for includes the work. This means that in, for example, a ship-building contract, once the work has

14 Ie, subject to the terms of the particular contract in question.
15 *Rowland v Divall* [1923] 2 KB 500.
16 See below, pp 329–331, 339–341.
17 [1943] AC 32.
18 Ibid, at p 55. See also p 61 (per Lord Macmillan).
19 Ibid, at p 72.

commenced, the failure will be merely partial, even though the payor does not receive any part of the ship.

This is clearly illustrated by the leading case on the meaning of total failure of consideration, *Stocznia Gdanska SA v Latvia Shipping Co.*[20] The claimant shipbuilders entered into a contract with the defendants, to design, build and deliver a ship. The claimants terminated the contract for the defendants' repudiatory breach in failing to pay the second instalment due under the contract. At this stage, the keel of the ship had been constructed but no part of the ship had been delivered to the claimant. The defendants argued that they were not bound to pay the second instalment because, if paid, it was immediately recoverable for total failure of consideration. The House of Lords held that, apart from any liability in damages for their repudiatory breach, the defendants were bound to pay the second instalment and that there was no total failure of consideration. The earlier decision of their Lordships, on very similar facts, of *Hyundai Heavy Industries Co Ltd v Papadopoulos*[1] was applied and approved. The House of Lords rejected the defendants' argument that the test for total failure of consideration was whether the buyers had received the benefit of any part of that which they had bargained for. Although no property in the ship had passed to the buyers, there was no total failure of consideration because this contract was not merely one of sale but was also for design and construction; and the design work, and some of the construction work, had already been carried out.

Lord Goff, giving the leading speech, said:

'In truth, the test is not whether the promisee has received a specific benefit, but rather whether the promisor has performed any part of the contractual duties in respect of which the payment is due. The present case cannot, therefore, be approached by asking the simple question whether the property in the vessel or any part of it has passed to the buyers. That test would be apposite if the contract in question was a contract for the sale of goods (or indeed a contract for the sale of land) simpliciter, under which the consideration for the price would be the passing of the property in the goods (or land). However, before that test can be regarded as appropriate, the anterior question has to be asked: is the contract in question simply a contract for the sale of a ship? or is it rather a contract under which the design and construction of the vessel formed part of the yard's contractual duties, as well as the duty to transfer the finished object to the buyers? If it is the latter, the design and construction of the vessel form part of the consideration for which the price is to be paid, and the fact that the contract has been brought to an end before

20 [1998] 1 WLR 574.
1   [1980] 1 WLR 1129.

the property in the vessel or any part of it has passed to the buyers does not prevent the yard from asserting that there has been no total failure of consideration in respect of an instalment of the price .... '[2]

It follows from the *Stocznia* case that the statement made in several previous cases[3] – that total failure turns on whether the defendant has got or received any part of what he bargained for – must be treated with some caution and is probably best avoided altogether. Professor Treitel expresses the point by saying that, after *Stocznia,* 'the test is whether performance has been rendered not whether it has been received'.[4] Another way of looking at this is to say that *Stocznia* represents a clear acceptance that 'detrimental' as well as 'beneficial' performance can count as the relevant consideration bargained for.[5]

In *Stocznia* the claimant had received no benefits and yet, applying the correct meaning of total failure of consideration, there was held to be merely a partial and not a total failure. One might have thought that it would follow that, where a claimant has received some of the benefit which he bargained for, there would inevitably be only a partial, and not a total, failure of consideration. Unfortunately this is not borne out by all the cases.

For example, in *Rowland v Divall*[6] the Court of Appeal held that there was a total failure of consideration, despite the buyer's having had the use of the car for two months, because he had not been given good title to the car. Atkin LJ said, 'It seems to me that in this case there has been a total failure of consideration, that is to say that the buyer has not got any part of that for which he paid the purchase money. He paid the money in order that he might get the property and he has not got it.'[7]

In *Rover International Ltd v Cannon Film Sales Ltd (No 3)*[8] the Court of Appeal held that Rover's receipt, and use, of the films from Cannon (under a contract that was void because Rover had not been incorporated) did not prevent a claim for total failure of consideration. This was because Rover had bargained for making profits from the

---

2 [1998] 1 WLR 574, 588.
3 Eg, *Rowland v Divall* [1923] 2 KB 500, 506; *Rover International Ltd v Cannon Film Sales Ltd (No 3)* [1989] 1 WLR 912, 923–925.
4 *The Law of Contract* (10th edn, 1999), p 977, note 47.
5 *Stocznia* also means that there is now no necessary link between there being no total failure of consideration and the defendants being entitled to a restitutionary counterclaim. Detrimental, but non-beneficial, performance by the defendants plainly does not entitle them to restitution.
6 [1923] 2 KB 500. For the facts, see below, p 339.
7 Ibid, at p 506.
8 [1989] 1 WLR 912. The facts are explained in more detail below, at pp 393–396.

films so as to, at least, break even and this had not been achieved. Kerr LJ, with whom Nicholls LJ agreed, said:

> 'The question whether there has been a total failure of consideration is not answered by considering whether there was any consideration sufficient to support a contract or purported contract. The test is whether or not the party claiming total failure of consideration has in fact received any part of the benefit bargained for under the contract or purported contract. … Delivery and possession were not what Rover had bargained for. The relevant bargain … was the opportunity to earn a substantial share of the gross receipts … with the certainty of at least breaking even by recouping their advance. Due to the invalidity of the agreement Rover got nothing of what they had bargained for, and there was clearly a total failure of consideration.'[9]

In *DO Ferguson & Associates v Sohl*[10] builders, in repudiatory breach of contract, left a site having been paid £26,738 by the employers for work done that was actually worth only £22,065. The Court of Appeal held that the employers were entitled to restitution of the difference (£4,673) as money paid for a total failure of consideration. This was said to be because the £4,673 was paid for work that was never done at all. This is an extraordinary interpretation of what is meant by total failure of consideration and effectively emasculates the difference between total and partial failure.

Again in *Goss v Chilcott*,[11] it was held by the Privy Council that lenders of money (under an initially valid, but subsequently avoided, mortgage instrument) were entitled to restitution of the balance of the loan for total failure of consideration even though two repayments of interest had been made by the borrowers. Lord Goff separated the capital sum loaned and the interest on it and said that, as no part of the capital sum had been repaid, the failure of consideration was total (albeit that he then went on to say that, in any event, partial failure of consideration would ground restitution in a case like this where apportionment can be carried out without difficulty).

Applying the *Stocznia* test of whether there has been any rendering of the performance that the other party was paying for, it would seem that in *Rowland, Rover, Ferguson* and *Goss*, the failure of consideration was partial and not total. While recognising that this is a matter of interpreting the particular contract in question, these cases can be criticised for taking an artificial view of total failure.[12] The defendants had rendered part of the performance which the claimants had bargained for. In the light of such cases, Beatson has written that,

9   Ibid, at pp 923–925.
10   (1992) 62 BLR 95.
11   [1996] AC 788.
12   For this criticism, see also Birks, at pp 465, 476.

'The concept of total failure of consideration can be rather arbitrary ignoring real benefits received by the payer ...'[13]

It would seem that the best way forward is to purify total failure of consideration by re-interpreting *Rowland, Rover, Ferguson* and *Goss* and similar cases[14] as allowing restitution of money for *partial* failure of consideration.[15] Looked at in this way, they support the correct position of principle, argued for below, that there is no need for failure of consideration to be total.

(3) The *Thomas v Brown* requirement

A relevant contract must be ineffective before a claim for failure of consideration can be successful.[16] Is it therefore sufficient for failure of consideration that, in addition to this, the claimant has not been rendered what he bargained for?

Although authority is sparse the answer appears to be 'no'. The basis upon which the claimant has benefited the defendant is a promise by the defendant and, so long as the defendant is (and has been) ready, able and willing to perform his promise, the consideration does not fail even if that promise is legally ineffective.[17] Where the contract is discharged for breach or frustration the legal enforceability of the contract and the defendant's readiness and ability to perform are two sides of the same coin. But where the contract is unenforceable for lack of formality or is merely anticipated or incomplete, or is void for mistake or want of authority or non-incorporation or because ultra vires, the questions of the validity of the contract and of whether the defendant is ready, able, and willing to perform his bargained-for promise are distinct.

The most instructive case is *Thomas v Brown*.[18] The claimant contracted to buy a shop from the defendant and paid a deposit. The contract was unenforceable under the Statute of Frauds because it did not disclose the name of the vendor. Before conveyance the claimant withdrew from the contract and sought recovery of the deposit for total failure of consideration. The action failed. Quain J said:

13 'Discharge for Breach: The Position of Instalments, Deposits and Other Payments Due Before Completion' (1981) 98 LQR 389, 406.
14 See, eg, *Ebrahim Dawood Ltd v Heath (Est 1927) Ltd* [1961] 2 Lloyd's Rep 512 in which it was held that there was a total failure of consideration in respect of that part of a quantity of goods rejected under the Sale of Goods Act 1979, s 30.
15 This is not to suggest that the beneficial use of the car in *Rowland* should have grounded a restitutionary *quantum valebat* counterclaim by the seller. On the contrary, the seller's lack of title meant that the buyer's benefit was not at the expense of the seller. It was at the true owner's expense. See above, pp 34–35.
16 Above, p 323, n 1.
17 Goff and Jones, para 19-006, Birks, at p 301. Cf Birks, at pp 217, 244.
18 (1876) 1 QBD 714. Cf *Monnickendam v Leanse* (1923) 39 TLR 445.

'I decide this cause on the ground that it is an action by an unwilling vendee against a willing vendor, and that it cannot be said that the consideration has failed so as to entitle the plaintiff to recover ... it appears that the defendant has always been ready and willing to assign the purchased property to the plaintiff in pursuance of the contract; in short, to give the plaintiff all that was bargained for. Now where, upon a verbal contract for the sale of land the purchaser pays the deposit and the vendor is always ready and willing to complete, I know of no authority to support the purchaser in bringing an action to recover back the money.'[19]

If correct it follows that, although the first of these is generally assumed without comment, there are two ingredients of failure of consideration, which together establish that the claimant's basis for rendering benefits to the defendant has failed: (i) that the defendant is not (or has not been) ready, able and willing to perform his promise; and (ii) that the claimant has not been rendered any part (for total failure) or not substantially all (for partial failure) of what he bargained for. It is an initial separate requirement, before one can bring a claim for failure of consideration, that any relevant contract or purported contract is ineffective.

(4) The time lag between the receipt of the benefit and the failure of consideration

Having clarified the meaning of failure of consideration, this seems an appropriate juncture to point out that failure of consideration is a unique unjust factor in the sense that there can be a time lag between the defendant's receipt of the benefit and the failure of consideration.

If C pays D £100 by mistake, the injustice and the enrichment occur simultaneously. If C pays D £100 under a contract which is later discharged for breach or frustration or in anticipation of a contract that never materialises there is no failure of consideration and hence no injustice until the date that the contract is discharged or the anticipated contract falls through. The question that then follows is whether restitution is concerned only with benefits that the defendant still had after the failure of consideration; or whether it is concerned with the benefits that the defendant had prior to the failure of consideration. One might argue that the benefits received prior to the date of the failure of consideration are not *unjust* enrichments and irrelevant. Alternatively it can be said that, once the basis for the benefits has been removed, restitution is concerned with all benefits

---

19   Ibid, at p 723. See also Mellor J, at pp 722–723.

that have been rendered and received *on that basis*: that is, that while at the time when received the enrichments were not unjust, they have retrospectively become so.

The latter approach is the one that the courts have adopted. *Subject to defences* (now most importantly the defence of change of position) there has been no question of a claimant not being entitled to, for example, an action for money had and received on the ground that the money received was dissipated prior to the failure of consideration. This also underpins the restitutionary regime laid down in the Law Reform (Frustrated Contracts) Act 1943.

However, it should be noted that, as the cause of action for failure of consideration cannot accrue until the failure of consideration, and as interest under s 35A of the Supreme Court Act 1981 cannot be awarded for a time prior to the accrual of the cause of action,[20] the claimant cannot recover interest on a payment prior to the failure of consideration.

2. SHOULD IT BE NECESSARY FOR THE FAILURE OF CONSIDERATION TO BE TOTAL?

Although it can be argued that there are exceptions (in particular where restitution for benefits in kind is being sought) the predominant common law position is that the failure of consideration must be total in order to count. Why should this be so? Is there a valid objection to partial failure of consideration as a ground for restitution?

Two main reasons for the requirement of total failure may be suggested although neither is convincing. The first is that to insist on total failure limits subversion of contract by restitution: to allow restitution for partial failure would extensively undermine contract law. But while restitutionary principles are clearly different from, and can run counter to, contractual principles it is submitted that unwarranted subversion is already prevented by the insistence that the contract be ineffective before a restitutionary claim can succeed. For example, it is not being suggested that, for any minor breach of contract, the innocent party can switch to restitution. On the contrary, he is locked into the contractual regime unless the breach is of the sort that entitles him to terminate the contract and he does terminate it.

Secondly, it may be argued that total failure of consideration has the merit of rendering it unnecessary to consider counterclaims for restitution of benefits in kind, which tend to raise difficult problems

20 Above, p 55, esp n 14.

of valuation. Where there has been a total failure of consideration, the claimant has not been benefited. Assuming the claimant is seeking the return of money paid, restitution is therefore simple and essentially one-sided. However, simplicity is hardly justice. In any event, to seek to avoid the difficulties of restitution for benefits in kind runs counter to vast tracts of the law of restitution where a claimant is entitled to claim restitution for such benefits; for example, a claimant's right to a *quantum meruit* for beneficial services rendered by mistake or under necessity or under a contract discharged for the other's breach or under a void, unenforceable or anticipated contract. It is also not entirely consistent with the approach to rescission of a contract for, for example, misrepresentation or undue influence, where counter-restitution is required.

The arguments in favour of 'total failure' therefore lack force. Moreover, there are several strong positive arguments against the requirement:

(i) The explanation of the injustice underlying total failure of consideration, whether expressed as 'failure of basis' or 'qualification of the will', applies equally to partial failure of consideration. While one is more extreme than the other, both render the enrichment at the claimant's expense unjust.

(ii) The courts have not adopted a consistent approach as to what is meant by total failure of consideration. As we have seen, in important cases such as *Rowland v Divall*,[1] *Rover International Ltd v Cannon Film Sales Ltd (No 3)*,[2] *DO Ferguson & Associates v Sohl*[3] and *Goss v Chilcott*[4] an artificial interpretation has been taken of what constitutes total failure of consideration. The covert willingness to ignore the fact that part of the performance bargained for by the claimant has been rendered in effect amounts to an acceptance of partial failure of consideration.

(iii) The Law Reform (Frustrated Contracts) Act 1943, s 1(2), has moved the basis for the restitution of money paid following discharge of a contract for frustration from the total failure of consideration insisted on at common law in *Fibrosa Spolka Akcyjna v Fairbairn Lawson Combe Barbour Ltd*[5] to partial failure of consideration. There is no good

---

1   [1923] 2 KB 500.
2   [1989] 1 WLR 912.
3   (1992) 62 BLR 95.
4   [1996] AC 788.
5   [1943] AC 32. In *Fibrosa* itself the House of Lords recognised a principle, illustrated by *Rigg v Minett* (1809) 11 East 210, according to which the need for total failure of consideration may be applied to severable parts of the contract. In reality, this 'waters down' the need for the consideration to have totally failed.

reason for treating restitution after frustration any differently from restitution consequent on other grounds invalidating a contract. Indeed one can argue that, as the legislature has expressed a preference for partial failure in the frustration area, the common law should follow suit in other analogous areas.

(iv) There is a line of old annuity cases, for example *Hicks v Hicks,*[6] where the contract was void for failure to register the annuity, in which payments both ways had been made and yet restitution (through an action for money had and received) was granted. One interpretation of these cases is that they show that, at least where both parties' performance comprises making payments, restitution for partial failure of consideration will be granted. This line of cases was put before Hobhouse J, at first instance, in *Westdeutsche Landesbank Girozentrale v Islington London Borough Council.*[7] Unfortunately he interpreted them as being based on an unjust factor of 'absence of consideration'.[8] Somewhat similarly, Lord Browne-Wilkinson in the House of Lords in that case, and the Court of Appeal in *Guinness Mahon v Kensington and Chelsea Royal London Borough Council,*[9] have taken the view, criticised below,[10] that in a void contract there is automatically a total failure of consideration.

(v) Although the courts have not traditionally used the language of failure of consideration where restitution of benefits in kind is in issue,[11] it is submitted that symmetry (between different types of benefit) dictates that the same unjust factor must apply to benefits in kind as to money. And yet it is clear that, where the claimant seeks restitution of benefits in kind rendered under an ineffective contract, a part payment of the contract price does not bar restitution. For example, if the claimant renders services under a contract that it discharges for the defendant's failure to pay the agreed price, the fact that the claimant was paid a small sum in advance cannot rule out its restitutionary claim. This is clearly illustrated by the United States case of *Boomer v Muir*[12] where the claimants were held able to recover a *quantum meruit* for the value of

---

6   (1802) 3 East 16; cf *Davis v Bryan* (1827) 6 B & C 651. See similarly *North Central Wagon Finance Co Ltd v Brailsford* [1962] 1 WLR 1288 (hire-purchase agreement void for non-registration; creditor entitled to restitution of full sum loaned even though there had been some repayments).
7   [1994] 4 All ER 890.
8   See below, pp 386–387, 399.
9   [1999] QB 215. See above, p 325.
10 See below pp 386–388, 397–401.
11 An exception was *Pearce v Brain* [1929] 2 KB 310. This decision is criticised on other grounds, below, chapter 11.
12 24 P 2d 570 (1933).

work done in building a dam even though they had been paid all but $20,000 of the contract price. Cast in terms of failure of consideration, therefore, the law on the restitution of benefits in kind already recognises that the failure need only be partial and not total.

The conclusion is that the law ought to move to partial failure of consideration as an unjust factor triggering the restitution of money as well as benefits in kind.[13]

This now derives strong support from the Privy Council's reasoning in *Goss v Chilcott*.[14] Restitution of money loaned by the claimant to the defendants was awarded despite the fact that two repayments of interest had been made. The Privy Council considered that there had been a total failure of consideration,[15] but Lord Goff went on to say: '[E]ven if part of the capital sum had been repaid, the law would not hesitate to hold that the balance of the loan outstanding would be recoverable on the ground of failure of consideration, for at least in those cases in which apportionment can be carried out without difficulty, the law will allow partial recovery on this ground.'[16]

One can also pray in aid obiter dicta of Lord Goff in *Westdeutsche Landesbank Girozentrale v Islington London Borough Council*[17] (although unfortunately, as we have seen,[18] Lord Browne-Wilkinson giving the leading speech in that case regarded there as having been a total failure of consideration merely because the contract was void). Lord Goff said, 'There has long been a desire among restitution lawyers to escape from the unfortunate effects of the so-called rule that money is only recoverable at common law on the ground of failure of consideration where the failure is total, by reformulating the rule upon a more principled basis; and signs that this will in due course be done are appearing in judgments throughout the common law world, as appropriate cases arise for decision.'[19]

---

13 See also McKendrick, 'Total Failure of Consideration and Counter-Restitution: Two Issues or One?' in *Laundering and Tracing* (ed Birks, 1995), pp 217–242; Birks, 'Failure of Consideration' in *Consensus Ad Idem* (ed Rose, 1996), pp 179–202; Virgo, *The Principles of the Law of Restitution* (1999), pp 341–344. It is a major disappointment that the Law Commission in its Report No 121 (1983) on 'Pecuniary Restitution on Breach of Contract' decided not to endorse its provisional recommendation (in Working Paper No 65 (1975)) that an innocent party should be entitled to restitution of money paid to a contract breaker for partial as well as total failure of consideration.

14 [1996] AC 788.

15 See above, p 330.

16 [1996] AC 788, 798.

17 [1996] AC 669.

18 See above, p 325 and below, pp 399–400.

19 [1996] AC 669, 682. The judgment in *Goss v Chilcott* was handed down the day after that in the *Westdeutsche* case.

3. APPLICATION OF FAILURE OF CONSIDERATION

This is a long section. Its examination of the application of failure of consideration is subdivided into contracts discharged for breach, contracts discharged by frustration, incomplete or anticipated contracts, contracts unenforceable for want of formality, void contracts, contracts that are invalid for infancy and illegal contracts.

Restitution for a claimant consequent on rescission of a contract is not examined in this section and chapter because the difficulty of separating the sweeping away of the contract from the claimant's consequent restitution means that the relevant unjust factor is best viewed as being, for example, mistake, duress or undue influence rather than failure of consideration.

(1) Contracts discharged for breach[20]

It is submitted that failure of consideration is the unjust factor whether the enrichment in question is money or benefits in kind and whether it is the innocent party or the contract breaker who seeks restitution. Symmetry is therefore the key idea unlocking the mysteries of this area.

As regards establishing that the defendant is enriched where benefits in kind are in issue then, even if there is no incontrovertible benefit,[1] subjective devaluation can be overcome by the fact that the defendant has bargained for the services or goods. So long as the defendant receives part of what he bargained for, there is a rebuttable presumption that he is benefited. It is argued below that the question of whether the defendant is entitled to rely on the contract price, to establish that he values the benefit in kind at a lower price than the market price, turns on which test of benefit applies.

'At the expense of the claimant' here always means that there is a subtraction from the claimant and not wrongdoing by the defendant. Here one is not concerned with the use of breach of contract as a wrong. This must be so where it is a contract breaker who seeks

---

20 See, generally, Skelton, *Restitution and Contract* (1998).
1 The notion of a *positive* incontrovertible benefit is virtually redundant in the context of ineffective contracts because, subject to very rare exceptions, the defendant can realistically argue that he would have been willing to pay for the lower cost of creating or acquiring that positive benefit either because commercially necessary or, more commonly, because he has bargained for that benefit. Even where unusually the cost of producing or acquiring the positive benefit is higher than its realised or realisable value the defendant cannot deny that he has been saved that cost where he has bargained for the positive benefit (although he may only be bound to pay a lower market price: above, p 24).

restitution but it is also so where it is the innocent party who wants restitution. Locating the case law within unjust enrichment by subtraction helps to explain two of its features. First, it can explain why the innocent party is able to escape from a bad bargain by claiming restitution. If one were concerned with restitution for the wrong of breach of contract one would presumably allow the defendant to keep the gains that it would have made if the contract had been properly performed. Secondly, it can explain why essentially the same pattern of restitution applies whether there has been a breach of contract or not: ie essentially the same approach to restitution is taken where a contract has been discharged for frustration, or is void or unenforceable or incomplete, as where the contract is discharged for breach. The question of whether there can be restitution for breach of contract as a wrong (that is, where breach of contract is the cause of action) is discussed in chapter 15.

(a) Innocent party seeking restitution of money paid

(i)   Total failure of consideration

An innocent party is entitled to the restitution of money paid, in an action for money had and received, provided there has been a total failure of consideration. A standard illustration is *Giles v Edwards*,[2] where the claimants had contracted to buy wood from the defendant. The defendant was to cord the wood that had been cut before collection by the claimants. The claimants paid the contract price of 20 guineas but the defendant corded only one sixth of the wood. The claimants discharged the contract for breach and were held entitled to recover the 20 guineas paid for failure of consideration. Although not mentioned in the judgment, one can assume that the claimants rejected the one hundred and twentieth of the wood which they had, in a technical sense, collected so that there was, indisputably, a *total* failure of consideration.

　　An important Australian case which went the other way, because there had been only a partial and not a total failure of consideration, is *Baltic Shipping Co v Dillon, The Mikhail Lermontov*.[3] The claimant had paid for a fourteen-day cruise but after eight days of the cruise the ship sank. The defendant shipowners were thereby in breach of contract. The claimant sued for damages for breach of contract and for restitution of the cruise fare. Restitution was refused by the High Court of Australia because there was no total failure of consideration

2   (1797) 7 Term Rep 181.
3   (1993) 176 CLR 344.

in that the claimant had had eight days of the cruise. In Mason CJ's words, 'The consequence of the respondent's enjoyment of the benefits provided under the contract during the first eight full days of the cruise is that the failure of consideration was partial, not total.'[4]

Does the claimant's intermediate use and enjoyment of property, which is the subject matter of a contract that he subsequently terminates for breach, prevent his establishing that the consideration has totally failed?

As regards the purchase (or hire-purchase) of goods the view taken is that where the claimant is not given good title to the goods the consideration totally fails irrespective of intermediate use of them. The leading case is *Rowland v Divall.*[5] The claimant had bought a car from the defendant and had resold it two months later. Two months after that the police seized the car as stolen property. The claimant refunded the purchase price to his purchaser and sought to recover from the defendant the price he had paid on the ground of total failure of consideration. His claim succeeded. According to the Court of Appeal the claimant had 'not received any part of that which he had contracted to receive'[6] because he had not been given good title and the right to possession. The same approach was taken and same result reached in *Butterworth v Kingsway Motors Ltd*[7] and *Barber v NWS Bank plc*[8] where, respectively, a hire-purchaser had used a car for eleven months, and a conditional purchaser had used a car for twenty-two months, before finding out about the defect in title and terminating for breach.

On the other hand, if the purchaser is given good title to the goods and they are defective in quality, the purchaser's possession and use

---

4   Ibid, at 353. Although the reasoning of the High Court appears to support the traditional insistence that the failure of consideration must be total, not partial, it is significant that the claimant had already been returned a proportionate part of the fare. In other words, an acceptance of restitution for partial failure of consideration (subject to counter-restitution) would merely have given the claimant what she had already been repaid. She was alleging a total failure of consideration in order to recover the whole fare without giving any counter-restitution. The High Court of Australia also decided that the claimant could not combine a claim for restitution of the fare with damages for breach of contract. Rather the must elect between them. The better view (supported, eg, by Treitel, *The Law of Contract* (10th edn, 1999), p 878) is that, so long as one avoids 'double recovery', there should be no objection to an award of both restitution and damages. For criticism of this aspect of the High Court's decision, as well as its failure to reconsider the rule denying restitution for a partial failure of consideration, see Kit Barker, 'Restitution of Passenger Fare' [1994] LMCLQ 291.
5   [1923] 2 KB 500.
6   Ibid, at p 507 (per Atkin LJ).
7   [1954] 1 WLR 1286. See also the reasoning in *Warman v Southern Counties Car Finance Corpn Ltd* [1949] 2 KB 576 where the claim was for damages for breach of a hire-purchase agreement.
8   [1996] 1 WLR 641, CA.

of the goods prevents a claim for total failure of consideration. In *Yeoman Credit Ltd v Apps*[9] the defendant had hire-purchased a car which was in an unroadworthy condition. He kept it for six months before rejecting it. The Court of Appeal held that he was not entitled to the instalments paid on the ground of total failure of consideration because he had had the possession and use of the car albeit that that was of little value. Holroyd Pearce LJ said, 'This is not a case like *Rowland v Divall* where title was lacking and the defendant never had lawful possession.'[10]

Again, if the property in question is land, rather than goods, it appears that intermediate use and enjoyment rules out a claim for total failure of consideration even if the contracted-for title has not been conveyed. The leading case is *Hunt v Silk.*[11] Under an agreement for a lease of a house the lease was to be executed, and the landlord was to carry out certain repairs to the house, within ten days. The tenant, who was to pay £10 on execution of the lease, was let into the house immediately and paid the £10. However, despite the tenant's protests, the landlord failed to execute the lease or to carry out the agreed repair work. After staying a few days beyond the ten, the tenant terminated the contract, left the house, and sought restitution of the £10. The claim failed and the most straightforward interpretation of the judgments is that this was because the few days' occupation of the land beyond the ten prevented the tenant establishing a total failure of consideration. He had got a small part of what he had bargained for. Goff and Jones, however, regard the case as turning on the affirmation of the contract by the tenant by staying on knowing of the breach.[12] Although that interpretation is supported by some of the reasoning of the judges, it would contradict normal principles of affirmation in that the occupation, after the initial ten days, was for no more than a few days and throughout the tenant had made clear by his frequent requests for the work to be carried out that he was not prepared to tolerate the breach.

The law on the effect of the intermediate enjoyment of property is therefore inconsistent. Even if one could accept treating serious defects of quality differently from defects of title there is no reason to distinguish title defects in land from title defects in goods. So long as one insists on a total failure of consideration, the *Rowland v Divall* line of cases should be regarded as wrong in taking an artificial view of total failure. But the best approach would be to re-interpret those cases as recognising that

9   [1962] 2 QB 508.
10   Ibid, at p 521.
11   (1804) 5 East 449.
12   Goff and Jones, at para 20-013.

money can be recovered for partial failure of consideration and that the defendants had no valid restitutionary counterclaim for the use and enjoyment of the property because the loss of use was not at their expense but rather at the expense of the true owner. This last point is supported by the Law Commission in its Report on 'The Sale and Supply of Goods'[13] rejecting its earlier provisional recommendation[14] that credit should be given by the restitution-seeking purchaser to the non-owning vendor for his use and possession of the goods. On the other hand, it is unfortunate that in neither that Report, nor in its report on 'Pecuniary Restitution on Breach of Contract',[15] did the Law Commission put forward any criticism of the reasoning on total failure of consideration in *Rowland v Divall*.

(ii) Escape from a bad bargain and other advantages

Say the claimant contracts to buy a car from the defendant for £900 and pays £100 deposit; the defendant fails to deliver the car; the market price is £700. Is the claimant entitled to restitution of £100 for total failure of consideration even though its expectation damages for breach of contract would be nil?

As shown by *Wilkinson v Lloyd*[16] and obiter dicta in *Ebrahim Dawood Ltd v Heath Ltd*[17] the answer to this question is 'yes', albeit that the scenario will be rare as it will not usually be in the defendant's interests to break what, for it, is a good contract. In the former case, the defendant contracted to sell shares in a mining company to the claimant but, in breach of contract,[18] failed to have the shares transferred into the claimant's name. On discharge, the claimant was held able to recover the purchase price paid on the ground of total failure of consideration even though the value of the shares had subsequently fallen below the contract price. In the latter case, McNair J said that the buyer was entitled to restitution for total failure

---

13 No 160 (1987), paras 6.1–6.5.
14 Working Paper No 65 (1975) 'Pecuniary Restitution on Breach of Contract', paras 57–78. See also the possible solutions put forward in Working Paper No 85 (1983) 'Sale and Supply of Goods', paras 6.11–6.13.
15 No 121 (1983). Cf Working Paper No 65 (1975), para 62 where *Rowland v Divall* was criticised.
16 (1845) 7 QB 27.
17 [1961] 2 Lloyd's Rep 512. This may also be supported by *DO Ferguson & Associates v Sohl* (1992) 62 BLR 95, CA, where employers were able to recover in restitution part of the price paid for building work even though overall (and taking into account that they had had to pay other builders for the work to be completed) this appeared to put them into a better position than if the contract had been performed. See also on this case, above, p 330.
18 On an alternative interpretation there was no breach but rather the failure of a (non-promissory) contingent condition.

of consideration of part of the purchase price for goods that it had validly rejected; and that the importance of this was that it might entitle the buyer to a higher sum than damages for breach of contract. He said:

> 'The next point is whether the plaintiff's right to recover the money which they have paid ... stands as a claim to recover the money as money paid to the use of the plaintiffs or paid for a consideration which has wholly failed. The contrary view is that the remedy only stands in damages so that if ... the market price at the time of the delivery conformed to £70 against the contract price of £73 10s, there would be recovered on this argument only £70 per ton and not £73 10s per ton, leaving a profit of £3 10s in the pockets of the seller... The buyers' right ... is clearly ... the right to recover money for a consideration which has wholly failed and which, accordingly, must be regarded as money paid to the buyers' use.'[19]

Similarly in the famous United States case of *Bush v Canfield*[20] the claimant purchaser contracted to buy flour from the defendant seller for $14,000. Although the market price dropped to $11,000 the seller, peculiarly, failed to deliver the flour. The purchaser terminated the contract and sought recovery of the $5,000 part payment that he had made. Although the action was not expressed as being one for money had and received for total failure of consideration restitution of the $5,000 was ordered (Hosmer J dissenting). This was so even though the claimant buyer would have lost $3,000 on the transaction (and his expectation damages would, therefore, have been $2,000).

This state of the law seems entirely correct. Expectation damages are awarded in an action for breach of contract and aim to put the claimant into as good a position as if the contract had been performed. Hence expectation damages, and even reliance damages (albeit that with the latter the defendant has the burden of proving that the claimant would not have recouped his reliance losses under the contract)[1] do not allow the claimant to escape from a known bad bargain. But a claim for the restitution of money for total failure of consideration is a separate cause of action from breach of contract and lies within unjust enrichment by subtraction. Whether the bargain was a good or a bad one is irrelevant. Once the contract has been discharged, and subject to the claimant having contracted-out of restitution, there is no need for the law of restitution to bow to contract.

Escape from a bad bargain is the major advantage to be gained by an innocent party claiming restitution of money paid rather than

19   [1961] 2 Lloyd's Rep 512, 518–520.
20   2 Conn 485 (1818). See also *Mobil Oil Exploration v United States* 530 US 604 (2000).
1   *C & P Haulage (a firm) v Middleton* [1983] 1 WLR 1461; *CCC Films (London) Ltd v Impact Quadrant Films Ltd* [1985] QB 16. See also *Anglia Television Ltd v Reed* [1972] 1 QB 60.

suing for expectation or reliance damages. Three additional advantages may be suggested.

First, the claimant avoids the need to prove the position he would have been in if the contract had been performed. This may explain why restitution, rather than expectation damages, was claimed in, for example, *Giles v Edwards*.[2] However, in this respect, restitution offers no advantage over claiming reliance damages.

Secondly, where the claimant has had the use and enjoyment of goods bought from the defendant, which did not belong to the defendant, the defendant has no restitutionary counterclaim for that benefit because it was not gained 'at his expense'. Whether one follows the *Rowland v Divall* interpretation of total failure of consideration or, preferably, one regards the cause of action as being partial failure of consideration, the claimant is therefore entitled to restitution of the full purchase price paid. In contrast, a claim for expectation or reliance damages should in principle give credit for the use and enjoyment of the goods received.[3]

Thirdly, although not suggested in any of the cases, there may conceivably be situations in which restrictions on damages, for example, the duty to mitigate, or remoteness, or particularly worded exclusion clauses, may mean that the claimant stands to gain more by claiming restitution of money paid than by suing for damages.

(b) Innocent party seeking restitution for benefits in kind

(i) *Failure of consideration and an incontrovertible or bargained-for benefit*

The primary restitutionary remedy in play here is a *quantum meruit* for services rendered. In principle if the innocent party has validly terminated the contract for breach it should be entitled to restitution provided there has been a total or partial failure of consideration and provided it can establish, whether by showing an incontrovertible benefit or by the 'bargained-for' test, that the defendant has been benefited.

As Goff and Jones point out,[4] there are few relevant authorities. What there are, are consistent with the above principled approach albeit that the judges did not use the language of failure of consideration or bargained-for benefit.

In *De Bernardy v Harding*[5] the defendant was in control of letting seats to see the funeral procession of the Duke of Wellington. He

2   (1797) 7 Term Rep 181.
3   Cf *Warman v Southern Counties Car Finance Corpn Ltd* [1949] 2 KB 576.
4   Goff and Jones, para 20-020. The well-known case of *Planché v Colburn* (1831) 8 Bing 14 is better viewed as non-restitutionary with the *quantum meruit* awarded being the equivalent of contractual damages (whether expectation or reliance): above, p 17.
5   (1853) 8 Exch 822.

made a contract with the claimant to deal with sales overseas. The claimant had accordingly advertised abroad and had arranged accommodation for overseas visitors. The defendant then repudiated the contract by insisting that he would sell the tickets on the spot and, although the claimant sent applicants for tickets to him, he refused to pay the claimant anything. Alderson B said, 'Where one party has absolutely refused to perform, or has rendered himself incapable of performing his part of the contract, he puts it in the power of the other party either to sue for breach of it, or to rescind the contract and sue on a *quantum meruit* for the work actually done.'[6] Although the actual decision was to order a retrial, the *quantum meruit* recognised by Alderson B was fully justified according to restitutionary principles. There had been a failure of consideration in that the claimant had not been paid. And the defendant had received part of the bargained-for services (eg by being sent applicants) so that presumptively he was benefited (by being saved some of the expense he would otherwise have incurred) and, on the facts, that presumption was not rebutted.

Again in *Chandler Bros Ltd v Boswell*,[7] where the defendant head contractors were held to be in breach of contract in repudiating a sub-contract under which the claimants were excavating for a tunnel, the claimants were held entitled on terminating the contract to recover a *quantum meruit* for the work they had done. In Greer LJ's words, '... it has long been well settled that the plaintiff whose contract is broken is entitled, if he so chooses, to claim damages or claim on a *quantum meruit* basis'.[8]

(ii) Escape from a bad bargain?

Once one recognises that an innocent party does have a restitutionary claim for benefits in kind, the crucial question is can it thereby escape from a bad bargain? Or, on the contrary, is the restitutionary award limited by the claimant's expectation loss? This is closely linked to, but not precisely the same as, the question often asked in this context of whether restitution is limited by the pro rata contract price. While both questions can be said to be concerned with 'contract ceilings' on restitution, they subtly differ in that even to award the claimant the pro rata contract price can allow it some escape from a bad bargain. This is because the pro rata contract price relates only to the beneficial performance already carried out rather than to the full (losing) performance and, therefore, on a losing contract, it will be greater than the claimant's expectation loss.

6   Ibid, at p 824.
7   [1936] 3 All ER 179.
8   Ibid, at p 186.

In *Lodder v Slowey*[9] the Privy Council upheld the decision of the Court of Appeal of New Zealand that the claimant, who had partly completed a tunnel in accordance with a contract repudiated by the defendant, was entitled to a *quantum meruit* for the work done. And in expressing agreement with the lower court's approach to the *quantum meruit* the Privy Council implicitly approved the view that there is no contract ceiling on restitution. Williams J had said, 'As the defendant has abandoned the special contract, and as the plaintiff has accepted that abandonment, what would have happened if the special contract had continued in existence is entirely irrelevant.'[10] The vast majority of cases in the United States also take this line. The best known is *Boomer v Muir*[11] in which the claimants recovered a *quantum meruit* of $257,000 for work in building a dam even though they were entitled to only another $20,000 under the contract.

This was also the position taken by the Court of Appeal of New South Wales in *Renard Constructions (ME) Pty Ltd v Minister for Public Works.*[12] The claimant builder was held entitled to a *quantum meruit* which exceeded the sum that it would have been entitled to under the contract, which the employer had wrongfully repudiated. In a powerful statement, Meagher JA referred with approval to *Lodder v Slowey* and *Boomer v Muir* and went on:

> 'There is nothing anomalous in the notion that two different remedies, proceeding on entirely different principles, might yield different results ... Nor is there anything anomalous in the prospect that a figure arrived at on a *quantum meruit* might exceed, or even far exceed, the profit which would have been made if the contract had been fully performed... The most that one can say is that the amount contractually agreed is evidence of the reasonableness of the remuneration claimed on a *quantum meruit;* strong evidence perhaps, but certainly not conclusive evidence. On the other hand, it would be extremely anomalous if the defaulting party when sued on a *quantum meruit* could invoke the contract which he has repudiated in order to impose a ceiling on amounts otherwise recoverable.'[13]

Goff and Jones argue that the claimant should not be able to recover more than the contract price because otherwise contracts would be subverted by restitution.[14] Initially Birks tentatively took a similar view

---

9   [1904] AC 442, affirming (1900) 20 NZLR 321.
10 (1900) 20 NZLR 321, 358.
11 24 P 2d 570 (1933). It is also the view taken in the Restatement of Contracts, s 347(1). See generally Palmer, *Law of Restitution* (1978) Vol 1, para 4.4; and Palmer, 'The Contract Price as a Limit on Restitution for Defendant's Breach' (1959) 20 Ohio St LJ 264.
12 (1992) 26 NSWLR 234.
13 Ibid, at 267–268.
14 Goff and Jones, paras 20-021 to 20-022. See also Jones, *Restitution in Public and Private Law* (1991), pp 119–121; and *Keating on Building Contracts* (7th edn, 2001), para 8.61. Goff and Jones' earlier, and slightly different view, was that the pro rata contract price (rather then the contract price) should be the ceiling: see Goff and Jones, (3rd edn, 1986), pp 467–468.

but he has since changed his mind.[15] Goff and Jones' reasoning is puzzling for two main reasons. First, it is inconsistent with their approach to the restitution of money where they are happy for the innocent party to escape from a bad bargain by claiming restitution for total failure of consideration. Secondly, unwarranted subversion of contract by restitution is already prevented by the insistence that the contract be discharged before restitution can be claimed.

It is submitted therefore that, as with money, there is and should be no objection to the claimant escaping from a bad bargain by claiming restitution. The cause of action in unjust enrichment by subtraction is distinct from, and need not bow down to, contract.

Having said that, the pro rata contract price may be important not in avoiding a conflict with contract but as an inherent element of the unjust enrichment claim: more specifically, in establishing the defendant's benefit. A central theme throughout the law of restitution is that a crucial difference between money and benefits in kind is that the latter may be subjectively devalued. If one overcomes subjective devaluation by regarding the defendant as having been benefited because he received part of what he bargained for, the pro rata contract price should form the upper limit in assessing the defendant's benefit: for to allow the claimant the objective market price in excess of this would be to re-encounter subjective devaluation in that the defendant can validly argue that it was only willing to pay at the contractual rate. In contrast if one regards the defendant as having been incontrovertibly benefited by 'necessary expense saved' there should be no restriction to the pro rata contract price, for this would be contradictory: if the expense saved were really necessary the defendant would have been prepared to pay at the market price rather than merely at the particular contract price.

So, unless one takes the extreme and unconvincing view that the contract price is irrelevant because a contract breaker, as a wrongdoer, cannot appeal to subjective devaluation,[16] the whole issue of a pro rata contract price should turn on how the defendant's benefit is established. Birks, in agreeing with this reasoning, expresses the point by saying that the contract price is a 'valuation ceiling' not a 'contract ceiling'.[17]

---

15 Compare Birks, p 288 with Birks, 'In Defence of Free Acceptance' in *Essays on the Law of Restitution* (ed Burrows, 1991), p 105 at p 136.

16 The 'reprehensible seeking-out' test – see above, chapter 1 – would only apply (rendering the defendant liable to pay the objective market price) in an exceptional case where the defendant intends from the outset to break the contract (ie he is fraudulent).

17 Birks, 'In Defence of Free Acceptance' in *Essays on the Law of Restitution* (ed Burrows 1991), pp 105, 135–137. For a different approach to rejecting the pro rata or full contract price limit, see Beatson, *The Use and Abuse of Unjust Enrichment* (1991), pp 12–15.

In most situations the claimant cannot establish that the defendant was incontrovertibly benefited and instead must rely on the bargained-for test. Generally, therefore, the pro rata contract price ought to act as the true measure of restitution. In the light of this, *Lodder v Slowey*, *Boomer v Muir*, and *Renard Constructions Pty Ltd v Minister for Public Works* seem wrong. In none of them were the defendants incontrovertibly benefited.

Apart from the possibility of escaping from a bad bargain, are there any other possible advantages to an innocent party in claiming a restitutionary *quantum meruit*? There appear to be two. First, while presenting its own problems in establishing a benefit, restitution does avoid the difficulties of proving one's expectation interest (although this would offer no advantage over reliance damages). Secondly, restitution avoids restrictions on damages, such as the duty to mitigate.

Goff and Jones argue that, where the claimant has fully or substantially performed, by rendering services or supplying goods, its action lies on the contract alone – for recovery of the contract debt – and not for restitution. They consider this to be 'historically sound' and 'correct in principle'[18] and point out that there is no English authority suggesting the contrary. But there is also no English authority denying the contrary and assuming the claimant can, and has elected to, terminate the contract it seems illogical to deny restitution in the more extreme case of substantial performance, while allowing it for partial performance. Moreover, no one suggests that a similar restriction applies to deny restitution to the claimant who has paid the full purchase price for a total failure of consideration.

(iii) Restitution from a third party beneficiary of a contract

A question on which there is little authority is whether an innocent party can ever rely on failure of consideration[19] to ground restitution from a third party beneficiary of a contract.[20]

---

18 Goff and Jones, para 20-019. See also Maddaugh and McCamus, *The Law of Restitution* (1st edn, 1990), pp 428–429.
19 The same question could also arise with regard to other unjust factors: eg, the contract for the third party's benefit may be void for common mistake or voidable for misrepresentation or undue influence. An analogous answer to that suggested in the text applies: ie restitution may be possible.
20 See Goff and Jones, paras 1-074 to 1-078; Friedmann, 'Valid, Voidable, Qualified and Non-Existing Obligations: An Alternative Perspective on the Law of Restitution' in *Essays on the Law of Restitution* (ed Burrows, 1991), pp 247, 273–275. Cf the Law Reform (Frustrated Contracts) Act 1943, s 1 (6) which allows the courts to award restitution against the other contracting party for benefits conferred on a third party beneficiary. Similarly, the Law Commission's Report No 121 'Pecuniary Restitution on Breach of Contract' (1983), para 2.47 proposing restitution from the other contracting party for benefits conferred on the intended third party beneficiary.

Say, for example, a sub-contracting joiner under a building contract to erect a house for an owner performs work which, in breach of the head contractor's contract with him, he is not paid for. Could the joiner, as an alternative to suing the head contractor (who may be insolvent) for breach of contract or in restitution, sue the owner in restitution?

In most circumstances the answer is clearly 'no'.[1] The owner would already be paying for the work through the head contract so that the restitutionary claim would be undermining the contractual relationship between the head contractor and the owner. There will also often be genuine difficulties in establishing the defendant's enrichment because, although he may have bargained for the work, it was under a bargain with someone other than the claimant.

However, where the head contract has been terminated (or in a situation where the beneficiary has not made any contract to receive the benefit) and the defendant's benefit can be established (eg because it is incontrovertible) it may be that there is no objection to restitution.[2] In particular there seems no necessary reason why a failure of consideration should only operate between two parties. In the above example, the joiner is certainly not a risk-taker vis-à-vis the head contractor, and it would seem to beg the question to assert that, nonetheless, he is a risk-taker vis-à-vis the owner. The 'at the expense of' requirement may be regarded as straightforwardly satisfied in the sense that the joiner has performed the work on the owner's property (albeit under a contract with the head-contractor not the owner). A requirement of accounting over to the first defendant who paid for the work in the event of the claimant recovering from a second defendant would ensure that the claimant does not recover twice over for the work it has done. And the defence of change of position (or a specific rule against double actionability) can ensure that the defendant is not bound to pay twice over for the same benefit. Certainly 'privity of contract' cannot be a necessary restriction on restitution which commonly operates outside contractual relationships.

The most important case on this issue, where the third party beneficiary was an assignee of the benefit of a contract, is *Pan Ocean Shipping Ltd v Creditcorp Ltd, The Trident Beauty*.[3] The House of Lords denied a restitutionary claim against the assignee. While that result seems correct, it is only in Lord Goff's speech, and then only in his

---

1   See, eg, *Brown and Davies Ltd v Galbraith* [1972] 1 WLR 997.
2   Very tentative support for this may be gleaned by drawing an analogy with the subrogation rights of creditors of a business carried on by trustees (above, p 113).
3   [1994] 1 WLR 161; noted by Burrows, 'Restitution from Assignees' [1994] RLR 52; Barker, 'Restitution and Third Parties' [1994] LMCLQ 305.

secondary reasoning, that one finds the true explanation for the denial of recovery. Pan Ocean had time-chartered a ship from Trident. Trident had assigned its right to hire to Creditcorp for valuable consideration. A third instalment of hire was paid in advance by Pan Ocean to Creditcorp for a period during which, as it transpired, the ship was off-hire. Pan Ocean subsequently terminated the contract for Trident's repudiatory breach in failing to pay for repair of the ship. As Trident was not worth suing, Pan Ocean sought restitution of the third advance payment of hire from Creditcorp on the ground that it had been paid for a consideration (use of the ship) that had totally failed (ie, the ship was off-hire).

Lord Woolf, giving the leading speech, thought that a claim for failure of consideration could only be made against the contracting party responsible for that failure. But, as has been argued above,[4] there seems no good reason in principle for this restriction, especially as failure of consideration can be a valid ground of restitution even where there has never been a valid contract between the parties. Lord Goff preferred to leave open as being still 'a matter of debate' whether 'a plaintiff may have a claim in restitution when he has conferred a benefit on the defendant in the course of performing an obligation to a third party'.[5]

Lord Goff's primary reason for denying restitution was that, had the money been paid to Trident, rather than Creditcorp, restitution would have been unnecessary and inappropriate because there was an express contractual term governing the recovery of overpaid hire. However, as restitution would not have been in conflict with that clause, it is far from clear why the agreed contractual regime should have ousted restitution to Trident, let alone Creditcorp. More persuasive was Lord Goff's secondary reasoning to the effect that it would be unjust to grant restitution where this would undermine the contract of assignment according to which Creditcorp had 'bought' the right to the payment of hire free from any condition as to repayment. His Lordship said:

'[I]t would in any event be unjust [to grant restitution] in a case such as the present where the defendant, Creditcorp, is not the mere recipient of a windfall but is an assignee who has purchased from Trident the right to receive the contractual debt which the plaintiff, Pan Ocean, is now seeking to recover from Creditcorp in restitution, despite the fact ... that there is nothing in the assignment which even contemplates, still less imposes, any additional obligation on the assignee (Creditcorp) to repay. This is the point which, as I understand it,

4   Above, p 348.
5   [1994] 1 WLR 161, 166.

concerned Neill LJ in the Court of Appeal when he said that "Creditcorp were in a position analogous to that of a bona fide purchaser for value."[6]

To have allowed restitution would have been analogous to allowing restitution to the sub-contracting joiner against the house-owner in the hypothetical example set out above. Just as restitution for the joiner should normally be denied, because it would undermine the valid contract between the owner and the head-contractor, so in *The Trident Beauty* the true justification for denying restitution was that this would undermine the valid contract of assignment.

(c) Party in breach seeking restitution of money paid

(i) The position in principle

To be consistent with the position of the innocent party, a contract breaker ought to be entitled to restitution of money paid (in an action for money had and received) for at least total failure of consideration under a contract discharged by the innocent party.

Of course, on this side of the line one can counter-argue that, as the contract breaker has himself been responsible for the failure of consideration, he has debarred himself from claiming that the enrichment is unjust. Put another way, one can counter-argue that, while failure of consideration is normally an unjust factor, it is not so here because it is self-induced. But the wrongfulness of the defendant's breach is adequately dealt with by the innocent party's right to damages by which he is entitled to be put into as good a position as if the contract had been performed. The crucial effect of denying restitution may be to leave the innocent party in a far better position than if the contract had been performed: ie, with a windfall. Restitution should therefore be permitted for the contract breaker provided one recognises the innocent party's right to set off damages for breach.

One should also recognise the innocent party's entitlement to contract out of restitution. Analogous to the right to insert a liquidated damages clause, the parties should be free to insert contractual terms by which they deal with the restitutionary consequences if the contract is not performed. This can be regarded as a further example, alongside the need for the contract to be ineffective, of restitution rightly giving way to contract. In theory contracting out of restitution should be possible whatever the restitutionary context or claim but, in practice, it is in respect of a claim by a contract breaker for money paid that contracting out – through forfeiture clauses – is most prevalent. This is not to deny that, in a somewhat similar way to the control of penalty

6   Ibid, citing [1993] 1 Lloyd's Rep 443, 449.

clauses, equitable principles *of contract law* may grant relief against forfeiture by striking out penal forfeiture clauses or giving the contract breaker extra time to perform.[7] However, equitable relief against forfeiture does not enable the contract breaker to recover money paid unless, having escaped the forfeiture clause, he can go on to establish a normal restitutionary ground, such as failure of consideration. Indeed, if it were otherwise, a contract breaker would be treated more favourably vis-à-vis restitution than an innocent party.

Birks' analysis of restitution to the party in breach avoids talking of contracting out of restitution. On his view, if the payment is construed as a valid sanction against the payor's withdrawal, the consideration does not fail.[8] There is therefore no restitutionary cause of action.

Birks' analysis ought to produce the same result as the 'contracting out' view. The debate seems analogous to the well-known dispute as to whether an exclusion clause is better regarded as qualifying the primary obligation under the contract or as a defence once a breach has been established.[9] The latter view is now largely accepted as being the more straightforward and it is for the same reason that the similar 'contracting out of restitution' view of forfeiture clauses is preferred here.

(ii) The case law

A leading case allowing a contract breaker restitution of money paid is *Dies v British and International Mining and Finance Corpn*.[10] The claimant purchaser had contracted to buy rifles and ammunition for £270,000. Having paid £100,000 to the defendant vendor he failed to take delivery of any of the rifles and sought restitution of

---

7   The most discussed case on forfeiture of money paid is *Stockloser v Johnson* [1954] 1 QB 476: see also *Galbraith v Mitchenhall Estates Ltd* [1965] 2 QB 473; *Workers Trust and Merchant Bank Ltd v Dojap Investments Ltd* [1993] AC 573. In most other cases the question of relief against forfeiture has arisen outside the restitutionary context: eg as to whether to relieve against a clause permitting termination of a contract granting proprietary or possessory rights; see, eg, *The Scaptrade* [1983] 2 AC 694; *Sport International Bussum BV v Inter-Footwear Ltd* [1984] 1 WLR 776; *BICC plc v Burndy Corpn* [1985] Ch 232; *On Demand Information plc v Michael Ferson (Finance) plc* [2002] UKHL 13, [2002] 2 WLR 919. See generally Goff and Jones, paras 20-041 to 20-046, Treitel (10th edn, 1999), pp 937–973. L Smith, 'Relief against Forfeiture: a Restatement' [2001] CLJ 178. Birks, pp 213–216, 236 argues that relief against forfeiture is itself restitutionary triggered by the unjust factor of inequality or a miscellaneous policy ground. The preferable view is that the restitutionary cause of action is total failure of consideration and that relief against forfeiture is simply a contractual doctrine concerned with knocking out contractual terms. See above, p 269, n 20. See similarly above, p 59, n 11.
8   Birks, at pp 235–238.
9   *Cheshire, Fifoot and Furmston's Law of Contract* (14th edn, 2001), p 172.
10 [1939] 1 KB 724. Restitution was also awarded to a contract breaker in, eg, *Palmer v Temple* (1839) 9 Ad & El 508; *Mayson v Clouet* [1924] AC 980 (as regards the instalments); *McDonald v Dennys Lascelles Ltd* (1933) 48 CLR 457.

the part payment. He succeeded. Unfortunately Stable J's reasoning failed to pinpoint the reason for restitution and specifically rejected failure of consideration as the ground. 'In my judgment, the real foundation of the right which I hold exists in the present case is not a total failure of consideration but the right of the purchaser, derived from the terms of the contract and the principle of law applicable, to recover back his money.'[11] To regard the right to restitution as somehow implicit in the contract is to adopt the out-dated and fictional 'implied contract' analysis. The better view is that restitution was based on a total failure of consideration. The claimant had received no guns and the defendant had elected to terminate the contract for that breach. Stable J's express rejection of failure of consideration reasoning is perhaps explicable by the fact that *Dies* was decided before the House of Lords in *Fibrosa*[12] had clarified that total failure of consideration is not dependent on the contract being rescinded *ab initio*. In other words, Stable J was following the *Chandler v Webster*[13] heresy, as he was bound to do.

The approach through total failure of consideration is supported by the Court of Appeal's decision, on Proper's claim, in *Rover International Ltd v Cannon Film Sales Ltd (No 3)*.[14] For a fee of £1,000,000 payable in three instalments Proper had been granted a licence by Cannon to show various films on Italian television. After paying the first two instalments Proper refused to pay the third and, as a consequence, Cannon elected to terminate the contract. It was held that Proper were not bound to pay the remaining instalment because, had they already paid it, they would have been entitled to restitution of it for total failure of consideration. Kerr LJ said that the question at issue was whether Cannon had 'provided any consideration under the contract for which the instalment of US $900,000 was payable, or was this instalment payable merely as an advance for the obligation which [Cannon] had agreed to perform thereafter'.[15] And in Dillon LJ's words, 'The crux, therefore, as I see it on the cases, is whether [at the date of termination] the Proper agreement was wholly executory on the part of Cannon or, to put it another way, whether by that date Proper had received any of the consideration moving from Cannon under the

---

11 Ibid, at p 744. See a similar stress on contract as the basis of the right to restitution in the *McDonald* case, op cit, at p 479 (per Dixon J). Beatson also appears to favour this 'implied contract' approach: 'Discharge for Breach: The Position of Instalments, Deposits and Other Payments Due Before Completion' (1981) LQR 389, 417; cf *The Use and Abuse of Unjust Enrichment* (1991), pp 70–77.

12 [1943] AC 32.

13 [1904] 1 KB 493.

14 [1989] 1 WLR 912. See also *Clough Mill Ltd v Martin* [1985] 1 WLR 111, 117–118.

15 Ibid, at p 932.

Proper agreement.'[16] As the consideration had totally failed – Proper had not received any of the films from Cannon – Proper was held not liable to pay the remaining instalment. Indeed by the same token, it would seem that Proper would have been prima facie entitled to restitution of the first two instalments had they claimed for them.

In reaching this decision the Court of Appeal approved *Dies* and distinguished *Hyundai Heavy Industries Co Ltd v Papadopoulos*[17] on the ground that the facts of *Rover* were more akin to a contract of sale than a continuing building contract. In *Hyundai* the House of Lords had itself distinguished *Dies* on that sort of ground and had held that an instalment payable under a contract for the building and purchase of a ship remained payable (there being no total failure of consideration).

Hyundai has since been applied and approved by the House of Lords in *Stocznia Gdanska SA v Latvian Shipping Co*[18] which concerned very similar facts. It is important for the theme of this section that the House of Lords analysed the purchasing contract-breaker's defence to the shipbuilders' claim for the second instalment in terms of total failure of consideration; and decided that the design and construction work carried out by the shipbuilders meant that there had been no total failure.

Even if there is a total failure of consideration a contract breaker has quite commonly contracted out of his right to restitution by a forfeiture clause or by agreeing to pay a non-refundable deposit. For example, in *Mayson v Clouet*[19] a term of a contract for the sale of land provided that, if the purchasers were in default, they were to forfeit the deposit paid. The purchaser paid a deposit plus two instalments amounting to 10% of the rest of the contract price but then defaulted. The vendor, as he was entitled to do, terminated the contract and resold the land. Although the purchaser had clearly received no part of the consideration, he was able to recover only the two instalments. The terms of the contract had expressly laid down that the deposit (and, as held by the Privy Council, only the deposit) was to be forfeited on default. In the earlier leading case of *Howe v Smith*[20] it was in effect held that the use of the word 'deposit' should be construed as meaning 'non-refundable deposit' (hence countering restitution) in the absence of an express indication to the contrary.

---

16 Ibid, at p 936.
17 [1980] 1 WLR 1129.
18 [1998] 1 WLR 574. See above, pp 328–329.
19 [1924] AC 980.
20 (1884) 27 Ch D 89. For further examples of express forfeiture clauses ruling out restitution see *Mussen v Van Diemen's Land Co* [1938] Ch 253 and *Stockloser v Johnson* [1954] 1 QB 476.

Unfortunately many of the cases on forfeiture clauses, including the above two, have not been as clearly reasoned as one would have hoped in that the courts have taken an implied contract approach whereby the parties' intentions have been relied on to explain not only the denial of restitution but also, fictitiously, the reason *for* restitution.[1] The important point lost has been that, while the parties may sometimes deal in the contract with a forfeiture of money by a contract breaker, it will be very unusual for them to deal with giving restitution to each other. Quite simply, the parties' intentions run out on this issue and one needs to turn to the imposed obligations of unjust enrichment based on failure of consideration to find the true explanation for restitution.

(d) Party in breach seeking restitution for benefits in kind[2]

Symmetry with restitutionary claims by the innocent party, and with the preferred approach to a contract breaker's claim for the restitution of money, requires the following: that, provided the innocent party has terminated the contract, the contract breaker should be entitled to restitution where there has been a partial or total failure of consideration and where it can establish that the innocent party has been benefited.

In practice, however, the contract breaker has been denied a restitutionary remedy whether a *quantum meruit* for the value of services rendered or a *quantum valebat* for the value of goods supplied. This is shown by the leading Court of Appeal decisions of *Sumpter v Hedges*[3] and *Bolton v Mahadeva*.[4] In the former the claimant had contracted with the defendant to build two homes and stables on the defendant's land. The claimant did a good deal of the building work but later became insolvent and was unable to continue. His claim for a *quantum meruit* for the work done was denied.[5] In the latter, Bolton agreed to install a heating system in Mahadeva's home for £560. He broke the contract by installing a system that did not heat adequately and gave out fumes. Although he was requested to remedy the defects he did

1   See analogously above, p 352.
2   See generally Waddams, 'Restitution for the Part Performer' *Studies in Contract Law* (ed Reiter and Swan, 1980), pp 151–179; McFarlane and Stevens, 'In Defence of *Sumpter v Hedges*' (2002) 118 LQR 569.
3   [1898] 1 QB 673.
4   [1972] 1 WLR 1009. See also *Boston Deep Sea Fishing and Ice Co v Ansell* (1888) 39 Ch D 339.
5   At first instance he was given judgment for the value of the materials left behind and used by the owner to complete the buildings. The most straightforward view is that that constituted compensatory damages for the tort of conversion. Cf Goff and Jones, para 20-051 and Birks, p 239 who regard this as an example of free acceptance and hence as an exception to no restitution.

not do so. The cost of putting the system into satisfactory working order was £174.50. It was held that Bolton was not entitled to the contract price nor any part of it.

In each of these cases the innocent party was presumptively benefited by receiving part – and a considerable part – of what he had bargained for. The consequence of denying restitution was that he ended up paying significantly less for the buildings and heating system respectively than he had contracted for. That windfall, combined with the fact that the contract breaker was obviously only carrying out the work on the basis of the innocent party's promised payment (so that there was a failure of consideration), constituted an unjust enrichment of the innocent party at the contract breaker's expense. Prima facie, therefore, the contract breaker should have been granted restitution, subject to the innocent party's right to set off damages for the breach.

What are the arguments in favour of the present law's denial of restitution?

First, it may be argued that breach cancels out the injustice of the innocent party's enrichment: that, in other words, self-induced failure of consideration should not count as an unjust factor. But, as has been suggested above, the contract breaker's wrongdoing is adequately dealt with by his liability to pay damages and should not bar an unjust enrichment claim. To deny restitution in order to punish the contract breaker seems out of place in a system which rejects exemplary damages for breach of contract.

Secondly, one might argue that in entire contracts, like those in *Sumpter* and *Bolton* – or, analogously, where the claimant has performed only part of an entire stage of a severable contract – the defendant can only be said to have been benefited where he has received the full performance (or 'substantial performance')[6] that he bargained for. The defendant did not promise to pay for partly completed buildings or a heating system that did not work properly. This argument turns on one's approach to benefit. Throughout this book the view has been taken that, once the defendant has received part of what he bargained for, he can be presumed to have been benefited. The presumption can, of course, be rebutted. For example, if at the time of the dispute it was as expensive to complete the building as the original full contract price, the defendant would not have been benefited. He would have been saved no expense. Similarly if the defendant says that the half building is of no use to him and does not in fact go on to make use of it (eg, he may destroy it) the presumption

6   See *Hoenig v Isaacs* [1952] 2 All ER 176.

of benefit could be rebutted. On the facts of the two leading cases there were no such extraordinary facts. In *Sumpter* the owner went on to complete the buildings and there was no suggestion that the owner would not rectify and use the heating system in *Bolton*. It is submitted therefore that it flies in the face of common sense to deny the enrichment in those cases. Furthermore it would be inconsistent with the innocent party's right to a restitutionary *quantum meruit* against the contract breaker to deny that part performance of an entire contract can be beneficial to the payor.[7]

Thirdly, it may be thought that an entire contract (or obligation) is the equivalent of a forfeiture clause. By saying that the builder in *Sumpter* would only be paid on completion the parties were deciding that, in the event of the builder's breach, work done would be forfeited. In short, an entire contract constitutes a contracting-out of restitution.[8] But this is surely to exaggerate the position. While it may be true that sometimes that is the best interpretation of what was meant by the contract, in many and probably most entire contracts the parties have not thought about the restitutionary consequences for the part performer. A contract may be entire, not because the parties intend the payor to get something for nothing in the event of non-completion of the work, but because, for example, the payor fears that he will be unable to recover an advance payment in the event of bankruptcy or abandonment of the job by the other party or simply because his financial circumstances make it more convenient for him to pay at the end. The correct approach, therefore, is prima facie to allow restitution to the part performer while recognising that, where on its true construction, an entire contract does constitute contracting-out of restitution by the parties, the will of the parties (subject, possibly to equitable rules relieving against the forfeiture) should override restitution.

Fourthly, one can argue that to allow restitution to the part performing contract breaker would encourage breach. It has been said, for example, that this would remove the one self-help 'lever' a householder has against a builder to compel complete performance.[9] This again underplays (or ignores) the contract breaker's liability to

---

7   Contra is Birks, pp 126–127, 229–234, 238–242, who argues that what is generally the only relevant test of benefit for part performance – 'limited acceptance' – is valid against a contract breaker but not against an innocent party. See also Tettenborn, *The Law of Restitution in England and Ireland* (3rd edn, 2002), pp 144–145. For Birks' later views see *Essays on the Law of Restitution* (ed Burrows, 1991), pp 105, 139–140.

8   This lies at the heart of the suggested rejection of restitution in this context by McFarlane and Stevens, 'In Defence of *Sumpter v Hedges*' (2002) 118 LQR 569, esp 577.

9   This was the thrust of Brian Davenport's dissent from the Law Commission's Report No 121 (1983).

pay damages and the payor's self-help right to set off those damages against the restitutionary claim. They should act as a sufficient sanction against breach.

A final possible argument is that the denial of restitution is justified because it makes up for inadequacies in the assessment of expectation (and reliance) damages. It may be said that the theoretical aim of putting the claimant into as good a position as if the contract had been performed is not achieved because, for example, the courts have traditionally been reluctant to award contractual damages for mental distress and the assessment of such non-pecuniary loss is, in any event, non-scientific. Legal costs are also irrecoverable as damages. Allowing the innocent party to keep the contract breaker's work without paying for it is a rough-and-ready way of making up for the shortfall left by compensatory damages. However, even if one were to accept that the law on contractual damages is defective, the answer in principle is to reform it directly and openly. Only pragmatism in an extreme and untenable form could allow an unrelated measure of restitution to act as a surrogate for compensation.

The conclusion is that the case against restitution for the part performing contract breaker is not sufficiently strong to outweigh the argument of principle for it.

A further argument in favour of reform is that, in addition to *contractual* doctrines that counteract the harshness of denying restitution,[10] there are dicta of the House of Lords in two cases, in completely separate fields, supporting restitution for the contract breaker.

In *Hain Steamship Co Ltd v Tate and Lyle Ltd*,[11] the question was discussed whether a shipowner who deviates – thereby committing a repudiatory breach of contract – but delivers goods to the cargo owner at the agreed port of discharge is entitled to a *quantum meruit*. The question was posited on the assumption that the contractual entitlement to freight had been lost because the cargo owner had terminated the contract for the breach.[12] On the facts the discussion was obiter dicta because all the parties had intended that the charterers, and not the cargo owners, were to pay the freight. Nevertheless, while leaving the matter open, Lords Wright and Maugham indicated that,

---

10 Eg, 'substantial performance'; Sale of Goods Act 1979, s 30(1); and, on the face of it, the Apportionment Act 1870 (although in *Moriarty v Regent's Garage Co Ltd* [1921] 1 KB 423 Lush J, at 434–435, denied that this Act could assist a contract breaking employee; cf McCardie J at 449). These examples are best viewed as contractual and not restitutionary in that, while the sum awarded may be consistent with either an expectation or restitutionary measure, there is no requirement that the contract has been terminated.

11 [1936] 2 All ER 597.

12 This is only made absolutely clear by Lord Maugham, ibid, at p 616.

at least in certain circumstances, the cargo owner would be liable to pay a *quantum meruit* and the views of the Court of Appeal to the contrary were doubted. Lord Wright said:

> 'Let me put a quite possible case: a steamer carrying a cargo of frozen meat from Australia to England deviates by calling at a port outside the usual or permitted route: it is only the matter of a few hours extra steaming: no trouble ensues except the trifling delay. The cargo is duly delivered in England at the agreed port. The goods' owner has had for all practical purposes the benefit of all that his contract required; he has had the advantages of the use of a valuable ship, her crew, fuel, refrigeration and appliances, canal dues, port charges, stevedoring ... [I cannot] help feeling that the court would not be slow to infer an obligation when the goods are received at destination to pay, not indeed the contract freight, but a reasonable remuneration.'[13]

In *Miles v Wakefield Metropolitan District Council*[14] the claimant, a registrar of births, deaths, and marriages, as part of industrial action, refused in breach of contract to conduct marriage ceremonies on Saturday mornings. It was held that, without terminating his contract of employment, his employer was entitled to deduct 3/37ths of his salary. Lords Templeman and Brightman went on to consider what the position would be, if, rather than a refusal to perform particular duties, the industrial action took the form of a 'go slow'. They thought that, while the employee would not be entitled to any wages, he would be entitled to a *quantum meruit* for the value of the reduced work. Unfortunately the strength of those dicta is weakened because it was not made clear that a restitutionary analysis could only come into play once the employer had elected to terminate the contract.[15] Until then the contract should govern. Furthermore Lord Bridge doubted whether a *quantum meruit* could be awarded although it would appear that his doubts were based purely on a contractual and not a restitutionary analysis of the *quantum meruit*.

Finally, the case for reform is strengthened by the fact that it has received the backing of the Law Commission. In its Report on 'Pecuniary Restitution on Breach of Contract'[16] the Commission

13   [1936] 2 All ER 597, 612.
14   [1987] AC 539. In *Wiluszynski v Tower Hamlets London Borough Council* [1989] IRLR 259 an employee was held disentitled to any wages by refusing to perform part of his contractual duties. Restitution was not discussed and rightly not because (i) the contract had not been terminated and (ii) the employers had made clear that they would not pay for any of the work (ie on the facts the presumption of benefit, raised by bargaining for the work, was rebutted). As a matter of contractual principle, the Court of Appeal's reasoning is confused and confusing; see Mead, 'Employer's Right to Withhold Wages' (1990) 106 LQR 192, 'Restitution Within Contract?' (1991) 11 Legal Studies 172.
15   Above, p 323, n 1.
16   No 121 (1983).

recommended that a part performer in breach should be entitled to the value to the benefited party of what it has done under the contract, subject to a pro rata contract price ceiling and to the innocent party's right to set off (or counterclaim) damages. The new remedy would not be available if the contract was 'on foot' or the parties had contracted out of it. The reason put forward for the pro rata contract price ceiling was that otherwise a party in breach might be better off by breach than by full performance. In practice, however, the same result would, in any event, be achieved by applying pure restitutionary principles for valuing benefits (which may, or may not, reflect the contract price)[17] because the innocent party's right to set off damages would ensure that the contract breaker ends up no better off by breach.

Although this aspect of the report was unique in not commanding the unanimous support of the Law Commissioners (Brian Davenport QC dissented), it is unfortunate that Lord Hailsham – the then Lord Chancellor – chose not to take it further. Restitutionary principle demands reform and, subject to some minor criticisms,[18] the Law Commission's detailed proposals and draft bill represent an acceptable way forward.

(2) Contracts discharged by frustration

(a) The defects of the common law

The Law Reform (Frustrated Contracts) Act 1943, which governs restitution following discharge for frustration, is the most important statute in the law of restitution. To understand fully the effect of its provisions, it is helpful to look first at the position prior to the Act. In any event the common law continues to apply in the areas excluded from the Act.[19]

The common law of restitution suffered from three defects, two of which have already been encountered in relation to contracts discharged for breach. First, restitution of money was possible only if there had been a total failure of consideration. Restitution of an advance payment was therefore allowed in *Fibrosa Spolka Akcyjna v Fairbairn Lawson Combe*

---

17 Above, pp 346–347.
18 For detailed consideration of the proposals, see Burrows 'Law Commission Report on Pecuniary Restitution on Breach of Contract' (1984) 47 MLR 76, 79–83. Note that the Law Commission proposed to allow restitution from *the other contracting party* for benefits conferred on an intended third party. This is criticised in the aforementioned article at p 81. Restitution from the third party would be more in line with principle. Cf above, pp 347–350.
19 By s 2(5), the Act does not apply to contracts for the carriage of goods by sea, many charterparties, contracts of insurance, and contracts for the sale of goods where the goods have perished. It is difficult to justify those exclusions.

Barbour Ltd[20] where the purchasers had received none of the contracted-for machinery. In contrast in *Whincup v Hughes*,[1] where a claimant had paid to have his son apprenticed to a watchmaker for six years and the watchmaker had died after one year, restitution of the 'premium' paid was denied because the consideration had only partially failed.

Secondly, a *quantum meruit* for work done was generally denied. The classic case is *Cutter v Powell*.[2] Cutter, who was a member of the crew on a voyage from Jamaica to Liverpool, was to be paid on arrival in Liverpool but died when the voyage was nearly complete. His administratrix failed in her claim for a *quantum meruit* for the services he had rendered before his death. This was followed in *Appleby v Myers*[3] where the claimant had contracted to erect certain machinery on the defendant's premises. The price was to be paid upon completion of the whole. After some, but not substantially all, of the work had been finished the premises with all the machinery and materials were destroyed by an accidental fire which frustrated the contract. The claimant was denied a *quantum meruit* and a contrast was drawn with the *quantum meruit* available to an innocent party where a contract has been discharged for breach. Blackburn J said, 'We think that where, as in the present case, the premises are destroyed without fault on either side, it is a misfortune equally affecting both parties: excusing both parties from further performance of the contract, but giving a cause of action to neither.'[4]

One exceptional case, allowing a *quantum meruit*, was *Société Franco Tunisienne D'Armement v Sidermar Spa, The Massalia*,[5] in which a charterparty had been frustrated by the blocking of the Suez Canal. The cargo had nonetheless been delivered by the claimant shipowners, albeit by a different route, to the agreed port of discharge. It was held that the charterers were bound to pay a *quantum meruit* even though this could not be based on the intention of the parties. In support of this, Pearson J relied on the dicta of Lords Wright and Maugham in the *Hain Steamship Co Ltd* case which, as we have seen,[6] examined the same essential facts but from a contract breaker's perspective; and on *Craven-Ellis v Canons Ltd*[7] where the contract was void for want of authority.

On the unjust enrichment principle the unjust factor in play in frustration cases is failure of consideration. The defendant has not

---

20   [1943] AC 32.
1   (1871) LR 6 CP 78.
2   (1795) 6 Term Rep 320.
3   (1867) LR 2 CP 651.
4   Ibid, at p 659.
5   [1961] 2 QB 278.
6   Above, pp 357–358.
7   [1936] 2 KB 403. Below, pp 390–391.

substantially performed his promise to the claimant which was the basis upon which the claimant transferred a benefit to the defendant. There should be no necessity for the failure to be total: hence the objection to *Whincup v Hughes.* 'At the expense of the claimant' causes no difficulty: as the contract has been discharged for frustration, not breach, it is clear that one can only be concerned with subtraction from the claimant and not wrongdoing by the defendant. The benefit question is non-problematic where money has been transferred. Where benefits in kind have been rendered the subjective devaluation objection can be overcome either, exceptionally, because the benefits were incontrovertibly (negatively) beneficial or, more commonly, because, subject to rebuttal, the defendant has received part of what it bargained for. It follows that, unless the parties could be said to have contracted out of restitution for part performance in *Cutter v Powell* and *Appleby v Myers*, both decisions were prima facie (subject to defences) contrary to the principle of reversing unjust enrichment.

A third defect of the common law was that it did not recognise a defence of change of position.[8] If in *Fibrosa* the defendants, consequent on the advance payment, had incurred considerable loss in manufacturing the machinery (on the facts it appears that two machines had been completed but were realisable without loss) that would have afforded them no defence to the claimant's restitutionary action for the return of the advance purchase money paid.

It has been argued that a further defect of the common law – albeit not a defect within the law of restitution – was that there was no method by which losses incurred under the contract (ie reliance expenses) could be apportioned.[9] As again illustrated by *Fibrosa* (and now leaving aside the defence of change of position) the defendants would have had no remedy to recoup loss incurred in manufacturing the machinery. It should be stressed, however, that the case for loss apportionment must be made out and not merely assumed. It does not rest on a principle of unjust enrichment and there is little, if any, precedent for it in any area of the common law.

(b) The Law Reform (Frustrated Contracts) Act 1943

The 1943 Act has largely – but not entirely or perfectly – remedied the defects of the common law. The Act is best examined by dividing between the restitution of money (s 1(2)) and the restitution of benefits in kind (s 1(3)).

---

8 See generally below, chapter 15.
9 Williams, *Law Reform (Frustrated Contracts) Act 1943* at pp 7–10.

(i)   Restitution of money: s 1(2)

Section 1(2) reads:

'All sums paid or payable to any party in pursuance of the contract before the time when the parties were so discharged (in this Act referred to as "the time of discharge") shall, in the case of sums so paid, be recoverable from him as money received by him for the use of the party by whom the sums were paid, and, in the case of sums so payable, cease to be so payable: provided that, if the party to whom the sums were so paid or payable incurred expenses before the time of discharge in, or for the purpose of the performance of the contract, the court may, if it considers it just to do so, having regard to all the circumstances of the case, allow him to retain or, as the case may be, recover the whole or any part of the sums so paid or payable, not being an amount in excess of the expenses so incurred.'

The crucial importance of the main part of this is that there is no requirement that money can only be recovered where the failure of consideration is total. On the contrary, it recognises that money can also be recovered for partial failure of consideration. *Whincup v Hughes*[10] is therefore no longer good law. This is an enlightened move forward and a lead which the common law ought to follow outside the realm of frustration.

As at common law under *Fibrosa* – and in line with the position of an innocent party seeking restitution of money paid under a contract discharged for breach[11] – the payor can recover his money under s 1(2) even though this enables him to escape from a bad bargain. The independent cause of action in unjust enrichment by subtraction should not be, and is not, restricted by the claimant's expectation interest. In Robert Goff J's words, at first instance, in *BP Exploration Co (Libya) Ltd v Hunt (No 2)*:[12]

'An award under the Act may have the effect of rescuing the plaintiff from an unprofitable bargain. This may certainly be true under s 1(2), if the plaintiff has paid the price in advance for an expected return which, if furnished, would have proved unprofitable; if the contract is frustrated before any part of that expected return is received, and before any expenditure is incurred by the defendant, the plaintiff is entitled to the return of the price he has paid, irrespective of the consideration he would have recovered had the contract been performed.'

Much more problematic is the proviso in s 1(2). What is its aim?

In *BP Exploration Co (Libya) Ltd v Hunt (No 2)* Robert Goff J, in obiter dicta, thought that it was 'probably best rationalised as a statutory

10   (1871) LR 6 CP 78.
11   Above, pp 341–343.
12   [1979] 1 WLR 783, 800.

recognition of the defence of change of position'.[13] On that interpretation, s 1(2) is wholly concerned with the law of restitution and has not introduced any novel scheme of loss apportionment.

Certainly the proviso enables the courts to recognise a limited change of position defence: limited in the sense that the detriment in question must comprise expenses incurred 'in, or for the purpose of, the performance of the contract'. A defendant who, believing the money to be his, buys a holiday, which he would otherwise not have done, would be covered by a true defence of change of position but is outside the proviso to s 1(2). However, one might have thought that a problem with regarding the proviso as purely concerned with a change of position defence is that it does not require the expenses to have been incurred subsequent to the receipt of a benefit. Indeed by reason of the phrase 'for the purpose of the performance' even pre-contractual expenses are included within the ambit of s 1(2). But although there has been doubt about this, the preferable view is that a change of position counts even though it is anticipatory provided there is a causal link between the change of position and the benefit.[14] And that necessary causal link would seem to be inherent in s 1(2) given its insistence that the expenses must be incurred for the purpose of the performance of the contract (which will, of course, be the same contract under which the payment has been made for which restitution is sought).

On the other hand, an apparently insurmountable difficulty for the 'change of position interpretation' of the proviso is that the defendant's expenses can be recovered even though no money was ever paid by the claimant, so long as the money was payable before the time of discharge. This situation cannot be one of change of position (ie a defence to restitution) because the defendant has not received any benefit against which the loss can be off-set.

Hence, although the courts are given an overall discretion to do what is just within the powers entrusted to them, it seems that the proviso to s 1(2) is intended to go beyond a limited change of position defence and to encompass loss apportionment.

This is supported by the only English case which has had to apply the proviso, *Gamerco SA v ICM/Fair Warning (Agency) Ltd.*[15] A contract for a rock concert in Spain to be given by the defendants, the Guns N' Roses, was held to be frustrated when the stadium, where the concert was to be held, was declared unsafe a few days before the concert. The claimants had paid the defendants $412,500 and owed them a

13 Ibid, at p 800.
14 See below, pp 517–519.
15 [1995] 1 WLR 1226.

further $362,500 at the date of the frustration. Both the claimants and defendants had incurred expenses prior to the frustration in preparation for the concert. These expenses were found to be $450,000 by the claimants and $50,000 by the defendants. Garland J held that the claimants were entitled to restitution of the $412,500 under s 1(2) of the 1943 Act and that there should be no deduction for the defendants' expenses under the proviso.

In looking at the purpose of s 1(2) Garland J implicitly rejected the change of position interpretation. He said that he derived no specific assistance from the obiter dicta of Robert Goff J in *BP Exploration v Hunt*; and on the facts he said that there was 'no question of any change of position as a result of the plaintiff's advance payment'.[16] Having also rejected the view that he should seek equal division of all losses, Garland J went on to favour the view that the proviso simply conferred a broad discretion to do what was just. His decision that there should be no deduction for the defendants' expenses in fact meant that the claimants were left to bear $37,500 wasted expenses and the defendants $50,000. He further stressed that the burden of proof in relation to the proviso lay with the defendants.

In rejecting the change of position interpretation, Garland J was in effect accepting that, within its conferral of a broad discretion to achieve justice, the proviso to s 1(2) encompasses loss apportionment. But while this seems correct, it should be realised that the scope for loss apportionment is severely restricted. Most significantly, the proviso only bites if money was paid or payable before the time of discharge to the party who has incurred expenses: receipt of an advance payment, or an entitlement to be paid in advance, is a necessary pre-condition for the recovery of expenses under s 1(2). For example, the proviso would only have applied to the facts of *Fibrosa*, empowering the courts to compensate the manufacturers' reliance expenses, because the purchasers were bound to pay £1,600 in advance (of which £1,000 had been paid). Furthermore, the amount of recoverable expenses is limited by the advance payment paid or payable before the time of discharge. In *Fibrosa* the maximum the manufacturers could have recovered was, therefore, £1,600, even if their expenses 'in, or for the purpose of, the performance of the contract' had exceeded that sum. Haycroft and Waksman regard these limitations as defects of the Act.[17] The fact remains that, as it stands, s 1(2) empowers only limited loss apportionment.

The proviso to s 1(2) therefore empowers the courts both to allow a limited change of position defence and, within limits, to apportion

16 Ibid, at 1236.
17 'Frustration and Restitution' [1984] JBL 207, 217.

reliance expenses. One may criticise this as a muddle. From a purely restitutionary perspective a full-blown defence of change of position would be preferable. The inadequacies of the statutory formulation of the defence are particularly glaring, and ironically backward, now that *Lipkin Gorman v Karpnale Ltd* [18] has recognised the defence at common law. And if one is going to recognise loss apportionment – novel as that may be – there seems no sense in imposing the arbitrary limits embodied in s 1(2).

In several other Commonwealth jurisdictions full loss apportionment schemes have been enacted for frustration. [19] Loss apportionment is supported by McKendrick [20] principally on the ground that, where there are two innocent parties involved in a joint enterprise, and loss is suffered by one of them, and it has not taken the risk of the joint enterprise failing, the just solution would be for the loss to be shared rather than falling entirely on the one party's shoulders. He writes:

'... the frustrating event which has occurred is one which neither party has foreseen and neither party has assumed the risk of its occurrence. Moreover, neither party has been at fault. The expenditure was incurred justifiably in the pursuance of what was at the time a valid and subsisting contract. Justice and reasonableness surely demands that such expenditure be brought into account so that, on the frustration of a contract ... benefits conferred must be paid for (thus protecting the restitution interest) and losses suffered as a result of wasted expenditure be apportioned between the parties (thus taking account of the reliance interest).' [1]

If one were to recognise loss apportionment in the sphere of frustration there would be no good reason for not extending it to other areas where the contract fails without the fault of either party and where it may be difficult to accept that the loss sufferer has taken the risk of its loss: for example, where the contract is void for common mistake, or even where the contract is merely anticipated or void for lack of formality. Moreover, it has to be recognised that loss splitting contradicts the basic individualistic tradition of contract law whereby contracting parties are viewed as pursuing their own self interest and taking their own risk. Unless there is a breach by the other party (or tortious wrongdoing) – and subject to the availability of restitutionary

---

18 [1991] 2 AC 548. The statutory scheme of course supplants the common law. *Lipkin Gorman* cannot therefore be applied to frustrated contracts covered by the Act.
19 British Columbian Frustrated Contracts Act 1974, New South Wales Frustrated Contracts Act 1978, South Australian Frustrated Contracts Act 1988.
20 'Frustration, Restitution and Loss Apportionment' in *Essays on the Law of Restitution* (ed Burrows, 1991), pp 147–170. See also, eg, Maddaugh and McCamus, *The Law of Restitution* (1st edn, 1990), p 408.
1 Ibid, at pp 168–169.

relief – a party is traditionally regarded as taking the risk of loss in preparing for and performing a contract. Another problem is the uncertainty that loss apportionment brings. Although frustration may require that the event is not the fault of either party this is not to say that one party may not share more of the blame for the reliance loss than the other. A true loss apportionment approach would seek to weigh the relative fault of the parties. The complexities and uncertainties of this are obvious.

It may be argued, therefore, that the case for loss apportionment is as yet unproven and that restitution achieves sufficient justice following frustration.[2] Even if one favours loss apportionment it seems only sensible to go through the restitutionary analysis (including change of position) first. This will enable one to isolate clearly the losses which a loss apportionment scheme alone would reallocate. In other words, it is a sensible discipline to clarify where the firm land of restitution runs out and the shifting sands of loss apportionment begin.

By s 2(3) of the 1943 Act the parties may contract out of the statutory scheme. Just as an innocent party can, and commonly does, contract out of its liability to make restitution to a contract breaker for failure of consideration, so the contracting parties can contract out of restitution following frustration. In *BP Exploration Co (Libya) Ltd v Hunt (No 2)*,[3] the facts of which are set out below, the primary ground of appeal to the House of Lords was that by reason of clause 6 of the contract (which stated, inter alia, that 'Hunt shall have no personal liability to repay the sums required') s 2(3) applied to rule out any award under s 1(2) and s 1(3). In an approach reminiscent of the courts' traditional reluctance to construe contractual terms as ousting the doctrine of frustration in the first place,[4] the House of Lords (upholding the decisions of Robert Goff J and the Court of Appeal) held that the clause was not intended to deal with expropriation, as had occurred, but with the different risk that no oil might be found.

(ii) Restitution of benefits in kind: s 1(3)

By s 1(3):

> 'Where any party to the contract has, by reason of anything done by any other party thereto in, or for the purpose of, the performance of the contract, obtained a valuable benefit (other than a payment of money to which the last foregoing subsection applies) before the time of discharge, there shall be recoverable

2   This is strongly supported by Stewart and Carter, 'Frustrated Contracts and Statutory Adjustment: The Case for a Reappraisal' (1992) 51 CLJ 66.
3   [1983] 2 AC 352.
4   As in, eg, *Jackson v Union Marine Insurance Co Ltd* (1874) LR 10 CP 125 and *Metropolitan Water Board v Dick Kerr & Co* [1918] AC 119.

from him by the said other party such sum (if any), not exceeding the value of the said benefit to the party obtaining it, as the court considers just, having regard to all the circumstances of the case and, in particular – (a) the amount of any expenses incurred before the time of discharge by the benefited party in, or for the purpose of, the performance of the contract, including any sums paid or payable by him to any other party in pursuance of the contract and retained or recoverable by that party under the last foregoing subsection, and (b) the effect, in relation to the said benefit, of the circumstances giving rise to the frustration of the contract.'

As ever, the argument of subjective devaluation means that restitution for non-money benefits is more problematic than the restitution of money. In Robert Goff J's words in *BP Exploration Co (Libya) Ltd v Hunt (No 2)*:[5]

'By their nature services cannot be restored; nor in many cases can goods be restored, for example where they have been consumed or transferred to another. Furthermore the identity and value of the resulting benefit to the recipient may be debatable. From the very nature of things, therefore, the problem of restitution in respect of such benefits is more complex than in cases where the benefit takes the form of a money payment.'

The legislature's approach to this problem through s 1(3) has been criticised, most notably by Robert Goff J in *BP v Hunt*.[6] With respect, s 1(3) can be straightforwardly interpreted as being consistent with s 1(2) and, subject to not allowing a full defence of change of position, as resting on true restitutionary principle, while also empowering some loss apportionment.

The key words in the first part of s 1(3) are 'obtained a valuable benefit'. This corresponds to the 'receipt of money' in s 1(2). Apart from rightly dictating that the defendant must have obtained or received the services or goods before it can be said to have been benefited, the subsection leaves it to the courts to decide how the problem of subjective devaluation should be overcome. It is therefore open to the courts to adopt the 'incontrovertible benefit' and 'bargained-for' tests of benefit advocated in this book. It is also open to them to adopt the argument that, while there is no objection to an innocent party (which includes both parties under a contract discharged for frustration) escaping from a bad bargain by claiming in restitution, the pro rata contract price will normally be a ceiling because, under the 'bargained-for' test, the defendant is only benefited at the contract rate. And while the unjust factor is not spelt

5   [1979] 1 WLR 783, 799.
6   See also McKendrick, 'Frustration, Restitution and Loss Apportionment' in *Essays on the Law of Restitution* (ed Burrows, 1991), pp 147, 159–165.

out in s 1(3), any more than in s 1(2), it can again be said to be (partial) failure of consideration.

Section 1(3)(a) then corresponds to the proviso to s 1(2). That is, by its very similar wording, it empowers the courts to allow a limited defence of change of position (limited for the reasons explained in the last subsection) and, within limits (as also explained above), to apportion reliance expenses.

The only significant difference from the scheme of s 1(2) is s 1(3)(b) which deals with the problem, not encountered in relation to money, of the frustrating event affecting the non-money benefit. A restitutionary interpretation is that it empowers the courts to apply a change of position defence not only to reliance expenses but also to where a benefit is lost by reason of the frustration. The classic example is of a building under construction being destroyed by fire. In accordance with restitutionary principle, the builder should prima facie be entitled to restitution from the owner because once the building has been started the owner has received part of what it bargained for and is therefore (presumptively) benefited. The main part of s 1(3) empowers the courts to adhere to this restitutionary principle because it focuses on the obtaining of the benefit 'before the time of discharge'. However, on a wide view of the defence,[7] the subsequent burning down of the building would constitute a change of position by the owner so that, within a purely restitutionary regime, at the defence stage, application of s 1(3)(b) ought to result in a refusal of a remedy.[8] Alternatively one may consider that, as with s 1(2) and s 1(3)(a), the discretion conferred under s 1(3)(b) should be interpreted as also allowing loss apportionment.[9]

However, the above interpretation was not taken by Robert Goff J in *BP v Hunt*. Mr Hunt was the owner of an oil concession granted by the Libyan government. As he did not have the resources to exploit the concession himself he entered into a joint venture with BP. Under the terms of the contract BP was to carry out the exploration for, and extraction of, oil and was to pay Hunt money and oil (called 'farm-in' contributions). In return Hunt granted BP one half of his concession and, if an oil field were found, agreed to repay 125% of BP's farm-in contributions and half the exploration and extraction costs. Payment was to be by transferring three-eighths of his half share of the oil extracted until such a time as the agreed repayment had been made. The thinking behind the contract, therefore, was that BP should bear

---

7   See below, chapter 15.
8   If the owner were insured against fire it would suffer no loss and hence no change of position. But by s 1(5) insurance is usually to be ignored.
9   This is supported by Treitel (10th edn, 1999), pp 853–854.

the risk of there being no oil but that, if an oilfield were found, BP was to be generously remunerated from the oil. In the event, a giant oilfield was found and the field came on stream in 1967. In 1971 the contract was frustrated when the Libyan government expropriated BP's half share in the concession. Later, in 1973, Hunt's interest was also taken over. BP claimed the award of a just sum under s 1(3).

Robert Goff J's approach to s 1(3) (which was upheld on appeal albeit that the Court of Appeal said that it found no help from the concept of unjust enrichment given that that wording was not used in the Act)[10] can be summarised in the following points:

(i) There are three distinct stages to the inquiry under s 1(3): identification of the defendant's benefit, valuing the benefit, and assessment of the just sum.

(ii) Although he thought it 'contrary to principle and capable of producing injustice',[11] Robert Goff J considered that the wording of s 1(3) dictates that 'in an appropriate case'[12] (ie, where there is a valuable end product) the defendant's benefit should be identified as the end product of services rather than the services themselves. The valuable benefit Hunt obtained was therefore the enhancement in the value of his concession, not the work carried out by BP in exploring for, and extracting, the oil.[13]

(iii) Consequently in valuing the benefit one is generally concerned to value the end product and not the services, even though a small service may create an enormously valuable end product and a large service may create a worthless end product.

(iv) Section 1(3)(b) is relevant at the 'identification of the benefit' stage. Where the frustrating event destroys the end product, and hence the benefit (for example, a building is destroyed by fire), there can be no award at all under s 1(3).[14] *Appleby v Myers* is therefore still good law. In *BP v Hunt* the frustrating event and its consequences (the expropriation of BP's interests) had greatly reduced the enhancement in value of Hunt's concession. By reason of s 1(3)(b) the 'valuable benefit' obtained was reduced, in broad terms, to half the oil Hunt had obtained from the concession (net of the reimbursement oil 'paid' to BP) plus the benefit of his settlement with the Libyan government.[15]

---

10 [1981] 1 WLR 232, 243, CA; [1983] 2 AC 352, HL.
11 [1979] 1 WLR 783, 834.
12 Ibid, at p 801.
13 Ibid, at pp 816–817.
14 Given his wide approach to the change of position defence (see below, pp 513–514), it is peculiar that Lord Goff did not regard this as an issue of change of position.
15 [1979] 1 WLR 783, 816.

(v) Section 1(3)(a) is a statutory recognition of the defence of 'change of position'.[16] It should be brought into account at the valuation stage: ie the expenses are deductible from the value of the benefit. In *BP v Hunt*, therefore, Hunt's expenses were taken into account in valuing the benefit.[17]

(vi) The benefit should be valued at the date of frustration but the time value of money is not to be taken into account.[18]

(vii) The valuation of the benefit acts as a ceiling to the assessment of the just sum. In assessing the just sum the courts should apply restitutionary principle (reversing unjust enrichment) so that the services themselves, rather than the end product, are valued: ie the courts should go about the task of assessing the just sum in the same way as they would assess a restitutionary *quantum meruit* or *quantum valebat*. Although the Act is silent on the point, the pro rata contract price should probably be a limit on recovery.

(viii) As will commonly be the case, valuing the benefit (at nearly $85 million) in *BP v Hunt* turned out not to be decisive because the just sum (which was the sum awarded, plus interest, under s 1(3)) was assessed at a lower amount (around $35m subject to currency adjustments).

The primary feature of Robert Goff J's interpretation therefore was that the central thrust of s 1(3) is the assessment of the just sum which, in contrast to the rest of the subsection, can and should be interpreted in line with true restitutionary principle. In contrast, and despite its emphasis on the 'obtaining of a valuable benefit', most of the wording of s 1(3) was thought to be contrary to correct restitutionary principle.

This interpretation contrasts sharply with the view tendered above, whereby s 1(3) can be straightforwardly interpreted as consistent with s 1(2) and with true restitutionary principle.

With great respect, it is possible that Robert Goff J took a false step in regarding there as being a crucial difference, so far as restitution is concerned, between the end product of contracted-for services and the services (or performance of the services) themselves.[19] *Even if there is an end product produced by the services the defendant's benefit comprises his saving of expense in paying for the services producing that end product.*[20] And

---

16   Ibid, at p 804.
17   Ibid, at p 821.
18   Ibid, at pp 803–804.
19   For a similar criticism, see Haycroft and Waksman, 'Frustration and Restitution' [1984] JBL 207, 218–219; Dickson, 'An Action for Unjust Enrichment' (1983) 34 NILQ 106, 113–115. Contra, supporting Robert Goff J, is McKendrick, 'Frustration, Restitution and Loss Apportionment' in *Essays on the Law of Restitution* (ed Burrows, 1991), pp 147, 163.
20   Cf above, p 337, n 1.

the crucial line between when services constitute mere reliance loss to the performer and when they become objectively beneficial to the other party (and hence, subject to subjective devaluation, belong within restitution) is, it is submitted, when the other party receives the services.[1] Where the purpose of the services is to produce an end product (eg, building work) it is true that one regards the owner as receiving the services at the time when it receives part of the end product (eg, when the first part of the building is erected). But the same notion of receipt explains why a theatregoer is only objectively benefited when the play begins or why a home owner who engages a gardener to mow the lawn is only objectively benefited when the gardener starts to cut the lawn. On a restitutionary interpretation of s 1(3) the important distinction is therefore between services that are not received and services that are received and not between services and the end product of those services.

Once one excises the distinction between end product and services the acute problems encountered by Robert Goff J in interpreting s 1(3) disappear. For example, there is now no problem of a small service producing very substantial end products and vice versa; there is no need to carve out inconsistent 'exceptions' where there is no end product or an end product of no objective value; there is no reason to confine a true restitutionary analysis to the assessment of the just sum; and, while the same conclusion may be reached by applying 'change of position' reasoning, s 1(3)(b) does not have to be interpreted as meaning that no valuable benefit was obtained where a building under construction is destroyed by fire. Indeed on this last point Treitel's more specific criticisms of Robert Goff J's interpretation of s 1(3)(b) seem irrefutable.[2] His interpretation does contradict the emphasis in s 1(3) on a valuable benefit having been obtained 'before the time of discharge' and also cuts across the natural structure of s 1(3) whereby s 1(3)(b) goes to the exercise of the court's discretion as to what is a just sum to award rather than to the prior non-discretionary question of whether a valuable benefit has been obtained.

There are two final points on s 1(3).

First, for the reasons expressed above vis-à-vis the proviso to s 1(2), Robert Goff J's view that s 1(3)(a) is a statutory recognition of change of position seems too narrow. Section 1(3)(a) (and s 1(3)(b)) empowers in addition, and within limits, loss apportionment. Although the case in principle for loss apportionment may be unproven, the 1943 Act is not concerned solely with the reversal of unjust enrichment.

---

1   Above, pp 16–18.
2   *Law of Contract* (10th edn, 1999), pp 853–854. See also Haycroft and Waksman, 'Frustration and Restitution' [1984] JBL 207, 220–221.

Secondly, the discussion above of s 2(3) of the 1943 Act in the context of s 1(2), applies *mutatis mutandis* to contracting out of s 1(3). It should be noted that the argument made in relation to a contract breaker's claim for a restitutionary *quantum meruit* – that an entire contract should not generally be regarded as a contracting-out of restitution – applies equally in the realm of frustration. As Robert Goff J said in *BP v Hunt*:

> 'In most frustrated contracts under which the claim is made in respect of a benefit other than money, the time for payment will not yet have come; the contract, or a severable part of it, will be "entire" in the old strict sense of that term. I do not, however, consider that such a provision should automatically preclude an award under s 1(3). If it were intended to do so, there would be few awards under s 1(3) and the matter would surely be the subject of an express provision if it was the intention that so fundamental a qualification was to be imposed on the power of the court under this subsection.'[3]

(3) Incomplete or anticipated contracts

The question of what remedies are available for work done by a party leading up to a contract that then falls through is not only of great importance to practitioners but is also of immense theoretical interest.[4] Indeed, and perhaps because all the main cases concern services rather than money paid, this is the major battleground between the restitutionary and 'unjust sacrifice' schools of thought.[5] Within restitution the cases are also central to those who support the concept of 'free acceptance'.[6]

There are three introductory points.

First, as it is not so much the lack of consideration that invalidates contracts in this sphere but rather the lack of certainty or of an intention to create legal relations, one can talk here of a failure of consideration in the traditional sense of a defendant failing to perform his bargained-for promise to the claimant. In so doing it is being accepted that parties carrying on pre-contractual negotiations can often be said to have reached some kind of bargain before a binding contract is struck.[7]

---

3   [1979] 1 WLR 783, 807.
4   For useful discussions see, eg, Jones, 'Claims Arising Out of Anticipated Contracts Which Do Not Materialise' (1980) 18 U W Ont LR 447; Carter, 'Services Rendered Under Ineffective Contracts' [1990] LMCLQ 495–506; McKendrick, 'Work Done in Anticipation of a Contract which does not Materialise' in *Restitution, Past Present and Future* (eds Cornish et al, 1998), pp 163–194; Giliker, 'Uncertain or Anticipated Contracts' in *The Law of Restitution* (eds Hedley and Halliwell, 2002), ch 13.
5   Above, pp 10–11.
6   Below, pp 402–407.
7   If this is thought strained an alternative interpretation is that the promised performance is not a *bargained-for* counter-performance: above, p 326, n 12.

Secondly, the signs are that, in time, and probably through developing promissory estoppel 'as a sword', the contractual requirements of certainty and intention to create legal relations will be watered down so that the realm of contract and protection of the expectation interest will expand to swallow up what are, at present, pre-contractual bargains. If that development were to take place, this subsection would be subsumed within that on contracts discharged for breach. As, according to the analysis adopted here, the pattern of restitution is consistent between the two subsections such a development would create no major upheavals so far as restitution is concerned.

Thirdly, Goff and Jones subdivide into different chapters incomplete and anticipated contracts.[8] The distinction seems so thin that they are better treated together.

It is submitted that, contrary to those advocating an 'unjust sacrifice' interpretation or a restitutionary analysis dependent on free acceptance, the leading cases can be straightforwardly analysed as based on failure of consideration within unjust enrichment by subtraction.[9] The defendant has refused to perform its bargained-for promise (partially or totally) which was the claimant's basis for rendering a benefit to the defendant. The defendant's benefit is most obviously presumptively established where it has received part of what it bargained for (valued at the anticipated contract rate): exceptionally a defendant may have been incontrovertibly benefited. And the defendant's gain is 'at the claimant's expense' in the subtractive sense. The failure of consideration analysis would be equally applicable to where money was paid under an incomplete contract although, in accordance with the traditional view at common law, the courts would probably insist that the failure of consideration be total. Implicit in the restitutionary analysis is an acceptance that the fact that contract law does not impose liability should not rule out the independent cause of action in unjust enrichment by subtraction.

The five leading cases are *Way v Latilla*,[10] *William Lacey (Hounslow) Ltd v Davis*,[11] *British Steel Corpn v Cleveland Bridge and Engineering Co Ltd*[12] and *Countrywide Communications Ltd v ICL Pathway*[13] in each of

---

8 Chapters 23 and 26.
9 Cf the restitutionary analysis of the battle of the forms by McKendrick 'The Battle of the Forms and the Law of Restitution' (1988) OJLS 197.
10 [1937] 3 All ER 759.
11 [1957] 1 WLR 932.
12 [1984] 1 All ER 504.
13 [2000] CLC 324. See also *Lamb v Bunce* (1815) 4 M & S 275; *Paynter v Williams* (1833) 1 Cr & M 810; *Alexander v Vane* (1836) 1 M & W 511 (which are discussed below, pp 405–406): *Marston Construction Co Ltd v Kigass Ltd* (1989) 15 Con LR 116; *Easat Antennas Ltd v Racal Defence Electronics Ltd* (28 March 2000, unreported); *Vedatech Corp v Crystal Decisions (UK) Ltd* [2002] EWHC 818 (Ch).

which restitution was granted; and *Regalian Properties Ltd v London Docklands Development Corporation*[14] in which restitution was refused.

In the first of these, the claimant maintained that his services had been rendered pursuant to a contract by which the defendant had agreed to give him a share in a gold mining concession. This was rejected by the House of Lords on the ground that there had been no concluded agreement as to the amount of the share which the claimant was to receive. But the claimant was granted a *quantum meruit* of £5,000 in respect of the work he had done for the defendant.[15] The House of Lords sought to justify this on the grounds of a second contract of employment between the parties, but Birks and Goff and Jones criticise this as artificial and regard the decision as restitutionary, based on free acceptance.[16] However, even if one does reject the reasoning based on contract as artificial, there is no need to resort to free acceptance to explain restitution. Rather, the unjust factor can be regarded as the (total) failure of consideration in that the claimant did not receive the share in the concession which he had been 'promised' (ie reasonably led to expect) and which was the basis for his work: and the defendant was negatively benefited by receiving the work for which he had bargained.

In *William Lacey (Hounslow) Ltd v Davis* – the most important of the cases – the claimants submitted a tender for building work in relation to premises which had suffered war damage. They were 'promised' (ie reasonably led to believe) by the defendant owner of the land that the contract would be theirs. Subsequently at the defendant's request the claimants submitted detailed and revised estimates of the proposed work (which the defendants were then able to use and did use in making a war damage claim to the War Damages Commission). But then the building contract, which would have included a term reimbursing the claimants, fell through and the defendant sold the land. It was held by Barry J that the claimants were entitled to a restitutionary *quantum meruit* for the work done at the defendant's request. Comparing the instant case with *Craven-Ellis v Canons Ltd*[17] he said:

'I am unable to see any valid distinction between work done which was to be paid for under the terms of a contract erroneously believed to be in existence, and work done which was to be paid for out of the proceeds of a contract which

---

14   [1995] 1 WLR 212.
15   This included 'commission' based on his success in relation to the concession. See similarly *Vedatech Corp v Crystal Decsions (UK) Ltd* [2002] EWHC 818 (Ch) in which Jacobs J held that the *quantum meruit* was to be assessed on a 'time and success' basis.
16   Birks, p 272, Goff and Jones, paras 23-002 to 23-003.
17   [1936] 2 KB 403. Below, pp 390–391.

both parties erroneously believed was about to be made. In neither case was the work to be done gratuitously and, in both cases, the party from whom payment was sought requested the work and obtained the benefit of it. In neither case did the parties actually intend to pay for the work otherwise than under the supposed contract, or as part of the total price which would become payable when the expected contract was made. In both cases, when the beliefs of the parties were falsified, the law implied an obligation – and, in this case, I think the law should imply an obligation – to pay a reasonable price for the services which had been obtained.'[18]

This passage fits easily into the restitutionary scheme presented in this chapter, with the 'falsification of belief' correlating to failure of consideration (that is the failure of the 'promised' payment through the main contract) and the 'request' and 'obtaining of benefit' indicating that the defendant had been negatively benefited by receiving part of what he had bargained for.

The claimants in the *British Steel* case manufactured and delivered steel nodes to the defendants following a letter of intent sent by the defendants. Robert Goff J found that there was no concluded contract between the parties (and hence no possible counterclaim for damages for late delivery) but that the claimants were entitled to a *quantum meruit* for the reasonable value of their work, carried out at the request of the defendants and in anticipation of a contract. He relied on *William Lacey (Hounslow) Ltd v Davies* and it is submitted that the same 'failure of consideration' and 'bargained-for benefit' elements of unjust enrichment underpin his reasoning. The central passage in the judgment is as follows:

'Both parties confidently expected a formal contract to eventuate. In these circumstances, to expedite performance under that anticipated contract, one requested the other to commence the contract work, and the other complied with that request. If thereafter, as anticipated, a contract was entered into, the work done as requested will be treated as having been performed under that contract; if, contrary to their expectation, no contract was entered into, then the performance of the work is not referable to any contract the terms of which can be ascertained, and the law simply imposes an obligation on the party who made the request to pay a reasonable sum for such work as has been done pursuant to that request, such an obligation sounding in quasi contract or, as we now say, in restitution.'[19]

In the *British Steel* case, the negotiations between the parties had not reached the stage of there being an agreement as to the liability

18   [1957] 1 WLR 932, 939.
19   [1984] 1 All ER 504, 511.

(if any) of the sellers for late delivery. And Robert Goff J considered that, even if the sellers had assumed liability for failure to deliver within a reasonable time, that time had not expired on the facts. In such circumstances it can be accepted that, apart from failing in their contractual counterclaim, the buyers did not merit protection against allegedly late delivery by a reduction of the restitutionary award. In any event the amount of that award had been agreed between the parties. It would therefore be misleading to conclude from this case that, in the context of anticipated contracts, the law of restitution ignores the legitimate interests of defendants. On the contrary, the restitutionary approach to 'benefit' is designed to allow for the defendant's argument that he is not benefited by an objective benefit. Applying the 'bargained-for' test, if the performance does not match what the defendant bargained for, by being late or defective, the *quantum meruit* should be reduced because the defendant has only received a part of what he bargained for: and in some cases the restitutionary award should be further reduced (or eliminated) because loss caused by the late or defective performance means that the presumption of benefit, generated by the defendant having received part of what he bargained for, is partly (or wholly) rebutted.[20]

In contrast to the above three cases, in which a *quantum meruit* was awarded, restitution was refused in *Regalian Properties Ltd v London Docklands Development Corpn.*[1] Here the claimant property developers submitted to the defendants a tender of £18.5 million for residential development of part of the docklands area of London. The defendants accepted this tender in a letter headed 'subject to contract'. As a consequence of the defendants' difficulties in obtaining vacant possession and fluctuations in the property market, the parties were ultimately unable to conclude a contract and the site was not developed. The claimants had incurred considerable expense in paying architects and other professionals for detailed designs and site investigations. They now sought reimbursement, in the law of restitution, of the £2,891 million they had so paid. Their claim was refused because the work had been carried out on a 'subject to contract' basis. That is, the claimants knew that either party was free to walk away from the negotiations even though they confidently expected that this would not happen. The case was therefore held to be significantly different from *William Lacey v Davies* and *British Steel*

---

20   This sentence answers the question left open in *Crown House Engineering Ltd v Amec Projects Ltd* (1989) 48 BLR 37. For a criticism of the restitutionary approach as being unfair to defendants, see Ball 'Work Carried Out in Pursuance of Letters of Intent — Contract or Restitution?' (1983) 99 LQR 572.

1   [1995] 1 WLR 212.

Corpn v Cleveland Bridge and Engineering Co Ltd. Moreover, Rattee J was not satisfied that the defendants had been benefited by the work paid for by the claimants because the project had fallen through and the defendants did not, and were not entitled to, make use of the designs for developing the land. Furthermore, in contrast to both the *William Lacey* and *British Steel* cases, the work was not expressly requested by the defendants; and in contrast to the *British Steel* case, the work was not an accelerated performance of the anticipated contract but was carried out for the purpose of putting the claimants in a position to obtain and then perform the contract.

In the words of Rattee J:

> 'I appreciate that the English law of restitution should be flexible and capable of continuous development. However, I see no good reason to extend it to apply ... to facts such as those of the present case where, however much the parties expect a contract between them to materialise, both enter negotiations expressly (whether by use of the words 'subject to contract' or otherwise) on terms that each party is free to withdraw from the negotiations at any time. Each party to such negotiations must be taken to know (as in my judgment Regalian did in the present case) that pending the conclusion of a binding contract any cost incurred by him in preparation for the intended contract will be incurred at his own risk in the sense that he will have no recompense for those costs if no contract results.'[2]

Analysed in terms of unjust enrichment, Rattee J's decision is to be explained because, first, the defendants may not have been benefited; and, secondly, there was no injustice. Although there was in one sense a failure of consideration any injustice was displaced by the parties' understanding that costs incurred by the claimant were at its own risk and would not be reimbursed if no contract was concluded. While the 'subject to contract' letter was not decisive, it was helpful in construing the parties' understanding of the risks.[3]

The *Regalian* case was distinguished in *Countrywide Communications Ltd v ICL Pathway*.[4] The claimants had provided advice and assistance to the defendants regarding public relations and communications, in relation to the defendants' successful tender to supply a computerised payment system to the Benefits Agency. There was an agreement that if the bid succeeded the claimants would be

---

2   Ibid, at 231. Although not cited to Rattee J, *A-G of Hong Kong v Humphreys Estate Ltd* [1987] AC 114, PC, may be thought to lend tangential support to his decision. There it was held that, despite the 'promisee's' detrimental reliance, proprietary estoppel did not operate to prevent the 'promisor' withdrawing from an agreement made 'subject to contract'.

3   For a useful discussion, drawing a contrast with *Chillingworth v Esche* [1924] 1 Ch 97 (see below, p 408) see Virgo, *The Principles of the Law of Restitution* (1999), pp 363–365.

4   [2000] CLC 324.

offered by the defendants the public relations and communications contract for the operation of the system on terms to be negotiated. However, after the defendants won the tender, they appointed another company to carry out the public relations and communications work. The claim for damages for breach of contract failed on the ground that no binding contract had been concluded, it being trite law that an agreement to negotiate is not a valid contract. But the claim for a *quantum meruit* was granted. Nicholas Stauss QC explained that this was essentially because the defendants had been benefited by being provided with services which they would otherwise have had to pay for; and because they were induced to provide those services by an assurance that the defendants ultimately dishonoured. The facts were therefore far removed from the 'subject to contract' situation in the *Regalian* case, and that case was also distinguishable because it may have been that no benefit had been conferred on the defendants. The facts of *Countrywide Communications Ltd* were thought to be closest to *William Lacey v Davies*, which was followed.

Nicholas Strauss QC, sitting as a Deputy High Court judge, said:

'Undoubtedly the court may impose an obligation to pay for benefits resulting from services performed in the course of a contract which is expected to, but does not, come into existence. This is so, even though, in all cases, the defendant is *ex hypothesi* free to withdraw from the proposed contract, whether the negotiations were expressly made 'subject to contract' or not. Undoubtedly, such an obligation will be imposed only if justice requires it or, which comes to much the same thing, if it would be unconscionable for the plaintiff not to be recompensed. Beyond that, I do not think that it is possible to go further than to say that, in deciding whether to impose an obligation and if so its extent, the court will take into account and give appropriate weight to a number of considerations which can be identified in the authorities. The first is whether the services were of a kind which would normally be given free of charge. Secondly, the terms in which the request to perform the services was made may be important in establishing the extent of the risk (if any) which the plaintiffs may fairly be said to have taken that such services would in the end be unrecompensed ... Thirdly, the nature of the benefit which has resulted to the defendants is important ... Fourthly, what may often be decisive are the circumstances in which the anticipated contract does not materialise and in particular whether they can be said to involve "fault" on the part of the defendant, or (perhaps of more relevance) to be outside the scope of the risk undertaken by the plaintiff at the outset.'[5]

---

5   Ibid, at 349.

Two further, albeit troublesome cases, deserve mention: *Jennings and Chapman Ltd v Woodman, Matthews & Co*[6] and *Brewer Street Investments Ltd v Barclays Woollen Co Ltd*.[7] In each, landlords had carried out alterations to their property at the request of potential tenants but the anticipated lease between them had subsequently fallen through. In the former case, payment for the landlords' work was refused, whereas it was ordered in the latter case. The majority of the Court of Appeal in each case (Somervell and Romer LJJ) appeared to use contractual expectation reasoning: and the cases can be easily reconciled on that view. For the defendants had a lawful excuse for non-performance in *Jennings and Chapman* since the landlords should have sought permission for the conversion from the head lessee (in accordance with covenants in the head lease); whereas there was no such excuse in *Brewer Street* – rather, negotiations for a new lease simply broke down because of disagreement between the parties concerning the right to purchase the reversion.

Denning LJ, however, preferred restitutionary reasoning at least in the *Brewer Street* case. But a restitutionary analysis runs into two difficulties. First, on that analysis, the two cases seem indistinguishable and should therefore have been decided the same way. Secondly, while there is no problem in finding the unjust factor – there was a total failure of consideration in that the landlords had carried out the work on the basis of the tenants' 'promises' to pay which were not performed – there is a real problem in establishing that the tenants were benefited. In particular although they had bargained for the work to be carried out, could they be said to have received the services given that they had no right to the property? It would seem not. The majority's apparent preference for contractual rather than restitutionary reasoning therefore seems justified.

Alternatively as, on the face of it, no main contract was concluded one could perhaps interpret the judges as implicitly applying promissory estoppel as a cause of action. That is, the claimants had detrimentally relied on the defendants' promise to pay and in *Brewer Street* that promise had been broken by the defendants thereby entitling the claimants to recover at least their reliance loss. The objection to this is that it is well-established in English law that promissory estoppel can only be used as a shield and not a sword.[8] Although the landmark Australian case of *Waltons Stores (Interstate) Ltd v Maher*[9] – in which the High Court allowed

---

6   [1952] 2 TLR 409.
7   [1954] 1 QB 428.
8   Eg, *Combe v Combe* [1951] 2 KB 215. See also *Baird Textile Holdings Ltd v Marks and Spencer plc* [2001] EWCA Civ 274, [2002] 1 All ER (Comm) 737.
9   (1988) 164 CLR 387. See also *Commonwealth of Australia v Verwayen* (1990) 170 CLR 394; *Guimelli v Guimelli* (1999) 161 ALJ 473.

promissory estoppel to be used as a sword in the context of pre-contractual negotiations for a lease from which the defendants decided to withdraw – may act as a catalyst for reform of the unnecessarily restrictive English rule, it is clearly a strained interpretation to regard *Brewer Street*, decades earlier, as departing from that restriction without even mentioning promissory estoppel.

Many of the above cases were considered in the much discussed judgment of Sheppard J in the Supreme Court of New South Wales in *Sabemo Pty Ltd v North Sydney Municipal Council*.[10] Sabemo had won a 'tender' from the defendant council for the development of a civic centre. The parties' understanding was that a firm contract would not be made until the plans had been agreed. At the council's request Sabemo submitted several sets of estimates and plans. Ultimately, however, the council chose to abandon the project. Sheppard J's central reasoning was as follows:

> '... where two parties proceed upon the joint assumption that a contract will be entered into between them, and one does work beneficial for the project, and thus in the interests of the two parties, which work he would not be expected, in other circumstances, to do gratuitously, he will be entitled to compensation or restitution, if the other party unilaterally decides to abandon the project, not for any reason associated with bona fide disagreement concerning the terms of the contract to be entered into, but for reasons which, however valid, pertain only to his own position and do not relate at all to that of the other party.'[11]

Sheppard J was inclined to see his decision as awarding expectation or reliance loss rather than restitution. For example, he explicitly denied that the case was one of unjust enrichment[12] and he specifically rejected the view that it was important in *William Lacey* that the defendant had benefited in the sense of being left with a valuable end product.[13]

The difficulty lies in pinpointing the principle justifying expectation or reliance loss given that first, no contract had been formed and hence a claim for breach of contract was out of the question; and secondly, promissory estoppel has traditionally been available only as a defence and not a cause of action. In contrast, the facts of *Sabemo* are susceptible to a straightforward restitutionary analysis. The claimants

---

10   (1977) 2 NSWLR 880.
11   Ibid, at pp 902–903. In *Regalian Properties Ltd v London Docklands Development Corpn* [1995] 1 WLR 212 Rattee J primarily distinguished the *Sabemo* case because, in contrast to the facts in *Sabemo*, the defendants had not unilaterally decided to abandon the project. But, in any event, Rattee J thought that a principle such as that applied in *Sabemo* was inapplicable where the parties were negotiating on the express terms that both were free to withdraw. See above, pp 376–377.
12   Ibid, at p 897.
13   Ibid, at p 902.

had carried out the work in producing estimates and plans on the basis of being remunerated through a main contract for the building of the civic centre. When the defendant refused to remunerate them, there was a failure of consideration. And the defendant council was benefited when it received the requested estimates and plans. Sheppard J's apparent rejection of the view that the defendant had been benefited seems incorrect. Although the defendant had changed its mind about developing the site, the relevant date for examining whether there was a benefit was, subject to a change of position defence, the date of the defendant's receipt of the services not some subsequent date.

Those scholars who propose an unjust sacrifice analysis of anticipated contracts find comfort in the reasoning in *Sabemo*. But unless one is advocating promissory estoppel as a cause of action – which is justifiable in principle but runs counter to the English authorities – there seems no obvious compelling reason in justice to compensate one party's loss where there has been no unjust enrichment of the defendant by reason of that loss. The major challenge facing the 'loss only' school is to pinpoint precisely the force of its position where wrongdoing is not involved. Even if one were to accept an unjust sacrifice approach, it would seem only sensible to go through a restitutionary analysis first so as to isolate clearly the parties' net losses.

(4) Contracts unenforceable for want of formality

A few types of contract are valid only if they comply with statutory formalities. Most importantly, under s 2 of the Law of Property (Miscellaneous Provisions) Act 1989 contracts for the sale or other disposition of an interest in land must be in writing and signed. Where the necessary formalities are not complied with, so that the contract is unenforceable, the parties' restitutionary remedies become important. Certainly there is no reason to think – unless the relevant statute clearly indicates the contrary – that the formalities applicable to contract should carry over to rule out the independent cause of action in unjust enrichment by subtraction.

Discussion of this area is dominated by the Canadian case of *Deglman v Guaranty Trust Co of Canada and Constantineau*[14] and the Australian case of *Pavey & Matthews Pty Ltd v Paul*.[15] Each concerned want of formality. However, they are so important not because of that, per se, but because each represented the acceptance by the highest court of

14 [1954] 3 DLR 785.
15 (1986) 162 CLR 221.

their respective countries of a law of restitution founded on the principle of reversing unjust enrichment.[16]

In *Deglman* the claimant entered into an oral agreement with his aunt by which in return for his performing various personal services for her (for example, doing odd jobs, taking her out on trips, and running errands) she promised to leave him a house in her will. He performed the services but she failed to leave him the house. It was held by the Supreme Court of Canada that while the contract was unenforceable because not evidenced in writing as required by the Ontario Statute of Frauds 1950 the claimant was entitled to a *quantum meruit* from the deceased's estate. Rand J said:

> 'The statute in such a case does not touch the principle of restitution against what would otherwise be an unjust enrichment of the defendant at the expense of the plaintiff. This is exemplified in the simple case of part or full payment in money as the price under an oral contract; it would be inequitable to allow the promisor to keep both the land and the money and the other party to the bargain is entitled to recover what he has paid. Similarly is it in the case of services given'.[17]

And Cartwright J, giving the leading judgment, cited with approval Lord Wright's comments on unjust enrichment and restitution in *Fibrosa* and went on to say, 'The deceased having received the benefits of the full performance of the contract by the respondent, the law imposed on her, and so on her estate, the obligation to pay the fair value of the services rendered to her.'[18]

Although no precise breakdown of the unjust enrichment was attempted, the reasoning and facts clearly fit a failure of consideration model. The claimant had rendered the services on the basis of a promise that the aunt had refused to perform. And the aunt had been negatively benefited either on the ground that she had received (all) the services which she had bargained for or possibly because the services received were necessities and hence incontrovertibly beneficial.

In *Pavey and Matthews Pty Ltd v Paul* the claimant builders had renovated a cottage for the defendant pursuant to a contract by which they were to be remunerated according to prevailing rates. When the work was done the defendant paid $36,000. The claimants maintained that she should pay nearly twice that sum. The contract was unenforceable because it was not in writing as required for building

---

16 Cf Gummow J's attack on the 'theory' of unjust enrichment in *Roxborough v Rothmans of Pall Mall Australia Ltd* [2001] HCA 68. See above, p 7, n 12.

17 [1954] 3 DLR 785, 788.

18 Ibid, at p 795.

contracts to be enforceable by builders under the New South Wales Builders Licensing Act 1971. It was held by the High Court of Australia (Brennan J dissenting) that the claimants were entitled to a restitutionary *quantum meruit*. The majority emphasised the independence of restitution (based on unjust enrichment) from contract and that the *quantum meruit* did not constitute indirect enforcement of the contract so that the statutory formalites were inapplicable to it. For example, Dawson J said, '... were the plaintiffs to succeed in its action in this case, the result would be, not the enforcement, directly or indirectly, of the contract, but the enforcement of an obligation which, whilst it arose from the performance of the contract, was separate and distinct from it'.[19]

Unfortunately the leading judgments, given by Mason and Wilson JJ jointly and by Deane J, chose to stress that a key feature of the restitutionary action was that the benefit of the building work had been *accepted* by the defendant. So Deane J talked of the need for a benefit to have been 'actually or constructively accepted'.[20] And Mason and Wilson JJ said:

> 'If all the plaintiff had to prove was that he had fully executed the contract on his part and that he had not been paid the contract price, there would be some force in the suggestion that the proceeding amounted to an indirect enforcement of the contractual cause of action. However, when success in a *quantum meruit* depends, not only on the plaintiff proving that he did the work but also on the defendant's acceptance of the work without paying the agreed remuneration, it is evident that the court is enforcing against the defendant an obligation that differs in character from the contractual obligation had it been enforceable.'[1]

In what sense had Mrs Paul accepted the benefit of the building work? After the work had been completed, she clearly had no choice but to accept it. In Pollock CB's oft-cited dictum in *Taylor v Laird*,[2] 'One cleans another's shoes; what can the other do but put them on?'. Nor, even if one believes in free acceptance, can it be said that she accepted the work by allowing it to carry on when in all conscience she ought to have rejected it: as she was perfectly willing to pay what she thought was a reasonable sum for the work there was no 'unconscientiousness' in her allowing it to continue.[3]

It is submitted, therefore, that the High Court of Australia was wrong to place any importance on Mrs Paul's 'acceptance' of the

19   (1986) 162 CLR 221 at p 269.
20   Ibid, at p 263.
1   Ibid, at p 228.
2   (1856) 25 LJ Ex 329, 332.
3   Birks, 'In Defence of Free Acceptance' in *Essays on the Law of Restitution* (ed Burrows, 1991), pp 105, 111–112. Surprisingly Birks does not discuss how the benefit could be made out in *Pavey*.

benefit. The key distinguishing feature of restitution was rather that she had been benefited because she had received the building work. Moreover, she could not subjectively devalue the work because she had bargained for it at prevailing contract rates and had received all that she had bargained for.

Nor did the High Court clarify the unjust factor. But given that, as just explained, one must rule out free acceptance, even if one believes in it, it is clear that failure of consideration offers the only convincing rationale.[4] The builders had not been paid at the prevailing rate as promised which was their basis for doing the work.

The few relevant English cases lack the central prominence of the above two Commonwealth authorities. One, which has already been considered in detail, is *Thomas v Brown*,[5] which concerned the recovery of money rather than a *quantum meruit*. It stands as the best illustration of the proposition that failure of consideration cannot be made out by a claimant where the defendant is ready, able and willing to perform its promise.

Another is *Scarisbrick v Parkinson*[6] in which the claimant was held entitled to a *quantum meruit* for three years' services as a clerk performed for the defendant under an oral contract that was unenforceable by reason of the Statute of Frauds (as not being one to be performed within a year). Consistently with the bargained-for test of benefit, the contractual salary of £20 a year was relied on in awarding a *quantum meruit* of £60.

Two other main cases, both concerning a *quantum meruit*, present certain difficulties for a restitutionary analysis. In *Pulbrook v Lawes*[7] the claimant tenant had entered into an oral agreement for a lease of a house and, with the defendant landlord's consent and in anticipation of his occupation, had paid to have a room of the house painted and to have gas pipes laid. When the defendant failed to complete the agreement it was held that, while the claimant could not enforce it, because it was not evidenced in writing, he could recover on a *quantum meruit* for the 'improvements' carried out. Both judges (Blackburn and Lush JJ) expressly used failure of consideration reasoning and drew an analogy with money paid to the landlord.[8] This would be helpful to the central theme of this chapter were it not for the fact that, on a restitutionary analysis, there are serious difficulties over the

---

4   Birks, ibid.
5   (1876) 1 QBD 714: above, pp 331–332. See also *Hicks v Hicks* (1802) 3 East 16; *Bradford Advance Co v Ayers* [1924] WN 152; *North Central Wagon Finance Co Ltd v Brailsford* [1962] 1 WLR 1288 (restitution of payments under contracts void for non-registration).
6   (1869) 20 LT 175.
7   (1876) 1 QBD 284.
8   This was to use failure of consideration in the rare sense of a promised performance not given in return for the claimant's services: above, p 326, n 12.

landlord's benefit. How was the landlord benefited by the 'improvements'? He did not bargain for them but merely permitted the claimant to carry them out at his own expense. Nor was there any evidence that he was incontrovertibly benefited by realising, or being very likely to realise, the value of the improvements (by, for example, letting the house at a higher value). *Pulbrook v Lawes* therefore belongs alongside several other cases in which the courts have apparently ignored subjective devaluation in treating land improvement as beneficial.[9]

In *Scott v Pattison*[10] the claimant was employed for one year as a farm labourer at a fixed weekly wage under an oral contract that was unenforceable because contrary to the Statute of Frauds. The claimant was paid for all the weeks that he worked but not for those 19 weeks when he was off ill. The Divisional Court held that, even though the contract was not enforceable, there was an implied contractual obligation on the defendant to pay a *quantum meruit* for the services rendered and, in calculating that fair sum, it might be relevant to take account of a local custom whereby wages were to be paid during sickness. Salter J said:

'If a party to a contract, which is unenforceable under the Statute of Frauds, has rendered services under that contract to the other party, and the other party has accepted and benefited by those services, then I think that the party who has rendered the services can sue the other party in debt or an implied contract to pay him according to his deserts. That is not enforcing the unenforceable contract ...'[11]

One would nowadays reject Salter J's fictional 'implied contract' reasoning and, as has been said in relation to *Pavey v Paul*, the stress on 'acceptance' was misplaced. But even if one sees in the reasoning the seeds of the modern independent view of restitution the major obstacle faced by a restitutionary analysis of the case is that the claimant had been paid at the agreed rate for all the services he had rendered. It is very hard to see how one could justify, in restitution, additional payments for when no services were rendered. On the face of it the decision allows the protection of the expectation interest based on terms implied by custom. As such it would appear to have run directly contrary to the Statute of Frauds.

The most recent case concerned with these issues is *Dimond v Lovell*.[12] Here a contract for the hire of a car was held by the House of Lords to

---

9   Above, pp 165–166. Even if one believes in it there was no free acceptance because at the time the improvements were made the landlord no doubt intended to perform.
10   [1923] 2 KB 723.
11   Ibid, at pp 727–728.
12   [2000] 2 WLR 1121.

be unenforceable by the creditor under s 65(1) of the Consumer Credit Act 1974 as an improperly-executed regulated consumer credit agreement. This was because all the prescribed terms had not been included in a written document signed by the debtor. Although the creditor could not therefore recover the agreed hire from the debtor in contract, the question was whether the statutory bar to contractual enforcement also applied to rule out a restitutionary (*quantum valebat*) claim by the creditor for the benefit the debtor had had from using the car. In other words, did the policy of s 65(1) dictate that the debtor should pay nothing for the use of the car? The House of Lords held that that indeed was the case. In Lord Hoffmann's words, '[T]o treat Mrs Dimond as having been unjustly enriched would be inconsistent with the purpose of s 65(1). Parliament intended that if a consumer credit agreement was improperly executed, then subject to the enforcement powers of the court, the debtor should not have to pay. This meant that Parliament contemplated that he might be enriched and I do not see how it is open to the court to say that this consequence is unjust and should be reversed by a remedy at common law.'[13] It should be noted that that interpretation of s 65(1) is strengthened because in other circumstances of improper execution the court has a discretion under s 127 to allow enforcement of the contract by the creditor; but by s 127(3) there is no such discretion when there is no signed document containing all the prescribed terms.[14]

(5) Void contracts

There is on-going controversy about the correct approach to restitution of benefits conferred (almost invariably money) under a void contract. Professor Treitel, for example, has long presented the law as being that the restitution of money follows simply because the contract is void.[15] In the interest-rate swap cases, where the contracts were void because ultra vires the public authorities, a similar approach to Professor Treitel's has, in effect, been applied. Hobhouse J at first instance in *Westdeutsche Landesbank Girozentrale v Islington London Borough Council*[16] saw the ground for restitution under void contracts as 'absence of

---

13   Ibid, at 1131.
14   Interestingly s 127(3) was regarded as incompatible with the European Convention on Human Rights in *Wilson v First County Trust Ltd (No 2)* [2001] EWCA Civ 633, [2001] 2 QB 74, CA, because it can leave a debtor unjustly enriched at the creditor's expense and yet the creditor has no redress.
15   *The Law of Contract* (10th edn, 1999), pp 985–988. See, similarly, Cremer, 'Recovering Money Paid Under Void Contracts: Absence of Consideration and Failure of Consideration' [2001] JCL 37.
16   [1994] 4 All ER 890. See below, p 399.

consideration'. And in *Guinness Mahon & Co Ltd v Kensington and Chelsea Royal London Borough Council*,[17] while the traditional language of 'total failure of consideration' rather than 'absence of consideration' was applied, the Court of Appeal held that there was inevitably a total failure of consideration where the contract was void. Restitution was therefore awarded even though the contract was fully executed on both sides.

It is submitted that, while the decisions in these cases were correct, the reasoning was not. 'Absence of consideration' carries with it a host of problems, not least that, without qualification, it would mean that all gifts were recoverable. But the notion that there is a total failure of consideration wherever a contract is void is also problematic. First, it is contrary to authority. Past cases have not treated the voidness of the contract as automatically triggering a total failure.[18] Moreover, the classic statement of the meaning of total failure of consideration has precisely distinguished the validity of the promise from its performance, stressing that failure of consideration is concerned with the latter not the former.[19] Secondly, to treat void contracts as inevitably triggering a total failure of consideration will, in rare situations, lead to incorrect decisions. This will be so where there has been full performance on both sides *and* the parties were not mistaken in believing that the contract was valid when it was, in truth, void (and there is no other unjust factor in play). In that situation, there ought to be no restitution. Yet the automatic total failure of consideration approach would dictate that there would be restitution. As I have written before, '[That approach] if valid, would mean that a [claimant] who made no mistake in entering into a void contract which is then fully executed on both sides would still be entitled to restitution. Surely that cannot be right. If the swap in *Westdeutsche* had been "closed" (ie, fully executed over the ten year period), there is no good reason why Westdeutsche should have been entitled to restitution if it had known from the start that the contract was void.'[20]

It is submitted, therefore, that reliance on automatic total failure of consideration (and absence of consideration) merely serves to hide the true grounds for restitution in play in void contract cases.[1] Leaving

17 [1999] QB 215. This is supported by obiter dicta of Lord Browne-Wilkinson in the *Westdeutsche* case [1999] AC 669, 710. See below, pp 399–400.
18 See, eg, *Valentini v Canali* (1889) 24 QBD 166, as interpreted in *Pearce v Brain* [1929] 2 KB 310; *Rover International Ltd v Cannon Film Sales Ltd (No 3)* [1989] 1 WLR 912.
19 Viscount Simon's in *Fibrosa* [1943] AC 32, 48. See above, p 325.
20 'Swaps and the Friction between Common Law and Equity' [1994] RLR 15, 17.
1 See also Birks, 'No Consideration: Restitution after Void Contracts' (1993) 23 UWALR 195; McInnes, 'Bases for Restitution: A Call for Clarity with Unjust Factors' [1996] JCL 73; Virgo, *The Principles of the Law of Restitution* (1999), pp 403–408.

to one side that a policy reason for the contract being void (eg, incapacity) may itself be an unjust factor allowing restitution,[2] the true grounds are failure of consideration (which in principle should extend to partial failure but has traditionally been limited to total failure) and mistake. Only the latter can apply where the void contract has been fully executed.

In this section, we shall therefore examine restitution under void contracts on the basis that absence of consideration is not a ground for restitution; that traditionally in respect of restitution of money, but not of benefits in kind, the failure of consideration must have been total; that the notion that there is automatically a total failure of consideration in void contracts is unsound; and that while, after *Kleinwort Benson v Lincoln City Council*,[3] a claimant will very commonly be able to found a claim for restitution under a void contract on mistake of law, that was not possible prior to the abrogation of the mistake of law bar by the House of Lords in that case.

Each of the four main types of void contract will be considered in turn. It is only in relation to the last (ultra vires contracts) that there is any question of the policy that renders the contract void carrying over to form a defence to restitution.

(a) Contracts void for mistake

Two old cases in which the contracts can be regarded as void for common mistake at common law illustrate the restitutionary consequences. In *Strickland v Turner*[4] the claimant had bought a life annuity. Before the contract was made, and unknown to both parties, the annuitant had died. The claimant was held entitled to restitution of the purchase money because the consideration for the money had wholly failed. In *Pritchard v Merchant's and Tradesman's Mutual Life Assurance Society*[5] the claimant had renewed a life insurance policy with the defendant on the life of X. Unknown to both parties, X had already died. It was held that the claimant could recover the premiums paid for the renewal 'on the ground of it having been paid and received under a mistake of fact'.[6]

The mistake of fact approach adopted in the *Pritchard* case – whereby the (common) mistake of fact that rendered the contract void can be used to found a mistake of fact claim in restitution – appears to be more advantageous for the claimant than the failure of

---

2　See below, chapter 11.
3　[1999] 2 AC 349.
4　(1852) 7 Exch 208.
5　(1858) 3 CBNS 622.
6　Ibid, at p 645.

consideration approach adopted in the *Strickland* case because it avoids the need to show that the failure of consideration was total.[7] After *Kleinwort Benson v Lincoln City Council*[8] there is also now no need for the restitution-claimant to establish that the mistake was one of fact rather than law.

The advantage of founding one's claim on mistake rather than failure of consideration will be less clear-cut where benefits in kind are in issue, simply because there has been no traditional insistence that the failure of consideration be total.

Moreover, where the contract is void for the *unilateral* mistake of the party receiving the benefit (the defendant) the claimant's only obvious ground for restitution is (total) failure of consideration. By definition the claimant has made no mistake. On the contrary he knew or ought to have known of the defendant's mistake. An illustrative case is *Boulton v Jones*.[9] Jones 'consumed' hose pipe ordered from Brocklehurst, with whom he had a set-off, but supplied by Boulton, who had taken over Brocklehurst's business. Boulton was held to have no contractual right to payment because any purported contract was void for Jones' unilateral mistake as to identity. A restitutionary remedy was also impliedly ruled out.

Should a restitutionary claim have succeeded on those facts? Goff and Jones suggest that Jones' mistake which made the contract void also undermined the inference that he had freely accepted the goods.[10] Birks does not dissent from that approach although he leaves open the possibility that, if Boulton had also been mistaken, restitution might have been justified on the ground that Boulton would then have been relying on free acceptance solely to establish benefit, and in such a 'mixed claim' acceptance need not be as free – and hence may not be nullified by mistake – as where it is being relied on to establish both injustice and enrichment.[11]

The implication of this reasoning is that had Jones not 'consumed' the hose pipe before he found out that the supplier was Boulton and not Brocklehurst, Boulton would have been entitled to a restitutionary *quantum valebat* because then the objection to free acceptance would have been removed. The strength of this reasoning is that it provides an explanation for why one judge, Channell B, did indeed leave open the question whether 'the plaintiff might not have had a right of action on an implied contract'[12] had the demand for payment been received

7   See above, p 129.
8   [1999] 2 AC 349.
9   (1857) 27 LJ Ex 117.
10 Goff and Jones, para 23-005.
11 Birks, pp 115–116. See also p 280.
12 (1857) 27 LJ Ex 117, 119.

by Jones while he still had the goods. But if Jones had known of the identity of the vendor before 'consuming' the goods, surely there would have been a valid contract constituted by Boulton's offer to sell and Jones' acceptance by conduct, and Boulton would have therefore had a valid contractual claim for the agreed price. In other words, Channell B's dicta is perfectly explicable on normal contractual principles without resort to free acceptance restitutionary thinking.

To dispute the importance of the leading scholars' free acceptance analysis does not mean that no restitutionary claim should have succeeded on the facts of *Boulton v Jones*. There was no difficulty over an unjust factor because the consideration for Boulton's supplying the hose pipe had (totally) failed: Jones refused to perform his apparent contractual promise to pay. The sole problem in establishing unjust enrichment was therefore one of benefit. Jones was incontrovertibly benefited if he was saved expenses necessary to his business (ie if he would have had to buy the pipe elsewhere). Alternatively one can argue that Jones was prima facie negatively benefited in that he had received the goods he had bargained for: the set-off would then be taken into account, as if a contract price, in fixing the value of the goods to Jones so that there would be no benefit at all if the set-off was intended to cover the whole price.

(b) Contracts void for want of authority

The two leading cases on restitution in respect of a contract void for want of authority have both concerned a contract purportedly made between a director and his company where, in making the contract, the directors were acting outside their authority. By s 35A of the Companies Act 1985 contracts made by directors acting outside their powers with parties acting in good faith are now valid except, inter alia, where the other party is a director of the company in which case, by s 322A, the contract is voidable at the company's option.[13]

Those provisions mean that the restitutionary principles laid down in the two leading cases would no longer be in issue on the same facts. Of course, they remain of direct practical importance to other types of agency contract rendered void for want of authority (including contracts with companies if the statutory provisions do not apply).

In *Craven-Ellis v Canons Ltd*[14] the defendant company under a purported contract with the claimant agreed to pay him a certain remuneration for work to be done. When the defendant company

---

13 Section 322A is analogous to breach of a fiduciary duty by self-dealing: see below, p 493, n 5.
14 [1936] 2 KB 403.

refused to pay as agreed for the work done the claimant brought an action in contract or alternatively for a non-contractual *quantum meruit*. It was held that the contract was void for want of authority.[15] The 'directors' who had made the agreement, including the claimant, were not qualified to do so, not having obtained qualification shares as required by the articles of association. However, a *quantum meruit* was awarded.

The unjust factor can be regarded as (total) failure of consideration. The claimant had received none of the money he had been promised by his fellow directors in return for rendering the services.[16] One might think that a mistake analysis was also possible but the claimant's mistake would seem to have been one of law not fact in believing that the directors had authority to make the contract on behalf of the company; and prior to *Kleinwort Benson Ltd v Lincoln City Council*[17] a mistake of law would not have counted.

Was the company benefited by the claimant's work? In the first edition of their work, but not thereafter, Goff and Jones regarded the decision as a leading example of restitution based on free acceptance.[18] However, in an influential article in 1971,[19] Birks challenged this view on the ground that the impediment to there being a valid contract also prevented there being a free acceptance: ie, there were no directors qualified to accept freely. The same objection probably also applies to thwart any attempt to use the 'bargained-for' test of benefit in this context. However, as Birks explained, the decision was still justified because there was an express finding that the claimant's services were of a kind 'which, if they had not been performed by the plaintiff, they [the company] would have had to get some other agent to carry out'.[20] In other words there was an incontrovertible benefit in the sense of a saving of necessary business expense.

A similar claim – but in this case made by a qualified company director – was dealt with in disappointing fashion by Lord Templeman, giving the leading speech of the House of Lords, in *Guinness plc v Saunders*.[1] The defendant director had been paid £5.2 million for services rendered to his claimant company in connection with a successful take-over bid by the company. The defendant claimed that

---

15 Greene LJ suggested the contract might alternatively be void for common mistake. But the mistake was surely one of law not fact.
16 Strictly speaking, the *company* was a third party beneficiary of the services.
17 [1999] 2 AC 349.
18 Goff and Jones (1st edn, 1966), pp 31, 269–270, 278. See also Denning, '*Quantum Meruit: The Case of Craven-Ellis v Canons Ltd*' (1939) 55 LQR 54.
19 '*Negotiorum Gestio* and the Common Law' (1971) 24 CLP 110.
20 [1936] 2 KB 403, 412.
1 [1990] 2 AC 663.

the money had been paid under a valid contract with the company and that, even if this was not so, he was nevertheless entitled to some payment for his services either on a *quantum meruit* or by virtue of the allowance for skill and effort that equity may allow fiduciaries required to account for profits following *Boardman v Phipps*.[2]

The House of Lords held that the contract was void for want of authority as the directors who had entered into it had done so contrary to the procedures in the company's articles of association. The claimant was therefore prima facie entitled to restitution of the £5.2 million. The exact ground for this was not made clear. Birks suggests mistake[3] but, prior to *Kleinwort Benson v Lincoln City Council*,[4] this would probably have fallen foul of the mistake of law bar. Another possibility within unjust enrichment by subtraction was the claimant's ignorance (or powerlessness) in having its money transferred to the defendant.[5] In contrast *total* failure of consideration could not have been the ground because the services had been rendered and were conceded by Guinness to have been beneficial.[6] Alternatively, and in line with the emphasis in the pleadings on a constructive trust, the defendant's payment may be better viewed as wrongfully acquired: he had made an unauthorised profit out of his position as director and hence had to account as fiduciary for his gain.

On the central issue, it was held that the claimant's prima facie entitlement to restitution should not be reduced because the defendant was not entitled to a *quantum meruit* or equitable allowance. Unfortunately Lord Templeman dealt with the *quantum meruit* argument by relying on the discredited implied contract view of restitution. 'The short answer to a *quantum meruit* claim based on an implied contract by Guinness to pay reasonable remuneration for services rendered is that there can be no contract by Guinness to pay special remuneration for the services of a director unless that contract is entered into by the board pursuant to article 91'.[7] This observation provides no valid explanation for the denial of the restitutionary *quantum meruit* precisely because its basis is non-contractual.

A more satisfactory explanation is provided by Lord Goff (and later, as one of his reasons for distinguishing *Craven-Ellis v Canons Ltd,* by Lord Templeman). A restitutionary *quantum meruit* could not be granted to the company director for work done for the company

---

2   [1967] 2 AC 46. Below, pp 495–496.
3   'Restitution Without Counter-Restitution' [1990] LMCLQ 330, 332.
4   [1999] 2 AC 349, HL.
5   Birks, ibid. Above, chapter 4.
6   Cf [1990] 2 AC 663, 698 (per Lord Goff).
7   [1990] 2 AC 663, 689. See also the criticism by Beatson and Prentice, 'Restitutionary Claims by Company Directors' (1990) 106 LQR 365.

because that would have contradicted the long-established principle that a director may not make an unauthorised profit out of his position. That principle therefore overrode the defendant's prima facie right to restitution (Guinness conceded that it had been benefited by the defendant's services) based on (total) failure of consideration.

One can argue, however, that the 'no unauthorised profit' principle should be flexibly applied so as not to rule out a *quantum meruit* to a company director in all cases. *Guinness* was a weak case for a departure from the usual principle because the defendant had plainly placed himself in a position where his interests were in stark conflict with his duty as a director. Support for a flexible approach is found in Lord Goff's speech but apparently only in relation to whether there should be an equitable allowance deducted from the account of profits following *Boardman v Phipps* and not in relation to the *quantum meruit* claim.

Although the House of Lords suggested otherwise, consistency dictates that, had the contract been voidable not void, the good reason for denying the *quantum meruit* on the facts would have equally ruled out the defendant's normal right to counter-restitution on rescission.[8]

Neither of the above two leading cases touched on the restitution of money paid *to* the purported principal[9] but, in line with other void contracts, the primary ground of recovery would be total failure of consideration or, after *Kleinwort Benson v Lincoln City Council*,[10] mistake (of law).

(c) Contracts void for non-incorporation of a company at the time of contracting

The important case of *Rover International Ltd v Cannon Film Sales Ltd (No 3)*[11] largely concerned a contract that was void because at the time it was made one of the contracting companies was non-incorporated. Rover had entered into a purported contract with Cannon (initially Thorn EMI) whereby Rover would dub and distribute in Italy films owned by Cannon. Rover would also make substantial advance payments to Cannon. Box office receipts would then reimburse Rover and, in any event, at the end of the agreement, Cannon was to repay to Rover any difference between the total advance paid by Rover and the net

---

8 See Birks, 'Restitution Without Counter-Restitution' [1990] LMCLQ 330.
9 If the payor pays the purported agent the restitutionary claim lies against him. If the purported agent pays the money over to the purported principal, the latter's retention of the money will presumably normally constitute ratification so that the contract will be validated and any restitutionary claim would be governed by the principles discussed below, pp 599–608.
10 [1999] 2 AC 349.
11 [1989] 1 WLR 912.

receipts recouped by it. After the advance payments had been made, and much work had been done, it was discovered that the contract was void as it ante-dated the incorporation of Rover by about a month. Cannon was therefore able to end the deal without being in breach to Rover. Rover sought to recover the money paid and a *quantum meruit* for the dubbing and distribution work carried out. It succeeded on both claims.

On the claim for restitution of money paid, the Court of Appeal held that Rover should succeed because it had paid under a mistake of fact. Nor was there any defence. Kerr LJ said that Cannon had no defence of change of position because its delivery of the films was not detrimental as it ended up better off by the abandoning of the purported contract. Dillon LJ, taking the traditional view prior to *Lipkin Gorman v Karpnale Ltd*,[12] argued that estoppel alone, and not change of position, was a valid defence and on the facts there was no basis for any estoppel.

One would have thought that, being prior to *Kleinwort Benson Ltd v Lincoln City Council*,[13] a problem with the mistake analysis was that the mistake was one of law not fact: that is, Rover did not realise that, as a matter of law, it did not technically exist until after the contract was made and that, therefore, there was no valid contract. But this was lightly dismissed by Kerr LJ: '[Counsel for Cannon] rightly did not suggest that this mistaken belief involved a mistake of law.'[14]

Kerr LJ alternatively thought that the claimant could succeed on the ground of total failure of consideration. As we have seen,[15] Kerr LJ's approach to the requirement of a total failure is controversial. There was plainly a failure of consideration in that Rover had been promised by a term of the agreement that, at its conclusion, Cannon would repay any net loss suffered by Rover (ie if the net receipts did not match the advance payments made to Cannon). As it was, Rover was left out of pocket: contrary to its bargain it had not at least broken even. But Rover had received films which it had dubbed and distributed and from which it had reaped profits. It is therefore hard to agree with Kerr LJ that it had not received *any part* of what it had bargained for. Like *Rowland v Divall*,[16] on which Kerr LJ relied, it is best to interpret his judgment as support for a move to *partial* failure of consideration being a sufficient ground for restitution of money paid.

---

12 [1991] 2 AC 548. Below, chapter 15.
13 [1999] 2 AC 349.
14 [1989] 1 WLR 912, 925.
15 Above, pp 329–331.
16 [1923] 2 KB 500.

Kerr LJ (but, peculiarly, not Dillon LJ) went on to discuss Rover's claim to a *quantum meruit* for the dubbing and distribution work carried out. Cannon had conceded that Rover was entitled to a *quantum meruit* but there was a dispute between the parties as to whether the terms of the purported contract should act as a ceiling on the *quantum meruit*. Had the contract been valid Rover would have been in breach by its unauthorised early release of one of the films. The question was therefore whether Rover was limited to the low amount of gross receipts that it would have been entitled to retain under an 'extremely draconian'[17] clause allowing Cannon, in the event of Rover's breach, to terminate and take most of the profits.

Kerr LJ held that there should be no such limit (as did Dillon LJ but he was looking at that question in relation to the restitution of money) for two main reasons. First, reference to the contract was unfounded because it was void *ab initio*. 'It would involve the application of provisions of a void contract to the assessment of a *quantum meruit* which only arises due to the non-existence of the supposed contract.'[18] Somewhat similarly he thought that Cannon could not both insist on the contract being void and then seek to rely on its terms. This would be to have its cake and eat it. Secondly, he opined that to impose a contract ceiling would be inconsistent with the restitutionary position where contracts are ineffective for, for example, frustration.

The question of whether a contract price should act as a ceiling on restitution has already been discussed.[19] It has been submitted that, while there is no need per se for the independent restitutionary cause of action to bow to contract, the contract price should limit restitution where the defendant's benefit is established by the 'bargained-for' test. The same argument is applicable where a contract is void *ab initio*.

The unusual feature of *Rover International*, however, is that the contract ceiling in question was not the contract price. That is, the relevant clause was not in any sense a valuation of Rover's work; rather it was a clause that came into operation once the parties' primary obligations had been terminated for breach.[20] In effect the issue was whether Rover's restitution should be limited in line with what Cannon would have been entitled to under what was a kind of 'forfeiture' or 'liquidated damages' clause. Kerr LJ's decision was therefore unsurprising and clearly correct. Even if the contract had been valid,

17   [1989] 1 WLR 912, 918.
18   Ibid, at p 927.
19   Above, pp 344–347.
20   Analogously one can say that the question of escaping from a bad bargain in restitution was not in issue.

and the contract had been discharged for breach, the relevance of the clause to a restitutionary *quantum meruit* would have been questionable and would have turned on whether there was a 'contracting out' of restitution. But as the clause was void it could not constitute a valid 'contracting-out' and had no possible relevance to restitution.

Cannon's concession as to Rover's entitlement to a *quantum meruit* meant that it was unnecessary for Kerr LJ to clarify the unjust enrichment involved. Nevertheless, as has been discussed in chapter 3,[1] his view that the concession was rightly made was clearly correct. As with the money claim the unjust factor can be regarded as being either mistake or failure of consideration: and, as regards the latter, the controversy over whether the receipt of the films negated a *total* failure of consideration would not arise because, for restitution in respect of benefits in kind, even partial failure of consideration has been implicitly accepted as sufficient.[2]

By s 36C(1) of the Companies Act 1985 a contract which purports to be made by, or on behalf of, a company at a time when it has not been formed, shall have effect as one made with the purported agent, subject to any agreement to the contrary. That section (or, rather, its forerunner) was inapplicable in *Rover International* because Rover was a foreign company.[3]

Even non-incorporated English companies can fall outside that provision so that restitution is brought into play as is shown by *Cotronic (UK) Ltd v Dezonie*.[4] The purported contract between a building company and a Mrs Osborne was held void by the Court of Appeal because the company had existed but had been dissolved before the making of the contract. The statutory words 'at a time when the company has not been formed' were thought inapplicable where the agent purported to act on behalf of a company that had been formed long before. Although, therefore, no contractual action could succeed, it was held that the building company could be entitled to a restitutionary *quantum meruit* for the work done for Mrs Osborne so that her application to have its action struck out failed. Although there was no discussion of the ingredients of the *quantum meruit,* it is susceptible to the same analysis as the *quantum meruit* in *Rover International:* mistake or failure of consideration would be the unjust factor and the benefit could be established by the 'bargained-for' test.

---

1   Above, p 166.
2   Above, pp 335–336.
3   As explained by Harman J at first instance [1987] BCLC 540, 543–544.
4   [1991] BCC 200.

(d) Contracts void because ultra vires a company or public authority

The cases concerned with restitution of money paid to a company[5] under contracts void because ultra vires the company[6] are now merely of historical interest for two reasons. First, the leading case of *Sinclair v Bougham*[7] has been overruled by the House of Lords in *Westdeutsche Landesbank Girozentrale v Islington London Borough Council*.[8] In *Sinclair v Brougham* the House of Lords held that, at least for borrowing contracts, the ultra vires incapacity preventing there being a valid contract was also a defence to restitution for total failure of consideration. This flawed approach – recognised to be flawed in the *Westdeutsche* case – is discussed in chapter 15. Secondly, by reason of s 35(1) of the Companies Act 1985 ultra vires contracts made by (non-charitable) companies are no longer void.

In contrast, the question of restitution of money paid to a public authority under a contract that is void because ultra vires the public authority remains of significant practical importance[9] and was at the centre of a mass of fascinating and ground-breaking litigation in the 1990s in the context of interest rate swap transactions.[10]

In *Hazell v Hammersmith and Fulham London Borough Council*[11] the House of Lords held that a public authority was acting ultra vires in concluding interest rate swap transactions and that such contracts were therefore void. An interest rate swap transaction is an agreement under which each party agrees to pay to the other on specified dates the interest which would have accrued over a given period on the same notional principal sum assuming that each party agrees to pay a different rate of interest. Usually one party (the fixed rate payer) will agree to pay a fixed rate of interest while the other party (the floating rate payer) agrees to pay a rate of interest determined by reference to an index, for example the six month London Inter-Bank Offered

---

5 For restitutionary claims brought by a company, the primary unjust factor was the incapacity (by reason of ultra vires) itself rather than a total failure of consideration: see, eg, *Brougham v Dyer* (1913) 108 LT 504. This is discussed in chapter 11.

6 See, eg, *Re Pheonix Life Assurance Co, Burgess and Stock's Case* (1862) 2 John & H 441; *Sinclair v Brougham* [1914] AC 398.

7 [1914] AC 398.

8 [1996] AC 669.

9 This is so even though the practical importance has been narrowed by the Local Government (Contracts) Act 1997. That Act does not remove the starting point that contracts made by local authorities ultra vires are void. But it allows a local authority to certify that a contract is intra vires, subject to judicial review; and, on such an application for judicial review, a court can decide that the contract should be treated as intra vires having regard 'to the likely consequences for the financial provision of the local authority, and for the provision of services to the public, of a decision that the contract should not have effect' (s 5(3)(b)).

10 See generally *Lessons of the Swaps Litigation* (eds Birks and Rose, 2000).

11 [1992] 2 AC 1, HL.

Rate (LIBOR). The decision in *Hazell* spawned much litigation – and several important decided cases – dealing with the restitution of money paid under a contract that is void as being ultra vires a public authority.

Leaving until chapter 11, the possibility that money paid *by* the public authority could be recovered on the basis of the incapacity (by reason of ultra vires) itself, there were two main possible grounds for restitution in these cases. One possible ground was mistake. The difficulty was that the mistake was one of law (the parties incorrectly believed that the contract was valid) and, traditionally, only mistakes of fact grounded restitution. As we have seen in chapter 3, it was in one of these swaps cases *Kleinwort Benson Ltd v Lincoln City Council*[12] that the House of Lords finally removed the mistake of law rule. The other main possible ground for restitution in these cases was failure of consideration. The claimants had paid money on the expectation, induced by the other party's promise, that it would receive net counter-payments over several years; and in the so-called 'open' swaps the other party had made some but not all of the counter-payments. A difficulty with this ground was that traditionally a total failure of consideration was required. And so long as some counter-payments had been made it would appear that the consideration for the claimants' payments had partially, but not totally, failed.

However, in *Westdeutsche Landesbank Girozentrale v Islington London Borough Council*[13] the House of Lords thought that there was a total failure of consideration, despite the receipt of some counter-payments by the claimant. Although the decision was particularly important in rejecting a claim for *proprietary* restitution,[14] there were also important statements made on the approach to total failure of consideration in personal restitutionary claims under void contracts.

The facts were these. The claimant bank had entered into an interest rate swap transaction with the defendant local authority on 18 June 1987. Under that agreement the claimant bank was the fixed rate payer and the defendant local authority was the floating rate payer. Additionally the bank had agreed to pay, and had paid, £2.5 million to the local authority on the commencement of the contract. Interest rates had favoured the bank (that is, the floating rate had been higher than the fixed rate) so that, prior to the first instance decision[15] in the *Hazell* case, the local authority had made four payments to the bank totalling £1,354,474. The bank brought an action against the local authority claiming restitution of £1,145,526 (being the initial lump

---

12   [1999] 2 AC 349.
13   [1996] AC 669.
14   See below, pp 409–410.
15   [1990] 2 WLR 17, upheld [1992] 2 AC 1, HL.

sum minus the four payments received from the local authority) plus interest from 18 June 1987.

At first instance,[16] Hobhouse J held that the bank was entitled to restitution on the ground that the money had been paid for no consideration; that is, there was an 'absence of consideration'. This was upheld by the Court of Appeal.[17] Both Hobhouse J and the Court of Appeal also added compound interest (although from different dates). The defendant local authority appealed to the House of Lords purely against the award of compound, as opposed to simple, interest. That appeal was successful. Although most of the speeches in the House of Lords were concerned with proprietary restitution and compound interest, their Lordships (with the exception of Lord Woolf) did consider the justification for personal restitution in a swaps case.

In the leading speech for the majority, Lord Browne-Wilkinson, with whom Lords Slynn and Lloyd agreed, said that the bank was entitled to (personal) restitution because there had been a total failure of consideration. There was a total failure because the counter-promise for the payments was void. In Lord Browne-Wilkinson's words, referring to *Sinclair v Brougham* (and overruling its rejection of a personal restitutionary claim),[18] 'The failure of consideration was *not* partial: the depositors had paid over their money in consideration of a promise to repay. That promise was ultra vires and void; therefore the consideration for the payment of the money wholly failed. So in the present swaps case (although the point is not one under appeal) ... the swap moneys were paid on a consideration that wholly failed.'[19]

In contrast, Lord Goff referred to academic criticisms of Hobhouse J's reliance on 'absence of consideration' as a ground for restitution and said that he thought there was 'considerable force'[20] in those criticisms. His view was that the correct ground for restitution might well therefore be failure of consideration. He studiously avoided saying that the failure of consideration had to be total.

One difficulty with Lord Browne-Wilkinson's approach is that, contrary to the traditional view, it treats the failure of consideration as turning on the validity of the promise rather than its performance.[1] On his Lordship's approach, there will be a total failure of consideration wherever a contract is void and despite the fact that, in a contract

16 [1994] 4 All ER 890.
17 [1994] 1 WLR 938. For criticism of 'absence of consideration' as an unjust factor, see above, pp 325, 386–388.
18 See below, chapter 11.
19 [1996] AC 669, 710.
20 Ibid, at 683.
1   See above, pp 325, 386–388.

where there are payments both ways, many (and indeed perhaps all) counter-payments have been made. It is submitted that Lord Browne-Wilkinson here joins a number of other judges in adopting an artificial view of what constitutes a total failure of consideration.[2] He should instead have recognised, more straightforwardly, that restitution should be available for a partial failure of consideration.

One must not think that this question of articulating the correct ground for restitution, and interpreting total failure of consideration correctly, is merely a matter of terminology. It has practical consequences. An important example came before the Court of Appeal in another swaps case, *Guinness Mahon & Co Ltd v Kensington and Chelsea Royal London Borough Council.*[3] The issue in that case was whether there could be restitution where the swap was a closed rather than an open one; that is, where the void contract had been fully executed on both sides so that all promised payments had been made. In line with Lord Browne-Wilkinson's reasoning in the *Westdeutsche* case, the Court of Appeal held that there should be restitution in a closed swap because there was a total failure of consideration. In Morritt LJ's words:

> 'A contract which is ultra vires one of the parties to it is and always has been devoid of any legal contractual effect. ... Payments made in purported performance thereof are necessarily made for a consideration which has totally failed and are therefore recoverable as money had and received ... The fact that the swap contract, though ultra vires and void, has been fully performed does not constitute a defence or bar to the recovery of the net payment as money had and received for the recipient had no more right to receive or retain the payment at the conclusion of the contract than he did before.'[4]

Significantly, however, Waller LJ, while concurring in the result and the reasoning, was troubled by the idea that the appropriate ground was total failure of consideration; and he referred to Lord Goff's obiter dicta in the *Westdeutsche* case, where Lord Goff had apparently approved criticisms of Hobhouse J's reliance on 'absence of consideration'. Waller LJ correctly pointed out that a possible ground for restitution in a closed swap would have been mistake of law were that not barred by the traditional English rule. Since *Guinness Mahon*, English law has been developed by the House of Lords in *Kleinwort Benson Ltd v Lincoln City Council*[5] so as to allow restitution for mistakes of law. *Kleinwort Benson* was itself a closed swap case where mistake,

---

2   Ibid. See also above, pp 327–331
3   [1999] QB 215. See above, pp 325, 386–388.
4   Ibid at 230.
5   [1999] 2 AC 349. See above, chapter 3.

rather than failure or absence of consideration, was being relied on because of its advantageous limitation period.

It is submitted that Waller LJ's doubts are justified and that, in a closed swap, the correct ground for restitution is mistake of law not failure of consideration. In an open swap, both (partial) failure of consideration and mistake of law are valid grounds for restitution. Contrary to the Court of Appeal in *Guinness Mahon* and the majority of the House of Lords in the *Westdeutsche* case, it distorts the meaning of total failure of consideration to regard restitution in a closed swap as resting on failure of consideration. Had the claimant banks in *Guinness Mahon* and *Kleinwort Benson Ltd v Lincoln City Council* made no mistake – that is, if they had known that the transaction was ultra vires the local authority and void – there should have been no restitution. By distorting 'failure of consideration' one would arrive at the wrong decision in that situation.[6]

(6) Contracts invalid because of infancy

In chapter 11 the question is examined whether a minor's incapacity is a ground for restitution. The answer on the authorities is that it is but only to a very limited extent. That is, the law unsatisfactorily insists that where a contract is invalid because of infancy, the minor's restitutionary remedies are dependent on whether there has been a total failure of consideration in the sense of the minor not having been rendered any part of what he bargained for.[7] The only distinction from a restitutionary claim by an adult is that the *Thomas v Brown*[8] requirement for total failure of consideration is not applied so that the minor can claim restitution even though the other contracting party (the adult) is ready, able and willing to perform.

Infancy operating as a defence to a claim for total failure of consideration by an adult under a contract invalid for infancy is discussed, and criticised, in chapter 15.[9]

(7) Illegal contracts

Where a contract is invalid because illegal, the illegality carries over to act as a defence to a restitutionary claim for total failure of consideration. The case law is examined – and criticised as being too restrictive of restitution – in chapter 15.

---

6   See above, p 387.
7   Eg *Steinberg v Scala (Leeds) Ltd* [1923] 2 Ch 452. Below, p 413.
8   (1876) 1 QBD 714: above, pp 331–332.
9   The leading case is *R Leslie Ltd v Sheill* [1914] 3 KB 607. Below, pp 559–562.

4. IS FREE ACCEPTANCE AN UNJUST FACTOR?

For Birks and Goff and Jones free acceptance is a central concept in the law of restitution. A free acceptance occurs 'where a recipient knows that a benefit is being offered to him non-gratuitously and where he, having the opportunity to reject, elects to accept'.[10] In Birks' structure in *An Introduction to the Law of Restitution,* free acceptance is unique in showing both that there is an enrichment and that it is unjust. Its role in establishing enrichment has been rejected in chapter 1. The focus in this section is on whether free acceptance is an unjust factor. This is conveniently considered in this chapter because the primary authorities relied on by Birks as showing free acceptance as an unjust factor are ones that have been analysed above as resting on failure of consideration.[11] Indeed the question can be centrally presented as one of whether the factor negativing the claimant's voluntariness of failure of consideration goes far enough or whether it requires supplementation by the 'defendant-sided'[12] ground of free acceptance.

Birks explained that the injustice outside non-voluntary transfer of a benefit, which free acceptance picks up, is that of refusing restitution to a disappointed risk-taker who has conferred a benefit on the free acceptor. 'This ... is the essential point: volunteers who are disappointed risk-takers can get restitution on the basis of free acceptance.'[13]

To illustrate this, Birks put forward the following example. 'Suppose that I see a window-cleaner beginning to clean the windows of my house. I know that he will expect to be paid. So I hang back unseen till he has finished the job; then I emerge and maintain that I will not pay for work which I never ordered. It is too late, I have freely accepted the service. I had the opportunity to send him away. I chose instead to let him go on. I must pay the reasonable value of his work.'[14]

Although he subsequently withdrew this description, he initially regarded the window-cleaning example as 'clear and simple'.[15] For the present author, however, it was the start of the feeling that something was amiss. I explained my unease as follows:

---

10   Birks, at p 104.
11   Most importantly *William Lacey (Hounslow) Ltd v Davis* [1957] 1 WLR 932: see Birks, at pp 272–274.
12   Birks, 'In Defence of Free Acceptance' in *Essays on the Law of Restitution* (ed Burrows, 1991), at pp 105, 144–145.
13   Birks, at p 266.
14   Birks, at p 265.
15   Ibid.

'... the crucial importance of free acceptance for Birks is that it would allow restitution to the window-cleaner even if he had been acting merely in the hope that I would pay; that is, even if the window-cleaner was a disappointed risk-taker. Yet surely on any common sense view there would be no injustice in my not paying a risk-taker. For even if I can be said to have acted shabbily, this is matched by the fact that the plaintiff was a risk-taker – without any inducement, he gambled on my willingness to pay. Why should we now want to protect him against the very risk that he undertook? In short, the plaintiff's risk-taking cancels out any shabbiness in my free acceptance. As such, free acceptance cannot be regarded in principle as an unjust factor.'[16]

Having challenged free acceptance as a matter of principle, I went on to argue that the major authorities relied on by Birks and Goff and Jones for free acceptance were explicable on other grounds, most importantly failure of consideration (combined with the bargained-for test of benefit).

Mead too has rejected free acceptance as an unjust factor.[17] He argues that it is inconsistent with other well-established common law principles, for example, the general antipathy to liability for omissions and the contractual rule of 'no acceptance by silence'. He also regards the doctrine as unacceptably uncertain in its practical application: would it, for example, impose liability on a person who did not stop the work because old or timid or simply because it was inconvenient to do so?

Birks responded with an essay entitled 'In Defence of Free Acceptance'[18] which, while conceding some points to his critics, kept free acceptance intact. Confining ourselves to the debate on free acceptance as an unjust factor, the thrust of this defence may be summarised as follows:

(i) As a matter of authority free acceptance was espoused and relied on in several common law cases: ie, *Lamb v Bunce*,[19] *Weatherby v Banham*,[20] *Paynter v Williams*,[1] *Alexander v Vane*,[2] *Leigh v Dickeson*,[3] *Falcke v Scottish Imperial Insurance Co*[4] and *Re Cleadon Trust Ltd*.[5]

(ii)   Where a benefit has been conferred by the claimant at the request of the defendant (for example, under a contract discharged for breach

---

16 'Free Acceptance and the Law of Restitution' (1988) 104 LQR 576, 578.
17 'Free Acceptance: Some Further Considerations' (1989) 105 LQR 460.
18 In *Essays on the Law of Restitution* (ed Burrows, 1991), pp 105–146.
19 (1815) 4 M & S 275.
20 (1832) 5 C & P 228.
1   (1833) 1 Cr & M 810.
2   (1836) 1 M & W 511.
3   (1884) 15 QBD 60.
4   (1886) 34 Ch D 234.
5   [1939] 1 Ch 286.

or frustration or under an anticipated contract) the primary unjust factor is failure of consideration. The unjust factor may be, but hardly ever is, free acceptance because this requires 'initial unconscionability' and a defendant who requests a benefit but later refuses to pay is generally guilty of only 'supervening' and not 'initial' unconscionability. 'Free acceptance, if it works at all, works because of the unconscientiousness of the recipient in not availing himself of the opportunity to save the intervener from the risk... It is obvious that "supervening unconscionability" has little or no weight in breaking the balance between a risk-taking intervener and the initially innocent recipient.'[6] So, for example, in *Pavey & Matthews Pty Ltd v Paul*[7] free acceptance was not the unjust factor because the defendant was not behaving unconscionably in allowing the building work to continue. She was intending to pay what she thought was a reasonable rate. The correct explanation for the decision was that the builders recovered the reasonable value of their work on the ground of failure of consideration. The same applies, for example, to the *'William Lacey* family of cases'.[8]

(iii)   Where a benefit has been conferred by the claimant without the request of the defendant, failure of consideration can explain those cases where the claimant knows that the defendant knows that he (the claimant) expects to be paid. Where there is initial unconscionability free acceptance offers an alternative explanation. But free acceptance alone could explain restitution in a situation of 'secret acceptance'.[9] That is, where the defendant knows that the claimant expects to be paid but the claimant is a risk-taker because he does not know that the defendant knows that he expects to be paid. However, there has been no case in which restitution has been awarded for secret acceptance.

(iv)   The window-cleaning example was not a good one on which to concentrate attention. The facts would only illustrate free acceptance if the window-cleaner would have desisted if the householder had told him that he would not be paid and if the householder had already made up his mind that he would not pay the window-cleaner. Without this combination of facts the householder would not be 'unequivocally unconscientious in not speaking out'.[10]

(v)   A good test for whether there is free acceptance (that is, for the particular species of unconscientiousness required) is, 'Did the

---

6   'In Defence of Free Acceptance' in *Essays on the Law of Restitution* (ed Burrows, 1991), at pp 105, 111.
7   (1986) 162 CLR 221, discussed above, pp 382–384.
8   'In Defence of Free Acceptance' in *Essays on the Law of Restitution* (ed Burrows 1991), at pp 105, 114.
9   Ibid, at p 119.
10   Ibid, at p 124.

defendant have reason to believe that, if the plaintiff knew what it was in his power to tell him, the plaintiff would desist?'[11] There is no free acceptance, for example, where a defendant stops to watch a street show at which, periodically, a hat is passed round: although the players have a certain expectation of payment they would not have desisted from continuing the show even if the defendant had told them in advance that he would not pay. 'The mean by-stander can therefore stop and watch with a defensibly clean conscience. He is not called upon to speak out because he knows that they would not be influenced by the knowledge of his intention not to pay.'[12] But that test is not foolproof. One does not freely accept by riding in a London taxi resolving to pay only the fare and no tip even if one knows that the taxi driver would have refused to take you had you told him that he would not be tipped.

(vi) Free acceptance should be used as a last resort. Where possible, other less controversial justifications, like failure of consideration, should be adopted. 'Free acceptance ... should be regarded as a long-stop, not to be called upon until the inquiry into the plaintiff-sided factors has produced a negative result.'[13]

Two main comments can be made on this defence of free acceptance.

First, the cases Birks referred to indisputably do contain statements broadly supporting free acceptance. But in the three latest cases, in which the statements were the strongest – *Leigh, Falcke* and *Cleadon* – restitution was denied on the facts. And in the four earlier cases, there were other 'claimant-sided' unjust factors justifying restitution, namely mistake of fact in *Weatherby v Banham* (the claimant had continued to supply a racing magazine to his customer who had died), necessity or failure of consideration in *Lamb v Bunce,* and failure of consideration in *Paynter v Williams* and *Alexander v Vane.* In line with point (vi) above, Birks would presumably agree that free acceptance was not the best explanation of those four cases.

That *Lamb, Paynter,* and *Alexander* can be explained on the ground of failure of consideration requires further elaboration. The central point is that, while in each the terms were not clearly spelt out, so that it was artificial to regard there as being such a sufficiently certain or complete bargain as to constitute a valid contract, there was a loose bargain in the sense that the claimant was reasonably led to expect by the defendant that he would be paid for the services conferred.

---

11 Ibid, at p 121.
12 Ibid.
13 Ibid, at pp 144–145.

In the first two cases, doctors performed necessitous medical services for paupers. Both successfully sued for payment from the parish whose officers had passively induced the claimants to believe that they would be paid for their services. The passive inducement was constituted in *Lamb* by the overseer not repudiating the claimant's continued treatment of the sick man; and in *Paynter* by the parish not replying to the claimant's letter explaining the position.[14] In *Alexander v Vane* the claimant, without the express request of the defendant but in his presence, undertook to the supplier of harnesses being bought by the defendant that, if the defendant did not pay the contract price, he would. After paying off the price, the claimant was held able to recover the money from the defendant. On the face of it this looks like an example of restitution for payment of another's debt under legal compulsion. But even ignoring *Owen v Tate*,[15] the problem with that analysis is that the guarantee given by the claimant was oral and therefore 'binding in honour' only. However, one can say that in the circumstances the defendant passively engendered the expectation in the claimant that he would be reimbursed if he did pay off the debt. Failure to reimburse therefore constituted a failure of consideration.

By slightly different reasoning Birks reached the same conclusion on those three cases. For him there was a failure of consideration in each because, although the claimant did not expressly communicate the basis for his services to the defendant, the claimant was not a risk-taker because he knew that the defendant knew his terms:

> 'If I do work for you, privately determined that you shall pay, I shall not by that alone persuade any court that I worked only in consideration that you would pay. I shall seem merely to have taken a risk. To avoid that charge I must communicate my intention to you so that you know the basis upon which I am working and can repudiate it if you wish. But if I know that you know my terms, I will be excused the need to tell you what they are.'[16]

Birks' reasoning is equivalent to saying (in line with the suggested analysis above) that the claimant is a risk-taker unless he has been reasonably led to expect, by the defendant's active or passive conduct, that he would be paid for his services.

The second comment is that in defending free acceptance as a matter of principle Birks resorted to a high degree of fine tuning for

---

14   The court's reasoning in this case was clearly not based on the unjust factor of necessity as shown by the denial of the claimant's claim for the nine weeks' services rendered before the letter was sent. Note also that the liability to provide services to the pauper was that of the different parish where the pauper was residing.

15   [1976] QB 402, criticised above, chapter 8.

16   'In Defence of Free Acceptance' in *Essays on the Law of Restitution* (ed Burrows, 1991), pp 105, 115.

which there is clearly no direct authority. At this point unjust enrichment is in danger of floating down from the sky on a mist of subjective intuition. Moreover, the distinctions drawn are complex and, arguably, unworkable in practice. For example, the initially unconscientious recipient will nearly always be able to argue plausibly that he was absolved from speaking out (ie that the unconscientiousness was subsequent only) because he did not firmly decide not to pay for the work until it was complete. In addition Birks gave no convincing explanation for his taxi driver 'exception'. It seems a classic case of free acceptance: the taxi driver's claim to a tip is no more, and no less, appealing than the window-cleaner's claim for full payment.

It is submitted, therefore, that while free acceptance does have some support in the cases that support is not sufficiently strong to avoid marginalisation and reclassification; and, as a matter of principle, even a minor and 'last resort' role for free acceptance as an unjust factor seems overgenerous. At least at the present time burial is more apt for Birks' troublesome creature than imprisonment in a tiny cell.

Indeed it may be that even Birks has come to accept these criticisms. In his most recent writings, the unjust factors have been divided into factors negativing voluntariness and a residual class of policy-motivated factors. No room has been found for an unjust factor of free acceptance or unconscientious receipt. In a work co-authored with Mitchell,[17] he writes, 'Attempts have been made to divide that residue between "unconscientious receipt" and "policy reasons". However, it turns out that every supposed case of unconscientious receipt is no more than a weak or otherwise special case of non-voluntary transfer.'

5.   FAILURE OF CONSIDERATION AS THE FAILURE OF AN UNPROMISED FUTURE EVENT

It was explained at the start of this chapter that failure of consideration can be, and has been, used to include the failure of an *unpromised* future event. Whether the event was promised or not, the injustice of the defendant's enrichment is the same in that, where the future event does not occur, the basis for the claimant's conferral of the benefit is undermined.

---

17 'Unjust Enrichment' in *English Private Law* (ed Birks, 2000), para 15.47. See also Virgo, *The Principles of the Law of Restitution* (1999), pp 121–124. In contrast, Tettenborn, *The Law of Restitution in England and Ireland* (3rd edn, 2002), ch 5 continues to defend free acceptance as an unjust factor: see also Tolhurst and Carter, 'Acceptance of Benefit as a Basis for Restitution' (2002) 18 JCL 52; *Andrew Shelton & Co Pty Ltd v Alpha Healthcare Ltd* [2002] VSC 248, Supreme Court of Victoria.

In line with the standard meaning of failure of consideration, the claimant alleging that the rendering of the benefit was conditional on an unpromised future event can only avoid being treated as a risk-taker not entitled to restitution if he either expressly communicated the contingent condition to the defendant or was reasonably led to believe by the defendant that he (the defendant) knew that that contingent condition was the basis for the benefit being rendered.

The leading case is *Chillingworth v Esche*.[18] The claimant purchasers agreed to purchase certain land from the defendant vendor 'subject to contract', and paid over £240 as a deposit and in part payment. Subsequently the claimants refused to go ahead and sign the written contract and claimed the return of the £240. The Court of Appeal held that the claimants were entitled to restitution of the £240. The money was not paid under a valid contract. Rather it was paid on condition that a binding contract would subsequently be entered into between the parties. When that contingent condition (which was not promised by either party) failed to eventuate the claimants were entitled to recover their money. And as there was no binding contract there was no question of applying the 'contracting-out of restitution' rule normally associated with deposits.[19]

Counsel for the defendant had argued that the claimants could not recover because to do so they would have to show a failure of consideration and this they could not do because, applying *Thomas v Brown*,[20] the defendant was always ready, able and willing to convey the land. But as the ground for restitution was the failure of an unpromised future event, that objection could not hold sway and was rightly rejected.

In *Roxborough v Rothmans of Pall Mall Australia Ltd*[1] the High Court of Australia (Kirby J dissenting), in allowing restitution of money paid for total failure of consideration, regarded the failure as the failure of an unpromised future event. That is, the basis of a severable part of the payment made by retailers to wholesalers for tobacco was that that sum would be payable by the wholesalers to the state as tax. The consideration failed when the statute imposing the tax was declared invalid.[2]

---

18   [1924] 1 Ch 97. See also *Guardian Ocean Cargoes Ltd v Banco do Brasil SA* [1991] 2 Lloyd's Rep 68 (Hirst J applying *Chillingworth v Esche*). Hirst J's alternative ground of reasoning, applying a *Quistclose* trust, was reversed by the Court of Appeal as, consequentially, was the award of compound interest . [1994] 2 Lloyd's Rep 152.

19   Above, p 353.

20   (1876) 1 QBD 714: above, pp 331–332.

1   [2001] HCA 68.

2   A major difficulty, which was the reason for Kirby J's dissent, was that the contract between the retailers and wholesalers was valid. See above, p 323, n 1. On the face of it mistake of law (by analogy to *Kleinwort Benson Ltd v Lincoln City Council* [1999] 2 AC 349) was the more obvious ground for restitution than failure of consideration: the retailers paid mistakenly thinking that the tax was legally owing. But mistake is mentioned only in the dissenting judgment of Kirby J.

6. PROPRIETARY RESTITUTION IN RESPECT OF PAYMENTS MADE FOR A FAILED CONSIDERATION

The above discussion of restitution consequent on a failure of consideration has been dealing with the usual situation where the claimant seeks *personal* restitution. But if, by reason of the failure of consideration, an unjust enrichment at the claimant's expense is established and the defendant retains the payment (whether in the same form or, by the rules of tracing, in a substitute) is the claimant entitled to *proprietary* restitution?[3] This will be of vital importance if the defendant has become insolvent because proprietary restitution gives priority on the defendant's insolvency.

The general answer to this is clear. The claimant is not entitled to proprietary restitution. If a debtor fails to repay a loan to its creditor, the creditor is not entitled to proprietary restitution for failure of consideration even if the debtor retains the loaned money (or its traceable substitute). If that were not so, many unsecured creditors would automatically be given security through proprietary restitution.

So, for example, in *Re Goldcorp Exchange Ltd*[4] the Privy Council was concerned with claims, by two separate sets of investors, in respect of the purchase of gold bullion held by the defendant insolvent company. In contrast to the so-called 'Walker and Hall claimants', the 'non-allocated claimants' were in the same position as general creditors. That is, they had paid in advance for goods (the gold) and title to the goods had not passed to them prior to the defendant's insolvency. The Privy Council therefore dismissed their claims to a proprietary interest in the purchase money. As regards misrepresentation by the defendant (or mistake), the claimants had not rescinded the contracts: and, as regards failure of consideration, there was no immediate failure of consideration and 'there was nothing in the express agreement to require, and nothing in their Lordships' view can be implied, which constrained in any way the company's freedom to spend the purchase money as it chose.'[5]

Similarly, in *Westdeutsche Landesbank Girozentrale v Islington London Borough Council*,[6] one of the interest-rate swap cases, the House of Lords decided that the money paid by the bank under the void partly-executed contract was not held on (resulting) trust by the defendant (this being regarded as important in deciding whether the bank was

---

3 For general discussion see, eg, Chambers, *Resulting Trusts* (1997), pp 143–170; Birks, 'Restitution and Resulting Trusts' in *Equity and Contemporary Legal Developments* (eg Goldstein, 1992), pp 335–373.
4 [1995] 1 AC 74. See also *Guardian Ocean Cargoes Ltd v Banco do Brasil SA* [1994] 2 Lloyd's Rep 152.
5 Ibid, at 101 (*per* Lord Mustill).
6 [1996] AC 669.

entitled to compound, rather than merely simple, interest on the repayment). Prior to the removal of the mistake of law bar, the unjust factor was most obviously, and was treated by their Lordships as being, failure of consideration. In Lord Goff's words:

> 'The question has ... arisen whether the bank should also have the benefit of an equitable proprietary claim in the form of a resulting trust. The immediate reaction must be – why should it? Take the present case. The parties have entered into a commercial transaction. The transaction has, for technical reasons, been held to be void from the beginning. Each party is entitled to recover its money, with the result that the balance must be repaid. But why should the plaintiff bank be given the additional benefits which flow from a proprietary claim, for example the benefit of achieving priority in the event of the defendant's insolvency? After all, it has entered into a commercial transaction, and so taken the risk of the defendant's insolvency, just like the defendant's other creditors who have contracted with it.'[7]

In rejecting a trust, the House of Lords overruled *Sinclair v Brougham*.[8] In that long-controversial decision, it had been held that money paid to a company under a contract that was void because ultra vires the company was held on a (resulting) trust for the payor.

In line with the discussion of proprietary restitution in chapter 1, proprietary restitution in respect of failure of consideration is indeed generally not justified and the overruling of *Sinclair Brougham* by *Westdeutsche* seems correct. On one approach, this is because the claimant's consent is qualified rather than vitiated. Therefore, prior to the failure of consideration, the defendant is generally entitled to the enrichment and free to deal with it as its own. On an alternative approach, one can say that a claimant alleging failure of consideration has generally taken the risk of the defendant's insolvency.

However, this will not always be so. Exceptionally, proprietary restitution for a failure of consideration is justified and has been granted. Two examples can be given.[9]

First, and most importantly, there is the so-called *Quistclose* trust. In *Barclays Bank Ltd v Quistclose Investments Ltd*[10] the claimant loaned money

---

7   Ibid, at 683–684.
8   [1914] AC 398. See also below, pp 566–568. Peculiarly, Lord Goff, unlike their other Lordships, preferred not to overrule *Sinclair v Brougham* but rather regarded it as laying down no principle of general application.
9   Another illustration is subrogation to securities. In chapter 2 some examples of this have been discussed where the unjust factor is best viewed as failure of consideration: eg, *Butler v Rice* [1910] 2 Ch 277; *Boscawen v Bajwa* [1996] 1 WLR 328. It has been submitted in that chapter that that proprietary restitution can in most cases (but not all, see especially *Lord Napier and Ettrick v Hunter* [1993] AC 713) be justified because the claimant has not taken the risk of the payee's insolvency.
10   [1970] AC 567.

to the defendant for the exclusive purpose of paying a dividend to shareholders. When that purpose failed, because of the defendant's insolvency, the House of Lords decided that the money paid was held on trust for the claimant.[11] This result is justified even if the payor did not create an express purpose trust. Applying Chambers' approach,[12] this is because the payee never obtained the unrestricted use of the money before the failure of consideration; or, on the alternative approach discussed in chapter 1,[13] the express restriction on the use of the money meant that the claimant was unlike other unsecured creditors and had not taken the risk of the defendant's insolvency. The *Quistclose* exception explains why in *Re Goldcorp Exchange Ltd* the Privy Council was at pains to clarify that the money paid by the 'unallocated claimants' fell within the general fund of the defendant's assets and did not have to be applied for a special designated purpose.[14] Wherever failure of consideration is the unjust factor, and proprietary rather than merely personal restitution is sought, a court will always need to construe the terms of the payment in order to ascertain whether the *Quistclose* exception to the general rule of no proprietary restitution applies.

Secondly, a resulting trust imposed where an express trust fails because events do not turn out as specified may perhaps exemplify proprietary restitution for a failure of consideration (using failure of consideration in its non-promissory sense).[15] The trust can be regarded as imposed to reverse the unjust enrichment of the beneficiaries or the trustee. Proprietary restitution in this situation can be justified either because the recipient never had the unrestricted use of the property or because, by setting up the trust, the transferor had not taken the risk of the recipient's insolvency.

---

11 The correct analysis of the *Quistclose* trust has long been a matter of debate: see, eg, Lord Millett's speech in *Twinsectra Ltd v Yardley* [2002] UKHL 12, [2002] 2 AC 164.

12 See above, p 68, esp n 4.

13 See above, pp 70–71, esp n 14.

14 [1995] 1 AC 74, 101. See above, p 409.

15 Eg, *Re Ames' Settlement* [1946] Ch 217 (trust set up on son's marriage which was subsequently annulled); *Re Abbott Fund Trusts* [1900] 2 Ch 326; *Re Gillingham Bus Disaster Fund* [1958] Ch 300; *Re West Sussex Constabulary Widows' Children and Benevolent (1930) Fund Trust* [1971] Ch 1 (subsequent failure of purpose trusts).

Chapter 11

Incapacity as a ground for restitution

An individual who, at the time of conferring a benefit, is a minor (under 18) or insane or drunk, may be regarded by the law as entitled to restitution (within unjust enrichment by subtraction) on the ground of incapacity. Such mental incapacity is clearly similar to the unjust factor that we have labelled 'exploitation of mental weakness'.[1] But the distinguishing requirement of exploitation is that the terms of the transaction must be substantively unfair whereas, in principle, the procedural unfairness of incapacity ought to be sufficient in itself to render substantive unfairness irrelevant. Instead the closest analogy to incapacity should lie with mistake for the claimant who lacks capacity does not truly intend to benefit the defendant.

Consideration is also given in this chapter to the incapacity of non-human legal persons.[2] Can a company or public authority be granted restitution on the basis that its transfer of benefits to the defendant was ultra vires?

Most of this chapter concerns personal restitution. But, as we shall see, proprietary restitution through rescission has been granted for insanity.[3] In principle, the same approach to proprietary restitution should probably be taken as is taken in relation to the closest analogous area of mistake.[4]

Incapacity may also operate as a defence to restitution (ie, to other grounds for restitution). That is examined in chapter 15.

1. INFANCY

Our primary focus is on benefits rendered under *contracts* invalidated for infancy.

---

1   Above, pp 261–267.
2   For a general consideration of incapacity as a ground for restitution, see O'Dell, 'Incapacity' in *Lessons of the Swaps Litigation* (eds Birks and Rose, 2000), pp 113–167.
3   See below, p 418.
4   See generally above, pp 64–75. For proprietary restitution for mistaken payments, see above pp 159–162. For discussion of whether incapacity does and should trigger restitution through a resulting trust, see Chambers, *Resulting Trusts* (1997), pp 118–125.

The contractual rules on minors' contracts are complex, despite the repeal of the Infants Relief Act 1874 by the Minors' Contracts Act 1987. Basically, contracts fall into three categories:[5] first, those that are valid (eg, contracts for necessaries or beneficial contracts of service); secondly, those that can be 'repudiated' by the infant before or within a short time after reaching adulthood (eg, contracts for shares in companies or partnership agreements); and, thirdly, the most common category, those that are unenforceable against the minor unless he ratifies them on reaching adulthood. In none of the three categories is it relevant whether the adult knew or not that the other party was under 18.

The question at issue is whether the incapacity invalidating the contract carries through to constitute an unjust factor grounding a claim by the minor for restitution of the benefits conferred. In other words, is a minor entitled to restitution if he chooses to repudiate under category 2 or chooses not to ratify under category 3?

The unsatisfactory but predominant view in the authorities is that, in order to recover money, or even specific goods, the minor must establish a total failure of consideration.

In *Steinberg v Scala (Leeds) Ltd*,[6] for example, the infant claimant had bought shares in a company (a category 2 contract). Some 18 months later she repudiated the contract and had her allotment of shares cancelled. But she was denied restitution of the purchase price paid on the ground that there had been no total failure of consideration. She had had the benefit of her shareholding (ie, the right to dividends, although she had not received any, and the right to attend meetings, although she had not attended any). Lord Sterndale MR said:

> 'I think the argument for the respondent has rather proceeded upon the assumption that the question whether she can rescind and the question whether she can recover her money back are the same. They are two quite different questions ... although the contract may be rescinded the money paid cannot be recovered back unless there has been an entire failure of the consideration for which the money has been paid.'[7]

In *Pearce v Brain*[8] a minor exchanged his motorcycle and sidecar for a car (a category 3 contract). After driving the car for 70 miles it broke down owing to a serious defect. It was held that the minor's claim to recover the motorcycle and sidecar[9] should fail because there

---

5   Treitel, *The Law of Contract* (10th edn), pp 498–510.
6   [1923] 2 Ch 452.
7   Ibid, at p 458.
8   [1929] 2 KB 310.
9   It appears that the claim was being brought in the tort of detinue.

had been no total failure of consideration and there was no sensible distinction between the recovery of a specific chattel and the recovery of money.

One difficulty is that the court envisaged title to the motorcycle and sidecar revesting in the minor had there been a total failure of consideration. On that view, the adult's title to the goods could not be accurately described as void or voidable. Instead it would be *sui generis*: ie, void unless some consideration passed to the minor (or, under a category 2 contract, unless the minor chose not to repudiate). Given the emphasis on total failure of consideration the more obvious view would probably have been that good title to the motorcycle had passed to the adult and could not be revested in the minor. And the relevant remedy for total failure of consideration would then have been the personal restitutionary remedy of a *quantum valebat*. This is supported by the majority's judgment (Lord Denning dissenting) in *Chaplin v Leslie Frewin Publishers Ltd* [10] which held that, even if the contract in question was invalid (within category 3) rather than, as it preferred, valid within category 1, the infant claimant could not recover the copyright assigned to the defendants. In Danckwerts LJ's words, 'If an infant revokes a contract, the property and interests which have previously been transferred by him cannot be recovered by the infant ... the transfers of property made by the plaintiff remain effective against him even if the contract is otherwise revocable.' [11]

A further difficulty of *Pearce v Brain* is that *Valentini v Canali* [12] was treated as binding authority for there being a requirement of total failure of consideration vis-à-vis the restitution of money. In that case the infant claimant agreed to buy furniture from the defendant for £102 and paid £68 on account (a category 3 contract). Having used the furniture for several months he sought restitution of the £68. Lord Coleridge CJ said, 'Here the infant plaintiff who claimed to recover back the money which he had paid to the defendant had had the use of a quantity of furniture for some months. He could not give back his benefit or replace the defendant in the position in which he was before the contract.' [13]

Goff and Jones tentatively criticise the interpretation of *Valentini* in *Pearce v Brain* on the ground that the language used by Lord Coleridge CJ suggested that the relevant bar to restitution was the impossibility of *restitutio in integrum* and not that there had been no *total*

10   [1966] Ch 71.
11   Ibid, at p 94.
12   (1889) 24 QBD 166
13   Ibid, at p 167.

failure of consideration.[14] This seems a valid criticism and links in with the major thrust of Goff and Jones' approach, which is that, contrary to the predominant insistence on total failure of consideration, infancy *should* trigger restitution subject to the minor giving counter-restitution. This proposal should be supported.[15] The present approach of the courts means that infancy is only being treated as an unjust factor, triggering restitution of contractual benefits, to the limited extent that a minor can claim restitution for total failure of consideration even though the other contracting party (the adult) is ready, able and willing to perform (ie, the normal *Thomas v Brown* requirement[16] is ignored).[17] It is to this limited extent only that, in the context of contractual benefits, the law of restitution treats minors differently from adults.[18] To confine the impact of infancy so is unsatisfactory. The policy justification for allowing minors out of contracts – protecting the young against foolishness and poor judgment – should surely be fully carried over to restitution. Restitutionary remedies, subject to the adult's rights to counter-restitution (for failure of consideration),[19] should be triggered by infancy and there should be no requirement that the infant claimant establishes a total failure of consideration in the sense of showing that he has not been rendered any part of what he bargained-for.[20] Admittedly the peculiar contractual regime for infancy means that there is no straightforward restitutionary precedent to which one can turn. To describe the contracts in categories 2 and 3 as voidable so that infancy (like, for example, undue influence) triggers rescission might at first sight seem the neatest solution[1] but it could carry some disadvantages to minors as against the present law: for example, title to goods would undoubtedly pass to a bona fide purchaser for value without notice whereas, if the approach in *Pearce v Brain* is correct, good title does not pass under the present law; and the burden of effecting rescission would fall on the minor even in what is now a category 3 case. Even if reformed in the way suggested by Goff and Jones the law on infancy may therefore have to remain *sui generis*.

---

14 Goff and Jones, at para 25-006.
15 This is also supported by Treitel, 'The Infants Relief Act 1874' (1957) 73 LQR 194, 202–204; and by Maddaugh and McCamus, *The Law of Restitution* (1st edn, 1990), pp 338–339.
16 Above, pp 331–332.
17 See *Corpe v Overton* (1833) 10 Bing 252.
18 Birks at p 217, Treitel, *The Law of Contract* (10th edn), p 507. Cf Lord Sterndale in *Steinberg v Scala (Leeds) Ltd* [1923] 2 Ch 452, 459.
19 In chapter 15 it is argued that infancy should not be a defence to an adult's restitutionary claim.
20 An alternative restitutionary analysis based on mistake could not generally have helped minors in the reported cases because they rarely made causative mistakes (especially of fact).
1 Lord Denning's dissent in *Chaplin v Leslie Frewin (Publishers) Ltd* [1966] Ch 71 offers some support for this.

Although there appear to be no clear authorities on the point, it seems that gifts cannot be set aside and are not invalidated by infancy. In the words of the Latey Committee, 'There is ... no legal restriction upon the power of infants to make a gift of property which they can lawfully hold save that in certain cases the law relating to ... undue influence may be applied more as a matter of presumption.'[2] If correct, this is surprising. By analogy to the restitution of contractual benefits one would have expected a minor to be able to repudiate a gift, and to have restitution, within a short time after becoming 18.

2.   INSANITY AND DRUNKENNESS

By s 94 of the Mental Health Act 1983, where 'a person is incapable, by reason of mental disorder, of managing and administering his property and affairs' they may be brought under the control of the Court of Protection. If so, a non-testamentary gift by the *incapax* is void[3] (and presumably restitution follows)[4] and a contract is voidable at the option of the *incapax* represented by the Court of Protection (subject presumably to the usual bars to rescission).[5] This applies even if the gift or contract was made during a period when the *incapax* knew what he was doing for the invalidity is at root based on avoiding a conflict with the court's control over the affairs of the *incapax*.

Where a person of unsound mind retains control of his own affairs and concludes a contract, he can set it aside if he did not know what he was doing provided the other party knew of his insanity. This contrasts with the law on minors' contracts where, as we have seen in the previous section, it is irrelevant whether or not the adult contracting party knew that the claimant was a minor. The leading case is *Imperial Loan Co v Stone*[6] in which the Court of Appeal refused to allow the defendant to avoid his contractual obligations as a surety because he had not proved that the sane party knew of his insanity. Lord Esher MR said:

> 'When a person enters into a contract, and afterwards alleges that he was so insane at the time that he did not know what he was doing, and proves the allegation, the contract is as binding on him in every respect, whether it is executory

---

2   'Report of the Committee on the Age of Majority' (1967) Cmnd 3342, p 98. A minor cannot hold a legal estate in land: Law of Property Act 1925, s 1(6). With a few exceptions, no person under 18 can make a valid will: Wills Act 1837, s 7 as amended by s 3, Family Law Reform Act 1969.
3   *Re Walker* [1905] 1 Ch 160.
4   See *Rourke v Halford* (1916) 31 DLR 371 where tracing was also talked about.
5   *Baldwyn v Smith* [1900] 1 Ch 588.
6   [1892] 1 QB 599.

or executed, as if he had been sane when he made it, unless he can prove further that the person with whom he contracted knew him to be so insane as not to be capable of understanding what he was about.'[7]

This was reaffirmed by the Privy Council in *Hart v O'Connor*[8] in overruling the New Zealand case of *Archer v Cutler*,[9] in which McMullin J had held that an unfair contract entered into by an insane person would be set aside irrespective of the sane party's knowledge of that insanity. Lord Brightman said:

'The validity of a contract entered into by a lunatic who is ostensibly sane is to be judged by the same standards as a contract by a person of sound mind, and is not voidable by the lunatic or his representatives by reason of "unfairness" unless such unfairness amounts to equitable fraud which would have enabled the complaining party to avoid the contract even if he had been sane.'[10]

On the facts in *Hart*, a contract made by an 83 year-old man of unsound mind was held valid on the ground that, as the purchaser did not know of the vendor's insanity, the contract could not be set aside either for incapacity or as an 'unconscionable bargain'.

The approach in *Imperial Loan Co v Stone* and *Hart v O'Connor* has been criticised on the ground that it is too harsh to the insane party and is out of line with the law on infancy, where knowledge of the incapacity is irrelevant.[11] A tentative counter-argument is that while both are concerned with the policy of protecting those who are likely to enter foolish and ill-considered transactions, one can justify treating insanity (and drunkenness) differently from infancy because there is no objective test of insanity (or drunkenness) that corresponds to the simple 'under or over 18' distinction. Put another way, it is perhaps understandable that the law is less willing to intervene where the incapacity is a matter of opinion rather than verifiable fact.

What is perhaps more disappointing is that the Privy Council in *Hart v O'Connor* did not make more of the opportunity opened up by *Archer v Cutler* to apply 'exploitation' rules – where 'substantive fairness' is traditionally important – to supplement the restrictive incapacity rules. That is, the Privy Council not only followed *Imperial Loan Co v Stone* but also insisted on knowledge and hence 'bad faith' by the sane party in order for the contract to be set aside as an 'unconscionable bargain'. Arguably, this was to take an unnecessarily restrictive interpretation of the principles of exploitation.[12]

---

7   Ibid, at p 601.
8   [1985] AC 1000.
9   [1980] 1 NZLR 386. This case was welcomed by Hudson (1984) Conv 32.
10 [1985] AC 1000, 1027.
11 Eg, Goudy, 'Contracts by Lunatics' (1901) 17 LQR 147.
12 Above, pp 265–266.

The relevant remedy for incapacity by reason of insanity is rescission of the contract which will presumably be subject to its usual four bars of lapse of time, affirmation, third party rights and *restitutio in integrum* being impossible. Rescission was non-restitutionary (being simply concerned to allow escape from a contract) in *Imperial Loan Co v Stone* whereas it operated as a proprietary restitutionary remedy in *Archer v Cutler* and *Hart v O'Connor*.[13]

That rescission is the relevant remedy in respect of contracts entered into by a person of unsound mind constitutes a further difference from the infancy regime where the minor needs to establish a total failure of consideration and the questions of contractual invalidity and restitution are sharply differentiated. This difference is puzzling and adds weight to the call for the reform of the law on restitution for infancy advocated in the last section. As it is, while the rules on a minor's incapacity are in one sense more liberal to the minor – the other contracting party does not need to know of his infancy – they are more restrictive to the extent that a total failure of consideration is insisted on for restitution.

In contrast to the contractual position, a gift will be void (presumably entitling the *incapax* to a personal restitutionary remedy for the value of the benefit conferred) or, on another view, voidable, where effected by an insane person who did not know what he was doing, *irrespective of the donee's knowledge of the insanity*.[14] As in other areas (eg mistake) this contrast shows the courts' greater reluctance to intervene where bargained-for expectations would be destroyed. A more puzzling contrast is between the willingness of the courts to hold gifts void (or voidable) for insanity but not for infancy.

There is very little, and no modern, authority on drunkenness. What there is supports the view that, apart from the Court of Protection having no role, the law examined above on insanity applies equally to drunkenness.[15]

---

13 Restitutionary and counter-restitutionary consequences following rescission were carefully considered in the second of the New Zealand Court of Appeal's judgments in *O'Connor v Hart* [1984] 1 NZLR 754.

14 *Daily Telegraph Newspaper Co Ltd v McLoughlin* [1904] AC 776; *Re Beaney* [1978] 1 WLR 770 (where it was left open whether the gift was rendered void or voidable); *Simpson v Simpson* [1992] 1 FLR 601. In *Gibbons v Wright* (1954) 91 CLR 423 the High Court of Australia thought that gifts were voidable not void. In *Re Beaney* it was said that the degree of understanding required varies according to the type of transaction and its content.

15 *Gore v Gibson* (1845) 13 M & W 623; *Matthews v Baxter* (1873) LR 8 Exch 132; Treitel, *The Law of Contract* (10th edn), pp 518–519. In the *Gore* case Alderson B at 627 also equated somnambulism with drunkenness.

3. A COMPANY ACTING ULTRA VIRES

If a company (other than a public authority as dealt with in the next section) acts ultra vires in rendering a benefit to the defendant, is it entitled to restitution on the ground that it had no capacity to transfer that benefit?

That question is now of little practical importance because, by s 35 of the Companies Act 1985, the ultra vires doctrine has largely been abolished. Although there are exceptions to it, s 35(1) reads, 'The validity of an act done by a company shall not be called into question on the ground of lack of capacity by reason of anything in the company's memorandum.'

A leading authority on the position at common law is *Brougham v Dwyer*.[16] The Birkbeck Permanent Benefit Building Society had been carrying on an ultra vires banking business. Its lending contracts were void because ultra vires.[17] Nevertheless it was held that the Society's liquidator could recover money loaned to the defendant customer in an action for money had and received. Lush J said, 'The case appears to me to be on all fours with one in which money has been advanced on something which was thought to be a contract, but as to which it turns out there has been a total failure of consideration'.[18]

There is also dicta of Mocatta J at first instance in *Bell Houses Ltd v City Wall Properties Ltd*[19] suggesting that, while a company cannot enforce an ultra vires contract, it is entitled to the restitutionary remedies of money had and received and *quantum meruit*. And, as regards the latter, an analogy was drawn with the want of authority case of *Craven-Ellis v Canons Ltd*.[20] This is further supported by Lawson J in *International Sales and Agencies Ltd v Marcus*,[1] where a director, in breach of his fiduciary duty to the claimant company, had used £30,000 of company money to pay off personal debts of a friend to the defendant moneylender. While the judge's primary reasoning in allowing the company restitution was the defendant's intermeddling by knowing receipt and dealing,[2] he thought that the company was in any event entitled to restitution simply

---

16 (1913) 108 LT 504. See also *Re Halt Garage (1964) Ltd* [1982] 3 All ER 1016, 1044–1045, which concerned non-contractual benefits.

17 That a contract is void if ultra vires is laid down by *Ashbury Railway Carriage and Iron Co Ltd v Roche* (1875) LR 7 HL 653. Cf Salmon LJ in *Bell Houses Ltd v City Wall Properties Ltd* [1966] 2 QB 656, 694, who hinted that an *executed* contract may be enforceable by a company and is not void.

18 (1913) 108 LT 504, 565.

19 [1966] 1 QB 207. His decision that the contract was ultra vires was reversed by the Court of Appeal: [1966] 2 QB 656.

20 [1936] 2 KB 403. Above, pp 390–391.

1 [1982] 3 All ER 551, 560. Above, p 200.

2 See similarly *Precision Dippings Ltd v Precision Dippings Marketing Ltd* [1986] Ch 447. On 'knowing receipt', see above, pp 194–206.

on the ground that, through the director, the company had become a party to the transaction that was ultra vires the company and under which the company paid money to the defendant.

What was the unjust factor in the above cases?[3] Although no clear view was expressed, and although failure of consideration and mistake were both possibilities, the most natural and straightforward view is that the ultra vires doctrine, which nullified the contract, carried on through to allow the company restitution. That is, that the policy of protecting shareholders and creditors of the company which lay behind the contractual invalidity also justified restitution for the company, so that the ground for restitution was, straightforwardly, the incapacity of the company.[4]

4. A PUBLIC AUTHORITY ACTING ULTRA VIRES[5]

If a public authority confers a benefit ultra vires, is it entitled to restitution on the ground of lack of capacity?

The main case on point is *Auckland Harbour Board v R*[6] where the Privy Council held that £7,500 paid by the Ministry of Railways ultra vires was recoverable. Viscount Haldane said, 'Any payment out of the consolidated fund made without parliamentary authority is simply illegal and ultra vires, and may be recovered by the government if it can, as here, be traced.'[7] Presumably the public authority paid the money under a mistake (whether of law or fact). But the decision was based on the policy of protecting public funds and thereby recognised that the incapacity (by reason of ultra vires) was itself an unjust factor. In this it mirrors *Woolwich Equitable Building Society v IRC.*[8] Just as that decision protects the public from the raising of money by public authorities ultra vires, *Auckland Harbour Board* protects the public from the spending of funds by public authorities ultra vires. The policy in

---

3   Birks, pp 309–310.
4   A defendant's entitlement to counterclaim for restitution depends in principle on whether incapacity, by reason of ultra vires, is a good *defence* to failure of consideration or, possibly, mistake: see below, pp 565–568.
5   See the Law Commission's Report, *Restitution: Mistakes of Law and Ultra Vires Public Authority Receipts and Payments*, Law Com No 227 (1994) Part XVII. A state has EC rights entitling it prima facie (ie, subject to defences) to restitution of overpaid EC subsidies and grants. Indeed EC law may require restitution to be sought. See, eg, *H Ferwerda BV v Producktschap voor Vee en Vlees* Case 265/78 [1980] ECR 617; *Deutsche Milchkontor GmbH v Germany* Cases 205–215/82 [1983] ECR 2633. This requirement of restitution appears to be satisfied in English law by the application of incapacity as a ground for restitution (ie, the application of *Auckland Harbour Board v R* [1924] AC 318). See generally Alison Jones, *Restitution and European Community Law* (2000), chapter 5.
6   [1924] AC 318.
7   Ibid, at p 327.
8   [1993] AC 70. Below, chapter 13.

question is directly analogous to the policy of protecting shareholders and investors that lies behind the company law ultra vires ground for restitution discussed in the previous section.

There are two puzzling features of Viscount Haldane's reasoning. The first is his reference to tracing. Although Lord Goff in *Woolwich* interpreted that as meaning that the claim was 'proprietary in nature'[9] there was nothing either in the facts or in the rest of Viscount Haldane's judgment to suggest that tracing in the strict sense was what was meant. Such a restriction would be anomolous. With respect therefore, the better interpretation is that taken by the Supreme Court of Victoria in *Commonwealth of Australia v Burns*[10] to the effect that the reference to tracing was not to 'tracing in the equitable or proprietary sense but to tracing the identity of the recipient of the money ... there was no evidence that the sum of £7,500 there in question was at any relevant time still identifiable in the hands of the recipient'.

The second puzzle is the emphasis on the money being paid out of the consolidated fund. While this may be the paradigm case, the same policy must apply to all moneys administered by public authorities.[11]

In the *Burns* case, the claimant public authority was given restitution of the money that, by a mistake of fact, it had continued to pay to the defendant under her father's pension after his death. Newton J made clear that the payment was ultra vires and, in following *Auckland Harbour Board v R*, his reasoning was clearly based on the policy of protecting public funds. He said:

> 'The authorities establish that money paid out of Consolidated Revenue without statutory or other lawful authority is recoverable by the Crown from the recipient, at all events if paid without any consideration ... I consider that the principle, which I have just stated, is a special overriding principle applicable to public moneys in the sense of moneys of the Crown forming part of Consolidated Revenue; the principle is of wider scope than the principles relating to the recovery as between subject and subject of moneys paid under a mistake of fact or for a consideration which has failed.[12] The principle is, in my view, based on public policy.'[13]

---

9   Ibid, at p 177.

10 [1971] VR 825, 828.

11 Peculiarly, the Law Commission in its Report Law Com No 224, at para 17.11, suggests that the rule 'is probably limited to payments made by Central Government' and 'would be unlikely ... to apply to expenditure by local authorities ...'.

12 Along with mistake, (total) failure of consideration could be an alternative possible ground for a public authority's restitutionary claim. But it will be rare because a public authority does not usually pay on the basis of a counter-promise or the occurrence of a subsequent event.

13 [1971] VR 825, 827. *Auckland Harbour Board* and *Burns* were relied on by the Federal Court of Australia in *Sandvik Australia Pty Ltd v Commonwealth of Australia* (1989) 89 ALR 213 in allowing the state restitution of money paid under an invalid ministerial order.

Unfortunately Newton J went on to hold that the defendant was not entitled to rely on an estoppel defence based on her detrimental reliance on the public authority's representation that she was entitled to the money. His view was that an ultra vires payment cannot be cured by an estoppel. It is submitted that that was to carry the desire to protect public funds to unacceptable lengths. Normal unjust enrichment defences should be applied. In particular there cannot even be a technical argument against allowing the payee the defence of change of position.[14]

To recognise that a public authority's incapacity is a ground for restitution may mean that in well-known mistake cases like *Holt v Markham*[15] and *Avon County Council v Howlett*[16] the public authorities' claims for restitution could have alternatively been framed simply on the payments being ultra vires. This turns on the difficult question of the scope of the ultra vires doctrine and the extent to which a public authority can make intra vires mistakes whether of fact or law.[17] On the face of it, if *Burns* involved an ultra vires mistake so did *Holt* and *Avon*.

One might have expected that this ground for restitution would have featured in the interest-rate swap cases,[18] where the swaps had been disadvantageous for the local authorities so that restitution was being sought by them rather than by the banks.[19] That is, the ground for restitution of money paid by local authorities, under the contracts that were void because ultra vires the local authorities, could be said to have been the policy of protecting public funds (ie the incapacity itself). This would appear to have justified restitution for a public authority even if the other main grounds in play (eg mistake or failure of consideration) could not have been made out. But the courts in the swaps cases made very little reference to this possibility;[20] *Auckland Harbour Authority v R* was not relied on; and the same grounds for restitution were applied irrespective of whether restitution was being sought by the public authorities or by the banks.

As regards social security payments made ultra vires by public authorities, to what extent is the common law affected by s 71 of the Social Security Administration Act 1992?

14 Change of position, but not estoppel, succeeded in *Eastbourne Borough Council v Foster*, (20 December 2000, unreported); varied on a different point [2001] EWCA Civ 1091.
15 [1923] 1 KB 504.
16 [1983] 1 WLR 605.
17 Below, pp 443–444.
18 See above, pp 397–401.
19 As, eg, in *South Tyneside Metropolitan Borough Council v Svenska International plc* [1995] 1 All ER 545.
20 An exception was Morritt LJ in *Guinness Mahon & Co Ltd v Kensington and Chelsea London Borough Council* [1999] QB 215, 225.

That section allows recovery by the Secretary of State of overpaid social security benefits but only where induced by the payee's misrepresentation, or non-disclosure, of fact or where materially due to the payment being made by direct credit transfer. Statutory restitution is therefore based, and then only partially, on the public authority's mistake of fact. In contrast overpayments can be offset against other benefits payable which appears to rest on the public authority's incapacity being the unjust factor. The Act does not expressly lay down that any common law right to restitution of overpaid social security benefits is replaced. But it is probably accurate to say that, given its inconsistency with the common law, it is implicitly intended to be exclusive.

Chapter 12

Illegality as a ground for restitution

1. ILLEGALITY AS A GROUND FOR RESTITUTION AND ILLEGALITY AS A DEFENCE

In this book a broad view of what is meant by illegality is adopted, which includes not only conduct involving a crime or civil wrong but also conduct which is sometimes described as 'contrary to public policy'. In particular it is believed that, in line with Anson and Treitel, the distinction drawn by Cheshire, Fifoot and Furmston between illegal contracts and contracts that are void on grounds of public policy is unhelpful.[1]

Confining ourselves to unjust enrichment by subtraction, the traditional approach to illegality in the law of restitution, as set out, for example, in Goff and Jones,[2] is as follows. First, for similar reasons to those which make the contract unenforceable, restitution of benefits conferred under illegal contracts is generally denied: the general maxims governing restitution are *ex turpi causa non oritur actio* ('no court will lend its aid to a man who founds his action upon an immoral or an illegal act') and *in pari delicto potior est conditio defendentis* ('where both parties are equally wrongful the position of the defendant is the stronger'). Secondly, there are three main exceptions to this general denial of restitution: where the parties are *non in pari delicto*; withdrawal during the *locus poenitentiae*; and where the claimant can establish a proprietary claim[3] against the defendant without relying on the illegality or the illegal transaction.

The major problem with that approach is that it does not explain what are the relevant grounds for restitution. Put another way, it does

---

1   See *Anson's Law of Contract* (28th edn, 2002), p 348; Treitel, *The Law of Contract* (10th edn), p 393. Cf *Cheshire, Fifoot and Furmston's Law of Contract* (14th edn, 2001), pp 405–410. Using the broad meaning of illegality, invalid gaming and wagering contracts can be described as illegal: cf Treitel (10th edn), chapter 24. On changes in the law, see Treitel, pp 401–402.

2   Goff and Jones, chapter 24. See also *Cheshire, Fifoot and Furmston's Law of Contract*, pp 429–436; Treitel, *The Law of Contract*, pp 452–465; *Anson's Law of Contract*, pp 402–412.

3   Strictly speaking, this book is concerned only with restitutionary proprietary rights (ie, proprietary restitution) and not pure proprietary rights. Many of the illegality cases have concerned the latter.

not clarify whether illegality is an unjust factor itself or a defence to claims based on other unjust factors.

The great strength of Birks' treatment of illegality is that he confronts that central question head on.[4] His conclusion is that illegality is generally operating as a possible defence to standard restitutionary grounds, whether total failure of consideration or, as shown in the *non in pari delicto* cases, factors based on the vitiation of a claimant's will, such as mistake and duress. The one general exception is withdrawal during the *locus poenitentiae* which, for Birks, is a restitutionary claim (within unjust enrichment by subtraction) based on the policy of discouraging unlawful conduct.[5]

This book follows Birks' approach. So in this chapter we are concerned with encouraging the abandonment of an illegal purpose by allowing withdrawal during the *locus poenitentiae*. The usual role of illegality – as a defence – is examined in chapter 15.

2. ENCOURAGING THE ABANDONMENT OF AN ILLEGAL PURPOSE: WITHDRAWAL IN THE *LOCUS POENITENTIAE*

(1) Introduction

It may be tempting at first sight to regard even withdrawal in the *locus poenitentiae* as concerned with illegality as a defence. That is, one might argue that the ground of action triggering restitution is total failure of consideration and that withdrawal merely allows the claimant to avoid the normal illegality defence to a claim based on total failure of consideration.[6]

On closer inspection it is clear that Birks is right to argue that withdrawal during the *locus poenitentiae* is based on illegality as a ground of action. Even if it were the law (which is unclear) that the claimant cannot withdraw once it has received some part of the benefit (which would be consistent with the traditional general insistence that a

---

4 Birks, at pp 299–303, 424–432.
5 A further illegality ground for restitution, albeit specialised, is where the illegality is designed to protect those who might otherwise unjustifiably lose out as a result of transactions to which they are not parties. For examples, see ss 238–241, 339–342, and 423–425 of the Insolvency Act 1986 (transactions at an undervalue, preferences, and transactions defrauding creditors); and s 37 of the Matrimonial Causes Act 1973 (a spouse's disposal of assets to frustrate a claim for financial relief by the other spouse). There may be other specialised examples of illegality operating as a ground for restitution laid down in particular statutes. On the question of whether change of position operates as a defence under the statutory 'clawback' insolvency provisions, see *Re Ernst and Young Inc* (1997) 147 DLR (4th) 229; O'Sullivan, 'Defending a Liquidator's Claim for Repayment of a Voidable Transaction' (1997) 9 Otago LR 111.
6 See, eg, Tettenborn, *The Law of Restitution in England and Ireland* (3rd edn, 2002), p 284.

failure of consideration has to be total) the fact remains that the claimant can withdraw even though the defendant is ready, able and willing to perform his promise. Indeed the claimant can withdraw even in advance of the time fixed for the defendant's performance. Say, for example, the claimant has paid £1,000 in advance for illegal services to be rendered by the defendant in the following week. The claimant has an immediate entitlement to withdraw and to recover the £1,000. This restitutionary right cannot simply be said to be based on total failure of consideration because until the defendant is unable or unwilling to perform as promised, the consideration – the basis upon which the claimant transferred the money – does not fail.[7]

The difficulty then faced is in pin-pointing the precise injustice (assuming an enrichment) to which withdrawal during the *locus poenitentiae* responds. The answer must be that the law wishes to discourage illegal conduct and hence wishes to encourage the abandonment of illegal contracts. There would be no incentive for the claimant to withdraw if the defendant were allowed to retain, without payment, the benefits received at the claimant's expense.

The Law Commission in its Consultation Paper on *Illegal Transactions: The Effect of Illegality on Contracts and Trusts*[8] summarises the position as follows: 'Illegality is being used to found a claim in restitution when the plaintiff relies on the doctrine of *locus poenitentiae*, that is, where the plaintiff claims to withdraw from the illegal contract during "the time for repentance." Here one cannot analyse the illegality as constituting a defence to a standard restitutionary claim: rather the law grants restitution, where it otherwise would not, precisely in order to discourage illegality.'

Like rescission, withdrawal does not necessarily involve any restitution. One may be seeking to withdraw from an illegal contract even though no benefits have been conferred under it. But as an illegal contract is generally unenforceable, a claimant seeking withdrawal usually wants personal or proprietary restitution.[9]

In examining the case law it should be said at once that it is notoriously uncertain and much academic ink has been spilt in an

---

7   *Thomas v Brown* (1876) 1 QBD 714; above, pp 331–332.
8   Consultation Paper No 154 (1999), para 2.49.
9   Withdrawal is analogous to rescission and may, therefore, effect proprietary, as well as merely personal, restitution. The justification for this cannot rest on the vitiation of the claimant's intention or that the claimant has not taken the risk of the defendant's insolvency (cf above, pp 67–73). Rather it must rest on both personal and proprietary restitution being thought desirable in order to encourage the abandonment of an illegal contract.

attempt at clarification.[10] In the most important recent decision of *Tribe v Tribe*,[11] which clarified that the *locus poenitentiae* doctrine applies to equity and trusts as well as at common law, the Court of Appeal accepted that it was impossible to reconcile all the relevant cases. Perhaps the clearest picture that emerges is that, while this doctrine was interpreted liberally so as to allow restitution until around the turn of the nineteenth century, it was then restrictively interpreted for most of the twentieth century until *Tribe v Tribe*.

(2) The liberal approach to withdrawal

The classic statement on withdrawal is in the judgment of Buller J in *Lowry v Bourdieu*.[12] The claimants paid a premium under an illegal contract of insurance. Buller J held that they could not recover the premium paid because the contract had been executed before the action to rescind the contract had started. That is, the ship's voyage (the subject matter of the insurance) had been completed before the claimants sought to withdraw. Buller J said:

> 'There is a sound distinction between contracts executed and executory, and if an action is brought with a view to rescind a contract, you must do it while the contract remains executory, and then it can only be done on the terms of restoring the other party to his original situation ... So, if the plaintiffs in the present case had brought their action before the risk was over, and the voyage finished, they might have had a ground for their demand; but they waited till the risk ... had been completely run.'[13]

Several of the early cases in which restitution was ordered on the basis of withdrawal concerned gaming and wagering contracts. For example, in *Hastelow v Jackson*[14] the claimant and one Wilcoxon, had each deposited £20 with the defendant, the £40 to be paid over to the winner of a boxing match between them. After Wilcoxon had won, the claimant told the defendant not to pay over the £40 to

---

10 Eg, Grodecki, 'In Pari Delicto Potior Est Conditio Defendentis' (1955) LQR 254, 261–263; Beatson, 'Repudiation of Illegal Purpose as a Ground for Restitution' (1975) 91 LQR 313; Merkin, 'Restitution by Withdrawal from Executory Illegal Contracts' (1981) 97 LQR 420; Rose, 'Restitutionary and Proprietary Consequences of Illegality' in *Consensus Ad Idem* (ed Rose, 1996), pp 203, 226–234; Buckley, *Illegality and Public Policy* (2002), chapter 18.
11 [1996] Ch 107, 121, 135.
12 (1780) 2 Doug KB 468.
13 Ibid, at p 471.
14 (1828) 8 B & C 221. See also, eg, *Tappenden v Randall* (1801) 2 Bos & P 467; *Aubert v Walsh* (1810) 3 Taunt 277; *Varney v Hickman* (1847) 5 CB 271; and later *Hampden v Walsh* (1876) 1 QBD 189; *Strachan v Universal Stock Exchange Ltd (No 2)* [1895] 2 QB 697; *Re Cronmire, ex p Waud* [1898] 2 QB 383.

Wilcoxon and when he did so brought an action to recover his £20. It was held that the claimant was entitled to restitution of the £20 because the contract was not completely executed in the sense that, when he sought to withdraw, the defendant had not yet paid the money over to Wilcoxon.[15]

The leading case in which the doctrine was successfully invoked was *Taylor v Bowers*.[16] To prevent his creditors seizing his business goods, the claimant and his nephew, Alcock, entered into an agreement whereby, inter alia, the claimant delivered his goods to Alcock. Although the content of the agreement was not entirely clear, the idea was presumably that Alcock should reconvey the goods to the claimant after settlement had been reached with the creditors. Instead Alcock sold the goods to the defendant. The claimant demanded their return from the defendant, who refused. Mellish and Baggallay LJJ held that the claimant was entitled to recover the goods because he had withdrawn from the illegal contract – the agreement with Alcock to defraud the claimant's creditors – before any settlement with the creditors. Hence proprietary rights to the goods had revested in him.[17] In Mellish LJ's words, 'If money is paid or goods delivered for an illegal purpose, the person who had so paid the money or delivered the goods may recover them back before the illegal purpose is carried out.'[18] This confirmed the reasoning of the court below. In contrast James LJ, and arguably Grove J, did not rely on withdrawal and instead reasoned that the claimant could establish his title to the goods independently of the illegal contract.

In the light of subsequent developments it is important to emphasise two points about this and several other cases[19] in which the doctrine was successfully invoked.

First, the requirement that the contract be executory and not executed was not interpreted to mean that there should have been no performance of the contract nor that no part of the contractual purpose should have been achieved. Rather the idea seemed to be that the contract must not have been fully performed and that not all the purpose must have been achieved. In other words, the courts were happy to allow withdrawal at quite a late stage.

---

15 Judgments in the last two cases in the previous note indicate that where money is deposited with the other party to the wager (rather than with a stakeholder) withdrawal is allowed until the other party wins the wager and appropriates the deposit accordingly. See also *Re Futures Index Ltd* [1985] FLR 147.

16 (1876) 1 QBD 291.

17 The revesting of proprietary rights is itself restitutionary. But the delivery up of goods, which was not actually sought in *Taylor*, is a remedy, allied to compensation, for the tort of conversion.

18 (1876) 1 QBD 291, 300.

19 Eg, *Bone v Ekless* (1860) 5 H & N 925; *Wilson v Strugnell* (1881) 7 QBD 548; *Hermann v Charlesworth* [1905] 2 KB 123; *Petherpermal Chetty v Muniandy Servai* (1908) 24 TLR 462.

Secondly, there was no requirement that the claimant's reason for withdrawal was genuine repentance rather than a thwarting of the purpose by, for example, the defendant's breach of promise.

(3) The restrictive approach to withdrawal

The first case to signal a more conservative approach to withdrawal was *Kearley v Thomson*.[20] The claimant, a friend of a bankrupt, agreed with the defendants, who were the solicitors representing the petitioning creditor, that in return for payment of £40 the defendants would not appear at the bankrupt's public examination and would not oppose his discharge. That contract was illegal as interfering with the course of justice. The defendants having duly absented themselves, the bankrupt passed his public examination. But before he had applied for his order of discharge, the claimant sought restitution of the £40 paid. This was denied. Fry LJ, giving the judgment of the Court of Appeal, expressed doubts as to whether the reasoning and decision in *Taylor v Bowers* were correct. However, on the assumption that the withdrawal principle did exist, he held that it was not made out on the facts because the contract had been partly performed: ie the defendants had performed the first part of the two part contract. He said, 'Where there has been a partial carrying into effect of an illegal purpose in a substantial manner, it is impossible, though there remains something not performed, that the money paid under that illegal contract can be recovered back.'[1] It would seem that *Taylor v Bowers* was therefore being distinguished on the ground that in that case no part of the illegal purpose had been achieved – despite partial performance – because no creditor had been defrauded.[2]

Even if that distinction is thought convincing, further doubt was cast on *Taylor v Bowers* by twentieth century cases which imposed a new restrictive requirement for withdrawal, namely that the claimant's reason for withdrawal must be repentance rather than frustration of purpose. That restriction was first articulated in *Parkinson v College of Ambulance Ltd and Harrison*[3] where Lush J said that the claimant was not withdrawing from the illegal contract to purchase a knighthood because of repentance but rather because he had not obtained the promised title.

20 (1890) 24 QBD 742.
1   Ibid, at p 747. See also Millett LJ in *Taylor v Bhail* (1996) 50 Con LR 70: 'He may [repudiate the illegal contract] only if no part of the illegal purpose has been carried out.' See further on this case, below, p 572, n 15. Although the insurance company had not been successfully defrauded, much of the building work had been carried out.
2   That ground of distinction was expressly articulated in *Bigos v Bousted* [1951] 1 All ER 92, 97.
3   [1925] 2 KB 1. In addition to the cases cited in this and the following paragraph see *Harry Parker Ltd v Mason* [1940] 2 KB 590.

The restriction was referred to in very clear terms in *Alexander v Rayson*,[4] which concerned enforcement of an illegal contract rather than restitution. And in *Berg v Sadler and Moore*[5] it was arguably applied by the Court of Appeal to deny restitution to a stop-listed purchaser of cigarettes, even though he had not received any cigarettes.

However the leading case imposing this requirement is *Bigos v Bousted*.[6] The claimant agreed to supply the defendant's wife and daughter, who were to holiday in Italy, with £150 worth of Italian lire for which the defendant was to pay the claimant in sterling in England. The defendant gave the claimant a share certificate as security for repayment of the loan. That agreement was illegal under exchange control regulations. The claimant failed to supply the lire as promised and the wife and daughter therefore returned to England sooner than planned. In an action by the claimant, the defendant counterclaimed to recover the share certificate on the ground that, as the contract was executory, he was within the *locus poenitentiae*.[7] Pritchard J refused that counterclaim on the ground that, as in *Alexander v Rayson* and *Berg v Sadler and Moore*, the defendant had not withdrawn because of repentance but rather because the illegal contract had been frustrated by the claimant. The question of whether the defendant was within the *locus poenitentiae* was therefore irrelevant. He said:

> '[The authorities] show ... that there is a distinction between what may, for convenience, be called the repentance cases, on the one hand, and the frustration cases, on the other hand. If a particular case may be held to fall within the category of repentance cases, I think the law is that the court will help a person who repents, provided his repentance comes before the illegal purpose has been substantially performed ... this case falls within the category of cases which I call the frustration cases.'[8]

Pritchard J purported to distinguish *Taylor v Bowers* as a repentance case. This seems incorrect. The claimant in *Taylor* only sought to withdraw from defrauding the creditors once he knew that Alcock had departed from the scheme by selling his goods to the defendant.

It appears therefore that for most of the twentieth century the predominant approach to withdrawal, with its emphasis on genuine repentance and withdrawal at an early stage (at the latest before any part of the contractual purpose had been achieved), was a rejection of *Taylor v Bowers* and the earlier liberal cases.

(4) *Tribe v Tribe*[9]

In this case, the claimant, in order to make himself judgment-proof in the face of a potential liability, transferred the shares in his company to the defendant, who was his son. The transfer was expressed to be for a consideration that was never intended to be paid. In fact the liability did not materialise and the claimant therefore called for a retransfer of the shares. The defendant refused, arguing that the shares were his and that the claimant could not rely on an illegal agreement, designed to conceal the claimant's assets from his creditors, to rebut the presumption of advancement.

The Court of Appeal held that the claimant was entitled to a retransfer of the shares. He could rebut the presumption of advancement and establish that the shares were held on resulting trust because he had withdrawn from the illegality during the *locus poenitentiae* (although Nourse LJ, unlike Millett LJ, preferred to avoid that term).[10] The *locus poenitentiae*, or withdrawal, doctrine was not an exclusively common law doctrine but also applied to equity and trusts. Here the claimant had withdrawn in time because deceiving the creditors had, in the event, been unnecessary; although the shares had been transferred, the potential liability went away before any creditor had been deceived. Therefore, no part of the illegal purpose had been carried out. In Nourse LJ's words, 'It is the purpose which has to be carried into effect and that would only have happened if and when a creditor or creditors of the plaintiff had been deceived by the transaction.'[11]

Millett LJ further emphasised that genuine repentance was not needed.[12] While the claimant must withdraw voluntarily, so that being forced to withdraw because a plan has been discovered would not

9   [1996] Ch 107. It is not clear that one can regard the *locus poenitentiae* doctrine in *Tribe v Tribe* as operating: (i) within the law of restitution (because the resulting trust was triggered by unjust enrichment) as opposed to within the law of 'pure' property; (ii) as a *ground* for restitution as opposed to merely knocking out the 'reliance on illegality' defence applied to proprietary claims in, eg, *Tinsley v Milligan* [1994] 1 AC 340 (see below, chapter 15). But whatever the correct analysis, it has been considered most convenient to consider the case here not least because of the general observations on the *locus poenitentiae* doctrine made by Millett LJ. Cf Burrows and McKendrick *Cases and Materials on the Law of Restitution* (1997), p 885.
10 Ibid, at 121.
11 Ibid, at 122. But it should be noted that Nourse LJ, unlike Millett LJ, did not analyse the contract cases as well as the equity and trusts cases and, at 121, said, 'I do not propose to distinguish between law and equity, or to become embroiled in the many irreconcilable authorities which deal with the exception in its application to executory contracts ... *In a property transfer case* the [withdrawal] exception applies if the illegal purpose has not been carried into effect in any way.' (Author's italics).
12 See also *McDonald v Fellows* (1980) 105 DLR (3d) 434.

count, 'voluntary withdrawal from an illegal transaction when it has ceased to be needed is sufficient'.[13]

It can be seen, therefore, that *Tribe v Tribe* favours the more liberal approach to withdrawal adopted in the early cases rather than the more restrictive approach favoured for most of the twentieth century. This is in line with the consensus of academic opinion to which we now turn.

(5) Academic views

In a well-known article,[14] Grodecki argued that withdrawal should be allowed as long as the illegal purpose has not been fully carried out and irrespective of genuine repentance. This was on the ground that the law should give every encouragement to stop any illegal purpose being pursued. However this reasoning can be criticised to the extent that, if the illegal purpose has been frustrated irrespective of the law allowing withdrawal, it is hard to see any point in legal intervention.

For this reason Beatson's subtly different thesis seems more attractive.[15] Like Grodecki he regards genuine repentance as an unnecessary requirement but differs in arguing that recovery should only be allowed where it will increase the chance of thwarting the illegal purpose. Hence there can be no withdrawal where the purpose has already been fully achieved or where it has been frustrated. Admittedly this approach finds no explicit support in the cases but Beatson argues that it is consistent with the *results* in all the leading cases. In particular even though there had been some thwarting of the purpose in *Taylor v Bowers* irrespective of legal intervention, the purpose would be most perfectly thwarted by the law allowing the claimant to recover his goods so that they would be available for the creditors. A similar argument could also perhaps now be made in relation to *Tribe v Tribe*. It is respectfully submitted, however, that, applying Beatson's thesis, *Kearley v Thomson* should have been decided the other way, so that, while Beatson's approach can be accepted as a sensible way forward, his claim that it is already inherent in the results of the leading cases must, sadly, be rejected.

Birks differs from both Grodecki and Beatson in supporting the genuine repentance requirement essentially on the ground that 'it

---

13   [1996] Ch 107, 135.
14   'In Pari Delicto Potior Est Conditio Defendentis' (1955) LQR 254, 263.
15   'Repudiation of Illegal Purpose as a Ground for Restitution' (1975) 91 LQR 313. Cf Law Commission Consultation Paper No 154 *Illegal Transactions: The Effect of Illegality on Contracts and Trusts* (1999), paras 7.58–7.69.

clears away the taint of turpitude, putting the plaintiff outside the category of persons unworthy to invoke the court's assistance'.[16] This seems to go too far in assuming that all parties to illegal contracts are, without repentance, too wicked to deserve the help of the courts. Many illegal contracts are innocently entered into and involve relatively minor offences or no crimes or civil wrongs at all. In contrast, can it really be said that a claimant who genuinely repents from a contract for the murder of A and B, after B has been murdered thereby 'clears away the taint of turpitude'? And, in any event, the general objection to aiding a wicked party is surely outweighed where intervention will encourage abandonment of the illegal purpose. The consensus of academic opinion rejecting this requirement, now supported by *Tribe v Tribe*, is to be preferred.[17]

(6) Bars to withdrawal

Finally, it is unclear how far normal bars to rescission apply to bar withdrawal during the *locus poenitentiae*. Affirmation appears not to be a relevant bar given that, even a person who knew of the illegality from the start, is entitled to withdraw and to do so, on the view preferred above, even after part performance. Similarly it is hard to see that laches has any relevance given the need to act within the *locus poenitentiae*. In contrast if, as seems to be the law,[18] title does pass under an illegal contract, withdrawal may not be possible once a bona fide purchaser for value without notice has acquired the property. During the *locus poenitentiae*, therefore, the title under an illegal contract is probably accurately described as voidable.[19]

What about the bar of *restitutio in integrum* being impossible? This bar is concerned with the defence of counter-restitution; and one explanation for it, as discussed in chapter 15, is that it recognises that a defendant could counterclaim for restitution based on total failure of consideration.[20] If that is correct, it logically follows that, as traditionally illegality is a defence to a claim for total failure of consideration, counter-restitution should not be required (subject to the rare situation of the defendant being able to found its counterclaim on a mistake) and it should be no bar to withdrawal that *restitutio in*

---

16 Birks, at p 301.
17 In addition to Beatson and Grodecki, the need for genuine repentance is rejected, albeit regarded as helpful in some cases, by Merkin, 'Restitution by Withdrawal from Executory Illegal Contracts' (1981) 97 LQR 420, esp 430–431, 444. See also Law Commission Consultation Paper No 154, paras 7.67–7.69.
18 Below, pp 578–583.
19 Birks, at p 303.
20 Below, pp 538–542.

integrum is impossible.[1] This is supported by, for example, *Hermann v Charlesworth*[2] where the claimant was held entitled to withdraw from a marriage brokage contract even though she had been given various introductions by the defendants during the four months that the contract had been on foot. On the other hand, Buller J's classic dictum in *Lowry v Bourdieu*, cited above, insists that withdrawal is only permitted 'on the terms of restoring the other party to his original situation'. And Goff and Jones cite a decision of Cross J[3] (which does not in terms mention withdrawal during the *locus poenitentiae*) for the requirement that '"some sort of *restitutio in integrum* on equitable terms" must still be possible'.[4]

---

1   This is an argument based on consistency in the law. The position would be different if, as is advocated below, pp 572–574, illegality were not usually a defence to restitution for failure of consideration. For general criticism of there being a bar that '*restitutio in integrum* is impossible', as opposed to there being an insistence on counter-restitution, see below, pp 541–542.
2   [1905] 2 KB 123.
3   *South Western Mineral Water Co v Ashmore* [1967] 1 WLR 1110.
4   Goff and Jones, at para 24-008.

Chapter 13

Ultra vires demands by public authorities

Until the decision in *Woolwich Equitable Building Society v IRC*,[1] English law did not recognise that an ultra vires demand by a public authority was itself a ground for restitution. Rather the standard 'private law' grounds of mistake of fact or, more commonly, duress were required to be established if the payor was to succeed in an action for money had and received:[2] the aspect of duress often labelled 'demands made *colore officii*' was of particular relevance.

In *An Introduction to the Law of Restitution*[3] and in a powerful and highly influential essay entitled 'Restitution from the Executive: A Tercentenary Footnote to the Bill of Rights'[4] Birks argued that that traditional approach was unsound. Starting from the principle of 'no taxation without Parliament' enshrined in the Bill of Rights, Birks coupled flaws in the duress analysis with flashes of judicial support for a wider view to preach the case for recognition of a special public law ground for restitution based simply on the ultra vires nature of the demand. In essence it is that thesis that the House of Lords, by a 3–2 majority, accepted in *Woolwich*. In Lord Goff's words (hereinafter referred to as 'the *Woolwich* principle'), '... money paid by a citizen to a public authority in the form of taxes or other levies paid pursuant to an ultra vires demand by the authority is prima facie recoverable by the citizen as of right'.[5]

While primarily concentrating on the *Woolwich* principle, this chapter first examines the traditional approach which, although presumably no longer of practical importance,[6] is the necessary starting point in understanding the major step taken by the House of Lords.

---

1   [1993] AC 70.
2   This chapter, reflecting the case law, focuses entirely on payments. The same principles apply to other benefits. Subjective devaluation would be overcome because the ultra vires demand would fall within the 'reprehensible seeking-out' test.
3   Birks, pp 294–299.
4   In *Essays on Restitution* (ed Finn, 1990), pp 164–205.
5   [1993] AC 70, 177.
6   Cf below, p 454.

1. THE DURESS APPROACH: ILLEGITIMATE THREATS BY PUBLIC AUTHORITIES MADE IN SUPPORT OF ULTRA VIRES DEMANDS

A public authority that has made ultra vires demands for payment is as susceptible to restitution on the basis of standard unjust factors as is any other person. Examples of successful claims based on mistake are rare.[7] This is because the mistakes in question have usually been ones of law, not fact, and hence, until *Kleinwort Benson Ltd v Lincoln City Council*,[8] restitution was taken to be barred.[9] Although there was potential for using the *non in pari delicto* exception to the mistake of law bar in an action against a public authority, only the Canadian case of *Eadie v Township of Brantford*[10] directly supported that possibility.

The primary ground for restitution in this context has therefore traditionally been regarded as duress. Assuming causation, duress in principle required the claimant to establish that the demand carried with it an illegitimate threat, which was usually implied rather than express.

In addition to duress of the person and goods, illegitimate threats by a public authority centrally comprise threats to a person's entitlement. In *Woolwich* Lord Goff explained that head of compulsion in the following way: 'Money paid to a person in a public or quasi-public position to obtain the performance by him of a duty which he is bound to perform for nothing or for less than the sum demanded by him is recoverable to the extent that he is not entitled to it.'[11] Similarly Birks described this type of case as one in which 'the demand is made in respect of something which the applicant wants and which it is the duty of the authority to provide, where the potentiality for duress consists in the withholding of the applicant's entitlement.'[12] This is also what is normally meant when demands are described as having been made *colore officii* although that terminology can be used in wider senses and hence tends to cause confusion. It is best avoided wherever possible.

Several cases illustrate restitution being granted on the basis of an entitlement threat.[13] In *Morgan v Palmer*[14] restitution of 4s was awarded

---

7   An example is *Meadows v Grand Junction Waterworks Co* (1905) 21 TLR 538.
8   [1999] 2 AC 349.
9   Above, pp 147–159.
10 (1967) 63 DLR (2d) 561. Above, p 148.
11 [1993] AC 70, 164.
12 'Restitution from Public Authorities' (1980) 33 CLP 191, 198.
13 In addition to the cases in this paragraph, see eg *Hooper v Exeter Corpn* (1887) 56 LJQB 457; *Queens of the River Steamship Co Ltd v River Thames Conservators* (1899) 15 TLR 474; *South of Scotland Electricity Board v British Oxygen Co Ltd (No 2)* [1959] 2 All ER 225.
14 (1824) 2 B & C 729.

following an implied threat by a mayor not to renew the claimant's pub licence unless the mayor was paid that sum. He had no power to make that demand. In *Steele v Williams*[15] restitution was given where a threat had been made not to allow the claimant's clerk to copy extracts from the Parish Register of Burials and Baptisms unless he paid the same rate as for certificates. No charge at all should have been made. In *T and J Brocklebank Ltd v R*[16] restitution would have been awarded (had it not been for the Indemnity Act 1920) because of the shipping controller's implied threat to withhold a licence, permitting the claimants to sell a ship to a foreign firm, unless the Ministry of Defence was paid a percentage of the price. The shipping controller had no power to make that demand.

In the light of such cases it appears that *Slater v Burnley Corpn*[17] and *Twyford v Manchester Corpn*[18] were incorrectly reasoned in denying restitution. In each the judges ignored the *implied* entitlement threat lying behind the ultra vires demand (to cut off a water supply and to bar entry to a cemetery respectively).[19]

On the other hand, short of extending the notion of an entitlement threat beyond that outlined by Lord Goff, the influential Australian case of *Mason v New South Wales*[20] is best viewed as an example of duress of goods. The public authority was acting ultra vires in requiring lorries to have permits for inter-state journeys. The High Court of Australia granted restitution of money paid for such a permit, the reasoning being that, as the public authority had the power (without coming to court) to seize vehicles without permits, the demand for payment carried with it an implied threat to seize the payor's lorries.

Contrasting with illegitimate threats are where the public authority's ultra vires demand is backed merely by a threat to sue. That type of threat is normally legitimate and does not ground duress.[1] It was for that reason that restitution was denied in *William Whitely Ltd v R*[2] and was denied *on the basis of duress* in *Woolwich*. In both, taxes that were not due had been demanded (and paid) but, in the ultimate analysis, all that the Inland Revenue was threatening was to sue to recover the unpaid tax and penalties for non-payment. In the former Walton J said:

---

15 (1853) 8 Exch 625.
16 [1925] 1 KB 52.
17 (1888) 59 LT 636.
18 [1946] Ch 236.
19 Burrows, 'Public Authorities, Ultra Vires and Restitution' in *Essays on the Law of Restitution* (ed Burrows, 1991), pp 39, 47–50. Cf *Woolwich Equitable Building Society v IRC* [1993] AC 70, 165 (per Lord Goff).
20 (1959) 102 CLR 108.
1   Above, pp 239–240.
2   (1909) 101 LT 741.

'The plaintiffs must have known that if proceedings were taken for penalties it would be open to them in such proceedings to raise the question as to whether the duties were payable or not, as they did, in fact, in 1906 ... They knew that the Commissioners of the Inland Revenue could not determine whether the duties were payable or not. They could take no action if the duties were not paid except by legal proceedings ... In the circumstances I have come to the conclusion that there was nothing in this case which amounted to compulsion.'[3]

And in *Woolwich* Lord Goff said, '... since the possibility of distraint by the Revenue was very remote, the concept of compulsion would have to be stretched to the utmost to embrace the circumstances of such a case as this. It is for this reason that Woolwich's alternative claim founded on compulsion did not loom large in the argument, and is difficult to sustain'.[4]

This leads us on to the decision in *Woolwich* which, in allowing restitution despite there being no duress, has subsumed the traditional duress approach. Although not expressly spelt out, it is submitted that *Slater*, *William Whitely*, and *Twyford* have all been overruled.[5]

2.   *WOOLWICH EQUITABLE BUILDING SOCIETY V IRC*

If *Lipkin Gorman v Karpnale Ltd*[6] is the *Donoghue v Stevenson*[7] of the law of restitution, *Woolwich* is its *Hedley Byrne & Co Ltd v Heller & Partners Ltd*.[8]

The claimant had been charged composite rate tax which, from the start, it objected to paying on the ground that the regulation authorising it was ultra vires the Inland Revenue. Although it paid the tax demanded (some £57 million) the claimant straightaway issued judicial review proceedings to establish the invalidity of the charge and, shortly thereafter, issued a writ claiming restitution. Having succeeded before the House of Lords in establishing that the demand was ultra vires,[9] the claimant was repaid the principal sum of tax. But the Revenue refused to pay interest on that sum (agreed by the parties to be £6.73 million). Under s 35A of the Supreme Court Act 1981 the claimant would only be entitled to interest at the court's discretion (it being assumed that that discretion would be exercised in favour of the claimant) if the claimant could establish that it was legally entitled

---

3   Ibid, p 745.
4   [1993] AC 70, 173.
5   Cf Lord Slynn, at p 204.
6   [1991] 2 AC 548.
7   [1932] AC 562.
8   [1964] AC 465.
9   *R v IRC, ex p Woolwich Equitable Building Society* [1990] 1 WLR 1400.

(as a debt) to restitution of the principal sum. So although relating to a dispute over interest the question at issue was whether the claimant was entitled as of right to restitution of the principal sum.[10]

It is important to add that the facts raised a pure matter of common law because, in contrast to most incorrect tax demands, the question of repayment was not governed by statute. In particular s 33 of the Taxes Management Act 1970 is inapplicable where the basis for the charge is an ultra vires regulation.

The difficulty facing the claimant was that it appeared to fall just outside the standard 'private law' grounds for restitution. As it had no real doubt that the tax was invalidly demanded it had made no mistake in paying and, even if it had made a mistake, it was one of law not fact. More crucially the Inland Revenue's demands appeared not to have been supported by any illegitimate threats so as to constitute duress. The only obvious implied threat was the legitimate one of suing to recover the tax demanded plus the penalties for non-payment. Hence Nolan J at first instance,[11] and Ralph Gibson LJ, dissenting in the Court of Appeal,[12] and Lords Keith and Jauncey, dissenting in the House of Lords, thought that the claimant should fail.

In contrast the majority of the Court of Appeal (Glidewell and Butler-Sloss LJJ), albeit with some untenable restrictions, and the majority of the Lords (Lords Goff, Browne-Wilkinson, and Slynn) departed from the traditional approach in holding that the claimant should succeed simply on the basis that the demand had been made ultra vires.

The leading speech was given by Lord Goff. His reasoning was expressly agreed with by Lord Browne-Wilkinson and was in essence agreed with by Lord Slynn. Lord Goff's enlightened and masterly analysis merits the careful attention of all students of the law. It can be said to have five key stages.

First, Lord Goff accepted that, while the ultra vires ground for restitution was supported by some dicta (eg Lord Atkin's in *A-G v Wilts United Dairies Ltd*[13] and Dixon CJ's in *Mason v New South Wales*)[14] and by the reasoning of some dissenting or minority judges (eg, Martin B in *Steele v Williams*[15] and Wilson J in *Air Canada v British Columbia*)[16] and by

---

10 See also *SCI Operations Pty Ltd v Commonwealth of Australia* (1996) 139 ALR 595 in which the Federal Court of Australia applied *Woolwich* in a decision that similarly turned on whether, and from when, interest on overpaid duty should be payable.
11 [1989] 1 WLR 137.
12 [1991] 3 WLR 790.
13 (1921) 37 TLR 884, 887.
14 (1959) 102 CLR 108, 117.
15 (1853) 8 Exch 625.
16 (1989) 59 DLR (4th) 161.

possible interpretations of cases such as *Campbell v Hall,*[17] *Dew v Parsons,*[18] and *Hooper v Exeter Corpn,*[19] the weight of authority showed that the law had become settled in rejecting that wide unjust factor and in requiring the narrower grounds of mistake of fact and duress. However, that understanding of the law had never been cemented at a level higher than the Court of Appeal.

Secondly, Lord Goff thought that the step forward to the wide ground for restitution should be made for a number of positive reasons. (i) The justice underpinning Woolwich's claim was plain to see. (ii) It is a constitutional principle, enshrined in the Bill of Rights, that taxes should not be levied without the authority of Parliament. (iii) A demand for tax is implicitly backed by the coercive powers of the state so that the taxpayer knows that unpleasant economic and social consequences may be entailed if he does not pay. (iv) The traditional law is unattractively weighted against the citizen in that it is well-established that, if the Crown pays money out of the consolidated fund without authority, it can recover it (provided traceable) simply on the ground that it was paid ultra vires.[20] (v) The European Court of Justice in *Amministrazione delle Finanze dello Stato v San Giorgio SpA*[1] established that an individual is prima facie entitled to restitution of money demanded by a state in contravention of his directly effective EC rights. In Lord Goff's words, '... at a time when Community law is becoming increasingly important, it would be strange if the right of the citizen to recover overpaid charges were to be more restricted under domestic law than it is under European law'.[2]

Thirdly, while accepting that the step forward would be an example of judicial legislation Lord Goff did not think that that in itself was a valid objection. If it were, many of the major judicial developments of the twentieth century (eg *Donoghue v Stevenson,* judicial review, freezing injunctions) would never have taken place.

Fourthly, it was emphasised by Lord Goff (and Lord Slynn) that it was unnecessary in the instant case to consider whether particular defences (eg, passing on or a short limitation period) should be introduced to protect public authorities from restitutionary claims. Such matters could be dealt with by legislation and would presumably be considered by the Law Commission in its then on-going review of this area.[3] But, contrary to

---

17 (1774) 1 Cowp 204.
18 (1819) 2 B & Ald 562.
19 (1887) 56 LJQB 457.
20 Above, pp 420–423.
1   Case 199/82 [1983] ECR 3595.
2   [1993] AC 70, 177.
3   Lord Goff described as 'most valuable' the Law Commission's Consultation Paper No 120, 'Restitution of Payments made under a Mistake of Law' (1991). Subsequent to *Woolwich,* the Law Commission published its Report entitled *Restitution: Mistakes of Law and Ultra Vires Public Authority Receipts and Payments,* Law Com No 227 (1994).

the majority's view in the Court of Appeal, it was no *defence* that the payor had made a mistake of law. That was irrelevant given that the ground for restitution was not mistake but the ultra vires demand.

Finally, Lord Goff turned round the Revenue's argument that the existing welter of statutory provisions dealing with levies demanded ultra vires made common law development inappropriate. On the contrary the statutory regimes meant that cases turning on the ultra vires unjust factor would be rare. Moreover, the fact that the Law Commission was working in the area made it a peculiarly appropriate time to develop the common law. For in consultation with the Law Commission the Revenue could press for limits to the common law right of recovery and there could be a rationalisation of the existing, often inconsistent, statutory provisions.[4]

The power of the case put by Lord Goff is overwhelming. And his strategy of developing the ground for restitution, while leaving possible defences to be worked out subsequently does seem an appropriate way forward.

There are just two minor features of the majority's reasoning that are disappointing.

First, in two passages Lord Goff relied on the idea that restitution followed because there was no consideration for the payment. That approach was given greater prominence in the speech of Lord Browne-Wilkinson. He thought that the stream of authority based on the concept of want of consideration was 'attractive'.[5] 'The money was demanded and paid for tax, yet no tax was due: there was a payment for no consideration.'[6]

With respect, that approach is unhelpful.[7] Want of consideration, as opposed to failure of consideration, is not a recognised unjust factor and it is unclear what is meant by it. If the idea is that there should be restitution where nothing is given in return for a payment, all gifts would be recoverable. If on the other hand all it means is that there is no good reason for the defendant to keep the payment, it is circular and begs the question of whether there is an unjust factor: all clarity in the law of restitution would be lost if the inquiry into the injustice of an enrichment were reduced to the single question of whether there was want of consideration. Even if the role of want of

---

4   A measure of rationalisation of the statutory taxation provisions with some defences (including, most significantly, the defence of 'passing on' or 'unjust enrichment of the claimant') applying to all the repayment provisions was proposed by the Law Commission in its final Report, Law Com No 227. These recommendations have not been implemented. At paras 16.9–16.10, no special defences were recommended for the residual *Woolwich* principle itself: these would be for the common law to develop if thought necessary.
5   [1993] AC 70, 197.
6   Ibid, at p 198.
7   See similarly above, pp 325, 386–388, 397–401.

consideration could somehow be confined to *demands* for payment, acceptance of it would appear to transform the present law of mistake and duress irrespective of whether the defendant is a public authority. To take just one example, all those who paid the unwarranted toll demands in *Maskell v Horner*[8] (where the defendant was not a public authority) would be entitled to restitution irrespective of whether they paid under duress of goods or by reason of a mistake.

Secondly, Lord Goff generously and rightly paid tribute to the writings of Cornish[9] and, particularly, Birks. Yet he implicitly rejected Birks' view that the authorities could be interpreted as having already established that an ultra vires demand was an unjust factor. Birks argued this not only in terms of what was expressly said in past cases but also, in an earlier article,[10] by exposing a serious flaw in the duress (ie entitlement threat) analysis of the *colore officii* cases. For he showed that in licensing cases the duress analysis would mean that the greater the invalidity the lower the chance of restitution:

> 'If the whole scheme is ultra vires, fees paid for licences cannot be recovered in the absence of some collateral duress ... The withholding of the licence itself is not duress for the citizen can have no entitlement to a nullity. If, however, the power to issue licences is itself valid and only the demand for fees is ultra vires the fees can be recovered. For here ... he is entitled to have the licence without charge and its withholding is itself duress.'[11]

Birks concluded that that was 'intolerable ... [for] his hope of restitution diminishes as the illegality established against the agency becomes more radical'.[12] Although presumably now of mere academic interest[13] it is a slight disappointment that that forceful argument was not referred to by the Lords in the examination of the so-called *colore officii* cases.

3.   WHAT SHOULD BE THE SCOPE OF THE *WOOLWICH* PRINCIPLE?

Now that a public authority's ultra vires demand has been authoritatively established as an unjust factor, the focus of attention must switch to its precise ambit.[14] Twelve main issues arise here for

8   [1915] 3 KB 106. Above, p 222.
9   '"Colour of Office": Restitutionary Redress Against Public Authority' (1987) 14 JMCL 41.
10   'Restitution from Public Authorities' (1980) 33 CLP 191.
11   Ibid, pp 196–197.
12   Ibid, p 197.
13   Cf below, p 454.
14   See Beatson, 'Restitution of Taxes, Levies and Other Imposts: Defining the Limits of the *Woolwich* Principle' (1993) 109 LQR 401.

consideration including the burning question, left open by the House of Lords, of whether special public law defences are needed to counter the width of the *Woolwich* principle.

(i) Does the *Woolwich* principle apply if the reason a payment was incorrectly exacted by the public authority was because it misconstrued or misapplied a relevant statute or regulation rather than, as in *Woolwich*, because the demand was based on an invalid regulation? The majority Law Lords left that question open while inclining to the view that it did so apply.

In general terms that provisional view seems right. The key question is whether or not the demand for payment, even if based on a valid regulation, is ultra vires. If the demand is intra vires, even though based on a mistake, it is authorised by Parliament and does not constitute an unjust factor. The scope of the doctrine of ultra vires is a controversial issue of public law but it appears that all, or nearly all, mistakes of law are regarded as going to jurisdiction.[15] Mistakes of fact may be more problematic but again one would expect that serious mistakes of fact (eg, demanding tax from the wrong person) would render the demand ultra vires.

This is now supported by *British Steel plc v Customs and Excise Comrs*.[16] Between 1988 and 1993, British Steel had paid excise duty (of over £25 million) on oil delivered to its blast furnaces. For some time previously, and again in this period, British Steel had argued that it was not liable to pay the tax demanded. It argued that it qualified for relief from duty because it was not using the oil in its blast furnaces as fuel. On a preliminary issue, it was assumed that the Commissioners were mistaken in their construction of the qualifying relief or on how it applied to the facts and that British Steel should, therefore, have been granted that relief. On that assumption the Court of Appeal held that, applying the *Woolwich* principle, British Steel was entitled at common law to restitution of the excise tax paid. Sir Richard Scott V-C said:

'An unlawful demand must, in a sense, always be an ultra vires demand. Whether the demand is based on ultra vires regulations, or on a mistaken view of the facts of the case, it will, as it seems to me, be bound to be a demand outside the taxing power conferred by the empowering legislation. If, for any of these reasons, a demand for tax is an unlawful demand, it seems to me to follow from the speeches of the majority in the *Woolwich* case that the taxpayer would, prima facie, become entitled, on making payment

15 Craig, *Administrative Law* (4th edn, 1999), pp 485–487.
16 [1997] 2 All ER 366.

pursuant to the unlawful demand, to a common law restitutionary right to repayment.'[17]

Paradoxically the majority of the Supreme Court of Canada in *Air Canada v British Columbia*[18] rejected a right to restitution of tax paid under a mistake of law where the tax is exacted under invalid legislation as opposed to being based on a misconstruction or misapplication of a statute. Wilson J's dissenting judgment is to be preferred.

It is also worth mentioning here that one important general area of public authorities making payment demands ultra vires is where charges are demanded by the state that are contrary to the payor's directly effective EC rights. European Community law requires that prima facie (ie, subject to defences) the payor is entitled to restitution of such charges.[19] That requirement of restitution appears to be satisfied in English law (leaving aside any statutory right to restitution)[20] by the application of the *Woolwich* principle.[1]

(ii) To which bodies or types of payment demand does the *Woolwich* principle apply?

This turns on where one draws the divide between public and private law in this context. The House of Lords did not elaborate on this beyond talking of public authorities, taxes or levies, and ultra vires demands. In contrast Glidewell LJ in the Court of Appeal regarded public law for these purposes as concerning 'cases in which the defendant is an instrument or officer of central or local government, exercising a power

---

17 Ibid, at 376. The *Woolwich* principle was held inapplicable in *Norwich City Council v Stringer* (2001) 33 HLR 158, CA, where the claimant had paid back housing benefit that the defendant local authority had overpaid him. Although the local authority had not complied with the correct procedure for reclaiming overpaid housing benefit, it was not making a demand for tax (or an equivalent) but was rather 'demanding' repayment of what it was entitled to. In refusing the claim for restitution Buxton LJ said, 'I find it wholly artificial to equiparate this case, where the reality is that the Council was saying, "You have received public money to which you were not entitled. Would you please return it?", with a case where a public authority is demanding a citizen's own money from him under powers that it does not have.'

18 (1989) 59 DLR (4th) 161.

19 *Amministrazione delle Finanze dello Stato v SpA San Giorgio* Case 199/82 [1983] ECR 3595; *Société Comateb v Director Général des Douanes et Droits Indirects* Cases C–192–218/95 [1997] ECR I-165; *GT Link A/S v De Dankse Statsbaner (DSB)* Case C–242/95 [1997] ECR I-4349; *Fantask A/S v Industriministeriet* Case C–188/95 [1997] ECR I-6783; *Metallgesellschaft Ltd v IRC, Hoescht AG v IRC* Cases C–397–410/98 [2001] Ch 620 (in the *Hoescht* case, where in effect corporation tax had been demanded and paid earlier than it should have been, in contravention of Art 52 of the EC Treaty on freedom of establishment, the claimant companies were held entitled to a remedy, best rationalised as restitutionary reversing the defendants' unjust enrichment, for the lost 'interest': such interest would be recoverable in English law under, or by close analogy to, the *Woolwich* principle). See generally, Alison Jones, *Restitution and European Community Law* (2000), chapter 3.

20 Below, pp 447–448.

1 Alison Jones, *Restitution and European Community Law* (2000), chapter 4.

to require payment of a tax, customs duty, licence fee or other similar impost'.[2] Similarly Butler-Sloss LJ said, 'In the category of public law, someone with actual or ostensible authority to require payment in respect of tax, duty, licence fee or other payment on behalf of central or local government makes the demand for payment ...'[3] Both emphasised that ordinary commercial transactions for consideration, even though concluded by a public authority, were not within the ambit of their decision.

The obvious hard case is that of a privatised company making a payment demand beyond what is permitted by statute. Is that caught by the *Woolwich* principle? This ought to turn on general principles of public law and is not a direct matter for the law of restitution. In other words, as with issue (i), the key is the doctrine of ultra vires.[4] If and in so far as the payment demand falls within that doctrine and is hence susceptible to judicial review under s 31 of the Supreme Court Act 1981 and CPR Part 54 the *Woolwich* principle applies: otherwise not.

There is the merest of hints that Lord Goff may have regarded public utilities as falling outside the wide principle. For in his discussion of duress he treated *South of Scotland Electicity Board v British Oxygen Co Ltd (No 2)*,[5] which involved alleged overcharging by an electricity board, as lying outside the *colore officii* category and as lying instead within the same category as the indisputably private law decision in *Great Western Rly v Sutton*.[6]

(iii) Does a restitutionary claim based on the *Woolwich* principle require the claimant to go through the public law judicial review procedure (CPR Part 54, formerly RSC Order 53)? In *Woolwich* the claimant had issued two sets of proceedings. One seeking a declaration under RSC Order 53 that the tax demand was ultra vires; and a second claiming restitution through an ordinary writ action.

It is first necessary to point out that, in allowing restitution by an ordinary claim even though the unjust factor was rooted in public law, the House of Lords implicitly rejected any procedural objection to the claim arising from *O'Reilly v Mackman*.[7] That decision laid

2   [1991] 3 WLR 790, 797.
3   Ibid, p 852.
4   That doctrine can include levies demanded contrary to EC law as well as domestic public law.
5   [1959] 2 All ER 225.
6   (1869) LR 4 HL 226. Above, pp 223–224.
7   [1983] 2 AC 237. Alder, 'Restitution in Public Law: Bearing the Cost of Unlawful State Action' (2002) 2 LS 165 controversially argues that restitution of money demanded ultra vires should be seen as an exclusively public law right. Restitution (which he suggests could be effected by a 'mandatory order' under CPR Part 54) would be a matter for the standard discretionary decision-making of the administrative court, which would be able to take into account the need to avoid restitution disrupting public services. With respect, this approach adopts too sharp a distinction between public and private law and would produce unhelpful incentives for claimants to found their restitutionary claims on 'private law' grounds such as duress and mistake.

down that RSC Order 53 (with its short limitation period), now CPR Part 54, provides the exclusive procedure for public law claims. Had it been applied in *Woolwich* that principle of exclusivity might have had the drastic consequence of ruling out the development of the ultra vires ground for restitution because the only remedies allowed under Order 53 were certiorari, prohibition, mandamus, injunctions, and damages.[8] On the face of it, restitutionary remedies were not included. The case for rejecting the exclusivity principle was therefore particularly strong. It may be that the House of Lords was in any event unconvinced by the strict division between public and private law drawn in *O'Reilly v Mackman*. Or perhaps it considered that all restitutionary claims should be treated for procedural purposes as private. After all, there is a very close analogy between a public authority's ultra vires demand and the 'private law' unjust factor of exploitation of weakness.[9]

Clearly therefore there is no objection to proceeding as the claimant did in *Woolwich*. But the House of Lords gave no indication as to whether judicial review is a necessary preliminary to restitution. In the Court of Appeal both Glidewell and Ralph Gibson JJ hinted that at least one payor would first need to bring judicial review proceedings to establish that the demand was ultra vires.[10] However, as Ralph Gibson LJ went on to say, it is hard to see thereafter why other payors would not be entitled through ordinary writ actions to claim restitution based on the ultra vires demands.

Whether one should insist, somewhat artificially, that *all* payors first issue judicial review proceedings ties in with the question of whether a short limitation period should be introduced. For, subject to judicial discretion, an application for judicial review must be brought within three months from the time at which the ground of challenge arises. It is argued below (issue xii) that the call for shorter limitation periods should be rejected. It is submitted therefore that, even if judicial review by one payor is a necessary preliminary, all payors should not be first forced down that route. But the better view is that judicial review proceedings are not a necessary preliminary to the operation of the *Woolwich* principle. This is in line with the approach taken to the tort of misfeasance in public office which treats the procedure for that

---

8   CPR Part 54, which has replaced RSC Order 53, renames the prerogative remedies, as a 'mandatory order' (mandamus), a 'prohibiting order' (prohibition) and a 'quashing order' (certiorari). An injunction and a declaration may also be sought under CPR Part 54, as may damages where claimed in addition to one of the other remedies. But, as with RSC Order 53, there is no mention in CPR Part 54 of restitution.

9   Above, pp 269–271. Cf Birks, 'Restitution from the Executive: A Tercentenary Footnote to the Bill of Rights' in *Essays on Restitution* (ed Finn, 1990), pp 175, 204, note 184.

10 [1991] 3 WLR 790, 817, 835.

'public law' tort no differently than any other tort. This is also now supported by *British Steel plc v Customs and Excise Comrs*[11] where British Steel was held entitled to restitution of excise duty demanded unlawfully and ultra vires even though it had not first taken judicial review proceedings.

At present it is a distraction that CPR Part 54 does not expressly include restitutionary remedies. On any view that defect should be removed. Costs and time would be saved if in a single action a claimant were able to claim restitution having established that the public authority's demand was ultra vires. If that reform were made, the case for forcing all payors through the public law procedure would be given added strength. Even then the better view is that an ordinary claim for restitution, governed by ordinary limitation periods, should still be possible.

(iv) To what extent is the *Woolwich* principle overriden by the various statutory provisions that deal with overpaid taxes and levies?

In *Woolwich* Lord Goff's view was that 'most cases will continue for the time being to be regulated by the various statutory regimes now in force'.[12] In conformity with that, the picture appears to be as follows: some provisions expressly exclude the common law (eg, s 80(7) of the Value Added Tax Act 1994 dealing with overpaid VAT);[13] others (eg, s 33 of the Taxes Management Act 1970 dealing with overpaid income tax, corporation tax and capital gains tax)[14] do so by necessary implication, except that the statutory provisions may be inapplicable where the regulation under which the tax has been charged is itself ultra vires as on the facts of *Woolwich*. And, presumably, there are also some taxes and levies demanded by public authorities for which there are no statutory repayment provisions.

Whatever their impact on the common law, the present statutory restrictions are unsatisfactorily inconsistent with one another. For example, the Taxes Management Act 1970, s 33[15] dealing with overpaid income tax, corporation tax and capital gains tax gives the Inland Revenue a discretionary power whether to make restitution of mistakenly paid tax; there is no unjust enrichment or passing on defence; but there is a defence where the tax was paid in accordance with a prevailing practice or a settled understanding of the law. In

---

11 [1997] 2 All ER 366. See above, p 443. For a useful note on this case, see Bamforth, 'Restitution and the Scope of Judicial Review' [1997] PL 603.
12 [1993] AC 70, 176.
13 See also, eg, Customs and Excise Management Act 1979, s 137A, as inserted by the Finance Act 1995, s 20 and as amended by the Finance Act 1997, s 50 and Sch 5 (overpaid excise duty).
14 See also, eg, Inheritance Tax Act 1984, s 241 (overpaid inheritance tax).
15 As amended by the Finance Act 1998, s 117(3) and Sch 19.

contrast, the Value Added Tax Act 1994, s 80[16] gives the taxpayer a right to restitution of VAT that was not due; there is an unjust enrichment or passing on defence;[17] but there is no settled practice defence. The Law Commission recommended some (but not total) rationalisation of the statutory taxation provisions, including the suggested application to all the statutory repayment provisions of the defence of passing on or unjust enrichment of the claimant. But those recommendations have not been implemented.[18]

(v) What is the causation test for restitution under the *Woolwich* principle?

This should be consistent with the rest of the law of restitution and, in accordance with the general approach advocated in chapter 1, it should normally be the 'but for' test. It will be for the claimant to show that but for the ultra vires demand by the public authority he would not have made the payment. Satisfying that test should rarely produce problems for a claimant in this context.

(vi) Does the *Woolwich* principle extend to cases where the public authority has made no demand for payment? Say, for example, an ultra vires tax is paid in reasonable anticipation of a demand: is the payor entitled to restitution?

The answer should surely be 'yes'.[19] The policy of 'no taxation without Parliament' applies equally whether there has been a demand or not. The expression 'ultra vires demands' can therefore be taken to be shorthand for demands or reasonably anticipated demands that are, or will be, ultra vires. The stress on 'reasonable anticipation' is designed to exclude the person who pays where there is no prospect of the tax being demanded. It would seem that he should have to rely on the ground of mistake if he is to recover.

(vii) Is restitution ruled out where the payor compromises the ultra vires demand (ie enters into a contractual settlement) or otherwise 'submits to an honest claim' or pays 'to close the transaction'?

Following the theory that there should be no taxation without Parliament to its absolute limits it could be argued that a payor should even be able to unwind a contractual settlement of an ultra vires demand. That extreme position ignores the policy, so important for the proper administration of justice, of encouraging the self-help

16　As amended by the Finance Act 1997, ss 46–47. See similarly the Customs and Excise Management Act 1979, s 137A, as inserted by the Finance Act 1995, s 20 and as amended by the Finance Act 1997, s 50 and Sch 5 (overpaid excise duty).
17　On overpaid VAT and the defence of unjust enrichment, see *Marks & Spencer plc v Customs and Excise Comrs* [2000] STC 16: below, p 595, n 16.
18　Above, p 441, n 4.
19　This is supported by the Law Commission Consultation Paper (No 120), para 3.90.

resolution of disputes. As the Law Commission commented in its Consultation Paper on *Restitution of Payments Made Under a Mistake of Law*, 'The public interest in avoiding litigation is as important in the context of tax claims and other claims by public authorities as in other contexts.'[20] Contractual settlements should be binding subject to the normal contractual rules governing their validity. This links to saying that an ultra vires demand is a ground for restitution of a non-contractual payment only. It does not render a contract void or voidable.

In contrast, the notions of a non-contractual submission to an honest claim and a payment to close a transaction are vague and confusing. Contrary to the view of the majority in the Court of Appeal they should not be restrictions on the *Woolwich* principle.[1] In chapter 5 it was suggested that in the context of duress those concepts are probably synonymous with saying that causation has not been satisfied or that a threat to sue is not illegitimate. The latter plainly has no force where the unjust factor is an ultra vires demand as *Woolwich* itself shows. And causation must always be made out if the restitutionary claim is to succeed as has been discussed above (issue v). In the context of mistake it was suggested in chapter 3 that what the submission concept might be referring to is that a payor cannot recover where he pays believing that the money is probably not owed (or in extreme cases recklessly chooses not to check the true position). Again, as *Woolwich* shows, there is no scope for that restriction where the ground for restitution is an ultra vires demand and not mistake.

(viii) What is the position on changes in the law? Albeit rare it is possible for a demand that was intra vires (or was generally so regarded) at the time of payment to become ultra vires as a result of legislation or of a judicial decision being overruled.

The question mirrors that debated in respect of mistakes of law in chapter 3.[2] In accordance with the conclusion reached there the best view seems to be that, subject to statutory provision to the contrary, there should be restitution in the above situation where there has been a judicial change in the law (or a retrospective legislative change).[3] Similarly, if a demand that was ultra vires has been declared intra vires by reason of a judicial change in the law (or a retrospective legislative change) restitution should surely be denied.

---

20 Consultation Paper No 120, para 3.69. See also Law Commission Report, Law Com No 227, paras 2.25–2.28, 10.31–10.35.

1 Contrast *res judicata* and the linked idea that, generally, payment is irrecoverable where made following proceedings by the payee. These are discussed, alongside contractual compromise, as aspects of the general defence of 'dispute resolved', below, at pp 556–559.

2 Above, pp 150–158.

3 This derives some support from *SCI Operations Pty Ltd v Commonwealth of Australia* (1996) 139 ALR 595.

(ix) Can there be proprietary restitution in respect of payments demanded ultra vires by public authorities?

It has been assumed so far in this chapter that the claimant is seeking personal restitution from the public authority. But if, by reason of the ultra vires demand, an unjust enrichment at the claimant's expense is established and the defendant retains the payment (whether in the same form or, by the rules of tracing, in a substitute) is the claimant entitled to proprietary restitution? In practice, this is unlikely to be an important question because a public authority is unlikely to become insolvent and the main practical importance of proprietary restitution is in respect of a defendant's insolvency.

However this question was raised in the Canadian case of *Zaidan Group Ltd v City of London*[4] in the context of whether a claimant was entitled to interest on restitution of overpaid tax. This was thought to turn on whether the public authority was a trustee of the overpaid tax. At first instance Barr J, relying on *Chase Manhattan Bank NA v Israel-British Bank (London) Ltd*,[5] decided that the tax was held on a constructive trust so that interest (and presumably compound interest) was payable. While this decision was overturned by the Ontario Court of Appeal, this was on the ground that the question of whether there should be restitution of overpaid tax and interest thereon was entirely dealt with by statute and there was no room for restitution at common law. The constructive trust reasoning at first instance was not, therefore, directly addressed.

Although the claimant's intention may not be vitiated by an ultra vires demand, it would seem that, if proprietary restitution for mistake and duress is justified,[6] the same should follow in respect of ultra vires demands.

(x) Should the defence of change of position be available to a public authority to resist restitution based on an ultra vires demand?

Certainly a public authority would have great difficulties proving that it had changed its position as a result of the particular payment made by the claimant. And even if, in line with the rough-and-ready approach to that defence applied in *Lipkin Gorman v Karpnale Ltd*,[7] it is legitimate to take account of the defendant's reliance on a number of payments by different payors, it can usually be argued that a public authority can raise additional money from the public to compensate for any shortfall that disrupts its spending plans. In any event it is

---

4   (1987) 36 DLR (4th) 443; revsd (1990) 64 DLR (4th) 514.
5   [1981] Ch 105.
6   See above, pp 60–75, 159–162, 218–219. For discussion, including of the *Zaidan* case, see Maddaugh and McCamus, *The Law of Restitution* (1st edn, 1990), pp 95–96.
7   [1991] 2 AC 548. Below, p 514.

arguable that a public authority making an ultra vires demand is more at fault than the payor so that, if one were to apply the 'relative fault' approach to change of position discussed in chapter 15, it could not avail itself of the defence.[8]

(xi) Should a defence of passing on (otherwise referred to as 'unjust enrichment of the claimant') be open to a public authority?

This is examined in detail in chapter 15. While that chapter looks at the defence from the perspective of defendants generally, there seems no good reason (see issue xii below) for affording public authorities special protection. Passing on should hold good for all defendants or for none. But this is not the present law in that, while passing on has been rejected as a general common law defence,[9] several of the taxing statutes do apply that defence under the language of 'unjust enrichment of the claimant.'[10]

(xii) Should there be special defences open to a public authority because of the disruption to public finances that the *Woolwich* principle might otherwise cause? In particular should restitution based on an ultra vires demand be subject to a short limitation period or to a defence of 'extreme disruption of public funds'?[11]

It was the policy objection of disrupting public funds that led the majority of the Supreme Court of Canada in *Air Canada v British Columbia*[12] to reject an abolition of the mistake of law bar in respect of levies based on ultra vires legislation or regulations. La Forest J said, '... fiscal chaos would result if the general rule favoured recovery, particularly where a longstanding taxation measure is involved'.[13] Isaacs J spoke in similar fashion in his dissenting judgment in *Sargood Bros v Commonwealth*:[14] 'After several years, questions might be raised which, on some suddenly discovered interpretation of a taxing Act, whether internal revenue or Customs, would unexpectedly require the return of enormous sums of money and quite disorganise the public treasury.'

As an argument against recognising a wide unjust factor that approach has already been rejected by the decision in *Woolwich*. But

---

8　That the defence should not apply appears to be supported by the Law Commission: see Report No 227, paras 11.10–11.17.
9　*Kleinwort Benson Ltd v Birmingham City Council* [1997] QB 380, CA.
10　See above, p 448 and below, p 595.
11　A more radical, unappealing, and hence most unlikely, alternative special defence would be to imitate EC law by allowing only those to succeed who have already brought restitutionary claims at the time of the declaration of the invalidity of the demand. See Law Commission Report No 227, paras 11.8–11.9, 11.26–11.30; Birks, 'Restitution from the Executive: A Tercentenary Footnote to the Bill of Rights' in *Essays on Restitution* (ed Finn 1990), pp 197–198. Cf Lord Slynn in *Woolwich* [1993] AC 70, 200.
12　(1989) 59 DLR (4th) 161, 193.
13　Ibid, p 195.
14　(1910–11) 11 CLR 258, 303.

those concerns could re-emerge to dictate the creation of special defences to the *Woolwich* principle. That would accord with McCamus' strategy for, while advocating reform of the mistake of law bar, he feared that 'In an extreme case the granting of recovery could have a seriously disruptive effect on public finances.'[15] He therefore suggested that a special defence of 'extreme disruption of public finances'[16] should be recognised along with careful fashioning of normal defences like change of position and limitation.

On the other side of the fence stand Cornish and, slightly more tentatively, Birks.[17] Cornish finds 'unattractive' the notion of a special defence of 'extreme disruption of public finances'. 'It would confer a discretion inherently difficult to exercise: and it seems to contain the imperative that, if governments are to exceed their taxing powers, this should be done on the grandest scale.'[18] But the most forthright statement in favour of this position is Wilson J's dissenting judgment in the *Air Canada* case:

'What is the policy that requires such a dramatic reversal of principle? Why should the individual taxpayer, as opposed to taxpayers as a whole, bear the burden of government's mistake? I would respectfully suggest that it is grossly unfair that X, who may not be (as in this case) a large corporate enterprise, should absorb the cost of government's unconstitutional act. If it is appropriate for the courts to adopt some kind of policy in order to protect the government against itself (and I cannot say that the idea particularly appeals to me) it should be one which distributes the loss fairly across the public. The loss should not fall on the totally innocent taxpayer whose only fault is that it paid what the legislature improperly said was due. I find it quite ironic to describe such a person as "asserting a right to disrupt the government by demanding a refund" or "creating fiscal chaos" or "requiring a new generation to pay for the expenditures of the old". By refusing to adopt such a policy the courts are not "visiting the sins of the fathers on the children". The "sin" in this case (if it can be so described) is that of government and only government and government has means available to it to protect against the consequences of it. It should not, in my opinion, be done by the courts and certainly not at the expense of individual taxpayers.'[19]

15 'Restitutionary Recovery of Moneys Paid to a Public Authority under a Mistake of Law' (1983) 17 UBCLR 233, 273. Cf Maddaugh and McCamus, *The Law of Restitution* (1st edn, 1990), pp 274–275.
16 Jones, *Restitution in Public and Private Law* (1991), pp 24–28 argues that this is essentially an illustration of the defence of change of position. But the latter seems narrower in requiring a causal link between the overpayment and the defendant's change of position.
17 Birks, 'Restitution from the Executive: A Tercentary Footnote to the Bill of Rights' in *Essays on Restitution* (ed Finn, 1990), pp 195–204.
18 '"Colour of Office": Restitutionary Redress Against Public Authority' (1987) JMCL 41, 52. See also Collins, 'Restitution from Government Officials' (1984) 29 McGill LJ 407, 436–437; Law Commission Report No 227, paras 11.6, 11.23.
19 (1989) 59 DLR (4th) 161, 169.

It is submitted that there is no convincing counter-argument to the powerful logic and fairness of Wilson J's words. In *Woolwich* Lord Goff found her reasoning 'most attractive' and, while he earlier adverted sympathetically to the possibility of shorter limitation periods, he agreed with Wilson J in doubting 'the advisability of imposing special limits upon recovery in the case of "unconstitutional or ultra vires levies"'.[20]

Moreover, a defence of 'extreme disruption of public funds' would be hopelessly vague and arbitrary. And, in any event, why should it be confined to public authorities when, leaving aside change of position, fiscal disruption to other defendants would be happily judged an unacceptable defence to a restitutionary claim? There is also the point that, even if it were correct that in an extreme case restitutionary claims would threaten the public interest, Parliament can react on an ad hoc basis by legislation barring restitution.

In similar vein, and with respect to Lord Goff who showed some interest in this idea, there seems no justification for shortening the limitation periods for restitution under the *Woolwich* principle.[1] The spirit of Wilson J's dissent again requires a rejection of this. Although it is true that judicial review under CPR Part 54 is subject to very short time limits that is because the procedure is designed for remedies that would nullify, stop, or enjoin the action of a public authority. There is no reason why monetary claims based on invalid governmental action should be so restricted. In sum, a public authority should be treated no differently in respect of limitation periods than any other defendant. Indeed that has already been accepted in modern times by the Law Reform (Limitation of Actions, &c) Act 1954, which abolished the special short limitation period for actions (in, eg, contract, tort, and restitution) against public authorities.

Even if such arguments against a special defence are rejected, advocates of the need for a special defence may find themselves caught on the horns of a dilemma in deciding the range of that special

---

20   [1993] AC 70, 176. In *Kleinwort Benson Ltd v Lincoln City Council* [1999] 2 AC 349, 382, Lord Goff left open whether the restitution of overpaid tax should be denied where the tax was paid in accordance with a prevailing practice or a settled understanding of the law: see above, pp 152, 157. Certainly this type of restriction is embodied in various tax statutes: see, eg, the proviso to s 33(2) of the Taxes Management Act 1970.

1   Shorter limitation periods were also rejected by the Law Commission in its Report No 227, paras 10.36–10.41. But shorter limitation periods (of three years) have been introduced for several of the statutory repayment provisions. See, eg, Value Added Tax Act 1994, s 80, as amended by the Finance Act 1997, ss 46–47. See similarly the Customs and Excise Management Act 1979, s 137A, as inserted by the Finance Act 1995, s 20 and as amended by the Finance Act 1997, s 50 and Sch 5 (overpaid excise duty). For a general rejection of shorter limitation periods against public authorities see Law Commission Consultation Paper No 151 *Limitation of Actions* (1998), paras 13.142–13.153 and Report No 270 *Limitation of Actions* (2001), para 4.203.

defence. Would it only apply, as one might at first blush expect, where the unjust factor is the public authority's ultra vires demand? Or would it apply wherever the defendant to a restitutionary action (for the return of a payment demanded) is a public authority? If the former, the traditional law would live on for it might be to a claimant's advantage to establish duress (or mistake) so as to avoid the special defence: the thin (and, on one view, flawed)[2] distinction between the *colore officii* cases and other cases within the *Woolwich* principle would be of crucial practical significance. If the latter, the paradoxical and unfortunate overall effect of *Woolwich* might be to diminish a citizen's restitutionary rights against public authorities. Those who in the past would have succeeded in a restitutionary claim might run up against the new special defence.

2   Above, p 442.

Chapter 14

Restitution for wrongs

1. INTRODUCTION

At this point we cross the central divide in the law of restitution.[1] Chapters 3–13 have all been concerned with unjust enrichment by subtraction. In this chapter 'at the expense of the claimant' is instead established by showing that the defendant has committed a wrong to the claimant. The cause of action in restitution for wrongs is the wrong. The cause of action in unjust enrichment by subtraction is the unjust enrichment.

In many cases – but not all – a further distinguishing feature of restitution for wrongs, as against unjust enrichment by subtraction, will be the measure of restitution.[2] In relation to restitution for wrongs, it is clear that the claimant can recover more than its loss. This will often be the primary reason why the claimant seeks restitution rather than the standard remedy of compensation for the wrong. In contrast, in unjust enrichment by subtraction the claimant must establish that the defendant's gain has come from the claimant's wealth. And normally, but not always, there will be an equivalence between the gain to the defendant and the loss to the claimant.

At a deeper level, the distinction between restitution for wrongs and unjust enrichment by subtraction reflects different moral ideas. The former rests on the notion that 'no man shall profit from his wrong'. The latter principally reflects the idea of restoring the status quo for both claimant and defendant to the extent that the claimant's loss has unjustifiably become the defendant's gain.

---

1 For detailed discussion, see above, pp 25–31. For general discussion of restitution for wrongs, see Law Commission Report No 247 *Aggravated, Exemplary and Restitutionary Damages* (1997), paras 3.1–3.84. The essential approach recommended by the Law Commission was to leave development of restitution for wrongs to the courts. But some minimal legislative proposals, consequent on the recommended statutory reform of punitive damages, were recommended. For consideration of these reforms, and of some specific points on restitution for wrongs (eg the problems of multiple defendants and multiple claimants) see Burrows, 'Reforming Non-Compensatory Damages' in *The Search for Principle* (eds Swadling and Jones, 1999), pp 295–312.

2 For a detailed examination of the measure of restitution for wrongs see Friedmann, 'Restitution for Wrongs: The Measure of Recovery' (2001) 79 Texas LR 1879.

Another distinguishing feature is that bars and rules expressed as applying to actions for a wrong are prima facie applicable to restitution for the wrong just as much as to compensation for the wrong. In contrast such bars and rules do not prima facie apply to unjust enrichment by subtraction. But again this is not a necessary (any may in practice be an insignificant) distinction because, applying a purposive construction, a court may disapply the bars or rules to restitution, as opposed to compensation, for a wrong; and may extend a bar or rule to unjust enrichment by subtraction that is expressed as applying to restitution (and compensation) for wrongs.

A further difference is shown in cases where another's conduct induces the claimant to render a benefit. In unjust enrichment by subtraction restitution can be obtained from a 'third party' recipient for, for example, mistake induced by misrepresentation, duress, or undue influence. In contrast in relation to restitution for wrongs restitution is available against the wrongdoer only.

Although of no importance to the law of restitution itself, restitution for wrongs also obviously differs from unjust enrichment by subtraction in that other remedies (for example, compensatory damages or injunctions) may be available for the wrong apart from restitution.

Recognition of the law of restitution's central divide leads to the phenomenon which Birks has labelled 'alternative analysis'.[3] That is, one must recognise that, even if the defendant has made a gain by committing a wrong to the claimant, the same facts may alternatively give rise to a claim in unjust enrichment by subtraction. Say, for example, the defendant induces the claimant to pay him £1,000 by a fraudulent misrepresentation. The claimant may seek restitution for the wrong based on the argument that the defendant made the £1,000 by committing the tort of deceit. Alternatively the tort could be ignored and restitution of the £1,000 sought within unjust enrichment by subtraction on the basis that it was paid by a mistake of fact as dealt with in chapter 3. Or say the defendant detains the claimant and refuses to release him unless he pays the defendant £50. If the claimant complies, he may try to claim restitution of the £50 for the tort of trespass to the person (false imprisonment). Alternatively he could recover within unjust enrichment by subtraction for duress of the person as covered in chapter 5.

To recognise alternative analysis is to accept that, on a given set of facts, it may be to the claimant's advantage or disadvantage to formulate the restitutionary claim in unjust enrichment by subtraction as opposed to basing it on the wrong. The possibility of alternative analysis also

---

3   Birks, at pp 44, 314.

means that, in interpreting past decisions, one cannot assume that restitution has been triggered by the wrong just because, on facts involving a gain caused by a wrong, restitution has been granted: the true explanation for the restitution may be unjust enrichment by subtraction not that the wrong has triggered restitution.

Not every instance of enrichment by wrongdoing triggers restitution. On the contrary, the bulk of this chapter will be concerned to isolate when the law permits a claimant to choose restitution (rather than compensation) for a wrong. In other words, our primary concern will be to clarify when the law considers there to be *unjust* enrichment by wrongdoing. But the preliminary question – which is crucial, given the importance of the central division of the law of restitution – is, what is meant by a wrong?

Certainly the term must not be a vague indicator of individual morality. As with the term unjust enrichment, one is concerned with what the law means by a wrong. It is clear that the law does not equate reprehensible conduct with wrongdoing. If this were otherwise many torts or instances of breach of contract could not be classified as wrongs because the basis of the liability is strict.

Birks argues that a wrong means 'conduct ... whose effect in creating legal consequences is attributable to its being characterised as a breach of duty'.[4] And he also points out that the division between restitution for wrongs and for unjust enrichment by subtraction 'corresponds exactly to the Austinian distinction between remedial (or secondary) rights and primary rights'.[5] Similarly *Winfield and Jolowicz on Tort*, in distinguishing tort from unjust enrichment (by subtraction) emphasise that the remedial duty in tort springs from the breach of a primary duty of some kind whereas that is not so in respect of unjust enrichment. So, for example, if I pay D £100 by mistake it cannot be said that D's remedial duty to repay the money is the result of the breach of some primary duty. In the words of *Winfield and Jolowicz*, '[I]t would be meaningless to say that [D] was under a duty not to accept the money from me or that he was under a duty of any kind save the remedial duty to return the money to me ...'[6]

But, given that judicial or statutory language may not make it clear, is there any straightforward way of telling whether the law characterises particular conduct as constituting the breach of a (primary) duty? With the conceivable exception of some statutory duties, a sure test appears to be that compensation must be an available remedial

---

4   Birks, at p 313. See also the excellent discussion by Edelman, *Gain-Based Damages* (2002), ch 2.

5   Birks, at p 43.

6   (16th edn, 2002), p 12.

measure for the conduct in question if loss is caused to the claimant by that conduct. Applying this test, the common law civil wrongs are torts[7] and breach of contract; and the equitable civil wrongs are breach of fiduciary duty, breach of confidence,[8] dishonestly procuring or assisting a breach of fiduciary duty,[9] and those forms of estoppel that constitute causes of action, in particular proprietary estoppel. Duress, undue influence, exploitation of weakness and ultra vires demands by public authorities are, in contrast, not wrongs. They fall within unjust enrichment by subtraction and have been dealt with in earlier chapters. The central question being examined in this chapter, therefore, is when is it that a victim of those civil wrongs can recover restitution reversing benefits made by the wrongdoer rather than compensation?

There are six final introductory points. First, there is little if any difficulty in this context in establishing that the defendant is enriched. It appears that in all the cases the defendant was incontrovertibly benefited, either because it realised a profit from the wrong[10] or because it saved itself a necessary expense.[11] Even if this is not so, the 'reprehensible seeking-out test' can usually be satisfied: a wrongdoer who, for example, steals another's chattel or intentionally uses another's land without permission indicates by its positive conduct that the chattel or use of land is of value to it; and its reprehensible conduct debars it from relying on the argument that it was not willing to pay.

---

7   Torts include the tort of breach of statutory duty and what may be termed 'statutory torts': the breach of duties under, eg, the Occupiers' Liability Act 1957, the Nuclear Installations Act 1965, the Misrepresentation Act 1967, s 2(1), the Sex Discrimination Act 1975. See Stanton, *Breach of Statutory Duty in Tort* (1986), pp 8–12. For a general examination of civil wrongs arising under statute, see Law Commission Report No 247, *Aggravated, Exemplary and Restitutionary Damages* (1997), paras 5.57–5.70. Sections 382–386 of the Financial Services and Markets Act 2000 are difficult to classify. They are probably best viewed as creating an express statutory tort for which restitution (irrespective of loss) can be awarded to the 'victims' and yet, uniquely, the claimant must be the Financial Services Authority or the Secretary of State. See generally *Securities and Investments Board v Pantell SA (No 2)* [1992] 3 WLR 896 in which Steyn LJ described proceedings under an equivalent section of an earlier Act as 'a type of representative action for the benefit of investors.'

8   This is still treated as an equitable wrong rather than a tort: *A-G v Guardian Newspapers (No 2)* [1990] 1 AC 109, 286 (per Lord Goff). See Burrows, *Remedies for Torts and Breach of Contract* (2nd edn, 1994), p 11. Cf *Aquaculture Corpn v New Zealand Mussel Co Ltd* [1990] 3 NZLR 299.

9   This was the wrong recognised in *Royal Brunei Airlines Sdn Bhd v Tan* [1995] 2 AC 378. More traditionally, it has been called 'knowing assistance'. Lord Nicholls has also suggested that dishonest receipt of property transferred in breach of fiduciary duty should be recognised as an equitable wrong and that both these wrongs should be regarded as embraced by the single wrong of 'dishonest participation in a breach of fiduciary duty'. See 'Knowing Receipt: The Need for a New Landmark' in *Restitution, Past, Present and Future* (eds Cornish, Nolan, O'Sullivan and Virgo, 1998), pp 231–245, esp 243–244. See above ch 4.

10   Eg, *Lamine v Dorrell* (1705) 2 Ld Raym 1216; *Lister & Co v Stubbs* (1890) 45 Ch D 1.

11   Eg, *Phillips v Homfray* (1883) 24 Ch D 439; *Penarth Dock Engineering Co Ltd v Pounds* [1963] 1 Lloyd's Rep 359.

Secondly, restitution for a wrong can be equally well classified as part of the law concerning the wrong or as part of the law of restitution. To take the example of restitution for a tort, one can equally happily say that one is dealing with the law of tort or the law of restitution. Nothing of substantive importance should turn on that classification. It follows that, just as nominal and exemplary damages, as well as central compensatory damages, are discussed in tort textbooks, so should be restitutionary remedies for torts. Some tort books have now recognised this but three main reasons may be suggested for why this has traditionally not been so. First, there has traditionally been a lack of acceptance, awareness and understanding of the law of restitution. Secondly, it is still comparatively rare for a claimant to be awarded restitution for a tort. Indeed the compensatory ideal is so dominant that, even where restitution has been awarded, some commentators have re-analysed the award as compensatory. Thirdly, there is the difficulty of alternative analysis. Just because restitution has been awarded against a tortfeasor does not mean that the tort has triggered restitution. The decision may be explicable on the basis of unjust enrichment by subtraction in which case it rightly has no place within tort.

Thirdly, some texts[12] on the law of restitution include alongside chapters on restitution for civil wrongs a chapter on benefits made from crimes. Indeed in recent years there has been increased interest in two aspects of this general topic. First, there has been the narrower question (looked at in the 'public law' claim in *A-G v Blake*[13] but also raised by the alleged payments made to Mary Bell for co-operation in the writing of a book about her life)[14] as to whether criminals should be allowed to profit from their memoirs. Secondly, there has been legislation widening the scope of the criminal courts' powers to confiscate the proceeds of crime.[15] In addition to 'confiscation', discussion of this topic in the texts principally looks at the law which prevents a murderer or, subject to the courts' discretion under the

---

12 Eg Goff and Jones, ch 38; Virgo, *The Principles of the Law of Restitution* (1999) ch 19; Maddaugh and McCamus, *The Law of Restitution* (1st edn, 1990), ch 22. See also Jones, 'Stripping a Criminal of the Profits of Crime' (2000) 1 Theoretical Inquiries in Law 59.

13 [2001] 1 AC 268.

14 Mary Bell was eleven when found guilty in 1968 of manslaughter of two young children. In 1998, newspapers claimed that she was paid money in relation to a new book about her by Gitta Sereny, *Cries Unheard*.

15 Criminal Justice Act, 1988, Part VI. The Proceeds of Crime Act 2002 (which at the time of writing in September 2002 is not yet in force) deals not only with confiscation by the criminal courts but introduces in Part 5 a civil remedy allowing the Director of the Assets Recovery Agency to recover property which is, or represents, property obtained through criminal conduct. For reasons explained in the text below (eg, the gain is not 'at the expense of the claimant') this new civil remedy, like a confiscation order, is outside the ambit of the unjust enrichment principle used in this book.

Forfeiture Act 1982,[16] other unlawful killer from profiting from his victim's death. For example, a murderer is not entitled to benefit under the will or intestacy of the deceased,[17] nor from an insurance policy that would otherwise have inured in his favour.[18] Nor can social security benefits (eg, a widow's allowance) be recovered.[19]

Certainly this area constitutes an obvious application of the maxim 'no man shall profit from his own wrong'. But crimes are plainly significantly different from civil wrongs and this area falls outside the ambit of the unjust enrichment principle used in this book. More specifically, the principle against unjust enrichment that we are concerned with needs the 'at the expense of the claimant' requirement to be satisfied and furthermore results in the enrichment being given back, or given up, to the claimant (whether by personal or proprietary restitution). In contrast, confiscation orders do not give the victim of the crime the criminal's ill-gotten gains. Similarly, in relation to forfeiture, it is irrelevant whether the person benefiting from the law's intervention is or is not the victim of the crime. Indeed, a crime cannot in itself be a relevant restitution – yielding wrong because a crime is a 'wrong' against the state and is not 'at the expense of' any particular person. It follows that a victim of a crime cannot assert a claim to restitution of the gains made by the criminal from that crime without basing his or her claim on a civil wrong (or on an unjust enrichment by subtraction). Civil wrongs only fall within the ambit of the law of restitution although, of course, many crimes also constitute civil wrongs.

Fourthly, as will become plain, there are several differently labelled remedies, both common law (eg, award of money had and received, and restitutionary damages) and equitable (eg, an account of profits), which are doing the same job of effecting personal restitution for wrongs. It would simplify and improve the law if, as the Law Commission has recommended, one here moved to a single remedy or, as one might otherwise view it, a single label; and, in the context of wrongs, the most obvious single personal remedy/label to choose seems to be 'restitutionary damages'.[20]

---

16 On this discretion see *Re K* [1986] Ch 180. By the Forfeiture Act 1982, s 1(1): 'In this Act, the "forfeiture rule" means the rule of public policy which in certain circumstances precludes a person who has unlawfully killed another from acquiring a benefit in consequence of the killing.' Note that a constructive trust is generally considered not to be in issue on the ground that the killer does not acquire legal title.

17 *Re Sigsworth, Bedford v Bedford* [1935] Ch 89.

18 *Cleaver v Mutual Reserve Fund Life Association* [1892] 1 QB 147.

19 *R v Chief National Insurance Comr, ex p Connor* [1981] QB 758.

20 Law Commission Report No 247 (1997), paras 3.82–3.84. Unfortunately Lord Nicholls in *A-G v Blake* [2001] 1 AC 268, 284 said that he preferred to avoid the unhappy expression 'restitutionary damages'.

Fifthly, as we shall see, for equitable wrongs, although not common law wrongs, proprietary rather than merely personal restitution has been granted. That is, the wrongdoer has been held to be a constructive trustee for the victim of gains made from the wrong. This is controversial.[1] In terms of policy, it is very hard to see why a claim for restitution for a wrong, in contrast to restitution of an unjust enrichment by subtraction, should have priority on the wrongdoer's insolvency. Certainly one would have thought that, as a claim for compensation for a wrong does not give priority on the wrongdoer's insolvency, it cannot be correct to give priority to a claim for restitution, which is a less obvious measure of recovery for a wrong.

Finally, James Edelman in his stimulating and superbly-argued book *Gain-Based Damages*[2] has put forward the novel thesis that so-called restitution for wrongs in fact embodies two different remedial measures which should be kept distinct. The first is the reversal of a wrongful transfer of value from a claimant to a defendant. He terms this measure 'restitutionary damages'. The second is the stripping away of profits made by the defendant committing a wrong to the claimant. He calls this measure 'disgorgement damages'. The importance of this distinction, according to Edelman, is that the former rests on corrective justice, is analogous to unjust enrichment by subtraction, is relatively uncontroversial and should be available for every type of wrong. The latter, in contrast, is designed to deter a wrong where compensatory damages are inadequate to do so. Disgorgement damages are, and should therefore be, restricted to two main circumstances. First, where a wrong is committed cynically with a view to making material gain and the profit made exceeds the compensation payable; and, secondly, for breach of fiduciary duty in order to protect the institution of trust inherent in the fiduciary relationship.

One difficulty with this thesis is that, in every situation of what Edelman calls restitutionary damages for a wrong, there appears to be an alternative cause of action based on unjust enrichment by subtraction.[3] In the light of this, it may be doubted whether the wrong adds anything to the justification for restitution. In contrast, the wrong is normatively crucial if the claimant seeks compensation or a gain-based measure that goes beyond compensation (or beyond reversing a transfer of value). Another difficulty is that to draw a rigid line between restitution and disgorgement

1 See above, p 72.
2 (2002). See esp pp 2–3 and ch 3.
3 Birks, p 41 writes, '[T]here could, as a matter of logic, be causes within the subtraction sense of "at the expense of" in which the plaintiff would still have to base himself on a wrong in order to establish that the enrichment was "unjust" ie reversible. But as a matter of actual observation there are no such cases.' Cf Edelman, *Gain-Based Damages* (2002), pp 93–99.

for a wrong does not sit well with the range of factors and range of measures that courts seem to apply. Gain-based measures awarded have ranged from stripping away all profits to stripping away some profits through to thinking in terms of 'expense saved' rather than 'profit'.[4] Similarly, allowances for skill and labour have sometimes been granted. The state of mind of the wrongdoer appears sometimes to be a relevant factor as, perhaps, is how far the gain exceeds the claimant's loss. It is not obvious that this diversity is satisfactorily explained by Edelman's sharp distinction. A final problem is that, even after *A-G v Blake*,[5] Edelman's thesis is particularly hard to reconcile with the law on restitution for breach of contract. No distinction was drawn by the House of Lords between 'disgorgement damages' and 'restitutionary damages' and, contrary to Edelman's thesis, there was no indication that different less restrictive criteria should apply in determining the availability of the latter than the former. On the contrary, restitution for breach of contract, whatever the measure, is treated as highly exceptional and available only where compensatory damages, and other remedies, are inadequate.

2. RESTITUTION FOR TORTS

(1) Meaning of 'waiver of tort'

The first difficulty we encounter is the phrase 'waiver of tort'. This is usually taken to refer to where a claimant claims restitution for a tort rather than, for example, usual compensatory damages and this was certainly how the phrase was interpreted in *United Australia Ltd v Barclays Bank Ltd*.[6] There a claim was initially brought for money had and received by conversion of a cheque. The actual decision of the House of Lords was that, when that initial claim was abandoned before judgment, there was nothing to stop the claimant bringing an action to recover compensatory damages for conversion of the cheque by another party. The tort had not been extinguished and the claimant's election between different remedies for the tort was open until judgment or, possibly, satisfaction of judgment. Viscount Simon LC said:

> 'When the plaintiff "waived the tort" and brought assumpsit he did not thereby elect to be treated from that time forward on the basis that no tort had been committed; indeed, if it were to be understood that no tort had been committed, how could an action in assumpsit lie? It lies only because the acquisition of the defendant is wrongful and there is thus an obligation to make restitution... The

4   Cf Edelman, *Gain-Based Damages* (2002), pp 73–76.
5   [2001] 1 AC 268. See below, pp 486–491. Cf Edelman, *Gain-Based Damages* (2002), pp 186–187.
6   [1941] AC 1.

substance of the matter is that on certain facts he is claiming redress either in the form of compensation, ie damages as for a tort, or in the form of restitution of money to which he is entitled, but which the defendant has wrongfully received. The same set of facts entitles the plaintiff to claim either form of redress. At some stage of the proceedings the plaintiff must elect which remedy he will have.'[7]

If 'waiver of tort' were always used in this way, to mean claiming restitution for a tort, it would be a perfectly usable shorthand phrase albeit not very apt given that waiver implies that the claimant is forgoing its right to sue on the tort whereas in reality one would be describing a claim based on the tort.

Unfortunately there are two other meanings that can be and have been given to the phrase. The first is what Birks calls 'extinctive ratification'.[8] This refers to a principle of agency law whereby the victim of a tort may choose to forgo its right to sue for the tort by *ex post facto* treating the tortfeasor – provided it committed the tort purporting to act as the claimant's agent – as indeed authorised to act as its agent and then relying on the standard remedies against an agent to recover the profits made. A rare example of this is provided by *Verschures Creameries Ltd v Hull and Netherlands Steamship Co Ltd*[9] which was approved in the *United Australia* case. In this situation the tort is truly extinguished. What was wrongful becomes non-wrongful.

The second meaning recognises the phenomenon of alternative analysis and refers to where the claimant ignores the tort and brings its restitutionary claim in unjust enrichment by subtraction. This appears to have been the meaning in Lord Diplock's mind in *The Universe Sentinel*[10] when he said that it would be inappropriate, by the simple expedient of waiving the tort and claiming restitution for economic duress, that the statutory trade dispute defence applicable to torts would be ignored.

Given its three possible meanings, it seems preferable to avoid confusion by managing, wherever possible, without the phrase 'waiver of tort'. If one does use the phrase it should be confined, unless one explains otherwise, to its standard, albeit inapt, first meaning.

---

7 Ibid, at pp 18–19. The need for the claimant to elect between restitution and compensation for a wrong is shown in a number of other cases. See, eg, on the need to elect between an account of profits and compensatory damages, *Neilson v Betts* (1871) LR 5 HL 1, HL; *De Vitre v Betts* (1873) LR 6 HL 319, HL; *Island Records Ltd v Tring International plc* [1996] 1 WLR 1256; *Tang Min Sit v Capacious Investments Ltd* [1996] AC 514, PC. See also *Mahesan S/O Thambiah v Malaysian Government Officers Co-operative Housing Society* [1979] AC 374 (a claimant cannot recover both a bribe and compensation for loss caused by the bribed party's deceit or breach of fiduciary duty). For criticism of the 'election' requirement, see Burrows, *Understanding the Law of Obligations* (1998), pp 40–44.

8 Birks at pp 315–316.

9 [1921] 2 KB 608.

10 [1983] 1 AC 366, 385: see above, p 236.

(2) Case law supporting restitution for torts

There are a number of cases which are most naturally analysed as awarding restitution *for* a tort rather than the more usual compensatory measure. These cases can be classified in several different ways. The one chosen here is to divide the cases according to whether the remedy given for the tort was money had and received, an account of profits, or damages.

(a) Money had and received

An award of money had and received is automatically restitutionary: ie by its very nature it is looking at the defendant's receipt and not just the claimant's loss (if any). It is submitted, therefore, that it would be sufficient in proving that restitution may be awarded for a tort to point to cases in which this remedy has been awarded (or, as in *United Australia*, recognised as being available) *for* a tort. But if the defendant's gain correlates to the claimant's loss, as is usually the case with this remedy in unjust enrichment by subtraction, there is the conceivable re-interpretation that one is concerned with the well-established principle of compensating for wrongful loss. It follows that the best proof lies in the fact that in several cases awarding money had and received it is at least strained to regard the measure of recovery as corresponding to the claimant's loss and it is more natural, either in the light of the amount awarded or the court's reasoning or both, to regard the measure as solely concerned to strip the tortfeasor of some or all of the gains made by the tort.

First, there are the cases of *Lamine v Dorrell*[11] and *Chesworth v Farrar*[12] on the tort of conversion. In the former, the defendant had wrongfully converted the claimant's Irish debentures by selling them off. It was held that the claimant could recover the actual sale price of the debentures. No investigation was made as to whether that sale had been at the market price. Had the claim been for compensatory damages the normal measure would have been the value of the goods assessed according to the market price at the date of the tort. It must be admitted, however, that the actual reasoning in the case weakens its authority as an example of restitution for the tort because Holt CJ relied on extending the 'extinctive ratification' agency reasoning in a way which was later disapproved by the House of Lords in *United Australia*.

In *Chesworth v Farrar* the deceased landlord had wrongfully converted, by selling off, property belonging to his tenant. The tenant successfully recovered the sale price of the goods from the deceased's

11 (1701) 2 Ld Raym 1216.
12 [1967] 1 QB 407.

administrators again without any investigation of their value at the date of conversion. The central issue in the case concerned whether the claim was time barred by the statutory remnant of the *actio personalis* rule laying down a six month limitation period for an action in tort where the tortfeasor had died. In holding that it was not so time barred Edmund Davies J reasoned that that limitation period only applied to an action for damages for the tort and not to a quasi-contractual or, as we would now say, restitutionary remedy. In an important passage he said, 'A person upon whom a tort has been committed has at times a choice of alternative remedies, even though it is a *sine qua non* regarding each that he must establish that a tort has been committed. He may sue to recover damages for the tort, or he may waive the tort and sue in quasi-contract to recover the benefit received by the wrongdoer.'[13]

Turning to the tort of trespass to goods, in *Oughton v Seppings*[14] a sheriff's officer in executing a writ of *fieri facias* against a Mr Winslove had seized a horse belonging to the claimant. That horse had subsequently been sold by the sheriff and the proceeds of sale paid to the officer. Again, without any investigation of the loss to the claimant, it was held that he could recover the sale proceeds from the officer in an action for money had and received.

Finally, there is *Powell v Rees*[15] which concerned the tort of trespass to land by the extraction of coal from the claimant's land. The claimant was held able to evade the *actio personalis* bar by suing the deceased tortfeasor's estate in an action for money had and received to recover the sale proceeds of the coal. But this case is somewhat weaker than the above three in that Lord Denman CJ did not seem concerned by the lack of direct evidence of the sale price and also indicated that a compensatory award would have yielded the same sum.

One complication in interpreting *Lamine v Dorrell, Chesworth v Farrar,* and *Oughton v Seppings* as unequivocally accepting restitution for the torts of conversion and trespass to goods is the possibility, in principle, that the claimants were tracing their goods into the sale proceeds as substitute products. It was explained in chapter 2 that, through tracing, the claimant may be able to recover (by an action for money had and received) more than its *initial* loss even within unjust enrichment by subtraction.[16] On that analysis the autonomous unjust factors in play would be, for example, ignorance or powerlessness. But while a complication in theory the judgments do not mention tracing. The interpretation in terms of restitution for wrongdoing is undoubtedly the more obvious.

---

13   Ibid, at p 417.
14   (1830) 1 B & Ad 241.
15   (1837) 7 Ad & El 426.
16   Above, pp 28, 80.

(b) Account of profits

An account of profits is necessarily a restitutionary remedy. It is a remedy by which the defendant is required to draw up an account of, and then to pay over, the net profits it has acquired by a wrong.[17] There has never been any question of an account of profits being limited to the claimant's loss. That an account of profits is restitutionary and not compensatory was most clearly stressed by Windeyer J in the Australian infringement of trademark case of *Colbeam Palmer Ltd v Stock Affiliates Property Ltd.*[18] He said:

> 'The distinction between an account of profits and damages is that by the former the infringer is required to give up his ill-gotten gains to the party whose rights he has infringed: by the latter he is required to compensate the party wronged for the loss he has suffered. The two computations can obviously yield different results, for a plaintiff's loss is not to be measured by the defendant's gain, nor a defendant's gain by the plaintiff's loss. Either may be greater, or less, than the other. If a plaintiff elects to take an inquiry as to damages the loss to him of profits that he might have made may be a substantial element of his claim... But what a plaintiff might have made had the defendant not invaded his rights is by no means the same thing as what the defendant did make by doing so.'

The restitutionary nature of an account of profits was also made clear at first instance (the decision on liability was reversed on appeal) in *My Kinda Town Ltd v Soll,*[19] in which the claim was that the defendants were passing off their chain of restaurants as the claimants'. Slade J said, 'The purpose of ordering an account of profits in favour of a successful plaintiff in a passing off case ... is to prevent an unjust enrichment of the defendant.'[20]

The profits to be awarded are those factually caused by the wrong applying the usual 'but for' test.[1] However, in *Celanese International Corpn v BP Chemicals Ltd*[2] Laddie J controversially held that, in assessing the sum to be awarded under an account of profits for patent

---

17 There appears to be no example of an account of profits having been measured by the 'expense saved' by the wrong. See below, n 2 and p 489, n 7.

18 (1968) 122 CLR 25, 32. See also *Dart Industries Inc v Decor Corp Pty Ltd* (1993) 179 CLR 101, 111, 123.

19 [1982] FSR 147; revsd [1983] RPC 407, CA.

20 [1982] FSR 147, 156. See also *Potton Ltd v Yorkclose Ltd* [1990] FSR 11.

1   Eg, *Siddell v Vickers* (1892) 9 RPC 152 (patent infringement); *Colbeam Palmer v Stock Affiliates Pty Ltd* (1968) 122 CLR 25, 37 (trade mark infringement); Burrows, *Remedies for Torts and Breach of Contract* (2nd edn, 1994), pp 302–303.

2   [1999] RPC 203. Edelman, *Gain-Based Damages* (2002), pp 75–76 interprets the case as favouring a measure which strips profits rather than reverses 'expense saved'. But, with respect, Laddie J did not appear to discuss 'expense saved'. Rather he rejected the method of assessing profits that compares the profits (or losses) that would have been made had there been no infringement with profits (or losses) that were actually made.

infringement, no sum could be awarded if no profits (but instead losses) were made (even though the losses would have been greater but for the infringement); and while causation was important, so that the profits must be ones made by the infringement, it was inappropriate to consider what profits the defendant would have made had it adopted the most likely non-infringing method of production.

In *Redwood Music Ltd v Chappell & Co Ltd*,[3] a case of innocent copyright infringement, Robert Goff J thought that, by analogy to the allowance afforded to a fiduciary in *Boardman v Phipps*,[4] the courts could make an allowance for the defendant's skill and effort in making the profits. Such an allowance has the effect of cutting back the amount of recoverable profit.

Given that an account of profits is restitutionary, the question becomes, for what torts can it be awarded?

As yet the remedy is only available for torts protecting intellectual property rights. Historically the reason for this is that these are the torts that started life as equitable wrongs and an account of profits is an equitable remedy. So at common law an account of profits may be ordered for the torts of passing off[5] or infringement of trademark[6] although it appears that dishonesty is here a pre-condition of the restitutionary remedy[7] (albeit not of a claim for damages).[8] By s 61(1)(d) of the Patents Act 1977 an account of profits may be ordered for infringement of a patent,[9] although by s 62(1) it is a defence to both damages and an account of profits that the defendant 'was not aware, and had no reasonable grounds for supposing, that the patent existed'. Section 96(2) of the Copyright, Designs and Patents Act 1988 lays down that an account of profits may be ordered for infringement of copyright.[10] By s 97(1) it is a defence to damages but not to any other remedy that the defendant 'did not know, and had no reason to believe, that copyright existed in the work to which the action relates'. That an account of profits may be ordered for infringement of a design right and infringement of performer's property right is

---

3   [1982] RPC 109, 132.

4   [1967] 2 AC 46. Below, pp 495–496.

5   *Lever v Goodwin* (1887) 36 Ch D 1; *My Kinda Town Ltd v Soll* [1982] FSR 147, reversed on liablity [1983] RPC 407.

6   *Edelsten v Edelsten* (1863) 1 De G J & Sm 185; *Slazenger & Sons v Spalding & Bros* [1910] 1 Ch 257; *Colbeam Palmer Ltd v Stock Affiliates Pty Ltd* (1968) 122 CLR 25. Cf Trade Marks Act 1994, s 14(2): 'In an action for infringement [of a registered trade mark] all such relief by way of damages, injunctions, accounts or otherwise is available to him as is available in respect of the infringement of any other property right.'

7   *Colbeam Palmer Ltd v Stock Affiliates Pty Ltd* (1968) 122 CLR 25.

8   *Gillette UK Ltd v Edenwest Ltd* [1994] RPC 279.

9   See also *Siddell v Vickers* (1892) 9 RPC 152.

10 See also *Delfe v Delamotte* (1857) 3 K & J 581; *Potton v Yorkclose Ltd* [1990] FSR 11.

embodied respectively in s 229(2) and s 191I(2) of the Copyright, Designs and Patents Act 1988. By s 233(1) and s 191J(1) it is a defence to damages for a primary infringement of a design right[11] and infringement of performer's property right, but not to any other remedy, that the defendant did not know, and had no reason to believe, that the design right or performer's right subsisted in the work to which the action relates.

It is therefore indisputable that for the intellectual property torts restitution, through an account of profits, can be and will be awarded. However, there is inconsistency as to the effect of the wrongdoing being innocent. For infringement of copyright, primary design infringement and infringement of performer's property right, an account of profits but not damages can be ordered on a strict liability basis, whereas for patent infringement one needs at least negligence for both damages and an account of profits: and in the purely common law areas of passing off and infringement of trademark the indications are that, while strict liability applies to damages, a defendant is only liable for an account of profits if the wrong was dishonestly committed. There seems no good reason for this inconsistency.

(c) Damages

As damages are indisputably normally compensatory, it might be thought especially controversial to argue that they are sometimes restitutionary. But just as the law accepts nominal or exemplary damages, which are not concerned to compensate the claimant's loss, it also recognises restitutionary damages. As with the action for money had and received, the approach adopted here is to isolate cases where it is more natural, either in the light of the amount awarded or the courts' reasoning or both, to regard the measure as restitutionary stripping the tortfeasor of some or all of the gains made by the tort.

There are seven main cases to consider.[12] They cover the torts of trespass to land,[13] wrongful interference with goods, and nuisance.

Taking them chronologically, the first case was *Whitwham v Westminster Brymbo Coal & Coke Co.*[14] The defendants had trespassed

---

11 For secondary infringement of a design right where the defendant did not know, and had no reason to believe, that the article was an infringing one the only remedy is damages not exceeding a reasonable royalty: s 233(2) of the 1988 Act.

12 See also the dicta of Lord Shaw in *Watson, Laidlaw & Co Ltd v Pott, Cassels & Williamson* (1914) 31 RPC 104, 120 (patent infringement).

13 Damages for the use and occupation of land are sometimes referred to as 'mesne profits'. That historical label appears to have no significance for the question of whether such damages are ever restitutionary. Note that by adding them to an action for the recovery of land it seems that mesne profits can be recovered without establishing the tort of trespass. See *Clerk and Lindsell on Torts* (18th edn, 2000), paras 18-78 to 18-79.

14 [1896] 2 Ch 538.

on the claimants' land by tipping spoil from their colliery onto a part of it. In awarding damages the judgments, by and large, adopted normal compensatory reasoning, although it is not at all clear what the claimants' loss was. It is, however, just about realistic to think that, had they been approached, the claimants would have granted the defendants the right to tip the spoil for a fee and that the damages therefore compensated for loss of that fee: ie the damages compensated for loss of the opportunity to bargain with the defendants. However there are passages in the judgments supporting a restitutionary interpretation by which the damages awarded stripped the defendants of the expense saved by not having to dispose of the spoil elsewhere. For example Lindley LJ said, 'If one person has without leave of another been using that other's land for his own purposes, he ought to pay for such user.'[15]

In *Strand Electric and Engineering Co Ltd v Brisford Entertainments Ltd*[16] the defendant had wrongly kept and used the claimant's theatre equipment after the conclusion of a period of hire. In an action for detinue, which would now be an action for conversion under the Torts (Interference with Goods) Act 1977, the claimant was awarded damages which the majority of the Court of Appeal clearly regarded as compensatory. The loss being compensated was presumably the loss of the fee that the claimant would have charged either a third party or the defendant itself for the hire of the equipment during the extended time that it was kept. However the case is particularly interesting because of Denning LJ's judgment. He clearly took a restitutionary approach:

> 'If a wrongdoer has made use of goods for his own purposes, then he must pay a reasonable hire for them, even though the owner has in fact suffered no loss. It may be that the owner would not have used the goods himself or that he had a substitute readily available which he used without extra cost to himself. Nevertheless the owner is entitled to a reasonable hire ... The claim for a hiring charge is therefore not based on loss to the plaintiff but on the fact that the defendant has used the goods for his own purposes. It is an action against him because he has had the benefit of the goods. It resembles therefore an action for restitution, rather than an action for tort.'[17]

On a restitutionary analysis the most obvious benefit to the tortfeasor was the saving of expense of hiring the equipment from someone else.

Neither of the above two cases could be regarded as, in themselves, establishing the notion of restitutionary damages but the third case

15 Ibid, at pp 541–542.
16 [1952] 2 QB 246.
17 Ibid, at pp 254–255.

cannot be so marginalised. In *Penarth Dock Engineering Co Ltd v Pounds*[18] Lord Denning, sitting as a first instance judge, awarded restitutionary damages where the defendants were trespassers in the claimants' dock in failing to remove their pontoon. The important point is that there is no question of realistically analysing the damages awarded as compensatory because the claimants were trying to empty their dock and would not have let it out to the defendants or any other party (subject presumably to being paid a huge price). Lord Denning relied on the *Whitwham* case and on his own judgment in *Strand Electric* and awarded damages to reverse the defendant's benefit. He said:

> 'The Penarth company would not seem to have suffered any damage to speak of. They have not had to pay any extra rent to the British Transport Commission. The dock is no use to them: they would not have made any money out of it. But ... in a case of this kind ... the test of the measure of damages is not what the plaintiffs have lost, but what benefit the defendant has obtained by having the use of the berth.'[19]

The damages were assessed at £32 5s a week. This was apparently based on the evidence that £37 10s a week was what the defendants would have had to pay for an alternative dock of that kind. There is no indication of why some reduction was made but perhaps, for example, the claimants' berth was inferior to the alternative. *Penarth Dock* therefore stands as a decision where the sole judicial reasoning is restitutionary and, on the facts, the damages could not be realistically re-analysed as compensatory.

In *Bracewell v Appleby*[20] the claimant sought an injunction to prevent the defendant continuing to trespass over his road to reach his (the defendant's) newly built house. Although the injunction was refused, damages in lieu were awarded. These were assessed on a 'hypothetical bargain' basis: on what would have been a fair sum for the claimant to have accepted for granting the defendant a right of way over the road. On the facts it is clear that, subject presumably to being paid a huge fee, the claimant would not have been willing to grant the defendant such a right of way and it is therefore fictional to regard the hypothetical bargain as corresponding to a real loss of fee for the claimant. On the other hand, one could regard the award as compensating the claimant for the loss of the value of his property or even as compensating for the mental distress consequent on the

---

18 [1963] 1 Lloyd's Rep 359.
19 Ibid, at pp 361–362.
20 [1975] Ch 408. See also the somewhat similar case of *Jaggard v Sawyer* [1995] 1 WLR 269. The claim there was for damages for breach of covenant and trespass to land. The Court of Appeal rejected a restitutionary analysis.

increased user of the road. It is significant, however, that Graham J thought it crucial to look at what profit the defendant had made from building the house, which would be irrelevant on a compensatory approach. Ultimately he awarded £2,000 damages from a notional profit estimated at £5,000. It may therefore be that a restitutionary analysis is the best interpretation. This is supported by the judge's reliance on the contract case of *Wrotham Park Estates Co v Parkside Homes Ltd*[1] which, as we shall see shortly, is best viewed as awarding restitutionary damages.

Swordheath Properties Ltd v Tabet[2] is a further case of trespass to land. Tenants remained in the claimant's property after the expiration of their lease. The Court of Appeal held that they were liable to pay the ordinary letting value of the property, irrespective of whether the claimant would have let the property to someone else. Although one could analyse those damages as compensatory, on the ground that the claimant would have allowed the tenants to stay on by paying the rent, it is significant that the Court of Appeal cited with approval *Penarth Dock v Pounds* and also relied on the *Whitwham* case.

The hypothetical bargain approach of *Bracewell v Appleby* was applied in assessing damages in lieu of a mandatory injunction in *Carr-Saunders v Dick McNeil Associates Ltd*,[3] where the defendants were liable in the tort of nuisance for having erected extra storeys to their buildings which interfered with the claimant's light. The importance of the case for present purposes was Millett J's dicta that he was 'entitled to take account of ... the amount of profit which the defendants would look to in the development of their site'.[4] This indicated his willingness to adopt a restitutionary approach. However, since no evidence of profit was available, the damages awarded are most naturally viewed as compensating for the claimant's loss of use and amenity.

Finally, and perhaps most importantly, in *Ministry of Defence v Ashman*,[5] a tenant had wrongfully ignored a notice to quit RAF accommodation because she and her children had nowhere else to go. A majority of the Court of Appeal (Kennedy and Hoffmann LJJ) accepted that the claimant landlord was entitled to restitutionary damages for the trespass. The *Swordheath* and *Penarth Dock* cases were relied on: and it was held that the damages should be assessed

---

1   [1974] 1 WLR 798.
2   [1979] 1 WLR 285.
3   [1986] 1 WLR 922.
4   Ibid, at 931.
5   (1993) 66 P & CR 195. See also *Ministry of Defence v Thompson* [1993] 40 EG 148, CA; *Gondall v Dillon Newsagents Ltd* [2001] RLR 221, CA. See generally Cooke, 'Trespass, Mesne Profits and Restitution' [1994] 110 LQR 420. Cf *Inverugie Investments v Hackett* [1995] 1 WLR 713, PC.

according to what it would have cost the tenant to rent alternative local authority accommodation had any been available.[6] Hoffmann LJ said:

> 'A person entitled to possession of land can make a claim against a person who has been in occupation without his consent on two alternative bases. The first is for the loss which he has suffered in consequence of the defendant's trespass. This is the normal measure of damages in the law of tort. The second is the value of the benefit which the occupier has received. This is a claim for restitution. The two bases of claim are mutually exclusive and the plaintiff must elect before judgment which of them he wishes to pursue. These principles are not only fair but, as Kennedy LJ demonstrated, also well established by authority. It is true that in earlier cases it has not been expressly stated that a claim for mesne profit for trespass can be a claim for restitution. Nowadays I do not see why we should not call a spade a spade. In this case the Ministry of Defence elected for the restitutionary remedy.'[7]

It is submitted, therefore, that in the above seven cases there are indications of an acceptance of restitutionary damages and that *Penarth Dock, Ministry of Defence v Ashman* and probably *Bracewell v Appleby* are decisions actually awarding restitutionary damages.

This restitutionary interpretation now also derives some support from *A-G v Blake*[8] in which, as we shall see below, the House of Lords for the first time awarded an account of profits for breach of contract. Lord Nicholls drew on cases such as *Whitwham, Penarth Dock, Strand Electric* and *Bracewell v Appleby* to show that, for tortious interference with property, the normal compensatory measure of damages is not always applied and that damages may be measured by reference to the benefits obtained (or to be obtained) by the defendant.

It is also important to bear in mind the second of the three categories of exemplary damages recognised in *Rookes v Barnard*.[9] This category is where 'the defendant's conduct has been calculated to make a profit for himself which may well exceed the compensation payable to the plaintiff'. Exemplary damages go beyond restitution. But if the courts are willing to go to the lengths of punishing the profit- seeking deliberate tortfeasor, it arguably follows that they ought to be prepared to go to the lesser length of awarding a restitutionary remedy stripping the deliberate tortfeasor of some or all of his ill-gotten gains.

---

6   This can be interpreted as an acceptance that an incontrovertible benefit (the market value of the property) can be subjectively devalued: see above, p 20.
7   (1993) 66 P & CR 195, 200–201.
8   [2001] 1 AC 268.
9   [1964] AC 1129, 1226.

(3) Three significant anti-restitution cases?

Three Court of Appeal decisions stand as possible obstacles to the full or wide acceptance of restitution as a remedial measure for a tort.[10] In *Phillips v Homfray*[11] the deceased had trespassed by using roads and passages under the claimants' land to transport coal. In an earlier action the claimants had won a judgment for 'damages' to be assessed against the then living tortfeasor.[12] After his death, the question at issue was whether the claimants could treat the judgment for damages for use of their land as one for a restitutionary remedy which would survive against the deceased's executors despite the *actio personalis* rule. The majority held not on the ground that for a restitutionary remedy, at least one that is to survive against the deceased's executors, it is necessary for the gain made by the tortfeasor to comprise the claimant's property or the proceeds of that property. On the facts that was not so: the deceased had gained by saving himself the expense of not paying the claimant for using the underground roads or alternatively by not paying for other methods of transporting the coal. Baggallay LJ, in a powerful dissenting judgment, could not see why the type of benefit should matter. He said, 'I feel bound to say that I cannot appreciate the reasons upon which it is insisted that although executors are bound to account for any accretions to the property of their testator derived directly from his wrongful act, they are not liable for the amount or value of any other benefit which may be derived by his estate from or by reason of such wrongful act.'[13]

This case can be, and has been, analysed in many different ways. Goff and Jones in their first three editions regarded it as an unfortunate decision on restitution for the tort of trespass to land which should be overruled. They wrote, 'In our view the principle of Baggallay LJ's dissent should be adopted and *Phillips v Homfray* overruled.'[14] Similarly in the first edition of this book, I wrote, 'It is probably preferable ... to go along with Goff and Jones' approach and to fight *Phillips v Homfray* head on as a problem case for tortious restitution. As its restrictive approach to the type of relevant benefit has no validity in principle and may confuse personal and proprietary remedies the decision

10 One could add *Re Simms, ex p Trustee* [1934] Ch 1 (receiver who had converted bankrupt's goods held not liable, in damages or in an action for money had and received, to disgorge profits made by using those goods). But the reasoning is plainly unsound resting on the implied contract fallacy and the pre-*United Australia* analysis of waiver of tort. Moreover the decision can perhaps be justified on the ground that the net profit from using the goods was matched by the value of the receiver's own skill.
11 (1883) 24 Ch D 439.
12 (1871) 6 Ch App 770.
13 (1883) 24 Ch D 439, 471–472.
14 Goff and Jones (3rd edn, 1986) at p 611.

should be overruled.'[15] Underpinning this view was that, while the issue in point was whether an action could be brought against the deceased's executors and was therefore bound up with the *actio personalis* rule which no longer applies, the reasoning appeared to be also directed to claims against the wrongdoer himself. For example, Bowen LJ said, 'The true test to be applied in the present case is whether the plaintiffs' claim against the deceased... belongs to the category of actions *ex delicto* or whether any form of action against the executors of the deceased, *or the deceased man in his lifetime,* can be based upon any implied contract or duty.'[16]

Birks has argued that the case presents no obstacle to restitution for wrongdoing because, given the *actio personalis* bar to tort actions then existing, the case could only be concerned with 'waiver of tort' in its third sense of 'alternative analysis'.[17] But while it would be *possible* to analyse the decision as concerned purely with unjust enrichment by subtraction – the unjust factor being ignorance – the judgments seemed principally geared towards enrichment by wrongdoing.

On another view, favoured more recently by Goff and Jones[18] and in a forceful article by Swadling, while the decision does deal with restitution for wrongs, it should be regarded as posing no difficulty for the modern law because of the abolition of the *actio personalis* rule. Swadling persuasively contends that, taking into account the earlier 1871 decision (which he calls *Phillips v Homfray (No 1)*), the 1883 decision (which he calls *Phillips v Homfray (No 2)*) was not denying that a court can award restitution for negative benefits against a living trespasser.[19] He writes:

> '*Phillips & Homfray (No 2)* is not the anti-restitutionary case it is painted to be. It should not be overruled, or banished to a dark corner of our law, but instead set out in lights. It is a decision concerned only with the operation of the maxim *actio personalis moritur cum persona*, and therefore tells us nothing of the restitutionary liability of living wrongdoers. And when read in conjunction with *Phillips v Homfray (No 1)*, it is in fact authority *against* the very proposition for which it is said to stand, namely, that a restitutionary claim in respect of the wrong of trespass to land yields only positive benefits, for in the first stage of the litigation Stuart V-C

---

15   *The Law of Restitution* (1st edn, 1993), p 391.
16   (1883) 24 Ch D 439, 460–461 (author's italics).
17   Birks at p 323. See similarly Virgo, *The Principles of the Law of Restitution* (1999), pp 481–484.
18   Goff and Jones, para 36-003: the reasoning 'may have been then valid but ... can no longer be supported'. See also Hedley, 'Unjust enrichment as the basis of Restitution – an overworked concept' (1985) 5 LS 56, 64; Gummow, 'Unjust Enrichment, Restitution and Proprietary Remedies' in *Essays on Restitution* (ed Finn, 1990), pp 60–67.
19   'The Myth of *Phillips v Homfray*' in *The Search for Principle* (eds Swadling and Jones, 1999), pp 277–294.

at first instance, and Lord Hatherley LC on appeal, allowed a restitutionary claim for expense saved by the then living defendants ... The only thing which needs to be buried is the myth in *Phillips v Homfray*, not the decision itself.'[20]

Even if one treats *Phillips v Homfray* as a problem case it must not be forgotten that it was not totally anti-restitution in that it indisputably did recognise that restitution could be given for a tort where the gain comprised the claimant's property or its proceeds.[1] It was therefore implicit in the majority's reasoning that the first part of the 'damages' to be assessed for the value of the coal taken (which the Court of Appeal in the later *Phillips v Homfray* appeal[2] construed as being for an equitable account of profits so that no interest could be added) was maintainable against the deceased's executors despite the *actio personalis* rule.

Moreover, it is noteworthy that the decision has had no impact outside actions for money had and received: the granting of an account of profits for intellectual property torts accepted at common law and in statutes and, most directly, the restitutionary damages cases, such as *Penarth Dock v Pounds* and *Bracewell v Appleby*, conflict with, while ignoring, the *Phillips v Homfray* restriction.

A second problematic Court of Appeal case is *Stoke-on-Trent City Council v W & J Wass Ltd*.[3] The defendants had deliberately committed the tort of nuisance by operating a market within a distance infringing the claimant's proprietary market right. The claimant was granted an injunction to restrain further infringement of its right. On the question of damages it was accepted by the claimant that it had not suffered any loss, in the sense of loss of custom. But at first instance Peter Gibson J awarded damages on the basis of an appropriate licence fee that the claimant could have charged the defendant for lawful operation of its market: that is, he awarded damages applying the 'hypothetical bargain' approach of *Bracewell v Appleby*. On the facts this could have constituted a compensatory measure because the claimant might well have granted such a licence. Alternatively those damages could have been restitutionary stripping the defendant of some of the profits made.

In contrast the Court of Appeal restricted the claimant to nominal damages. The damages cases considered above were distinguished on, with respect, unconvincing grounds. Most alarming was that the

---

20 Ibid, at p 294.
1   Taking account of all the stages of the litigation, Birks regards the case as 'indisputably authority in favour of the proposition that an account does lie for the profits of a trespass': 'Civil Wrongs: A New World' (*Butterworths Lectures 1990–91*), pp 64–67.
2   [1892] 1 Ch 465.
3   [1988] 1 WLR 1406.

whole question was approached as if only compensatory damages could be awarded. It was only at the very end of Nourse LJ's judgment that there was any reference to restitution. He said, 'It is possible that the English law of tort, more especially of the so-called "proprietary torts" will in due course make a more deliberate move towards recovery based not on loss suffered by the plaintiff but on the unjust enrichment of the defendant – see Goff and Jones *The Law of Restitution* (3rd edn), pp 612–614. But I do not think that that process can begin in this case and I doubt whether it can begin at all at this level of decision.'[4] The contrast to Lord Denning's judgment in *Penarth Dock*, at first instance, could not be more clear. It should have been plain that restitution for a tort is not a novel concept beyond the reach of the Court of Appeal.

In the final case of the problematic trio, *Halifax Building Society v Thomas*,[5] the defendant fraudulently misrepresented his identity and creditworthiness to obtain a loan from the claimant to finance the purchase of a flat. The loan was secured by a mortgage over the flat. When the defendant defaulted on the repayments, the claimant exercised its right to sell off the flat. The proceeds of sale exceeded the loan. The claimant sought a declaration that it was entitled to keep all the proceeds of sale (ie including the surplus of £10,504.90 plus interest) as restitution for the tort of deceit. If made out, such a restitutionary claim would have defeated the Crown's competing claim to confiscate the surplus in execution of a criminal confiscation order made when the defendant was found guilty of conspiring to obtain mortgage advances by deception.

The Court of Appeal held that the claimant was not entitled to restitution (whether personal or proprietary) for the tort of deceit. The primary reasoning was that this was not a proprietary tort case. Nor did it involve a breach of fiduciary duty. Moreover, the claimant had affirmed the mortgage and had recovered all that, as a secured creditor, it was contractually entitled to under the loan agreement.

One may interpret this case as a significant block on restitution for a personal, non-proprietary tort. But especially in the light of *A-G v Blake*,[6] which awarded an account of profits for a 'non-proprietary' breach of contract, the case is best interpreted narrowly as being dependent on the criminal convictions and confiscation order. They ensured that the defendant would not profit from his wrong and there was therefore no work needing to be done by the civil law of restitution.

---

4   Ibid, at p 1415.
5   [1996] Ch 217.
6   [2001] 1 AC 268.

(4) The anti-restitution analysis of Sharpe and Waddams

In 'Damages for Lost Opportunity to Bargain'[7] Sharpe and Waddams argue that the damages cases examined above can be justified on compensatory rather than restitutionary grounds. Their theory is that what a claimant loses in such cases is the opportunity to bargain with the defendant for the use of the claimant's property.

It can be conceded immediately that, to a large extent, Sharpe and Waddams' view is correct. Indeed it has been adopted above in the analysis of several of the cases. But in some cases, for example *Penarth Dock* and *Bracewell v Appleby*, it has been seen to be fictional to imagine that the claimant would have accepted a fee (or at least a fee equivalent to the amount of damages awarded) for the defendant's legitimate use of his property. Sharpe and Waddams' theory goes too far in requiring one to reanalyse all the above cases as awarding compensatory rather than restitutionary damages.

The fiction becomes even more obvious when Sharpe and Waddams go on to argue that even the account of profits granted in respect of intellectual property torts can be viewed as compensatory. It cannot be realistic to say that, in advance of the amount of profit being known, the claimant would have charged the defendant as a fee the precise amount of gain that the defendant is required to give up by the account of profits remedy.

Although they do not specifically deal with the conversion and trespass to goods cases awarding money had and received, like *Lamine v Dorrell*, *Chesworth v Farrar* and *Oughton v Seppings*, it is probable, in view of their discussion of 'waiver of tort', that Sharpe and Waddams would seek to reanalyse those cases as awarding compensation rather than restitution. This would again be to make a strained use of the notion of a loss of opportunity to bargain.

In short, the all-embracing use to which Sharpe and Waddams put the hypothetical bargain analysis means that it ends up as a fiction similar to the outdated implied contract theory of restitution.

(5) Are the pro-restitution cases justified?

A common feature of the cases that have awarded a restitutionary remedy is that the torts in question have been 'proprietary torts'

---

7   (1982) 2 OJLS 290. See also Stoljar 'Restitutionary Relief for Breach of Contract' (1989) 2 JCL 1, 4–5. For explicit judicial discussion of damages for loss of bargaining opportunity see, eg, *Surrey County Council v Bredero Homes Ltd* [1993] 1 WLR 1361 (*per* Steyn LJ); *Jaggard v Sawyer* [1995] 1 WLR 269, CA; *A-G v Blake* [2001] 1 AC 268 (*per* Lord Nicholls).

(conversion, trespass to goods, trespass to land, and the intellectual property torts) as opposed to 'personal torts' such as libel, slander, assault, malicious prosecution and most types of negligence.

An alternative characteristic of a few of the cases is that, in line with the second category of exemplary damages in *Rookes v Barnard*, restitution has been given where the tort has been committed cynically. So as regards the passing off and infringement of trademark cases (but not other intellectual property cases) the indications are that a defendant is only liable for an account of profits (or damages) if it is a conscious wrongdoer. It may also be significant that in the breach of contract case of *A-G v Blake*,[8] as we shall see, the House of Lords awarded an account of profits in respect of a cynically committed, but 'non-proprietary', breach of contract.

This description of the law leads conveniently to the main views put forward by commentators as to what the law on restitution for torts ought to be.

Jackman in his excellent article 'Restitution for Wrongs'[9] has argued that restitution is justified as a means of protecting 'facilitative institutions'. He defines these as 'power conferring facilities for the creation of private arrangements between individuals, such as contracts, trusts and private property'.[10] They presumably differ from, for example, bodily integrity or reputation because the latter are natural assets which exist irrespective of rights given by law and do not therefore require the same type of protection.[11] On his theory, to infringe proprietary rights is to harm the facilitative institution of private property and it is to instill proper respect for that institution, and to deter harm to it, that restitution is given. For Jackman the moral quality of the wrongdoing – whether deliberate or not – is merely a secondary factor that the courts may wish to take into account in deciding the quantum of restitution: '... once the infringement of a private legal facility is shown, there may be scope for applying different measures of relief according to different degrees of wrongfulness.'[12]

---

8   [2001] 1 AC 268. See below, pp 486–491. But Lord Nicholls did say, at p 286, that the fact that the breach of contract was cynical and deliberate was not, by itself, a good reason for ordering restitution.

9   [1989] CLJ 302.

10   Ibid, at p 304.

11   Jackman's discussion of 'economic torts' is brief: ibid, at pp 310–311. While he does not reach any firm conclusion his reasoning suggests that restitution for most economic torts could be justified on the need to protect the facilitative institution of contract from a third party's interference. Tentative support for restitution in this context is provided by cases on 'waiver' of the old tort of seduction: *Lightly v Clouston* (1808) 1 Taunt 112 and *Foster v Stewart* (1814) 3 M & S 191. Cf the position in the United States: *Federal Sugar Refining Co v United States Equalisation Bd* 286 F 575 (1920) (restitution for inducing breach of contract).

12   [1989] CLJ 302, 317.

In *An Introduction to the Law of Restitution* Birks expressed the view that restitution for wrongs is justified in three situations.[13] First, where there has been deliberate exploitation of wrongdoing. Secondly, where the wrong is an anti-enrichment, as opposed to an anti-harm, wrong. And thirdly, where deterrence of the mere possibility of harm being caused is sought ('prophylaxis').

Birks seems to regard the third of these as a rarity confined to the restitution of secret profits made in breach of fiduciary duty. And he has subsequently abandoned his second suggestion[14] which was flawed in assuming that a clear division can be made between anti-enrichment and anti-harm wrongs. On the contrary, it can be strongly argued that all common law and equitable civil wrongs are primarily concerned to avoid or compensate harm.

This leaves Birks' first test, focusing on the moral quality of the wrongdoing, as his most valuable contribution. Applying this approach to the tort area, it should be irrelevant whether the tort is proprietary or personal. Although this flies in the face of the main feature of the cases it does derive support from, what has been called above, their alternative characteristic and, not surprisingly, Birks relies heavily on the second category of exemplary damages. This is also now supported by the Law Commission. Irrespective of any other power to award restitution for torts (eg for proprietary torts) the Commission has recommended that a claimant may be awarded restitutionary damages for any tort if the defendant's conduct shows a deliberate and outrageous disregard of the claimant's rights.[15]

The widest approach of all is that taken by Goff and Jones.[16] For them the present picture of restitution sometimes being awarded for a tort, and sometimes not, cannot be rendered coherent short of saying that restitution should be granted whenever the defendant's gain would not have been made but for his commission of a tort. They are therefore adopting a causation test.

Which of these views is to be preferred? It is submitted that restitution for wrongs is more difficult to justify than compensation for wrongs (assuming that one is referring to restitution of gains irrespective of the claimant's loss). Compensation is readily explained by the basic utilitarian liberal philosophy that a person can do what he likes so long as he does not *harm* others. In contrast there are two

---

13   Birks, at pp 326–333.
14   Birks, 'Civil Wrongs: A New World', p 97. In cases not covered by the other two tests he uncharacteristically suggests that one can give no more guidance than that the courts should consider case by case whether there is a justification for giving the claimant a windfall profit and for suppressing the defendant's economic activity.
15   Law Commission Report No 247, para 3.51 and Draft Bill, clause 12.
16   Goff and Jones, para 36-006. This is also supported by Virgo, *The Principles of the Law of Restitution* (1999), pp 496–497.

conflicting relevant ideas where restitution for a wrong is in issue. One is that the defendant should not keep a gain that he has wrongfully acquired (no man shall profit from his wrong). Why should a wrongdoing defendant end up better off, for example, than a competitor who has taken care not to infringe another's legal rights? On the other hand it can be argued that there is no good reason why the wrongfully acquired gain should be transferred to the claimant because he will then end up better off than he otherwise would have done. The gain should instead be paid to the state.

Followed to their logical conclusions those two sides of the argument would lead to restitution either always being available for enrichment by wrongdoing (the Goff and Jones approach to torts) or never being available. The law takes neither extreme position. By accepting that restitution is sometimes available it is recognising that there is no mechanism within civil law by which gains can be made payable to the state rather than to the claimant and that overcompensating the claimant is a lesser evil than leaving the defendant with ill-gotten gains. On the other hand, its enthusiasm for this departure from the compensatory ideal is lukewarm so that *additional* reasons for restitution over and above simply profiting from wrongdoing are looked for.

Jackman's thesis and Birks' first test are important in providing additional reasons for restitution. Any development in the law is therefore likely to centre on the two ideas of, first, protecting facilitative institutions (hence the emphasis on proprietary torts) and, secondly, deterring cynical wrongdoing. On either view, the denial of restitution in, for example, *Stoke-on-Trent City Council v W & J Wass Ltd* was unwarranted for the tort in question was not only proprietary but was also committed cynically.

3. RESTITUTION FOR BREACH OF CONTRACT

(1) Restitution for a wrong and unjust enrichment by subtraction

It is important to distinguish restitution *for* breach of contract, where the claimant is basing its claim on the defendant's wrong, from restitution (through, eg, an action for money had and received or a *quantum meruit*) after a contract has been terminated for breach. The latter belongs within unjust enrichment by subtraction with the unjust factor being (total) failure of consideration. It has been fully examined in chapter 10.

This distinction is not just an academically convenient one. It helps to explain two features of the law. First, an innocent party may be able to escape from a bad bargain by claiming restitution on the basis of failure of consideration. If one was concerned with restitution for the wrong of breach of contract one would presumably allow the defendant to keep the gains that it would have made if the contract had been properly performed. Say, for example, the claimant contracts to buy a car from the defendant for £500 and pays £50 in advance; the defendant fails to deliver the car; the market price is £400. The claimant can recover £50 in an action for money had and received. This cannot be sensibly explained if restitution is regarded as a remedy for the breach since if there had been no breach the defendant would still have made that gain from the contract.[17]

Secondly, rooting the law on failure of consideration in unjust enrichment by subtraction explains why the pattern of restitution is very similar whether there has been a breach of contract or not. That is, the basic pattern is the same whether the contract has been discharged for breach or frustration or is void, unenforceable, or merely anticipated.

(2) The law prior to *Blake*: no restitution subject to a rare exception

The traditional view, prior to *A-G v Blake*,[18] was that there can be no restitution *for* breach of contract. One of the best known illustrations is the Scottish case of *Teacher v Calder*.[19] The defendant financier broke a contract to invest £15,000 in the claimant's timber business and instead invested the same sum in a distillery. In his claim for damages it was held that the claimant was entitled to compensation for the loss to his business (ie his expectation interest was protected) but he was not entitled to a disgorgement of the much higher profits that the defendant had made from the distillery investment. In other words, restitution was denied.

The same view applied in England, as is shown by *Tito v Waddell (No 2)*.[20] The case concerned mining operations on Ocean Island in the Pacific. The defendant English company had promised to replant the island after mining but in breach of covenant failed to do so. The claimant islanders sued, inter alia, for damages. Megarry V-C awarded merely nominal damages because the difference in value of the land with and without the replanting was trivial and, as the claimant islanders

---

17 For a contrary view, see Edelman, *Gain-Based Damages* (2002), pp 186–187.
18 [2001] 1 AC 268.
19 [1899] AC 451.
20 [1977] Ch 106. See also the much-discussed Louisiana case of *City of New Orleans v Fireman's Charitable Association* 9 So 486 (1891).

had now set up home elsewhere, there was no prospect of their using a higher 'cost of cure' measure of damages to replant the island. He expressly rejected an alternative restitutionary measure of damages saying, 'The question is not one of making the defendant disgorge what he has saved by committing the wrong, but one of compensating the plaintiff.'[1]

Similarly in *Surrey County Council v Bredero Homes Ltd*[2] the Court of Appeal refused to award restitutionary damages for a breach of contract, whether assessed according to the full profits made by the breach by the contract-breaker or according to the expense saved by the contract-breaker in not seeking a release from its contractual undertaking. The claimant councils had sold two adjoining parcels of land to the defendant for the development of a housing estate. The defendant covenanted to develop the land in accordance with the scheme approved by the claimants. In breach of that covenant it built more houses on the site than under the approved scheme thereby making extra profit. Although aware of the breach, the claimants did not seek an injunction or specific performance but waited until the defendant had sold all the houses on the estate and then sought damages. Nominal damages only were awarded on the ground that the claimants had suffered no loss and restitutionary damages were inappropriate because this was an action for ordinary common law damages for breach of contract: it did not involve either a tort or an invasion of proprietary rights or equitable damages.

The traditional position, therefore, was that, while the claimant could recover compensatory damages, whether measured on an expectation or reliance basis, it could not recover restitution for a breach of contract.

The one clear exception – 'a solitary beacon' as Lord Nicholls referred to it in *A-G v Blake*[3] – was the decision in *Wrotham Park Estate Co v Parkside Homes Ltd*.[4] The defendants had built a number of houses on land in breach of a restrictive covenant enforceable in equity by the claimant neighbouring landowner. Brightman J refused an injunction ordering the demolition of the houses but held that,

---

1   Ibid, at p 332.
2   [1993] 1 WLR 1361. See O'Dair, 'Remedies for Breach of Contract: A Wrong Turn' [1993] RLR 31; Birks, 'Profits of Breach of Contract' [1993] 109 LQR 518; Burrows, 'No Restitutionary Damages for Breach of Contract' [1993] LMCLQ 453; Stephen Smith, 'Of Remedies and Restrictive Covenants' [1994] JCL 164.
3   [2001] 1 AC 268, 283.
4   [1974] 1 WLR 798. See also, subsequent to *A-G v Blake* [2001] 1 AC 268, the award of restitutionary damages for breach of a restrictive covenant, assessed applying the 'hypothetical bargain' approach, in *AMEC Developments Ltd v Jury's Hotel Management (UK) Ltd* (2000) 82 P & CR 286.

although the claimant's land had not been diminished in value, the defendants were liable to pay substantial damages assessed using the 'hypothetical bargain' approach. That is, he asked what would have been a reasonable contract price for the claimant to have accepted for relaxation of the covenant. In working out the price, the major factor taken into account was the defendants' profits from the housing development. That emphasis on the defendants' profits, in addition to Brightman J's acceptance that it was artificial to pretend that the claimant would ever have relaxed the covenant, means that the damages are most naturally viewed as restitutionary, stripping the defendants of part (5%) of their profits, not compensatory. It is therefore not at all surprising that the authorities relied on by Brightman J were those examined above under restitution for a tort: *Whitwham v Westminster Brymbo Coal and Coke Co*, Denning LJ's judgment in *Strand Electric Engineering Co v Brisford Entertainments*, and *Penarth Dock Engineering Co Ltd v Pounds*.[5]

Looked at alongside the tort cases *Wrotham Park* can be easily justified. Not only was the breach apparently cynical but it also constituted a 'proprietary' wrong. Breach of a restrictive covenant, albeit an action for breach of contract, is enforceable by third parties, contrary to normal privity restrictions, and is closely akin to a 'proprietary tort'.

Not everyone agrees that the *Wrotham Park* decision was an example of restitution for breach of contract. Applying their 'loss of opportunity to bargain' approach, Sharpe and Waddams argue that the case was simply explicable as awarding compensation for loss.[6] This can again be criticised as fictional.[7] Brightman J accepted that the claimant would never have relaxed the covenant.

Were there any other exceptions? One could perhaps point to *Penarth Dock* where the claim was brought for both the tort of trespass to land and breach of contract but it is difficult to believe that without the trespass claim restitutionary damages would have been awarded. Similarly it requires the radical step of treating the label of 'fiduciary'

---

5   Brightman J also relied on Lord Shaw's dicta in the *Watson* case: above, p 468, n 12.
6   'Damages for Lost Opportunity to Bargain' (1982) 2 OJLS 290, 292. See also Stoljar, 'Restitutionary Relief for Breach of Contract' (1989) 2 JCL 1, 4–5.
7   In *Surrey County Council v Bredero Homes Ltd* [1993] 1 WLR 1361, 1369, Steyn LJ said, 'The plaintiff's argument that the *Wrotham Park* case can be justified on the basis of a loss of bargaining opportunity is a fiction. The object of the award in the *Wrotham Park* case was not to compensate the plaintiffs for financial injury, but to deprive the defendants of an unjustly acquired gain.' But these comments were expressly disagreed with by Millett LJ in *Jaggard v Sawyer* [1995] 1 WLR 269: in that case, which concerned damages for breach of covenant and trespass to land, the Court of Appeal applied compensatory 'hypothetical bargain' reasoning and rejected a restitutionary analysis.

as meaningless to argue that cases where restitution was given for breach of a fiduciary duty arising from a contractual relationship were in reality examples of restitution for breach of contract.[8]

(3) Was the traditional denial of restitution satisfactory?

Prior to *A-G v Blake*,[9] much academic ink had been spilt in debating whether the law should be more willing to award restitution for breach of contract, and, if so, when.[10] As Lord Nicholls said in the *Blake* case, 'This is a subject on which there is a surprising dearth of judicial decision. By way of contrast, over the last 20 years there has been no lack of academic writing.'[11]

Jackman suggested that there may be no need for restitution to protect the facilitative institution of contract because protection is sufficiently afforded by the standard award of expectation damages.[12] In other words, one of the justifications for awarding expectation, rather than reliance, damages is to protect the institution of contract. On his view, *Wrotham Park* was a rare and acceptable exception because it was not a pure contract case. Breach of a restrictive covenant constitutes the infringement of a proprietary right and falls to be treated like a 'proprietary tort'.

Support for the denial of restitution is also derived from the 'efficient breach' theory that it is more economically efficient to allow breach of contract than to deter it, as restitution would prima facie do.[13] The difficulty with presenting the idea of not deterring breach as an economic argument, rather than simply saying that it flows from the desire to leave parties free to pursue their own self-interest so far

---

8　See, eg, *Reid-Newfoundland Co v Anglo-American Telegraph Ltd* [1912] AC 555; *Lake v Bayliss* [1974] 1 WLR 1073. The High Court of Australia (Mason and Deane JJ dissenting) in *Hospital Products Ltd v United States Surgical Corpn* (1985) 156 CLR 41 denied restitution precisely because there was no fiduciary relationship only a contractual one.

9　[2001] 1 AC 268.

10　In addition to the articles cited elsewhere in this chapter, see, eg, Farnsworth, 'Your Loss or my Gain? The Dilemma of the Disgorgement Principle in Breach of Contract' (1985) 94 Yale LJ 1339; O'Dair, 'Restitutionary Damages for Breach of Contract and the Theory of Efficient Breach' (1993) 46(2) CLP 113; Lionel Smith, 'Disgorgement of the Profits of Breach of Contract: Property, Contract and Efficient Breach' (1994) 24 Can Bus LJ 121; Dagan, 'Restitutionary Damages for Breach of Contract: An Exercise in Private Law Theory' (2000) 1 Theoretical Inquiries in Law 115.

11　[2001] 1 AC 268 at 277.

12　'Restitution for Wrongs' [1989] CLJ 302, 318–321. However at the end of his analysis of breach of contract he very tentatively suggests that his secondary principle of the moral quality of the wrongdoing might justify restitution for cynical breach.

13　For this general theory, see Posner *Economic Analysis of Law* (5th edn, 1998), at pp 130–135. For criticism see, eg, Friedmann, 'The Efficient Breach Fallacy' (1989) 18 Jo of Legal Studies 1.

as possible without harming others, is that economic theory postulates that parties will bargain round the remedies provided by the courts. To establish that restitution is economically inefficient ultimately, therefore, requires proof, presumably by empirical data, that the transaction costs associated with bargaining round restitution outweigh, by more than a trivial amount, the costs associated with a normal award of expectation damages. Yet empirical data is not usually offered to support the 'efficient breach' theory.

In contrast Birks, applying his cynical wrongdoing test, argued that restitution should be more widely available as a remedy for breach of contract.[14] As an example of cynical wrongdoing he pointed to *Tito v Waddell (No 2)* as a case in which restitutionary damages, rather than nominal or a small sum of compensatory damages, should have been awarded. It was also a theme of Birks' work that sometimes the label 'breach of fiduciary duty' is merely acting as a mask for what are in reality already examples of restitution for breach of contract.[15]

Some expansion of restitution was also advocated by Beatson.[16] He saw restitution as 'in reality a monetised form of specific performance'. This is because if a person knows he will be stripped of his profits from breach there is no advantage for him in breaking the contract. Restitution is therefore justified in the rare cases where specific performance is available (or would have been available were it not now too late for such an order); most obviously where damages are inadequate. This theory has the attraction of building on existing principles of contract law. However, on closer inspection it is far from clear that one would want to apply principles of specific performance to restitution. For example, would general bars to specific performance, such as the bar to specific performance in contracts of personal service or the severe hardship bar, apply also to rule out restitution? And how would the theory apply to negative contractual promises where the prohibitory injunction is the primary remedy and damages are generally regarded as inadequate. It would be odd if restitution were widely available for the breach of negative but not positive promises.

14 'Restitutionary Damages for Breach of Contract: Snepp and the Fusion of Law and Equity' [1987] LMCLQ 421.
15 Apart from the two cases cited above, p 484, n 8, Birks relies on *Reading v A-G* [1951] AC 507 and the dissenting judgment of Deane J in *Hospital Products Ltd v United States Surgical Corpn* (1985) 156 CLR 41.
16 *The Use and Abuse of Unjust Enrichment* (1991), at pp 15–17. See similarly Maddaugh and McCamus, *The Law of Restitution* (1st edn, 1990), pp 432–438 tentatively favouring restitution where compensatory damages are inadequate and yet equitable relief is not available.

As with tort, the most radical approach was put forward by Goff and Jones.[17] They basically argued that restitution (through an account of profits) should be available wherever the defendant has made a gain that it would not have made but for the breach of contract. However, in contrast to their approach to tort, they also emphasised that the courts should have a general discretion whether to allow restitution or not taking into account factors such as the nature of the contract, whether the breach was cynical, and any delay by the claimant in suing for restitution.

(4) *A-G v Blake*[18]

All previous writings and case law on restitution for breach of contract must now be read in the light of the fascinating and controversial decision of the House of Lords in *A-G v Blake*.

The notorious spy, George Blake, had written his autobiography in 1989. The publishers had agreed to pay him, as an advance against royalties, three sums of £50,000 on signing the contract, delivery of the manuscript and on publication. They had paid him £60,000 so that £90,000 was still owing. The Crown sought to stop him being paid that £90,000 and for that sum, instead, to be paid to the Crown. Their claims were brought in both public and private law. The Court of Appeal had upheld Sir Richard Scott V-C's decision at first instance that Blake was not acting in breach of fiduciary duty in publishing the book because there was no fiduciary duty owed by an ex-employee to the Crown. There was also no question of a breach of confidence claim succeeding because, by the time of publication, the information in the book was in the public domain and no longer confidential. But the Court of Appeal had decided that a public law claim should succeed: the Attorney General, as an extension of his power to obtain injunctions in aid of the criminal law in furtherance of the public interest, was entitled to an order for payment so as to prevent Blake receiving money from his breach of the Official Secrets Act 1989.

---

17 See, eg, Goff and Jones (4th edn, 1993), at pp 414–417; Jones 'The Recovery of Benefits Gained from a Breach of Contract' (1983) 99 LQR 443. Cf Goff and Jones (6th edn, 2002), paras 20-024 to 20-034.

18 [2001] 1 AC 268. For analysis of this case see, eg, Edelman, *Gain-Based Damages* (2002), ch 5. Campbell and Harris, 'In Defence of Breach: a Critique of Restitution and the Performance Interest' (2002) 2 LS 208 are highly critical of the reasoning in *Blake*: but their argument is directed against restitution for breach of contract as a generally-available remedy whereas the House of Lords stressed that it should be an exceptional remedy only. In *Hospitality Group Pty Ltd v Australian Rugby Union* [2001] FCA 1040 the Federal Court of Australia considered that, unless and until *Blake* was approved by the High Court of Australia, an account of profits or 'disgorgement damages' could not be awarded for breach of contract in Australia.

The House of Lords firmly rejected that novel public law order on the ground that, without any established private law claim, it constituted a criminal confiscatory order that had not been expressly authorised by Parliament. Nevertheless the House of Lords (Lord Hobhouse dissenting) found in favour of the Crown not in public law but by revisiting *obiter dicta* of the Court of Appeal in relation to whether the Crown was entitled to the private law remedy of 'restitutionary damages' for breach of contract.

The argument that succeeded was based on the fact that, while there was no cause of action for breach of fiduciary duty or for breach of confidence, there was a cause of action for breach of contract. Blake had expressly undertaken at the beginning of his employment not to publish, during or after his employment with the Secret Service, any official information gained by him as a result of that employment. And, although the normal remedy for breach of contract is damages, compensating the claimant, this was regarded as an exceptional case where an account of profits, aimed at a disgorgement of the gains made from the breach of contract, could, and should, be awarded.

Lord Nicholls, giving the leading speech, elegantly drew together the cases awarding restitution for, for example, proprietary torts and breach of fiduciary duty, and concluded that there was no good reason in principle why an account of profits (or as one might otherwise term it, although Lord Nicholls did not like this term,[19] 'restitutionary damages') should not be awarded for breach of contract. However, as to when such an order would be made, his Lordship's speech is rather thin on detail and relies heavily on this being at the discretion of the court. He stressed that an award would be exceptional and should only be made where the standard remedies for breach of contract of compensatory damages or specific performance or an injunction were inadequate. He said:

> 'An account of profits will be appropriate only in exceptional circumstances. Normally the remedies of damages, specific performance and injunction, coupled with the characterisation of some contractual obligations as fiduciary, will provide an adequate response to a breach of contract. It will be only in exceptional cases, where those remedies are inadequate, that any question of accounting for profits will arise. No fixed rules can be prescribed. The court will have regard to all the circumstances, including the subject matter of the contract, the purpose of the contractual provision which has been breached, the circumstances in which the breach occurred, the consequences of the breach and the circumstances in which relief is being sought. A useful general guide, although

---

19   See also, eg, Doyle and Wright, 'Restitutionary Damages – The Unnecessary Remedy?' (2001) 25 MULR 1.

not exhaustive, is whether the plaintiff had a legitimate interest in preventing the defendant's profit-making activity and, hence, in depriving him of his profit.'[20]

Later in his speech his Lordship said that three facts which, individually, would *not* constitute a good reason for ordering an account of profits are: 'the fact that the breach was cynical and deliberate; the fact that the breach enabled the defendant to enter into a more profitable contract elsewhere; and the fact that by entering into a new and more profitable contract the defendant put it out of his power to perform his contract with the plaintiff.'[1]

It is obvious that phrases like 'inadequacy'[2] and 'legitimate interest' are open-ended and import a wide degree of judicial discretion. They could be used to justify an account of profits in a wide or a narrow range of cases. The crucial point, therefore, is that the House of Lords regarded restitution as an exceptional remedy reserved for rare cases. However, we must then ask, how exceptional and how rare?

The *Blake* case itself was unusual.[3] What Blake had done came very close to being, but was not quite, a breach of fiduciary duty and a breach of confidence. Moreover, the courts had no sympathy with a notorious traitor whose book profits would to some extent have derived from his crime of breaking the Official Secrets Act. One might therefore be tempted to dismiss this case as so exceptional that it is a 'one-off' that will not be repeated. That would be a mistake. It is submitted that there will be a limited range of cases where an account of profits or restitutionary damages will be awarded for a breach of contract. Certainly from now on one must bear this in mind as a possibility whenever one is concerned with remedies for breach of contract. So, for example, although perhaps not formally overruled, it is clear that the House of Lords did not like the decision in *Surrey County Council v Bredero.*[4] If similar facts were to reoccur after *Blake*, the defendant would surely be held liable to the claimant to account for the profits made from building the extra houses. Although the

---

20   [2001] 1 AC 268, 285.

1   Ibid, at 286.

2   It is noteworthy that the inadequacy referred to is in respect of specific remedies as well as damages. But if compensatory damages are considered inadequate, and profits have been made from a past breach, it is likely to be rare for an injunction or specific performance to be 'adequate' (given that they can only ensure that there is no future or continuing breach).

3   But see similarly *A-G for England and Wales v R* [2002] 2 NZLR 91 in which the New Zealand Court of Appeal held that the defendant, an ex-member of the SAS, would be liable to an account of profits and damages (but an injunction was refused) for breach of contract if he published, without the Crown's consent, a book about his experiences in the Gulf War. An account of profits was thought appropriate because of a clause by which the defendant promised to assign to the Crown any rights acquired in breach of the confidentiality clauses. One of the three judges (McGrath J) cited the *Blake* case.

4   [1993] 1 WLR 1361. See above, p 482.

loss to the claimant from the breach may have been minimal, *Blake* means that the claimant need not be limited to nominal damages. Again, one may draw on cases, which have traditionally been rationalised on the basis of a breach of fiduciary duty but which Lord Nicholls indicated are, in substance, examples of an account of profits being granted for breach of contract. For example, in *Reid-Newfoundland Co v Anglo-American Telegraph Co Ltd*[5] the defendant company agreed not to transmit any commercial messages over a particular telegraph wire except for the claimant. The Privy Council held the defendant liable to account for the profits made in breach of that agreement. Similarly, Lord Nicholls indicated that the award of damages in *British Motor Trade Association v Gilbert*,[6] for breach of a covenant not to resell a car within a certain period of time, was in reality concerned to strip the defendant of the profits he had made by breaking that covenant.

Again, although in a difficult passage Lord Nicholls seemed to regard this as rather different,[7] restitutionary damages can provide a satisfactory solution to the 'skimped performance' situation exemplified by *Tito v Waddell* (which we have examined above)[8] and, particularly notoriously, by *Ruxley Electronics and Construction Ltd v Forsyth.*[9] In the latter case, the defendant had built a swimming-pool but had failed to build it to the specified depth. The House of Lords refused to award the cost of replacing the pool to its specified depth because the claimant did not intend to rebuild the pool and it would be unreasonable to do so. It instead awarded £2,500 as damages for 'loss of amenity.' An alternative, after *Blake*, would be to award the claimant the cost the defendant saved by the breach of contract.

In contrast, it is unlikely that the courts would wish to strip away the gains made by a defendant breaking one contract in order to enter into another more lucrative contract. Indeed, as we have seen, Lord Nicholls expressly said that such a fact alone would not justify an account of profits. To lock parties into less profitable contracts would

5   [1912] AC 555. See also *Lake v Bayliss* [1974] 1 WLR 1073 (breach of a contract to sell land); and *CMS Dolphin Ltd v Simonet* [2001] 2 BCLC 704 in which Lawrence Collins J said that, had an account of profits for breach of fiduciary duty not been available, he would have awarded an account of profits for breach of the contractual duty of fidelity in line with *Blake.*

6   [1951] 2 All ER 641.

7   [2001] 1 AC 268, 286. Lord Nicholls indicated that 'expense saved' is not within the scope of an account of profits as ordinarily understood. He suggested that 'skimped performance' should lead to damages based on the difference between the price paid and the value of the services received or contracted-for. It is unclear whether he had in mind expectation (or reliance) damages for breach of contract; or restitution for (partial) failure of consideration subject to counter-restitution.

8   See above, pp 481–482.

9   [1996] AC 344, HL.

be inconsistent with the general approach in English law whereby specific performance is not the primary remedy for breach of contract.

That *Blake* was far from being a one-off has been shown by *Esso Petroleum Co Ltd v Niad*[10] in which Sir Andrew Morritt V-C decided that the claimants were entitled, at their election, to compensatory damages or an account of profits or a 'restitutionary remedy' for breach of contract. Niad, who owned a petrol station, had entered into a pricing agreement (called 'Pricewatch') with Esso who supplied Niad with petrol. In breach of that agreement, Niad charged higher prices to its customers than had been agreed. This in turn meant that Niad was given 'price support' by Esso to which Niad was not entitled: that is, Niad paid less to Esso for its petrol than it would have done had Esso known that Niad was over-charging its customers. Applying *Blake*, Morritt V-C held that Esso was here entitled to an account of profits aimed at stripping away the gains Niad had made from breaking the contract. Compensatory damages were inadequate because it was almost impossible for Esso to establish that sales had been lost as a result of the breach by Niad. The breach undermined the whole Pricewatch scheme that Esso had agreed with all retailers in the area. Esso had complained to Niad on several occasions. And Esso had a legitimate interest in preventing Niad from profiting from its breach. Alternatively Morritt V-C said that Esso was entitled to a 'restitutionary remedy' for the amount of the price support that, in breach of contract, it had obtained from Esso.

Although the distinction between an account of profits and the so-called 'restitutionary remedy' is a difficult one to draw on these facts (ie, it is not clear what the difference is between the two) the great importance of the case is that it shows *Blake* being applied to a commercial contract far removed from the peculiar facts of *Blake* itself.

On the other hand in *WWF World Wide Fund for Nature v World Wrestling Federation Entertainment Inc*,[11] where one might have thought that an account of profits would be appropriate, not least because of the close link to trade-mark infringement, Jacobs J refused to allow an amendment to the Particulars of Claim to add an account of profits. The case concerned the alleged deliberate and repeated breach of a contract concerning the use of the initials WWF. Jacobs J said, 'I can

10 (22 November 2001, unreported). See also the comments of the Supreme Court of Canada in *Bank of America Canada v Mutual Trust Co* [2002] SCC 43 to the effect that restitutionary damages for breach of contract can be awarded but not where this would discourage efficient breach.

11 [2002] FSR 32; affd, without considering this point, [2002] FSR 33, CA. See also *AB Corporation v CD Company, The Sine Nomine* [2002] 1 Lloyd's Rep 805 in which an account of profits was refused by arbitrators for the withdrawal, and use of, a ship in breach of a charterparty.

see nothing which makes this case of the exceptional character called for by the decision in *Blake*. All one really has here is a negative covenant. The fact that it relates to use of initials and so is a bit "trademarkish" or "IPish" does not mean the common law should provide what Parliament provides by statute for an infringement of a registered mark or intellectual property right.'[12]

It will be apparent from this discussion that, as could readily have been predicted from the academic ferment prior to *Blake*, the precise scope of *Blake* is proving controversial. But while a degree of initial uncertainty seems inevitable, that is not a good reason for regarding the development in *Blake* as fundamentally flawed. On the contrary it serves to support Lord Steyn's observation that 'Exceptions to the general principle that there is no remedy for disgorgement of profits against a contract breaker are best hammered out on the anvil of concrete cases.'[13]

4. RESTITUTION FOR EQUITABLE WRONGS

As explained in the introduction to this chapter, there are four main types of equitable wrong: breach of fiduciary duty, breach of confidence, dishonestly procuring or assisting a breach of fiduciary duty, and proprietary estoppel.

There is little to say on restitution for the last two types of wrong as there appears to be no English case in which restitution has been awarded. The standard remedy for dishonestly procuring or assisting a breach of fiduciary duty (for which the standard of liability has now been settled in favour of dishonesty rather than negligence)[14] is equitable compensation (sometimes alternatively referred to as accounting for loss). Should this equitable wrong ever trigger restitution?: ie should it be a restitution-yielding wrong? Although one might argue that it is closely akin to the proprietary torts the closest analogy is with the economic torts for which restitution is not traditionally available, although arguments can be put forward that it ought to be. For example, on Birks' view, that it is the moral quality of the wrongdoing that is particularly important, it would appear that, given their standard of liability,

---

12 Ibid, at para 63.
13 [2001] 1 AC 268, 291.
14 In earlier cases the negligence standard was favoured: see, eg, *Selangor United Rubber Estates Ltd v Craddock (No 3)* [1968] 1 WLR 1555; *Karak Rubber Co Ltd v Burden (No 2)* [1972] 1 WLR 602. But dishonesty was established as the correct standard by *Royal Brunei Airlines Sdn Bhd v Tan* [1995] 2 AC 378; *Twinsectra Ltd v Yardley* [2002] UKHL 12, [2002] 2 AC 164. See above, pp 194–196.

restitution should generally be available for the economic torts and for dishonestly procuring or assisting a breach of fiduciary duty.[15]

Similarly, the remedies for the wrong of proprietary estoppel, whether specific or substitutional, have not been restitutionary but have been concerned to protect the claimant's expectation interest or, occasionally, reliance interest.[16] That is not surprising given that proprietary estoppel is closely akin to breach of contract in resting on a breach of promise or conduct equivalent to a promise; and restitution has not traditionally been available for breach of contract. Whether following *A-G v Blake*[17] it will be and *should* be more widely available turns on the issues concerning restitution for breach of contract considered in the last section.

In contrast, restitution is the standard response to breach of fiduciary duty and breach of confidence through the remedy of accounting for profits. Indeed it has sometimes been assumed that restitution is so central to these wrongs that the claimant cannot alternatively claim compensation for them. That is incorrect.[18] Compensation, through the remedies of equitable compensation (sometimes referred to as accounting for loss) or equitable damages in lieu of or in addition to an injunction, is readily available. For example, as regards breach of fiduciary duty, there are many cases where trustees have been held bound to compensate beneficiaries for loss caused to the trust by reason of their failure to carry out their duties properly.[19] *Nocton v Lord Ashburton*,[20] in which a fiduciary was held

---

15   This is supported by *Warman International v Dwyer* (1995) 182 CLR 544 (account of profits ordered for 'dishonest assistance' of Dwyer's breach of fiduciary duty). It was also accepted as regards 'dishonest assistance' (by a briber) in obiter dicta of Toulson J in *Fyffes Group Ltd v Templeman* [2000] 2 Lloyd's Rep 643. It is further supported by the Law Commission. In Report No 247, para 3.51 and Draft Bill, clause 12, it recommends that, irrespective of any other power to award restitutionary damages, they may be awarded to a claimant for an equitable wrong where the defendant's conduct shows a deliberate and outrageous disregard of the claimant's rights. An equitable wrong is defined as a breach of fiduciary duty, breach of confidence, or procuring or assisting a breach of fiduciary duty: paras 5.44, 5.54–5.55, and Draft Bill, clause 15(4).

16   *Dillwyn v Llewellyn* (1862) 4 De GF & J 517; *Inwards v Baker* [1965] 2 QB 29; *Crabb v Arun District Council* [1976] Ch 179; *Pascoe v Turner* [1979] 1 WLR 431; *Baker v Baker* [1993] 2 FLR 247; *Gillett v Holt* [2001] Ch 210 (all awarding the expectation interest) and *Dodsworth v Dodsworth* (1973) 228 *Estates Gazette* 1115 (in effect protecting the reliance interest). See also *Jennings v Rice* [2002] EWCA Civ 159 (expectations protected if 'proportionate'). It is a separate issue whether there may be a claim in unjust enrichment by subtraction based, eg, on mistake: see above, pp 164–166.

17   [2001] 1 AC 268, HL.

18   See Davidson 'The Equitable Remedy of Compensation' (1982) 13 Melb Univ LR 349; Gummow, 'Compensation for Breach of Fiduciary Duty' in *Equity, Fiduciaries and Trusts* (ed Youdan, 1989), pp 57–92; Rickett, 'Compensating for Loss in Equity – Choosing the Right Horse for Each Course' in *Restitution and Equity* (eds Birks and Rose, 2000), pp 173–191; Getzler, 'Equitable Compensation and the Regulation of Fiduciary Relationships', ibid, pp 235–257.

19   Eg, *Fry v Fry* (1859) 27 Beav 144; *Bartlett v Barclays Bank Trust Co Ltd* [1980] Ch 515; *Target Holdings Ltd v Redfern* [1996] AC 421, HL.

20   [1914] AC 932.

liable for a negligent misrepresentation 50 years prior to *Hedley Byrne & Co Ltd v Heller & Partners Ltd,*[1] awarded equitable compensation. More recently, there have been high profile 'professional negligence' cases awarding equitable compensation for breach of fiduciary duty against solicitors.[2] And on breach of confidence the Court of Appeal in *Dowson and Mason Ltd v Potter*[3] adopted a straightforward compensatory approach in awarding damages to the claimant manufacturers who had lost sales profit as a result of the defendants' wrong. Indeed it is because compensation is available that one can clearly say that breach of fiduciary duty and breach of confidence are wrongs.

(1) Restitution for breach of fiduciary duty

One can first hive off cases where a fiduciary has misappropriated his beneficiary's equitable property and the beneficiary seeks proprietary restitution of the traceable property. In such cases there is no need to found one's claim on the wrong of breach of fiduciary duty. The claim can be seen as lying within unjust enrichment by subtraction with the unjust factor being ignorance (or powerlessness).Examples of such cases have been looked at in chapter 2.[4]

In analysing the rest (forming the bulk) of the case law awarding restitution, it is helpful for the purposes of exposition, to divide between secret or unauthorised profits made by a fiduciary and bribes taken by a fiduciary.[5]

1   [1964] AC 465.
2   Eg, *Bristol and West Building Society v Mothew* [1998] Ch 1, CA; *Swindle v Harrison* [1997] 4 All ER 705, CA. See also *Canson Enterprises Ltd v Boughton & Co* (1991) 85 DLR (4th) 129, Supreme Court of Canada; *Day v Mead* [1987] 2 NZLR 443; *Bank of New Zealand v New Zealand Guardian Trust Ltd* [1991] 1 NZLR 664; *Pilmer v The Duke Group Ltd* [2001] HCA 31.
3   [1986] 1 WLR 1419. There was no mention of how *equitable* damages could be justified.
4   See, eg, *Re Hallett's Estate* (1880) 13 Ch D 696; *Re Oatway* [1903] 2 Ch 356; *James Roscoe (Bolton) Ltd v Winder* [1915] 1 Ch 62.
5   A further possible example of restitution (or compensation) for breach of fiduciary duty is provided by cases laying down that a beneficiary can rescind a sale of trust property to his fiduciary unless, perhaps, the fiduciary has fully disclosed all material facts to the beneficiary and the beneficiary has consented. It is irrelevant whether the terms are substantively fair. See, eg, *Ex p Lacey* (1802) 6 Ves 625; *Ex p James* (1803) 8 Ves 337; *Wright v Morgan* [1926] AC 788; *Re Thompson's Settlement* [1986] 1 Ch 99. (Cf the less strict approach in *Holder v Holder* [1968] Ch 353.) (See also, analogously, ss 330 and 341 of the Companies Act 1985 which render a loan to a director voidable at the instance of the company.) If the uncertainty in the law were to be firmly resolved in favour of full disclosure and consent absolving the fiduciary, this line of authority would lie within the law on non-disclosure (covered in chapter 3). This 'self dealing rule' is traditionally to be contrasted with the 'fair dealing rule': with what is in effect the application of presumed undue influence principles to transactions between a fiduciary and his beneficiary where substantive unfairness may be crucial; above, p 254. See generally *Tito v Waddell (No 2)* [1977] Ch 106, 238–250, Hanbury and Martin, *Modern Equity* (16th edn, 2001), pp 606–608, Pettit, *Equity and the Law of Trusts* (9th edn, 2001), pp 441–444; Nolan, 'Conflicts of Interest, Unjust Enrichment, and Wrongdoing' in *Restitution, Past, Present and Future* (eds Cornish et al, 1998), pp 87–125.

(a) Secret or unauthorised profit

There have been many cases of fiduciaries, usually trustees or company directors, being required by the remedy of an account of profits to disgorge unauthorised profits made out of their position as fiduciaries.[6] The duty is a strict one: no unauthorised profit can be made. Although the courts do have a discretion to give the fiduciary an allowance out of the profits made to remunerate him for his skill and time, it is no defence for the fiduciary to establish that he was acting bona fide and in the best interests of the beneficiary. The leading cases are *Regal (Hastings) Ltd v Gulliver*[7] and *Boardman v Phipps*.[8]

In the former, the claimant company, Regal, owned a cinema and wanted to acquire two other cinemas. The directors found that Regal could not itself afford to buy the cinemas so they put up much of the money themselves by creating a subsidiary company in which they themselves took 2,000 £1 shares, the company's solicitor took 500 £1 shares, outside purchasers took 500 £1 shares and Regal took 2,000 £1 shares. The two cinemas were bought and subsequently the shares in the subsidiary company were sold at a considerable profit (£2 16s 1d profit per share). Regal, now under new directors, sought to recover the profits made by the former directors from the sale of the shares in the subsidiary company. The House of Lords held that the former directors were liable to account to Regal for the profits made. Although they had been acting bona fide, the fact remained that they had personally made unauthorised profits out of their fiduciary position as directors.

Viscount Sankey said:

'... the respondents were in a fiduciary position and their liability to account does not depend upon proof of *mala fides*. The general rule of equity is that no one who has duties of a fiduciary nature to perform is allowed to enter into engagements in which he has or can have a personal interest conflicting with the interests of those whom he is bound to protect.'[9]

In Lord Russell's words:

6   In addition to the two leading cases examined in the text, see *Keech v Sandford* (1726) Sel Cas temp King 61; *Parker v McKenna* (1874) 10 Ch App 96; *Boston Deep Sea Fishing & Ice Co v Ansell* (1888) 39 Ch D 339; *Re North Australian Territory Co, Archer's Case* [1892] 1 Ch 322; *Cook v Deeks* [1916] 1 AC 554 (for an 'enrichment by subtraction' analysis, see Birks, pp 137, 144–145); *Williams v Barton* [1927] 2 Ch 9; *Industrial Development Consultants v Cooley* [1972] 1 WLR 443; *Canadian Aero Services v O'Malley* (1974) 40 DLR (3d) 371; *English v Dedham Vale Properties Ltd* [1978] 1 WLR 93; *Queensland Mines Ltd v Hudson* (1978) 52 ALJR 399; *Hospital Products Ltd v United States Surgical Corpn* (1985) 156 CLR 41; *Guinness plc v Saunders* [1990] 2 AC 663 (above, pp 391–393); *Warman International Ltd v Dwyer* (1995) 182 CLR 544; *Nottingham University v Fishel* [2000] ICR 1462; *CMS Dolphin Ltd v Simonet* [2001] 2 BCLC 704.
7   [1967] 2 AC 134n.
8   [1967] 2 AC 46.
9   [1942] 1 All ER 378, 381.

'The rule of equity which insists on those, who by use of a fiduciary position make a profit, being liable to account for that profit, in no way depends on fraud or absence of bona fides; or upon such questions or considerations as whether the profit would or should otherwise have gone to the plaintiff, or whether the profiteer was under a duty to obtain the source of the profit for the plaintiff or whether he took a risk or acted as he did for the benefit of the plaintiff, or whether the plaintiff had in fact been damaged or benefited by his actions. The liability arises from the mere fact of a profit having, in the stated circumstances, been made. The profiteer, however honest and well-intentioned, cannot escape the risk of being called upon to account.'[10]

And according to Lord Wright:

'... both in law and equity, it has been held that, if a person in a fiduciary relationship makes a secret profit out of the relationship, the court will not inquire whether the other person is damnified or has lost a profit which otherwise he would have got ... Nor can the court adequately investigate the matter in most cases. The facts are generally difficult to ascertain or are solely in the knowledge of the person who is being charged. They are ... hypothetical because the inquiry is as to what would have been the position ... or what he might have done if ... interest had not conflicted with duty.'[11]

In *Boardman v Phipps* the claimant was a beneficiary with a 5/18ths beneficial interest in the Phipps trust. The trust property, inter alia, comprised shares in a company. The defendants, who were another beneficiary and the solicitor to the trustees, sought to improve the value of the shares. Using information acquired while acting as agents for the trustees the defendants embarked on a skilful operation whereby they acquired for themselves the majority of shares in the company. The value of the shares in the company rose sharply so that the defendants' operations were profitable for themselves personally and for the trust holding. The claimant beneficiary nevertheless brought an action claiming a declaration that the defendants held 5/18ths of their shares on constructive trust for him and that they should account to him for 5/18ths of the profit they had personally made. The House of Lords by a 3–2 majority (Viscount Dilhorne and Lord Upjohn dissenting) granted the declaration sought and held the defendants liable to account as constructive trustees for the profit they had made. *Regal Hastings* was followed. Although the defendants had been acting bona fide, this did not alter the fact that they had made their gains out of their position as agents for the trustees and hence while acting as fiduciaries to the beneficiaries and the beneficiaries had not authorised their scheme.

---

10 Ibid, at p 386.
11 Ibid, at p 392.

However it was stressed that the defendants should be entitled to a liberal allowance for their work and skill.[12]

The minority's reasoning was that to order a disgorging of profits was too harsh. The normal strict rule against unauthorised profits acquired by a fiduciary ought not to apply here where the fiduciaries had acted in good faith and the trustees, on behalf of the beneficiaries, had made it clear that they were not interested in any scheme to obtain majority shares in the company.

Two points should be made on those two leading cases. First, it is clear that the account of profits remedy awarded was restitutionary. It cannot realistically be reanalysed as compensatory. If the fiduciaries had not gone ahead with their schemes because unauthorised, the beneficiaries would not have otherwise made the gains that were required to be disgorged. And even if the beneficiaries had given the necessary authority, they would probably have accepted that the fiduciaries should be allowed to keep their profits.

Secondly, in *Boardman v Phipps*, as is commonplace in this area of the law, constructive trust terminology was used. The personal liability to account was described as being a liability to account as a constructive trustee. The importance of imposing a constructive trust is that it makes the beneficiary the equitable owner of the unauthorised gains thereby affording priority if the fiduciary is insolvent. The terminology also appears to make clear, although this may follow in any event, that the trustee is under a personal liability to account for unauthorised gains made from the initial unauthorised gain. Whether a constructive trust should be imposed – and indeed whether it was being imposed in *Boardman v Phipps* – will be considered below in comparing bribe cases.

(b) Bribes or secret commissions

The law is most easily described by examining three leading cases, *Lister & Co v Stubbs*,[13] *Reading v A-G*,[14] and *A-G of Hong Kong v Reid*.[15]

---

12 See also *Nottingham University v Fishel* [2000] ICR 1462. No such allowance was given, and *Boardman v Phipps* was distinguished, in *Guinness plc v Saunders* [1990] 2 AC 663: above, pp 391–393.

13 (1890) 45 Ch D 1.

14 [1951] AC 507.

15 [1994] 1 AC 324.Other cases on bribes include *Metropolitan Bank v Heiron* (1880) 5 Ex D 319; *Boston Deep Sea Fishing & Ice Co v Ansell* (1888) 39 Ch D 339; *Mahesan S/O Thambiah v Malaysian Government Officers Cooperative Housing Society Ltd* [1979] AC 374; *Islamic Republic of Iran Shipping Lines v Denby* [1987] 1 Lloyd's Rep 367; *Logicrose Ltd v Southend United Football Club Ltd* [1988] 1 WLR 1256; *Petrotrade Inc v Smith* [2000] 1 Lloyd's Rep 486; *Fyffes Group Ltd v Templeman* [2000] 2 Lloyd's Rep 643. It is also well-established that the amount of the bribe or compensatory damages (for the tort of deceit or, more realistically, inducing a breach of contract or for the equitable wrong of dishonest assistance) can be recovered from the briber; see, eg, the *Mahesan*, *Logicrose* and *Fyffes* cases. Recovery of the bribe from the briber probably cannot be justified on restitutionary principle. Cf Birks, at pp 337–338.

Taking the second case first, Reading was a Sergeant in the British Army serving in Egypt and, in return for bribes totalling £20,000, he sat on several occasions in his military uniform on lorries illegally transporting alcohol thereby avoiding their inspection by the police. Ultimately he was found out, court martialled, sent to prison and £19,325 was seized by the Crown. He claimed recovery of that money. The House of Lords refused that claim. On the contrary, the Crown was held entitled to the money because in accepting bribes to sit in his military uniform Reading had been acting in breach of his fiduciary duty to the Crown as his employer. He was therefore liable to account for the bribe or to pay it over in an action for money had and received. The fact that the Crown had not lost anything was irrelevant: the measure of relief, as in all bribe cases, was therefore indisputably restitutionary.

One peculiarity of the bribe cases, as illustrated by *Reading*, is that, as an alternative to the equitable remedy of accounting for the bribe, the claimant has an action for money had and received. The latter is a common law remedy and, on the face of it, flouts the conventional dogma that common law remedies cannot be given for equitable wrongs.[16] One radical explanation would be that the common law remedy is responding to a breach of contract: ie, the breach of an implied term in the employment or agency contract. Support for this could be found in the vagueness of the fiduciary label. But this would then contradict the traditional view, prior to *A-G v Blake*,[17] that there could be no restitution for breach of contract. As there is no logical, as opposed to historical, reason why common law remedies should not be given for equitable wrongs, probably the better view is that the bribe cases represent a long-accepted, but little appreciated, exception to the 'no fusion' dogma.

The issue in *Lister v Stubbs* and *A-G of Hong Kong v Reid* can be expressed by asking, is the fiduciary a constructive trustee of the bribe?: that is, is the bribe owned in equity by the beneficiary?

Lister v Stubbs gave a negative answer to these questions. The defendant was the foreman buyer for the claimants. He accepted a bribe of £5,541 from particular suppliers in return for showing them favouritism in orders. The defendant had invested some of that bribe in land and other securities. What the claimants sought in this action was not restitution of £5,541 (which they were clearly entitled to) but rather an order that the defendant should stop dealing with the investments and should hold them for the claimants. That order was refused.

---

16 Hanbury and Martin, *Modern Equity* (16th edn, 2001), at pp 24–26.
17 [2001] 1 AC 268.

In a very clear statement, exploring the implications of accepting the claimants' argument, Lindley LJ said:

> 'One consequence, of course, would be that, if Stubbs were to become bankrupt, this property acquired by him with the money ... would be withdrawn from the mass of his creditors and be handed over bodily to Lister. Can that be right? Another consequence would be that, if the appellants are right, Lister could compel Stubbs to account to them, not only for the money with interest, but for all the profits which he might have made by embarking in trade with it. Can that be right? It appears to me that those consequences show that there is some flaw in the argument ... the unsoundness consists in confounding ownership with obligation.'[18]

On the face of it, therefore, *Lister v Stubbs* meant that the bribe cases were treated differently from the unauthorised profit cases in that the fiduciary did not hold bribes on constructive trust.[19] Goff and Jones criticised this distinction and suggested that *Lister v Stubbs* was wrongly decided. They wrote, 'This decision emphatically marks off the secret commission cases... an honest fiduciary, such as Mr Boardman, who is deemed to have abused his position of trust, is a constructive trustee of his profits, even though he acted in the best interests of the trust and his beneficiary gained over £20,000 from his intervention. In contrast the corrupt agent, or Sergeant Reading, is simply obliged to account for the value of his bribe.'[20]

That type of criticism has since been dispelled, and the remedial difference between the bribe and unauthorised profit cases removed, by the Privy Council in *A-G for Hong Kong v Reid*[1] which refused to follow *Lister v Stubbs*. The defendant, a Crown Prosecutor and ultimately Director of Public Prosecutions in Hong Kong, had accepted bribes so as to obstruct the prosecution of certain criminals. He was convicted of criminal offences and imprisoned. The Hong Kong Government successfully sought to establish that three properties in New Zealand, bought by the defendant using the bribe, were held on constructive trust for it so that its registration of caveats on the title of the three properties was valid. Lord Templeman contrasted the bribe cases with authorities on other unauthorised gains made by fiduciaries, such as *Keech v Sandford*,[2] and referred with approval to an article by Sir Peter

---

18 (1890) 45 Ch D 1, 15.

19 It was followed on this point in, eg, *Islamic Republic of Iran v Denby* [1987] 1 Lloyd's Rep 367; *A-G's Reference (No 1 of 1985)* [1986] QB 491.

20 Goff and Jones (4th edn, 1993), at pp 668–669. See also, eg, Needham 'Recovering the Profits of Bribery' (1979) 95 LQR 536, 540–545; Finn, *Fiduciary Obligations* (1977), para 513.

1 [1994] 1 AC 324. For a consideration of the consequences for criminal law, see J C Smith, '*Lister v Stubbs* and the Criminal Law' (1994) 110 LQR 180.

2 (1726) Sel Cas temp King 61.

Millett criticising *Lister v Stubbs*,[3] Lord Templeman said:

> 'The decision in *Lister & Co v Stubbs* is not consistent with the principles that a fiduciary must not be allowed to benefit from his own breach of duty, that the fiduciary should account for the bribe as soon as he receives it and that equity regards as done that which ought to be done. From these principles it would appear to follow that the bribe and the property from time to time representing the bribe are held on a constructive trust for the person injured. A fiduciary remains personally liable for the amount of the bribe if, in the event, the value of the property then recovered by the injured person proved to be less than that amount.'[4]

Although *A-G of Hong Kong v Reid* is technically of only persuasive authority, the very firm opinion of the Privy Council suggests that, in practice, *Lister v Stubbs* has been overruled.[5]

But not everyone disagrees with *Lister v Stubbs*. On the contrary, the powerful voices of Birks[6] and Goode[7] have long argued that the case was correct and that there is generally no justification for imposing proprietary, rather than personal, restitution to strip gains made by a wrongdoer. They principally argue that a proprietary restitutionary remedy is not justified other than where there has been a subtraction from the claimant's ownership. In Birks' terminology, the claimant must have a 'proprietary base'.[8] In contrast to where a trustee has misappropriated his beneficiary's equitable property, there is no such proprietary base here because a beneficiary does not own the bribe or the unauthorised gain before the (alleged) constructive trust takes effect.[9] With respect, an even more

---

3   'Bribes and Secret Commissions' [1993] RLR 7.
4   [1994] 1 AC 324, 336.
5   Cf *obiter dicta* of Sir Richard Scott V-C at first instance in *A-G v Blake* [1996] 3 All ER 903, 912.
6   Birks, *Introduction*, at pp 387–389, 473–474; 'Personal Restitution in Equity' [1988] LMCLQ 128.
7   Goode, 'Ownership and Obligation in Commercial Transactions' (1987) 103 LQR 433, 441–445; 'Property and Unjust Enrichment' in *Essays on the Law of Restitution* (ed Burrows, 1991), pp 215–246, esp 242; 'Proprietary Restitutionary Claims' in *Restitution, Past, Present and Future* (eds Cornish, Nolan, O'Sullivan and Virgo, 1998), pp 63–77. Finch and Worthington, 'The *Pari Passu* Principle and Ranking Restitutionary Rights' in *Restitution and Insolvency* (ed Rose, 2000), pp 1–20 reach the similar conclusion, at pp 19–20, that 'unjust enrichment claimants merit proprietary status but disgorgement claimants do not'. See also Crilley, 'A Case of Proprietary Overkill' [1994] RLR 57; Rotherham, 'The Recovery of the Profits of Wrongdoing and Insolvency' [1997] CFILR 43. Note that Goode also argues that a form of proprietary remedy (he labels it a 'remedial constructive trust') which protects the interests of D's creditors is justified where D makes a 'deemed agency gain' (ie a gain which D was bound in equity to make, if he made it at all, for C).
8   See above, p 72, n 18.
9   One could conceivably argue that *Boardman v Phipps* involved misappropriation of the beneficiaries' property, in the sense of information, and that the beneficiaries were therefore tracing through to the substitute product of that property. But three of their Lordships rejected the rather artificial idea that the information was trust property: Viscount Dilhorne, at pp 89–90, Lord Cohen, at p 102, Lord Upjohn, at pp 127–128; contra were Lord Hodson, at p 107 and Lord Guest, at p 115.

convincing objection to proprietary restitution for a wrong is that, without the subtraction inherent in unjust enrichment by subtraction, there seems no good reason why a victim claiming restitution for a wrong should have priority on the wrongdoer's insolvency given that a compensation-claimant does not have such priority.[10]

One would have expected it to follow that Birks considers *Boardman v Phipps* to be wrong. Not so. He argues that nothing turned in that case on the constructive trust terminology used: it was superfluous. *Boardman v Phipps* merely imposed a personal restitutionary remedy. Contrary to the common assumption the decision was, in his view, consistent with *Lister v Stubbs.*

It is hard to agree with Birks' startling re-interpretation. Admittedly the cases on the equitable wrong of dishonest assistance show that the courts do sometimes adopt constructive trust language that is indisputably unwarranted (clearly so in that area, as is well-recognised, because the defendant has commonly not received any property).[11] And it is true that no order was made in *Boardman v Phipps* that the defendants should transfer the shares to the claimant. But a declaration that the defendants held the shares on constructive trust was made[12] and it must follow that the claimants would have been entitled to priority had the defendants been insolvent. Even if Birks were right on *Boardman v Phipps* itself, he would be fighting against both the consistent use of constructive trust terminology by the judiciary and the widespread assumption of commentators that this means that a beneficiary is entitled to a proprietary restitutionary remedy for unauthorised profits.

It is a distinct policy question what the quantum of personal restitution for equitable wrongs should be. Even though factual causation is satisfied, in that the gain would not have been made but for the wrong, it may be too harsh to the defendant to strip it of all factually caused profits however far removed from the wrong. Reflecting the analogy to remoteness of loss principles, Birks has neatly labelled this the 'remoteness of gain' question.[13] Constructive trust terminology prima facie indicates that there is no cut-off point: the fiduciary is liable for any profit made from the initial gain. In contrast, it is clear from Lindley LJ's reasoning in *Lister v Stubbs* that he considered fiduciaries liable to account only for the bribe and not for gains made from investing that bribe. In fact the distinction is not quite as sharp as

---

10 See above, p 72.
11 Hanbury and Martin, *Modern Equity* (16th edn, 2001), at p 306. For the same argument vis-à-vis 'knowing receipt', see above, pp 196–197.
12 This is made clear by the report of Wilberforce J's judgment in *Phipps v Boardman* [1964] 2 All ER 187, 208.
13 Birks, at p 351.

may at first sight appear because of the judicial discretion – exercised in *Boardman v Phipps* – to afford a fiduciary an allowance for his time and skill in making the profit. It is tentatively submitted that that discretion is an important and adequate means of controlling remoteness of gain and that there is no need for an essentially arbitrary restriction to the initial gain received.

Birks disagrees. In his view *Lister v Stubbs* was correct on quantum because gains beyond the 'first non-subtractive receipt' are too remote.[14] Moreover, he again argues that, contrary to what is generally thought, *Boardman v Phipps* was consistent with his approach; and that the defendants were merely held liable to account for the first non-subtractive receipt rather than for all profits made from the shares (subject to the allowance for time and skill). However, it is not easy to apply Birks' 'first non-subtractive receipt' test to the unauthorised acquisition of shares that are themselves profit producing. The first non-subtractive receipt might be regarded as the initial value of the shares or the first capital distribution. Yet the defendants were apparently held liable to account for all capital distributions and for the existing value of the shares.

Before leaving the *Lister v Stubbs* debate it should be noted that, in the very difficult case of *Soulos v Korkontzilas*,[15] the Supreme Court of Canada imposed a constructive trust for breach of fiduciary duty apparently on the ground that the property acquired by the fiduciary was wanted by the claimant for non-financial reasons. The defendant estate agent, in breach of fiduciary duty to his client, the claimant, had failed to pass on important information from the vendor to the claimant and had bought the property in question himself. Although the property had fallen in value so that the defendant had made no 'profit' from the breach, and the claimant had suffered no financial loss, the claimant sought a constructive trust. This was sought, apparently, because the property was of special value to the claimant in that a bank was a tenant in the property and being a landlord of a bank would enhance the claimant's reputation in the Greek community. The majority of the Supreme Court granted the constructive trust and ordered the property to be conveyed to the claimant subject to his paying the defendant the purchase price and compensating for any other loss sustained from holding the property. This order seems analogous to specific performance for a breach of contact and, arguably, the primary justification was 'compensatory' – to put the claimant into as good a position as if the defendant had performed his fiduciary duty – rather than restitutionary reversing

---

14 Birks, at pp 351–355.
15 (1997) 146 DLR (4th) 214; noted by Lionel Smith (1997) 76 CBR 539.

the defendant's wrongful gain.[16] This is so despite the fact that the majority's reasoning (given by McLachlin J) marks an important clarification for the Canadian law of restitution that constructive trusts may be imposed not merely to reverse unjust enrichment (by subtraction) but also to effect restitution for an equitable wrong. Certainly it is hard to accept that difficulty in assessing the value of the defendant's enrichment provides a good justification for imposing proprietary, rather than personal, restitution.[17] Neither *Lister v Stubbs* nor *A-G for Hong Kong v Reid* was cited by the Supreme Court of Canada.

Whatever the correct answer to the *Lister v Stubbs* debate, one must not lose sight of the uncontroverted starting point, namely that restitution can be granted for breach of fiduciary duty. Is this justified?

Jackman argues that it is, because trusts and other fiduciary relationships are facilitative institutions that merit special protection.[18] The imposition of restitution for breach of a strict fiduciary duty is therefore no more surprising than restitution for strict liability in the proprietary torts. On his view, the judicial discretion to make an allowance for the fiduciary's skill and time will primarily be exercised where the fiduciary aims bona fide to make the beneficiaries (perhaps as well as himself) better off and is successful in so doing and reflects the consistent idea that the moral quality of the wrongdoing is a discretionary factor going to the quantum of restitution not to whether it is justified in the first place.

On Birks' approach, restitution is also justified. The bribe cases constitute deliberate exploitation of wrongdoing[19] and his 'prophylaxis' test explains, and indeed is specifically geared to, the unauthorised profit cases.[20]

In contrast to their analysis of restitution for torts and breach of contract, Goff and Jones do not specifically address the question whether restitution is justified here although it plainly fits the wide 'but for' causation test that they advocate for the common law wrongs. Their primary critical analysis focuses on the *Lister v Stubbs* controversy examined above and on arguing that the content of the fiduciary duty imposed in cases like *Boardman v Phipps* and *Regal (Hastings) Ltd v Gulliver* is too strict.[1]

---

16 Cf *LAC Minerals Ltd v International Corona Resources Ltd* (1989) 61 DLR (4th) 14: see below, pp 504–506.
17 See above, pp 74–75.
18 'Restitution for Wrongs' [1989] CLJ 302, 311–314.
19 See also Law Commission Report No 247, paras 3.51 and Draft Bill, clause 12. See above, p 479.
20 Birks, at pp 332–333, 338–343.
1   Goff and Jones at paras 33-014 to 33-026.

Goff and Jones' analysis reflects the fact that for breach of fiduciary duty the authorities leave no room for seriously disputing the appropriateness of restitution. Here history has afforded restitution prominence over compensation.

(2) Restitution for breach of confidence

It is clear that, apart from non-restitutionary remedies like an injunction or compensatory damages, a claimant is entitled to an account of profits for breach of confidence at least if that breach was deliberate. It is possible that he is alternatively entitled to restitutionary damages.

That an account of profits can be awarded is shown by, for example, *Peter Pan Manufacturing Corpn v Corsets Silhouette Ltd* [2] where the defendants had manufactured and sold brassieres knowingly using confidential information obtained from the claimants. And in *A-G v Guardian Newspapers Ltd (No 2)*,[3] the Sunday Times was held liable to account for profits made in publishing, in breach of confidence to the Crown, the first extract of Peter Wright's book *Spycatcher*, that publication having taken place before the information had reached the public domain. Lord Keith said of an account of profits, 'The remedy is, in my opinion ... to be attributed to the principle that no one should be permitted to gain from his own wrongdoing. Its availability may also, in general, serve a useful purpose in lessening the temptation for recipients of confidential information to misuse it for financial gain.'[4] And in Lord Brightman's words, 'The only remedy available to the Crown is the inadequate remedy of an account of profits, on the basis that the Sunday Times unjustly enriched itself and should therefore be stripped of the riches wrongfully acquired.'[5]

In none of the English cases has it been said that the gains are held on constructive trust.[6]

In principle, proprietary restitution would be justified if the correct analysis is that the confidential information is a form of property, owned

---

2   [1964] 1 WLR 96. See also *Ansell Rubber Co Pty Ltd v Allied Rubber Industries Pty Ltd* [1972] RPC 811; *AB Consolidated v Europe Strength Food Co Pty Ltd* [1978] 2 NZLR 515.
3   [1990] 1 AC 109.
4   Ibid, at p 262.
5   [1990] 1 AC 109, 266. Lord Goff's general comments on restitution for wrongs at p 286 are also of interest.
6   But in dicta in *A-G v Guardian Newspapers (No 2)* [1990] 1 AC 109, 288 Lord Goff tentatively suggested that the copyright in *Spycatcher* might be held on constructive trust for the Crown. See also *Service Corporation International plc v Channel Four Television Corpn* [1999] EMLR 83, 90–91.

in equity by the claimant,[7] and which the claimant can then trace in equity into its substitute product. Without that subtraction from the claimant's wealth there seems no justification for giving the claimant priority on the defendant's insolvency. If one were to take that analysis (which seems rather artificial) there would be no need to view the claim for proprietary restitution as based on the wrong of breach of confidence. It would be most naturally explained as lying within unjust enrichment by subtraction, with the unjust factor being ignorance or powerlessness.

The separate issue of whether the account of profits excludes secondary receipts has not been discussed in the English cases. As with breach of fiduciary duty it is tentatively suggested that, given the courts' discretion to afford the defendant a liberal allowance for work and skill, there is no need for an arbitrary cut-off point beyond factual causation.

In the difficult Canadian case of *LAC Minerals Ltd v International Corona Resources Ltd* [8] a constructive trust was imposed for breach of confidence. In negotiations for a joint venture between them, the defendants acquired from the claimant information about the mineral potential of some land. The defendants subsequently outbid the claimant in buying that land and set up a successful gold-mine on it. The majority of the Supreme Court of Canada held that the claimant was entitled to a constructive trust of the land as a remedy for the defendants' breach of confidence, subject to an allowance to the defendants, secured by a lien, for expenses in developing the mine that the claimant itself would have necessarily had to incur.

La Forest J, giving the main majority judgment, rejected the argument that a proprietary restitutionary remedy is only justified where the claimant had a pre-existing right of property. He said:

> '... it is not the case that a constructive trust should be reserved for situations where a right of property is recognised. That would limit the constructive trust to its institutional function and deny it the status of a remedy, its more important role. Thus, it is not in all cases that a pre-existing right of property will exist when a constructive trust is ordered ... it is not necessary, therefore, to determine whether confidential information is property ...'[9]

---

7   This was left open by Lord Goff in *A-G v Guardian Newspapers (No 2)* [1990] 1 AC 109, 281. In *Satnam Investments Ltd v Dunlop Heywood & Co Ltd* [1999] 3 All ER 652 it was held by the Court of Appeal that, even assuming that confidential information could be treated as property, it could not on the facts be traced into the land acquired by the recipient of that information. Cf above, p 499, n 9.

8   (1989) 61 DLR (4th) 14. In *Cadbury Schweppes Inc v FBI Foods Ltd* (1999) 167 DLR (4th) 577, the Supreme Court of Canada has subsequently stressed that, in Canada, the imposition of a constructive trust is discretionary and dependent on the particular facts of a case. It was there held that compensation for breach of confidence, and not a proprietary remedy, was appropriate (the claimants not having sought an account of profits). See Abdullah and Hang, 'To Make the Remedy Fit the Wrong' (1999) 115 LQR 376.

9   Ibid, at p 50.

The objection to this approach is that, to the extent that it imposes proprietary restitution for a wrong, it unjustifiably sacrifices the interests of a defendant's creditors.[10] And for what positive reasons? La Forest J suggests the following: 'Having specific regard to the uniqueness of the Williams property, to the fact that but for LAC's breaches of duty, Corona would have acquired it, and recognising the virtual impossibility of accurately valuing the property, I am of the view that it is appropriate to award Corona a constructive trust over the land.'[11]

It is hard to accept that difficulty of assessment is a valid reason for preferring a proprietary, as opposed to a personal, restitutionary remedy for a wrong.[12] And even if a justification for a constructive trust could lie in there having been an enrichment by interceptive subtraction, that should surely have meant that the constructive trust existed from the date when LAC acquired the property.

Wilson J appeared to think that the constructive trust was being imposed as a compensatory remedy:

'... the only sure way in which Corona can be fully compensated for the breach in this case is by the imposition of a constructive trust on LAC in favour of Corona with respect to the property. Full compensation may or may not have been achieved through an award of common law damages depending upon the accuracy of valuation techniques. It can most surely be achieved in this case through the award of an *in rem* remedy.'[13]

A merit of that approach is that the remedies of a mandatory injunction, specific performance, and delivery up, suggest that difficulty in assessing compensation for a wrong can constitute a valid ground for preferring a proprietary remedy. But on the facts to impose the constructive trust as a means of ensuring full compensation rested on the unrealistic assumption that, had there been no breach of confidence, not only would the claimant have developed the mine itself rather than jointly with the defendants but also would have developed it as profitably as the defendants had done.

The minority (Sopinka and McIntyre JJ) preferred to award compensatory damages. The remedy of an accounting of profits had not been in issue and they thought a constructive trust inappropriate because, on their view of the facts, the extent of the connection

10 Goode, 'Property and Unjust Enrichment' in *Essays on the Law of Restitution* (ed Burrows, 1991), pp 215, 239–240; Gummow, 'Unjust Enrichment, Restitution and Proprietary Remedies' in *Essays on Restitution* (ed Finn, 1990), pp 47, 78; Birks, 'The Remedies for Abuse of Confidential Information' [1990] LMCLQ 460, 463.
11 (1989) 61 DLR (4th) 14, 52.
12 Above, pp 74–75.
13 (1989) 61 DLR (4th) 14 at p 17.

between the confidential information and the acquisition of the property was uncertain.

The possibility of restitutionary damages being awarded for breach of confidence primarily derives from the Court of Appeal's judgment in *Seager v Copydex Ltd (No 2)*.[14] The defendants had inadvertently (ie subconsciously) used confidential information in manufacturing a new style carpet-grip. Lord Denning said that if there was nothing special about the confidential information, damages for breach of confidence should be based on the fee the defendant saved by not employing a consultant to acquire that information; whereas if the information was special, damages should be assessed according to what a willing buyer would have paid for it.

The former is restitutionary. The latter can be analysed as either compensatory or restitutionary: it represents either what the claimant has lost by not selling to the defendant or a third party, or what the defendant has gained by saving itself the expense of paying for the information.

The Court of Appeal appeared to think that an account of profits was not an appropriate remedy.[15] Although the reason for this was not given, the obvious explanation is that, in contrast to the *Peter Pan* and *Spycatcher* cases, the wrongdoing was not deliberate in *Seager v Copydex*.

There is further support for the award of restitutionary damages for breach of confidence in Sir Donald Nicholls V-C's judgment in *Universal Thermosensors Ltd v Hibben*.[16] In assessing the defendants' damages on the claimant's cross-undertaking supporting an interim injunction restraining the defendants' breach of confidence, the Vice-Chancellor deducted the damages the claimant was entitled to 'for the benefits they derived from the wrongful use of its confidential information, in particular (but not exclusively) by saving themselves the time, trouble, and expense of compiling their own list of contacts without reference to the plaintiff's records.'[17] He referred to *Seager v Copydex* and to the 'user principle' by which 'the plaintiff ought to be paid by the defendants for the use they made of the plaintiff's confidential information even if the plaintiff suffered no loss of profits in consequence'.[18] Although he thereby used clear restitutionary reasoning, the strength of this is weakened by the fact that the Vice-Chancellor also described the damages as compensatory; and, despite the wrongdoing being deliberate, he thought that the claimant was

---

14   [1969] 1 WLR 809. On the traditional view the damages were equitable.
15   *Seager v Copydex Ltd* [1967] 1 WLR 923, 932.
16   [1992] 1 WLR 840.
17   Ibid, at pp 858–859.
18   Ibid, at p 856.

not entitled to an injunction (nor, by inference, to an account of profits) because that would put the claimant in a better position than if there had been no breach of confidence.

Is restitution for breach of confidence justified? Jackman's 'facilitative institution' analysis neatly reconciles the main cases. A relationship of confidentiality (whether confidential information is property or not) is a facilitative institution which merits special protection by the courts. On this view, *Peter Pan*, the *Spycatcher* case, and *Seager* are all justifiably restitutionary with the difference between the remedy of an account of profits and restitutionary damages being one of quantum turning on the secondary factor of the deliberateness of the wrongdoing.

Birks analyses *Seager* as awarding compensation only which would leave the other leading cases as explicable on his primary test of cynical wrongdoing.[19]

As in their chapter on breach of fiduciary duty, Goff and Jones do not directly consider the justification for restitution for breach of confidence and do not refer back to their wide 'but for' test advocated for torts. They suggest that the standard of liability for breach of confidence extends beyond dishonesty[20] and that an account of profits for breach of confidence should not be confined to where the defendant was a conscious wrongdoer.[1]

5. CONCLUSION

Restitution for wrongs is as difficult as it is interesting. Nowhere is the blinkering effect of the historical divide between common law and equity more self-evident: for torts and breach of contract restitution is rare whereas for breach of fiduciary duty and breach of confidence it is commonplace. Nothing is more essential than that there is consistency across the whole area.

The main stance of this chapter has been that compensation is a more natural measure of recovery for a wrong than restitution and that the courts need a good reason to overcome the objection to restitution of giving the claimant a windfall. Two primary justificatory reasons have emerged: awarding restitution to protect facilitative institutions and awarding restitution against cynical wrongdoers. It may be that the best way forward is to regard them as alternative basic

---

19 See also Law Commission Report No 247, para 3.51 and Draft Bill, clause 12. See above, p 479. Cf Birks, at pp 345–346 which relies on his now abandoned 'anti-enrichment wrong' test.

20 Goff and Jones, at para 34-008.

1 Goff and Jones, at para 34-012.

tests, albeit that additional criteria may sometimes have to be satisfied (eg, that compensatory damages are inadequate). Certainly any idea that restitution is simply unavailable for certain types of wrong (eg, personal torts) is hard to maintain in the light of *A-G v Blake*.

Chapter 15

Defences

A claimant, who has established in accordance with the law examined in chapters 2–14 that the defendant has been (i) unjustly (ii) enriched (iii) at the claimant's expense, may still be denied a restitutionary remedy because of (iv) a restitutionary defence.

In recent years, the importance of the defences to restitution has increased. As the grounds for restitution have been expanded (for example, by the acceptance of the 'but for' causation test for mistakes of fact, by the abolition of the mistake of law bar, and by the willingness to evade the requirement of *total* failure of consideration) so it has fallen to the defences to ensure sufficient security of receipt and to avoid there being excessive restitution. Rather than the courts placing arbitrary restrictions on liability, the scope of restitution is now more satisfactorily and openly controlled by the defences, especially the change of position defence.

As is the case throughout the law, what counts as a defence rather than as going to the defendant's prima facie liability rests on common practice or understanding rather than clear-cut principle. For example, it would be possible in theory, albeit contrary to convention, to treat as a defence the traditional need for a failure of consideration to be total: one could say that a claimant who proves that he made a payment for a failed consideration establishes a prima facie case for restitution to which the defence is that the failure of consideration was partial and not total. Nevertheless the distinction between prima facie liability and defences does have practical significance in that the legal burden of proof switches to the defendant once prima facie liability is established.[1]

Some defences, for example, election,[2] and contracting out (ie, exclusion), will not be examined because the details of their application in the realm of restitution are not significantly different

---

1 However, the main authorities on tort claims suggest that, while the defendant must plead limitation, the claimant has the burden of proving that its claim falls within the limitation period. The Law Commission's Report No 270, *Limitation of Actions* (2001), paras 5.29–5.32 recommends a different burden of proof for different limitation defences.
2 Election can be regarded as including the bar to rescission of affirmation: see above, pp 175, 245.

than elsewhere in the civil law; and an agent's 'payment over' defence is considered in chapter 16.

This leaves nine main defences as the subject matter of this chapter: change of position, estoppel, counter-restitution, limitation, dispute resolved, incapacity, illegality, bona fide purchase and passing on. The first two of these (and possibly counter-restitution) essentially go to the question of the defendant's enrichment. The last goes to whether the enrichment was at the claimant's expense. The rest (including possibly counter-restitution) go to the injustice of an enrichment.

1. CHANGE OF POSITION[3]

(1) Acceptance of the defence

Although a defendant has been unjustly enriched his subsequent 'loss' of the benefit (his 'disenrichment') may render it unacceptable to order restitution. Traditionally in English law it was only where the claimant represented that the benefit was the defendant's and the defendant detrimentally relied (ie, changed its position) on the faith of that representation that a defence could be made out. That is, estoppel alone was a defence. This was notoriously unsatisfactory and in *Lipkin Gorman v Karpnale Ltd*[4] the House of Lords responded to the overwhelming arguments of principle by recognising a defence of change of position.

The leading case applying the traditional approach was *Baylis v Bishop of London*[5] in which the claimants had mistakenly paid to a bishop (who was acting as sequestrator for the parish on the bankruptcy of its rector) tithe rent-charges on certain property in which their leasehold interest had already expired. The bishop applied some of the money in providing for the needs of the parish and paid over the surplus to the rector's trustee in bankruptcy. It was held by the Court of Appeal that the defendant bishop had no defence to the claimant's restitutionary claim for money paid by mistake of fact. Payment over would have constituted a defence had the bishop been acting as an agent and had paid the money over to his principal but here the bishop received the money as principal.

But while the case law formally remained against a change of position defence there were ever-increasing indications of judicial

---

3   This section draws heavily on my forthcoming article in the Loyola of Los Angeles Law Review, 'Change of Position: The View from England'.
4   [1991] 2 AC 548.
5   [1913] 1 Ch 127. See also, eg, *Durrant v Ecclesiastical Comrs* (1880) 6 QBD 234; *Ministry of Health v Simpson* [1951] AC 251. For an agent's defence of 'payment over', see below, pp 599–608.

support for that defence. In *Larner v LCC*[6] Denning LJ thought that the defence he was discussing – and, on the facts, rejecting because of a breach of duty by the payee – was more accurately called 'change of circumstances' rather than estoppel and he made no reference to the need for any representation. In *Barclays Bank v WJ Simms, Son and Cooke (Southern) Ltd*[7] Robert Goff J referred to good faith change of position as one of his qualifications on the payor's prima facie right to restitution for a mistaken payment and he explained that he did not need to decide in the instant case whether the defence was dependent on a breach of duty or representation by the claimant. In *R v Tower Hamlets London Borough Council, ex p Chetnik Developments Ltd*[8] the same judge, by now Lord Goff, thought that the question of whether the defendant rating authority had spent overpayments in meeting precepts by other authorities was 'no more than an enquiry whether it would be right for the local authority to invoke the restitutionary defence of change of position'. Kerr LJ in *Rover International Ltd v Cannon Film Sales Ltd (No 3)*[9] ruled out a change of position defence merely on the facts (delivery of the films was not a *detrimental* change of position by Cannon).

Further impetus for a move to change of position came from the virtually unanimous support of commentators for this[10] and from the acceptance of the defence in the United States,[11] Canada,[12] New Zealand[13] and parts of Australia.[14]

So the scene was set for the momentous decision in *Lipkin Gorman* in which the House of Lords held that a bona fide change of position should itself be a good defence. In Lord Goff's words, 'The principle is widely recognised throughout the common law world ... The time for its recognition in this country is, in my opinion, long overdue.'[15]

There are several reasons of principle or policy for wholeheartedly supporting that acceptance of the defence.

6   [1949] 2 KB 683.
7   [1980] QB 677. See also Robert Goff J's controversial view in *BP Exploration Co (Libya) Ltd v Hunt (No 2)* [1979] 1 WLR 783 that the proviso to s 1(2) and 1(3)(a) of the Law Reform (Frustrated Contracts) Act 1943 is best rationalised as a statutory recognition of the change of position defence.
8   [1988] AC 858.
9   [1989] 1 WLR 912. See also his judgment, as Kerr J, in *National Westminster Bank Ltd v Barclays Bank International* [1975] QB 654, 675–676.
10 Eg, Goff and Jones (3rd edn, 1986), at pp 691–696; Birks, at pp 412–415. Cf Beatson and Bishop, 'Mistaken Payments in the Law of Restitution' (1986) 36 U Toronto LJ 149.
11 Restatement of Restitution, s 142.
12 *Storthoaks Rural Municipality v Mobil Oil Canada Ltd* (1975) 55 DLR (3d) 1.
13 New Zealand (Judicature) Act 1908, s 94B.
14 Eg, *Bank of New South Wales v Murphett* [1983] 1 VR 489. Subsequent to *Lipkin Gorman* the defence was accepted by the High Court of Australia in *David Securities Pty Ltd v Commonwealth of Australia* (1992) 109 ALR 57.
15 [1991] 2 AC 548, 579–580.

(i) The essential concern of the change of position defence is with the defendant's loss of enrichment (ie, 'disenrichment'). The law's traditional insistence, through the estoppel defence, that the loss had to be induced by the claimant's representation was too restrictive. For example, if the payee had in good faith detrimentally relied on a payment being his or hers it was hard to see why a representation by the payor was additionally insisted on. The granting of restitution in *Baylis v Bishop of London* was surely unacceptable.

(ii) According to *Avon County Council v Howlett*,[16] as we shall see, estoppel can operate only as an all or nothing defence. In contrast change of position, divorced from the rule of evidence strictures of estoppel, can operate in a *pro tanto* fashion. The latter is plainly more appropriate for restitution because it can be geared to the precise extent of the loss of enrichment. It is to be hoped that in time change of position will supplant estoppel completely. So long as estoppel remains it gives the defendant who can satisfy its more stringent requirements an unwarranted complete defence.[17]

(iii) Birks suggests that the strongest argument in principle for change of position lies 'in the logic of subjective devaluation'.[18] The argument runs as follows: if the defendant uses money received to buy benefits which he would not otherwise have bought, liability to make restitution to the payor in effect forces him to pay for benefits that he did not want; denial of change of position is therefore inconsistent with the acceptance in the law of restitution of the importance of a defendant's subjective devaluation.

(iv) The expansion of the grounds for restitution, (for example, to include mistake of law) requires counterbalancing by an expansion of the restitutionary defences to include change of position. For without that there might be too much restitution both in the 'floodgates of litigation' sense and from the perspective of giving adequate security of receipt to payees. Indeed an extreme version of this argument would say that the law of unjust enrichment by subtraction ought not to have been expanded until a change of position defence was firmly in place.

(2) The ingredients of the defence

(a) The narrow and wide versions of the defence

Since the acceptance of change of position in England, attention has shifted to the precise ingredients of the defence. This was expressly

---

16 [1983] 1 WLR 605.
17 See below, pp 533–538. Cf Maddaugh and McCamus, *The Law of Restitution* (1st edn, 1990), pp 235–236.
18 Birks, at p 413.

left open for case law development by the House of Lords in *Lipkin Gorman*. However, Lord Goff's tentative formulation was very broad. 'At present I do not wish to state the principle any less broadly than this: that the defence is available to a person whose position has so changed that it would be inequitable in all the circumstances to require him to make restitution, or alternatively to make restitution in full.'[19] Cases subsequent to *Lipkin Gorman* have slowly but surely been clarifying the ingredients of the defence.

Two main versions of the defence can be and have been articulated. The first and narrow view is that change of position is the same as estoppel minus the representation. The defendant must have detrimentally relied on the benefit being his to keep.[20] So Birks has written of change of position, 'This defence is like estoppel with the requirement of a representation struck out. In other words the enriched defendant succeeds if he can show that he acted to his detriment on the faith of the receipt.'[1] This version is embodied in the New Zealand Judicature Act 1908, s 94B according to which mistaken payments may not be recoverable 'if the person from whom the relief is sought received the payment in good faith and *has so altered his position in reliance on the validity of the payment* that in the opinion of the court, having regard to all possible implications in respect of other persons, it is inequitable to grant relief, or to grant relief in full, as the case may be.'[2] And this version derives further support from *Storthoaks Rural Municipality v Mobil Oil Canada Ltd*[3] in which the Supreme Court of Canada first accepted change of position as a defence. Martland J said, 'It should be open to the municipality to seek to avoid the obligation to repay the moneys it received if it can be established that it has materially changed its circumstances as a result of the receipt of the money.'

The alternative wide view is to say that detrimental reliance is not a necessary ingredient and that the defendant should have a defence where his position, consequent on the benefit, has so changed that it would be inequitable to order restitution. This is the version of the defence adopted by s 142(1) of the *Restatement of Restitution*.[4] This has also been Goff and Jones' preferred view. In the third edition of their book, they wrote:

---

19 [1991] 2 AC 548, 580.
20 For what is meant by 'detrimental reliance', see below, pp 532–533.
1   Birks, at p 410. Cf his later views in 'The English recognition of unjust enrichment' [1991] LMCLQ 473, 486–496 in which he sees change of position as encompassing 'counter-restitution essential' and bona fide purchase. See also Birks, *Restitution – The Future* (1992), ch 6.
2   Author's italics. See also the identical provision in the Western Australia Property Law Act 1969, s 125.
3   (1975) 55 DLR (3d) 1, 13. See also the High Court of Australia's acceptance of the defence in *David Securities Pty Ltd v Commonwealth Bank of Australia* (1992) 109 ALR 57.
4   See below, p 517.

'Unlike the legislature in New Zealand, we would not restrict the defence of change of position to cases where the defendant has "altered his position in reliance on the validity of the payment." No doubt, many cases of change in position will fall within that description. But there are others which do not, where it would be inequitable to order the defendant to make restitution ... The surest guide for the future is, we think, to be found in the broad general statement in s 142(1) of the Restatement of Restitution. Each case will have to be judged on its own facts in order to determine whether it is just and equitable to require the defendant to make restitution.'[5]

Of the two versions being considered, the wide view was also that tentatively supported by Lord Goff in *Lipkin Gorman*.

On the facts of *Lipkin Gorman* either version of the defence would have produced the same result. That is, the relevant change of position was paying out winnings to a thief on the assumption that the money he was using to bet with was untainted, and was hence the gaming club's to keep, whereas in fact it had been stolen from the claimant solicitors. Although the amount of stolen money staked was much higher, the overall enrichment received by the defendant club from the stolen money was about £151,000. It was this sum that was awarded in restitution. As is expressly recognised in Lord Goff's speech, the House of Lords took a rough-and-ready rather than a strictly logical approach to the acute factual difficulties in applying change of position to winnings paid out on bets: for on a strict approach winnings on a bet relate to, and cancel out only, the receipt of that particular bet and not other losing bets.

One implicit limitation on the wide view is that there is a sufficient causal link between the defendant's unjust enrichment and his change of position. In other words, the defence must be concerned with loss of benefit ('disenrichment') and not with general hardship suffered by the defendant. Say, for example, the unjustly enriched defendant, subsequent to receipt, is made redundant or is injured in a car crash. Or say, having received a mistaken payment of £100 the defendant has £500 stolen from him which would have been stolen irrespective of the mistaken payment. These changes of circumstance may make it more difficult for the defendant to repay the claimant. But they ought not to afford a defence to restitution. Unless the subject is to disintegrate into a case by case discretionary analysis of the justice of individual facts, far removed from principle, it is imperative that, even on the wide formulation, there is a sufficient causal link between the defendant's unjust enrichment and his pecuniary loss.

5   Goff and Jones, *The Law of Restitution* (3rd edn, 1986), pp 693–694. Cf Goff and Jones (6th edn, 2002), para 40-003.

That this should be so has now been expressly supported by the Court of Appeal in *Scottish Equitable plc v Derby*.[6] Robert Walker LJ said, 'The fact that the recipient may have suffered some misfortune (such as a breakdown in his health, or the loss of his job) is not a defence unless the misfortune is causally linked (at least on a 'but for' test) with the mistaken receipt.'

A crucial practical question is what the test for that sufficient causal link should be. As Robert Walker LJ said, it should at least be for the defendant to show that but for the enrichment received he would not have suffered the loss. However, by analogy to the parallel position in relation to compensatory damages, namely to what extent should subsequent benefits be taken into account to reduce the claimant's loss, one should probably add that, even if factually caused, the loss is irrelevant if too indirectly related to (ie, too far removed from or essentially coincidental to) the enrichment received.[7]

The main range of situations where the above narrow and wide versions of change of position may produce different results is where loss is brought about by a third party or a natural event. Say, for example, money mistakenly paid to the defendant is immediately stolen or destroyed by fire. Or let us assume that a building being erected by the claimant for the defendant is half complete when destroyed by fire. In those examples only the wider version of change of position would afford a defence because the defendant has not suffered the loss as a result of relying, in any meaningful sense, on the benefit being his.

Indeed, given Goff and Jones' and Lord Goff's preference for the wide view of change of position, it is surprising that Robert Goff J in *BP Exploration Co (Libya) Ltd v Hunt (No 2)*[8] did not treat the example of the burnt down building as raising a question of change of position. Moreover, he appeared to think that in principle the builder should be entitled to restitution and that it was only because of the wording of s 1(3)(b) of the Law Reform (Frustrated Contracts) Act 1943 that a judge would be required to refuse restitution.

Which of the two versions of change of position is to be preferred? Although one possible advantage of the narrower version is that it is more closely tied to the long-established defence of estoppel, the wider view is to be preferred.[9] For example, it seems grotesque that a

---

6 [2001] EWCA Civ 369, [2001] 3 All ER 818, para 31. For the facts of this case, see below, p 536.
7 Burrows, *Remedies for Torts and Breach of Contract* (2nd edn, 1994), pp 119–123. Even on the narrow version of the defence one may want some causal limitation over and above 'reliance'.
8 [1979] 1 WLR 783. Above, p 369.
9 At root, the wider view rejects reliance while insisting on causal detriment (ie, the payee must show that it will be pecuniarily worse off if now required to make restitution than if the benefit had not been conferred in the first place).

defendant who is paid £100,000 by the mistake of his bank (perhaps even negligently) which is immediately stolen[10] can be held (strictly) liable to make restitution of £100,000. Even though the subsequent loss of the benefit cannot be blamed on the bank the fact remains that the bank started the chain of events by first making the mistaken payment. It is also important that the wide view was tentatively supported by Lord Goff in *Lipkin Gorman.*

Furthermore there is much to be said, at this stage in its development, for holding the law of restitution in check by a wider, rather than a narrower, change of position defence. This was Goff and Jones' argument in relation to counterbalancing the expansion of the types of mistaken payments grounding restitution heralded by *Barclays Bank Ltd v WJ Simms, Son and Cooke (Southern) Ltd:*[11]

> 'It is important to interpret the defence generously, given that the litigation will generally arise in the context of payments made under a mistake of fact; for it now appears that a payer can recover his payment if he can prove that he would not have made the payment if he had known the true facts. That is a wide principle, which protects the payer, even though he was negligent in making the payment. In order to protect the bona fide recipient, it is then all the more necessary to accept a broad defence of change of position.'[12]

The wide view has now won the support of the Court of Appeal in *Scottish Equitable plc v Derby.*[13] Robert Walker LJ said:

> 'The judge noted the view, put forward by Andrew Burrows[14] that there is a narrow and a wide version of the defence of change of position, and that the wide view is to be preferred. The narrow view treats the defence as "the same as estoppel minus the representation" (so that detrimental reliance is still a necessary ingredient). The wide view looks to a change of position, causally linked to the mistaken receipt, which makes it inequitable for the recipient to be required to make restitution. In many cases either test produces the same result, but the wide view extends protection to (for instance) an innocent recipient of a payment which is later stolen from him ... In this court, Stephen Moriarty QC ... did not argue against the correctness of the wide view, provided that the need for a sufficient causal link is clearly recognised ... In my view, Mr Moriarty was right to make that concession. Taking a wide view of the defence facilitates "a more generous approach ... to the recognition of the right to restitution."'[15]

---

10 Ie, the defendant would not otherwise have lost £100,000.
11 [1980] QB 677.
12 Goff and Jones (3rd edn, 1986), p 694.
13 [2001] EWCA Civ 369, [2001] 3 All ER 818, paras 30–31.
14 *The Law of Restitution* (1st edn, 1993), pp 425–428.
15 Robert Walker LJ here cited Lord Goff in *Lipkin Gorman* [1991] 2 AC 548, 581.

The wide view has also been adopted by the New Zealand Court of Appeal in *National Bank of New Zealand Ltd v Waitaki International Processing (NI) Ltd.*[16] The defendant had there been mistakenly paid NZ $500,000 by the claimant bank. The defendant had told the bank of the mistake and, despite the bank's insistence, believed throughout that it was not entitled to the money. The defendant then lost the money by investing it, without security, in a company that became insolvent. The majority of the New Zealand Court of Appeal (Thomas and Tipping JJ) held that s 94B of the Judicature Act 1908 did not apply to these facts. Given the defendant's belief that he was not entitled to the money he could not be said to have 'altered his position in reliance on the validity of the payment'. In contrast, the defendant could rely on the non-statutory change of position defence put forward in *Lipkin Gorman*[17] because that was wider and was not dependent on detrimental reliance on the validity of the payment. Thomas J said that the wider version of change of position was 'obviously superior.'[18]

(b) Seven further issues

(i) Does change of position cover losses incurred prior to the receipt of the benefit? In other words, does it extend to anticipatory, as well as subsequent, change of position? Until recently, in almost all discussions of the defence[19] it was assumed that it only applies to subsequent losses. This was expressly spelt out in s 142(1) of the *Restatement of Restitution*: 'The right of a person to restitution from another because of a benefit received is terminated or diminished if, after the receipt of the benefit, circumstances have so changed that it would be inequitable to require the other to make full restitution.'[20] But there seems no significant distinction between the following two defendants. D1 who, having been paid £1,000 by the claimant by mistake, pays £100 to charity; and D2 who, having been mistakenly told that she has won £1,000, pays £100 to charity and the £1,000 is then mistakenly paid. Although D2's change of position was consequent on the expectation of payment, rather than on an actual payment, and although D2 could not have directly enforced such an expectation (absent a contract) that seems unimportant given that one is here concerned with a defence to restitution. As I have previously

---

16 [1999] 2 NZLR 211.
17 The Privy Council in *Goss v Chilcott* [1996] AC 788 accepted that the common law change of position defence could be applied in New Zealand despite s 94B of the Judicature Act 1908.
18 [1999] 2 NZLR 211, 229.
19 An exception was Robert Goff J's rationalisation of the proviso to s 1(2) and 1(3)(a) of the Law Reform (Frustrated Contracts) Act 1943 as 'a statutory recognition of the defence of change of position': *BP Exploration Co (Libya) Ltd v Hunt (No 2)* [1979] 1 WLR 783, 800. See above, pp 362–363. See also Birks, at p 257.
20 See also Palmer, *Law of Restitution* (1978), vol III, p 510.

written, '[T]he fact that the defendant would have no active claim to recoup particular losses, does not mean that those losses should not be taken into account as a defence to restitution.'[1] The crucial common feature is a clear causal link between the defendant's loss of £100 and the mistaken payment of £1,000. If the defendant were required to make restitution of £1,000, he or she would be worse off by £100 than if the payment, or the indication of payment, had never been made.

The contrary view – that anticipatory change of position does not count – was taken by Clarke J in *South Tyneside Metropolitan Borough Council v Svenska International plc*.[2] This was one of the many interest rate swap cases[3] but, unusually, it was the bank rather than the local authority that was the defendant. The defendant bank sought to establish that it had changed its position by incurring losses on 'hedging transactions' (including valid swap contracts with other banks) that had been entered into as a consequence of, and to limit the risk on, the void swap contract with South Tyneside. Those hedging contracts were entered into prior to the receipt of payments from South Tyneside. Clarke J said, '[S]ave perhaps in exceptional cases, the defence of change of position is designed to protect a person who receives money in good faith and who thereafter changes his position in good faith so that it would be inequitable to require him to repay part or all of the money to its rightful owner.'[4] More specifically, the defence was thought inapplicable on the facts because the bank's reliance in entering into the hedging contracts was upon the apparent contractual promise of South Tyneside rather than upon the receipt of any payments.

However, the better view has now been forcefully expressed – and Clarke J's decision regarded as dependent on the exceptional facts of that case[5] – by the Privy Council in *Dextra Bank & Trust Co*

1   Burrows, 'Swaps and the Friction between Common Law and Equity' [1994] RLR 15, 21. In that article I recanted from the tentative view, expressed in the first edition of this book, at p 424, that the defence applied only to a subsequent change of position.
2   [1995] 1 All ER 545. See also Hobhouse J's reasons, at first instance, for change of position not to include 'hedging contracts' in *Westdeutsche Landesbank Girozentrale v Islington London Borough Council* [1994] 4 All ER 890, 948–949.
3   See, generally, above, pp 397–398.
4   [1995] 1 All ER 545, 566.
5   It is hard to see that the decision can be reconciled with the Privy Council's reasoning. On the face of it, losses on 'hedging contracts' should have constituted change of position (unless, where those contracts were themselves void, the losses could have been avoided by claiming restitution). This is supported by Goff and Jones, para 40-004 who criticise Clarke J's reasoning and decision: '[I]t is inequitable to conclude that the bank should repay its gain on the swap but should not be allowed to set off its losses on the hedging transactions.' A conceivable justification for ignoring the hedging contracts might have been that to take them into account would have cut across the counter-restitution that was allowed in treating the claim as being merely for the net enrichment. Another possible justification is that, once one takes into account hedging contracts, there may be further consequential contracts to take account of, and to avoid endless enquiries it is preferable to treat all such losses as too remote.

Ltd v Bank of Jamaica.[6] The claimant, Dextra, drew a cheque for $2,999,000 on its bankers in favour of the defendant, the Bank of Jamaica (BOJ). Dextra drew the cheque on the assumption that it would constitute a loan to BOJ under a secured loan agreement with BOJ. But that loan agreement was never concluded. The cheque had been arranged on BOJ's behalf by agents whom BOJ reimbursed in advance of receiving the cheque. The Privy Council held that Dextra was not entitled to restitution of the money as money paid by mistake of fact because Dextra had paid the money on the basis of a misprediction (that a loan agreement would be entered into) and not a mistake. In any event, BOJ had the defence of change of position to the claim by virtue of their reimbursement of their agents. It did not matter that that change of position was anticipatory. In the words of Lords Goff and Bingham, giving the judgment of the Privy Council:

> 'Here what is in issue is the justice or injustice of enforcing a restitutionary claim in respect of a benefit conferred. In that context, it is difficult to see what relevant distinction can be drawn between (1) a case in which the defendant expends on some extraordinary expenditure all or part of a sum of money which he has received from the plaintiff, and (2) one in which the defendant incurs such expenditure in the expectation that he will receive the sum of money from the plaintiff, which he does in fact receive. Since ex hypothesi the defendant will in fact have received the expected payment, there is no question of the defendant using the defence of change of position to enforce, directly or indirectly, a claim to that money. It is surely no abuse of language to say, in the second case as in the first, that the defendant has incurred the expenditure in reliance on the plaintiff's payment or, as is sometimes said, on the faith of the payment.'[7]

(ii) It is sometimes said (as illustrated by the previous citation) that to count as a change of position expenses incurred by the defendant must be extraordinary.[8] The ambiguity of that term can cause confusion. All that is required is that the defendant would not otherwise have incurred those expenses (ie, that they are extraordinary *to the defendant*). Whether the expenses are extra-ordinary in the sense of being used to buy luxuries as opposed to everyday items, like food and drink, is not decisive.

---

6   [2002] 1 All ER (Comm) 193. See also obiter dicta of Jonathan Parker J in *Philip Collins Ltd v Davis* [2000] 3 All ER 808, 827: '[W]hether or not a change of position may be anticipatory, it must (as I see it) have been made as a consequence of the receipt of, or (it may be) the prospect of securing, the money sought to be recovered: in other words it must, on the evidence, be referable in some way to the payment of that money.' Jewell, 'The Boundaries of Change of Position – A Comparative Study' [2000] RLR 1 draws on German law in favouring the inclusion of anticipatory change of position.
7   Ibid at p 204.
8   See also Maddaugh and McCamus, *The Law of Restitution* (1st edn, 1990), pp 232–234; Jones, 'Change of Circumstances in Quasi-Contract' (1957) 78 LQR 48, 55.

(iii) What standard of proof does the defendant need to attain in establishing change of position?[9] It is submitted that, while there is no reason to depart from the normal balance of probabilities standard, a broad-brush approach should be taken which would tend to favour defendants. This is in line with the need for change of position to be a wide defence so as to prevent too much restitution and to ensure security of receipt. It would impose an excessively onerous burden on defendants to require them, for example, to show precisely how each item of money received had been spent. In *RBC Dominion Securities Inc v Dawson*[10] the Newfoundland Court of Appeal held that, in relation to change of position consequent on a mistaken payment, while the onus of proving change of position was on the defendant, detailed evidence of expenditure by the defendant was not required. Reasonable approximation was sufficient. The Court said:

> 'The appellant argues that the respondents should have been required to submit receipts, dates of purchase, and precise amounts rather than oral evidence and estimates. Certainly the best evidence available should be provided to the court. However, to require that a private individual, who believed that she was spending her own money, prove her expenditures as if she were claiming damages in an action for negligence would be most unfair. It was the plaintiff's error that put her in the funds in the first place and led her to believe the funds were hers to spend without having to account to anyone for her expenditures... In the circumstances, the trial judge was not in error to be satisfied with reasonable approximations.'[11]

A similar approach was taken by Jonathan Parker J in *Philip Collins Ltd v Davis*.[12] Two musicians forming a backing band to the pop-star Phil Collins had been mistakenly overpaid. They successfully raised a change of position defence as regards half the overpayment on the ground that their general philosophy of life was to alter their lifestyle according to their income. It was not necessary for them to account precisely for how they had spent the money. A broad approach was to be adopted. This was approved in obiter dicta of the Court of Appeal in *Scottish Equitable plc v Derby*.[13] Robert Walker LJ said, 'I would ... accept that it may be right for the court not to apply too demanding a standard of proof when an honest defendant says that he has spent an overpayment by improving his lifestyle, but cannot produce any detailed accounting: see the observations of Jonathan Parker J in *Philip Collins Ltd v Davis* ... with which I respectfully agree.'

9   For this issue in relation to estoppel, see below, pp 535–536.
10   (1994) 111 DLR (4th) 230.
11   Ibid, at p 240.
12   [2000] 3 All ER 808.
13   [2001] EWCA Civ 369, [2001] 3 All ER 818, para 33.

(iv) What if the defendant's expenses were incurred in purchasing property which he still retains? For example, the defendant uses an overpayment of £500 to buy a television. The television could now be sold for £300. Assuming that he would not otherwise have bought the property, there are two possible lines of argument. One is that the defendant is not pecuniarily worse off to the full extent of the money spent for he retains the pecuniary value of the property: he has changed his position to the extent of the difference between what the property cost him and, in the usual case, its resale value (ie his change of position is £200). Alternatively it might be argued that, applying the strict logic of subjective devaluation through to the defence of change of position, it is irrelevant that the defendant still retains the property unless he is reasonably certain to realise its value (ie his change of position is £500): otherwise to deny the defendant a full change of position defence would force him either to sell the property or to end up paying for property that he would not otherwise have chosen to buy.

The former argument is more attractive.[14] Subjective devaluation should carry less force once the claimant has established the defendant's prima facie restitutionary liability and the focus has switched to whether there is a defence. Moreover, the defendant seeking to establish his change of position is in an analogous position to a claimant who seeks to prove his loss in order to recover compensatory damages. And in that context the duty to mitigate one's loss dictates that the claimant cannot deny that he is benefited by property that should reasonably be realised. In addition the former argument is supported by dicta of Lord Templeman (whose reasoning on the application of change of position was agreed with by a majority of the Lords) in *Lipkin Gorman v Karpnale Ltd*:[15] '... if the donee spent £20,000 in the purchase of a motor car which he would not have purchased but for the gift, it seems to me that the donee has altered his position on the faith of the gift and has only been unjustly enriched to the extent of the secondhand value of the motor car at the date when the victim of the theft seeks restitution.'[16]

14 Birks, 'Overview: Tracing, Claiming and Defences' in *Laundering and Tracing* (ed Birks, 1995), pp 289–348, 331–332 appears to favour the latter 'subjective devaluation' argument.
15 [1991] 2 AC 548, 560. Cf *RBC Dominion Securities Inc v Dawson* (1994) 111 DLR (4th) 230 where the Newfoundland Court of Appeal ignored the fact that the defendant retained the furniture bought with (and which would not have been bought but for) the overpayment. But no explanation for that was given; and the major thrust of the court's reasoning was that a broad-brush, rather than a precise, approach to change of position was appropriate.
16 Where real property has been purchased, not as an investment but to live in, the position would be different. The defendant can deny that he is benefited by the property and it would be unreasonable to require him to realise it: ie his change of position should relate to the full expenditure without a deduction for the resale value of the property.

For the avoidance of doubt it must be stressed that this issue has nothing at all to do with tracing. The claimant is not seeking to establish that he can trace to the property bought.

(v) To what extent is the fault of the defendant (or the claimant) relevant to change of position? Certainly a defendant who has changed his position in bad faith is disqualified from raising the defence. Hence Lord Goff's emphasis in *Lipkin Gorman* on good faith change of position. But is it relevant that the defendant has merely been negligent in, for example, failing to realise that he was not entitled to the benefit or in foolishly changing his position? Given that change of position is not an all or nothing defence, the defendant's 'contributory negligence' could be taken into account to reduce the relevant loss. This is the position under the New Zealand statutory defence of change of position as laid down in *Thomas v Houston Corbett & Co.*[17] A solicitor's clerk fraudulently induced the claimant firm of solicitors to pay £1,381 into the defendant's bank account as part of a scheme to convince the defendant that he was making a profit from money paid to the clerk to invest. The defendant relied on that money being his by paying a further £840 to the clerk. On discovering the fraud the claimant sought to recover its mistaken payment of £1,381 from the defendant. Applying a causation test for restitution of mistaken payments – and rejecting the need for supposed liability between payor and payee – it was held that the claimant firm was prima facie entitled to recover the money subject to the change of position defence embodied in s 94 of the Judicature Act 1908.

In 'balancing the equities' and deciding which of the parties should have spotted the fraud the New Zealand Court of Appeal held that the defendant, as a young and inexperienced doctor, was one third at fault for his change of position compared to two thirds responsibility being on the claimant solicitors. The relevant change of position was therefore reduced by a third from £840 to £560. Restitution of £821 was therefore ordered.

To give a further simple example. Say C pays D £100 by mistake. D changes its position to the tune of £80. If both parties are equally at fault then a 'contributory negligence' approach to change of position means that C would have restitution of £60 (ie, £100 – 80 + 80/2).

The same 'contributory negligence' approach was applied to the non-statutory change of position defence by the New Zealand Court of Appeal in *National Bank of New Zealand Ltd v Waitaki International Processing (NI) Ltd.*[18] Here the defendant was held to have a 90% change

17 [1969] NZLR 151.
18 [1999] 2 NZLR 211. See Grantham and Rickett, 'Change of Position and Balancing the Equities' [1999] RLR 158.

of position defence. The court compared the fault of the parties: the claimant bank's fault in making the mistaken payment and the defendant's fault in losing the money in an imprudent unsecured investment. The bank's fault was assessed at 90% and the defendant's at 10%, so that the defendant's change of position defence was reduced by 10%.

Should the English version of change of position follow the approach in New Zealand? It is submitted that the introduction of contributory negligence would involve too much uncertainty and complexity and would hamper out of court settlements. One would not want most restitution cases descending into disputes about comparative blameworthiness.

Much more difficult is whether one would want a pragmatic all-or-nothing approach to fault under which the defendant would be disqualified from the change of position defence where clearly more at fault than the claimant.[19] This was the approach favoured in the first edition of this book, which also stressed that the relevant fault of the claimant and the defendant was, respectively, avoiding making payment (or avoiding conferring another type of benefit) and avoiding relying on it as one's own.[20] A possible problem with this is that all-or-nothing approaches, by definition, tend to be conducive of some injustice; and it can be argued that, provided the defendant was acting in good faith – thereby ruling out, for example, the defendant who silently knows of the claimant's mistake[1] or who founds his change of position on criminal expenditure – there is no principled reason to exclude negligently incurred change of position.

In *Dextra Bank and Trust Ltd v Bank of Jamaica*[2] the Privy Council has rejected the relevance of the defendant's fault short of bad faith.[3] Having looked at the New Zealand cases Lords Goff and Bingham thought that the introduction of what they termed 'relative fault' would render the defence of change of position too uncertain. Their central conclusion was expressed as follows: 'Their Lordships are ... most reluctant to recognise the propriety of introducing the concept of relative fault into this branch of the common law, and indeed

---

19 Beatson and Bishop, 'Mistaken Payments in the Law of Restitution' (1986) U Toronto LJ 149 label this 'relative fault' as distinct from 'comparative fault'. The Restatement of Restitution, s 142(2) also appears to adopt a relative fault approach.

20 *The Law of Restitution* (1st edn, 1993), pp 430–431.

1 In *National Bank of New Zealand v Waitaki International Processing (NI) Ltd* [1999] 2 NZLR 211 the defendant was acting in good faith even though it knew of the claimant's mistake because it had reluctantly kept the money having told the claimant of the mistake.

2 [2002] 1 All ER (Comm) 193.

3 See also Goff and Jones, para 40-006; Birks, 'Change of Position and Surviving Enrichment' in *The Limits of Restitutionary Claims: A Comparative Analysis* (ed Swadling, 1997), p 41; Jewell, 'The Boundaries of Change of Position – A Comparative Study' [2000] RLR 1.

decline to do so.'[4] Moreover, their Lordships thought it would be very strange to examine the fault of the parties given the well-established starting point for mistaken payments that restitutionary liability is strict so that the fault of the payor does not bar restitution. With respect, this latter point is unconvincing. Strict liability goes hand-in-glove with unjust enrichment. In contrast, the issue on change of position rests on the defendant having been disenriched and it is hard to see why the same considerations as to fault should necessarily apply in relation to that issue.

Dextra has been applied in *Niru Battery Manufacturing Co v Milestone Trading Ltd*[5] in which the defence was denied because, in paying away the mistakenly paid money, the defendant was not acting in good faith albeit that it was not subjectively dishonest. Moore-Bick J said that bad faith 'is capable of embracing a failure to act in a commercially acceptable way and sharp practice of a kind that falls short of outright dishonesty as well as dishonesty itself'.[6]

(vi) Change of position will no doubt be primarily applied to mistaken payments and to money paid to the defendant without the knowledge of its owner. However, there seems no reason in principle why it should not apply as a defence in respect of any type of benefit and in respect of other unjust factors *provided* the defendant does not fall foul of the bad faith disqualification (as he often will where the unjust factor is duress, undue influence or exploitation of weakness).[7] So, for example, in *Goss v Chilcott*[8] the Privy Council accepted that change of position was a possible defence to a claim for total failure of consideration albeit that, on the facts, that defence failed.[9] Similarly in the swaps cases,[10] change of position was regarded as a possible defence irrespective of whether the ground for restitution was treated as being total failure of consideration, absence of consideration or mistake of law.

What about restitution for wrongs? Clearly change of position is irrelevant to compensation for wrongs. But the position is not so obvious in relation to restitution for wrongs assuming that the wrongdoer was not dishonest and has therefore changed his position in good faith.

---

4   [2002] 1 All ER (Comm) 193, 207.
5   [2002] EWHC 1425 (Comm), [2002] 2 All ER (Comm) 705.
6   Ibid, at para 135.
7   For change of position in the context of rescission for misrepresentation and undue influence, see above, pp 178–179, 246–247.
8   [1996] AC 788. See above, p 330.
9   Clarifying the reason why the defence failed is not easy. The defendants had been loaned money under a mortgage instrument that had been avoided. They had in turn lent the money, without security, to a third party. One possible reason for denying change of position was that the defendants were no worse off because they would otherwise have taken out a valid loan, which they would have had to repay.
10   See above, pp 397–401.

The essence of change of position is that it allows a good faith defendant to say that, although on the face of it enriched, he has as a result of the enrichment suffered 'loss' which should be taken into account in arriving at the measure of restitution. And that reasoning may be thought relevant to restitution from an innocent wrongdoer just as it is in relation to unjust enrichment by subtraction. It is true that Article 141(2) of the United States *Restatement of Resititution* says that change of position is not available to a tortfeasor. And it may be that this is what Lord Goff had in mind when in *Lipkin Gorman v Karpnale Ltd*[11] he said that 'it is commonly accepted that the defence should not be open to a wrongdoer'. But it cannot be argued that Lord Goff was definitively laying that down as the law. In the next sentence he said, 'These are matters which can, in due course, be considered in depth in cases where they arise for consideration. They do not arise in the present case. Here there is no doubt that the respondents have acted in good faith throughout, and the action is not founded upon any wrongdoing of the respondents.'

Obiter dicta of Lord Nicholls in *Kuwait Airways Corpn v Iraqi Airways Co (Nos 4 and 5)*[12] are also inconclusive. While, on the face of it, his Lordship appeared to suggest that change of position applied to restitution for the tort of conversion, it is possible to interpret what he was saying as dealing with unjust enrichment by subtraction not restitution for wrongs.

In considering whether it is at least arguable that change of position is applicable in respect of restitution for wrongs, it might help to focus on an example. D buys a painting from X, who is a rogue and has stolen the painting from C. D has been honest and indeed has acted reasonably. She sells the painting at well above its market price for £10,000. She then uses that money to take a once-in-a-lifetime holiday. C brings an action in the tort of conversion against D and claims £10,000 in an action for money had and received. D wishes to raise the defence of change of position to the restitutionary claim for the conversion on the ground that she changed her position in honest reliance on that money being hers and has, therefore, 'lost' the enrichment.

The academic discussion of this question tends to the view that change of position should be available in this sort of situation.[13] For example, Goff and Jones[14] give as an illustration of where change of position may be invoked, other than in respect of mistaken payments, a claim based

11 [1991] 2 AC 548, 580.
12 [2002] UKHL 19, [2002] 2 WLR 1353, para 79.
13 In addition to the views cited below see Philip Hellwege, 'The Scope of Application of Change of Position in the Law of Unjust Enrichment: A Comparative Study' [1999] RLR 92, esp 96–100.
14 At para 40-002, n 26.

on an innocent breach of confidence. They write, 'A defendant who did not know and ought not to have known that he was betraying another's confidence acts honestly. In our view, a court should allow him to rely on the defence of change of position. A defendant who is honest but ought to have known of the breach of confidence should also be allowed to invoke the defence, for he has acted in good faith.'[15] And later they suggest that an innocent converter, who is sued for the proceeds of the conversion, should be able to invoke the defence.[16]

Richard Nolan, in his essay 'Change of Position', writes the following:[17]

> '[N]ot all ... wrongs involve fault, or some turpitude or want of probity on the part of the defendant: eg, a claim for an account of profits from a fiduciary does not necessarily entail any wickedness on the part of the fiduciary. Now if an innocent fiduciary, obliged to make restitution in respect of profits made in breach of duty, can be awarded an allowance for his skill by way of counter-restitution (as in *Boardman v Phipps*[18]) then, assuming Lord Goff has not ruled out any application of change of position in the context of restitution for wrongs, it would seem odd if the law could take into account the defendant's conferring of a benefit on the plaintiff, but be unable to take into account any other way in which the defendant had changed his position: both the allowance and the defence are directed to ensuring that the defendant is not worse off in consequence of making restitution to the plaintiff. Perhaps then, change of position may have a very limited role to play in the context of restitution for wrongs, where the wrong in question is a wrong as a matter of law only.'

Similarly, Virgo argues that change of position may be a defence to restitution for a wrong depending on whether the wrong was committed in bad faith or not.[19]

Finally, Andrew Tettenborn writes that he regards Lord Goff's statement in *Lipkin Gorman* as a little difficult to understand: and that a blanket refusal to apply change of position to restitution for wrongs is neither necessary nor desirable. He points to an innocent wrongdoer, such as the unwitting converter and continues, 'It is hard to see why he should not have the benefit of the defence if the claimant chooses to waive the tort and sue for money had and received.'[20]

Pitted against these views, is the argument that change of position is inextricably bound up with the cause of action of unjust enrichment

---

15   Ibid, at para 34-017.
16   Ibid, at para 40-009.
17   In *Laundering and Tracing* (ed Birks, 1995), p 135 at 154.
18   [1967] 2 AC 46.
19   Virgo, 'What is the Law of Restitution About?' in *Restitution: Past, Present and Future* (eds Cornish, Nolan, O'Sullivan and Virgo), p 305 at p 321 and *The Principles of the Law of Restitution* (1999), pp 470, 727.
20   *The Law of Restitution in England and Ireland* (3rd edn, 2002), p 278.

alone: that the security of receipt that change of position is designed to ensure is not relevant to restitution for wrongs. That, in other words, the cause of action of unjust enrichment requires a reversal of a transfer of wealth for reasons that do not relate to the need to 'remedy' a wrong. On this argument, change of position operates to counter the non-wrongful transfer of wealth but cannot ever outweigh the policies justifying restitution for a wrong.[1]

At the present stage in the law's development – and particularly in the light of the different possible arguments – the safest conclusion is that it is unclear whether change of position can ever apply to restitution for wrongs.

(vii) Although there has, as yet, been no case law on the point, in principle change of position should apply in respect of proprietary as well as personal restitutionary remedies.[2] Proprietary restitution is justifiably triggered by the defendant's unjust enrichment at the claimant's expense; therefore to ignore the defendant's change of position in relation to proprietary restitution would be to ignore a fundamental aspect of the explanation and justification of proprietary restitution. In other words, whether the response to unjust enrichment is personal or proprietary should not affect the central elements of the unjust enrichment enquiry. It would also produce the oddity that a claimant would be presented with the opportunity to outflank the change of position defence by invoking proprietary, rather than personal, restitution. Say, for example, C mistakenly pays D £5,000. D buys shares with that money. Relying on his new financial security, D then treats himself to a holiday for £1,000. D is clearly entitled to raise the change of position defence to C's personal claim for £5,000. It would be odd if C could avoid the change of position defence by instead bringing a proprietary claim to the shares. This is because the best explanation of that proprietary claim is that it is concerned to reverse D's unjust enrichment at C's expense.[3]

It is submitted that the position would be different if C was bringing a pure proprietary claim or was claiming compensatory damages for conversion. Such claims are not triggered by unjust enrichment and are therefore not diminished by the change of position defence. Indeed this is the most important practical reason why the House of Lords in *Foskett v McKeown*[4] can be criticised for relying on pure

---

1   This view is favoured by Birks, 'Overview: Tracing, Claiming and Defences' in *Laundering and Tracing* (ed Birks, 1995), pp 289, 325–326.

2   See Birks, 'Overview: Tracing, Claiming and Defences' in *Laundering and Tracing* (ed Birks, 1995), pp 289, 319–322, 326–327; Goff and Jones, paras 2-042 to 2-043, 40-006; Hanbury and Martin, *Modern Equity* (16th edn, 2001), pp 701–703. See also the discussion of *Re Diplock* [1948] Ch 465, above, pp 96–97.

3   See above, pp 64–66, 81, 207–210.

4   [2001] 1 AC 102. See above, pp 64–66, 81, 101–102, 207–210.

proprietary (rather than restitutionary proprietary) reasoning to explain the proprietary claim following tracing. That reasoning would produce the incorrect result in relation to the change of position defence.

How does one give effect to *pro tanto* change of position in relation to proprietary restitution? Where the remedy in question is an equitable lien there is no difficulty. The lien affords a security interest over particular property in relation to a particular sum of money and there is no difficulty in reducing the sum of money secured to take account of the change of position. In the example given above, the lien would therefore secure £4,000 rather than £5,000. More difficult is where the remedy in question is a (sole or proportionate) beneficial interest in property. For example, C may be given equitable ownership of shares. That interest cannot be reduced by a fixed amount to reflect the defendant's change of position. However, there seems no reason why the claim to a beneficial interest should not be made conditional on C paying D a fixed amount equivalent to D's change of position. So in the example above, C may be given beneficial ownership of the shares subject to his paying D £1,000. The imposition of terms on a claimant seeking a remedy is well-established in relation to equitable remedies, such as rescission[5] and specific performance,[6] and there seems no reason why it should not be applied here.

It follows that in *Re Diplock*,[7] if the claimants had been able to trace their money to new, or improved, buildings (it was held, incorrectly, that such tracing was not possible),[8] the defendant should have had a change of position defence.[9] But for the receipt of the money the buildings would not have been built or improved and the outlay could not now be recouped.

There is a final important point in relation to change of position and proprietary restitution. One must be careful to distinguish between two separate questions. The first is whether the enrichment traceably survives. This depends on the rules of tracing and has nothing to do with the defence of change of position. If the property has been lost or destroyed, tracing is not possible and one does not need to consider change of position as a defence to a proprietary claim. However, if the enrichment traceably survives, a second question is whether the defendant has a change of position defence to a proprietary claim to

---

5   Eg *Cooper v Phibbs* (1862) LR 2 HL 149.
6   Eg *Re Fawcett and Holmes' Contract* (1889) 42 Ch D 150; *Harvela Investments Ltd v Royal Trust Co of Canada Ltd* [1986] AC 207, HL. See generally Burrows, *Remedies for Torts and Breach of Contract* (2nd edn, 1994), pp 383–385.
7   [1948] Ch 465, 545–548, CA.
8   See above, pp 96–97.
9   Goff and Jones, para 2-042. See above, p 97.

that traced property. The fact that the enrichment traceably survives does not mean that no change of position defence is possible. So, in the example above, the enrichment traceably survives in the shares and yet D can still invoke the change of position defence because, in reliance on having the shares, he has spent money on a holiday that he would not otherwise have bought. The distinction between tracing and change of position is also shown by the fact that property may not be traceably surviving and yet the defendant may be unable to establish a change of position defence. For example, the money received by the defendant may have been expended by him on paying off debts that he would in any event have had to pay. Although there is then no traceably surviving property, the defendant cannot establish a change of position defence.

2. ESTOPPEL

The long-awaited recognition of a change of position defence has reduced the importance of estoppel, the essence of which is that the defendant has detrimentally relied on a representation by the claimant that the benefit is his to keep. Nevertheless estoppel still merits examination for two reasons. First, it has a long pedigree and the case law may be of assistance in working out what is meant by change of position for the 'straight' defence. Secondly, and more importantly, estoppel may afford a defendant a better defence than change of position because it has been laid down that it is an all or nothing, rather than a *pro tanto*, defence.

Estoppel has never been applied as a restitutionary defence other than to a mistaken payment. Factually it is no doubt extremely rare for a claimant to make a representation that a benefit belongs to a defendant outside the context of mistaken payments. Moreover, a defendant who has made his gain by wrongdoing or who has induced a payment by duress or undue influence or exploitation of weakness may be ruled out from relying on estoppel because of his bad faith. But there is no compelling reason why estoppel cannot be used as a defence to autonomous unjust factors, like failure of consideration or legal compulsion, and in respect of benefits in kind as well as money.

(1) Is a breach of duty necessary as well as a representation?

An initial and difficult question emerging from the case law on estoppel, is when, if at all, is it necessary to show a breach of a duty of accuracy (ie, special fault) by the claimant.

In *RE Jones Ltd v Waring and Gillow Ltd*[10] and *Weld-Blundell v Synott*[11] the estoppel defence failed on the ground that there was no such breach of duty. In the former, the claimants had been tricked by a rogue into paying £5,000 to the defendants under a contract with the rogue. In allowing the claimants restitution of the mistaken payment, the House of Lords (by a 3–2 majority) held that there could be no defence of estoppel because there was no breach of duty owed by the claimants to the defendants in making the overpayment. In the latter, the claimants, who were first mortgagees enforcing their security over mortgaged property, were bound after satisfying their own debt to pay over any surplus to the defendant, the second mortgagee, to go towards what the mortgagor owed to him. The claimants miscalculated their own entitlement and hence paid over too much surplus to the defendant. In allowing the claimants restitution and rejecting estoppel Asquith J said, 'When the decisions as to estoppel in connection with payment of money under a mistake of fact are closely examined, much seems to turn on whether the payor was subject to a duty as against the payee to inform him of the true state of the account – in effect, a duty not to make a mistake of fact in that regard.'[12]

In contrast in the earlier case of *Holt v Markham*[13] estoppel was successfully invoked without any requirement of a breach of duty. On the demobilisation of the RAF after the First World War the government paymasters overpaid the defendant officer because they failed to appreciate that those officers on the Emergency List, including the defendant, were entitled to less than if not on that list. Their restitutionary claim failed because the mistake was one of law not fact and, in any event, because of estoppel. Bankes and Warrington LJJ thought that the two and a half months' delay, before the claimants replied to a letter of the defendant's on a matter concerning the payment, constituted a sufficient representation that the money was the defendant's; while Scrutton LJ considered that, irrespective of the letter, the time lag since the original payment was itself a sufficient representation to that effect. None of the judges made any mention of there needing to be a breach of duty of accuracy by the payor, although on the facts there presumably was such a breach of duty: the paymasters had the better means of knowing the sum to which the defendant was entitled.

In other early cases breach of duty was regarded as an alternative to, rather than an essential ingredient of, estoppel. For example, in

10   [1926] AC 670.
11   [1940] 2 KB 107.
12   Ibid, pp 114–115.
13   [1923] 1 KB 504. See also Kerr J's dicta in *National Westminster Bank Ltd v Barclays Bank International Ltd* [1975] QB 654, 676.

Skyring v Greenwood[14] an army officer had for three years been paid too much by the army paymasters. On his death they deducted the overpayments from what was owed to him. The deceased's administratrix sought to recover the amount deducted and this in turn depended on whether the defendant paymasters could have recovered the overpayments from the deceased as money paid by mistake. It was held that they could not because the deceased had changed his mode of living in the induced belief that his income was higher than it was; and the defendants were in breach of duty in allowing the overpayments to continue for three years after they had been told by the Board of Ordnance that the deceased was not entitled to that extra money. However the court indicated that it did not regard that defence of the deceased as one of estoppel.

Similarly, in *Deutsche Bank v Beriro & Co*[15] the claimants, mistakenly believing that money payable under a bill of exchange in favour of one Benatar had been paid to their agents, informed the defendants (who were collecting the money for payment over to Benatar) that they had been paid the money and paid the amount to the defendants. The defendants in turn paid it to Benatar. It was held that the claimants could not recover the mistaken payment from the defendants either because they had been in breach of duty to the defendants *or* because of estoppel grounded on the claimants' representation that the bill had been met and the defendants' change of position on the faith of that representation.

The key to the reconciliation of those apparently conflicting authorities on whether a breach of duty is necessary is that where the payor owes a duty to the payee to pay over the correct money there is a factual representation inherent in the payment that that is money owed to the defendant. In contrast, most payments do not carry an inherent factual representation that the payee is entitled to the payment and the defendant therefore needs to show a representation collateral to the payment if he is to make out an estoppel.[16] The reconciling picture is therefore that there must be either a breach of duty, and hence an inherent representation, or a collateral representation.

It follows that in *Holt v Markham* and *Deutsche Bank v Beriro* there was no need to find a breach of duty because there were collateral representations on which to found the estoppel, whereas this was not so in *Weld-Blundell v Synott* and arguably not so in *Skyring v Greenwood* and *Jones v Waring*. And while the older cases treat as distinct breach

---

14   (1825) 4 B & C 281.
15   (1895) 73 LT 669.
16   Cf Birks, at pp 402–407.

of duty and estoppel, the view in the later cases that the one defence of estoppel is in issue is preferable; it is because the representation is inherent in the payment where there is a breach of duty that it may superficially appear that breach of duty alone is important.

What remains puzzling is the reasoning in *Weld-Blundell v Synott* to the effect that the first mortgagees were not in breach of duty in paying over the incorrect sum to the second mortgagee. As between the mortgagees what was owed to the first mortgagees by the mortgagor was in the exclusive knowledge of the first mortgagees. If the notion of a duty of accuracy is to be at all intelligible, there was surely a duty on the first mortgagees to pay over the correct amount to the second mortgagee.

(2) Detrimental reliance

Assuming that there is a representation that the defendant is entitled to the payment, whether inherent in or collateral to the payment, the other essential requirement of an estoppel is that the defendant has detrimentally relied (changed his position in reliance) on the representation.[17]

Beatson and Bishop have identified three meanings of detrimental reliance.[18] 'Conventional reliance' which requires simply that the defendant has spent or committed the money in a way which cannot be recouped. 'Out of pocket reliance' which requires that the defendant has spent or committed the money in a way which cannot be recouped and in a way which he would not otherwise have done. And 'real reliance' which brings into account against out of pocket reliance the additional benefit the defendant has derived from spending the money in the way in which he would not otherwise have done.

Of these the first ignores the need for loss to have been caused to the defendant by the representation: if he would have spent his money in the same way anyway he has been saved expense and therefore cannot be said to have suffered any detriment as a result of the representation. The third requires an impossible assessment into subjective values. Indeed, on one view, taking account of subjective values simply cancels out the expenditure on the reasoning that any exchange is worth to the defendant what he paid for it. It is clear therefore that the law must take the 'out of

---

17   As with the change of position defence, so with estoppel, the change of position/detrimental reliance must have been incurred in good faith: *United Overseas Bank v Jiwani* [1976] 1 WLR 964; below, p 533.

18   'Mistaken Payments in the Law of Restitution' (1986) 36 U Toronto LJ 149, 151–152.

pocket reliance' view.[19] So to establish an estoppel, the defendant must show that, if he were now required to pay back the money, he would be in a worse position *pecuniarily* than if the representation and payment had not been made to him in the first place.

Taking the main cases in which estoppel was successfully invoked to deny restitution the detrimental reliance was clear in *Holt v Markham* and *Deutsche Bank v Beriro*. In the former the defendant had used some of the money paid to make a bad investment and in the latter the defendant had paid the money over to Benatar and could not now recover it. In *Skyring v Greenwood* the detrimental reliance was less clear-cut but the court was prepared almost to presume it, Abbott CJ saying, 'Every prudent man accommodates his mode of living to what he supposes to be his income: it therefore works a great injustice to any man if, having been allowed to draw on his agent on the faith that those sums belonged to him, he may be called upon to pay them back.'[20]

On the other side of the fence stands *United Overseas Bank v Jiwani*.[1] The claimant bank had there mistakenly credited the defendant's account with $11,000. The defendant had used the money to pay for a hotel which he would in any event have bought and was, moreover, a good investment. It was therefore held that – even if the defendant had in good faith been misled by the representation that the money was his, which Mocatta J thought he had not been – he had not changed his position and hence must repay $11,000.

(3) All or nothing?

A controversial question – and one which may determine whether estoppel has any role to play in the post *Lipkin Gorman* world – is whether estoppel can operate as a partial rather than a total defence. That is, if the defendant's detrimental reliance on the representation is less than the money paid, can the claimant recover the surplus? Or does detrimental reliance on the representation to any degree (provided not *de minimis*) give the defendant a complete defence?

The leading case is *Avon County Council v Howlett*.[2] The defendant had been mistakenly overpaid £1,007 sick pay. Although the Court of Appeal was satisfied that the defendant had detrimentally relied on the claimant's representation to the extent of the full amount paid, his pleaded case – for the purpose of making this a test case – merely

19 This is also the approach for proprietary and promissory estoppel.
20 (1825) 4 B & C 281, 289.
1   [1976] 1 WLR 964.
2   [1983] 1 WLR 605.

alleged detrimental reliance of £546.61 based on the fact that the defendant had not claimed the additional social security benefits that he would otherwise have claimed and had bought a car on hire-purchase and a suit which he would not otherwise have done. Assuming a mistake of fact rather than law (which the Court of Appeal thought was narrowly established)[3] could the claimant recover the balance of £460.39?

Cumming-Bruce LJ refused to decide a question not raised by the true facts but Slade and Eveleigh LJJ held that estoppel operates as a total defence only so that, even on the facts as pleaded, the claimant could not recover any of its mistaken payment. Slade LJ argued that this followed as a matter of principle from the nature of estoppel by representation as a rule of evidence 'the consequence of which is simply to preclude the representor from averring facts contrary to his own representation'.[4] If the representation is 'this £500 is yours', estoppel prevents the payor denying that the £500 validly belongs to the payee. As the statement is non-divisible so must be the defence.

There are three possible counter-arguments to that line of reasoning. The first is that it may be doubted whether estoppel by representation should be seen as a rule of evidence rather than a substantive legal principle. One would surely not want to describe promissory estoppel, for example, as a rule of evidence whatever its historical origins. And as a substantive principle it is accepted by the judges in *Avon* that the just solution would be to allow estoppel to operate in a *pro tanto* way.

Secondly, even playing the artificial 'rule of evidence game' one can argue, somewhat artificially perhaps, that a single representation is divisible into separate internal representations or parts, so that while the claimant in *Avon* was estopped from denying the statement (or that part of the statement) that £546.61 belonged to the defendant, he should have been free to deny the statement (or that part of the statement) that £460.39 belonged to the defendant. The argument is less artificial where, as in *Avon*, there are continuing payments and hence clearly more than one possible representation.

Thirdly, there is what was referred to by Robert Walker LJ in *Scottish Equitable plc v Derby*[5] as the 'novel and ingenious argument' of junior counsel in that case. According to this, if the payor limits its restitutionary claim by deducting the payee's change of position – or if one applies a change of position defence alongside estoppel – the

---

3   After *Kleinwort Benson Ltd v Lincoln City Council* [1999] 2 AC 349, it would no longer matter whether the mistake was one of law or fact.
4   [1983] 1 WLR 605, 622.
5   [2001] EWCA Civ 369, [2001] 3 All ER 818, para 45.

payee cannot establish the *detrimental* reliance needed for estoppel. That is, if the payee's change of position has been deducted, the payee cannot establish that it will be any worse off if it is now required to make restitution than if the payment had not been made in the first place. The argument, as Robert Walker LJ put it, is that 'the defence of change of position pre-empts and disables the defence of estoppel by negativing detriment'.[6] While Robert Walker LJ preferred to rest his decision on other grounds, it is strongly arguable that he was correct to regard this argument as 'convincing'.[7]

Having knocked out a *pro tanto* estoppel in form Slade LJ in *Avon* left open the question whether estoppel could operate *pro tanto* in substance by making its application conditional on the defendant's undertaking to repay a certain sum to the claimant, a course considered appropriate by Viscount Cave LC, with whom Lord Atkinson agreed, in his dissenting judgment in *RE Jones Ltd v Waring and Gillow Ltd*.[8] And Eveleigh LJ, without explaining how this would fit in with his denial of a *pro tanto* estoppel, baldly said, '... there may be circumstances which would render it unconscionable for the defendant to retain a balance in his hands'.[9] Presumably it was the hypothetical nature of the facts which made it unnecessary for the judges to tie up those loose ends.

One other point touched on in the judgments in *Avon* is whether a *pro tanto* approach would be too harsh on a defendant in requiring him to prove the exact extent of his detrimental reliance in order to resist restitution. Indeed Cumming-Bruce LJ suggested in obiter that, once the defendant had proved any detrimental reliance on a representation, the burden of proof would switch to the claimant who would need to plead facts showing why it would be unjust for the defendant to retain part of the money paid by mistake. In terms of principle, however, it would seem only right that the defendant is put to the burden of proving the extent of his detrimental reliance. The starting point, after all, is that he has been unjustly enriched by the receipt of the money, and it should be for him to establish the extent to which he has lost that benefit. There is no reason to think that the

---

6   Ibid, at 830.
7   Ibid, at 831. For the counter-arguments, see Fung and Ho, 'Establishing Estoppel after the Recognition of Change of Position' [2001] RLR 52, 54–55. While it is true that the defendant cannot be prevented from raising only the defence of estoppel and not change of position, the real force of the argument is that the payor can itself deduct the payee's detriment from its claim. But note that this was possible even prior to the recognition of the change of position defence; and, if valid, it would also be a means for a promisor to restrict liability under proprietary or promissory estoppel to protection of the promisee's reliance (rather than expectation) interest.
8   [1926] AC 670. As we have seen above, the majority decided that there was no estoppel because there was no breach of duty.
9   [1983] 1 WLR 605, 612.

normal balance of probabilities standard would require the defendant to account precisely for every last penny in order to prove the extent of his detrimental reliance.

There is no doubt that the defence of change of position recognised in *Lipkin Gorman* can operate *pro tanto* and is therefore a more flexible and just defence. Indeed Lord Goff referred to the all or nothing reasoning of *Avon County Council v Howlett* as one argument for accepting change of position. But short of taking a very radical and forced interpretation of Lord Goff's speech, the House of Lords has not wiped out estoppel as a restitutionary defence. It follows that, unless ways round *Avon* are utilised – including the 'novel and ingenious' third counter-argument considered above – the unsatisfactory result remains that, despite *Lipkin Gorman*, a defendant can avoid *pro tanto* change of position by establishing estoppel.

Cases subsequent to *Lipkin Gorman* have accepted that all or nothing estoppel survives but have then relied on the unconscionability exception in *Avon* to escape from the consequences of that conclusion.

In *Scottish Equitable plc v Derby*[10] the defendant had a pension policy with the claimant, Scottish Equitable. In 1989 he had exercised an option to take early retirement benefit under that policy so that he was paid £36,588 and £4,655 per annum. This left about £50,000 to be paid under the pension. Five years later on his 65th birthday he was told by Scottish Equitable that his pension was worth £201,938. Scottish Equitable had mistakenly forgotten about his earlier exercise of the option. In truth, his pension was worth £29,486. The defendant queried the matter but the higher figure was confirmed to be correct, orally and in writing; and the Scottish Equitable went ahead and paid him the £201,938, which was an overpayment of £172,500. The defendant, who was held to be naïve but honest, spent £9,600 on modest improvements in his lifestyle; £41,700 in reducing his mortgage; and invested the £121,100 in a pension which would pay him annually £11,000 more than he would otherwise have been paid.

A year later, the Scottish Equitable realised its mistake and sought to recover the overpayment less the £9,600 which it conceded fell within the change of position defence. The Court of Appeal, upholding Harrison J, held that its claim to £162,900 should succeed. The £41,700 that the defendant used to pay the mortgage did not constitute a change of position because that was a debt that he had had to pay anyway. So he was no worse off by having paid it. And the £121,000 paid into the pension could now be unwound without difficulty leaving the defendant with the same pension entitlement he would have had had he not been overpaid.

10   [2001] EWCA Civ 369, [2001] 3 All ER 818.

Most importantly, the Court of Appeal held that the defendant could not here rely on estoppel – constituted by his detrimental reliance on the claimant's representation that he was entitled to the money – so as to give him a total defence. This was on the basis that, although *Avon* remained good law unless and until overruled by the House of Lords, the facts of this case fell comfortably within its unconscionability exception.

The same approach was taken in *National Westminster Bank plc v Somer International (UK) Ltd*[11] where the claimant bank mistakenly credited the defendant's account to the tune of some US$76,708. The defendant was expecting a payment from a customer called Mentor and was led to believe by the claimant's representation that that was the sum being credited to its account. As a result, the defendant despatched goods to Mentor to the value of £13,180. The Court of Appeal rejected the defendant's argument that it had a complete estoppel defence to the claim for restitution and instead awarded restitution of the difference between US$76,708 and £13,180. In line with *Scottish Equitable plc v Derby* the unconscionability exception in *Avon* was applied so that, in substance if not in form, the estoppel operated *pro tanto*. In the words of Peter Gibson LJ, '[T]he circumstances here … are such that the disparity between the $76,708 mistakenly credited to Somer and £13,180, being the value of goods dispatched by Somer in reliance on the Bank's representation, makes it unconscionable and inequitable for Somer to retain the balance.'[12]

But in practice – and leaving to one side where there is an insignificant, *de minimis*, difference between the value of the defendant's change of position and the payment received – it will surely *always* be unjust and unconscionable for the defendant to retain a balance. In other words, the *Avon* exception swallows up its all or nothing rule. Estoppel will always, by this means, operate in a *pro tanto* fashion. The cleaner approach would be to recognise this and to clarify that, in contrast to change of position, the all or nothing estoppel defence is in this context inapt and should be excised.

This was the approach favoured by the Newfoundland Court of Appeal in *RBC Dominion Securities v Dawson*.[13] In the light of the acceptance of change of position in Canada in *Storthoaks Rural Municipality v Mobil Oil Canada Ltd*[14] Cameron JA said, 'To make the estoppel defence one which operates pro tanto would be inconsistent with the most commonly accepted view of estoppel: that it is a rule of evidence which prevents evidence of the event which resulted in the change of circumstances

11 [2001] EWCA Civ 970, [2002] 1 All ER 198.
12 Ibid, at para 68.
13 (1994) 111 DLR (4th) 230. See also *Philip Collins Ltd v Davis* [2000] 3 All ER 808, 826.
14 (1975) 55 DLR (3d) 1.

from being considered. We conclude that estoppel is no longer an appropriate method of dealing with the problem.'[15]

One can regard this controversy about all or nothing estoppel as turning on which aspect of the unjust enrichment principle estoppel relates to. On the one hand, the requirement of detrimental reliance seems to be concerned with the defendant's loss of the benefit received (ie, *enrichment*). Viewed in this way estoppel should wither away because its all or nothing approach is too inflexible in comparison with change of position.

On the other hand, one could regard estoppel as relating to the *injustice* of an enrichment. The claimant's mistake, while prima facie rendering the enrichment *unjust*, is cancelled out by its detrimentally relied upon representation that the money belongs to the defendant. Hence the traditional explanation that estoppel prevents the claimant averring facts contrary to those represented. Ie, *the claimant cannot establish that it was mistaken.*

The former view is to be preferred. The latter resorts to artificiality in explaining why the unjust factor is overridden. No one suggests that the representation per se cancels out the injustice and it is submitted that by requiring detrimental reliance the essence of the defence is focused on the defendant's loss of benefit.

This, of course, is not to suggest that estoppel should disappear in the many other areas of law in which it applies. Rather the argument is that in the law of restitution, in contrast to those other areas, the injustice that estoppel is concerned to prevent is entirely, and more appropriately, achieved by another defence, namely change of position.

3.   COUNTER-RESTITUTION

(1) The nature of this defence

Where a contract is rescinded for, for example, undue influence or misrepresentation, the claimant's entitlement to restitution is subject to the claimant making 'counter-restitution' to the defendant for the benefits the claimant has received from the defendant.[16] Similarly, where restitution of money has been awarded under a void contract, there has been an insistence that the claimant gives counter-restitution of the money it has received from the defendant.[17]

---

15 (1994) 111 DLR (4th) 230, 237. See also Key, 'Excising Estoppel by Representation as a Defence to Restitution' [1995] CLJ 525.

16 See above, pp 176–178, 245–246.

17 As in, eg, *Westdeutsche Landesbank Girozentrale v Islington London Borough Council* [1996] AC 669: see above, pp 397–401.

This requirement of counter-restitution is probably best regarded as a defence. It has traditionally been viewed as a total defence where counter-restitution is impossible; and this will presumably also be so where the claimant refuses to make counter-restitution or where payments have passed both ways and the sum paid by the claimant to the defendant is matched by the sum paid by the defendant to the claimant. Counter-restitution will be a partial defence where sums paid by the claimant to the defendant are greater than the sums paid by the defendant to the claimant so that the claimant is entitled merely to the difference between the two.

The requirement of counter-restitution appears to be an unjust-related defence which rests on recognising that the defendant has a counter-claim for the claimant's unjust enrichment at the defendant's expense grounded most obviously on total failure of consideration. That is, the basis upon which the defendant rendered benefits to the claimant has been removed by the rescission and consequent restitution for the claimant or, in a void contract, by the restitution of money paid by the claimant to the defendant. On this approach, to treat counter-restitution as a defence may therefore be doing nothing more than applying the general law that a counter-claim may operate as a set-off defence.

An alternative approach is that counter-restitution is not an unjust-related defence but rather is an enrichment-related defence. It dictates that a claimant is merely entitled to restitution of the defendant's net enrichment having taken into account the enrichment the claimant has itself received from the defendant.

The difference between these two approaches turns on whether the defendant has to establish all the elements of a counter-claim for unjust enrichment against the claimant in order to be entitled to counter-restitution. At first instance in *Kleinwort Benson Ltd v Sandwell Borough Council*[18] Hobhouse J held that counter-restitution had to be made even in respect of payments that the defendant had made over six years before the commencement of proceedings. He said, 'As is implicit in the action for money had and received on the ground of unjust enrichment ... the claim cannot be asserted without at the same time giving credit for any payments received. As a matter of the principle of unjust enrichment, the defendant has only been enriched in the net sum and the enrichment has only been at the expense of the plaintiff in the net sum.'[19] Hobhouse J appeared, therefore, to think that counter-restitution was solely concerned with the enrichment element and he did not require the defendant to establish

18   [1994] 4 All ER 890.
19   Ibid, at 941.

that a counter-claim would have succeeded. It should be emphasised, however, that counter-claims and set-offs can be raised outside the limitation period by reason of section 35(3) of the Limitation Act 1980. In other words, it appears that seeing the counter-restitution as a standard set-off would have led to the same result.

The two alternative approaches would appear to give different results where there is a change of position defence to a restitutionary counterclaim. Take two situations where money has been mistakenly paid both ways. In situation one, C pays D £1,000 and D pays C £800. D has not changed its position. C has changed its position to the tune of £800. Applying the counter-claim approach, D has no counter-claim against C because C has a total defence of change of position. So C would be entitled to restitution of £1,000 from D and D would be left to bear the loss of £800. In contrast, if one regarded counter-restitution as concerned with D's net enrichment, in line with Hobhouse J's approach, C would be merely entitled to the net sum of £1,000 minus £800, that is £200. In situation two, C pays D £1,000 and D pays C £800. D has not changed its position. C has changed its position to the tune of £600. Applying the counter-claim approach, D has a counter-claim of £200 against C because C has a partial, but not a total, defence of change of position. So C would be entitled to restitution of £800 from D, and D would be left to bear the loss of £600. In contrast, on Hobhouse J's approach, C would again be merely entitled to the net sum of £1,000 minus £800, that is £200.

Perhaps the major difficulty with Hobhouse J's net enrichment approach is that, in itself, it lacks justificatory force. It fails to answer the question, why should the claimant be restricted to the defendant's net enrichment?

That question links closely to another. What is the relationship between the change of position defence and counter-restitution?[20] Change of position is in one sense wider than counter-restitution because it covers all loss to the defendant irrespective of whether that loss has comprised the conferring of a benefit on the claimant. Indeed once one accepts that even anticipatory change of position counts, it may appear that change of position is sufficiently wide to swallow up counter-restitution entirely. Even if that were true it may be thought to aid clarity to treat the defences separately and to consider whether, and how, counter-restitution applies before going on to the change of position defence.[1] But, in any event, there is one important respect in which counter-restitution is significantly different from, and in this sense wider than, change of position. Unlike change of position,

---

20 See above, pp 178–179, 246–247.
1   See, eg, the analysis of *Cheese v Thomas* [1994] 1 WLR 129, above, at pp 246–247.

counter-restitution applies irrespective of the bad faith of the defendant. For example, where a claimant rescinds a contract for the fraud of the defendant, the claimant is still bound to make counter-restitution of benefits received from the defendant even though the defendant was acting in bad faith. One explanation for this is that, contrary to Hobhouse J's approach and change of position, counter-restitution is concerned not only with the defendant's disenrichment but also with *the claimant's* unjust enrichment (ie it is unjust-related and recognises a restitutionary counterclaim).

(2) Counter-restitution impossible

We have seen that traditionally counter-restitution has been regarded as a total defence where counter-restitution is impossible: hence the traditional bar to rescission of *restitutio in integrum* being impossible.[2]

Strictly speaking, however, it is a nonsense to suggest that restitution may be impossible. Personal restitution is always possible. What seems traditionally to have been in mind is that to avoid having to make difficult restitutionary assessments for *non-money benefits* it is better for neither party to have restitution where such benefits are in issue. Leaving the parties as they stand achieves a rough-and-ready mutual restitution. This is similar to the main policy underlying the traditional insistence that failure of consideration be total not partial.

This is not an appealing approach.[3] The courts are capable of assessing non-money benefits and, while imprecision may save time, it is at the expense of justice. Since at least as far back as *Erlanger v New Sombero Phosphate Co*[4] the bar has in practice been applied so as to allow some monetary equivalent to be awarded where precise restitution was impossible. And in *O'Sullivan v Management Agency & Music Ltd*[5] this approach was taken even further, with complex monetary restitutionary assessments for both parties being made. This can be seen as mirroring the rejection of the need for a total failure of consideration, and the consequent introduction of a regime of complex mutual restitution, in the Law Reform (Frustrated Contracts) Act 1943. In reality, the notion of counter-restitution being impossible is no longer at the heart of this defence. Rather the defence (which may be total or partial) requires the claimant to make (or to deduct from its own claim) counter-restitution whether in specie or by money:

2   See above, pp 176–178, 245–246.
3   Ibid. See also the articles by McKendrick and Birks referred to above, p 336, n 13.
4   (1878) 3 App Cas 1218.
5   [1985] QB 428. Above, pp 245–246.

in exceptional circumstances the claimant should also compensate the defendant for a deterioration of the property restored.

As has been discussed in chapter 5, counter-restitution is generally not required – and hence it is usually no bar that *restitutio in integrum* is impossible – where the claimant rescinds a contract for duress. This is because it would generally contradict the basis for the claimant's restitution. If it was illegitimate for the defendant to demand a sum of money for a particular consideration, eg carrying out work, it would be plainly inconsistent to award the defendant counter-restitution for that work. Similarly, as has been fully discussed in chapters 7 and 12 respectively, counter-restitution may also not be required where a party is entitled to 'rescind' an illegal contract because he belongs to a vulnerable class that the illegality is designed to protect or by withdrawing during the *locus poenitentiae*.[6]

4. LIMITATION[7]

(1) Introduction

There are several justifications for a limitation defence. Fairness to the defendant requires that, after a certain period of time, he should be free from the worry of a legal action hanging over him and should be secure in the knowledge that what he has he can keep. Oral evidence becomes less reliable the longer the period since the event and this makes the decision-making process more prone to arbitrariness. Limitation periods also act as an incentive to claimants not to sit on their claims but to pursue them as quickly as possible.

Given the validity of these policies, what is the best general approach to limitation? The common law approach has basically been to provide fixed limitation periods running from the accrual of the cause of action. This has the merit of certainty. In contrast the traditional equitable approach, through the doctrine of laches, has been to assess the injustice caused by delay on a flexible case by case basis.

One fascination of limitation vis-à-vis restitution is that, as the Limitation Act 1980 does not *expressly* deal with most restitutionary claims, the question of which approach should be taken is largely open. Moreover, as the subject draws together common law and equitable rules and principles, the pull of both approaches is strongly felt.

---

6   See above, p 270; and above, pp 433–434.
7   See, generally, McLean 'Limitation of Action in Restitution' [1989] CLJ 472; Law Commission Consultation Paper No 151, *Limitation of Actions* (1998), Part V, paras 13.77–13.83; Law Commission Report No 270, *Limitation of Actions* (2001), paras 2.48–2.51, 4.76–4.79.

The certainty of the common law approach makes it attractive. Although fixing the precise time limit is, to an extent, arbitrary – there is no rational reason why the general preference for six years is better than, say, three years – the important requirement is to have a clear limit. Indeed it is significant that, even before the Limitation Act 1939 (which was the primary forerunner of the present statutory provisions laid down in the Limitation Act 1980) the traditional laches doctrine was cut into by applying common law limitation periods by analogy to closely related equitable claims.[8] Having said that, the traditional common law approach has taken too rigid a view of the time from when the fixed limitation periods run.[9] In line with the statutory reforms brought about in cases of latent personal injury or negligently caused latent economic loss,[10] fairness to claimants dictates that time should not start to run until the claimant knows, or reasonably should have known, of his cause of action; and in cases of duress or undue influence or exploitation of weakness time should perhaps not run until the claimant is able to exercise his own free choice.

The easiest approach to examining the present law on limitation for restitution is to take the central divide of the subject (between unjust enrichment by subtraction and restitution for wrongs) and to commence the discussion within each by looking at the extent to which limitation is clearly governed by the Limitation Act 1980. The overall picture of the law is depressingly uncertain and disordered for, far from having a coherent plan for restitution, the Act constitutes a limited patchwork.

(2) Unjust enrichment by subtraction

(a) Limitation periods

There is nothing in the 1980 Act which naturally provides a limitation period for the vast bulk of unjust enrichment by subtraction. There are four exceptions:[11]

(i) By s 9 of the 1980 Act (sums recoverable by virtue of any enactment) restitutionary actions under the Law Reform (Frustrated

---

8   Eg, actions for breach of trust were governed by the same time limits as for actions in tort.
9   See McLean 'Limitation of Action in Restitution' [1989] CLJ 472, 480–481. The Law Commission in its Report No 270, *Limitation of Actions* (2001) has recommended reform so that, in general, including for restitutionary claims, limitation should run from the date of knowledge subject to a ten-year long-stop.
10 Limitation Act 1980, ss 11, 14A.
11 By Merchant Shipping Act 1995, s 224, Sch 11, Art 23(1) there is a two year limitation period for claims in respect of salvage which runs from the date when the salvage operations terminated.

Contracts) Act 1943 have a limitation period of six years from the accrual of the cause of action.

(ii) By s 10(1) of the 1980 Act contribution claims under the Civil Liability (Contribution) Act 1978 have a two year limitation period running from when the right accrued (as defined in s 10(2)–(4)).[12] (iii) For personal or proprietary remedies claiming a share of a deceased's estate as in *Re Diplock*,[13] s 22(a) of the 1980 Act lays down a 12 year limitation period which runs from when the right to receive the share accrued. But by s 21, there is no statutory limitation period where the trustee was fraudulent (s 21(1)(a));[14] or where the claim is by a beneficiary 'to recover from the trustee trust property or the proceeds of trust property' (s 21(1)(b)).[15] (iv) Subject to (iii) above, s 21(3) lays down that an action by a beneficiary to recover trust property or in respect of any breach of trust is governed by a six-year limitation period (running from when the right of action accrued). A proprietary, and possibly a personal,[16] restitutionary remedy by a beneficiary against a third party who has received trust property transferred without the consent of the beneficiary[17] falls within this[18] (unless, by reason of s 21(1)(a), the trustee was fraudulent).

Where there is no express statutory limitation period, what is the position? One extreme argument would be that, while equitable remedies (for example, rescission) are subject to the laches doctrine, there is no limitation defence for the common law restitutionary

---

12　Above, p 291.
13　[1948] Ch 465; affd, in respect of an appeal on the personal claim, in *Ministry of Health v Simpson* [1951] AC 251.
14　It appears that s 21(1)(a) applies even though the trustee is not the defendant: see Danckwerts J at first instance in *Baker Ltd v Medway Building and Supplies Ltd* [1958] 1 WLR 1216.
15　Section 38 of the 1980 Act, in defining trustee, refers to s 68(17) of the Trustee Act 1925. As interpreted that subsection includes, eg, resulting and constructive trustees and personal representatives.
16　*Baker Ltd v Medway Building and Supplies Ltd* [1958] 1 WLR 1216 (*per* Danckwerts J).
17　See above, chapter 4.
18　A possible counter-argument is that because constructive trustees are included within the definition of trustee – above note 15 – and as knowing recipients of trust money have traditionally been held liable 'as constructive trustees', s 21(1)(b) applies so that there is no statutory limitation period. Although not mentioned in the judgment *Re Montagu's Settlement Trusts* [1987] Ch 264 may illustrate this. But in *Paragon Finance plc v DB Thakerar & Co* [1999] 1 All ER 400, 407–416 the Court of Appeal has helpfully clarified that, apart from where constructive trust terminology is inappropriate (see above, pp 196–197) a constructive trust imposed or recognised as a response to a wrong or an unjust enrichment does not fall within s 21(1). See also *Taylor v Davies* [1920] AC 636, 653; Harpum, 'The Stranger as Constructive Trustee' (1986) 102 LQR 267, 287–289. Note also that an equitable restitutionary proprietary remedy that falls outside s 21(3), because it is not concerned with the recovery of trust property, may still be subject to a six-year limitation period because the courts may apply the limitation period for a common law restitutionary claim by analogy under s 36(1) of the Limitation Act 1980. See *Kleinwort Benson Ltd v Sandwell Borough Council* [1994] 4 All ER 890, 943 (Hobhouse J).

remedies. However this would be very unsatisfactory in terms of policy and, not surprisingly, the courts have sought to avoid that conclusion.

The 'escape route' favoured by the judiciary has been to force common law restitution into s 5 of the 1980 Act so as to give a six year time period. Admittedly, this requires distorting the statutory words particularly when the independence of unjust enrichment by subtraction – and the fictional nature of the implied contract theory – is fully appreciated. Nevertheless this was the approach approved by the Court of Appeal in dicta in *Re Diplock.*[19] Lord Greene MR thought that the expression 'founded on simple contract' must 'be taken to cover actions for money had and received, formerly actions on the case ... though the words used cannot be regarded as felicitous.' This is also supported by s 3 of the Limitation Act 1623, which, until the Limitation Act 1939, provided a six year limitation period for all assumpsit claims. Although not mentioned in the judgments, that provision was presumably the basis in *Maskell v Horner*[20] for restricting restitution of payments under duress to those payments made in the six years before the writ was issued.

After a careful examination, the opinion in *Re Diplock* was followed by Hobhouse J in *Kleinwort Benson Ltd v Sandwell Borough Council.*[1] Confronted with the argument that there was no limitation period for quasi-contractual claims, Hobhouse J (applying *Pepper v Hart*)[2] looked to see whether the *obiter dicta* in *Re Diplock* was supported by Hansard. He found that it was. The parliamentary debates made clear that the Limitation Act 1939 was to give effect to the recommendations of the Law Revision Committee's Fifth Interim Report in 1936.[3] And that Committee had recommended, among other things, 'that the period for all actions founded in tort or simple contract (*including quasi-contract*) ... should be six years'.[4] That there is a six-year limitation period for the common law restitution of money paid was also implicitly accepted by the House of Lords in *Kleinwort Benson Ltd v Lincoln City Council*[5] in deciding that that limitation period was subject to the mistake exception in s 32(1)(c) of the Limitation Act 1980.

(b) Accrual of the cause of action

Under the Limitation Act 1980, limitation periods normally run from the accrual of the cause of action. The important question therefore

19   [1948] Ch 465, 514.
20   [1915] 3 KB 106.
1   [1994] 4 All ER 890, 942-943.
2   [1993] AC 593.
3   Cmd 5334.
4   Para 37. Author's emphasis.
5   [1999] 2 AC 349.

becomes, when does a cause of action in unjust enrichment by subtraction accrue?

In relation to claims for contribution the 1980 Act defines when the right of action accrues. But otherwise the matter is essentially governed by the common law so that there is no need here to force restitution into inappropriately worded statutory provisions.

In *Kleinwort Benson v South Tyneside Borough Council,*[6] another of the swaps cases, Hobhouse J said, 'The cause of action in money had and received arises when the relevant money is paid by the plaintiff to the claimant.'[7] But while this, no doubt, is generally accurate it is not clear that it is correct where the ground for restitution is failure of consideration and at the time of payment there has been no such failure. Probably, therefore, it is more accurate to say that an action in unjust enrichment by subtraction accrues at the date when the enrichment is received or the date of the unjust factor, whichever is the later.[8] This is consistent with past decisions.[9] It is also supported by cases concerned with when a restitutionary cause of action accrues for the purposes of an award of interest under s 35A of the Supreme Court Act 1981. In *BP Exploration Co (Libya) Ltd v Hunt (No 2)*[10] it was held by the House of Lords that a cause of action under s 1(3) of the Law Reform (Frustrated Contracts) Act 1943 accrues at the date of the frustration (the date of the failure of consideration). And in *Guardian Ocean Cargoes Ltd v Banco do Brasil*[11] the Court of Appeal held that the cause of action for the restitution of money for total failure of consideration (in the sense of an unpromised future event) accrues only at the date of the failure of the consideration (here when the negotiations finally failed).

One complicating case is *Freeman v Jeffries.*[12] Here the defendant assigned his leasehold interest in a farm to the claimant for a consideration that was to be fixed by an independent valuation of the

6   [1994] 4 All ER 972. See also the *obiter dicta* of Lord Hope in *Kleinwort Benson Ltd v Lincoln City Council* [1999] 2 AC 349, 409, '[T]he right to recover the amount paid by mistake accrues at the moment when the sum is received by the payee....'

7   At p 978. Hobhouse J was concerned with the difficult question of whether restitution of payments made more than six years before the commencement of proceedings was time-barred where there had been payments both ways by the parties prior to, and during, those six years. The overall principle he applied was that the restitutionary cause of action was a continuing one for the net (unjust) enrichment on each swap contract; but that the limitation defence meant that the claimant could not recover more than the total of the payments it had made under that contract in the six years before the issue of the writ.

8   McLean, 'Limitation of Action in Restitution' [1989] CLJ 472, 476.

9   Eg, *Maskell v Horner* [1915] 3 KB 106; *Deglman v Guaranty Trust Co of Canada* [1954] 3 DLR 785.

10   [1983] 2 AC 352.

11   [1994] 2 Lloyd's Rep 152.

12   (1869) LR 4 Exch 189.

farm. The valuers included certain items within the valuation that should have been excluded. The claimant, having paid the full valuation sum, sought to recover part or all of it as money had and received paid by mistake of fact. The reasoning of two of the judges of the Court of Exchequer (Bramwell and Martin BB) was that the action failed because the claimant had made no demand for the money before bringing the action. This is incorrect in principle. The defendant is unjustly enriched as soon as he receives money paid by mistake. The law is not responding to a wrongful refusal to return money. The decision is better explained either on one of the main grounds relied on by the other two judges (Pigott B and Kelly CB) – namely that the claimant, as opposed to the valuers, had made no mistake in that he had agreed to pay and paid the sum fixed by the valuers – or, more obviously, because restitution cannot override a valid contract and there was no ground on which the contract could be held void or voidable.

The need for a demand before action was correctly denied in *Baker v Courage & Co*[13] where a brewery company successfully counterclaimed that it had mistakenly paid £1,000 too much to the vendor for the purchase of a pub because it had forgotten to take into account £1,000 already owed to it by the vendor. Hamilton J said:

'It was said that the cause of action is in the nature of a breach by the payee of a duty to hand over money which *ex aequo et bono* does not belong to him, but belongs to the payor, and that there can be no breach of that duty where the facts which give rise to the duty have not been brought to the payee's attention. It is clear that if that is right the payor might postpone the notification of his discovery and the making of his demand for an unlimited time and yet not have the [Statute of Limitations] run against him. But I think that the contention is fallacious. It seems to me that the cause of action in this case was complete independently of any notification of the discovery.'[14]

Freeman v Jeffries was distinguished on the ground that that was a case of a unilateral rather than a shared mistake. That is unconvincing not least because there would be no logic in requiring a demand in a case of unilateral mistake but not shared mistake. The weakness of the distinction shows how determined Hamilton J was not to follow the unsatisfactory earlier decision.

Most recently, in *Fuller v Happy Shopper Ltd*[15] Lightman J has distinguished *Freeman v Jeffries* as a case where rescission of the contract was sought; and to effect rescission a notice or demand must be given

13 [1910] 1 KB 56.
14 Ibid, at p 65.
15 [2001] 2 Lloyd's Rep 49.

to the other contracting party. That is to be distinguished from a simple claim to repayment of money. Lightman J said:[16]

> 'As a matter of principle there is no reason why a demand for payment of moneys had and received should be required before a right to repayment arises, for the right of restitution arises at the moment that unjust enrichment takes place ... But the case of *Freeman v Jeffries* is cited as authority in support of the proposition that a demand is necessary ... In my view, when the case of *Freeman v Jeffries* is properly understood, the law is clear; if the rescission of a contract gives rise to a right on the part of a party to repayment of moneys had and received, the due exercise of the right of rescission by giving notice of rescission must precede the accrual of the right of action for money had and received. But in the absence of some such special consideration, and in particular where no question of rescission arises as, for example, where the contract is void or (as on the facts of this case) where there is an overpayment, the general rule is that no notice or demand is required... There is a good reason why this should be so which is hinted at by Mr Justice Hamilton in *Baker v Courage*, and spelt out by Graham Virgo: "Despite certain dicta [in *Freeman v Jeffries*] that a restitutionary cause of action will accrue only once the plaintiff has demanded return of the enrichment, the better view is that there is no such requirement, for otherwise the plaintiff would be able to postpone the date from which the limitation period begins to run until it suits him or her to inform the defendant of the restitutionary claim."'[17]

(c) Statutory provisions delaying the running of time

In a few situations the 1980 Act pushes back from the accrual date the starting point for the limitation periods prescribed by the Act. So, for example, there are provisions delaying the running of time for those who are under a disability (s 28) or where the action is based upon the claimant's fraud (s 32(1)(a)) or where any fact relevant to the claimant's right of action has been deliberately concealed from him by the defendant (s 32(1)(b)).

Of special relevance to restitution is s 32(1)(c) which lays down that where the action is for relief from the consequences of a mistake the period of limitation shall not begin to run until the claimant has discovered the mistake or could with reasonable diligence have discovered it.[18] Assuming that the Act is regarded as having laid down a six year time bar for common law restitution, s 32(1)(c) means that an action for money had and received paid by mistake or for money

---

16   Ibid at 54.
17   Virgo, *The Principles of the Law of Restitution* (1999) p 770.
18   This departs from the position at common law applied in, eg, *Baker v Courage & Co* [1910] 1 KB 56.

mistakenly paid to the defendant's use or for a *quantum meruit* for services mistakenly rendered or a *quantum valebat* for goods mistakenly transferred will not be time barred until six years after the claimant knows or should have known of his mistake.

This subsection was of central importance in *Kleinwort Benson Ltd v Lincoln City Council*,[19] in which the House of Lords abrogated the mistake of law bar to restitution. The case concerned the restitution of money paid under a fully-executed void interest-rate swap transaction. The reason why the claim was formulated as one for mistake of law was precisely to invoke s 32(1)(c) so as to avoid the six-year limitation period applicable to the restitution of money paid. The majority of their Lordships decided that the claimants had made a mistake of law that grounded restitution and that restitution of money paid under a mistake of law fell within s 32(1)(c). As the claimants had commenced proceedings within six years of the House of Lords decision in *Hazell v Hammersmith and Fulham London Borough Council*,[20] laying down that swap transactions are ultra vires local authorities and void, they were entitled to restitution of all payments made under the void contracts even if paid more than six years before the issue of proceedings. Any problems with the potentially indefinite extension of a limitation period for mistakes of law, where judges 'develop' or 'change' the law by overruling past decisions, were felt to be matters for legislative reform after consideration by the Law Commission.

Although not mentioned by their Lordships, the Law Commission had in fact already provisionally recommended that to balance its proposed general 'date of knowledge' starting date for limitation, there should be a general ten-year long-stop.[1] Applying this to restitution of mistaken payments, it would mean that payments made more than ten years before the issue of proceedings would be statute-barred, irrespective of the date of the claimant's mistake or discovery of that mistake. This recommended reform of limitation is to be welcomed generally; and in the specific context with which we are here concerned of restitution for mistakes of law, it would serve to meet the concerns of there being indefinite claims for restitution expressed particularly forcefully by the two dissenting law lords (Lords Browne-Wilkinson and Lloyd).

Prior to the *Kleinwort Benson* case, the only restitution case in which s 32(1)(c) had been examined was *Peco Arts Inc v Hazlitt Gallery Ltd*[2]

---

19 [1999] 2 AC 349. See above, pp 149–158.
20 [1992] 2 AC 1.
1   Law Commission Consultation Paper No 151, *Limitation of Actions* (1998). See now Law Commission Report No 270, *Limitation of Actions* (2001), esp paras 4.76–4.79.
2   [1983] 1 WLR 1315. Cf *Phillips-Higgins v Harper* [1954] 1 QB 411. Goff and Jones, para 43-005 interpret dicta in *Re Diplock* [1948] Ch 465, 514–516 as supporting the view that an equitable personal claim against a third party can fall within s 32(1)(c).

which concerned a mistake as to whether a painting bought by the claimant from the defendant was an original. It is doubtful, however, whether s 32(1)(c) should have been in play: as the contract was probably not void at common law the relevant remedy should probably have been equitable rescission to which laches and not s 32(1)(c) applies. It was conceded, however, that s 32(1)(c) applied and the sole question for Webster J (which he decided in the claimant's favour so that the action was not time barred) was the essentially factual one of whether the claimant could have reasonably discovered the mistake more than six years before the legal proceedings were commenced. In any event there would seem to be no difference on this point between laches and s 32(1)(c): time does not run under the laches doctrine until the claimant knew or should reasonably have known of his claim.

A further provision of the 1980 Act of importance to restitutionary claims is s 29(5). By this, where an action has accrued to recover '(a) any debt or other liquidated pecuniary claim or (b) any claim to the personal estate of a deceased person or to any share or interest in any such estate' the action is to be treated as having accrued on the date of the defendant's acknowledgement of the claim (provided in writing and signed)[3] or part payment of the claim. Actions for money had and received and money paid to the defendant's use clearly fall within this subsection.[4] The personal equitable order to account for money received in, for example, *Re Diplock* also probably falls within s 29(5)(a) but, in any event, is covered by s 29(5)(b). In contrast restitutionary damages and contribution clearly fall outside s 29(5)(a).

Whether an account of profits, a *quantum meruit* and a *quantum valebat* fall within s 29(5)(a) is more difficult. At first blush one might imagine that those claims would fall outside the subsection as the amount to be awarded is dependent on an assessment by the court. However in *Amantilla Ltd v Telefusion plc*[5] it was held that a *quantum meruit* for extra building work carried out at the request of the owner over and above the contracted-for work constituted a debt or liquidated pecuniary claim for the purposes of s 29(5)(a). Judge John Davies QC's reasoning was that the *quantum meruit* was a contractual remedy and, being based on the parties' intentions, had a sufficiently certain description. The decision can therefore be interpreted as being inapplicable to a restitutionary *quantum meruit*. Whether a restrictive

---

3   Section 30.
4   The argument that, in relation to a claim for money had and received, payments under a void interest-rate swap transaction were 'part payments of the claim', so as to start time running again under s 29(5), was rejected by Hobhouse J in *Kleinwort Benson v South Tyneside Borough Council* [1994] 4 All ER 972, 980-981.
5   (1987) 9 Con LR 139.

interpretation should be taken may rest on what one sees as the policy underlying the postponement of the start of limitation periods for acknowledgement or part payment. Presumably the idea, akin to waiver, is that the claimant must not be misled into not issuing a claim form by the defendant's apparent acceptance of his claim. If this is the policy there seems no justification for having excluded unliquidated damages from its scope[6] and every good reason to construe the subsection as widely as possible. On this purposive construction the *quantum meruit, quantum valebat* and account of profits should be regarded as within s 29(5)(a).[7]

(d) Laches

It remains to examine the laches doctrine (also commonly referred to as the lapse of time bar) which applies to equitable remedies[8] like equitable contribution and rescission (eg, for misrepresentation[9] or undue influence). Under laches there are no fixed limitation periods. The doctrine is a flexible one which assesses whether the claimant's delay should bar its claim judged against any potential injustice to the defendant if the claim were allowed. It is closely linked to the bar to rescission of affirmation (and indeed to the general equitable doctrine of acquiescence) and in many situations lapse of time is evidence of affirmation.[10]

The classic formulation of the doctrine is that of Sir Barnes Peacock, giving the Privy Council's judgment in *Lindsay Petroleum Co v Hurd*.[11] The case concerned a fraudulent misrepresentation by the defendant vendor leading to the claimant's purchase of land. The claimant was allowed rescission even though the action was brought 15 months after the conveyance, as it had acted promptly once it had discovered the truth. Sir Barnes Peacock said:

> 'The doctrine of laches in Courts of Equity is not an arbitrary or a technical doctrine. Where it would be practically unjust to give a remedy, either because the party has, by his conduct, done that which might fairly be regarded as equivalent to a waiver of it, or where by his conduct and neglect he has, though

---

6 The Law Commission has recommended that s 29(5) should be extended to all claims, whether liquidated or not: Law Commission Report No 270, *Limitation of Actions* (2001), paras 3.146–3.155.

7 See also above, pp 54–55 (statutory interest on debts).

8 In some old cases, eg, *Mills v Drewitt* (1855) 20 Beav 632, laches was held not to apply to equitable proprietary claims to property in the hands of trustees.

9 Irrespective of laches, rescission for fraudulent misrepresentation may be barred, by the exercise of the power in s 36(1) of the 1980 Act, six years after the claimant knew of the fraud by analogy to the statutory limitation period for the tort of deceit; *Molloy v Mutual Reserve Life Insurance Co* (1906) 94 LT 756.

10 *Clough v London and North Western Rly Co* (1871) LR 7 Exch 26, 35.

11 (1874) LR 5 PC 221.

perhaps not waiving that remedy, yet put the other party in a situation in which it would not be reasonable to place him if the remedy were afterwards to be asserted, in either of these cases, lapse of time and delay are most material.'[12]

Under laches, time generally only starts to run once the claimant knew or could reasonably have known of his claim.[13] In a case of undue influence (and presumably also, eg, duress) it appears that time only starts running once the claimant is free to make a choice. For example, in *Allcard v Skinner*,[14] where a delay of six years was held to constitute affirmation and hence to bar rescission of a gift for undue influence, Lindley LJ said, '... if the donor desires to have his gift declared invalid and set aside he ought, in my opinion, to seek relief within a reasonable time after the removal of the influence under which the gift was made'.[15]

One decision that runs counter to this postponement of the starting point is *Leaf v International Galleries*.[16] The claim for rescission of a contract for the purchase of a painting was held to be barred because five years had passed since the contract was executed. The ground for rescission was the vendor's innocent misrepresentation that the painting was a Constable which the claimant only discovered to be untrue – and could only have been reasonably expected to discover as untrue – a short time before he sought rescission. If the decision is correct it marks off laches (or lapse of time) in respect of non-fraudulent misrepresentations from all other applications of the doctrine.

(3) Restitution for wrongs

(a) Restitution for torts or breach of contract

The natural interpretation of the 1980 Act is that, by ss 2 and 5 respectively, it provides a six year limitation period from the accrual of the cause of action for gains made by a tort or breach of contract.[17]

---

12 Ibid, at pp 239–240.
13 See, eg, *Lindsay Petrolem Co v Hurd* (1874) LR 5 PC 221 (misrepresentation); *Erlanger v New Sombrero Phosphate Co* (1878) 3 App Cas 1218 (non-disclosure); *Alec Lobb (Garages) Ltd v Total Oil (GB) Ltd* [1985] 1 WLR 173 (exploitation of weakness).
14 (1887) 36 Ch D 145.
15 Ibid, at p 187.
16 [1950] 2 KB 86.
17 Special limitation periods apply to some torts. For example, by s 4A of the Limitation Act 1980 the limitation period for defamation and malicious falsehood is one year from the date on which the cause of action accrued but by s 32A the courts have a discretion to exclude that period. Under ss 3–4 of the 1980 Act, special provisions also apply in respect of conversion dealing with successive conversions and theft. By s 8 of the 1980 Act the limitation period for breach of a contract that is a specialty (ie, a contract made by deed) is twelve years not six years.

However, this may not be a necessary interpretation. One might alternatively argue that an action for restitution for a tort or breach of contract is not 'an action founded on tort' or 'an action founded on simple contract' so that ss 2 and 5 do not apply. That is, one might say that, while standard compensatory damages are within ss 2 and 5, restitution was not intended to be covered and that, on a purposive construction, the six year time bar does not apply to restitution.

That kind of approach was taken in the leading case of *Chesworth v Farrar*[18] which concerned whether an action for money had and received to recover the proceeds of sale of converted goods was 'a cause of action in tort' for the purposes of the old six month time limit for tort actions against the deceased tortfeasor's estate (the remnant of the common law *actio personalis* rule for tort actions). Edmund Davies J held that it was not and should rather be regarded as analogous to a contractual action so that a six year time limit applied. It is clear that Edmund Davies J did not regard the action as lying within unjust enrichment by subtraction (on the basis, for example, of the claimant's ignorance). Rather he thought it essential that the claimant established the tort of conversion.[19]

Birks argues that the decision must be wrong because a bar expressed as applying to a tort must bar restitution for a tort.[20] This is clearly the natural starting point but *Chesworth v Farrar* shows that, contrary to Birks' view, the courts are willing on a purposive construction – the policy there being to evade the much criticised *actio personalis* rule – to disregard a tort bar in respect of restitution for a tort.

As a matter of policy, however, there is no good reason for the courts to reject, in respect of restitution for a tort or breach of contract, the modern six year time limit laid down for causes of action in tort or contract. In particular there is no other obvious time limit to which they can turn. Nor is there any suggestion of this in the cases. Indeed, as we have seen, the courts are only too anxious to force claims in unjust enrichment by subtraction into the six year statutory bar. No such distortion is needed here. It would seem therefore that, whether taking the most natural or a purposive construction, a six year time limit applies to restitution for a tort or breach of contract.

Under ss 2 and 5, the six years runs from the accrual of the cause of action. When does the cause of action accrue for restitution for torts or breach of contract? As the cause of action is the wrong (and

18 [1967] 1 QB 407.
19 The crucial passage from his judgment (ibid, at p 417) is set out above, p 465.
20 Dicta of Denning J at first instance in *Beaman v ARTS Ltd* [1949] 1 KB 550 are sometimes cited in support of this. But Denning J was not confronted with the consequences of such a view.

not the wrongful enrichment), the cause of action for restitution accrues, as for compensation, at the date of the tort or breach of contract. The law is well-established on how one determines the date of accrual for tort or breach of contract.[1] The most important factors are whether the wrong is actionable per se or actionable only on proof of damage, and whether the wrong is a continuing one or not.

Indeed it is the law on limitation that most clearly shows that the cause of action in respect of restitution for wrongs is the wrong and not the wrongful enrichment.[2] Say, for example, a defendant publishes a book that contains libellous comments about the claimant. The royalties on the book are not paid to the defendant until one year after publication. If restitutionary damages were available for the tort of libel the limitation period applicable to a claim for restitutionary damages for libel running under s 4A of the 1980 Act from accrual of the cause of action would, as for compensatory and punitive damages, start on the publication of the book and not on the date that the defendant first receives royalties. In other words, the cause of action is the wrong, the libel, not the wrongful enrichment. Similarly, if restitutionary damages were claimed for breach of contract, the limitation period under s 5 of the 1980 Act would start running from the date of the breach of contract and not from when the first gains were made by the defendant as a result of the breach of contract. If this were not so – and if the cause of action were to accrue only on the date of the wrongful enrichment – the peculiar position would apparently be that a new cause of action would accrue each time gains were received from the wrong.

(b) Restitution for equitable wrongs

As regards breach of trust, the crucial section of the 1980 Act is the tortuous s 21. The basic regime of that section is that there is a six year limitation period, running from the date when the right of action accrued,[3] for a breach of trust (s 21(3)) but that actions for fraudulent breach of trust or to recover trust property or its proceeds are excluded and have no statutory limitation period (s 21(1)).[4]

The position in relation to accounting for profits for a breach of fiduciary duty (other than by an express trustee) has recently been

---

1   See Law Commission Consultation Paper No 151, *Limitation of Actions* (1998), paras 3.1–3.28.
2   See above, pp 26, 455.
3   This is the date of the breach of trust: *Thorne v Heard and Marsh* [1894] 1 Ch 599.
4   Rescission of property sales to a trustee will normally fall within s 21(1)(b) and therefore have no limitation period. But where not so governed Megarry V-C in *Tito v Waddell (No 2)* [1977] Ch 106, 246–250 controversially thought that what is now s 21(3) would not apply because the trustee's conduct does not constitute a breach of trust. See also *A-G v Cocke* [1988] Ch 414.

the subject of judicial controversy. In *Nelson v Rye*[5] Laddie J held that, while laches applied, no statutory limitation period applied to a claim by a musician for an account of profits for his manager's breach of fiduciary duty. His reasoning was that a breach of fiduciary duty per se has no statutory limitation period; and a breach of fiduciary duty that gives rise to a constructive trust, which he thought was the position on the facts of the case, falls within s 21(1)(b) which says that there shall be no limitation period. However, in *Paragon Finance plc v DB Thakerar & Co*,[6] which was actually concerned with the remedy of equitable compensation not restitution, the Court of Appeal regarded that reasoning as incorrect. It was helpfully explained that a constructive trust imposed or recognised as a response to a wrong or an unjust enrichment does not bring a claim within s 21.[7] That is, on the facts of *Nelson v Rye* there was no breach of trust within the meaning of s 21. But nor was it correct that breach of fiduciary duty per se had no statutory limitation period because historically the six-year period laid down for breach of contract had been applied by analogy to a non-contractual breach of fiduciary duty under the power now contained in s 36(1) of the Limitation Act 1980.

Where there is no statutory limitation period (as, eg, in relation to breach of confidence) the equitable doctrine of laches, as discussed above in relation to unjust enrichment by subtraction, applies to equitable wrongs.

(4) Conclusion

The law on limitation as a defence to restitution is ripe for statutory reform. It cannot be sensible for there to be no provisions in the 1980 Act expressly dealing with most restitutionary claims. Even if reform suggestions, such as the introduction of a general discoverability date for the starting of limitation periods for common law restitution, do not win favour there is a clear need for clarification of the present law. As Brooke LJ said in *obiter dicta* in *Portman Building Society v Hamlyn Taylor Neck*,[8] '[There is a] need for Parliament to bring appropriate limitation rules relating to restitutionary remedies within a coherent, principled limitation statute as suggested by the Law Commission ... Everyone would then be able to understand clearly where they stand and what the relevant rules are ... .'

5 [1996] 1 WLR 1378.
6 [1999] 1 All ER 400.
7 See above, p 544, n 18. But a director who has acquired the company's property in breach of duty is a constructive trustee of that property within s 21: *Harrison (Properties) Ltd v Harrison* [2001] EWCA Civ 1467, [2002] 1 BCLC 162.
8 [1998] 4 All ER 202, 209.

5.   DISPUTE RESOLVED

Even though a claimant may once have been entitled to a restitutionary remedy, that entitlement may have been lost because the dispute has been resolved and cannot be reopened. We can therefore refer to a general defence of 'dispute resolved' which covers the law that has traditionally been treated under labels such as *res judicata* and compromise. While it is not a defence exclusive to the law of restitution, within the law of restitution we can say that it is an unjust-related defence. It rests on the sound policy of ensuring finality to disputes that have already been resolved.

As we have seen in chapter 3,[9] it is this defence, along with change of position, that ensures that, contrary to the fears of some, abolition of the mistake of law bar will not open the floodgates of litigation. There will commonly be a 'dispute resolved' defence which will operate to prevent the claimant seeking restitution of payments made after, for example, a judicial 'change' in the law.

There are three main aspects to (or specific defences within) this general defence. First, a payment made in accordance with a judgment cannot be recovered unless and until the judgment is set aside.[10] There are rules laid down as to the grounds, and time limits, for appealing against, or otherwise setting aside, judgments. Until the judgment is set aside, any question of restitution is *res judicata.* On the face of it, the well-known case of *Moses v Macferlan,*[11] with its influential *obiter dicta* of Lord Mansfield on unjust enrichment, appears to be inconsistent with this. The defendant had sued, and recovered judgment for £6 against, the claimant on four promissory notes despite an agreement between the parties that the defendant would not sue the claimant on the notes. Having paid the £6, the claimant sought to recover it in an action for money had and received. On the face of it, such a restitutionary claim was barred by the earlier judgment which was not set aside. But the Court of King's Bench, while referring to the *res judicata* defence, allowed the claim. This is puzzling and the decision has been rejected in some subsequent cases.[12] However, it has been suggested[13] that the case can be justified as awarding restitution for breach of contract rather than restitution for unjust enrichment by subtraction; and restitution for the former would not have been *res judicata.*

9   See above, p 154.
10   For consideration of the ground for restitution of money paid under reversed judgments, see McFarlane, 'The Recovery of Money Paid Under Judgments Later Reversed' [2001] RLR 1: above, p 240, n 7.
11   (1760) 2 Burr 1005. See above, p 2.
12   Eg, *Phillips v Hunter* (1795) 2 Hy Bl 402.
13   Birks and Mitchell, *English Private Law* (ed Birks, 2000), para 15.274.

Secondly, even though no judgment has to be set aside, there can be no restitution of a payment made after legal proceedings have been initiated in good faith demanding that payment. Restitution is here ruled out because of the need to respect the due process of litigation. So, for example, in *Marriot v Hampton*[14] the claimant paid for goods bought from the defendant. The defendant demanded payment again alleging that he had not been paid and brought an action for the price. The claimant could not find the receipt for the first payment and paid again. When he later found the receipt, he sought restitution of the second payment. This was refused. Similarly in *Moore v Vestry of Fulham*[15] the defendant demanded payment from the claimant for street improvements and a summons was issued. The claimant paid but then discovered that a mistake had been made because his house did not abut the street in question so that he should not have been liable to pay. He therefore sought restitution of the money paid on the ground that it was paid by a mistake of fact. This was refused. Lord Halsbury said, '[M]oney paid under the pressure of legal process cannot be recovered. The principle is based upon this, that when a person has had an opportunity of defending an action if he chose, but has thought proper to pay the money claimed by the action, the law will not allow him to try in a second action what he might have set up in the defence to the original action.'[16]

It is important to appreciate two points here. First, it has been explained in earlier chapters[17] that money paid under a threat to sue cannot be recovered for duress because such a threat is not illegitimate. But the defence we are here dealing with goes beyond the unjust factor of duress (ie, it is not merely the corollary of there being no duress) and rules out restitution for other unjust factors, such as mistake (as illustrated by *Moore v Vestry of Fulham*). Secondly, this aspect of the 'dispute resolved' defence requires that legal proceedings have been initiated. Prior to that, a payment made following a demand, in the mistaken belief that one is liable to pay, can be recovered on the ground of the mistake (unless, as we shall see, there has been a compromise).

The third aspect of the general defence of 'dispute resolved' is where the parties have entered into a contract to close the matter. Such a contract is called a compromise, a settlement or a release, although for shorthand we shall here refer to all these variants as a 'contract of compromise'. This rules out restitution even prior to the

---

14 (1797) Term Rep 269.
15 [1895] 1 QB 399. See also *Hamlet v Richardson* (1833) 9 Bing 644.
16 Ibid, at 401–402.
17 See above, pp 239–240, 273, 437.

initiation of legal proceedings let alone a judgment. While it is convenient to treat such a contract within the 'dispute resolved' defence, it is a general theme throughout the law of restitution that a valid contract that is inconsistent with restitution rules out restitution.[18] This is not to deny that a contract of compromise may be invalid thereby opening the way to restitution. Of particular importance is the extent to which mistake in entering into a contract of compromise may lead to it being treated as void or voidable.[19] In general, one would expect that the courts would be particularly reluctant to upset such contracts for mistake given that the very purpose of such a contract is to resolve the dispute even though one or other of the parties may be mistaken as to the facts or the law. However, in *Magee v Pennine Insurance Co Ltd*[20] a majority of the Court of Appeal set aside a contract of compromise for (equitable) common mistake. The claimant had sought £600 from the defendant insurers for damage to a car that was being driven by his son. The defendants had offered £385 in settlement which the claimant had accepted. The defendants then found out that the claimant had made an innocent misrepresentation in that he had signed the insurance proposal form stating that his son held a provisional licence which was untrue. This misrepresentation would have entitled the defendants to rescind the contract of insurance. The common mistake thought to justify setting aside a contract was therefore that both parties thought that the policy was binding whereas it was in truth voidable. This should be regarded as an exceptional decision. Referring to it, Birks and Mitchell write, '[T]his should not be regarded as a common case, for once the exercise of construction concludes that there was a contract of finality, a court will be reluctant to avoid it and will certainly not do so simply on the ground that the claim which was given up could later be shown to be bad or, vice versa, more valuable than was thought.'[1]

It should finally be stressed that one is here talking about a *contract of compromise*. A mere payment of a disputed claim does not constitute a contract of compromise. This goes to explain why the mistake claim in, for example, *Kelly v Solari*[2] was not ruled out by the defence of 'dispute resolved.' It also explains why in earlier chapters the distinction was drawn between a contractual submission to an

18 See above, p 323.
19 See Andrews, 'Mistaken Settlements of Disputable Claims' [1989] LMCLQ 431.
20 [1969] 2 QB 507. This decision has been overruled, on the ground that there is no equitable jurisdiction to rescind a contract for common mistake, by *Great Peace Shipping Ltd v Tsavliris (International) Ltd* [2002] EWCA Civ 1407; see above, p 169, n 12a.
1   *English Private Law* (ed Birks, 2000), para 15.278. They here cite, eg, *Callisher v Bischoffsheim* (1870) LR 5 QB 449. For an important case on the construction of a contract of compromise, see *Bank of Credit and Commerce International v Ali* [2001] UKHL 8, [2001] 2 WLR 735.
2   (1841) 9 M & W 54: see above, p 131.

honest claim (ie, a contractual compromise) which is a useful concept, and a non-contractual submission to an honest claim which, it was submitted, is not a useful concept.[3]

6. INCAPACITY AS A DEFENCE

We have seen in chapter 11 that human incapacity (infancy, insanity and drunkenness) and incapacity by reason of a company or a public authority acting ultra vires can be an unjust factor grounding restitution.[4] In this section we are asking the converse question; does the defendant's incapacity act as a defence to a standard ground for restitution?

(1) Infancy as a defence

(a) Unjust enrichment by subtraction

A useful starting point is the supply of necessaries to a minor. As explained in chapter 9, a contractual analysis of the minor's liability is normally possible rather than recasting it as restitutionary. However, the close link to restitution indicates that infancy would not afford a defence to a restitutionary claim (most obviously grounded on the unjust factor of necessity) for supplying necessaries. And in terms of policy this must be correct: the need to protect minors against their own foolish judgments and from unscrupulous adults, which is the thinking behind the infancy defence, has no impact where the minor has been supplied with necessaries at a reasonable price.

Turning aside from necessaries, the major controversy in this area has been whether an adult is entitled to restitution of money paid to a minor (under a contract that is unenforceable against the minor or has been repudiated by him on reaching adulthood)[5] on the ground of total failure of consideration.[6] In the two leading cases a negative answer has been given: that is, infancy has been held to be a defence.

In *Cowern v Nield*[7] the infant defendant carried on business as a hay and straw merchant. The claimant ordered some clover and hay from him and paid £35 19s in advance. The hay was never delivered and the claimant properly refused to take delivery of the clover because it

---

3   See above, pp 138–140, 212, 448–449.
4   It is obvious from chapter 11 that the incapacity cannot be a defence to a claim by an *incapax* for restitution.
5   For these categories, see above, p 413.
6   Or mistake: in the two cases that follow the adult could equally well have based his restitutionary claim on a supposed liability mistake of fact (as to the minor's age).
7   [1912] 2 KB 419.

was rotten. In holding that the claimant was not entitled to recover the £35 19s for total failure of consideration the Divisional Court's wholly inadequate reasoning was simply that only tortious claims (as in *Bristow v Eastman*)[8] and not contractual claims escaped the infancy defence so that, in the absence of fraud, the action for money had and received should fail.

In *R Leslie Ltd v Sheill*[9] the infant defendant had induced the claimant to lend him £400 by a fraudulent misrepresentation that he was of full age. In denying restitution of the £400 the Court of Appeal's reasoning was similar to that of the Lords in *Sinclair v Brougham*[10] which Lord Sumner, sitting in both, not surprisingly cited with approval as a 'closely analogous case'.[11] It was held that a tort action for deceit and an action for money had and received (and an equitable personal claim) should all fail because they would 'enforce in a roundabout way an unenforceable contract'.[12] In AT Lawrence J's words:

> 'I do not think that it is correct to say that the action for money had and received is wholly independent of contract. It arises wherever money has been received which *ex aequo et bono* belongs to the plaintiff. In such case the law implies a promise to pay it to the plaintiff, but where the express promise to repay the money is by statute "absolutely void" it is impossible to imply a promise to pay the same money ... To do so would be to (in large part) defeat the policy of the statute, and would violate the well-established principle that where there is an express promise no other like promise can be implied.'[13]

This reasoning must be criticised not only because it is based on the implied contract fallacy but also because it fails to pinpoint why the action for money had and received would contradict the infancy bar to contractual enforcement of the loan: for, although both are personal remedies for the recovery of money, the amounts recoverable would not necessarily be the same. The contractual terms would surely have entitled the claimant adult to an agreed rate of interest so that the contractual remedy would have yielded more than the principal sum lent. In contrast no interest could have been awarded on the restitutionary claim the case having been decided before the Law Reform (Miscellaneous Provisions) Act 1934. Even if that Act had been in force the awarding of interest and its rate would have been at the discretion of the court. Above all, the policies behind the infancy bar

8   (1744) 1 Esp 172.
9   [1914] 3 KB 607.
10   [1914] AC 398; discussed below, pp 566–568.
11   [1914] 3 KB 607, 613.
12   Ibid, per Lord Sumner. Nor was there thought to be any possibility of an equitable proprietary remedy because there was no fiduciary relationship between the minor and the adult.
13   Ibid, at p 626.

of protecting minors from squandering assets or being taken advantage of by unscrupulous adults (including by high interest loans) would not be infringed by reversing the minor's unjust enrichment on the ground of total failure of consideration. Instead of a blanket infancy defence minors would have been adequately protected by affording them a defence of change of position. Now that that general defence has been established the case for overruling *Cowern v Nield* and *Leslie v Sheill* is overwhelming. Indeed one might argue that the recent overruling of *Sinclair v Brougham*[14] by the House of Lords in *Westdeutsche Landesbank Girozentrale v Islington London Borough Council*[15] means that *Leslie v Sheill* has been implicitly overruled.

Although there are no clear authorities, the same argument for rejecting infancy as a defence to unjust enrichment by subtraction can be extended to allow restitution against minors grounded on all other autonomous unjust factors (most importantly, mistake) and in respect of all incontrovertible benefits (whether money or not). However, benefits in kind must be approached with care because the 'bargained-for' test of benefit is presumably inapplicable against a minor. His infancy means that he cannot be said to have validly chosen the benefit. That is, the contractual invalidity carries through to allowing the minor to 'devalue subjectively' the benefit despite his having bargained for it.[16]

This approach of regarding infancy as no defence to unjust enrichment by subtraction is largely supported by Goff and Jones, although they tentatively accept *Leslie v Sheill* on the ground that borrowing contracts should probably be treated differently as they more clearly contradict contractual non-enforcement.[17] The Latey Committee thought that prima facie an adult should be entitled to restitution from a minor but that the courts should have a residual discretion to relieve the minor from his liability.[18] Birks, while supporting the approach suggested above on, for example, mistake, thinks that *Cowern v Nield* and *Leslie v Sheill* were correct in denying restitution for value received. On the other hand, he propounds the novel view, that the adult claimant should have a personal restitutionary claim for value traceably surviving.[19]

The Law Commission took the view that the adult's existing restitutionary remedies (whatever they might be) should be

14 [1914] AC 398.
15 [1996] AC 669. See below, pp 566–568.
16 Birks at p 436. Contra is Arrowsmith, 'Ineffective Transactions, Unjust Enrichment and Problems of Policy' (1989) 9 LS 307, 310–311, 318.
17 Goff and Jones, at para 25-008.
18 'Report of the Committee on the Age of Majority', Cmnd 3342 (1967), paras 306–309. This is also the preferred view of Arrowsmith, 'Ineffective Transactions, Unjust Enrichment and Problems of Policy' (1989) 9 LS 307, 318–319.
19 Birks, at pp 399–400, 436–438. See above, p 82.

supplemented by allowing the court a discretion to order the transfer of any property acquired by the minor under the contract (ie, a contract that is unenforceable against a minor or repudiated by him) or any property representing it.[20] This was to take a peculiar proprietary approach. It may not have been intended to affect personal restitution and can be strongly criticised for being obscure in its purpose and effect, for introducing an uncertain judicial discretion, and for being too limited a reform. Unfortunately it has been adopted in s 3(1) of the Minors' Contracts Act 1987 whereby if a contract is unenforceable against the defendant, or he repudiates it, because he was a minor when it was made 'the court may, if it is just and equitable to do so, require the defendant to transfer to the plaintiff any property acquired by the defendant under the contract, or any property representing it.' It is a major disappointment that the golden opportunity was not taken to rid the law of *Cowern v Nield* and *Leslie v Sheill* and to declare statutorily that infancy should not be a defence to unjust enrichment by subtraction.

(b) Restitution for wrongs

In contrast to an action for breach of contract (including, probably, a claim for restitution for the breach)[1] and provided the contractual regime is not undermined, infancy is not a defence to a tort; although, of course, if the defendant cannot be shown to have had the necessary state of mind or to have fallen below the required standard of liability (eg negligence is judged according to the standards of a reasonable child of the defendant's age) he cannot be liable for the tort.[2] The same appears to apply to equitable wrongs.[3]

It follows naturally (and is also the obvious result in terms of policy) that, at least where there is no possible contradiction of contractual infancy rules, infancy should not be a defence to restitution for a tort or equitable wrong. This is borne out in the case law. For example, in *Bristow v Eastman*,[4] the infant defendant was held liable in an action for money had and received for having embezzled money from his

---

20   Report No 134, 'The Law of Contracts: Minors' Contracts' (1984).
1   In terms of policy a strong argument can be made, as developed in this subsection, that while there is a need to protect a minor against enforcement or compensation there is no reason why he should be allowed to keep the profits of his wrong. The difficulty in applying that argument to breach of contract is that the infancy may be construed as meaning that there is no valid contract and hence no possible breach.
2   *Winfield and Jolowicz on Tort* (16th edn, 2002), p 832, *Salmond and Heuston on The Law of Torts* (21st edn, 1996), pp 411–413.
3   Hanbury and Martin, *Modern Equity* (16th edn, 2001), p 505.
4   (1794) 1 Esp 172. Followed in *Re Seager* (1889) 60 LT 665. One could 'alternatively analyse' the decision in *Bristow*, albeit not its reasoning, to show that infancy is not a defence to ignorance within unjust enrichment by subtraction; see Birks, at p 438.

employer (ie, for the tort of conversion or, possibly, deceit). Lord Kenyon was of the opinion:

'... that infancy was no defence to the action; that infants were liable to actions *ex delicto*, though not *ex contractu*, and though the present action was in its form an action of the latter description, yet it was of the former in point of substance; that if the [employers' assignees in bankruptcy] had brought an action of trover for any part of the property embezzled, or an action grounded on the fraud, that unquestionably infancy would have been no defence; and as the object of the present action was precisely the same, that ... the same rule of law should apply, and that infancy was no bar to the action.'[5]

But where the tort is connected with a contract that is unenforceable because of infancy the courts have held, as we have seen in *Leslie v Sheill*, that a tort action for compensatory damages (in that case, for deceit) is also barred by the infancy so as to avoid indirectly undermining the contractual rules. This seems correct. Whether by expectation damages for a breach of contract or reliance damages for deceit inducing a contract (which will often, although not always, render the same amount) the infant defendant is being required to pay compensation so that, as a result of his foolishness, against which the law seeks to protect him, he ends up worse off than before the contract was made.

However there seems no equivalent policy reason why connection with an unenforceable contract should mean that *restitution* for the tort (or equitable wrong) is barred. No court should sanction a minor's profiting by wrongdoing (although the policy of protecting the minor against squandering his assets probably means that his change of position should be a defence despite his wrongdoing). This was supported by *Stocks v Wilson*.[6] The infant defendant by fraudulently misrepresenting his age had induced the claimant to sell and deliver to him all the furniture, pictures and artefacts from her house for £300. After delivery of the goods, the defendant sold some of them for £30 and used the rest as security for a loan of £100. But he failed to pay the agreed contract price to the claimant. Lush J held that, while the defendant had an infancy defence to the contract action, and was similarly not liable in damages for the tort of deceit because of its connection to the contract, the defendant was liable to account in equity for the benefit gained by the deceit (ie, £130). He said:

'For the more complete protection of the infant, the law prevents the other contracting party not only from suing on the contract, but also from suing for

---

5   Ibid, at p 173.
6   [1913] 2 KB 235. See also *Re King* (1858) 3 De G & J 63 and the reasoning in *Cowern v Nield* [1912] 2 KB 419.

> damages, if the fraud is connected with and forms the inducement to the contract
> ... What the Court of Equity has done in cases of this kind is to prevent the infant
> from retaining the benefit of what he has obtained by reason of his fraud. It has
> done no more than this, and this is a very different thing from making him liable
> to pay damages or compensation for the loss of the other party's bargain.'[7]

Three further points on *Stocks v Wilson* are noteworthy. First, there
is no logical reason why the remedy awarded was the equitable remedy
of accounting for gain rather than the common law remedy of the
recovery of money had and received. Both can be remedies *for* the
tort of deceit. Secondly, Lush J made clear that a tort action for
conversion of the goods would not lie because title to the goods passed
under the contract albeit that that contract was unenforceable against
the infant. The relevant tort in issue was therefore deceit. Thirdly,
and with respect to Birks,[8] there is nothing in Lush J's judgment to
suggest that he was striving for a personal remedy for 'value surviving'
against the minor. On the contrary, it is submitted that he was
concerned with a straightforward value received measure of restitution
for a wrong.

Unfortunately the proposition that infancy should not be a defence
to restitution for a wrong, any more than to unjust enrichment by
subtraction, was contradicted by *Leslie v Sheill* in which, inter alia, and
as we have already noted, the Court of Appeal refused to award an
equitable personal remedy or money had and received for a minor's
tortious deceit on the ground that this would indirectly enforce an
invalid contract. *Stocks v Wilson* was, to all intents and purposes,
overruled.

It is unclear whether the courts are likely to exercise their discretion
under s 3(1) of the Minors' Contracts Act 1987 to support the *Stocks v
Wilson* approach. Nor does the Report of the Law Commission, which
was the basis for that Act, provide any clear guidance on this issue.[9]

(2) Insanity and drunkenness as defences

For two reasons these defences can be dealt with very briefly. First,
with the exception of necessitous intervention there are no authorities
touching on insanity and drunkenness as defences to grounds for
restitution.[10] Secondly, in accordance with the approach preferred

---

7   Ibid, at p 242.
8   Birks, at pp 399–400.
9   No 134 (1984).
10   As regards restitution for wrongs, insanity and drunkenness are not defences to torts:
     Winfield and Jolowicz on Tort (16th edn, 2002), pp 840–842; *Salmond and Heuston on the Law
     of Torts* (21st edn, 1996), pp 415–417.

above vis-à-vis infancy, it is submitted that in principle insanity and drunkenness should not be restitutionary defences (although the claimant may not be able to use the 'bargained-for' test to establish the enrichment of the *incapax*). Protection of the *incapax* does not justify sanctioning his unjust enrichment.

As has been said in relation to the defence of infancy, the close link to restitution of what is usually best viewed as a *contractual* liability of an *incapax* to pay a reasonable price for necessary goods or services indicates that insanity and drunkenness would not be defences to a restitutionary claim for supplying necessaries. This is supported by *Re Rhodes*,[11] a necessitous intervention case, in which the claimant relatives had paid for some of the deceased's mental asylum charges. Although the claimants were denied recovery from the deceased's estate, that was because they had not established that they intended to be repaid. The denial was not based on any defence that the deceased had been insane.

(3) Ultra vires as a company's defence

If a claimant has conferred benefits on a company under a contract that is void because ultra vires the company, is the claimant entitled to restitution from the company on the standard grounds, most obviously for total failure of consideration or mistake? This question cannot now arise vis-à-vis a non-charitable company (because of s 35(1) of the Companies Act 1985). Moreover, the leading case at common law of *Sinclair v Brougham*[12] – in which the ultra vires incapacity was held to be a defence to restitution for total failure of consideration – has recently been overruled by the House of Lords in *Westdeutsche Landesbank Girozentrale v Islington London Borough Council*.[13] Our discussion of ultra vires as a company's defence is therefore included not because of its practical importance today but because it is useful background in understanding the incapacity defence generally and ultra vires as a public authority's defence particularly.

Consistently with the approach that has so far been advocated in this section, a company's incapacity should not have been a defence to unjust enrichment. The policy behind the contract being invalid because ultra vires – protecting shareholders and creditors of the company – provided no justification for leaving the company unjustly enriched. Unfortunately, as with *Cowern v Nield* and *Leslie v Sheill* on

---

11 (1890) 44 Ch D 94. Above, p 311.
12 [1914] AC 398.
13 [1996] AC 669.

infancy, the case law was not committed to this approach and the House of Lords in *Sinclair v Brougham* took a wrong turn in believing that to allow a restitutionary remedy, at least in borrowing contracts, would constitute indirect enforcement of an invalid contract.

We start, however, with a case applying the correct approach. In *Re Pheonix Life Assurance Co*[14] a company's objects entitled it to issue life assurance policies. It was acting ultra vires when it issued marine insurance policies to the claimants who, on the winding up of the company, sought to enforce claims on the policies. It was held that their claims were barred by the ultra vires doctrine but that the claimants could recover the premiums paid in an action for money had and received on the grounds of total failure of consideration. In other words, the incapacity of the company did not provide it with a defence to restitution. Sir Page Wood V-C said:

> 'They have had no consideration for the premiums they paid. The directors, it is true, had no power to issue marine policies, but they had power to receive money, and apply it for the benefit of the company. It is proved that they did so receive and apply these premiums and the amount might have been recovered, even at law, as money had and received. The proof must therefore be allowed for the amount of the premiums paid.'[15]

Contrasting with that award of restitution was the decision in *Sinclair v Brougham*. Here a building society acted ultra vires by carrying on a banking business. On the winding up of the society the question arose, inter alia, as to whether those who had loaned money under the ultra vires banking facilities (the 'depositors') could recover that money in an action for money had and received. In other words, while it was accepted that the ultra vires doctrine meant that the depositors could not succeed in contractual actions to enforce repayment of their loans, could they succeed in restitution on the grounds of total failure of consideration?

The House of Lords held that they could not. The primary reasoning was that to allow an action for money had and received would indirectly contradict the ultra vires bar by producing the same loan repayment as if the contract had been valid. This was linked to what the Lords saw as the theoretical basis for the action for money had and received, namely an implied contract. If an express contract was invalid so must be an implied contract to the same effect. However, it was left open whether this objection was confined to borrowing contracts and hence whether *Re Pheonix Life Assurance Co*

---

14   (1862) 2 John & H 441. This was followed in *Flood v Irish Provident Assurance Co Ltd* (1912) 46 ILT 214.
15   Ibid, at p 448.

was good law; and the depositors were held to have an equitable proprietary remedy to recover money that could be traceably identified as their property.

Apart from its reliance on the implied contract fallacy, the major difficulty with this decision was in pinpointing why it was thought that to allow the personal action for money had and received would contradict the ultra vires bar whereas granting an equitable proprietary remedy did not do so and ordering the return of the premiums paid in *Re Pheonix Life Assurance Co* might not do so. Three possible explanations could be put forward.

The first was that the action for money had and received would require payment of the same monetary *amount* as the contractual remedy: ie if the loan to the bank was £500 both the contractual and restitutionary remedy would be for £500. In contrast an equitable proprietary remedy would merely give depositors the value of their traceably surviving property and in an insurance contract, as in *Re Pheonix Life Assurance Co*, there is clearly no equivalence between the premium paid and the amount payable by the insurer on the policy. But this explanation was not convincing for the reasons that have been put forward above in criticising *Leslie v Sheill*: the contractual remedy would have yielded the principal sum lent plus the agreed rate of interest whereas no interest could have been awarded on the restitutionary claim, the case having been decided before the Law Reform (Miscellaneous Provisions) Act 1934.

Secondly, the crucial link between the contractual remedy and the action for money had and received might have been thought to be that both require the *repayment* of money. But while this explanation offered a satisfactory distinction between *Sinclair v Brougham* and *Re Pheonix Life Assurance Co* – the latter being concerned with a non-borrowing contract – it did not explain why the House of Lords thought it acceptable to order the equitable proprietary remedy.

A third explanation was that both the contractual remedy and the action for money had and received are *personal* remedies whereas the equitable remedy is proprietary: that is, the ultra vires rule barred the creation of debtor-creditor relationships but did not affect proprietary remedies. However, on that approach, the House of Lords should have held that *Re Pheonix Life Assurance Co* was indisputably wrongly decided. In any event it was not made clear why in terms of policy the ultra vires bar should be regarded as affecting only personal and not proprietary remedies and it is probable that the reasoning was linked to the implied contract theory of the action for money had and received.

Therefore, none of the three explanations was convincing and the reasoning in *Sinclair v Brougham* was unsatisfactory. In line with the views of a number of other commentators,[16] it was said in the first edition of this book that, 'The case should be regarded as wrongly decided in rejecting the depositors' actions for money had and received'.[17] This is what the House of Lords has subsequently accepted in *Westdeutsche Landesbank Girozentrale v Islington London Borough Council*.[18] Lord Browne-Wilkinson, with whom Lords Slynn and Lloyd agreed said:[19]

> 'The House of Lords [in *Sinclair v Brougham*] was unanimous in rejecting the claim by the ultra vires depositors to recover in quasi-contract on the basis of moneys had and received. In their view, the claim in quasi-contract was based on an implied contract. To imply a contract to repay would be to imply a contract to exactly the same effect as the express ultra vires contract of loan. Any such implied contract would itself be void as being ultra vires. Subsequent developments in the law of restitution demonstrate that this reasoning is no longer sound. The common law restitutionary claim is based not on implied contract but on unjust enrichment: in the circumstances the law imposes an obligation to repay rather than implying an entirely fictitious agreement to repay ... In my judgment, your Lordships should now unequivocally and finally reject the concept that the claim for moneys had and received is based on a implied contract. I would overrule *Sinclair v Brougham* on this point. It follows that in *Sinclair v Brougham* the depositors should have had a personal claim to recover the moneys at law based on a total failure of consideration.'

Although not dealt with in the authorities, a company that enters into a contract ultra vires ought also to be liable in restitution for receiving an incontrovertible benefit in kind (assuming an unjust factor) although its ultra vires conduct probably prevents the claimant relying on the 'bargained-for' test of enrichment.

It should be added for completeness that, even before statutory reform of the ultra vires doctrine, ultra vires was not a defence to a tort action against a company[20] – and hence, as a natural consequence, would not bar restitution for a tort – although, admittedly, the question of possible conflict with the contractual position has never been judicially considered.

---

16 Goff and Jones (4th edn, 1993), p 63; (6th edn, 2002), para 1-085 (who also there criticise the proprietary aspect of the decision: see above p 410); Arrowsmith, 'Ineffective Transactions, Unjust Enrichment and Problems of Policy' (1989) 9 LS 307–316; Maddaugh and McCamus, *The Law of Restitution* (1st edn, 1990), pp 325–333. Cf Birks, at pp 86, 396–397.

17 *The Law of Restitution* (1st edn, 1993), p 459.

18 [1996] AC 669.

19 Ibid, at 710. Lord Goff preferred to distinguish, not to overrule, *Sinclair v Brougham*.

20 *Winfield and Jolowicz on Tort* (16th edn, 2002), pp 836–837; *Salmond and Heuston on the Law of Torts* (21st edn, 1996), pp 407–408. The same presumably applies to equitable wrongs.

(4) Ultra vires as a public authority's defence

It was established in *Woolwich Equitable Building Society v IRC*,[1] that an ultra vires *demand* by a public authority should be a ground for restitution from the public authority. The concern has been to protect individuals against the abuse of public power. That the ultra vires doctrine can also be viewed as a defence based on the incapacity policy of *protecting the public authority* – or, more specifically, public funds – has been pushed into the background to re-emerge, if at all, at the secondary stage of whether there are special defences (eg, 'disruption of public finances', short limitation periods) to the (special) prima facie right to restitution. It would be a nonsense in relation to the *Woolwich* case to suggest that, by analogy to *Sinclair v Brougham*, the incapacity of a public authority rules out the restitution of money demanded by it.

It is therefore only when one moves away from ultra vires *demands* by public authorities to contracts entered into ultra vires by public authorities (eg, interest rate swap transactions) that incapacity as a defence can play a leading role. Is a claimant who has conferred benefits on a public authority under a contract that is void because ultra vires the public authority entitled to restitution (most obviously for failure of consideration or mistake)? Or is such a claim met by a public authority's ultra vires defence?

It is submitted that, in principle and consistently with the argument put forward regarding the other forms of incapacity, the answer should be that the ultra vires doctrine does not afford a public authority a defence. The policy of protecting public funds does not justify sanctioning the unjust enrichment of the public authority.[2]

That principled position is now strongly supported by the decisions in the swaps cases, especially *Westdeutsche Landesbank Girozentrale v Islington London Borough Council*.[3] In none of the swaps cases were the public authorities afforded an ultra vires defence. The precise policy behind the ultra vires doctrine here – of protecting public funds from being squandered in highly speculative transactions – would plainly not be furthered by allowing the local authorities to be unjustly enriched at the banks' expense.[4] Moreover, as we have seen in the *Westdeutsche* case,[5]

---

1   [1993] AC 70. Above, chapter 13.
2   This is supported by Arrowsmith 'Ineffective Transactions, Unjust Enrichment and Problems of Policy' (1989) 9 LS 307, 311.
3   [1996] AC 669, HL.
4   In the Court of Appeal in the *Westdeutsche* case, [1994] 1 WLR 938, 951, Leggatt LJ specifically made this point when he indicated that there was no good policy reason for refusing restitution. He said, 'Protection of council taxpayers from loss is to be distinguished from securing a windfall for them.'
5   See above, pp 566–568.

the majority of the House of Lords, led by Lord Browne-Wilkinson, thought that the claimant bank would have been entitled to personal restitution from the local authority and that *Sinclair v Brougham*, which recognised a defence to such a claim, should be overruled.[6]

As regards benefits in kind rendered to public authorities under a contract that is ultra vires the public authority, again, in principle, there should be no ultra vires defence. The most relevant cases concerned work done for, or goods transferred to, public authorities under contracts that were ultra vires the public authorities on the procedural ground that the contracts lacked the required corporate seals.[7] In some of the cases[8] (although, admittedly, this appears to have been rejected by the House of Lords in the leading case of *Young & Co v Royal Leamington Spa Corpn*)[9] an exception to the general rule of contractual unenforceability was recognised whereby a claimant was held able to recover the agreed price (or a reasonable price) if the contract was fully executed and especially if the work or goods were necessary. This approach shares some similarities with the liability of a minor or insane person to pay for necessaries. As with those cases, so here, the public authority's liability can probably be satisfactorily analysed on standard contractual grounds rather than recasting it as restitutionary (based, eg, on the unjust factor of failure of consideration).

Finally, it can safely be assumed that there is no question of incapacity affording a public authority a defence to restitution for a tort (or equitable wrong). On the contrary, the ultra vires nature of the public authority's conduct has traditionally served merely to render it more likely that a tort claim can be made out.[10] The theoretically possible defensive role of the ultra vires doctrine is not even deemed worthy of a mention in the standard tort textbooks.

7.   ILLEGALITY AS A DEFENCE

It was explained in chapter 12 that, while withdrawal during the *locus poenitentiae* shows illegality being used as a ground for restitution,

---

6   While preferring not to overrule *Sinclair v Brougham* Lord Goff was of the view that the public policy denying restitution in *Sinclair v Brougham* did not apply to swaps because they were not (void) *borrowing* contracts. At first instance Hobhouse J had also distinguished *Sinclair v Brougham* because it concerned a borrowing contract.

7   This requirement was abolished by the Corporate Bodies' Contracts Act 1960.

8   Eg, *Clarke v Cuckfield Union Guardians* (1852) 21 LJQB 349; *Nicholson v Bradfield Union* (1866) LR 1 QB 620; *Lawford v Billericay RDC* [1903] 1 KB 772.

9   (1883) 8 App Cas 517. See also *Hunt v Wimbledon Local Board* (1878) 40 LT 115; *Mackay & Co v Toronto City Corpn* [1920] AC 208; *Waterous Engine Works v Palmerston* (1892) 21 SCR 556.

10   Eg, *Home Office v Dorset Yacht Co Ltd* [1970] AC 1004.

illegality otherwise acts as a possible defence to restitution for standard unjust factors. This section is concerned with that defensive application of illegality. Just as illegality operates as a defence to actions in tort[11] and to actions for enforcement of a contract,[12] it may operate as a defence to restitution.[13]

This role of illegality as a possible defence to standard grounds for restitution is, arguably, somewhat obscured by the traditional approach to illegality which, applying the maxims *ex turpi causa non oritur actio* and *in pari delicto potior est conditio defendentis*, regards restitution as generally being denied subject to three exceptions: where the parties are *non in pari delicto*; withdrawal during the *locus poenitentiae* (which involves illegality as a ground for restitution and is therefore outside the scope of this section); and where the claimant can establish a proprietary claim against the defendant without relying on the illegality or the illegal transaction. The key to clarity lies in recognising that the *non in pari delicto* exception deals with standard unjust factors, most importantly, mistake, duress and exploitation of weakness (but it could also be, for example, undue influence or incapacity).

The picture on the *non in pari delicto* exception that then emerges is that illegality is generally only a defence to a claim based on total failure of consideration. Where the claim is based on mistake or duress or exploitation of weakness, illegality will rarely be a defence because usually the unjust factor means that, in contrast to the defendant, the claimant is innocent of the illegality. The structure adopted here, therefore, is to look at the operation of illegality as a defence, first, to restitution for total failure of consideration; secondly, to restitution for mistake, duress, and exploitation of weakness; and, thirdly, to proprietary claims. A final subsection looks at whether there should be statutory reform of illegality as a defence to restitution.

---

11 See, eg, *Thackwell v Barclays Bank plc* [1986] 1 All ER 676; *Pitts v Hunt* [1991] 1 QB 24. For examples of illegality as a defence to the tort of conversion, see below, pp 578–583. There have been no cases on illegality as a defence to restitution for wrongs. But, as a matter of policy, illegality should surely apply in the same way to restitution for a wrong as to compensation for a wrong.

12 *Re Mahmoud and Ispahani* [1921] 2 KB 716; *Re Cavalier Insurance Co Ltd* [1989] 2 Lloyd's Rep 430. The classic exposition of illegality as a defence to a contractual action was Lord Mansfield's in *Holman v Johnson* (1775) 1 Cowp 341, 343.

13 See, generally, Virgo, *The Principles of the Law of Restitution* (1999), ch 26; Rose, 'Restitutionary and Proprietary Consequences of Illegality' in *Consensus Ad Idem* (ed Rose, 1996), pp 203–234; Buckley, *Illegality and Public Policy* (2002), ch 17.

(1) Illegality as a defence to total failure of consideration

Illegality has usually constituted a defence to claims for total failure of consideration.[14] Three examples suffice.[15]

In *Parkinson v College of Ambulance Ltd and Harrison*,[16] the secretary of the defendant charity fraudulently represented to the claimant that, if the claimant made a large donation to the funds of the defendant charity, he would be able to arrange a knighthood for the claimant. The claimant paid £3,000. When his knighthood was not forthcoming, and realising that he had been fooled, the claimant sought restitution of the money paid. His action failed. Although there had clearly been a total failure of consideration, restitution on that ground was not justified because the contract was illegal and the parties were *in pari delicto*.

In *Berg v Sadler and Moore*[17] the claimant tobacconist had been placed on the Tobacco Trade Association's stop list so that he could not buy cigarettes from any member. Through an agent he contracted to purchase cigarettes from the defendant member and paid for them. The defendant was suspicious and refused to deliver any cigarettes or to return the purchase price. The claimant's action for restitution of the purchase price was denied. Although there had been a total failure of consideration, the contract was illegal as being a criminal attempt to obtain goods by false pretences. The *ex turpi causa* maxim was invoked to rule out restitution.

In *Awwad v Geraghty & Co*[18] the claimant solicitors entered into a conditional fee agreement with the defendant in relation to libel proceedings. When those proceedings were settled, the defendant refused to pay the solicitors' fees contrary to the agreement and argued

---

14 An apparent exception is the restitution of premiums paid under a marine insurance contract that is deemed to be a gaming or wagering contract: see ss 4 and 84 of the Marine Insurance Act 1906. In *Re London County Commercial Reinsurance Office* [1922] 2 Ch 67, Lawrence J allowed restitution because the contracts were not illegal (in the narrow sense).

15 In *Aratra Potato Co Ltd v Taylor Johnson Garrett* [1995] 4 All ER 695 both the solicitors and their clients, who were parties to a partly executed champertous agreement, were denied restitution. The solicitors were denied a *quantum meruit* for their unpaid services and the clients were denied restitution of payments already made. One can treat this as an illustration of illegality being a defence to failure of consideration: but as regards the money paid, the primary explanation was that the consideration had not totally failed because services had been rendered by the solicitors. A further case that can be interpreted as applying illegality as a defence to failure of consideration is *Taylor v Bhail* (1995) 50 Con LR 70 where a builder was denied enforcement of a contract or a restitutionary *quantum meruit* for building work done because the contract was illegal. The price fixed for the work had been inflated so as to defraud the insurance company who would ultimately pay for the work.

16 [1925] 2 KB 1.

17 [1937] 2 KB 158.

18 [2000] 1 All ER 608.

that the agreement was illegal. At the time of the agreement such agreements were illegal both at common law and under the Solicitors' Practice Rules (although the law was subsequently changed, and conditional fee agreements made legal, by the Access to Justice Act 1999). The claim to enforce the agreement therefore failed; as did a *quantum meruit* claim for the value of the services rendered (with the ground for restitution being best viewed as failure of consideration). The policy that prevented enforcement of the agreement also prevented a *quantum meruit*. In Schiemann LJ's words, 'If the court, for reasons of public policy, refuses to enforce an agreement that a solicitor should be paid, it must follow that he cannot claim on a *quantum meruit*.'[19]

The primary policy behind illegality as a defence to restitution – and, as the above three cases illustrate, the two Latin maxims *in pari delicto* and *ex turpi causa* can be used more or less interchangeably to deny restitution – is that the courts ought not to lend assistance to wicked claimants. The dignity of the court would otherwise be sullied. A secondary reason for not allowing restitution for failure of consideration is that otherwise the law might be encouraging performance of the illegal contract.[20] For example, if A contracts to pay B £10,000 to murder C, to allow A to recover money paid in advance if the murder is not carried out might encourage B to commit the murder.

It may be doubted how strong those policies are and hence whether illegality should be a rigid bar to a claim for total failure of consideration. Many illegalities do not involve wickedness and comprise the breach of relatively trivial statutory regulations. Within the law of contract, the courts in recent years, following the lead of Devlin J in *St John Shipping Corpn v Joseph Rank Ltd*,[1] have shown themselves more reluctant to bar enforcement of an illegal contract.[2] Indeed, one might argue that the position now reached in contract is that, unless the purpose of the relevant statute (or common law crime or civil wrong or rule of public policy) clearly dictates non-enforcement, or unless there is gross turpitude on behalf of the claimant, an illegal contract will be enforceable.[3] The case is even stronger for a less rigid

---

19 Ibid, at 630–631. At p 631, *Mohamed v Alaga & Co* [1999] 3 All ER 699 was distinguished because 'The interpreter was blameless and no public policy was infringed by allowing him to recover a fair fee for interpreting; the public policy element in the case only affected fees for the introduction of clients.' See below, pp 576–577.

20 Birks, at p 300 further subdivides this policy into first, giving the defendant an incentive not to perform, and secondly, depriving the claimant of a lever for compelling performance.

1   [1957] 1 QB 267.

2   See, eg, *Shaw v Groom* [1970] 2 QB 504; *Euro-Diam Ltd v Bathurst* [1990] 1 QB 1; *Howard v Shirlstar Container Transport* [1990] 1 WLR 1292.

3   If the illegal contract were enforceable the claimant would as usual need to discharge the contract (for breach) before being able to claim restitution for total failure of consideration.

application of illegality as a defence to restitution, given that it directly involves 'undoing', rather than performance of, the illegality.[4]

(2) Illegality as a defence to mistake, duress, and exploitation of weakness

Illegality is rarely a defence to these grounds of restitution for the claimant can usually bring himself within the *non in pari delicto* exception. This will most obviously not be so where the unjust factor is a mistake which does not mask (ie relate to) the illegality. For example, in *Parkinson v College of Ambulance Ltd and Harrison*[5] restitution of the claimant's donation was denied because, inter alia, the claimant's mistake in believing that the defendant had the power to arrange a knighthood for him, did not mask the illegality. The claimant knew he was entering into an illegal contract. Similarly, in *Morgan v Ashcroft*[6] the claimant bookmaker had mistakenly paid too much in settling bets with the defendant 'punter'. As we saw in chapter 3, one ground for the denial of restitution of the overpayment was that the mistake of fact was not one as to supposed liability. Irrespective of that, restitution was denied because of the illegality of the wagering contract. Again the claimant's mistake did not render him innocent of the illegality.

But in the vast majority of cases the unjust factor means that the claimant, in contrast to the defendant, is innocent of the illegality and within the *non in pari delicto* exception. Some of the leading cases allowing restitution, despite illegality, have already been touched on in the chapters dealing with mistake, duress and exploitation of weakness.

(a) Mistake[7]

That illegality generally does not afford a defence to restitution for mistake of fact is well-illustrated by the old case of *Oom v Bruce*.[8] The claimant, as agent for a Russian subject abroad, had insured goods on

---

4   Tentative support for this is offered by *Cotronic (UK) Ltd v Dezonie* [1991] BCC 200 in which the Court of Appeal allowed a *quantum meruit*, despite the builder's illegal conduct, because the statutory penalty was thought sufficient. But the ground for restitution was not discussed and one might argue that it was mistake rather than failure of consideration. Above, p 396.

5   [1925] 2 KB 1.

6   [1938] 1 KB 49. Above, p 134.

7   If the 'illegal' contract were enforceable, and the claimant's mistake was in entering the contract, the contractual rules on mistake, would need to be satisfied before the restitution could be awarded.

8   (1810) 12 East 225. See also *Clay v Yates* (1856) 1 H & N 73.

board a ship sailing from St Petersburg to London. Unknown to the claimant, war had already broken out between Russia and England and the contract was therefore illegal and unenforceable. The claimant was nevertheless able to recover the premiums paid. The illegality was no defence to the claim based on the claimant's supposed liability mistake of fact. To the defendant's argument that illegality barred the claim, Lord Ellenborough CJ said:

'[Illegality is a defence] ... if the party making the insurance knows it to be illegal at the time: but here, the plaintiffs had no knowledge of the commencement of hostilities by Russia, when they effected this insurance; and, therefore, no fault is imputable to them for entering into the contract; and there is no reason why they should not recover back the premiums which they have paid ...'[9]

A significant feature of the reasoning is that no importance was placed on the defendant's knowledge and it was probably the case, although the facts are not entirely clear, that the defendant shared the claimant's mistake of fact. If so the parties were *in pari delicto* and the decision shows that a restitution-yielding mistake, masking illegality, is itself sufficient to defeat the defence of illegality. In other words, mistake may be a separate exception to the illegality defence outside the *non in pari delicto* framework and based simply on the claimant's innocence irrespective of the corresponding innocence of the defendant.[10]

Turning to mistake of law, the leading authority is *Kiriri Cotton Co v Dewani*[11] where the claimant tenant had paid the defendant landlord 'key money' as part of the consideration for the lease of a flat, contrary to the provisions of the Uganda Rent Restriction Ordinance 1949. The tenant was held able to recover the key money paid. Lord Denning's classic judgment emphasised that, despite illegality, money paid under a mistake of law could be recovered provided the parties were *non in pari delicto*. And on the facts this was so because, although the tenant's mistake of law was shared by the landlord, the purpose of the statute was to protect tenants. 'The duty of observing the law is firmly placed by the Ordinance on the shoulders of the landlord for the protection of the tenant.'[12]

This was followed in *Re Cavalier Insurance Co Ltd*[13] where an insurance company had been offering certain types of insurance

---

9   Ibid, at p 226.
10 See also *Cotronic (UK) Ltd v Dezonie* [1991] BCC 200: above, p 574, n 4.
11 [1960] AC 192.
12 Ibid, at p 205 (per Lord Denning). Prior to *Kleinwort Benson Ltd v Lincoln City Council* [1999] 2 AC 349, the fact that the mistaken payor was *non in pari delicto* was treated as an exception to the normal mistake of law bar; see above, p 148. After the removal of that bar, the parties being *non in pari delicto* is relevant simply to the defence of illegality.
13 [1989] 2 Lloyd's Rep 430.

without licence to do so. In allowing the claimants restitution of the premiums they had paid by mistake of law, Knox J said:

> 'In my judgment the circumstances of this case where the statutory duty was laid exclusively on the shoulders of the insurer for the protection of insured persons and the insured had no reason to suspect that he was being asked to enter into a void contract amply justify treating the insured as not equally delictual as the insurer and therefore entitled to recover the premiums.'[14]

A further example is provided by *Hughes v Liverpool Victoria Friendly Society*[15] where the defendant's agent fraudulently misrepresented to the claimant that certain insurance policies were legal. Restitution of the premiums was granted to the claimant because, despite the illegality, the mistake of law of the claimant was induced by the defendant's fraud and hence the parties were *non in pari delicto*.

As yet, however, a negligent misrepresentation as to the law has not sufficed to ground restitution for the misrepresentee. For example, in *Harse v Pearl Life Assurance Co*[16] the facts were similar to those in *Hughes*, except that the defendant's agent made the misrepresentation in good faith. The parties were held to be *in pari delicto*. Romer LJ said, 'Nor do I think that agents of insurance companies must be treated as under a greater obligation to know the law than ordinary persons whom they approach in order to effect insurances'.[17] This is difficult to accept. In Grodecki's words, 'It can be argued that in [*Harse*] ... the maxim *in pari delicto* was applied with unnecessary harshness.'[18]

Mistake of law and the *non in pari delicto* exception may offer the best explanation of the difficult case of *Mohamed v Alaga & Co*.[19] The claimant entered into an agreement with the defendant solicitors under which the claimant would refer Somali refugees to the solicitors and assist them in preparing the clients' asylum applications in return for a share of the solicitors' fees. The sharing of fees was prohibited by the Solicitors' Practice Rules, which were treated as having the force of subordinate legislation. The contractual claim for the agreed share of the fees was refused because of illegality. But the Court of Appeal allowed the claim for a restitutionary *quantum meruit* for the services

---

14   Ibid, at p 450.
15   [1916] 2 KB 482. See also *Shelley v Paddock* [1980] QB 348.
16   [1904] 1 KB 558. See also *Beattie v Lord Ebury* (1872) 7 Ch App 777; *Eaglesfield v Marquis of Londonderry* (1876) 4 Ch D 693.
17   Ibid, at p 564.
18   'In Pari Delicto Potior Est Conditio Defendentis' (1955) LQR 254, 264.
19   [1999] 3 All ER 699. For an analysis indicating the difficulties in this case, see Enonchong, 'Restitution Following Illegal Fee-Sharing Agreement with Solicitor' [2000] RLR 241. This case was distinguished in *Awwad v Geraghty & Co* [2000] 1 All ER 608; see above, pp 572–573.

rendered by the claimant to the solicitors in assisting with the clients' applications. It was thought important that, in contrast to the solicitors, the claimant was ignorant of the prohibition on fee-sharing. In Lord Bingham CJ's words, 'It is ... in my judgment relevant that the parties are not in a situation in which their blameworthiness is equal. The defendant is a solicitors' firm and bound by the rules. It should reasonably be assumed to know what the rules are and to comply with them ... By contrast, the plaintiff ... was ignorant that there was any reason why the defendant should not make the agreement which he says was made.'[20]

(b) Duress

Duress renders the claimant innocent of the illegality and *non in pari delicto* and illegality is therefore no defence to the restitutionary claim. In *Astley v Reynolds*,[1] for example, the claimant who had pawned his plate with the defendant was able to recover the interest demanded by the defendant over the legally permitted rate. The illegality of the interest demanded and paid did not therefore defeat restitution grounded on duress of goods. Again in *Davies v London and Provincial Marine Insurance Co*[2] friends of an agent of the claimant company paid money to the company to remove the threat to prosecute the agent for suspected embezzlement. Fry J held that the friends could recover the money paid because, although the contract was illegal as being one to stifle a prosecution, the friends paid under oppression (ie duress constituted by the illegitimate threat to prosecute) and were hence *non in pari delicto*.

And in a number of eighteenth and nineteenth century cases claimants, who had been induced to pay money by a creditor's threat to sue – such a threat being illegitimate because the payment demanded would illegally defraud other creditors – were held entitled to restitution. In *Smith v Bromley*,[3] for example, the defendant creditor, acting through an agent, refused to sign a bankrupt's certificate unless he was paid £40. The claimant, the bankrupt's sister, paid the £40 but after the defendant had signed the certificate, sought restitution. In allowing this claim, Lord Mansfield reasoned that the normal illegality defence did not apply here because of the 'oppression' and 'extortion' involved. Similarly, in *Smith v Cuff*,[4] a creditor who had entered into a

---

20 Ibid, at 707–708.
1   (1731) 2 Stra 915. Another possible example is *Great Western Rly Co v Sutton* (1869) LR 4 HL 226: above, pp 223–224.
2   (1878) 8 Ch D 469.
3   (1760) 2 Doug KB 696n.
4   (1817) 6 M & S 160. In *Atkinson v Denby* (1862) 7 H & N 934 both *Smith v Bromley* and *Smith v Cuff* were followed in awarding restitution.

composition agreement, while demanding extra money from the debtor, was held bound to repay that extra money. In Lord Ellenborough's words, 'This is not a case of *par delictum*; it is oppression on one side and submission on the other; it never can be predicated as *par delictum*, when one holds the rod and the other bows to it. There was an inequality of situation between these parties; one was creditor, the other debtor, who was driven to comply with the terms which the former chose to enforce.'[5]

(c) Exploitation of weakness

We have seen in chapter 7[6] that a contract may be rendered illegal, especially by statute, in order to protect a vulnerable class from exploitation. It then naturally follows that the illegality is no defence to a claim for restitution by the claimant as a member of that vulnerable class. The ground for restitution (exploitation of weakness) and illegality not being a defence to restitution (because the parties are *non in pari delicto*) here converge; they are two sides of the same coin. The relevant cases have been fully discussed in chapter 7.

(d) Limiting illegality?

It is clearly right that illegality should rarely be regarded as a defence to mistake, duress and exploitation of weakness. The twin policies behind the illegality defence – not tainting the courts' dignity and not encouraging illegal conduct – are not infringed by allowing restitution to such an innocent party. Indeed the law should go further by, at the very least, clearly breaking free of the emphasis on relative blameworthiness inherent in the phrase *non in pari delicto* and recognising that a party who makes a mistake masking the illegality should be entitled to restitution even if the defendant is equally mistaken. Moreover, even if the mistake does not mask the illegality, it can be strongly argued, in the same vein as has been argued vis-à-vis failure of consideration, that the courts should be willing to ignore illegality unless a denial of restitution is clearly dictated by the purpose behind the illegality or there is gross turpitude on the claimant's behalf. Applying this line of reasoning, restitution should have been awarded in, for example, *Morgan v Ashcroft*.

(3) Illegality as a defence to proprietary claims

Strictly speaking, this book is concerned only with restitutionary proprietary rights (ie, proprietary restitution) and not pure proprietary

---

5   Ibid, at p 165.
6   See above, pp 269–271.

rights.[7] Many of the illegality cases have concerned the latter and not the former. But as the same approach to illegality applies to both it seems appropriate to treat them both together.

Here the traditional approach to illegality as a defence turns on whether the claimant can establish the proprietary claim without relying on the illegality or the illegal transaction. This 'reliance' principle is slippery and its precise ambit and justification are difficult to pin down. However, in most cases it appears that the claimant will be able to establish its proprietary claim without relying on the illegality or the illegal transaction. In most cases, therefore, illegality will not be a defence to proprietary claims.

For example, in the early case of *Feret v Hill*[8] a tenant had used his rented premises for a brothel. On being evicted the tenant successfully brought an action for ejectment against the landlord. The tenant's right to possession during the currency of the lease was unaffected by the illegal purpose that he had been pursuing.

More recently in *Singh v Ali Sardara*[9] a lorry was sold and delivered to the claimant by the defendant under a contract that was illegal as designed to deceive the authorities into giving a haulage permit for the lorry. The defendant took back the lorry without the claimant's permission. In an action for detinue the claimant was awarded compensatory damages for the lorry's value. The illegality of the contract was irrelevant. In Lord Denning's words, giving the judgment of the Privy Council, 'Despite the illegality of the contract, the property has passed to him by the sale and delivery of the lorry.'[10]

He later repeated that approach in the Court of Appeal in *Belvoir Finance Co Ltd v Stapleton*.[11] The claimants, who had bought cars under an illegal contract of sale and hired them out to Belgravia Car Hire Co Ltd under an illegal hire-purchase agreement, were awarded compensatory damages for the conversion of the cars by Belgravia's assistant manager. Applying normal proprietary principles, title to the cars passed to the claimants even though possession of the cars passed directly from the sellers to Belgravia without going through the claimants.

The two latter cases were relied on by the Divisional Court in *Chief Constable of West Midlands v White*[12] in holding that title to the purchase money of alchohol sold under an illegal contract passed to the seller. And, as there was thought to be no reason of public policy to deprive

7   See above, pp 61–62.
8   (1854) 15 CB 207.
9   [1960] AC 167.
10 Ibid, at p 177.
11 [1971] 1 QB 210.
12 [1992] NLJR 455.

the seller of his rights because of his illegality, a magistrate's order for the money to be delivered by the police to the seller under s 1 of the Police (Property) Act 1897 was upheld.

In the nineteenth century case of *Taylor v Chester*,[13] where normal property rules meant that the claimant had no proprietary claim, the 'reliance' principle was expressly relied on in denying the claim. A half banknote was pledged as security for the cost of wine and food consumed in an orgy at a brothel. The claimant sought unsuccessfully to recover back the half note. In accordance with normal property rules, the pledgee had the right to keep the property pledged until payment was tendered. Mellor J, giving the judgment of the court, put to one side what the position would have been if the payment had been tendered and said that, on these facts, 'It was ... impossible for him to recover except through the medium and by the aid of an illegal transaction to which he himself was a party.'[14]

The two most important, and also controversial, cases to consider the 'reliance' principle are *Bowmakers Ltd v Barnet Instruments Ltd*[15] and *Tinsley v Milligan*.[16] In the former, the defendants had hire-purchased machine tools from the claimants under three separate agreements, each of those agreements being illegal because not authorised by the Ministry of Supply. In breach of the agreements, the defendants paid some but not all of the agreed instalments. Furthermore they sold off the tools which were the subject matter of the first and third agreement. They were held liable for the conversion of the tools under all three agreements.

This has been widely criticised vis-à-vis the tools under the second agreement.[17] As regards the first and third agreements, the defendants were clearly liable in conversion as they had no right, contractual or otherwise, to sell off the machines. The decision on the second agreement is, in contrast, hard to explain when one tries to make sense of the idea – expressly used in the Court of Appeal's reasoning – of 'not relying on the illegal contract'. The claimants were clearly relying on the second contract in the sense that they were exercising their contractual right to terminate for breach. To argue, as Coote does,[18] that the owners' rights of termination derived from the pre-existing proprietary rights and were not the creation of the illegal

13 (1869) LR 4 QB 309.
14 Ibid, at p 314.
15 [1945] KB 65.
16 [1994] 1 AC 340.
17 Eg, *Cheshire, Fifoot and Furmston's Law of Contract* (14th edn, 2001), pp 433–434; Hamson, 'Illegal Contracts and Limited Interests' (1949) 10 CLJ 249.
18 'Another Look at *Bowmakers v Barnet Instruments*' (1972) 35 MLR 38, esp at 48. Cf Birks, at pp 431–432.

agreement merely shows how malleable and unhelpful is the notion of 'no reliance on the contract'.

In *Tinsley v Milligan*[19] the parties were same-sex cohabitees, who had both contributed to the purchase of a house. By an arrangement between them, the house was solely registered in Miss Tinsley's name so as to enable Miss Milligan to make false benefits claims to the Department of Social Security. The parties subsequently fell out and Tinsley moved out of the house. She brought a claim against Milligan for possession of the house on the basis that it was hers alone. Milligan counter-claimed that the house was held by Tinsley on resulting trust for them both in equal shares. Tinsley contended that illegality operated as a defence to that counter-claim; because of the illegal scheme Milligan could not establish the resulting trust.

The majority (Lords Browne-Wilkinson, Jauncey and Lowry, Lords Goff and Keith dissenting) held that illegality did not here operate as a defence and that Milligan could establish a resulting trust. The majority's reasoning extended the 'reliance' principle applied in the *Bowmakers* case to equitable, as well as legal, proprietary claims. Applying normal trusts law, Milligan was entitled to an equitable interest under a presumed resulting trust. Illegality was not a defence because she did not need to rely on the illegality in order to establish that resulting trust. The position would have been different had there been a presumption of advancement that Milligan was seeking to rebut. Then she would have had to rely on her illegal purpose to rebut the presumption and illegality would therefore have been a defence preventing her doing so. In Lord Browne-Wilkinson's words:

> 'A party to an illegality can recover by virtue of a legal or equitable property interest if, but only if, he can establish his title without relying on his own illegality. In cases where the presumption of advancement applies, the plaintiff is faced with the presumption of gift and therefore cannot claim under a resulting trust unless and until he has rebutted that presumption of gift: for these purposes the plaintiff does have to rely on the underlying illegality and therefore fails.'[20]

And earlier he had said:

> 'In this case Miss Milligan as defendant simply pleaded the common intention that the property should belong to both of them and that she contributed to the purchase price: she claimed that in consequence the property belonged to them equally ... Therefore Miss Milligan was not forced to rely on the illegality to prove her equitable interest.'[1]

---

19   [1994] 1 AC 340.
20   Ibid, at 375.
1   Ibid, at 371–372.

In contrast, Lord Goff (with whom Lord Keith agreed) dissenting thought that the 'reliance' principle was confined to common law; and that in equity the illegality defence was more wide-ranging and was to the effect that equity will not assist a claimant who does not come to equity with clean hands. Therefore, on these facts, as the court knew of Miss Milligan's fraud, she would be denied its assistance.

A major difficulty with the majority's reasoning is that, even if one is clear what it means, the 'reliance' principle is hard to justify in terms of policy. What should primarily matter is the seriousness of the illegality involved, the possibility of deterrence, and what other sanctions will be brought to bear; and not the technical question of whether there is a presumption of advancement or a presumed resulting trust. But nor, with respect, is Lord Goff's approach satisfactory. Not only does it draw an unprincipled distinction between common law and equity (the 'reliance' principle applying to the former but not to the latter) but under the 'clean hands' doctrine it embraces a very wide illegality defence that, had the minority's reasoning prevailed, would have produced an unjust result on the facts of *Tinsley v Milligan* itself. Perhaps a better way forward would have been for the House of Lords to have adopted the broad discretionary 'public conscience' test favoured by Nicholls LJ in the Court of Appeal in the *Tinsley* case. However, their Lordships were unanimous in rejecting that test as being too vague and unsupported by authority.

It is not surprising that, while English courts have considered themselves bound to apply *Tinsley v Milligan*[2] – although, as shown by *Tribe v Tribe*[3] a way out can sometimes be found through the withdrawal doctrine – academics,[4] the Law Commission[5] and the High Court of Australia in *Nelson v Nelson*[6] have subjected *Tinsley* to fierce criticism. In the *Nelson* case, a presumption of advancement to her son and daughter was rebutted by a mother leading evidence of her illegal purpose (which was to claim subsidised housing under the Australian Defence Service Homes Act 1918). The High Court of Australia paid close attention to the policy of the relevant Act. McHugh J said that

---

2   See, eg, *Silverwood v Silverwood* (1997) 74 P & CR 453, CA (presumption of advancement, so illegality a defence); *Lawson v Coombes* [1999] Ch 373, CA (presumption of resulting trust, so illegality not a defence); *Collier v Collier* [2002] EWCA Civ 1095 (express trust so illegality a defence).

3   [1996] Ch 107: see above, chapter 12.

4   Berg, 'Illegality and Equitable Interests' [1993] JBL 513, 517–518; Enonchong, 'Illegaility: The Fading Flame of Public Policy' (1994) 14 OJLS 295, 299; Stowe, '"The Unruly Horse" has Bolted: *Tinsley v Milligan*' (1994) 57 MLR 441, 446; Buckley, 'Law's Boundaries and the Challenge of Illegality' in *Legal Structures* (ed Buckley, 1996), p 229 at pp 231–234; Davies, 'Presumptions and Illegality' in *Trends in Contemporary Trust Law* (ed Oakley, 1996), ch 2.

5   *Illegal Transactions*, Law Commission Consultation Paper No 154 (1999), esp paras 3.19–3.24.

6   (1995) 184 CLR 538.

the *Bowmakers* reliance principle, approved by the majority in *Tinsley*, would produce results that were 'essentially random.' He went on:

> 'The *Bowmakers* rule has no regard to the legal and equitable rights of the parties, the merits of the case, the effect of the transaction in undermining the policy of the relevant legislation or the question whether the sanctions imposed by the legislation sufficiently protect the purpose of the legislation. Regard is had only to the procedural issue; and it is that issue and not the policy of the legislation or the merits of the parties which determines the outcome. Basing the grant of legal remedies on an essentially procedural criterion which has nothing to do with the equitable positions of the parties or the policy of the legislation is unsatisfactory, particularly when implementing a doctrine that is founded on public policy.'[7]

Even if one largely adheres to the reliance principle, it appears that there will be some extreme examples where, despite the claimant not needing to rely on the illegality, the illegality will be a defence to a proprietary claim. It has been clarified in *Costello v Chief Constable of Derbyshire Constabulary*[8] that the range of these examples should be narrow and does not include where the claimant has stolen the property. They essentially comprise where it is unlawful for the claimant to be in possession of that type of property. Examples might be illegal weapons, prohibited drugs or obscene books.[9] In such cases an illegality defence is justified because a remedy is clearly barred by the purpose behind the illegality.

(4) Should there be statutory reform of illegality as a defence to restitution?

The law on illegality in relation to restitution has been subjected to wide-ranging criticism as has the law on illegal transactions generally. Even once one has put to one side the withdrawal doctrine (because there illegality is a ground for restitution), illegality as a defence to restitution is complex, technical, capable of producing injustice, and, in some respects, uncertain.[10] Claims based on failure of consideration are too readily being denied because of illegality; and the 'reliance' principle in the context of proprietary claims pushes the courts down

---

7   Ibid, at p 609.
8   [2001] 1 WLR 1437, 1451–1452, CA.
9   The last of these was an example given in the *Bowmakers* case: [1945] KB 65, 72. The first two were examples given in the *Costello* case.
10 But the defence of illegality (to a contractual or restitutionary claim) has been held by the Court of Appeal not to infringe the claimant's right to peaceful enjoyment of possessions under Art 1 of the First Protocol in the Human Rights Act 1998: *Shanshal v Al-Kishtaini* [2001] EWCA Civ 264, [2001] 2 All ER (Comm) 601.

a largely irrelevant enquiry that avoids addressing the central policy issues at stake.[11] While an argument can be mounted that a reformed approach is within the interpretative reach of the courts,[12] the better view (especially in the light of *Tinsley v Milligan*) is that legislation, introducing a structured discretion attuned to the policies in play, should be introduced.[13] This is what the Law Commission has provisionally recommended, with the emphasis being on the discretion being structured and tied to illegality as a defence and not (as, for example, in New Zealand)[14] open-ended. According to the Law Commission's central provisional recommendations, the courts would have a discretion to decide whether illegality should be a defence (whether, for example, to enforcement of a contract or to restitution of unjust enrichment). More specifically, it was provisionally recommended that: 'The proposed discretion should be structured so that the court should be required to take into account specific factors in reaching its decision; and that those factors should be: (1) the seriousness of the illegality involved; (2) the knowledge and intention of the plaintiff; (3) whether denying relief will act as a deterrent; (4) whether denying relief will further the purpose of the rule which renders the contract illegal; and (5) whether denying relief is proportionate to the illegality involved.'[15]

11 A further specific problem is that it is unclear whether English law on restitution under illegal contracts satisfies the need to protect a person's directly effective rights under Arts 81 and 82. A contract that is contrary to Art 81 of the EC Treaty as anti-competitive will be regarded as illegal: *Gibbs Mew plc v Gemmell* [1999] 1 EGLR 43, CA. The same probably also applies to a contract that is contrary to Art 82. In *Courage Ltd v Crehan* [2002] QB 507, the ECJ ruled that an absolute defence of illegality would here infringe EC law but that there was no objection to a rule barring a remedy to a party who had been significantly responsible for the distortion of competition. See, generally, Alison Jones, *Restitution and European Community Law* (2000), ch 6.

12 Birks, 'Recovering Value Transferred Under an Illegal Contract' (2000) 1 Theoretical Inquiries in Law 155 argues that there is no need for legislation and that the central question is one of 'stultification': ie would awarding restitution contradict the reason for the contract being illegal.

13 Supporters of legislative reform include Grodecki, 'In pari delicto potior est conditio defendentis' (1955) 71 LQR 254, 273–274; Merkin, 'Restitution by Withdrawal from Executory Illegal Contracts' (1981) 97 LQR 420; Dickson, 'Restitution and Illegal Transactions' in *Essays on the Law of Restitution* (ed Burrows, 1991), pp 170–195; Buckley, 'Illegal Transactions: Chaos or Discretion?' (2000) 20 Legal Studies 155; Enonchong, 'Illegal Transactions: The Future' [2000] RLR 82; Buckley, *Illegality and Public Policy* (2002), paras 21.34–21.35.

14 New Zealand Illegal Contracts Act 1970, s 7. Although certain factors are spelt out as having to be considered by the court (eg, the conduct of the parties, the object of any enactment that has been broken, and the gravity of the penalty for breach) the discretion is to award such relief as the courts think just. For the Law Commission's rejection of this broader discretion, that allows the courts in the context of illegality to invent new rights to restitution, see Law Commission Consultation Paper No 154 (1999), paras 7.73–7.87.

15 Law Commission Consultation Paper No 154 (1999), para 7.43.

8.   BONA FIDE PURCHASE FROM A THIRD PARTY

It is a matter of controversy as to what role, if any, the defence of bona fide purchase for value without notice[16] from a third party plays in the law of restitution. On one view, the bona fide purchase defence is concerned only with pure proprietary claims and has no role as a defence to the cause of action of unjust enrichment. According to this view, the defence is solely concerned with where a transfer of property by a third party (ie by someone other than the owner) confers good title to the property on the transferee so that the owner's pure proprietary claim fails. It should solely be seen as being the fundamental exception to the general rule (embodied in the maxim *nemo dat quod non habet*) that the title of the original owner is preserved where property is transferred without his consent. So, for example, Virgo writes, 'The function of the *bona fide* purchase defence is to make good defects in the defendant's title to property. The defence constitutes an exception to the ... principle by virtue of which the transferee cannot obtain rights to property which are better than those of the transferor.'[17] And later, in his book, '[W]hereas the change of position defence is a general defence which is applicable to all restitutionary claims, the *bona fide* purchase defence is a specific defence which applies only where the plaintiff's restitutionary claim is founded on the vindication of property rights. This is because the rationale of the *bona fide* purchase defence is to give the defendant indefeasible title to property in which the plaintiff had a proprietary interest.'[18]

Virgo's view is supported by the speech of Lord Millett in *Foskett v McKeown*.[19] Having argued that the tracing claim in question was one to vindicate property rights and not to reverse unjust enrichment, his Lordship later said:

> 'As I have already pointed out, the purchasers seek to vindicate their property
> rights, not to reverse unjust enrichment. The correct classification of the
> purchasers' cause of action may appear to be academic, but it has important
> consequences .... [A] claim in unjust enrichment is subject to a change of position
> defence, which usually operates by reducing or extinguishing the element of
> enrichment. An action like the present is subject to the bona fide purchaser for
> value defence, which operates to clear the defendant's title.'[20]

16 For the details on what is meant by notice and value, see standard texts on equity and
    trusts: eg, Hanbury and Martin *Modern Equity* (16th edn, 2001) pp 34–40.
17 *The Principles of the Law of Restitution*, p 674.
18 Ibid, at p 732.
19 [2001] 1 AC 102.
20 Ibid, at 129.

With respect, the better view – as has been argued in chapter 1 above – is that *Foskett v McKeown* was concerned with the reversal of unjust enrichment; and linked with that, and the important point to be made here, is that, in addition to its role in relation to the passing of title, bona fide purchase is a defence in unjust enrichment by subtraction both in respect of personal and proprietary restitution.[1]

The bona fide purchase defence operates as a defence in unjust enrichment by subtraction where the defendant is an indirect recipient. That is, the situation we are concerned with is where the claimant can establish a cause of action in unjust enrichment against a defendant who has received the enrichment from a third party rather than from the claimant. As we have seen in chapter 1, restitution of unjust enrichment by subtraction is generally restricted to direct providers so that, to establish prima facie liability against an indirect recipient, the claimant will need to invoke an exception to that general rule.[2] This will most commonly be the title and tracing exception which allows the claimant to establish that the defendant's enrichment was at the claimant's expense, rather than at the third party's expense, where it was the claimant's property, or its traceable substitute, that was transferred by the third party to the defendant. But having established prima facie liability, the claim will still fail where the defendant can invoke the defence that in good faith, without notice, it gave value for the enrichment to the third party.

The leading modern judicial discussion of bona fide purchase, as a defence to a claim for unjust enrichment, was in the context of a *personal* restitutionary claim in *Lipkin Gorman v Karpnale Ltd*.[3] As we have seen,[4] the defence there failed. The reason for this is that, although in one sense value was given by the defendant club to Cass – in exchanging money for 'chips' or in paying out winnings on money gambled – that value did not count, for the purposes of establishing that the club was a bona fide purchaser *for value*, because it was given under a void wagering contract. To be valuable consideration or value for the purposes of the defence the value must be given under a valid, not a void, contract. Had the contract been a valid one, the defence would have succeeded. So, if we alter the facts, and imagine that Cass used the claimant's traceable money to stay at the Ritz, rather than gambling it at the Playboy Club, the Ritz would have been able to invoke successfully the bona fide purchase defence (assuming that it

---

1   This is also the view of Birks and Mitchell, *English Private Law* (2000), paras 15.267, 15.291–15.294.
2   See above, pp 31–41.
3   [1991] 2 AC 548.
4   See above, pp 192–193.

was acting in good faith and without notice that the money had been taken from the claimant).

Similarly, although not expressly spelt out in the judgments, it is generally assumed to be indisputable[5] that, had the money in *Ministry of Health v Simpson*[6] been mistakenly paid by the personal representative to bona fide purchasers for value rather than to innocent volunteers the next of kin's personal equitable restitutionary remedy would have been defeated.

Indeed, were it not for equity's traditional erroneous emphasis on 'knowing receipt' in order to establish prima facie liability, it is submitted that some of the cases examined in chapter 4 (on ignorance) would have illustrated bona fide purchase operating as a defence to personal restitution.[7]

Bona fide purchase has more commonly been recognised and applied as a defence to a proprietary, rather than a personal, restitutionary remedy. It is well-established as a defence to proprietary restitution following tracing;[8] and as a bar to rescission of a contract (for example, for misrepresentation or undue influence)[9] so as to prevent the claimant revesting its proprietary rights in property that has subsequently been transferred by a third party to the defendant.

What is the rationale for the bona fide purchase defence and how does it relate to change of position?

If we continue with the Ritz example, we can see the difference between the bona fide purchase and change of position defences. Let us assume that Cass drew £10,000 from the claimant's account and used it all to pay for ten nights at the Ritz. If the Ritz invoked the change of position defence, it would have to show that it would be worse off if now required to pay back the £10,000 than if it had never received it. Let us assume that the hotel was only part-full so that a similar contract with another customer would not have been entered into had Cass not stayed there. In that situation, the change of position defence would require an examination of the cost to the Ritz of providing the services to Cass. If the cost was, say, £6,000, so that the bargain for the Ritz was a good one, the change of position defence would be a partial defence only; the Ritz would have changed its position to the extent of £6,000 only and it would be bound to repay

---

5   See, eg, *GL Baker Ltd v Medway Building and Supplies Ltd* [1958] 2 All ER 532; on appeal [1958] 3 All ER 540, 543; *Re J Leslie Engineers Co Ltd* [1976] 1 WLR 292, 299; Goff and Jones, chapter 30.

6   [1951] AC 251, HL; affirming *Re Diplock* [1948] Ch 465, CA.

7   Eg *BCCI (Overseas) Ltd v Akindele* [2001] Ch 437.

8   See, eg, Hanbury and Martin, *Modern Equity* (16th edn, 2001), p 701; *Foskett v McKeown* [2001] 1 AC 102, 130 (per Lord Millett).

9   Eg, *Cundy v Lindsay* (1878) 3 App Cas 459, 463–464; *Morley v Loughnan* [1893] 1 Ch 736.

the claimant £4,000. But the bona fide purchase defence would succeed to bar entirely the claim for £10,000 because it is not concerned to quantify the value of what was rendered by the defendant; any value is sufficient. At a deeper level this is because, unlike change of position, bona fide purchase is not a disenrichment defence.

To give another example: say the recipient of £1,000 stolen money has 'bought' the money by selling the thief a car worth £400. He is a purchaser for value and provided innocent has an absolute defence to a restitutionary claim for £1,000. In contrast a change of position defence would only operate to prevent him having to pay back £400 (assuming no other loss consequent on the receipt of the £1,000). In short, bona fide purchase is not rooted in loss of benefit so that it is irrelevant whether the bona fide purchaser has made a good or a bad bargain.

It is for this reason that the House of Lords in *Lipkin Gorman v Karpnale Ltd* rejected the suggestion made[10] that bona fide purchase is simply an aspect of the change of position defence. Lord Goff said, 'The defence of change of position is akin to the defence of bona fide purchase: but we cannot simply say that bona fide purchase is a species of change of position. This is because change of position will only avail a defendant to the extent that his position has been changed; whereas, where bona fide purchase is invoked, no inquiry is made (in most cases) into the adequacy of the consideration.'[11]

But if the bona fide purchase defence is not a disenrichment defence, what is its rationale as a defence to unjust enrichment? Why is it that one is not concerned to quantify and compare the values rendered?

The best explanation is the policy of maintaining the sanctity of contract. Where there is a valid contract between a third party and the defendant, the courts will not undermine that contract, by allowing the claimant an unjust enrichment action against the defendant, unless the defendant was dishonest or had notice of the facts entitling the claimant to restitution of the benefit transferred under the contract. The bona fide purchase defence plays an analogous role in three-party cases to that played in two-party cases by the principle that one cannot have restitution of benefits transferred under a contract where that contract is valid. So, for example, in *Barclays Bank Ltd v WJ Simms, Son and Cooke (Southern) Ltd*[12] Robert Goff J's exclusion from his prima

---

10 Birks, 'Misdirected Funds: Restitution from the Recipient' [1991] LMCLQ 473; Millett, 'Tracing the Proceeds of Fraud' (1991) 107 LQR 71, 82.

11 [1991] 2 AC 548, 580–581.

12 [1980] QB 677.

facie causation test of payments made for consideration is the direct equivalent in a two-party mistake case of the bona fide purchaser defence in a three-party mistake case. There is therefore a coherent policy running through two-party and three-party cases (in the latter through the bona fide purchase defence) that restitution should not undermine the sanctity of contract.

That this is the rationale for the bona fide purchase defence in the law of restitution is carefully explained by Kit Barker in his seminal article on this topic.[13] He writes:

> '[T]he policy of transactional security underpinning the bona fide purchase defence need only be invoked where the defendant has received a benefit by way of exchange with a party other than the plaintiff. The defence exists in that type of case because the defendant is otherwise unprotected against the claims of the plaintiff who, in contract law, is immune from risk-allocations in contracts to which he is not party. Where, as in the typical two-party case, the receipt occurs as part of an agreement with the plaintiff himself ..., no defence of bona fide purchase is needed. A valid contract for the receipt and retention of the benefit remains in being, thereby ousting the plaintiff's restitutionary rights. The defendant's good faith is relevant, not because it fits into the defence of bona fide purchase, but because it is a precondition of his entitlement to invoke the "objective" principle of contract law ... Viewed in this light, the objective principle of contract law and the restitutionary defence of bona fide purchase pursue the same aim (security for those engaged in exchange-transactions) but in different contexts. The latter operates where the former cannot: where the exchange that has taken place is not one between the parties to the dispute.'

A useful case in seeing the coherence of the 'sanctity of contract' policy across the law of restitution, which bridges the gap between two-party and three-party cases, is *Pan Ocean Shipping Ltd v Creditcorp Ltd, The Trident Beauty*.[14] This case has been examined in chapter 10. As we saw, the House of Lords there denied a restitutionary claim against the assignee of a time-charter who had been paid hire by the claimant-charterer for a period when the ship was off-hire. The best explanation of this – albeit that only Lord Goff relied on this and then only as his secondary reasoning – is that to have awarded restitution for failure of consideration against the assignee would have undermined the contract of assignment by which the assignee had bought the right to payment of hire free from any condition as to repayment. Although the hire had been paid by the claimant to the

---

13 'After Change of Position: Good Faith Exchange in the Modern Law of Restitution' in *Laundering and Tracing* (ed Birks, 1995), pp 191, 200–201.
14 [1994] 1 WLR 161. See above, pp 348–350.

defendant assignee, so that this was not a case of payment by a third party and did not therefore involve the bona fide purchase defence, it was somewhat analogous; and indeed the analogy to the bona fide purchase defence was, as we saw in chapter 10, explicitly referred to by Lord Goff. The basis of the analogy was that the policy of restitution not undermining the sanctity of contract was being applied not to a contract between the restitution-claimant and the defendant but to a contract between a third party (the assignor) and the defendant (the assignee). This case is therefore a useful and important bridge between standard two-party cases, where the parties are in a contractual relationship and where sanctity of contract normally requires the contract to be invalid before restitution can be awarded; and three-party cases, where the benefit has been transferred by a third party to the defendant and where the sanctity of contract policy is upheld by the bona fide purchase defence.

One possible difficulty with the sanctity of contract explanation of the bona fide purchase defence is the meaning of purchaser for value.[15] If one were upholding sanctity of contract one would expect purchase for value to include where the defendant, in return for the benefit, has made a binding promise. Yet in the context of title rules the purchaser for value must have performed the promise. A promise to pay is insufficient.[16] There are obiter dicta in *Lipkin Gorman v Karpnale Ltd*[17] which may be interpreted as indicating that the same applies to the bona fide purchase defence in the context of restitution. If so, the sanctity of contract explanation would hold good only in a watered-down version, namely that, vis-à-vis a third party, the policy of respecting the sanctity of contracts applies only where the contract is fully executed.

A final point is that, contrary to earlier doubts,[18] it is now clear that the bona fide purchase defence in restitution applies only to where

---

15 For discussion, see Barker, 'Bona Fide Purchase as a Defence to Unjust Enrichment Claims: A Concise Restatement' [1999] RLR 75, 83. Another difficulty is that a bona fide purchaser of an equitable, rather than a legal interest, does not take priority over earlier equitable interests. In the context of restitution reversing unjust enrichment, the better view is that such a purchaser should have priority. There is no rationale in this context in favouring the bona fide purchaser of a legal but not an equitable interest. It is noteworthy that the bona fide purchase defence, expanded in this way, would meet the concerns to protect secured creditors expressed by Lord Browne-Wilkinson in *Westdeutsche Landesbank Girozentrale v Islington London Borough Council* [1996] AC 669: see above p 74, n 3.

16 *Story v Lord Windsor* (1743) 2 Atk 630. So in the Ritz example referred to at p 587 above, if Cass had pre-paid but the Ritz had not yet performed at the time when informed of the claim, the Ritz would have no bona fide purchase defence to the solicitors' restitutionary claim.

17 [1991] 2 AC 548, 562 (per Lord Templeman) and 577 (per Lord Goff): both said that a bank does not provide consideration for the payment of money by accepting the money on deposit (ie, the promise to repay the money does not constitute the giving of value).

18 See the 1st edn of this book, at pp 472, 474.

the defendant has received a benefit from a third party (ie, the defendant is an indirect recipient). It does not apply where the claimant was induced to enter into a contract with the defendant (a direct recipient) induced by the conduct of a third party, such as misrepresentation, duress or undue influence. The question as to whether the claimant can rescind such a contract generally turns on whether the defendant had actual or constructive notice of the third party's conduct.[19] That insistence on notice (so that the contract cannot be rescinded if the defendant had no notice) may be similar to, but is not a direct application of, the bona fide purchase defence. This was clarified by the House of Lords in *Barclays Bank plc v Boulter*[20] in deciding that, in contrast to the bona fide purchase defence, the burden of proof in relation to the defendant's notice is on the claimant (the person seeking to set aside the transaction) and not on the defendant. The underlying explanation for this had already been forcibly and fully expounded by Kit Barker. In his words, '[W]here a defendant pays for a benefit under an exchange transaction with the plaintiff himself ... as in ... cases such as *Bainbrigge v Browne*[1] and *Barclays Bank v O'Brien*[2] ... the requisite guarantees of transactional security are provided by the law of contract itself, in particular by the principle of contract known as the "objective principle." Although the good faith of the defendant is relevant in these cases, the defence of bona fide purchase has no part to play'.[3] And later on he continued, '[T]he defence only applies (is only needed) where the defendant has received a benefit under a contract with a third party, not where he receives it under a (voidable) contract with the plaintiff himself.'[4]

9. PASSING ON

There has been controversy as to whether passing on (or, as one might otherwise term it, mitigation of loss) is a defence to the cause of action

---

19 See above, pp 248–251.
20 [1999] 4 All ER 513.
1 (1881) 18 Ch D 188. See also *Bridgeman v Green* (1757) Wilm 58; *Lancashire Loans Ltd v Black* [1934] 1 KB 380.
2 [1994] 1 AC 180.
3 'After Change of Position: Good Faith Exchange in the Modern Law of Restitution' in Birks (ed), *Laundering and Tracing* (1995), p 193.
4 Ibid, at p 199. For similar reasons, it is submitted that the refusal of restitution against the creditor for the mistaken discharge of another's debt, as in *Aiken v Short* (1856) 1 H & N 210, is not an example of the bona fide purchase defence. Cf Goff and Jones, paras 4-042 to 4-043, chapter 41. The Restatement of Restitution, s 14 prefers to talk of a defence of discharge for value in that situation. The better view is that, as there is consideration, rules for wiping away a contract need to be satisfied and that, even then, normal defences (eg, change of position) would tend to rule out restitution. See Barker, ibid, at pp 199–202. See above, pp 131, 295.

of unjust enrichment.[5] If it does exist it goes to whether the enrichment was 'at the claimant's expense'.

The argument in favour of recognising the defence is that, leaving aside restitution for wrongs, 'at the expense of the claimant' requires the gain to the defendant to have been subtracted from the claimant's wealth. This suggests that the gain to the defendant must be a loss to the claimant (while not necessitating that there be an equivalence or correspondence of loss and gain).[6] Yet if the claimant has passed on or mitigated the loss, the 'at the expense of' element of the unjust enrichment principle is nullified. To reverse the unjust enrichment would leave the claimant better off (ie with a windfall) than if the defendant had not been unjustly enriched in the first place. That is, the restitution would leave *the claimant* unjustly enriched.

It should be stressed that, to have any merit, the defence of passing on could not be made out simply by the defendant showing that the claimant had 'passed on' the loss by, for example, increasing the prices charged to its customers. The reason for this is that spreading the loss does not necessarily mean that the claimant has mitigated its loss. For example, the charging of higher prices ought in theory to reduce the number of customers. So to have any merit as a defence, the defendant would need to show that the claimant has passed on, *and thereby avoided,* its loss.

An argument for rejecting the defence of passing on runs as follows. A windfall must go to either the defendant (by allowing this defence against the defendant's prima facie liability to make restitution of its unjust enrichment) or to the claimant (by rejecting this defence even though the claimant has mitigated its loss). As between the two, it is preferable to leave the claimant with the windfall because there is plainly no *duty to mitigate* in relation to the cause of action of unjust enrichment, and it would therefore be odd to treat actual mitigation as important. Put another way, there would be no incentive on the claimant to mitigate its loss because it would simply benefit the defendant.

A further argument against the defence is that it may be too simplistic to say that denying the defence will necessarily leave the claimant with a windfall (and itself unjustly enriched). This is because the claimant, who has had a direct link with the person to whom the loss has been passed on, may itself be liable to a restitutionary claim from that person. Indeed, where the loss has been passed on, instead of giving the defendant a defence, one

5   See, generally, Rose, 'Passing On' in *Laundering and Tracing* (ed Birks, 1995), pp 261–287.
6   See above, pp 28–29.

might require the claimant to pay over the amount recovered from the defendant to the third party to whom the loss has been passed on. Rather than unjustly enriching the claimant, the effect of denying the defence of passing on may therefore be to channel the restitutionary award down to the person who has really suffered the loss.

So perhaps the best approach in principle and policy is first, to deny the passing on defence: but, secondly, to require the successful claimant to pay over the amount recovered to a third party where that third party can establish that it is the third party, rather than the claimant, which suffered the loss that became the defendant's unjust gain.[7]

What is the approach of the English courts? The leading case is *Kleinwort Benson Ltd v Birmingham City Council*,[8] another of the swaps cases. Here the claimant bank sought restitution of payments (£353,322) which it had made to the defendant local authority under a void interest rate swap contract. The local authority argued that it was entitled to rely on the defence of passing on, and that that defence was here made out because the claimant bank had made hedging transactions with third parties to cover any losses on the swap contract. The defendant was, therefore, not unjustly enriched *at the claimant's expense*. But the Court of Appeal rejected this argument. It said that the idea of mitigating one's loss was concerned with the law of compensation and had no application to the law of restitution. The use of the phrase 'at the expense of the claimant' and the idea that there must be a subtraction from the wealth of the claimant did not mean that one should import the concept of mitigation of loss into the law of restitution. In any event, the hedging transactions were too remote from the unjust enrichment. The reasoning in *Kleinwort Benson Ltd v South Tyneside Metropolitan Borough Council*,[9] in which Hobhouse J had rejected passing on (by hedging) as a defence to restitution in another swaps case, was upheld.

The Court of Appeal also approved, and relied on, the reasoning of two great Australian judges. In *Mason v New South Wales*[10] the High Court of Australia rejected a defence of passing on to a claim for restitution of money paid under duress to a public authority. Windeyer J said:

---

7   This is supported by Michell, 'Restitution, Passing On and the Recovery of Unlawfully Demanded Taxes: Why *Air Canada* Doesn't Fly' (1995) 53 University of Toronto Faculty LR 130.
8   [1998] 3 WLR 1095.
9   [1994] 4 All ER 972, 984–987.
10 (1959) 102 CLR 108.

'It was argued that ... the plaintiffs were in some way [prevented] from recovering because they had "passed on" to their customers the amount paid for permits and are thus, it was said, not themselves at a loss. I can see no basis for this contention ... If the defendant be improperly enriched on what legal principle can it claim to retain its ill-gotten gains merely because the plaintiffs have not, it is said, been correspondingly impoverished? The concept of impoverishment as a correlative of enrichment may have some place in some fields of continental law. It is foreign to our law. Even if there were any equity in favour of third parties attaching to the fruits of any judgment the plaintiffs might recover – and there is nothing proved at all remotely suggesting that there is – this circumstance would be quite irrelevant to the present proceedings. Certainly it would not enable the defendant to refuse to return moneys which it was not in law entitled to collect and which *ex hypothesi* it got by extortion.'[11]

In *Commissioner of State Revenue v Royal Insurance Australia Ltd*[12] the High Court of Australia rejected a passing on defence to a claim for restitution of mistakenly overpaid stamp duty. Mason CJ said:

'Restitutionary relief, as it has developed to this point in our law, does not seek to provide compensation for loss. Instead, it operates to restore to the plaintiff what has been transferred from the plaintiff to the defendant whereby the defendant has been unjustly enriched. ... The subtraction from the plaintiff's wealth enables one to say that the defendant's unjust enrichment has been "at the expense of the plaintiff", notwithstanding that the plaintiff may recoup the outgoing by means of transactions with third parties. On this approach, it would not matter that the plaintiff is or will be overcompensated because he or she has passed on the tax or charge to someone else. And it seems that there is no recorded instance of a court engaging in the daunting exercise of working out the actual loss sustained by the plaintiff and restricting the amount of an award to that measure.'[13]

It should not, however, be thought that in rejecting passing on, the Court of Appeal in *Kleinwort Benson v Birmingham City Council* was simply following the clear consensus of opinion elsewhere. On the contrary, the position in Canada, as laid down by the majority of the Supreme Court in *Air Canada v British Columbia*,[14] is that passing on is a defence available at least to a public authority. In La Forest J's words, '... the law of restitution is not intended to provide windfalls to plaintiffs who have suffered no loss'.[15]

---

11 Ibid, at 146.
12 (1994) 126 ALR 1. See also *Roxborough v Rothmans of Pall Mall Australia Ltd* [2001] HCA 68.
13 Ibid, at 15.
14 (1989) 59 DLR (4th) 161.
15 Ibid, at 193. Wilson J dissenting considered that there should be no defence of passing on.

Moreover, a number of English tax statutes (eg, for the recovery of overpaid VAT[16] or excise duty[17]) lay down the defence of passing on or, as it is usually termed, that restitution would unjustly enrich the claimant. And the Law Commission has recommended that this should be a general defence to restitutionary claims against a public authority for overpaid taxes.[18] Moreover, it is established European Community Law that passing on is a permissible defence open to a public authority against whom restitution of taxes or charges is sought (the taxes or charges having been levied contrary to an individual's directly effective rights). This is subject to the proviso that the evidential burden of disproving that defence is not a practically impossible one for the payor to discharge.[19]

It is significant that the Court of Appeal in *Kleinwort Benson Ltd v Birmingham City Council* put to one side taxation cases. The swaps contracts with which it was dealing did not involve taxes or other charges levied by a public authority. But in principle it is hard to see how passing on can be rejected as a general defence to restitution while being allowed as a special defence to claims for restitution of overpaid tax. Indeed one can strongly argue that the relevant legislative provisions in the tax statutes which provide for a passing on defence are cynically designed by the Revenue authorities to override the taxpayer's legitimate right to restitution so as not to disrupt a public authority's finances. It is submitted that, in principle, all such provisions should be repealed. Passing on, or unjust enrichment of the claimant, should not be a defence to restitution.

As we have seen,[20] however, this should not necessarily mean that the defendant is left with a windfall. After referring to several United States cases on overpaid taxes, Mason CJ in *Commissioner of State Revenue v Royal Insurance Ltd* went on to suggest that the claimant might hold the recovered moneys as a constructive trustee for those to whom the tax had been passed on. This would be so where the claimant had

---

16 Value Added Tax Act 1994, s 80, as amended by the Finance Act 1997, ss 46–47. The Court of Appeal held that, applying s 80 of the 1994 Act, passing on was a defence as to 90% of Marks and Spencer's claim for restitution of overpaid VAT in *Marks & Spencer plc v Customs and Excise Comrs* [2000] STC 16.

17 Customs and Excise Management Act 1979, s 137A, as inserted by the Finance Act 1995, s 20 and as amended by the Finance Act 1997, s 50 and Sch 5.

18 *Restitution: Mistakes of Law and Ultra Vires Public Authority Receipts and Payments* (Law Com No 227, 1994), paras 10.44–10.48.

19 See, eg, *Hans Just I/S v Danish Ministry of Fiscal Affairs* Case 68/79 [1980] ECR 501; *Amministrazione delle Finanze delle Stato v San Georgio SpA* Case 199/82 [1983] ECR 3595; *EC Commission v Italy* Case 104/86 [1988] ECR 1799; Rudden and Bishop, 'Gritz and Quellmehl: Pass it On' (1981) 6 ELR 243; Alison Jones, *Restitution and European Community Law* (2000), pp 87–92.

20 Above, pp 592–593.

charged the tax as a separate item to its customers so that it was, in effect, acting as a tax collector in respect of the overpaid sums. One can therefore say that Mason CJ's approach was one of denying passing on as a defence while recognising that, where the passing on was clearly identified and quantifiable, the successful claimant would be bound to account for the moneys received to the third party. That seems an entirely principled approach and could be applied 'across the board' to all restitutionary claims, albeit that in practice it may only be in tax cases where the necessary identification and certainty of the passing on will be found. Given the approval afforded to Mason CJ's judgment by the Court of Appeal in *Kleinwort Benson Ltd v Birmingham City Council*, it is submitted that that is an approach that remains open to the English courts.

Chapter 16

Miscellaneous issues: agency and the conflict of laws

This chapter considers two unrelated areas: agency and the conflict of laws. Traditionally very little attention was paid by commentators to these topics in the context of the law of restitution. In recent years, that has changed especially in relation to the conflict of laws.

1. AGENCY

Apart from its great practical importance, agency in the law of restitution is of central theoretical significance for three main reasons. First, agency is one of the main exceptions to the 'direct providers only' principle that in unjust enrichment by subtraction a claimant cannot have restitution for benefits rendered on a defendant by a third party.[1] Secondly, and uniquely, a principal can be held liable in restitution even though he has not himself received a benefit. Thirdly, it is arguable that an agent has a unique 'payment over' defence.

There are two aspects of agency to consider. Confining ourselves, for ease of exposition, to the payment of money (while recognising that the same principles are applicable whatever the benefit) A may be C's agent in paying D; or A may be D's agent in being paid by C.

(1) A is C's agent in paying D

This situation can be dealt with relatively briefly. Assuming that A is C's agent in paying D, which is determined by the normal principles of the law of agency governing the creation of agency and an agent's authority,[2] both C (the principal) and A (the agent) normally have the right to sue D in restitution where there is an unjust factor.

The leading case is *Stevenson v Mortimer*.[3] A custom-house officer had demanded, and been paid, excessive fees from the master of a ship. The ship's owner, as principal of the master, successfully brought

---

1   Above, pp 31–41, esp p 35.
2   See, eg, *Bowstead and Reynolds on Agency* (17th edn, 2001), chs 2–3.
3   (1778) 2 Cowp 805.

an action for money had and received to recover the excessive fees (the unjust factor being, most obviously, duress). Lord Mansfield said, 'Where a man pays money by his agent, which ought not to have been paid, either the agent, or principal, may bring an action to recover it back.'[4]

Again in *Holt v Ely*[5] where an agent in paying off his principal's creditors was deceived by the defendant's fraud into paying him money to which he was not entitled, the agent was held able to recover the money paid in an action for money had and received. The court recognised that if it had been the principal who had sued for mistaken payment he too would have been successful.

In both those cases the principal was disclosed. The same principle applics where he is undisclosed.[6]

Clearly a principal will often have no knowledge, at the time of payment, of what the agent is doing. But a question that has arisen, in relation to an agent's payment by mistake, is what if the principal (or another of his agents), while not knowing of his agent's mistake, knew all the facts so that the principal (or other agent) would not have made the mistake?

In *Anglo-Scottish Beet Sugar Corpn v Spalding UDC 7*[7] the claimant's commercial manager drew up cheques paying the defendants at a higher old contract rate for water supplied even though a new lower contract rate had been agreed. The claimant's managing director had negotiated the new rate but had failed to inform the commercial manager. The managing director himself signed the over-paying cheques but without considering whether they were accurate or not. The claimant company was held entitled to restitution for mistake of fact, the key point being that the managing director did not know of the commercial manager's mistake.

The central principle was succinctly stated by Pilcher J in *Turvey v Dentons (1923) Ltd.*[8]

'Where ... a limited liability company is concerned and payments are made under a bona fide mistake of fact by an authorised agent of the company, the fact that some other agent of the company may have full knowledge of all the facts does not disentitle the company to recover the money so paid, provided that the agent with the full knowledge does not know that the payments are being made on an erroneous basis.'

---

4   Ibid, at p 806.
5   (1853) 1 E & B 795.
6   *Duke of Norfolk v Worthy* (1808) 1 Camp 337 is an example of a successful action by an undisclosed principal: below, pp 600–601.
7   [1937] 2 KB 607.
8   [1953] 1 QB 218, 224.

It also appears to follow from that principle that in the different situation where the agent knows all the true facts in paying and only the principal is mistaken there can be no restitution for mistake.

(2) A is D's agent in being paid by C

This raises more complex issues than the first situation, in particular because the agent may have paid over the money received to his principal. The case law is also more voluminous.[9]

Birks discusses these issues under the heading of a defence which he labels 'ministerial receipt'.[10] One might more straightforwardly talk of a defence of agency. Whatever one's label, it seems preferable to see this area not merely as a defence but also as raising the more general issue of which is the appropriate person to be sued (principal or agent or both).

(a) A receives the payment as agent not principal

The starting point is that A is D's agent in receiving a payment from C. Clearly if the payee receives the money *as principal* the claimant's entitlement to restitution is unaffected by special rules of agency. Whether a person receives money as an agent or a principal turns on the general principles of the law of agency governing the creation of agency and an agent's authority.

For example, in *Baylis v Bishop of London*[11] (which was overruled in so far as it rejected a change of position defence by *Lipkin Gorman v Karpnale Ltd*)[12] a bishop had received mistakenly paid tithe rent-charges from a payor and, after providing for the needs of the parish, had paid the surplus to the rector's trustee in bankruptcy. It was held that the bishop had received the money as principal and not as agent for the trustee in bankruptcy or anyone else. An agent's 'payment over' defence was therefore not open to him and he was bound to

---

9   For a general discussion, see *Bowstead & Reynolds on Agency* (17th edn, 2001), paras 9-098 to 9-106; Swadling, 'The Nature of Ministerial Receipt' in *Laundering and Tracing* (ed Birks, 1995), pp 243–260; Bryan, 'Recovering Misdirected Money from Banks: Ministerial Receipt at Law and in Equity' in *Restitution and Banking Law* (ed Rose, 1998), pp 161–188. With respect, Swadling's 'mandate' or 'estoppel' explanation of the agent's 'payment over' defence seems flawed not least because it fails to explain standard mistaken payment cases where, analogously to duress, the mistake would undermine the mandate.

10 See Birks, *Restitution – The Future* (1992), pp 139–141. See also Birks and Mitchell, 'Unjust Enrichment' in *English Private Law* (ed Birks, 2000), paras 15.255–15.259.

11 [1913] 1 Ch 127. In addition to the cases considered in this paragraph, see *Hudson v Robinson* (1816) 4 M & S 475 (failure of consideration); *Continental Caoutchouc and Gutta Percha Co v Kleinwort Sons & Co* (1904) 90 LT 474 (mistake).

12 [1991] 2 AC 548.

return the mistaken payment. In the early case of *Snowdon v Davis*[13] a bailiff exceeded his authority as agent of a sheriff by demanding more money than was due in executing a warrant for distress of goods. The owner of the goods was held entitled to recover the overpayment from the bailiff as paid under duress of goods. The fact that the bailiff had paid over the money to his principal, the sheriff, afforded him no defence and one explanation for this[14] is that in extracting the overpayment the bailiff had been acting outside the sheriff's authority and hence as his own principal. More recently in *Sorrell v Finch*[15] prospective house purchasers were held unable to recover from the vendor a pre-contractual deposit paid to his estate agent because the latter (who had since disappeared) had been acting outside the vendor's authority in demanding the deposit. Although the claim was framed in contract it is more realistic to regard it as restitutionary based on a total failure of consideration (in the sense of the non-occurrence of an unpromised future event).

Assuming that the payee has received the money as agent, and not as principal, and that the payor has a ground for restitution to reverse an unjust enrichment by subtraction[16] based on, for example, mistake, duress, or failure of consideration, who can be sued by the payor for restitution? The authorities are split.[17]

(b) One view: only the principal can be sued

One view is that only the principal can be sued in restitution: it does not matter whether the principal received the money or not because payment to the agent constitutes payment to the principal.

That was the view taken in the two early cases of *Sadler v Evans*[18] and *Duke of Norfolk v Worthy*.[19] In the former the claimant paid 1s 6d to Lady Windsor's agent in the mistaken belief that he owed her

---

13   (1808) 1 Taunt 359. This was followed in *Steele v Williams* (1853) 8 Exch 625. Cf *Brocklebank Ltd v R* [1925] 1 KB 52, 68.

14   An alternative explanation is that there was no *bona fide* payment over.

15   [1977] AC 728.

16   As regards restitution for wrongs, an agent is generally personally liable for wrongs committed even though acting with the authority of the principal: see *Bowstead & Reynolds on Agency* (17th edn, 2001), Art 115. And it would seem that any 'payment over' defence would, in any event, normally be ruled out because the agent would not be paying over the money in good faith. For a principal's liability for its agent's wrongs, see *Bowstead and Reynolds on Agency*, Art 92. The extent to which 'vicarious liability' applies in respect of restitution for wrongs is unclear: see Burrows, 'Reforming Non-Compensatory Damages' in *The Search for Principle* (eds Swadling and Jones, 1999), pp 295, 307.

17   For the argument that the first three cases set out below do not support the view that only the principal can be sued, see Swadling, 'The Nature of Ministerial Receipt' in *Laundering and Tracing* (ed Birks, 1995), pp 243, 247–250.

18   (1766) 4 Burr 1984.

19   (1808) 1 Camp 337.

that money. The claimant's action for money had and received was held to lie against Lady Windsor, as principal, and not against her agent, whether or not the agent had paid over the 1s 6d. In the latter the claimant purchaser (through his agent) paid a deposit under a contract for the sale of a country estate to the defendant vendor's agent, Richardson. After the claimant had terminated the contract for breach of a condition describing the property, he sought restitution of the deposit from the defendant (the ground being best viewed as total failure of consideration). The action succeeded, irrespective of whether Richardson had paid the deposit over to his principal. Lord Ellenborough said, 'It seems to make no difference whether it was actually paid over or not. Richardson here acted completely as the agent of the defendant. Therefore when the deposit was lodged with the agent this was in law *eo instanti* a payment to the principal.'[20]

Very similar reasoning was applied by the Court of Appeal in *Ellis v Goulton*[1] in refusing an action for total failure of consideration against a seller's agent, a solicitor, for recovery of a deposit under a contract for the purchase of land. Bowen LJ said, 'I am of the opinion that the payment of the money to the solicitor was equivalent to payment to his principal and that the money cannot be recovered from the solicitor, whether he had paid it over to his principal or not.'[2]

It appears that the same approach was being taken by Millett J at first instance in *Agip (Africa) Ltd v Jackson*[3] as regards the equitable claim for knowing receipt and dealing (but not the common law action for money had and received). He held that the defendants were not liable because they had not received the money for their own benefit, which seems to mean simply that they received it as agents.[4]

Indeed Millett J's judgment has led some commentators to suggest that this first view – that only the principal can be sued – is equity's approach to agency and contrasts with the alternative view, considered below, which is portrayed as the common law's approach.[5]

---

20 Ibid, at p 339.
1 [1893] 1 QB 350.
2 Ibid, at pp 353–354.
3 [1990] Ch 265, 292: upheld by the CA [1991] Ch 547. The unjust factor is best viewed as ignorance: above, chapter 4.
4 Millett J's mode of expression is, on the face of it, misleading because most agents, including banks, in one sense do receive money beneficially (ie they take legal and beneficial title to the money) albeit that they also receive for their principal. Millett J drew a distinction, in deciding whether a bank received beneficially, between overdrawn and in-credit bank accounts. Numerous commentators have criticised this distinction on the basis that a bank receives beneficially irrespective of the state of the account. See, eg, Bryan, 'Recovering Misdirected Money from Banks' in *Restitution and Banking Law* (ed Rose, 1998) pp 161, 181–187.
5 Birks and Mitchell, 'Unjust Enrichment' in *English Private Law* (ed Birks, 2000), paras 15.255–15.259.

However, as we have just seen, there are common law cases that have also taken this first view.

In principle, this first view has much to commend it (at least in respect of disclosed agents).[6] The standard effect of agency in contract law is that the agent, having concluded the contract, drops out of the picture. It is strongly arguable that, by analogy, the same should apply in relation to restitution of an unjust enrichment by subtraction. If this were accepted, one effect would be to limit the impact of strict restitutionary liability for commercial recipients, such as banks, who receive as disclosed agents for their customers.[7] By receiving as disclosed agents they would incur no restitutionary liability whether or not they could establish a defence of change of position.

(c) The alternative view: agent can be sued subject to the defence of 'payment over'

The majority of cases have taken the alternative view that a restitutionary claim does lie against the agent (or against the principal)[8] unless the agent has in good faith paid the money over to his principal, or done something equivalent, in which case only the principal is liable in restitution.

In several cases, therefore, a restitutionary action succeeded against an agent *because his purported payment over defence failed.* An early example is *Buller v Harrison*[9] in which the claimants mistakenly thought that they were bound to pay £2,100 under an insurance policy to their insured. They therefore paid the money to their insured's agent. The agent credited that sum against a debt of £3,000 owed to him by the insured. It was held that this did not afford a restitutionary defence to the agent. Lord Mansfield said:

> 'In this case, there was no new credit, no acceptance of new bills, no fresh goods bought or money advanced. In short, no alteration in the situation which the defendant and his principals stood in towards each other ... If there had been any new credit given it would have been proper to have left it to the jury to say

6   See below, pp 607–608.
7   See Birks, 'The Burden on the Bank' in *Restitution and Banking Law* (ed Rose, 1998), pp 189, 209–210; Jonathon Moore, 'Restitution from Banks' (unpublished Oxford D Phil thesis, 2000). Another consequence of this view is that it avoids the agent's dilemma of being potentially liable both to its principal for failure to pay the money over and to the payor in the law of restitution. Cf *Admiralty Comrs v National Provincial Bank* (1922) 127 LJ 452 which also avoided this dilemma by laying down that if the agent repays a mistaken payment it is not liable for failure to pay that money over to its principal.
8   Eg, *Coulthurst v Sweet* (1866) LR 1 CP 649 (principal liable to repay money even though agent had no defence).
9   (1777) 2 Cowp 565.

whether any prejudice had happened to the defendant by means of this payment; but here no prejudice at all is proved and none is to be inferred.'[10]

This was followed in *Cox v Prentice*,[11] another case involving a mistaken payment to an agent who had simply credited the amount to his principal. Lord Ellenborough said, 'I take it to be clear that an agent who receives money for his principal is liable as a principal so long as he stands in his original situation; and until there has been a change of circumstances by his having paid over the money to his principal, or done something equivalent to it.'[12]

The same approach underlies the reasoning of the Lords in *Kleinwort Sons & Co v Dunlop Rubber Co*[13] to the effect that it was unnecessary to decide whether the defendants were acting as agents, rather than principals, in receiving a mistaken payment because the defendants had not paid the money over or done anything equivalent to that. They were therefore liable even if agents. Lord Atkinson summarised the law as follows:

'... in an action brought to recover money paid to him under a mistake of fact, [the defendant] will be liable to refund it if it be established that he dealt as a principal with the person who paid it to him. Whether he would be liable if he dealt as agent with such a person will depend upon this, whether, before the mistake was discovered, he had paid over the money which he received to the principal, or settled such an account with the principal as amounts to payment, or did something which so prejudiced his position that it would be inequitable to require him to refund.'[14]

Finally there are cases in which an agent has extracted money from a claimant by duress of goods and yet payment over to his principal has afforded the agent no defence.[15] One explanation of those decisions is that, even if acting within their authority, the agents could not be said to have paid over the money *bona fide*.

In other cases an agent has defeated a restitutionary claim against it *by successfully establishing the payment over defence*. In *Holland v Russell*[16] the claimant insurer had paid money to the defendant as agent for the owner of a ship that had been lost. In fact the insurance policy with the owner was voidable for non-disclosure. The claimant sought to recover from the defendant the money mistakenly paid. The

---

10 Ibid, at p 568.
11 (1815) 3 M & S 344. See similarly *British American Continental Bank v British Bank for Foreign Trade* [1926] 1 KB 328, CA.
12 Ibid, at p 348.
13 (1907) 97 LT 263.
14 Ibid, at p 265.
15 *Snowdon v Davis* (1808) 1 Taunt 359; *Oates v Hudson* (1851) 6 Exch 346; *Keegan v Palmer* [1961] 2 Lloyd's Rep 449.
16 (1861) 1 B & S 424; affd (1863) 4 B & S 14.

defendant successfully resisted the action because in good faith he had paid over some of the money to his principal, had used part to settle a debt owed to him by the principal, and had spent the rest on his principal's behalf and with his authority.

Similarly in *Gower v Lloyds and National Provincial Foreign Bank Ltd*[17] pension payments mistakenly made to a former colonial officer's bank, for the benefit of the pensioner, who had died, were held irrecoverable from the bank. The bank had received the payments as agent and had bona fide paid them over, as it thought, to its principal.

A further example involving a mistaken payment is *Transvaal and Delagoa Bay Investment Co Ltd v Atkinson*[18] in which a husband defrauded the claimant company into paying his wife money which his wife, as agent for her husband and knowing nothing of the fraud, paid over to her husband or spent on his behalf. The claimant's restitutionary action against the wife for money mistakenly paid failed. Atkinson J said, 'Where money has been received by an agent for a principal he cannot be sued for its return if before notice he has paid it away to his principal or on his principal's instructions.'[19]

Turning away from restitution for mistake, in *Owen & Co v Cronk*[20] the manager of a company in receivership induced the claimant, under duress of goods, to pay money to the receiver of the company who, without notice of the duress, paid it over to his principals (the trustees of the company). The action for money had and received against the receiver failed. And at first instance in *Agip (Africa) Ltd v Jackson*[1] (in which, as we saw in chapter 4, the unjust factor is best viewed as ignorance) the defendants were held to have an agent's payment over defence to the common law action for money had and received (although, as we have seen above, Millett J appeared to prefer the wider version of the agency defence as regards the equitable claim). The bona fide (or 'without notice') requirement in the defence was held to be satisfied apparently because the defendants did not know of the claim when paying over the money (albeit that they had sufficient knowledge to render them liable for the equitable wrong of 'knowing assistance').

This alternative predominant view has recently been neatly summarised in obiter dicta of Millett LJ in *Portman Building Society v Hamlyn Taylor Neck*.[2] The claimant building society alleged that it had

---

17   [1938] 1 All ER 766.
18   [1944] 1 All ER 579.
19   Ibid, at p 585.
20   [1895] 1 QB 265.
1   [1990] Ch 265; affd [1991] Ch 547. Above, pp 87–89, 190. For a further example, see *Mara v Browne* [1896] 1 Ch 199: agent solicitor not liable for 'knowing receipt' because he had paid over funds received.
2   [1998] 4 All ER 202.

made a mistake of fact in lending money to a Mr Biggins. The money was paid to Mr Biggins' solicitors, the defendants, who had paid it on to Mr Biggins. The claim failed because the money was paid under a valid contract. However, had there been a restitutionary claim for the money and had the defendants been acting as agents for Mr Biggins (rather than, as the Court of Appeal thought, as agents for the claimant), Millett LJ clarified that, at common law, the defendants would have been able to resist the claim because they were agents who had paid over to their principal. In Millett LJ's words:

'I myself do not regard the agent's defence in such a case as a particular instance of the change of position defence, nor is it generally so regarded. At common law the agent recipient is regarded as a mere conduit for the money, which is treated as paid to the principal, not to the agent. The doctrine is therefore not so much a defence as a means of identifying the proper party to be sued. It does not, for example, avail the agent of an undisclosed principal; though today such an agent would be able to rely on a change of position defence. The true rule is that where the plaintiff has paid money under (for example) a mistake to the agent of a third party, he may sue the principal whether or not the agent has accounted to him, for in contemplation of law the payment is made to the principal and not to his agent. If the agent still retains the money, however, the plaintiff may elect to sue either the principal or the agent, and the agent remains liable if he pays the money over to his principal after notice of the claim... But once the agent has paid the money to his principal or to his order without notice of the claim, the plaintiff must sue the principal.'[3]

(d) Is payment over different from the change of position defence?

An agent's payment over defence was recognised long before the acceptance of a general change of position defence in *Lipkin Gorman v Karpnale Ltd*.[4] An important question is whether the payment over defence was merely an early recognition, in a specific context, of the change of position defence which has now been entirely swallowed up by the recognition of change of position as a general defence: or whether, on the contrary, and as Millett LJ indicated at the start of the passage just cited, it should be treated as distinct from change of position.

An initial point is that one must not allow the specific context in which the payment over defence applies to cloud the issue. That context can be accurately described as being concerned with identifying the proper party to be sued rather than as merely going to a defence.[5] That accurate description is not inconsistent with saying

3   Ibid, at 207.
4   [1991] 2 AC 548.
5   See above, p 599.

that payment over is an aspect of change of position. In other words, whether payment over is, or is not, an aspect of change of position, it is clear that, applying the predominant view, the principal and the agent are both prima facie liable (subject to defences).

Given that good faith is a requirement for both defences (albeit that, in the context of 'payment over', this is sometimes expressed as a 'without notice' requirement) it would seem that the central issue is whether the payment over defence necessitates the detriment or prejudice that is central to change of position. It is submitted that it does. As we have seen, some judges have expressly used the language of 'prejudice' in describing the agent's defence.[6] But whether that language has been used or not, the crucial point is that a payment over, unless it can be retrieved without prejudice, will itself constitute prejudice or detriment to the agent because the agent will be left worse off (pecuniarily) if it were now required to repay the money to the claimant than if the payment had never been made in the first place. And that is the meaning of prejudice or detriment that applies to the change of position defence.[7] Change of position therefore swallows up payment over.

This is consistent with the difficult Australian case of *Australia and New Zealand Banking Group Ltd v Westpac Banking Corp.*[8] Here the defendant bank had received a mistaken payment of $100,000 from the claimant bank for the credit of the defendant's customer, Jakes. After receipt of that payment, the defendant had irretrievably paid out nearly $83,000 in honouring cheques drawn on it by Jakes (which reduced Jakes' overdraft with the defendant). It was held that the defendant had a defence in respect of that $83,000 leaving the claimant with an entitlement to restitution of some $17,000. Although the High Court of Australia's judgment may be thought to suggest that the agent does not need to prove detriment or prejudice, it would seem that the better interpretation is that the Court was clarifying that, if irretrievable, the payment over itself constitutes the relevant detriment or prejudice. The central passage in the judgment is as follows:

> 'The rationale of ... [the payment over] rule can be identified in terms of the law
> of agency and of notions of unjust enrichment. If money is paid to an agent on
> behalf of a principal and the agent receives it in his capacity as such and, without

6   See the citations in the previous sub-section from *Buller v Harrison* (per Lord Mansfield)
     and *Kleinwort Sons & Co v Dunlop Rubber Co* (per Lord Atkinson).
7   It is irrelevant and confuses the issue to think in terms of the agent not being worse off
     because it was bound to pay the money over to its principal: cf Burrows, *The Law of
     Restitution* (1st edn, 1993), p 485.
8   (1988) 78 ALR 157.

notice of any mistake or irregularity in the payment, applies the money for the purpose for which it was paid to him, he has applied it in accordance with the mandate of the payer who must look to the principal for recovery ... If the matter needs to be expressed in terms of detriment or change of position, the payment by the agent to the principal of the money which he has received on the principal's behalf, of itself constitutes the relevant detriment or change of position.'[9]

If it is correct that payment over is swallowed up by change of position (rather than having to be considered separately alongside it) the law on an agent's receipt can be expressed very simply. On one view, only the principal can be sued; on the alternative (predominant) view, both the agent and the principal can be sued. On either view, the defendant(s) can invoke the change of position defence (as well as all other standard restitutionary defences).

(e) Does it make a difference if the principal is undisclosed?

Where the principal is undisclosed (or, as one may synonymously express it, the agent is an undisclosed agent) the payor thinks that the agent is the principal. Does this make a difference?

In nearly all the above cases the principal was disclosed. In *Holland v Russell*[10] it was left open whether the payment over defence would have applied had the principal been undisclosed. In dicta in *Agip (Africa) Ltd v Jackson*[11] Millett J at first instance thought that the payment over defence only applied if the principal was disclosed so that Baker Oil would not have been able to avail itself of the defence. Similarly in his obiter dicta in *Portman Building Society v Hamlyn Taylor Neck*[12] set out above, Millett LJ said that the payment over defence would not avail the agent of an undisclosed principal albeit that such an agent could rely on change of position. A contrary decision is that in *Transvaal and Delagoa Bay Investment Co Ltd v Atkinson*[13] where the payment over defence was applied even though the principal was undisclosed.

Whatever the merits of distinguishing between disclosed and undisclosed agents in relation to the alternative (predominant) view set out above (and if change of position swallows up payment over there will be no practical difference between the treatment of

---

9 Ibid, at p 168.
10 (1861) 1 B & S 424; affd (1863) 4 B & S 14.
11 [1990] Ch 265. See also Millett, 'Tracing the Proceeds of Fraud' (1991) 107 LQR 71, 76–77, where he relies for this point on *Newall v Tomlinson* (1871) LR 6 CP 405. But the decision in that case was that the supposed agents could not rely on a defence of payment over because they had received the money on their own account (ie, as principal).
12 [1998] 4 All ER 202, 207.
13 [1944] 1 All ER 579.

disclosed and undisclosed agents) that distinction would seem to be an important one in relation to the first view.[14] The analogy to agency in the law of contract – where the undisclosed agent does not drop out of the picture – suggests that the first view, that only the principal can be sued, applies only to disclosed, and not undisclosed, agents.

2. THE CONFLICT OF LAWS

The conflict of laws in relation to restitution is a topic of increasing practical importance and of immense theoretical interest. Having previously been neglected by commentators, it has recently spawned an ever-growing body of literature. Even for a blinkered restitution lawyer, who professes disinterest in disputes involving a foreign element, the topic merits consideration for it provides an important testing ground for the subject's structure, rules and principles.

Two aspects of the conflict of laws must be examined. First, the jurisdiction of the English courts to determine restitutionary actions with a foreign element; and secondly, the choice of law rules for restitutionary actions having a foreign element.[15]

(1) Jurisdiction

The rules for determining whether the English courts have jurisdiction over a civil claim are laid down in EC Council Regulation 44/2001[16] (which, as between Member States of the European Union except Denmark, replaces the Brussels Convention); in the Brussels Convention, given effect to by the Civil Jurisdiction and Judgments Act 1982[17] (which applies as between England and Denmark); in the Lugano Convention, given effect to by the Civil Jurisdiction and Judgments Act 1982 (which applies as between England, Poland, and the EFTA states); in the 'modified Regulation' in Schedule 4 to the Civil Jurisdiction and Judgments Act 1982[18] (which applies as between England and the other countries within the United Kingdom); and, if none of the above apply,[19] in the English 'domestic' rules.

The most important of the English 'domestic' rules is that there is jurisdiction where a claim form is served on a defendant within the

---

14 Set out above, at pp 600–602.
15 For the appropriate currency for a personal restitutionary remedy, see *BP Exploration Co (Libya) Ltd v Hunt (No 2)* [1979] 1 WLR 783, 838–845; affd [1981] 1 WLR 232, CA.
16 [2001] OJ L12/1.
17 As amended by the Civil Jurisdiction and Judgments Act 1991.
18 As inserted by SI 2001/3929, Sch 2, para 4.
19 Eg, where the defendant is domiciled outside the EU or EFTA states or Poland.

jurisdiction or where a claim form is served out of the jurisdiction with the permission of the court given under CPR r 6.20,[20] subject to the courts having discretion to refuse jurisdiction under the doctrine of *forum non conveniens.*

The special problems raised by restitution lie principally in determining which provision of Council Regulation 44/2001 (or analogously, of the Brussels or Lugano Conventions) and which paragraphs of CPR r 6.20 apply to restitution.

(a) Council Regulation 44/2001

The basic approach of Council Regulation 44/2001 (and of the Brussels Convention) is that, subject to wide-ranging exceptions, a person domiciled in a European Union State must be sued in that State. While there are exceptions for, eg, breach of trust[1] and salvage,[2] the main exceptions into which restitution must be fitted, if at all, are contained in arts 5(1) and 5(3).

Articles 5(1) and 5(3) read as follows:

'A person domiciled in a Member State may, in another Member State, be sued:

1(a) In matters relating to a contract, in the courts for the place of performance of the obligation in question;

1(b) for the purpose of this provision, and unless otherwise agreed, the place of performance of the obligation in question shall be:
  – in the case of the sale of goods, the place in a Member State where, under the contract, the goods were delivered or should have been delivered,
  – in the case of provision of services, the place in a Member State where, under the contract, the services were provided or should have been provided,

1(c) if subparagraph (b) does not apply then subparagraph (a) applies.

3 In matters relating to tort, delict or quasi-delict, in the courts for the place where the harmful event occurred or may occur.'

If one construes 'in matters relating to [contract or tort]' as meaning 'where the cause of action is based on [contract or tort]' these provisions cover restitution for wrongs but they do not apply to unjust enrichment by subtraction. That is, art 5(1) applies to restitution *for* breach of contract: and art 5(3) applies to restitution for torts. But, on this interpretation, they do not apply to the independent cause of action of unjust enrichment. That art 5(1) does not extend to unjust enrichment by subtraction is supported by the fact that 'the place of performance

---

20 This replaces what was Order 11 of the Rules of the Supreme Court.
1 Art 5(6).
2 Art 5(7).

of the obligation in question' is hardly apt given that the obligation to make restitution is imposed by law. On this interpretation, the obligation referred to appears to be the performance of the contract and not the performance of the obligation to make restitution.

Having said that, we have seen in chapter 1 how difficult it is to draw a sharp distinction between contract and restitution where rescission of a contract is the relevant remedy. For that reason, it is strongly arguable that rescission of a contract (including the consequential reversal of benefits) for, for example, duress or misrepresentation should fall within art 5(1).

One might argue for a still wider interpretation so that restitution (most obviously for failure of consideration) following the discharge of a contract for breach – or, yet wider still, restitution consequent on other grounds invalidating a contract (including where the contract is void) – should fall within art 5(1). This might be supported by the policy reasoning that it is inconvenient and wasteful to require a claimant to deal with the invalidity of the contract in one jurisdiction but the restitutionary consequences of that invalidity in another.

These questions of interpretation have not been resolved by the European Court of Justice. However, a narrow interpretation of art 5(1) is suggested by the jurisprudence of the Court. The Court has consistently emphasised that art 2 lays down the primary rule that defendants have the right to defend claims in their home courts and that the exceptions departing from that should be narrowly construed.[3]

The two leading English cases in which these issues have been considered are also consistent with a narrow interpretation of arts 5(1) and (3) which largely – albeit not entirely – excludes unjust enrichment by subtraction from those exceptions.[4]

Kleinwort Benson Ltd v Glasgow City Council[5] was another of the 'interest rate swap' cases. The claimant sought restitution of the payments it had made to the Scottish defendant under contracts that were void as being outside the powers of the defendant local authority. The claimant brought proceedings in England arguing that the equivalent to art 5(1) (under Schedule 4 to the Civil Jurisdiction and Judgments Act 1982 applicable to jurisdiction within the UK) applied. The defendant wished to defend the claim in Scotland where it was

3   See, eg, *Leathertex Divisione Sintetici Sp A v Bodotex BVBA* C–420/97, [1999] ECR I–6747, [1999] 2 All ER (Comm) 769.

4   A narrow interpretation of the exceptions may derive further support from the fact that the Brussels Convention was drafted by civilian lawyers who, being familiar with the independence of most unjust enrichment claims, might have been expected to mention them specifically if they were intended to be covered by the exceptions.

5   [1999] 1 AC 153. See Dickinson, 'Restitution and the Conflict of Laws in the House of Lords' [1998] RLR 104; Stevens, 'Conflict of Laws' in *Lessons of the Swaps Litigation* (eds Birks and Rose, 2000), pp 329, 329–341.

domiciled and sought a declaration that the English courts had no jurisdiction. A majority of the House of Lords (Lords Nicholls and Mustill dissenting) held that art 5(1) did not here apply. The restitutionary claim was independent of contract. Any purported contract was void. The place of performance of the obligation in question referred to the place of contractual performance and there was no such performance obligation under a void contract. The general rule in art 2 therefore applied and the claimant's restitutionary action against the defendant had to be brought in Scotland.

While not deciding the point, Lord Goff left open the possibility that restitution following the discharge of a contract for breach might fall within art 5(1).

Lord Nicholls in the leading dissenting speech interpreted art 5(1) in line with the policy of avoiding inconvenience and waste. He considered it unacceptable to have different courts dealing with the validity of a contract and its restitutionary consequences. In his view, art 5(1) should therefore be interpreted as including the claims for restitution.

None of their Lordships in the majority clarified what the position would be in relation to rescission of a contract; that is, where the contract was voidable rather than void. This arose for decision in *Agnew v Lansförsäkringsbolagens AB.*[6] The claimants, who were London reinsurers, sought a declaration that they were entitled to set aside a reinsurance contract with the defendant Swedish insurers for the latter's misrepresentation or non-disclosure during the negotiation of the reinsurance contract in London. All of their Lordships agreed that a claim to rescind or set aside a contract was a 'matter relating to contract' within the first part of art 5(1) (of the Lugano Convention). The majority (Lords Woolf, Nicholls and Cooke) went on to decide that the place of performance of the obligation in question referred to the obligation to disclose the correct information or (per Lords Cooke and Nicholls but not Lord Woolf) not to make a misrepresentation. Those were obligations owed during the pre-contractual negotiations which had taken place in London. The English courts therefore had jurisdiction under art 5(1).

Lords Hope and Millett dissenting did not think that the obligation referred to in art 5(1) could be a pre-contractual obligation. As neither party had contended that the relevant obligation was that which the claimant sought to be relieved of under the voidable contract, art 5(1) did not here apply and, applying the general rule under art 2, the claimants would have to commence proceedings in Sweden as the defendant's domicile.

6   [2001] 1 AC 223.

The minority's reasoning reached the odd result that, while they clearly accepted that the rescission sought was a matter relating to a contract, art 5(1) did not apply because there was no relevant obligation and hence no 'place of performance of the obligation in question'. Having said that, the minority's reasoning is persuasive in rejecting the majority's opinion that the relevant obligation is the obligation to disclose correct information.[7] Failure to disclose does not itself constitute an actionable wrong[8] and, where pre-contractual negotiations are carried on in different jurisdictions and over a period of time, it may be difficult to pinpoint the place where such an obligation should have been performed. Nor can it be rational to determine the ambit of art 5(1) by drawing the distinction suggested by Lord Woolf between the negative obligation not to misrepresent facts which he thought has no place of performance and the positive obligation to disclose information which he thought has a place of performance.[9] In any event, even if such a place of performance is identified (eg as being the only jurisdiction where contractual negotiations took place) it is far from clear that it is sufficiently significant to trigger jurisdiction.

The better view, therefore, is that art 5(1) does apply to a claim to rescind a contract (in that respect the majority should be supported) but that, in respect of such a claim, the relevant obligation, and hence place of performance, is the obligation from which the claimant seeks to be relieved.[10] In other words, art 5(1) applies where the claimant seeks to enforce performance of a contract, including by claiming damages, or where the claimant seeks to deny (whether by a claim for rescission or a declaration of non-liability) that it is liable to perform a contract. In either case, it seems acceptable to link jurisdiction to the place where one of the parties is alleging a contractual performance should have been carried out.

As regards art 5(3), the European Court of Justice in *Kalfelis v Bankhaus Schröder, Munchmeyer, Hengst & Co*[11] held that it included 'all claims which

---

7 Contrast Briggs and Rees, *Civil Jurisdiction and Judgments* (3rd edn, 2002), pp 72–73 who appear to favour the majority's approach to the relevant obligation.

8 See above, pp 457–458; *Banque Financière de la Cité v Westgate Insurance Co Ltd* [1990] 1 QB 665, 773–781; affd [1991] 2 AC 249, HL.

9 Cf the negative 'exclusivity' contractual obligation in *Besix SA v Wasserreinigungsbau Alfred Kretzschmar GmbH & Co* Case C-256/00 which, because it required 'performance' everywhere, was held by the European Court of Justice to fall outside art 5(1).

10 This is therefore consistent with the decision of the Court of Appeal in *Boss Group Ltd v Boss France SA* [1997] 1 WLR 351 where the claim for a declaration that no contract was concluded was held to fall within art 5(1) of the Brussels Convention. See also *Effer SpA v Kantner* Case 38/81 [1982] ECR 825. Indeed if such a declaration were not within art 5(1), it would appear that art 5(1) could always be outflanked by a party, who has not performed a contract, seeking a declaration of non-liability.

11 Case 189/87 [1988] ECR 5565.

seek to establish a defendant's liability and which are not related to a contract within art 5(1)'. At first blush, this could be taken to mean that all personal restitutionary claims not falling within art 5(1) fall within art 5(3). However, in *Kleinwort Benson Ltd v Glasgow City Council* their Lordships were unanimous in the view that art 5(3) does not apply to a claim based on unjust enrichment by subtraction because such a claim does not involve a harmful event or a wrong. In other words, *Kalfelis* should be interpreted as meaning that art 5(3) is concerned with liability for torts and other wrongs[12] (other than breach of contract) including restitution for wrongs, but not unjust enrichment by subtraction.

(b) CPR r 6.20[13]

The application to restitution of the English 'domestic rules' (on service out of the jurisdiction) was, until recently, very unsatisfactory.

The approach taken in the main English cases on the question, *Bowling v Cox*,[14] *Rousou's Trustee v Rousou*,[15] and *Re Jogia*[16] was to force restitutionary claims into the main contract head of Rules of the Supreme Court, Order 11. All three cases dealt with a specialised statutory example of restitution, namely a trustee in bankruptcy's right to recover money paid away by a bankrupt to the defendants.[17] In all of them it was reasoned that the trustee in bankruptcy's action for money had and received, albeit 'quasi-contractual', fell within the contract head of Order 11 so that one needed to determine whether the quasi-contractual obligation was 'made' (ie, arose) in England or whether the proper law of the quasi-contractual obligation was English. The former of these was inapt for restitution[18] and the whole approach was redolent of the outdated implied contract theory of restitution. It was concluded in the first edition of this book that, 'The situation cries out for the Supreme Court's Rules Committee to react to the existence of a law of restitution based on unjust enrichment.'[19]

---

12 This should include equitable wrongs analogous to torts such as breach of fiduciary duty, breach of confidence, and dishonestly assisting or procuring a breach of fiduciary duty. That 'dishonest assistance' falls within art 5(3) is established by *Casio Computer Co Ltd v Sayo* [2001] EWCA Civ 661.
13 See, generally, Panagopoulos, *Restitution in Private International Law* (2000), ch 10.
14 [1926] AC 751.
15 [1955] 3 All ER 486. See also *Re Intended Action, Rousou's Trustee v Rousou* [1955] 2 All ER 169.
16 [1988] 1 WLR 484. See also *Finnish Marine Insurance Co Ltd v Protective National Insurance Co* [1989] 2 Lloyd's Rep 99, 102–103; *The Olib* [1991] 2 Lloyd's Rep 108, 118–119.
17 The statutory provisions were previously laid down in the Bankruptcy Act 1914 and s 172 of the Law of Property Act 1925. The modern equivalents are contained in the Insolvency Act 1986. See above, p 425, n 5.
18 In *Re Jogia* [1988] 1 WLR 484 Sir Nicolas Browne-Wilkinson V-C took the view that the obligation arose where the enrichment was received and that this was generally the same as the proper law of the quasi-contract.
19 *The Law of Restitution* (1st edn, 1993), p 490.

This has now happened. The Civil Procedure Rule, CPR 6.20 (15), specifically deals with restitution. It reads, '[A] claim form may be served out of the jurisdiction with the permission of the court if ... (15) a claim is made for restitution where the defendant's alleged liability arises out of acts committed within the jurisdiction.'

As Briggs and Rees have written, 'It is to be expected that paragraph (15) will now provide the natural home for restitutionary claims, and that earlier authorities which had allowed a quasi-contractual claim to be brought, faute de mieux, within the contract head will not now need to be followed.'[20]

It is not entirely clear how paragraph 15 should be interpreted. Take a mistake case, where C in London sends a mistaken payment to D in New York. Does D's restitutionary liability arise out of acts committed within England? Presumably the answer is 'yes' albeit that those acts are entirely those of C (in making the payment) not D. What if it is C in the United States who sends a mistaken payment to D in London? Again one would expect this to be covered albeit that D's 'acts' are merely the passive receipt of a mistaken payment. So in a mistaken payment case, the English courts may give permission for service out of the jurisdiction, if the payment was either made from England or received in England.[1]

Certainly, there seems no good reason to take a narrow interpretation of paragraph 15 not least because the courts have an overriding discretion to refuse jurisdiction under the *forum non conveniens* doctrine.

In the light of paragraph 15, there should rarely be any need to agonise as to whether other paragraphs of CPR 6.20 cover a restitutionary claim (whether personal or proprietary). But it should be noted that, apart from paragraph 15, restitution for wrongs naturally falls within paragraph 6 (for breach of contract), paragraph 8 (for torts) and paragraph 14 (for equitable wrongs where the defendant is alleged to be a 'constructive trustee'). These paragraphs essentially allow service out where the wrong was committed within England. Potentially more significant – because they allow service out for reasons other than 'acts committed within the jurisdiction' – are paragraphs 5 and 7 which apply to claims in respect of a contract or for a declaration that no contract exists.[2] These allow service out if, for example, the contract is governed

---

20   *Civil Jurisdiction and Judgments* (3rd edn, 2002), para 4.48.

1   That not *all* the acts triggering liability have to take place within England is supported by, eg, *Polly Peck International Ltd v Nadir (No 3)* [1994] 1 BCLC 661, CA. This dealt with 'knowing assistance' and 'knowing receipt' under what is now CPR 6.20(14).

2   See also paragraph 10 under which English courts may grant permission for service outside the jurisdiction if 'the whole subject matter of a claim relates to property located within the jurisdiction'.

by English law or was made within the jurisdiction or has a clause conferring jurisdiction on the English courts. In general, however (and with the main possible exception of a claim for rescission where it is notoriously difficult to separate contract and restitution) courts should not seek to give paragraphs 5 and 7 a wide meaning so as to sweep up restitution. Restitution for unjust enrichment by subtraction should be dealt with through the more obvious paragraph 15.

(2) Choice of law

How one determines choice of law is a notoriously controversial question. Especially in the United States, the dispute between the formalist and realist schools of jurisprudence has surfaced very clearly in relation to whether one can develop satisfactory 'jurisdiction-selecting' choice of law rules or whether, in contrast, a case by case 'rule-selecting' approach is preferable. English law has continued to adhere to a traditional jurisdiction-selecting approach but the effect of the realist critique has been that, where possible, more flexible choice of law rules have been favoured (for example, the proper law of the contract) so that a degree of purposive analysis can be undertaken. Given the theoretical disputes that have also raged regarding the basis of the law of restitution, it is not surprising that the question of what are the correct choice of law rules for restitution does not admit of a straightforward or uncontroversial answer.

Relevant English case law is sparse and it is probably still true to say that 'the applicable choice of law rule or rules for restitutionary issues is … an open matter'.[3] Having said that, most cases have approved and applied what is now rule 200 in Dicey and Morris, *The Conflict of Laws*,[4] which is the leading text. We shall therefore begin by focusing on the approach in Dicey and Morris.

Before doing so, there is an important introductory point. Before applying a choice of law rule, one must first classify the issue with which one is concerned. This is known as the 'characterisation' question. In other words, if one has choice of law rules for the law of restitution, one first has to decide whether the issue with which one is concerned falls within the law of restitution. In general terms, characterisation in the conflict of laws is a matter for the *lex fori*. So the debates about the ambit of the English law of restitution resurface as being central to the conflict of laws. In this respect, it is worth reiterating

---

3   Panagopoulos, *Restitution in Private International Law* (2000), p 111, citing *Macmillan Inc v Bishopsgate Investment Trust plc (No 3)* [1996] 1 WLR 387, 408 (per Auld LJ).
4   (13th edn, 2000).

here two central features of the English law of restitution as viewed in this book. First, there is an important divide between unjust enrichment by subtraction and restitution for wrongs; in relation to the former, unjust enrichment is the cause of action whereas, in relation to the latter, the wrong is the cause of action.[5] Secondly, while most of the law of restitution concerns personal remedies, it also includes proprietary restitution; that is, it includes proprietary rights created to reverse unjust enrichment. But it excludes what have been termed 'pure proprietary claims' where the return of property to the claimant simply rests on pre-existing ownership.[6]

Rule 200 in Dicey and Morris reads as follows:

'(1) The obligation to restore the benefit of an enrichment obtained at another person's expense is governed by the proper law of the obligation.

(2) The proper law of the obligation is *(semble)* determined as follows:

(a) If the obligation arises in connection with a contract, its proper law is the law applicable to the contract;

(b) If it arises in connection with a transaction concerning an immovable (land), its proper law is the law of the country where the immovable is situated *(lex situs)*;

(c) If it arises in any other circumstances, its proper law is the law of the country where the enrichment occurs.'

It can be seen that Dicey and Morris' basic choice of law rule for restitution is the proper law of the obligation to make restitution. This basic rule has been accepted by the Court of Appeal in *Arab Monetary Fund v Hashim*.[7] But in itself it means very little albeit that it indicates that the question must always be approached with a degree of flexibility. The real thrust of Dicey and Morris' approach is therefore in rule 200(2). As restitutionary claims in relation to land are rare – and, in any event, where they do occur it is very likely that the place of enrichment and the *lex situs* are the same – the important sub-rules are 2(a) and 2(c). Although 2(a) has not been discussed in an English case, the default rule, 2(c), has been approved by the English courts.

In *Re Jogia*,[8] an action for money had and received was brought by a trustee in bankruptcy to recover money paid out by the bankrupt's

---

5   Above, pp 26, 455.

6   Above, pp 61–62. The claim in *Macmillan Inc v Bishopsgate Investment Trust plc (No 3)* [1996] 1 WLR 387 was purely proprietary – for the return of shares that had from the start belonged in equity to the claimant – so that the decision that the ownership of the shares should be decided by the *lex situs* should have been a straightforward one. There was no tracing into substitutes involved and the claim was not therefore a restitutionary proprietary one. See Panagopoulos, *Restitution in Private International Law* (2000), pp 44–45.

7   [1996] 1 Lloyd's Rep 589. This concerned restitution of a bribe acquired in breach of fiduciary duty.

8   [1988] 1 WLR 484.

agent to the defendant on or after the date of the receiving order. The central conflict of laws question was the jurisdictional one of whether leave to serve out should be granted. However, in determining this, Sir Nicolas Browne-Wilkinson V-C regarded the applicable choice of law rule for 'quasi-contract' as relevant; and he considered Dicey and Morris' residual rule – the place of enrichment – as 'sound in principle'.[9] Applying it, the relevant law was French because the enrichment was received in France. And he thought the two decisions in *Rousou*[10] (a similar bankruptcy case) had been wrong because the receipt of the moneys had occurred in Cyprus not in England. In *El Ajou v Dollar Land Holdings plc*,[11] which concerned a claim for 'knowing receipt', Millett J said that the law governing receipt-based restitutionary claims is 'the law of the country where the defendant received the money'[12] and he cited with approval rule 2(c) in Dicey and Morris. Finally in *Kuwait Oil Tanker Co v Al Bader*,[13] Nourse LJ giving the judgment of the Court of Appeal in relation to a claim, inter alia, for restitution for breach of fiduciary duty by directors to their companies, said, '[T]he rule of English private international law is that the obligation to restore the benefit of an enrichment such as was obtained by the defendants in this case is governed by the law of the country where the enrichment occurred.'[14] And he cited as 'authority' for that rule Dicey and Morris, rule 200 (2)(c).

However, the commentary to rule 200(2)(c) in Dicey and Morris is lukewarm in its support of that rule and suggests that the real question is which jurisdiction has the closest connection with the restitutionary claim; the place of enrichment may be a good indicator of that but it should be treated only as a starting point that can be displaced.[15] Moreover, the 'place of enrichment' rule has come under attack from

---

9 Ibid, at p 495.

10 *Re Intended Action, Rousou's Trustee v Rousou* [1955] 2 All ER 169; *Rousou's Trustee v Rousou* [1955] 3 All ER 486. But he considered that *Bowling v Cox* [1926] AC 751 had been correctly decided because, although the defendant was in the United States, the money had been received by the defendant, through his agent, in British Honduras.

11 [1993] 3 All ER 717; revsd on other grounds [1994] 2 All ER 685, CA.

12 Ibid, at p 736.

13 [2000] 2 All ER (Comm) 271. Two decisions in Singapore also applied Dicey and Morris' place of enrichment rule: *Hong Kong and Shanghai Banking Corp Ltd v United Overseas Bank Ltd* [1992] 2 SLR 495 (restitution for 'knowing receipt'); *Thahir v Pertamina* [1994] 3 SLR 257 (restitution of bribes acquired in breach of fiduciary duty). See also *Christopher v Zimmermann* (2001) 192 DLR (4th) 476, British Columbia CA. It has sometimes been suggested that *Chase Manhattan NA v Israel-British Bank (London) Ltd* [1981] Ch 105 supports the place of enrichment: but it was common ground between the parties that the law of New York governed (other than on matters of procedural law) as the 'lex causae'. In any event, Goulding J found that New York and English law were not in conflict on the facts.

14 Ibid, at p 338.

15 Dicey and Morris, paras 34-030, 34-036.

a number of commentators on the grounds that it may have relatively little to do with the claim in question and it may be difficult to determine in cases where funds are transferred through several jurisdictions. It is also conceivable that fraudsters may manipulate the place of enrichment so as to 'choose' laws that are more favourable to them. Panagopoulos summarises the arguments against the place of enrichment as follows: 'It is arbitrary; it gives a deceptively simple *locus*, yet it is often difficult to determine; it may not necessarily be connected with either of the parties, or events; and, finally, but most importantly, it can be manipulated by *mala fides* parties, who might ensure that they are "enriched" in jurisdictions with rules that will suit their aims.'[16]

A number of different suggestions have been made as to the appropriate choice of law rule.[17] For example, Bird would retain the place of enrichment as a residual rule (although even then it might be displaced). However, she suggests that the primary rule should be that of the contractual or other relationship that existed, or was assumed to exist, between the parties.[18] Similarly, Briggs favours the law of the contractual or other relationship that existed, or was assumed to exist, between the parties as the primary rule. But beyond that he suggests that one should choose, flexibly, the law which has the closest and most real connection with the alleged obligation to make restitution.[19] 'Any attempt to specify in advance what this means does not seem sensible.'[20] He would not apply the law of the place of enrichment 'even as an easily rebuttable presumption'.[1] More radically, Panagopoulos focuses on the unjust factor and attractively argues that restitutionary issues should be governed by the law, or the law of the place, with which the unjust factor has its closest and most real connection.[2] So, for example, in a mistaken payment case, the choice of law should be the law of the place where the mistake was made.

---

16 Panagopoulos, *Restitution in Private International Law* (2000), p 166. See also Briggs, *The Conflict of Laws* (2002), p 198.

17 In addition to the commentators referred to in this paragraph see, eg, Gutteridge and Lipstein, 'Conflicts of Law in Matters of Unjustifiable Enrichment' (1939) 7 CLJ 80; Hay, 'Unjust Enrichment in the Conflict of Laws' (1978) 26 AJ Comp L 3; Bennett, 'Choice of Law Rules in Claims of Unjust Enrichment' [1990] 39 ICLQ 136; Brereton, 'Restitution and Contract' in *Restitution in the Conflict of Laws* (ed Rose, 1995), pp 142–179; Stevens, 'The Choice of Law Rules of Restitutionary Obligations', ibid, pp 180–220. See also (Second) Restatement of the Conflict of Laws, s 221.

18 Bird, 'Choice of Law' in *Restitution and the Conflict of Laws* (ed Rose, 1995), pp 64–141, esp p 135. See also Bird, 'Conflict of Laws' in *The Law of Restitution* (eds Hedley and Halliwell, 2002), paras 22.63–22.106.

19 Briggs, *The Conflict of Laws* (2002), pp 194–199.

20 Ibid, at p 198.

1   Ibid.

2   Panagopoulos, *Restitution in Private International Law* (2000), ch 8. His approach is extensively criticised in a review essay by Lee, 'Choice of Law for Claims in Unjust Enrichment' (2002) 26 MULR 192.

It is noteworthy that a common feature of the approach of Dicey and Morris (rule 2(a)), Bird, Briggs and others is the reliance, in relation to restitution arising out of ineffective contracts, on the proper law or putative proper law of the contract. At first blush, this may be thought to reflect the old implied contract thinking about restitution. Where the claim is brought in unjust enrichment by subtraction following the discharge of a contract for breach or frustration – most obviously for failure of consideration – there is no good reason in principle why the proper law of the contract should govern the independent restitutionary claim rather than a specially thought out restitutionary choice of law rule.

It is precisely for this reason that Glanville Williams[3] criticised as a 'juristic blunder' the opening words of the Law Reform (Frustrated Contracts) Act 1943 which confine the Act's scope to where a contract is governed by English law. He explained, 'The situation ... is not a contractual but a quasi-contractual one. If so, the contract and its proper law are irrelevant considerations. When the quasi-contractual situation arises the contract has disappeared, and it is therefore illogical to make the rule governing the quasi-contractual situation depend upon the proper law of the contract.'

The argument in principle for applying the restitutionary choice of law rule rather than the contractual one can be expressed even more strongly when no valid contract has been concluded and it is the putative proper law that is being referred to: the putative proper law can be criticised as circular even where one is dealing with central contractual issues and perhaps is sometimes justified only because there is no other better solution. But, arguably, there is a better solution where a restitutionary claim is being brought, namely the choice of law rule for restitution.[4] Those advocating the (putative) proper law of the contract do not suggest that tort claims between parties who are in a contractual relationship should be governed by the proper law of the contract rather than the choice of law rules for tort.[5] The same deference to the independence of the claim should be shown for unjust enrichment by subtraction as for tort.

Indeed the heavy reliance on contract may run into a problem with the Contracts (Applicable Law) Act 1990. This has incorporated

3   *Law Reform (Frustrated Contracts) Act 1943* at pp 19–20.
4   The putative proper law of the contract was rejected for restitution consequent on a void interest rate swap transaction, in favour of the flexible proper law of the restitutionary claim, in the Scottish case of *Baring Bros & Co Ltd v Cunninghame District Council* [1997] CLC 108 (Ct of Sess). As it happened English law, which was the putative proper law of the contract, was decided to be the proper law of the restitutionary claim.
5   See, eg, Dicey and Morris, para 36-063.

into English law the Rome Convention which lays down uniform choice of law rules in the European Union for contract.[6] Nevertheless the choice of law rules for restitution dealing with 'the consequences of nullity of [a] contract' remain a matter for the English common law. This is because by s 2(2) of the 1990 Act, art 10(1)(e) of the Convention has been excluded so that, while 'the various ways of extinguishing [contractual] obligations' are governed by the statutory choice of law rules, 'the consequences of nullity' are not. The debates in the House of Lords indicate that the reason for s 2(2) is the distinction in English law between the law of contract and the law of restitution.[7]

The difficulty that then follows from applying the contractual choice of law rules to restitution arising out of ineffective contracts is that one appears to be contradicting the purpose of s 2(2). Dicey and Morris suggest that, while one cannot therefore apply the Rome Convention directly, there is no objection to the common law choice of law rules applying the law specified by the Rome Convention when this law happens to be that with which the obligation to make restitution has its closest connection.[8] Bird argues that there is not a problem here because the opt-out in s 2(2) leaves open whether the statutory rules should apply; it does not dictate that they do not apply. 'It is reading far too much into the Act to say that by inference it rejects application of the Rome Convention rules to unjust enrichment actions arising out of contracts.'[9] While largely agreeing with Bird's approach to s 2(2), Stevens goes further and argues that 'the consequences of nullity' in art 10(1)(e) should be narrowly construed and that 'nullity' does not refer to discharged, as opposed to void, contracts. On his interpretation, the reliance on the Rome Convention for determining the choice of law for restitution in respect of ineffective contracts is not merely possible but, in respect of restitution consequent on the discharge of a contract for breach or frustration, is dictated by the Rome Convention (because not within the opt-out).

Whatever the position generally, it is submitted that an express choice of law clause should be deferred to in a claim for restitution arising from a contract. The theory behind applying an express choice of law clause is that, while the parties may not have anticipated the

---

6   A choice of law rule for certain sorts of subrogation is also laid down in art 13.
7   Hansard HL, vol 513, cols 1259, 1262–1263, 1271.
8   Dicey and Morris, para 34–026.
9   Bird, 'Choice of Law' in *Restitution and the Conflict of Laws* (ed Rose, 1995), p 129. Certainly it is difficult to apply the opt-out to rescission of a contract because, as explained in chapter 1, it is notoriously difficult and unattractive to separate contractual and restitutionary issues where rescission is in play.

particular dispute in question, they can be taken to have chosen the law of a particular country to cover *all* disputes arising in relation to a contract. And this reasoning can be applied to restitutionary claims arising in connection with a contract as well as to 'pure' contract disputes. Certainly the difficulty in formulating fair choice of law rules suggests that an express indication of the parties' intentions should be seized upon with relief.[10] Of course, where the dispute in question includes a dispute as to whether there was true agreement as to the choice of law clause that clause cannot be determinative of the choice of law question. The normal choice of law rule for restitution must instead be applied.

It also seems tolerably clear that where the claim is for restitution *for* breach of contract, the Rome Convention applies. Restitutionary damages or an account of profits for breach of contract fall within art 10(1)(c) as concerning 'the consequences of breach, including the assessment of damages in so far as it is governed by rules of law'. Such a claim is not independent of the breach of contract (that is, the breach of contract is the cause of action) and there seems no pressing policy incentive to disapply the choice of law rules for contract even if that were possible.

What about restitution for wrongs other than breach of contract? As the wrong is the cause of action the most natural starting point is that the choice of law rule for the wrong should apply. So restitution for torts should be governed, at least prima facie, by the choice of law rule for torts which, with the exception of defamation, is laid down for 'issues relating to tort' in the Private International Law (Miscellaneous Provisions) Act 1995. The general rule under s 11 of the 1995 Act is that the applicable law is of the place where the events constituting the tort, or the most significant element of those events, occurred. By s 12 that general rule will be displaced if another country has a closer connection with the tort. Even if it were possible as a matter of statutory interpretation, there seems no good policy reason why this newly-reformulated choice of law rule for tort should not apply to where restitution, rather than the more usual compensation, is the remedy for the tort.[11] Put another way, the difficulty in formulating an appropriate special choice of law rule for restitution suggests that, whatever the position for unjust enrichment by subtraction, it is appropriate to apply the tort rule to restitution for torts. Although there is no English case directly on point, it is significant

---

10 In terms of principle it is equally arguable that tort claims arising out of a contract should be governed by an express choice of law clause. Admittedly, however, there is no case law support for this: see Dicey and Morris, *The Conflict of Laws* (13th edn, 2000), para 35-063.
11 Cf Goff and Jones, para 36-014.

that this is the conclusion agreed with by Dicey and Morris,[12] Bird,[13] Briggs,[14] Panagopoulos,[15] and Stevens.[16]

Similarly, one can strongly argue that restitution for equitable wrongs, such as breach of fiduciary duty, breach of confidence and dishonest assistance, should be governed by the choice of law rule applicable to the equitable wrong.[17] In line with this in *Grupo Torras SA v Al-Sabah (No 5),*[18] the Court of Appeal appeared to apply a version of the 'double actionability' tort rule to a claim for compensation for the equitable wrong of dishonest assistance. And in *Arab Monetary Fund v Hashim,*[19] the Court of Appeal applied the law of the place where the dishonesty took place (and not where the enrichment was received) to govern a claim for restitution of a bribe acquired in breach of fiduciary duty. But, as we have seen, in relation to a claim for restitution for breach of fiduciary duty the Court of Appeal in *Kuwait Oil Tanker Co SAK v Al Bader*[20] thought that the law of the place of enrichment was the applicable law.

Finally, whatever the choice of law rule for a restitutionary claim is decided to be, it will be subject to the well-recognised exceptional choice of law principle that, in Dicey and Morris' words, ' ... the courts of a country will not apply any foreign law if and in so far as its application would lead to results contrary to the fundamental principles of public policy of the *lex fori*'.[1] The most directly relevant discussion of this principle in relation to the law of restitution has been in the context of duress. Three cases merit consideration (although in only the second of them was restitution, rather than the validity of a contract, in issue).

In *Kaufman v Gerson*[2] Kaufman threatened Gerson that he would bring criminal charges against her husband unless she contracted to pay him a large sum of money. Both parties were domiciled in France which is where the purported contract was made. The contract was held unenforceable for undue influence or duress by the application of English law. Although no restitution was involved

12   Dicey and Morris, paras 34-007, 34-015, 34-031.
13   'Choice of Law' in *Restitution and the Conflict of Laws* (ed Rose, 1995), pp 92–99.
14   *The Conflict of Laws* (2002), pp 196–197.
15   *Restitution in Private International Law* (2000), pp 82–84, 174.
16   'The Choice of Law Rules of Restitutionary Obligations' in *Restitution and Conflict of Laws* (ed Rose, 1995), pp 187–188.
17   This is very tentatively supported by Dicey and Morris, para 34-032.
18   [2001] Lloyd's Rep Bank 36.
19   [1996] 1 Lloyd's Rep 589.
20   [2000] 2 All ER (Comm) 271. The law of the place of enrichment was also applied to restitution of a bribe acquired in breach of fiduciary duty in *Thahir v Pertamina* [1994] 3 SLR 257.
1   Para 32-227. This idea is embodied in art 16 of the Rome Convention.
2   [1904] 1 KB 591.

it can be assumed that the same approach would have been applied if Gerson had paid over the contractual sum and had then sought restitution of it.

At first sight the decision seems wrong in applying English law. All the events happened in France, the domicile of both parties was France, and the putative proper law was French. And by French law the contract was valid. Yet the Court of Appeal applied English law because to enforce the contract would infringe English public policy as being, so it was said, contrary to a moral principle that ought to be universally recognised. In other words, the above exceptional choice of law principle was applied. Having said that, it must be doubted whether the facts of this case were so extreme as to violate fundamental public policy.

In *Dimskal Shipping Co v International Transport Workers' Federation, The Evia Luck*[3] some of the issues concerning duress in private international law were confused in the lower courts; and the relevance of the House of Lords' decision to *Kaufman v Gerson* (which was not even mentioned in the speeches) is tangential. Nevertheless, the approaches in *The Evia Luck* and *Kaufman v Gerson* have subsequently been contrasted and it is therefore convenient to consider the conflict of laws aspect of that case. It concerned the long-running campaign by ITF of blacking ships sailing under flags of convenience. The question arose whether economic duress made a contract voidable, with consequent restitution, if the alleged illegitimate pressure took place in a country outside England, here Sweden, where the pressure was lawful.

One might have expected that the central issue would have been the correct choice of law rule governing the restitution of money paid under duress. But not so, for the defendants conceded that the questions of whether the contract was voidable and whether there should be consequent restitution were governed by English law.

Given that concession, it is hard to see that there was any case for not simply applying English (domestic) law according to which the pressure was illegitimate.[4] In particular it would be an entirely novel development if a court were to accept that, while the choice of law rule governing duress (for contractual invalidity and restitution) was English, there should be a backtracking so that a different choice of

---

3   [1992] 2 AC 152. See above, chapter 5.
4   Contra is O'Dair 'Restitution on the Grounds of Duress : Handle with Care' [1992] LMCLQ 145. His primary argument is that by analogy to taking account of the foreign illegality of a foreign performance in frustration cases, the legality in Sweden of the blacking should have dictated that, as a matter of English domestic law, the pressure was legitimate. With respect, that is not a convincing analogy.

law rule applied to a single issue (the legitimacy of the pressure) in the duress enquiry. Choice of law rules are not split in this way.[5]

Yet it took until the House of Lords, and Lord Goff's speech, for that answer to emerge and, even then, Lord Templeman dissented. In Lord Goff's words:

> '... we are left simply with an English contract which is voidable by the innocent party if the formation of the contract has been induced by duress in the form of blacking or the threat of blacking a vessel. The question then arises whether there is any basis in law for rejecting this simple approach, on the ground that the conduct in question was lawful by the law of the place where it occurred, viz Swedish law. Before your Lordships, it was the primary submission of Mr Burton on behalf of ITF that in relation to any duress abroad, in English law the court should, subject to overriding questions of public policy, look to the law of the place of duress to test its lawfulness or legitimacy ... I have to say that I know of no authority which supports his submission ...'[6]

The smokescreen put forward was the double actionability choice of law rule for tort. However, as Lord Goff stressed, duress need not be tortious and, even if it is, rescission of a contract (and consequent restitution) for duress is not (or, at least, need not be) a claim in tort. In other words, on the facts the claim was for restitution of an unjust enrichment by subtraction not restitution for a wrong so that the choice of law rule for tort did not directly apply. Nor was there any cogent reason for applying the tort rule by analogy.

The Evia Luck would have been far more interesting and important had the defendants' concession on choice of law not been made. Even then, however, it would seem that the same result – that English law governed the restitutionary claim – should have been reached. There was an express choice of law clause laying down that English law should govern; rescission (traditionally governed by the proper law or putative proper law of the contract) is perhaps not easy to separate clearly from the consequential restitution of the money paid; and the money was received in England and may have been paid out in England.

Although *Kaufman v Gerson* was not mentioned, Lord Goff indicated that the proper law of the contract would not be overriden by the exceptional principle of public policy applied in *Kaufman v Gerson*. This has led to the suggestion that *The Evia Luck* has narrowed the

---

5   Although an 'incidental question' can arise even having chosen a primary choice of law rule, the question of the legitimacy of the pressure can hardly be regarded as incidental to duress. Even if it were, the incidental question is normally determined according to the *lex causae* (the law governing the main question) or the *lex fori* both of which were English. See Dicey and Morris (13th edn, 2000), ch 2.

6   [1992] 2 AC 152, 168.

ambit of *Kaufman v Gerson* and that one must distinguish between some forms of duress, which invoke that exceptional principle, and others which do not.[7]

This suggestion was approved by Phillips LJ in *Royal Boskalis Westminster NV v Mountain*[8] in which the Court of Appeal decided that a waiver agreement would be unenforceable for duress of the person (comprising a threat to use a large number of people as 'human shields'). It was held that the exceptional principle of public policy laid down in *Kaufman v Gerson* here applied. Phillips LJ explored the issue in most detail and, after considering *Kaufman v Gerson* and *The Evia Luck,* said the following:

> '[Are there] two classes of duress – duress that is so shocking that the English court will not enforce the contract irrespective of whether it is valid under its governing law, and a lesser form of duress, whose legitimacy and effect falls to be determined by the proper law of the contract? Mr Aikens conceded implicitly that this must be so in that he submitted that the *Dimskal* case was not of such a type as to "violate some moral principle which, if it is not, ought to be universally respected."[9] It would be strange if duress of that [latter] type were to be rendered acceptable to the English court by virtue of the effect of a choice of law clause induced by the same duress, or because the law of the country with which the contract induced by duress had the closest connection regarded the duress as acceptable. My conclusion is that there remains a class of duress so unconscionable that it will cause the English court, as a matter of public policy, to override the proper law of contract.'[10]

It can be seen, therefore, that choice of law in relation to the law of restitution raises a number of difficult issues, several of which await authoritative resolution by the courts. Continuing litigation in this sphere seems inevitable.

---

7 Dicey and Morris, *The Conflict of Laws* (13th edn, 2000), p 1279.
8 [1999] QB 674.
9 Citing Collins MR in *Kaufman v Gerson* [1904] 1 KB 591, 598.
10 [1999] QB 674, 729.

Index